Eighth Edition

MEASUREMENT FOR EVALUATION

In Physical Education and Exercise Science

D0202612

Ted A. Baumgartner
University of Georgia

Andrew S. Jackson
University of Houston

Matthew T. Mahar
University of Glamorgan

David A. Rowe
University of Glamorgan

Boston   Burr Ridge, IL   Dubuque, IA   Madison, WI   New York   San Francisco   St. Louis
Bangkok   Bogotá   Caracas   Kuala Lumpur   Lisbon   London   Madrid   Mexico City
Milan   Montreal   New Delhi   Santiago   Seoul   Singapore   Sydney   Taipei   Toronto

Higher Education

Published by McGraw-Hill, an imprint of The McGraw-Hill Companies, Inc., 1221 Avenue of the Americas, New York, NY 10020. Copyright © 2007. All rights reserved. No part of this publication may be reproduced or distributed in any form or by any means, or stored in a database or retrieval system, without the prior written consent of The McGraw-Hill Companies, Inc., including, but not limited to, in any network or other electronic storage or transmission, or broadcast for distance learning.

1 2 3 4 5 6 7 8 9 0 DOC/DOC 0 9 8 7 6

ISBN-13: 978-0-07-304526-9
ISBN-10: 0-07-304526-8

Editor in Chief: *Emily Barrosse*
Publisher: *William R. Glass*
Executive Editor: *Christopher Johnson*
Director of Development: *Kathleen Engelberg*
Executive Marketing Manager: *Pamela S. Cooper*
Developmental Editor: *Beth Baugh, Carlisle Publishing Services*
Developmental Editor for Technology: *Julia D. Ersery*
Media Producer: *Michele Borrelli*
Project Manager: *Carey Eisner*
Manuscript Editor: *Jan McDearmon*
Senior Designer: *Cassandra Chu*
Text Designer: *Linda Robertson*
Lead Production Supervisor: *Randy Hurst*
Composition: *10/12 Times Roman by Carlisle Publishing Services*
Printing: *45# New Era Matte, R. R. Donnelley*

Library of Congress Cataloging-in-Publication Data

Measurement for evaluation in physical education and exercise science / Ted A.
    Baumgartner . . . [et al.].—8th ed.
      p. cm
    Includes bibliographical references and index.
    ISBN-13: 978-0-07-304526-9
    ISBN-10: 0-07-304526-8
      1. Physical fitness—Testing. 2. Physical education and training. I. Baumgartner, Ted A.

GV436.B33 2006
613.7—dc22   2006043639

The Internet addresses listed in the text were accurate at the time of publication. The inclusion of a Web site does not indicate an endorsement by the authors or McGraw-Hill, and McGraw-Hill does not guarantee the accuracy of the information presented at these sites.

www.mhhe.com

BRIEF CONTENTS

CONTENTS

CHAPTER 3

Reliability and Objectivity 69

CHAPTER 4

Validity 95

CHAPTER 5

**Test Characteristics, Administration,
and Interpretation   108**

**PART III
Measuring and Evaluating Physical
Attributes 121**

CHAPTER 6

School-Based Evaluation   122

CHAPTER 7

Authentic and Alternative Assessment   140

CHAPTER 8

Evaluating Skill Achievement   155

CHAPTER 9

Measuring Physical Activity   178

CHAPTER 10

Measuring Physical Abilities   222

CHAPTER 11

Evaluating Aerobic Fitness 262

CHAPTER 12

Evaluating Body Composition 297

CHAPTER 13

**Evaluating Youth Fitness
and Physical Activity   337**

CHAPTER 14

Adult and Older Adult Fitness   378

CHAPTER 15

**Applications to Persons with
Disabilities   415**

PART IV
Cognitive and Affective Testing 445

CHAPTER 16

Evaluating Knowledge   446

CHAPTER 17

Exercise Psychological Measurement   473

PREFACE

In previous editions we responded to changes in the field by adding information for students seeking careers in areas other than teaching, expanding the application of computers, and reorganizing the book. The result was a book that contained a solid foundation of the information needed by students in physical education or exercise science curricula.

In preparing this eighth edition, we revised the book based on suggestions from successful professionals in the field and from our own expertise. Information and references were updated throughout the book, new photos and graphs were added, and a major reorganization was undertaken. In addition, two new chapters are featured in this edition: Chapter 7, Authentic and Alternative Assessment, and Chapter 15, Applications to Persons with Disabilities. Two additional authors contributed their expertise and writing skills in creating these chapters.

We recognize that students using this text come from many backgrounds and with a great variety of interest areas (health, elementary or secondary physical education, fitness, adapted physical education, pre-physical therapy, athletic training, gerontology, exercise science, specialization areas, etc.). Sometimes we have roughly classified all students using the book as being in either physical education or exercise science. Thus, we have presented information that is important in most of the interest areas. Instructors should select from the information presented and supplement the book when necessary.

NEW TO THIS EDITION

Authentic and Alternative Assessment (Chapter 7) This new chapter expands on the topic of authentic assessment to include alternative assessment. It highlights the characteristics and types of authentic and alternative assessments and discusses various measurement concerns.

Applications to Persons with Disabilities (Chapter 15) This new chapter features physical fitness tests for both youth and adults with disabilities and considers assessments appropriate for field and clinical use. It includes discussion of the Individuals with Disabilities Education Act and provides the Wheelchair USA Medical Classification System Manual Muscle Test.

Reorganized and Revised Content The chapters were reorganized to increase their accessibility and to improve the flow of the book. Part II now concludes with a chapter on Test Characteristics, Administration, and Interpretation (Chapter 5), and Part III now includes the chapter on Evaluating Skill Achievement (Chapter 8), placed right before the chapters on Measuring Physical Activity

(Chapter 9) and Measuring Physical Abilities (Chapter 10). Extensive revisions were undertaken in the chapters on Measurement and Evaluation in a Changing Society (Chapter 1), Statistical Tools in Evaluation (Chapter 2), Test Characteristics, Administration, and Interpretation (Chapter 5), and Measuring Physical Activity (Chapter 9).

Broadened Scope   This edition offers a much expanded discussion of measurement and evaluation in persons with disabilities, measurement differences based on gender, and new measurement models for African Americans. Reliability and validity data are provided for all age ranges: children, adolescents, adults, and older adults.

NEW OR EXPANDED TOPICS

Chapter 1: Measurement and Evaluation in a Changing Society

- Accuracy of criterion-referenced standards
- FITNESSGRAM®/ACTIVITYGRAM®
- National Physical Activity Guidelines for Children
- Behavioral Risk Factor Surveillance System

Chapter 2: Statistical Tools in Evaluation

- Computer examples updated to SPSS 14.0
- Revised description of how to determine the median, standard deviation, and percentile ranks
- Instructions on how to determine percentile

Chapter 3: Reliability and Objectivity

- Relationship between reliability/objectivity and validity
- Formula revised for determining the coefficient alpha
- Discussion of one-way versus two-way ANOVA

Chapter 4: Validity

- Expanded example of the mile-run test
- Criterion-related validity evidence

Chapter 5: Test Characteristics, Administration, and Interpretation

- Additional material on administration and evaluation of measurement
- Expanded discussion of criterion-referenced standards

Chapter 6: School-Based Evaluation

- Rank order compared with grading on the curve
- Letter scores versus T-scores
- Incomplete grades

Chapter 7: Authentic and Alternative Assessment

- Characteristics of authentic assessments
- Types of authentic and alternative assessments
- Different types of scoring rubrics
- National Standards for Physical Education

Chapter 8: Evaluating Skill Achievement

- Added discussion of age, gender, and experience
- Additional considerations for formative and summative evaluation

Chapter 9: Measuring Physical Activity

- Measuring physical activity across the life span
- Latest reliability and validity evidence for children, adolescents, adults, and older adults
- Abundant new research

Chapter 10: Measuring Physical Abilities

- Updated information on testing NFL football draft prospects
- Expanded discussion of content validity of preemployment tests

Chapter 11: Evaluating Aerobic Fitness

- Latest ACSM (2006) guidelines
- Updated criteria for risk factors
- Single-stage treadmill walking test formulas for men and women

Chapter 12: Evaluating Body Composition

- Formulas for estimating percent fat from body density for African Americans
- Bioelectrical impedance analysis
- Discussion of android obesity and gynoid obesity
- Updated statistics and research

Chapter 13: Evaluating Youth Fitness and Physical Activity

- Updated information on FITNESSGRAM®/ACTIVITYGRAM®
- Website for training videos
- Using pedometers to assess physical activity in boys and girls

Chapter 14: Adult and Older Adult Fitness

- Updated YMCA and Army norms
- Army health and wellness website
- 1-minute half sit-up test

Chapter 15: Applications to Persons with Disabilities

- Youth and adult fitness assessments
- Motor function
- Assessments appropriate for field use and clinical use
- Individuals with Disabilities Education Act
- Wheelchair USA Medical Classification System
- Sport classification

Chapter 16: Evaluating Knowledge

- Discussion of Educational Testing Service
- Importance of planning ahead and reporting results promptly
- Revised sample problems

Chapter 17: Exercise Psychological Measurement

- Directory of psychological measurements
- New problem relating level of exercise to Self-Motivation Inventory

SUCCESSFUL FEATURES

Key words. The key words that are defined in every chapter are highlighted at the beginning of each chapter and boldfaced in the text. The definitions can also be found in the end-of-text glossary.

Objectives. The objectives at the opening of each chapter focus the students' attention on the key concepts that will be discussed in the chapter.

Formulas. Important formulas are numbered throughout the text to provide easy and quick reference to those used frequently in the course and in students' professional lives.

Tables and figures. Many of the graphics have been updated in this edition to give students a visual representation of the concepts discussed in the text.

Summary. The end-of-chapter summary provides a brief overview of what was discussed within the chapter.

Formative evaluation of objectives. This section at the close of each chapter helps to determine if the students have mastered the objectives set forth at the beginning of the chapter.

Additional learning activities. These activities provide students with a way to gain more experience with the concepts presented within the chapter.

ANCILLARIES

Instructor's resources to accompany the eighth edition of *Measurement for Evaluation in Physical*

Education and Exercise Science include an Instructor's Manual, a Computerized Testing Program, and PowerPoint slides. These resources may be downloaded from the Instructor's Resource website (www.mhhe.com/baumgartner8e).

Also available to accompany the text is the student version of SPSS 14.0. This comprehensive statistics package can perform any of the procedures discussed in the text. Contact your McGraw-Hill sales representative for information on packaging options.

ACKNOWLEDGMENTS

We would like to thank the reviewers of the eighth edition for their insightful comments:

Harry Beamon   *Tennessee State University*
Phil Bishop   *University of Alabama*
Lisa C. Colvin   *University of Louisiana-Monroe*
Trey Cone   *University of Central Oklahoma*
M. Allison Ford   *University of Mississippi*
Melissa Knight-Maloney   *Fort Lewis College*
Al Kornspan   *University of Akron*
Sally Schumacher   *Carroll College*
Nestor W. Sherman   *Texas A&M University-Kingsville*
Brent Walker   *Missouri Western State College*

TO THE STUDENT

The major goal of this text is to help you apply the principles of measurement and evaluation to your job. Often, measurement and evaluation are viewed as a necessary evil, not directly related to the real purpose of the job. However, appropriate measurement and evaluation techniques are essential for all professionals in the exercise and sport science and physical education fields who want to be excellent in the conduct of their job duties. This text was designed to help you learn how to use evaluation as an essential part of the total process.

We developed the text with two purposes in mind. First, we want to help you master the essential content, principles, and concepts you need to become an effective evaluator. We tried to provide the practical aspects, the "how" and the "why" of evaluation. We want this text to help you build a foundation based on theoretical concepts so that you can then apply these concepts in developing, using, and evaluating various tests.

Second, we designed the text to provide the practical skills and materials that you will need. We provide a wide assortment of tests, administrative instructions, and norms. We selected the tests, which provide the "how" of evaluation, either for their application to the job setting or for their value in teaching basic concepts discussed in the text.

The computer has become an essential tool for many physical educators and exercise science pro-fessionals. Practical computer applications are provided, by examples, with standard computer programs. As mentioned in the preface, an excellent computer program is available with the book (Student SPSS). Learn to use the computer and programs such as SPSS as a student while expert consultant help is available, and it will be easier to use whatever computer programs are available once you are on the job.

The approach we use in the text follows a teaching method that is an outgrowth of Benjamin Bloom's ideas on "mastery learning." The method stresses letting the student know what is to be learned, providing the material to accomplish the learning, and furnishing evaluation procedures to determine whether the learning has been achieved.

This approach, formative evaluation, is an essential feature of mastery learning. Psychologists maintain that feedback is one of the most important factors in learning. Formative evaluation is designed to provide that feedback. It enables you to diagnose weaknesses, and lets you know the content you have mastered, so that you can put more effort into problem areas.

Instructional objectives at the beginning of each chapter enable you to focus your attention on the concepts to be learned. The **text**—supplemented with class lectures, discussions, projects, and laboratory experiments—provides the information you need to help you achieve the objectives. The **evaluation of objectives** at the end of each chapter help you determine whether you have mastered the skills set forth.

The formative evaluation in this text offers two types of questions. The first, in **question/answer format**, is most appropriate for testing yourself on the statistics content. If you cannot calculate a statistic, you have not mastered the technique. The second type of question requires you to define, summarize, analyze, apply, or synthesize content. This is typical of an **essay-type** question and is more appropriate for testing yourself on basic content, principles, and concepts.

Many students dislike learning by rote. We hope that the use of instructional objectives and formative evaluation will help you to avoid that approach. The objectives and evaluation questions identify key points in a given chapter. Once you have read the chapter, you should be familiar with these points. Finally, we hope that by using this approach you will master important content.

Each student studies differently. However, the following suggestions may help you achieve mastery learning:

1. Before reading a chapter, review the instructional objectives and formative evaluation questions for the chapter. This gives you an overview and directs your attention to the important content areas.
2. Read the chapter, underlining important content. Also, underline material that you do not fully understand. After reading the entire chapter, return to the underlined parts to reinforce the important content and to try to grasp the material you do not fully understand.
3. Without referring to the text, answer the formative evaluation questions. After you have written your answers, go back to the material in the text and check your answers. Spend additional time on the questions that you did not answer correctly. If you do not feel comfortable with your answers to some questions, spend more time on these as well.
4. Practical learning activities are provided at the end of each chapter. Try them. We have found that these exercises help students gain further insight into the statistical or theoretical concepts being stressed. (Many of these suggested activities are enjoyable as well as helpful.)
5. When studying for summative exams, use the formative evaluation questions and your corrected answers as the basis for final review of the instructional objectives of each chapter. Examine the list of key words at the beginning of each chapter. They are a good second means for formative evaluation. If you find that you cannot think of a precise definition of a term, go back over the chapter until you find the term's definition.

We wish you good luck with your evaluating techniques.

T.A.B.
A.S.J.
M.T.M.
D.A.R.

PART

I

Introduction

1 Measurement and
Evaluation in
a Changing Society

1

MEASUREMENT AND EVALUATION IN A CHANGING SOCIETY

CONTENTS

KEY WORDS

age-appropriate physical activity

cardiovascular disease

coronary heart disease

criterion-referenced standard

evaluation

formative evaluation

health-related fitness

intermittent physical activity

measurement

moderate physical activity

norm-referenced standard

norms

obesity

objective

overweight

percentile rank

physical activity

prevalence

subjective

summative evaluation

vigorous physical activity

OBJECTIVES

Professions within the fields of physical education and exercise science are constantly changing. Graduates of exercise and sport science programs are becoming not only teachers and coaches, but also exercise specialists, physical and occupational therapists, personal trainers, sport psychologists, and consultants. Some are even starting or entering private business. Many colleges and universities are expanding their degree programs to include sport management. The process of measurement and evaluation is an integral component of all these professional efforts.

Obesity has reached epidemic proportions in the United States. Regular physical activity can have a positive effect on obesity and other cardiovascular disease risk factors. Strong scientific evidence exists to demonstrate that even moderate increases in physical activity can substantially impact public health. Thus, it is becoming more and more important for students in exercise and sport science programs to understand the construct of physical activity and how to measure it. We expect that exercise and sport science programs will adapt to societal needs by training students more thoroughly in the assessment and promotion of physical activity.

While many factors influence professional preparation in exercise and sport science programs, several contemporary social forces are especially salient. One major force pressuring our educational and public health institutions is demographic change. The American population is aging, and the ethnic mix is changing. Our occupations are becoming more sedentary, and medical and public health officials have concluded that inactivity and obesity are major public health problems. Increasing numbers of older adults and minorities, combined with increasing numbers of obese and sedentary individuals, are adding pressure to health care systems. These forces have led to the development of public health programs that promote establishing and maintaining health through physical activity and weight control. In November 2000, the U.S. Department of Health and Human Services published *Healthy People 2010: Understanding and*

Improving Health, and in 1996, the Surgeon General of the United States issued an important report on physical activity and health. This chapter reviews these historic public health initiatives and integrates them with K–12 physical education and adult fitness programming. These public health initiatives explain why many youth and adult programs have become health-related programs.

This chapter will help you understand the place of measurement and evaluation in our changing social and professional world. After reading Chapter 1, you should be able to

1. Define and differentiate between measurement and evaluation.
2. Define and differentiate between criterion- and norm-referenced standards.
3. Define and differentiate between formative and summative methods of evaluation.
4. Understand models of evaluation as they apply to teaching (K–12) and exercise science settings.
5. Describe the role of public health initiatives in physical education and exercise science.
6. Describe the physical activity guidelines for children.

MEASUREMENT AND EVALUATION

We tend to regard test results as a valid basis for decision making. They govern matters such as student promotions, college acceptances, and defining health-related levels of fitness. The terms *measurement* and *evaluation* are widely used, but often with little regard for their meanings. **Measurement** is the collection of information on which a decision is based; **evaluation** is the use of measurement in making decisions. This chapter clarifies these activities within the changing context of the fields of physical education, exercise science, and **health-related fitness** and introduces the procedures that have evolved to meet the challenges created by these dynamic fields.

Measurement and evaluation are interdependent concepts. Evaluation is a process that uses measurements, and the purpose of measurement is to collect information for evaluation. Tests are used to collect information. In the evaluation process, information is interpreted according to established standards so that decisions can be made. Clearly, the success of evaluation depends on the quality of the data collected. If test results are not consistent (or reliable) and truthful (or valid), accurate evaluation is impossible. The measurement process is an important step in evaluation; improved measurement leads to accurate evaluation. People are different. They vary in body size, shape, speed, strength, and many other respects. Measurement determines the degree to which an individual possesses a defined characteristic. It involves first defining the characteristic to be measured and then selecting the instrument with which to measure that characteristic (Ebel 1973). Stopwatches, tape measures, written tests, skill tests, attitude scales, pedometers, skinfold calipers, treadmills, and cycle ergometers are common instruments used by physical education teachers and exercise specialists to obtain measurements.

Test scores vary from highly **objective** to highly **subjective.** A test is objective when two or more people score the same test and assign similar scores. Tests that are most objective are those that have a defined scoring system and are administered by trained testers. A multiple-choice written test, a stopwatch, skinfold calipers, and an ECG heart rate tracing all have a defined scoring system. Testers need to be trained to secure objective measurements. For example, if percent body fat is to be measured by the skinfold method, the tester needs to be trained in the proper method of measuring a skinfold with a caliper. A highly subjective test lacks a standardized scoring system, which introduces a source of measurement error. We use objective measurements whenever possible because they are more reliable than subjective measurements.

Evaluation is a dynamic decision-making process that involves (1) collecting suitable data (measurement), (2) judging the value of these data according to some standard, and (3) making decisions based on these data. The function of evaluation is to facilitate rational decisions. For the teacher, this can be to facilitate student learning; for the exercise specialist, this could mean helping someone establish scientifically sound weight-reduction goals.

Functions of Measurement and Evaluation

Too often tests are administered with no definite purpose in mind. The ultimate purpose of testing is to enhance the decision-making process so that improvement can be made. Testing can have many purposes. Six general purposes that facilitate the decision-making process are presented below. These are equally applicable to K–12 teachers and exercise specialists.

Placement

Tests can be used to place students in classes or groups according to their abilities. Adult fitness tests are used to determine current status so that an individualized program can be prescribed.

Diagnosis

Tests can be used to diagnose weaknesses. While placement usually involves the status of the individual relative to others, diagnosis is used to isolate specific deficiencies that make for low or an undesirable status. In K–12 settings, tests can identify areas where students need to make improvements. In an exercise or health setting, test results are used to diagnose a problem. For example, a treadmill stress test is used to screen for heart disease.

Evaluation of Achievement

One goal of testing is to determine whether individuals have reached important objectives. Placement, diagnosis, and the evaluation of achievement together form the basis of individualized instruction. In K–12 settings, this can be the achievement of instructional objectives. In exercise settings, this can be meeting important goals or showing progress—for example, documenting changes made during rehabilitation.

Prediction

Test results can be used to predict an individual's level of achievement in future activities, or to predict one measure from another. Prediction often seeks information on future achievement from a measure of present status, and it may help students to select the activities they are most likely to master. For example, an individual found to have a high aerobic capacity may decide to engage in road racing or become a triathlete. The measurement and evaluation process is also used to predict hard-to-measure variables from measures that are more practical. For example, aerobic capacity ($\dot{V}O_2$ max) is estimated from distance run test performance, and percent body fat is estimated from skinfold measures.

Program Evaluation

Test results of participants can be used as one bit of evidence to evaluate the program. By comparing the results of tests for a school district against national norms or standards, or by comparing the yearly changes made within a school district, important decisions can be made. Comparing changes in fitness between tests can provide evidence of the effectiveness of an adult fitness program.

Motivation

Test scores can be motivating. Achievement of important standards can encourage one to achieve higher levels of performance or to participate regularly in physical activity.

Formative and Summative Evaluation

Summative evaluation is the judgment of achievement at the end of an instructional unit, and typically involves the administration of tests at the conclusion of an instructional unit or training period. **Formative evaluation** is the judgment of achievement during the formative stages of learning. Motor-learning research shows that feedback is one of the most powerful variables in learning. Formative evaluation is used to provide feedback to learners throughout the instructional process.

Formative evaluation was developed initially for use in classroom settings. Formative evaluation begins during the early stages and continues throughout instruction. It involves dividing instruction into smaller units of learning and evaluating the student's mastery of these subunits during instruction. Its main purpose is "to determine the degree of mastery of a given learning task and to pinpoint the part of the task not mastered" (Bloom et al. 1971, p. 61). The strength of formative evaluation is that it is used to provide feedback throughout the instructional unit.

Summative evaluation is used to decide whether broad objectives have been achieved. The similarities and differences between formative and summative evaluation identified by Bloom are summarized in Table 1.1.

Formative and summative evaluation and mastery learning were developed for use by classroom teachers (Bloom et al. 1971). However, the logic of the system can be applied to adult fitness programs. Helping adults set realistic fitness goals and using periodic testing to determine current

TABLE 1.1	**Similarities and Differences between Formative and Summative Evaluation**	
	Formative	**Summative**
Purpose	Feedback to student and teacher on student progress throughout an instructional unit	Certification or grading at the end of a unit, semester, or course
Time	During instruction	At the end of a unit, semester, or course
Emphasis in Evaluation	Explicitly defined behaviors	Broader categories of behaviors or combinations of several specific behaviors
Standard	Criterion-referenced	Norm-referenced or criterion-referenced

status can be used to provide feedback that facilitates achievement and motivation. A key element of a successful self-supervised fitness program for NASA executives was periodic fitness testing (Owen et al. 1980). Measuring body weight daily is a behavioral strategy used for weight-reduction programs (deBakey et al. 1984).

Both formative and summative evaluation processes are used for successful fitness training programs. Increases in intensity and/or duration of aerobic exercise can be used to provide feedback (i.e., formative evaluation) to the participant that he or she is improving, and can become a source of motivation to continue in the exercise program. A fitness test after training can be used for summative evaluation, to judge whether fitness goals have been met or whether the training program was successful.

You are encouraged to use the formative evaluation exercises provided after each chapter. After you have read the chapter, attempt to answer the questions. If you cannot answer a question or if you feel unsure of your answer, this is an indication that you need additional work. The key element of formative evaluation is the feedback it provides; it communicates to the participant what has been and what still needs to be achieved. For this course, your instructor probably will administer several major tests that will evaluate your ability to integrate and apply the readings. These would be an example of summative evaluation.

STANDARDS FOR EVALUATION

As previously explained, evaluation is the process of giving meaning to a measurement by judging it against some standard. The two most widely used types of standards are criterion- and norm-referenced. A **criterion-referenced standard** is used to determine if someone has attained a specified level. A **norm-referenced standard** is used to judge an individual's performance in relation to the performances of other members of a well-defined group—for example, 11-year-old boys. Criterionreferenced standards are useful for setting performance standards for all, whereas norm-referenced standards are valuable

for comparisons among individuals when the situation requires a degree of selectivity.

Criterion- and norm-referenced standards have application in a wide variety of settings. They are used extensively in K–12 educational settings, and there is a growing use of both standards in exercise and public health settings. Youth fitness tests have generally evolved from the use of norm-referenced standards to the use of criterion-referenced standards. The two national health-related youth fitness programs are the FITNESSGRAM®/ ACTIVITYGRAM® and the President's Challenge (see Chapter 13). The FITNESSGRAM®/ ACTIVITYGRAM® uses sound criterion-referenced standards. The President's Challenge uses criterion-referenced standards for its Health Fitness Test and has established standards for some of its awards based on normative comparisons. For example, to achieve the Presidential Physical Fitness Award and National Physical Fitness Award, students must achieve above the 85th and 50th percentiles, respectively, on all fitness tests. The popular YMCA program (Golding, Meyers & Sinning 1989) presented in Chapter 11 evaluates adult fitness with norm-referenced standards, but there is a growing trend to use criterion-referenced standards. The criterion-referenced fitness standards are evolving from medical research (Blair et al. 1989, 1995) showing that the relationship between health and aerobic fitness is not linear. Once a level of aerobic fitness is achieved, becoming more fit has little influence on health. These criterion-referenced aerobic standards are provided in Chapter 11.

Norm-Referenced Standards

Norm-referenced standards are developed by testing a large number of people of a defined group. Descriptive statistics are then used to develop standards. A common norming method is to use **percentile ranks.** This type of norm reflects the percentage of the group that can be expected to score below a given value. For example, a 1-mile run time of 11:31 for a boy 11 years of age is at the 25th percentile; only 25% ran slower, while 75% of the 11-year-old boys could be expected to exceed this time.

Percentile rank norms are commonly used to evaluate health status. For example, percentile norms are used at the Cooper Medical Clinic, Dallas, Texas, to communicate adult fitness and health status to patients (Pollock & Wilmore 1990). Procedures for developing percentile rank norms are presented in Chapter 2. Several examples of percentile rank norm-referenced standards are provided in the chapters that follow.

A major concern when using norm-referenced standards is the characteristics of the group on which the standards were developed. The **norm** does not always translate to a desirable level. This can be illustrated by examining blood cholesterol norms from the Cooper Clinic (Pollock & Wilmore 1990). The average cholesterol of men ages 40 to 49 is 214 mg/dl, but this average is not considered a desirable level. A serum cholesterol of less than 200 mg/dl is considered a desirable level for health. The average of the norms from the Cooper Clinic is typical of the general American population, and this elevated average can be traced to a diet high in calories from fats and cholesterol-rich foods. In contrast, blood cholesterol values are much lower in vegetarians, who consume less fat and cholesterol. In this instance, average is not desirable, because it has been shown that there is a powerful relationship between dietary high-fat, high-cholesterol animal products and risk of coronary heart disease mortality (Anderson, Castelli & Levy 1987; Castelli et al. 1977; Wood et al. 1988).

When making norm-referenced evaluations, a useful method is to consider the norms developed on the groups being evaluated as well as on other relevant groups. As an example, adult body composition standards are presented in Chapter 12. These were developed by examining normative data of adults and data published on many other groups, including defined atheletic groups.

Criterion-Referenced Standards

A criterion-referenced standard is a predetermined standard of performance that shows the individual has achieved a desired level of performance. It is unlike a norm-referenced standard in that the performance of the individual is not compared with that of other individuals, but rather just against the standard.

Many authors use the term "criterion-referenced test," suggesting that the difference is not just with the standard, but also with the method used to develop the test (Glaser & Nitko 1971; Safrit 1989). Glaser and Nitko define a criterion-referenced test as one developed to provide measurements that are directly interpretable in terms of explicit performance standards—that is, criterion-referenced. While it is true that some tests used in education were constructed to be criterion-referenced tests, the more common practice is to apply a criterion-referenced standard to a norm-referenced test. For example, the mile run is a common item of a youth fitness test. The mile run previously was norm-referenced, but now it is criterion-referenced. In this instance, the test itself has not changed, only the type of standard used to evaluate the aerobic fitness of youth. All the health-related youth fitness tests (Chapter 13) primarily use criterion-referenced standards.

Determining Accuracy of Criterion-Referenced Standards

Unlike a norm-referenced standard, which uses a continuous variable, a criterion-referenced standard is a dichotomy (a dichotomy is a division into two parts). Terms such as pass-fail, mastery-nonmastery, or positive-negative are used to describe the dichotomy. The validity of the criterion-referenced standard is examined by using a 2×2 contigency table. The accuracy of the criterion-referenced standard is analyzed by comparing the criterion-referenced standard and a criterion that represents the person's true state. This creates four possible options, which are illustrated in Figure 1-1.

Methods of determining the quality of a criterion-referenced standard by estimating its reliability and validity are provided in Chapters 3 and 4. For a more complete discussion, see Safrit (1989) and Looney (1989).

Criterion-referenced test reliability examines the consistency of classification. For example, what percentage of people were consistently classified as passing or failing a test that has been administered two times? Criterion-referenced test validity refers to the accuracy of the classification.

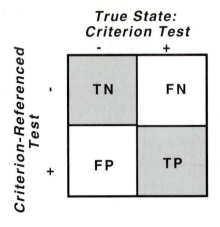

TN - True Negative -
The criterion-referenced test correctly indicates the failure to reach the criterion.

TP - True Positive -
The criterion-referenced test correctly indicates reaching the criterion.

FN - False Negative -
The criterion-referenced test incorrectly indicates the failure to reach the criterion.

FP - False Positive -
The criterion-referenced test incorrectly indicates reaching the criterion.

Figure 1-1

A 2 × 2 table is used to determine the accuracy of a criterion-referenced test. The criterion-referenced test can be wrong in two ways—false negative and a false positive evaluation.
(Source: CSI Software Company, Houston, TX. Reprinted by permission.)

That is, are the participants who are classified as passing or failing by the test classified correctly when compared to their true state?

When applied to youth fitness testing of aerobic fitness, a *true negative* would occur when a participant's performance does not reach the criterion-referenced standard and that participant's true aerobic fitness is considered too low for health purposes. A *true positive* test results when a person's performance reaches the criterion-referenced standard and his or her true aerobic fitness is at a level adequate for health promotion.

A positive test means the presence of the disease. For youth fitness tests, that means the participant does not reach the criterion-referenced standard (i.e., inadequate level of fitness for health purposes). A *false positive* test results when a student's performance does not reach the criterion-referenced standard, when in fact, the student has a true aerobic fitness adequate for health. A *false negative* test results when a student's performance reaches the criterion, when in reality he or she does not have an adequate level of aerobic fitness for health purposes.

When a criterion-referenced interpretation is applied to an exercise stress test that examines the electrical activity of the heart, a positive test indicates the presence of heart disease. The true coronary disease state is defined by a cardiac catheterization test, which involves passing a catheter into the coronary artery. The flow of dye is traced, with heart disease being defined as a coronary blood flow blockage of more than 70%. Because the catheterization test is dangerous, the exercise stress test is used first. A false positive test results when the stress test shows the person has heart disease, but the cardiac catheterization test shows the person is healthy. A false negative results when the stress test suggests that the person does not have heart disease, but the cardiac catheterization shows that heart disease is present.

Limitations of Criterion-Referenced Standards

A common and serious limitation of the criterion-referenced approach is that it is often not possible to find a criterion that explicitly defines mastery. Assume, for example, that a physical education teacher wants a criterion for the mastering of volleyball skills. Tests of mastery of complex motor skills are typically not readily available, and the criterion is then arbitrarily set. There are, however, situations where criterion-referenced standards can be easily set. For example, skill activities such as beginning swimming and tumbling lend themselves to the criterion-referenced approach. The successful execution of these defined skills can be clearly determined and judged.

Examples in Developing Health-Related Criterion-Referenced Standards

Health-related youth fitness tests (see Chapter 13) provide criterion-referenced standards, but the validity of the standards has not been determined because a criterion of true health-related fitness is presently not available. Then how were these standards developed? What may be most important in the development of criterion-referenced standards is the logic and data used to develop these standards. Provided next is the logic and data used to establish the standards for the aerobic fitness and body composition tests of the FITNESSGRAM®/ACTIVITYGRAM®.

Aerobic Fitness

The aerobic fitness tests for FITNESSGRAM®/ACTIVITYGRAM® include the *PACER* and 1-Mile Run tests (Meredith & Welk 2004). Different standards (see Chapter 13) were defined for boys and girls for different ages. The factors considered to establish the criterion-referenced standards were as follows:

1. Published distance run norms show performance times vary by age.
2. Different standards are needed for males and females because of gender differences in $\dot{V}O_2$ max. These differences can be traced to gender differences in blood hemoglobin, body composition, and rates of growth and development.
3. Published data (Blair et al. 1989, 1995) with adults showed that low aerobic fitness increases the risk of all-cause mortality. Chapter 11 provides a discussion of these data.
4. Data (Buskirk & Hodgson 1987) clearly show that aerobic fitness declines with age, but the rate of decline is related to one's lifestyle. Jackson et al. (1995, 1996) showed that rates of decline can be expected for

different levels of physical activity and body composition.
5. Standard equations are available to convert running speed into level of $\dot{V}O_2$ max (Cureton et al. 1995). These equations were used to convert 1-mile run performance into $\dot{V}O_2$ max estimates.

The FITNESSGRAM®/ACTIVITYGRAM® criterion-referenced standards were derived by (1) using the run performance $\dot{V}O_2$ max estimates, (2) considering the expected loss in $\dot{V}O_2$ max due to aging, and (3) considering levels of fitness needed for health promotion (Blair et al. 1989). Cureton & Warren (1990) provide a more detailed analysis of this process.

FITNESSGRAM®/ACTIVITYGRAM® standards are provided in Chapter 13. Youth who meet the FITNESSGRAM®/ACTIVITYGRAM® aerobic fitness standard have a good chance of maintaining a $\dot{V}O_2$ max at a healthy level if they control their weight and remain reasonably active during adulthood.

Body Composition

The FITNESSGRAM®/ACTIVITYGRAM® uses two methods to evaluate body composition of youth. The preferred method involves estimating percent body fat from the sum of triceps and calf skinfolds. The second method is with body mass index (BMI).

1. Research has repeatedly shown that skinfolds provide a valid index of body composition determined by the underwater weighing method (see Chapter 12). This is true for males and females, youths and adults.
2. The distributions of skinfolds and percent body fat of boys and girls differ.
3. Many Americans, especially young women, become overly concerned about being thin. Extreme thinness can cause health problems, such as eating disorders, which can even be fatal.
4. The body composition distributions of both boys and girls are positively skewed (see Chapter 2 for a discussion on skewness), which suggests that a small defined proportion are seriously overweight.

5. The mortality rates associated with body weight for a given height are J-shaped (see Chapter 12). These data show that mortality is associated with being either very thin or very much overweight, but a somewhat wide range of normalcy exists between these two extremes.

The public health data, skewed skinfold fat distribution, and J-shaped weight and mortality relationship were used to define the criterion-referenced standards. Lohman (1992) provides an authoritative discussion of the methods to consider when defining obesity and overweight standards for children and adolescents.

MODELS OF EVALUATION

While the professional environments of a K–12 physical education teacher and an exercise specialist are very different, the evaluation processes used are quite similar. Illustrated next are evaluation models commonly used in K–12 educational and adult fitness settings. The main difference between the two models is test selection.

Educational Model

A primary purpose of teaching is to produce a measurable change in behavior. Figure 1-2 is an evaluation model appropriate for use in K–12 educational settings. This dynamic model integrates measurement and evaluation with the instructional process. Each component of the model is briefly discussed next.

Objective

Preparation of the objective is the first step in the evaluation process, because objectives determine what we will seek to achieve. The objective gives direction to instruction and defines what behaviors we want to change.

Pretest

With some type of pretest, we can answer three questions: (1) How much has already been learned?

(2) What are the individual's current status and capabilities? (3) What type of activity should be prescribed to help achieve the objectives? Pretesting does not necessarily involve administering the same test that will be given after instruction; it can include any form of measurement that helps to answer these questions. For example, observing students swim a width of the pool can be an effective pretest.

Instruction

Sound instructional methods are needed to achieve the agreed-on objectives. Different instructional procedures may be needed to meet students' individual needs.

Measurement

This involves the selection or development of a test to gauge the achievement of the objectives. It is crucial that the test be designed to measure the behavior specified in the objectives. The objectives can be cognitive, affective, psychomotor, or fitness-related. These general types of tests are provided in this text. The key element is to select or develop a test that measures the objective. Often, teachers will need to develop their own tests, because standardized tests may not be consistent with their instructional objectives. Content validity (see Chapter 4) is achieved when the test is congruent with the instructional objective. This is a common method used to provide evidence of test validity in educational settings.

Evaluation

Once the instructional phase has been completed and achievement has been measured, test results are judged (i.e., evaluated) to find whether the desired changes achieved the stated objective.

What happens if students do not achieve the desired objective? Figure 1-2 shows a feedback loop from evaluation back to each component of the model. Failure to achieve the stated objective may be due to any segment of the model. First, it may be discovered that the objectives are not appropriate and may need to be altered. The instruction may not have been suitable for the group, or the selected test may not have been appropriate. The educational evaluation model is dynamic. The

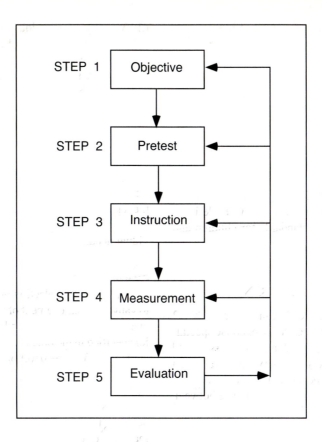

Figure 1-2

A systematic model of evaluation suitable for K–12 educational settings.

evaluation model provides information needed to alter any aspect of the educational process.

Adult Fitness Model

The exercise specialist and the teacher have a common goal: to produce changes in fitness. This may occur in many different settings, such as hospitals, physical therapy clinics, or fitness centers. Personal trainers depend a great deal on the ability to demonstrate improvements in their clients. Figure 1-3 shows how the evaluation model works in exercise settings.

Fitness Test

The first step in the development of an individualized fitness program is a fitness test. This may consist of more than one component. For some,

medical clearance may be needed before the person can start a fitness program. The American College of Sports Medicine has published guidelines (ACSM 2006) for exercise testing and prescription, which are detailed in Chapter 11. Once a person is cleared to engage in an exercise program, he or she is given a fitness assessment.

Exercise Prescription

Once the person's fitness level and goals are known, an exercise prescription is developed. The purpose of the exercise prescription is to define the individual's fitness needs and develop the exercise parameters that are consistent with scientific research (ACSM 1990, 2006). For example, the goal may be to exercise aerobically at 70% of $\dot{V}O_2$ max. In order to prescribe this level of aerobic

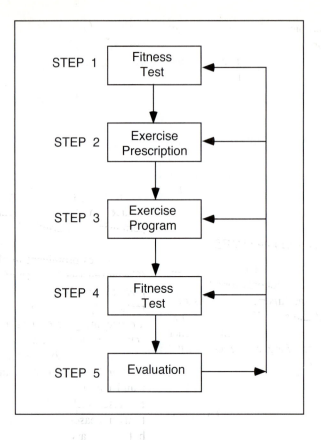

Figure 1-3

Evaluation model applied to adult fitness.
(Source: CSI Software Company, Houston, TX. Reprinted by permission.)

exercise, the person's $\dot{V}O_2$ max would need to be estimated.

Exercise Program

Once the exercise parameters are known, the next step is to develop the person's exercise program. This is based on the initial fitness assessment, exercise prescription, and interests and goals of the person. For example, a program for weight loss would be different from one designed to rehabilitate a knee or back.

Fitness Test

Once the program has been completed, a second fitness assessment is administered. The tests used will likely be the same as those used for the initial fitness assessment.

Evaluation

Once the training program has been completed and the fitness parameters of interest have been measured, test results are judged (i.e., evaluated) to find whether the desired changes have been made. Either norm- or criterion-referenced standards can be used to evaluate performance.

Like the educational model, the fitness evaluation model is dynamic. The model shows a loop from evaluation back to other components of the model. Once changes in fitness are made, the exercise prescription parameters also change. To illustrate: a common guideline for aerobic exercise is

70% of maximum aerobic capacity, or $\dot{V}O_2$ max (ACSM 2006, Jackson & Ross 1997). If the initial exercise program increased the person's aerobic capacity, a new exercise prescription would need to be prepared to maintain a suitable exercise intensity. Other feedback loops in this evaluation model suggest that sometimes the evaluation process can lead an exercise specialist to judge that the fitness tests that were originally chosen are not sensitive enough to document changes in fitness. If this occurs, other, more sensitive, fitness tests are adopted.

PUBLIC HEALTH INITIATIVES

Physical inactivity and obesity are major public health problems. This is true not only for adults, but also for youth. In 1992, the American Heart Association issued a medical and scientific position statement on exercise for health promotion (Fletcher et al. 1992). In 1996, the Surgeon General of the United States issued its historic report on physical activity and health (USDHHS 1996). In 2000, the U.S. Department of Health and Human Services published *Healthy People 2010: Understanding and Improving Health* (USDHHS, 2000).

There are two basic approaches to health promotion. The first attempts to change the behavior of the individual. The second targets a group. The public health approach is designed to change the behavior of the group. This, for example, has been used to alter tobacco use. Smoking cessation programs experience little success in changing the behavior of smokers, but public health programs have been highly successful in lowering the number of people who become smokers. A public health approach has the greatest possible impact when the prevalence is high. The prevalence of physical inactivity is high for both youth and adults. Provided next are overviews of two major public health initiatives: *Physical Activity and Health: A Report of the Surgeon General;* and *Healthy People 2010: Understanding and Improving Health.* As these reports show, public health professionals have targeted K–12 physical education and adult fitness programs as target groups for health promotion.

Surgeon General's Report— Physical Activity and Health

Throughout history people have believed that physical activity is beneficial, but it was not until the 1950s that scientific evidence began to accumulate confirming this belief. Many public health reports have documented that physical inactivity and obesity are major health problems for adults. Regular physical activity and exercise are critical elements of health promotion for older adults. Increased physical activity is associated with a reduced incidence of coronary heart disease, hypertension, noninsulin-dependent diabetes mellitus, colon cancer, depression, and anxiety. These are diseases prominent in older adult populations (Caspersen 1989). Much of adulthood obesity and physical inactivity has its roots in childhood. Unfortunately, youth fitness data show that children are becoming fatter, less aerobically fit, and less active (Hedley et al. 2004; USDHHS 1996).

Physical activity is a complex behavior and its relationship with health is multifaceted. The American Heart Association in its Position Statement on exercise concludes that regular aerobic physical activity increases exercise capacity and plays a role in both primary and secondary prevention of **cardiovascular disease** (Fletcher et al. 1992). In 1996, the Surgeon General of the United States published the report *Physical Activity and Health* (USDHHS 1996). The report was written by leading medical, public health, and exercise scientists. The major purpose of the report was to summarize the existing literature on the role of physical activity in preventing disease and on the status of interventions to increase physical activity. This review led to eight major conclusions (USDHHS 1996, p. 4). These conclusions are given next.

1. People of all ages, both male and female, benefit from regular physical activity.
2. Significant health benefits can be obtained by a moderate amount of physical activity . . . on most, if not all, days of the week. Through a modest increase in daily activity, most Americans can improve their health and quality of life.

3. Additional health benefits can be gained through greater amounts of physical activity. People who can maintain a regular regimen of activity that is of longer duration or of more vigorous intensity are likely to derive greater benefit.

4. Physical activity reduces the risk of premature mortality in general, and of coronary heart disease, hypertension, colon cancer, and diabetes mellitus in particular. Physical activity also improves mental health and is important for the health of muscles, bones, and joints.

5. More than 60% of American adults are not regularly physically active. In fact, 25% of all adults are not active at all.

6. Nearly half of American youths 12 to 21 years of age are not vigorously active on a regular basis. Moreover, physical activity declines dramatically during adolescence.

7. Daily enrollment in physical education classes has declined among high school students from 42% in 1991 to 25% in 1995.

8. Research on understanding and promoting physical activity is at an early stage, but some interventions to promote physical activity through schools, worksites, and health care settings have been evaluated and found to be successful.

The publication of the Surgeon General's report gives a clear signal that physical inactivity is a major health risk. Provided next is a brief discussion of selected public health studies that helped establish that physical inactivity is a major health risk. Provided first are studies that showed occupational physical activity was related to cardiovascular disease, the leading cause of death among Americans. Then the classic Harvard Alumni studies are briefly reviewed. They show the public health impact of a physically active lifestyle. Review of a few classic studies is designed to provide professionals in the broad field of physical activity with a historical perspective on the collection of scientific evidence that supports their profession.

Occupation and Coronary Heart Disease

In the 1950s, medical scientists started to suspect that leading a sedentary life increases the risk of heart disease. The first approach used to study exercise and health was to compare sedentary individuals with those who were physically active. This is a common approach used in physiology, where many studies compare physically active athletes to nonathlete controls. One of the first methods used to study exercise and health was to study occupational groups that varied in physical activity. The approach was to compare heart disease rates of workers who held physically active and less active jobs. The general conclusion of these studies was that individuals who had the most physically demanding jobs suffered fewer fatal heart attacks than their sedentary counterparts. For example, conductors who walked up and down the stairs of double-decker buses in London had fewer heart attacks than the more sedentary bus drivers (Morris et al. 1953). In the United States, postal workers who walked and delivered the mail were found to have a lower incidence of heart disease than those who just stood and sorted it.

One of the classic studies on the relationship of occupational physical activity to heart disease was conducted by medical scientists from the University of Minnesota (Taylor et al. 1962). They studied more than 191,000 American railroad workers. Because of union rules and benefits, railroad workers had excellent medical records, which provided the data for the study. In addition, union rules discourage shifting from one occupation class to another. A 55-year-old person with 20 years of service was likely to have spent all 20 years at the same job.

The occupational groups studied were (1) clerks, (2) switchmen, and (3) section men. The clerks represented men in jobs requiring little physical activity, while the work of the section men was the most physically demanding, and the work demands of the switchmen were moderate. Figure 1-4 presents the death rates ascribed to **coronary heart disease** for the age groups studied. The trends show the well-established influence of age on heart disease: older workers had a higher incidence of heart disease than younger workers. The data also showed that for each age group, the most physically active workers

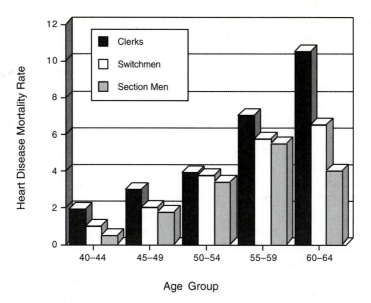

Figure 1-4

The relation between the specific job of railroad workers and death from heart disease. The heart disease death rate was related to the physical activity required by the occupation type. The clerks were most sedentary while the jobs of the section men were the most physically demanding.

(Source: Jackson, A. S. and Ross, R. M. *Understanding Exercise for Health and Fitness*, 1997. Reprinted by permission.)

(i.e., section men) had the lowest heart disease rate, while the least physically active (clerks) had the highest rates. The switchmen were between the two extremes. These data suggested that exercise reduced the risk of heart disease.

An accepted method of quantifying physical activity is by caloric expenditure (ACSM 2006; Ross & Jackson 1990). Paffenbarger and associates (1977) studied the role of caloric expenditure on fatal heart attacks of San Francisco longshoremen. This was an ideal group to study because most workers stayed in the same job throughout their working lives, and the amount of energy expended to perform a job could be determined. The study included a 22-year history of more than 3,500 longshoremen. Workers were divided into three general categories based on the energy expenditure of their jobs. The job categories were as follows:

- High—5.0 to 7.5 kilocalories per minute
- Intermediate—2.4 to 5.0 kilocalories per minute
- Light—1.5 to 2.0 kilocalories per minute

The data showed that for each of the heart disease risk factors, the longshoremen who expended the highest level of energy had the lowest rate of fatal heart attacks. Most impressive was the difference found between those active and inactive workers who had a history of diagnosed heart disease. The heart attack rate of the sedentary workers with a history of heart disease was about double the rate found for the physically active workers with previous heart problems. These data showed that it was not just occupation but energy expenditure that provided a margin of protection for these longshoremen.

Harvard Alumni Studies

The Harvard Alumni studies were surveys of the health and physical activity of nearly 17,000 Harvard alumni. Questionnaire data were used to quantify physical activity in terms of caloric expenditure. The forms of physical activity included various types of sports, stair climbing, and walking.

The researchers showed that caloric expenditure was related to heart attack rate (Paffenbarger et al. 1984) and all-cause mortality (Paffenbarger et al. 1986).

Harvard alumni who consistently exercised during their lifetimes had lower heart attack and mortality rates than their sedentary classmates. Walking regularly, climbing stairs, and playing either light or vigorous sports provided health benefits. The total amount of energy expended through all forms of exercise was highly related to heart disease and mortality rates. As total caloric expenditure increased, heart disease and mortality rates moved progressively lower. The highest heart disease and mortality rates were found in alumni who expended fewer than 500 kilocalories per week. The heart disease and mortality rates dropped steadily with a caloric expenditure up to about 2,000 kilocalories per week and then leveled off. Another study demonstrated that being a college athlete did not reduce risk unless the former athlete remained physically active after leaving college. The alumni at highest risk of a heart attack were those former athletes who were not physically active after college (Paffenbarger et al. 1984).

The key conclusion of the Harvard Alumni studies was that physical activity is a major determinant of public health. This was examined by calculating what public health researchers call community-attributable risk, an estimate of the potential reduction of heart attacks in the population if the risk factor were not present. This calculation considers the prevalence of the risk factor in the population. **Prevalence** in this context refers to the percentage of people in the group who have the risk factor. The higher the prevalence, the greater the potential improvement in public health if the risk factor were eliminated.

Figure 1-5 presents the community-attributable risk estimates for all the risk factors considered in the Harvard Alumni studies. Provided are community-attributable risk estimates for first heart attack and all-cause mortality. Eliminating physical inactivity had the greatest potential public health effect for preventing a heart attack. If all alumni were physically active, the heart attack rate of the Harvard Alumni could be expected to be reduced by nearly 25%. This effect is nearly twice as high as the effect of any other risk factor, including family history of heart disease.

Figure 1-5 also lists the community-attributable risk estimates for all-cause mortality. Elimination of smoking would have the greatest impact on the health of the alumni. Smoking is not only a primary risk factor for heart disease, but also the major cause of lung disease. By eliminating smoking, nearly 25% of the deaths could be prevented. The next most important adverse characteristic was physical inactivity: about 16% fewer deaths would be expected if all alumni were physically active. Since these estimates are additive, the death rate could be cut by nearly 40% if all alumni were physically active nonsmokers. Of least importance was early parental death, which was defined by the death of one or both parents before the age of 65. While the importance of genetics is well understood, these data demonstrate the importance of a physically active lifestyle. Genetics cannot be changed, but lifestyle can. Physical activity professionals, particularly those of you who are reading this book, have the opportunity to impact the health of the nation by encouraging your students and clients to adopt and maintain physically active lifestyles.

Exercising regularly extends life expectancy. Paffenbarger and associates (1986) estimated that at age 35, the physically active alumni could be expected to live about 2.5 years longer than their sedentary classmates. This may not sound like much. However, Paffenbarger[1] has made a rather startling comparison. If all forms of cancer deaths were eliminated (i.e., nobody died from cancer), the average increase in longevity would be just slightly *under* 2 years. In this context, regular forms of suitable exercise are potentially equally beneficial to public health as cancer prevention. The important role of physical activity on public health has been clearly established. Chapters 11 and 12 give additional research on the role of aerobic fitness and obesity in health.

---

[1]Communication with Dr. R. Paffenbarger Jr. at the Texas Chapter Meeting of the American College of Sports Medicine, Houston, Texas, December 1985.

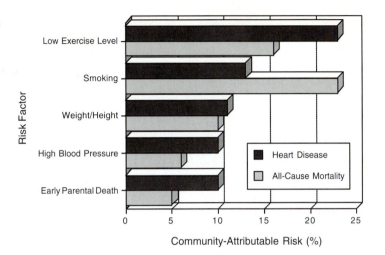

Figure 1-5

The community-attributable risks of first heart attack and all-cause mortality of Harvard alumni. The risk estimates the percentage reduction in heart attacks and deaths that could be expected in the total group if the adverse characteristic were not present. Elimination of sedentary lifestyle and smoking would provide the greatest improvement of public health of Harvard alumni. (Graph developed from published data in Paffenbarger, Wing, and Hyde 1978; Paffenbarger et al. 1984).

(Source: CSI Software Company, Houston, TX. Reprinted by permission.)

Healthy People 2010

Healthy People 2010: Understanding and Improving Health (USDHHS 2000) is a national strategy for significantly improving the health of Americans. It follows the work initiated in 1979 with the publication of *Healthy People: The Surgeon General's Report on Health Promotion and Disease Prevention* (USDHHS 1979), *Promoting Health/Preventing Disease: Objectives for the Nation* (USDHHS 1980), and *Healthy People 2000: National Health Promotion and Disease Prevention Objectives* (USDHHS 1990).

Healthy People 2010 has two major goals:

- to increase the quality and years of healthy life; and
- to eliminate health disparities among Americans.

These two goals reflect the changing demographics of society. The nation is growing older and becoming more diverse.

Healthy People 2010 is a comprehensive, national public health agenda that establishes health promotion and disease prevention objectives.

"Physical Activity" and "Overweight and Obesity" are two of the ten Leading Health Indicators identified in *Healthy People 2010*. The Leading Health Indicators are designed to help direct initiatives to improve health and to help measure the success of these initiatives.

Physical Activity Objectives

Of the 15 objectives in *Healthy People 2010* for Physical Activity, the two presented below were selected to measure progress.

- Increase the proportion of adolescents who engage in vigorous physical activity that promotes cardiorespiratory fitness three or more days per week for 20 or more minutes per occasion.
- Increase the proportion of adults who engage regularly, preferably daily, in moderate physical activity for at least 30 minutes per day.

Regular physical activity is associated with a lower risk of heart disease, diabetes, and colon cancer, as well as lower death rates. Benefits of regular physical activity include decreases in body fat, increases in the strength of muscle and bone, and enhanced psychological well-being. In addition, the improved strength and agility that results from regular physical activity in older adults can reduce the risk of falling and improve functional independence.

Relative to the first Physical Activity objective listed above, in 1999 it was estimated that 65% of high school students engaged in vigorous physical activity three or more days per week for 20 minutes or more per occasion. The goal for *Healthy People 2010* is to increase this to 85%. Regular physical activity for youth is important not only for the health benefits, but also because a physically active lifestyle during youth may continue into adulthood.

Relative to the second Physical Activity objective, it is estimated that 15% of adults engage in moderate physical activity for at least 30 minutes per day five or more days per week. The goal for *Healthy People 2010* is 30%. A brisk walk of 30 minutes per day would result in sufficient caloric expenditure to provide a significant health benefit.

The complete list of Physical Activity Objectives for *Healthy People 2010* is presented in Table 1.2.

TABLE 1.2   Physical Activity Objectives for *Healthy People 2010*

PHYSICAL ACTIVITY IN ADULTS
 1. Reduce the proportion of adults who engage in no leisure-time physical activity.
 2. Increase the proportion of adults who engage regularly, preferably daily, in moderate physical activity for at least 30 minutes per day.
 3. Increase the proportion of adults who engage in vigorous physical activity that promotes the development and maintenance of cardiorespiratory fitness 3 or more days per week for 20 or more minutes per occasion.

MUSCULAR STRENGTH/ENDURANCE AND FLEXIBILITY
 4. Increase the proportion of adults who perform physical activities that enhance and maintain muscular strength and endurance.
 5. Increase the proportion of adults who perform physical activities that enhance and maintain flexibility.

PHYSICAL ACTIVITY IN CHILDREN AND ADOLESCENTS
 6. Increase the proportion of adolescents who engage in moderate physical activity for at least 30 minutes on 5 or more of the previous 7 days.
 7. Increase the proportion of adolescents who engage in vigorous physical activity that promotes cardiorespiratory fitness 3 or more days per week for 20 or more minutes per occasion.
 8. Increase the proportion of the Nation's public and private schools that require daily physical education for all students.
 9. Increase the proportion of adolescents who participate in daily school physical education.
10. Increase the proportion of adolescents who spend as least 50% of school physical education class time being physically active.
11. Increase the proportion of adolescents who view television 2 or fewer hours on a school day.

ACCESS
12. Increase the proportion of the Nation's public and private schools that provide access to their physical activity spaces and facilities for all persons outside of normal school hours (that is, before and after the school day, on weekends, and during summer and other vacations).
13. Increase the proportion of worksites offering employer sponsored physical activity and fitness programs.
14. Increase the proportion of trips made by walking.
15. Increase the proportion of trips made by bicycling.

Source: *Healthy People 2010: Understanding and Improving Health* (USDHHS 2000).

Overweight and Obesity Objectives

One of the greatest challenges facing *Healthy People 2010* is the substantial increase in the proportion of people who are overweight or obese. The two objectives selected to measure progress are as follows:

- Reduce the proportion of children and adolescents who are overweight or obese.
- Reduce the proportion of adults who are obese.

Overweight and **obesity** are associated with an increased risk for coronary heart disease, high blood pressure, type 2 diabetes, stroke, respiratory problems, gallbladder disease, osteoarthritis, sleep apnea, and some forms of cancer. In addition, obesity is more common among particular ethnic groups. For example, Hispanic, African American, Native American, and Pacific Islander women all have higher rates of obesity than Caucasian women.

For adults, *Healthy People 2010* defined overweight as a body mass index (BMI) of ≥ 25 kg·m^{-2} and obesity as a BMI of ≥ 30 kg·m^{-2}. For youth age 6 to 19 years, overweight or obesity was defined as at or above the sex- and age-specific 95th percentile of BMI based on the Centers for Disease Control and Prevention (CDC) Growth Charts. Using these definitions, an alarming increase in the proportion of adults and youth categorized as overweight or obese has been seen over the last three decades. It is estimated that 66% of the adult population is overweight or obese (Hedley et al. 2004).

Relative to the first Overweight and Obesity objective presented above, it is estimated that 16% of children ages 6 to 19 years fall above the 95th percentile for BMI based on CDC Growth Charts. The goal established by *Healthy People 2010* is 5%. This is an important goal to consider not only because of the health problems and negative stigmatization associated with being overweight, but also because overweight and obesity during youth may persist into adulthood.

Relative to the second Overweight and Obesity objective, 30% of adults are categorized as obese (i.e., BMI ≥ 30 kg·m^{-2}). The goal for *Healthy People 2010* is 15%. Disparities exist between different sexes and ethnic groups with respect to the

TABLE 1.3	**Overweight and Obesity Objectives for *Healthy People 2010***

Weight Status and Growth

1. Increase the proportion of adults who are at a healthy weight.
2. Reduce the proportion of adults who are obese.
3. Reduce the proportion of children and adolescents who are overweight or obese.
4. Reduce growth retardation among low-income children under age 5 years.

Source: *Healthy People 2010: Understanding and Improving Health* (USDHHS 2000).

prevalence of overweight and obesity. These disparities should be considered when addressing the physical and social environmental changes that need to be made in order to make progress toward reaching the goal of fewer overweight and obese Americans. Recommended changes in the physical environment include better access to walkways and bicycle paths. Changes to the social environment might include increased social support and development of safe communities.

The complete list of objectives related to the Leading Health Indicator of Overweight and Obesity is presented in Table 1.3. Further information about *Healthy People 2010* can be found at the following website: www.health.gov/healthypeople.

NATIONAL PHYSICAL ACTIVITY GUIDELINES FOR CHILDREN

Charles B. (Chuck) Corbin has been one of the most influential people in the area of youth fitness and physical activity of the past half century. His research in the late 1960s was among the first to assess fatness among youth using skinfold calipers (Corbin 1969; Corbin & Pletcher 1968). Additional work showed the capacity of youth to do vigorous physical activity in an era when distance runs for children were limited to 600 yards. Corbin and his colleagues were influential in changing the focus of youth fitness from skill-related to health-related and provided the basis for many of the criterion-referenced health-related fitness standards in use today.

Corbin and Pangrazi (1998, 2004) authored the national physical activity guidelines for children. These guidelines are presented next.

Guideline 1: Children should accumulate at least 60 minutes, and up to several hours, of **age-appropriate physical activity** on all, or most, days of the week. This daily accumulation should include **moderate** and **vigorous physical activity**, the majority of which is intermittent in nature. Age-appropriate physical activity is activity of a frequency, intensity, duration, and type that leads to optimal growth and development in children and contributes to development of a physically active lifestyle. **Intermittent physical activity** refers to relatively short bursts of movement (several seconds or minutes) interspersed with periods of rest. Moderate physical activity is defined as an intensity equivalent to brisk walking. Moderate-intensity activities can be performed for relatively long periods. Vigorous physical activity is defined as movement that expends more energy than brisk walking. Figure 1-6 shows a computerized metabolic system assessing the exercise intensity for a youth.

Guideline 2: Children should participate in several bouts of physical activity lasting 15 minutes or more each day. It is typical for children that these bouts of activity will include both physical activity and time for rest and recovery. This recognizes that the physical activity needs of children are different from those of adults.

Guideline 3: Children should participate each day in a variety of age-appropriate physical activities designed to achieve optimal health, wellness, fitness, and performance benefits.

Guideline 4: Extended periods (periods of two hours or more) of inactivity are discouraged for children, especially during the daytime hours. This guideline recognizes that children should be active when opportunities to be active are available. Optimally, such opportunities would occur before school, after school, at appropriate times during school, and on weekends.

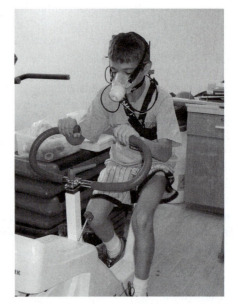

Figure 1-6
Exercise intensity and oxygen uptake in youth can be assessed with computerized metabolic systems.

SUMMARY

Measurement uses reliable and valid tests to secure the data essential to the evaluation process. Evaluation is a decision-making process with a goal for improved instruction. Tests can be used in six general ways: (1) placing students in homogeneous groups to facilitate instruction, (2) diagnosing weaknesses, (3) determining whether important objectives have been reached, (4) predicting performance levels in future activities, (5) comparing a program with others like it, and (6) motivating participants. The evaluation models appropriate for K–12 physical education teachers are quite similar to those used to evaluate adult fitness.

Evaluation is a means of determining whether objectives are being reached, and of facilitating achievement. Formative evaluation clarifies what remains to be achieved; summative evaluation determines whether general objectives have been reached. Evaluation, then, is the feedback system by which the quality of the instructional or training process is monitored. Criterion-referenced standards specify the level of performance necessary to achieve specific instructional objectives; norm-referenced standards identify a level of achievement within a group of individuals.

Medical and public health scientists acknowledge that physical activity and fitness promote health. The importance of exercise for health has been documented with the publication of *Physical Activity and Health: A Report of the Surgeon General*. This report shows that about 65% of high school students are not vigorously active and that physical activity declines during adolescence. Daily enrollment in K–12 physical education programs is declining. The K–12 physical education programs provide one vehicle for increasing the activity levels of Americans. Based on a national telephone survey conducted by the Centers for Disease Control and Prevention (CDC), called the Behavioral Risk Factor Surveillance System (BRFSS), 46% of adults participate in the recommended level of physical activity. Recommended physical activity is defined as at least 30 minutes per day, 5 days per week of moderate-intensity physical activity, or at least 20 minutes per day, 3 days per week of vigorous-intensity physical activity, or both. A relatively large percentage of adults (25%) report participation in no leisure-time physical activity. While activity levels of youth and adults are less than desirable, medical research shows that physical activity has a pos-

itive influence on health. Physical inactivity increases the risk of premature mortality in general, and of coronary heart disease, high blood pressure, colon cancer, and type 2 diabetes. Significant health benefits can be obtained from a moderate amount of daily physical activity. The demographic trends in America are increasing the need for exercise and weight-control programs. Our population is getting older, minorities are growing, and jobs are becoming more sedentary in nature. Older Americans and those from low-income groups have a higher prevalence of inactivity and overweight than the total population. The *Healthy People 2010* public health study identifies physical activity and fitness objectives to be reached by the year 2010. These objectives give direction to both K–12 physical education and adult fitness programs.

Physical activity guidelines for children emphasize that children should accumulate 60 minutes or more of physical activity on all, or most, days of the week. Recognizing that children are not little adults, the physical activity recommendations for children are different from those for adults. Children have unique needs and characteristics. Children will be physically active intermittently, interspersed with periods of rest. Children should participate in both moderate- and vigorous-intensity physical activity and should not be inactive for extended periods.

FORMATIVE EVALUATION OF OBJECTIVES

Objective 1 Define and differentiate between measurement and evaluation.

1. The terms *measurement* and *evaluation* often are used interchangeably. Define each term.
2. What are the key differences between measurement and evaluation?
3. Although measurement and evaluation are distinct functions, explain how they are related.

Objective 2 Define and differentiate between criterion- and norm-referenced standards.

1. What are the key differences between criterion- and norm-referenced standards?
2. Explain how a physical education teacher or exercise specialist could use both types of standards.

Objective 3 Define and differentiate between formative and summative methods of evaluation.

1. Many believe that greater achievement is possible if both formative and summative evaluation are used. Briefly describe formative and summative evaluation.
2. What are the key differences between formative and summative evaluation? Why could you expect to stimulate greater achievement by using both formative and summative evaluation?

Objective 4 Understand models of evaluation as they apply to teaching (K–12) and exercise science settings.

1. What are the steps of the K–12 evaluation model?
2. What are the steps of the exercise science evaluation model?
3. What are the similarities and differences of these two evaluation models?

Objective 5   Describe the role of public health initiatives in physical education and exercise science.

1. What are the major conclusions of the Surgeon General's report *Physical Activity and Health?*
2. What are the two main goals of *Healthy People 2010?*
3. List the fifteen physical activity objectives of *Healthy People 2010.* How do they affect physical educators and exercise scientists?

Objective 6   Describe the physical activity guidelines for children.

1. List characteristics of children's physical activity behavior.
2. How is children's physical activity different from physical activity of adults?

ADDITIONAL LEARNING ACTIVITIES

1. Visit physical education classes and determine if students meet the activity standards recommended in the *Healthy People 2010* report.
2. Visit a public school physical education program and discover the type of fitness test it is using. Many will not be using a health-related fitness test. Does the scientific evidence warrant its use?
3. Visit a facility that conducts an adult fitness program. Identify the types of tests that are administered and the type of program offered.
4. Visit a public school physical education program. Analyze the program and determine the students' level of physical activity.
5. Develop a unit of instruction showing how you could use both formative and summative evaluation procedures.
6. For the same unit of instruction, develop criterion-referenced standards for the tests. Explain your logic and sources of data used to establish the standards.

BIBLIOGRAPHY

American College of Sports Medicine (ACSM). 1990. The recommended quantity and quality of exercise for developing and maintaining cardiorespiratory and muscular fitness in healthy adults. *Medicine and Science in Sports and Exercise* 22: 265–274.

American College of Sports Medicine (ACSM). 2006. *ACSM's guidelines for exercise testing and prescription.* 7th ed. Philadelphia: Lippincott Williams & Wilkins.

Anderson, K. V., W. P. Castelli, and D. Levy. 1987. Cholesterol and mortality: 30 years of follow-up from the Framingham study. *Journal of the American Medical Association* 257: 2176–2180.

Blair, S. N., H. W. Kohl, C. E. Barlow, R. S. Paffenbarger, L. W. Gibbons, and C. A. Macera. 1995. Changes in physical fitness and all-cause mortality: A prospective study of healthy and unhealthy men. *Journal of the American Medical Association* 273: 1093–1098.

Blair, S. N., H. W., Kohl, R. S., Paffenbarger, D. G., Clark, K. H., Cooper, and L. W., Gibbons. 1989. Physical fitness and all-cause mortality: A prospective study of healthy men and women. *Journal of the American Medical Association* 262: 2395–2401.

Bloom, B. S., J. T. Hastings, and G. F., Madaus. 1971. *Handbook on formative and summative evaluation of student learning.* New York: McGraw-Hill.

Buskirk, E. R. and J. L. Hodgson. 1987. Age and aerobic power: The rate of change in men and women. *Federation Proceedings* 46: 1824–1829.

Caspersen, C. J. 1989. Physical activity epidemiology: Concepts, methods, and applications to exercise science. *Exercise and Sport Sciences Reviews* 17: 423–473.

Castelli, W. P., J. T. Doyle, T. Gordon, C. G. Hames, M. C. Hjortland, S. B. Hulley, A. Kagan, and W. J. Zukel. 1977. HDL-cholesterol and other lipids in coronary heart disease. The cooperative lipoprotein phenotyping study. *Circulation* 55: 767–772.

Corbin C. B. 1969. Standards of subcutaneous fat applied to percentile norms for elementary school children. *American Journal of Clinical Nutrition* 22: 836–841.

Corbin C. B. and R. P. Pangrazi. 2004. Guidelines for appropriate physical activity for elementary school children. 2003 update. A position statement. Council for Physical Education for Children (COPEC) of the National Association for Sport and Physical Education.

Corbin, C. and R. Pangrazi. (1998). *Physical activity for children: A statement of guidelines for children ages 5–12. National Association for Sport and Physical Education (NASPE)*. Reston, VA: NASPE.

Corbin, C. B. and P. Pletcher. 1968. Diet and physical activity patterns of obese and nonobese elementary school children. *Research Quarterly* 39: 922–928.

Cureton, K. J., M. A. Sloniger, J. P. O'Bannon, D. M. Black, and W. P. McCormack. 1995. A generalized equation for prediction of $\dot{V}O_2$ peak from 1-mile run/walk performance. *Medicine and Science in Sports and Exercise* 27: 445–451.

Cureton, K. J. and G. L. Warren. 1990. Criterion-referenced standards for youth health-related fitness tests: A tutorial. *Research Quarterly for Exercise and Sport* 61: 7–19.

deBakey, M. F., A. Gotto, L. W. Scott, and J. P. Foreyt. 1984. *The living heart diet*. New York: Simon and Schuster.

Ebel, R. L. 1973. *Measuring educational achievement*. Englewood-Cliffs, NJ: Prentice-Hall.

Fletcher, G. F., S. N. Blair, J. Blumenthal, C. Caspersen, B. Chaitman, S. Epstein, H. Falls, E. S. Froelicher, V. F. Froelicher, and I. K. Pina. 1992. Position statement: Statement on exercise: Benefits and recommendations for physical activity programs for all Americans. *Circulation* 86: 340–344.

Glaser, R. and A. J. Nitko. 1971. Measurement in learning and instruction. In R. L. Thorndike (Ed.). *Educational measurement*. pp. 625–670. Washington, DC: American Council on Education.

Golding, L. A., C. R. Meyers, and W. E. Sinning. 1989. *The Y's way to physical fitness*. 3rd ed. Chicago: National Board of YMCA.

Hedley, A. A., C. L. Ogden, C. L. Johnson, M. D. Carroll, L. R. Curtin, and K. M. Flegal. 2004.

Prevalence of overweight and obesity among U.S. children, adolescents, and adults, 1999–2002. *JAMA* 291: 2847–2850.

Jackson, A. S., E. F. Beard, L. T. Wier, R. M. Ross, J. E. Stuteville, and S. N. Blair. 1995. Changes in aerobic power of men ages 25–70 years. *Medicine and Science in Sports and Exercise* 27: 113–120.

Jackson, A. S. and R. M. Ross. 1997. *Understanding exercise for health and fitness*. 3rd ed. Dubuque, IA: Kendall/Hunt.

Jackson, A. S., L. T. Wier, G. W. Ayers, E. F. Beard, J. E. Stuteville, and S. N. Blair. 1996. Changes in aerobic power of women ages 20–64 years. *Medicine and Science in Sports and Exercise* 28: 884–891.

Lohman, T. G. 1992. *Advances in body composition assessment*. Champaign, IL: Human Kinetics.

Looney, M. A. 1989. Chapter 7. Criterion-referenced measurement: Reliability. In M. J. Safrit and T. M. Wood (Eds.). *Measurement concepts in physical education and exercise science*. Champaign, IL: Human Kinetics.

Meredith, M. D. and G. J. Welk. 2004. *FITNESSGRAM®/ACTIVITYGRAM® test administration manual*. 3rd ed. Champaign, IL: Human Kinetics.

Morris, J. N., J. A. Heady, P. A. B. Raffle, C. G. Roberts, and J. W. Parks. 1953. Coronary heart-disease and physical activity of work. *Lancet* 2: 1053–1057, 1111–1120.

Owen, C. A., E. F. Beard, A. S. Jackson, and B. W. Prior. 1980. Longitudinal evaluation of an exercise prescription intervention program with periodic ergometric testing: A ten-year appraisal. *Journal of Occupational Medicine* 22: 235–240.

Paffenbarger, R. S., W. E. Hale, R. J. Brand, and R. T. Hyde. 1977. Work-energy level, personal characteristics, and fatal heart attack: A birth cohort effect. *American Journal of Epidemiology* 105: 200–213.

Paffenbarger, R. S., R. T. Hyde, A. L. Wing, and C. C. Hsieh. 1986. Physical activity, all-cause mortality, and longevity of college alumni. *New England Journal of Medicine* 314: 605–613.

Paffenbarger, R. S., R. T. Hyde, A. L. Wing, and C. H. Steinmetz. 1984. A natural history of athleticism and cardiovascular health. *Journal of the American Medical Association* 252: 491–495.

Paffenbarger, R. S., A. L. Wing, and R. T. Hyde. 1978. Physical activity as an index of heart attack risk in college alumni. *American Journal of Epidemiology* 108: 161–175.

Pollock, M. L. and J. H. Wilmore. 1990. *Exercise in health and disease*. 2nd ed. Philadelphia: W. B. Saunders.

Ross, R. M. and A. S. Jackson. 1990. *Exercise concepts, calculations and computer applications*. Carmel, IN: Benchmark Press.

Safrit, M. J. 1989. Chapter 6. Criterion-referenced measurement: Validity. In M. J. Safrit and T. M. Wood (Eds.). *Measurement concepts in physical education and exercise science*. Champaign IL: Human Kinetics.

Taylor, H. L., E. Klepetar, A. Keys, et al. 1962. Death rates among physically active and sedentary employees of the railroad industry. *American Journal of Public Health* 52: 1692–1707.

USDHHS (U.S. Department of Health and Human Services). 1979. *Healthy people: The Surgeon General's report on health promotion and disease prevention*. Washington, DC: U.S. Department of Health and Human Services.

USDHHS (U.S. Department of Health and Human Services). 1980. *Promoting health/preventing disease: Objectives for the nation*. Washington, DC: U.S. Department of Health and Human Services.

USDHHS (U.S. Department of Health and Human Services). 1990. *Healthy People 2000: National health promotion and disease prevention objectives*. Washington, DC: U.S. Department of Health and Human Services.

USDHHS (U.S. Department of Health and Human Services). 1996. *Physical activity and health: A report of the Surgeon General*. Atlanta, GA: U.S. Department of Health and Human Services, Centers for Disease Control and Prevention, National Center of Chronic Disease Prevention and Health Promotion.

USDHHS (U.S. Department of Health and Human Services). November 2000. *Healthy People 2010: Understanding and improving health*. Washington, DC: U.S. Government Printing Office.

Wood, P. D., M. L. Stefanick, D. M. Dreon, B. Frey-Hewitt, S. C. Garay, P. T. Williams, H. R. Superko, et al. 1988. Changes in plasma lipids and lipoproteins in overweight men during weight loss through dieting as compared with exercise. *New England Journal of Medicine* 319: 1173–1179.

Quantitative Aspects of Measurement

STATISTICAL TOOLS IN EVALUATION

C O N T E N T S

K E Y   W O R D S

analysis of variance
bell-shaped curve
central tendency
coefficient of determination
continuous scores
correlation
correlation coefficient
cross-validation
curvilinear relationship

dependent variable
discrete scores
frequency polygon
independent variable
interval scores
linear relationship
line of best fit
mean
median
mode
multiple correlation
multiple prediction
negatively skewed curve
nominal scores
normal curve
ordinal scores
percentile
percentile rank

positively skewed curve
prediction
range
rank order correlation coefficient
ratio scores
regression
regression line
simple frequency distribution
simple prediction
standard deviation
standard error of the mean
standard error of prediction
standard score
T-scores
t-test
variability
variance
z-score

O B J E C T I V E S

Presented in this chapter are statistical techniques that can be applied to evaluate a set of scores. Not all techniques are used on every set of scores, but you should be familiar with all of them in order to select the appropriate one for a given situation.

After reading Chapter 2 you should be able to

1. Select the statistical technique that is correct for a given situation.
2. Calculate accurately with the formulas presented.
3. Interpret the statistical value selected or calculated.
4. Make decisions based on all available information about a given situation.
5. Utilize a computer to analyze data.

INTRODUCTION

Once test scores have been collected, they must be analyzed. You can use the data analysis techniques presented here to summarize the performance of a group and to interpret the scores of individuals within that group. Many of these techniques are used and discussed in later chapters. That is why they are presented at this time. Please think of the data analysis techniques as tools that will be used

throughout the book. You should not be anxious about the formulas presented, because most of the time you will use a computer to conduct the data analysis rather than using the formulas to do hand calculations.

You may find a good elementary statistics book, such as Ferguson and Takane (1989), Kuzma and Bohnenblust (2005), Runyon and associates (1996), Sanders (1995), or Vincent (2005), helpful when studying the material in this chapter.

ELEMENTS OF SCORE ANALYSIS

There are many reasons why we analyze sets of test scores. For a large group, a simple list of scores has no meaning. Only by condensing the information and applying descriptive terms to it can we interpret the overall performance of a group, its improvement from year to year or since the beginning of a teaching or training unit, or its performance in comparison to other groups of like background.

Score analysis is also used to evaluate individual achievement. Once information on the overall performance of a group has been obtained, an individual's achievement can be evaluated in relation to it. Analysis also helps the instructor or therapist develop performance standards, either for

09/07/10 Review

evaluative purposes or simply to let individuals know how they are doing.

Types of Scores

Presented in the next two sections is background information that is important to consider when collecting and recording test scores and when selecting a data analysis technique. Scores can be classified as either continuous or discrete. **Continuous scores**, as most are in physical education and exercise science, have a potentially infinite number of values because they can be measured with varying degrees of accuracy. Between any two values of a continuous score exist countless other values that may be expressed as fractions. For example, 100-yard dash scores are usually recorded to the nearest tenth of a second, but they could be recorded in hundredths or thousandths of a second if accurate timing equipment were available. The amount of weight a person can lift might be recorded in 5-, 1-, or 1/2-pound scores, depending on how precise a score is desired. **Discrete scores** are limited to a specific number of values and usually are not expressed as fractions. Scores on a throw or shot at a target numbered 5-4-3-2-1-0 are discrete, because one can receive a score of only 5, 4, 3, 2, 1, or 0. A score of 4.5 or 1.67 is impossible.

Most continuous scores are rounded off to the nearest unit of measurement when they are recorded. For example, the score of a student who runs the 100-yard dash in 10.57 seconds is recorded as 10.6 because 10.57 is closer to 10.6 than to 10.5. Usually when a number is rounded off to the nearest unit of measurement, it is increased only when the number being dropped is 5 or more. Thus, 11.45 is rounded off to 11.5, while 11.44 is recorded as 11.4. A less common method is to round off to the last unit of measure, awarding the next higher score only when that score is actually accomplished. For example, an individual who lifts a weight 8 times but cannot complete the 9th lift receives a score of 8.

We can also classify scores as ratio, interval, ordinal, or nominal (Ferguson & Takane 1989). How scores are classified influences whether calculations may be done on them. **Ratio scores** are the highest level of classification. They have a common unit of measurement between each score and a true zero point so that statements about equality of ratios can be made. Length and weight are examples, since one measurement may be referred to as two or three times that of another. **Interval scores** have a common unit of measurement between each score but do not have a true zero point. (A score of 0 as a measure of distance is a true zero, indicating no distance. However, a score of 0 on a knowledge test is not a true zero because it does not indicate a total lack of knowledge; it simply means that the respondent answered none of the questions correctly.) Most physical performance scores are either ratio or interval. **Ordinal scores** do not have a common unit of measurement between each score, but there is an order in the scores that makes it possible to characterize one score as higher than another. Class ranks, for example, are ordinal: if three students receive push-up scores of 16, 10, and 8, respectively, the first is ranked 1, the next 2, and the last 3. Notice that the number of push-ups necessary to change the class ranks of the second and third students differs. Thus there is not a common unit of measurement between consecutive scores. **Nominal scores** are the lowest level of classification. They cannot be rank ordered and are mutually exclusive. For example, individuals can be classified by sport preference, but we cannot say that one sport is better than another. Gender is another example. Scores may be treated as if they have a lower classification than their actual classification. Thus, interval scores may be treated like ordinal scores or nominal scores if so desired.

Common Unit of Measure

Many scores are recorded in feet and inches or in minutes and seconds. To analyze scores, they must be recorded in a single unit of measurement, usually the smaller one. Thus distances and heights are recorded in inches rather than feet and inches, and times are recorded in seconds rather than minutes and seconds. Recording scores in the smaller unit of measure as they are collected is less time-consuming than converting them into that form later.

Calculators and Computers

Much of the information presented in this section is background information concerning using the computer for data analysis. We are trying to convince students that data analysis is easy if a computer is used.

The analysis of a set of test scores is conducted in three steps: (1) selecting the appropriate analysis technique, (2) calculating with the analysis technique, and (3) interpreting the result of the analysis technique. Using a calculator or computer to quickly and accurately accomplish step 2 reduces the drudgery of analyzing a set of scores. In his classes the first author of this book has his students use a calculator or computer to accomplish step 2 whenever possible. Thus, his students seldom hand calculate the analysis technique.

Score analysis should be accurate and quick. Particularly when a set of scores is large, say, 50 or more, calculators and computers should be used to ensure both accuracy and speed. Today calculators are relatively inexpensive. A calculator will serve you well as a student and in your career. Your calculator should have the four basic mathematical operations, plus square root and squaring keys, a memory, and some of the basic statistical values.

Calculators work well to a point, but when the number of scores is very large, the use of a calculator is time-consuming and the user tends to make more errors. Computers are very fast and accurate and are available in school districts and universities, agencies, and businesses. Provided with each statistical example in this chapter is an example of the desktop computer application. Sometimes the output from the desktop computer program will have more on it than has been discussed in this chapter. In these cases, do not be concerned.

Throughout Chapter 2, we will reference computer programs from the SPSS version 14.0 (2005a) package of statistical programs. There are many reasons for selecting the SPSS package. It provides all of the statistical values and graphs you will ever

need as a teacher, exercise specialist, therapist, or researcher. The SPSS package is found in universities, secondary schools, businesses, industries, and agencies, and can be installed on a single computer or on all the computers in a computer lab. There are versions of SPSS for mainframe computers, and for desktop computers using the Windows operating system. Although the standard desktop computer version of SPSS is expensive, the SPSS Student Version 13.0 (2005b) is reasonably priced, and it will meet almost all of your statistical needs as a student and as a professional on the job. All desktop computer versions are similar; so if you learn one you can easily change to another version (e.g., change from student version to standard version). No one wants to have to enter a large set of data more than once. Another nice feature of SPSS is that data entered in the program can be used in another program (exported to another program), and data entered using another program can be imported into SPSS. A copy of the student version of SPSS Student Version 13.0 is available from the book publisher for about $15.00.

There are other packages of statistical computer programs very similar to SPSS, such as SAS version 9.1 for Windows (SAS 2005) and JMP version 5.1 (SAS 2004). There is a Macintosh version of SPSS version 14.0. JMP and SAS are available with both a Macintosh and a Windows version. On many campuses, SPSS or another good package of statistical computer programs will be installed on the computers to which you have access. In this case, use what is available. If it is SPSS, there is no reason to purchase the student version of SPSS unless you need it to work on your computer at home and/or you think it is a good professional investment. If there is not a good package of statistical computer programs installed on your campus computers, then installing the student version of SPSS on a computer or having each student purchasing a copy of the student version of SPSS may be the solution. The Excel program, which is part of Microsoft Office, can be used for statistical analysis. It may not be as versatile as SPSS, but it is available on most desktop computers.

The important thing is that what you learn to use as a student is either available or prepares you to use what is available when you become a professional. Learning to use a very expensive program while in college makes no sense if the program will not be available to you on the job. It is helpful to become computer proficient while in college, where there are many people to help you learn how to use the computer and answer your questions when you have problems. Once you are working, you may have to solve all of the problems yourself. Few students, once they are on the job, will be able to do an adequate job of data analysis using the statistical techniques presented in this book without using the computer to handle the large amount of data.

When entering data to be computer analyzed, always save the data on disk so that if you have to reanalyze the data because of a mistake in the original analysis or need to conduct a different analysis, the data do not have to be reentered. Additional analysis on the data is quite common, and for large amounts of data it is inconvenient to reenter it. If the data are saved on disk, the data has to be saved as a file with a name. The computer program will ask the name of the data file to be analyzed.

Versions of the SPSS package of statistical programs have changed rapidly. The examples of printouts from SPSS programs presented in this book were developed using version 14.0, but printouts from later versions are for all practical purposes the same.

Computer programs come with instruction manuals. The user must read the manual to learn how to use the program. There is a set of manuals for each version of SPSS. If there are few changes in SPSS from the older version to the newer version, the manuals for either version will be sufficient. A small manual, *Brief Guide* (SPSS 2005c), is excellent. The SPSS Student Version 13.0 (2005b) sold commercially has an excellent manual, but it is not part of the student version distributed with this book. Throughout Chapters 2 and 3 in this book, programs in the SPSS package will be referenced. Sufficient instructions on using SPSS are presented in Appendix A. More complete instructions are found in the manuals. Guides for using SPSS version 14.0 are available and quite helpful (Pavkov & Pierce 2007). Larose (1998) has a guide for using SAS.

The steps to follow in getting into SPSS, entering the data, saving the data, and editing the data are presented in sections 1 through 4 of the SPSS 14.0 for Windows Basics part of Appendix A. The steps used to analyze the data and print the output of the analysis are presented in sections 5 and 6 of the document. Sections 7 through 9 of this part of Appendix A have additional useful information. In the SPSS 14.0 for Windows Statistical Procedures part of Appendix A, there are directions for using the analysis procedures selected in section 5 of the SPSS 14.0 for Windows Basics part of Appendix A.

The most time-consuming part of analyzing a set of scores may be the data entry. If there are a limited number of computers available with SPSS installed on them, students may find that getting access to a computer is a problem. One solution is to have students install the student version of SPSS on their personal computer using the SPSS disk that is available with this book. A second solution is to have students enter and save their data using the Excel program (see Appendix B) and then analyze their data using SPSS. When getting into SPSS, you can indicate that the saved data file is from Excel.

ORGANIZING AND GRAPHING TEST SCORES

Simple Frequency Distribution

The 50 scores in Table 2.1 are not very useful in their present form. They become more meaningful if we know how many people received each score when we order the scores. To do this, we first find the lowest and highest scores in the table. Now we find the number of people who received each score between the lowest (46) and the highest (90) by making up a tally, as illustrated in Figure 2-1.

Notice that all possible scores between 40 and 99 appear on the chart. The first score in Table 2.1 is 66, so we make a mark in row 60 under column 6 (60 + 6 = 66). This mark indicates that one score of 66 has been tabulated. We continue through the table, making a mark in the appropriate row and column for each score.

Once the scores are ordered, it is easy to make a simple frequency distribution of the results, as *[handwritten margin notes: "09/02 Astros (are not in class)"; "several times"; "11 frequency"; "rank"; "called me art."; vertical left margin: "The number of score has been repeated"]*

TABLE 2.1		Standing Long Jump Scores for 50 Junior High School Boys		
66*	67	54	63	90
56	56	65	71	82
68	68	76	55	78
47	58	68	78	76
46	68	68	90	62
58	49	62	84	75
75	65	66	72	73
71	75	83	83	64
60	76	65	79	56
68	70	48	77	59

*66 inches

With a large number of scores, forming a simple frequency distribution is time-consuming without a computer. The computer allows you to enter the scores into the computer and to analyze them using any one of a number of programs. Most packages of statistical programs for mainframe and desktop computers have a frequency count program. The SPSS Frequencies program is such a program. The directions for using the Frequencies program are presented in section 1 of the SPSS 14.0 for Windows Statistical Procedures part of Appendix A. The output from the Frequencies program in SPSS for the data in Table 2.1 is presented in Table 2.2. The frequency count program in SPSS and many packages of statistical programs rank order the scores from smallest to largest (ascending order), which is desired if a large score is better than a small score. The Frequencies program in SPSS does have an option for listing the scores largest to smallest (decending order), which must be used if a small score is good. From Table 2.2 it can be seen that test scores were from 46 to 90, and six people scored 68. Other useful information provided is the percentage of the total group receiving each score (Percent column), and the cumulative summing of the percentage column (Cum.% column) starting at the top with the worst score and working downward to the best. For the score of 68, 6 boys received the score, 12% of all the scores were 68, and 58% of the scores were 68 or less.

shown in the first two columns of Table 2.2. We made Table 2.2 the way a computer program does it by listing the scores in rank order with the worst score first. In most cases, the lower scores are worse scores, but this is not true of running events, numbers of errors or accidents, and so on. A **simple frequency distribution** of a running event would list the higher scores first.

From a simple frequency distribution we can determine the spread of scores at a glance, as well as the most frequently received score and the number of people receiving each score. For example, from Table 2.2 we can see that the scores varied from 46 to 90, that the most frequently received score was 68, and that with one exception all scores had a frequency of 3 or less.

Grouping Scores for Graphing

We could present the information in Table 2.2 in the form of a graph. If there are many different

	0	1	2	3	4	5	6	7	8	9
40							/	/	/	/
50					/	/	///		//	/
60	/		//	/	/	///	//	/	⫶NHL I	
70	/	//	/	/		///	///	/	//	/
80			/	//	/					
90	//									

Figure 2-1

Ordering the set of scores in Table 2.1.

[handwritten: "Tally"]

TABLE 2.2	Simple Frequency Distribution of Standing Long Jump Scores of 50 Junior High School Boys in Table 2.1		
Score	**Frequency**	**Percent**	**Cum. %**
46.00	1	2.0	2.0
47.00	1	2.0	4.0
48.00	1	2.0	6.0
49.00	1	2.0	8.0
54.00	1	2.0	10.0
55.00	1	2.0	12.0
56.00	3	6.0	18.0
58.00	2	4.0	22.0
59.00	1	2.0	24.0
60.00	1	2.0	26.0
62.00	2	4.0	30.0
63.00	1	2.0	32.0
64.00	1	2.0	34.0
65.00	3	6.0	40.0
66.00	2	4.0	44.0
67.00	1	2.0	46.0
68.00	6	12.0	58.0
70.00	1	2.0	60.0
71.00	2	4.0	64.0
72.00	1	2.0	66.0
73.00	1	2.0	68.0
75.00	3	6.0	74.0
76.00	3	6.0	80.0
77.00	1	2.0	82.0
78.00	2	4.0	86.0
79.00	1	2.0	88.0
82.00	1	2.0	90.0
83.00	2	4.0	94.0
84.00	1	2.0	96.0
90.00	2	4.0	100.0

scores, the graph is usually formed by grouping like scores together. A graph shows the general shape of a score distribution. In grouping a set of scores, we try to form about 15 groupings. To do this, divide the difference between the largest and smallest scores by 15 and round off the result to the nearest whole number if necessary (Interval size = [largest score – smallest score]/15). This number, the interval size, tells us how many scores to group together. Design the first grouping to contain the best score.

Problem 2.1   Group the 50 standing long jump scores listed in Table 2.2.

Solution   Before we can determine the actual groupings, we must determine the interval size.

Step 1

From the table we see that the largest score is 90 and the smallest is 46, giving us an interval size of 3:

$$\text{Interval size} = \frac{90 - 46}{15} = \frac{44}{15} = 2.9 = 3$$

Grouping	Tally	Frequency
44–46	/	1
47–49	///	3
50–52		0
53–55	//	2
56–58	THL	5
59–61	//	2
62–64	////	4
65–67	THL /	6
68–70	THL //	7
71–73	////	4
74–76	THL /	6
77–79	////	4
80–82	/	1
83–85	///	3
86–88		0
89–91	//	2

Figure 2-2

Grouping of data in Table 2.1.

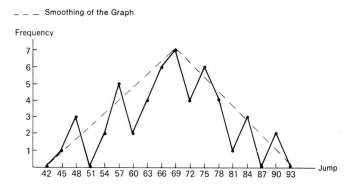

Figure 2-3

A graph of standing long jump scores recorded in inches from Figure 2-2.

Step 2

The first grouping must contain 3 possible scores, including the score 46 (the worst score). The first grouping of 44–46 was selected. Once the first grouping is established, it is easy to work up the rest as presented in Figure 2-2.

Figure 2-3 is a graph of the 50 scores in Figure 2-2. Test scores, in intervals of 3 (only midpoints are plotted), are listed along the horizontal axis, from low scores on the left to high scores on the right. The frequency is listed on the vertical axis, starting with 0 and increasing upward. We place a dot above each

score to indicate its frequency. For example, the dot above score 66 is opposite the frequency value 6, indicating that 6 students received scores in the grouping 65–67. By connecting the dots with straight lines, we complete the graph, forming an angled figure called a **frequency polygon**.

By smoothing out the frequency polygon, we create a curve that, by its shape, tells us the nature of the distribution. In Figure 2-3 the smoothing out is indicated by the broken line. If that line resembles the curve in Figure 2-4, the graph is called a **normal** or **bell-shaped curve**. The normal curve is

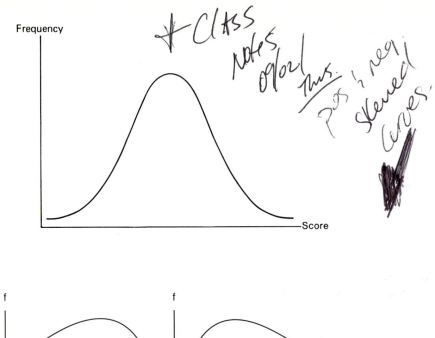

Figure 2-4

A normal curve.

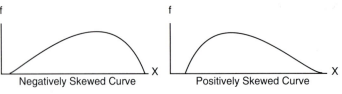

Figure 2-5

Negatively skewed and positively skewed curves.

discussed in detail later in the chapter and referenced in several other chapters.

When a smoothed graph has a long, low tail on the left, indicating that few students received low scores, it is called a **negatively skewed curve**. When the tail of the curve is on the right, the curve is called **positively skewed** (see Figure 2-5).

A computer can be used to create a graph. An option of most desktop computer programs is any number of groupings and several different types of graphs. The data in Table 2.1 was analyzed using the Line Chart program in SPSS. See section 18 of the SPSS 14.0 for Windows Statistical Procedures part of Appendix A for instructions on using it. The graph is presented in Figure 2-6. Another type of graph that is quite common is a *histogram*. Again, the frequencies for the intervals are plotted and bars are constructed at the height of the frequency running the full length of the interval. A histogram for the data in Table 2.1 is presented in Figure 2-7.

This was generated by the Histogram program in SPSS with the option that a normal curve be superimposed on the graph. See section 17 of the SPSS 14.0 for Windows Statistical Procedures part of Appendix A for instructions on using it. Notice that the intervals in Figures 2-3, 2-6, and 2-7 differ. This is because the desktop computer picked a different number of groupings.

DESCRIPTIVE VALUES

Once a large set of scores has been collected, certain descriptive values can be calculated—values that summarize or condense the set of scores, giving it meaning. Descriptive values are used, not only to evaluate individual performance by the person who administered the test, but also to describe the group's performance or compare its performance with that of another group.

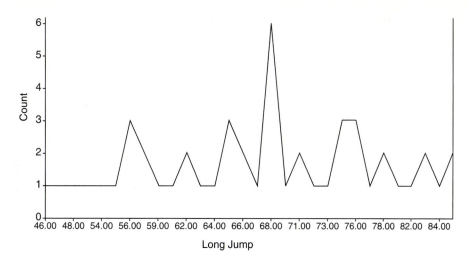

Figure 2-6
Computer-generated frequency polygon for the Table 2.1. data.

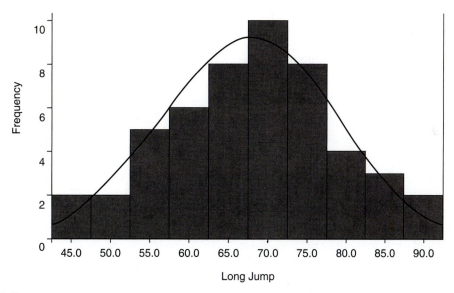

Figure 2-7
Computer-generated histogram for the Table 2.1. data with a normal curve superimposed.

Measures of Central Tendency

One type of descriptive value is the measure of **central tendency**, which indicates those points at which scores tend to be concentrated. There are three measures of central tendency: the mode, the median, and the mean.

Mode

The **mode** is the score most frequently received. It is used with nominal data. In Table 2.2 the mode is 68; more students received a score of 68 than any other one score in the set. It is possible to have several modes if several scores tie for most frequent. The mode is not a stable measure because the addition or deletion of a single score can change its value considerably. In Table 2.2, if two of the students who scored 68 had scored 66, the modes would be 66 and 68. Unless the data are nominal or the most frequent score is desired (e.g., most frequent injury or disease), other measures of central tendency are more appropriate.

Median

The **median** is the middle score; half the scores fall above the median and half below. It cannot be calculated unless the scores are listed in order from best to worst. Where n is the number of scores in the set, we can calculate the position of the approximate median using the following formula:

$$\text{Position of approximate median} = \frac{n + 1}{2} \quad \textbf{(2.1)}$$

Notice that the formula calculates the median's position, or rank, in the listing—not the median itself. The approximate value, always a whole or half number, is that score in the position determined by the equation.

Problem 2.2 Find the approximate median score for these 9 numbers: 4, 3, 1, 4, 10, 7, 7, 8, and 6.

Solution First, order the listing of scores. The approximate median score is the 5th score in the ordered listing, or the score 6.

Position of approximate median =

$$\frac{9 + 1}{2} = \frac{10}{2} = 5, \text{ or the 5th score}$$

10, 8, 7, 7, 6, 4, 4, 3, 1
          ⬆—Median

Problem 2.3 Find the approximate median score for these 6 numbers: 1, 3, 4, 5, 6, and 10.

Solution First, order the listing of scores. The approximate median score is that score that falls halfway between the 3rd and 4th scores in the ordered listing, or the score 4.5.

Position of approximate median =

$$\frac{6 + 1}{2} = \frac{7}{2} = 3.5, \text{ or the 3.5th score}$$

10, 6, 5, 4, 3, 1
         ⬆— Median

The approximate value of the median is often used by teachers, exercise specialists, and other practitioners in preference to the exact value, which is harder to obtain and unnecessarily precise. Notice that the value of the median is affected only by the position, not the value, of each score. If, in Problem 2.2, the scores were 10, 8, 7, 6, 6, 3, 2, 1, and 0, the approximate median would still be 6. This characteristic of the median is sometimes a limitation.

When scores are listed in a simple frequency distribution, we can obtain either an approximate or an exact value of the median. The approximate value of the median for the scores in Table 2.2 falls halfway between the 25th and 26th scores, at a median score of 68. Notice that we count down the frequency column from the worst score to the 25th and 26th scores received; we do not work in the score column until we have reached the approximate median value.

Researchers are likely to need an exact value of the median. When scores in a simple frequency distribution are listed from worst to best, we can calculate the exact value of the median.

The calculation of the median is a three-step process:

Step 1
Develop a simple frequency distribution like the one in Table 2.2, by hand or by using a computer, listing the worst score first.

Step 2
Go down the score column until a score (X) with a Cum. % of at least 50 is found.

Step 3
Calculate the median using the following formula:

$$\text{Median} = \text{lrl} + \left(\frac{50 - \text{Cum.\% above X}}{\text{Percent for X}} \right)(\text{UM}) \quad \textbf{(2.2)}$$

where X is the score that has a Cum. % of at least 50, lrl is the lower real limit (X − .5UM), Cum. % above X is the Cum. % for the score above X, and UM is the unit of measurement in which the scores are expressed.

Problem 2.4 Find the exact median score for the scores listed in Table 2.2.

Solution Because the scores in Table 2.2 are presented in a simple frequency distribution, [**Step 1**] has been done.

Step 2

Go down the score column and the score 68 is the first score with a Cum. % of at least 50.

Step 3

Where X is 68 (from Step 2), lrl is 67.5 (68 − .5), Cum. % for the score above X is 46, percent for X is 12, and UM is 1 (because the scores are recorded in whole numbers [inches], UM is 1), the exact median score is 67.83:

$$\text{Median} = 67.5 + \left(\frac{50 - 46}{12}\right)(1)$$

$$= 67.5 + \left(\frac{4}{12}\right)(1) = 67.5 + .33$$

$$= 67.83$$

Notice how close this is to the approximate median score, 68.

When a small score is a good score as in a running event, the score's in a simple frequency distribution are listed from worst (large score) to best (small score) as shown below and the median formula is correct.

Problem 2.5 Find the exact median score of the 100-yard dash times listed in the following frequency distribution.

Score	Frequency	Percent	Cum. %
11.0	2	5.00	5.00
10.7	5	12.50	17.50
10.5	9	22.50	40.00
10.4	8	20.00	60.00
10.3	7	17.50	77.50
10.2	4	10.00	87.50
10.1	3	7.50	95.00
10.0	2	5.00	100.00

Solution X is 10.4 since it has a Cum. % of at least 50, lrl is 10.35 (10.4 − .05), Cum. % for the score above X is 40, percent for X is 20, and UM is .1 (because the scores are in tenths of a second, UM is .1), so the exact median score is 10.4:

$$\text{Median} = 10.35 + \left(\frac{50 - 40}{20}\right)(.1)$$

$$= 10.35 + \left(\frac{10}{20}\right)(.1)$$

$$= 10.35 + (.5)(.1)$$

$$= 10.4$$

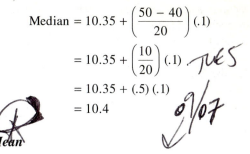

TUES 9/07

Mean

The mean is ordinarily the most appropriate measure of central tendency with interval or ratio data. It is affected by both the value and the position of each score. The **mean** is the sum of the scores divided by the number of scores.

$$\bar{X} = \frac{\Sigma X}{n} \qquad \qquad \textbf{(2.3)}$$

where $\bar{X}$ is the mean, ΣX is the sum of the scores, and n is the number of scores.

Problem 2.6 Calculate the mean of the following scores: 2, 3, 6, 7, 1, 5, and 10.

Solution Where ΣX is 34 and n is 7, the mean is 4.86:

$$\bar{X} = \frac{34}{7} = 4.857 = 4.86$$

Notice that the scores need not be ordered from highest to lowest to calculate the mean. For example, the mean for the scores in Table 2.1 is 67.78, the sum of the randomly ordered scores divided by 50.

When the graph of the scores is a normal curve, the mode, median, and mean are equal. When the graph is positively skewed, the mean is larger than the median; when it is negatively skewed, the mean is less than the median. For example, the graph for the scores 2, 3, 1, 4, 1, 8, and 10 is positively skewed, with the mean 4.14 and the median 3.

The mean is the most common measure of central tendency. But when scores are quite skewed or lack a common interval between consecutive scores (as do ordinal scores), the median is the best measure of central tendency. The mode is used only when the mean and median cannot be calculated (e.g., with nominal scores) or when the only information wanted is the most frequent score (e.g., most common uniform size, most frequent error).

Measures of Variability

A second type of descriptive value is the measure of **variability**, which describes the set of scores in terms of their spread, or heterogeneity. For example, consider these sit-up scores for two groups:

Group 1	Group 2
9	5
5	6
1	4

For both groups the mean and median are 5. If you simply report that the mean and median for both groups are identical without showing the scores, another person could conclude that the two groups have equal or similar ability. This is not true: Group 2 is more homogeneous in performance than is Group 1. A measure of variability is the descriptive term that indicates this difference in the spread, or heterogeneity, of a set of scores. There are two such measures: the range and the standard deviation.

Range

The range is the easiest measure of variability to obtain and the one that is used when the measure of central tendency is the mode or median. The **range** is the difference between the highest and lowest scores. For example, the range for the scores in Table 2.2 is 44 (90 – 46). The range is neither a precise nor a stable measure, because it depends on only two scores and is affected by a change in either of them. For example, the range of scores in Table 2.2 would have been 38 (84 – 46) if the students who scored 90 had been absent.

Standard Deviation

The **standard deviation** (symbolized s) is the measure of variability used with the mean. It indicates the amount that all the scores differ or deviate from the mean—the more the scores differ from the mean, the higher the standard deviation. The sum of the deviations of the scores from the mean is always 0. Provided are two types of formulas: (1) the definitional formula and (2) a calculational formula. The definitional formula illustrates what the standard deviation is, but is more difficult to use. The calculational formula is easier to use if you have only a simple calculator. They will both be illustrated by example.

The definitional formula for the standard deviation is this:

$$s = \sqrt{\frac{\Sigma\,(X - \bar{X})^2}{n - 1}} \quad \text{(definitional formula)}$$

$$(2.4)$$

where s is the standard deviation, X is the scores, $\bar{X}$ is the mean, and n is the number of scores.

Some books, calculators, and computer programs will use the term n rather than n – 1 in the denominator of the standard deviation formula. Many introductory statistics books have a comprehensive discussion of this point.

Problem 2.7a   Compute the standard deviation using the definitional formulas for the following set of scores: 7, 2, 7, 6, 5, 6, 2.

Solution   The process has four steps: calculate the mean, subtract the mean from each score, square the differences, and determine s. After calculating the mean, we can combine Steps 2 and 3 by creating a table, working across the rows, and then totaling the columns. Finally s is calculated.

Step 1

$$\bar{X} = \frac{\Sigma X}{n} = \frac{35}{7} = 5$$

Steps 2–3

X	$(X - \bar{X})$	$(X - \bar{X})^2$
7	(7 – 5) 2	4
2	(2 – 5) – 3	9
7	2	4
6	1	1
5	0	0
6	1	1
2	–3	9
$\Sigma = 35$	$\Sigma = 0$	$\Sigma = 28$

Step 4

$$s = \sqrt{28/(7-1)} = \sqrt{4.67} = 2.2$$

(by Formula 2.4)

Some calculators will calculate the standard deviation once the data is entered. These calculators provide the option of using n or n – 1 in the denominator. Desktop computer programs usually use n – 1 in the denominator.

The definitional formula is seldom used to calculate the standard deviation by hand, because it is cumbersome when the mean is a fraction. Instead, the following formula is used to calculate s:

$$s = \sqrt{\frac{\Sigma X^2 - (\Sigma X)^2 / n}{n - 1}}$$ (calculational formula)

(2.5)

where ΣX^2 is the sum of the squared scores, ΣX is the sum of the scores, and n is the number of scores.

Problem 2.7b Compute the standard deviation using the computational formulas for the following set of scores: 7, 2, 7, 6, 5, 6, 2.

Solution The process has three steps: calculate ΣX, calculate ΣX^2, and determine s. We can combine the first two steps by creating a table, working first across the rows and then totaling the columns:

X	X²
7	49
2	4
7	49
6	36
5	25
6	36
2	4
$\Sigma = 35$	$\Sigma = 203$

Where ΣX is 35, ΣX^2 is 203, and n is 7, the standard deviation is 2.2:

$$s = \sqrt{\frac{203 - 35^2 / 7}{7 - 1}} = \sqrt{\frac{203 - 1225 / 7}{6}}$$

$$= \sqrt{\frac{203 - 175}{6}} = \sqrt{4.67} = 2.2$$

Notice that with this formula the scores are listed in a column and the square of each score is listed in a second column. The sums of these two columns are needed to calculate the standard deviation.

Remember that the standard deviation indicates the variability of a set of scores around the mean. The larger the standard deviation, the more heterogeneous the scores. The minimum value of s is 0.

The calculations in Problem 2.7 are easy because the number of scores is small and the numbers we need to square are small whole numbers. Unhappily, you will usually be working with between 50 and 300 scores and large numbers. You can speed up the calculations using a calculator. In fact, there are calculators that, when the user pushes the appropriate key, compute the mean and standard deviation once the data are entered. Remember, though, that if the number of scores is very large, you may find a computer more accurate and faster than a calculator.

Computer programs that calculate means and standard deviations are very common. The Descriptives program in the SPSS package provides these statistics and other optional statistics. The optional statistics in the Frequencies program in the SPSS package provide the same statistics and, in addition, the median. See sections 1 and 2 of the SPSS 14.0 for Windows Statistical Procedures part of Appendix A for instructions on using either program. The output from Frequencies for the data in Table 2.1 is presented in Table 2.3. Computer programs that calculate the median are not numerous.

Variance

A third measure of variability that is commonly calculated is the **variance**. It is used not as a descriptive term like the range and standard deviation, but rather as a useful statistic in certain high-level statistical procedures like regression analysis or analysis of variance, which we will discuss later in this chapter. The variance is the square of the standard deviation. If, for example, the standard deviation is 5, the variance is 25 (5^2). The calculation of the variance is the same as that for the standard deviation, except the square root step is eliminated.

TABLE 2.3	Output from the Frequencies Program for the Data in Table 2.1						
Variable	Cases	Mean	Median	Mode	Std. Dev.	Min.	Max.
Score	50	67.78	68.00	68.00	10.74	46	90

MEASURING GROUP POSITION

Percentile Ranks

After a test session, most individuals want to know how their performance compares with those of others in the group. Ranks can be calculated by assigning the individual who earned the best score the rank of 1, the individual who earned the next best score the rank of 2, and so on. But rank has little meaning unless the number of individuals in the group is known. A rank of 35 is quite good when there are 250 individuals in the group; it is very poor when there are 37. **Percentile ranks** that indicate the relative position of an individual in a group indicate the percentage of the group that scored worse than a given score.

The calculation of percentile ranks is a three-step process:

Step 1

Order the scores in a simple frequency distribution, by hand or by using a computer, listing the worst score first (see Table 2.2).

Step 2

Calculate the percentile rank of a given score using the following formula:

$$PR_X = \text{Cum. \% above X} + \frac{\text{Percent for X}}{2} \quad \textbf{(2.6)}$$

where PR_X is the percentile rank of score X, and Cum. % above X is the Cum. % for the score above X.

Problem 2.8 Given the following simple frequency distribution, determine the percentile rank for a score of 6:

Score	Frequency	Percent	Cum. %
0	1	4.00	4.00
3	3	12.00	16.00
4	6	24.00	40.00
5	10	40.00	80.00
6	4	16.00	96.00
10	1	4.00	100.00

Solution   Because the scores are presented in a simple frequency distribution, [**Step 1**] has been done.

Step 2

The percentile rank of score 6 where Cum. % above X is 80 and percent for X is 16 is 88:

$$PR_6 = (80) + \left(\frac{16}{2}\right)$$
$$= 80 + 8 = 88$$

Of the scores received, 88% are worse than 6.

In the percentile rank formula (2.6), the term $\frac{\text{Percent for X}}{2}$ is the percent of the x scores in theory worse than the score (X). This is based on the assumption that half the individuals who have received a given score actually scored worse than that score before rounding off. That is, when four people receive a score of 10, we assume that two of them originally had scores between 9.5 and 10.0.

Usually the percentile rank of each score in a set of scores is calculated. Because the values in the Percent column of the simple frequency distribution are seldom whole numbers, computing percentile values can be tedious without a calculator (the easiest way to obtain the simple frequency distribution is to use a computer). When using a calculator, round off the Percent values to two digits to the right of the decimal point and round off the PR values to a whole number. For example, if n in our set of scores in Problem 2.8 had been 26 rather than 25 because there were two scores of 10, the Percent for a score with a frequency of 1 would have been 3.85 (1/26 = .03846 = 3.846% = 3.85%) and the percentile rank for score 3 would be 10:

$$PR_3 = 3.85 + \frac{11.54}{2} = 9.62 = 10$$

Disadvantages

Percentile ranks are ordinal scores. There is no common unit of measurement between consecutive percentile rank values because they are position measures, totally depending on the scores of the group. We can see this clearly in the following PR column, the percentile ranks for the complete set of scores with which we have been working.

Score	Frequency	Percent	Cum. %	PR
0	1	4.00	4.00	2
3	3	12.00	16.00	10
4	6	24.00	40.00	28
5	10	40.00	80.00	60
6	4	16.00	96.00	88
10	1	4.00	100.00	98

As the scores go up from 4 to 5 and from 5 to 6, notice that the percentile ranks rise at different rates: 32 and 28 respectively. For this reason, it is inappropriate to add, subtract, multiply, or divide percentile rank values.

Another disadvantage is that a small change in actual performance near the mean results in a disproportionate change in percentile rank; the opposite is true of changes at the extremes. We can see this in the columns above, where a change of 1 from X = 4 to X = 5 is a PR change of 32, while a

score change of 4 from 6 to 10 is a PR change of only 10.

Percentiles

We often express test standards, or norms, in percentile ranks that are multiples of 5 (5, 10, 15, and so on). Norms for nationally distributed physical fitness tests are an example. To develop these norms we must first determine the test score, or **percentile**, that corresponds to each rank. Here we have a percentile rank from which to calculate a test score (percentile). We use the following formula to calculate the test score that corresponds to a particular rank:

$$P = lrl + \left[\frac{PR - \text{Cum. \% above } X}{\text{Percent for } X} \right] (UM) \quad (2.7)$$

where P is the test score (percentile) that corresponds to the percentile rank (PR), X is the score that has a Cum. % of at least the PR value, lrl is the lower real limit [X − (.5)(UM)], Cum. % above X is the Cum. % for the score above X, and UM is the unit of measurement in which the test scores are expressed.

Note that the formula for calculating the median is a special case of this formula. The calculation of a percentile is a three-step process:

Step 1

Develop a simple frequency distribution like the one in Table 2.2 by hand or by using a computer, listing the worst score first.

Step 2

Go down the score column until a score (X) with a Cum. % of at least the PR value is found.

Step 3

Calculate the percentile (P) using the formula.

Problem 2.9 Given the scores and frequency distribution in Table 2.4, determine which score has a percentile rank of 45. (What is P for a PR of 45?)

TABLE 2.4	Sample Scores and Frequency Distribution		
Score	Frequency	Percent	Cum. %
1	1	2.00	2.00
5	1	2.00	4.00
6	2	4.00	8.00
7	5	10.00	18.00
8	6	12.00	30.00
9	4	8.00	38.00
10	7	14.00	52.00
11	10	20.00	72.00
13	4	8.00	80.00
14	4	8.00	88.00
15	3	6.00	94.00
18	3	6.00	100.00

Solution   Because the scores in Table 2.4 are presented in a simple frequency distribution, [**Step 1**] has been done.

Step 2

Go down the score column and the score 10 is the first score with a Cum. % of at least 45 (the PR value).

Step 3

Where X = 10 (from Step 2), lrl is 9.5 (10 − .5), Cum. % for the score above X is 38, Percent is 14, and UM is 1 (because the scores are recorded in whole numbers), the P is 10:

$$P = 9.5 + \frac{45 - 38}{14} (1) = 9.5 + .5 = 10.0$$

The score below which 45% of the scores fall is 10; it has a percentile rank of 45.

Using the Computer

With a large number of scores, percentile ranks and percentiles should be obtained by using the computer. Some packages of statistical programs have these programs. Percentiles can be obtained in the SPSS package by using the Frequencies program. See section 13 of the SPSS 14.0 for Windows Sta-

tistical Procedures part of Appendix A for the procedures. SPSS does not have a percentile rank program. In the absence of a percentile rank program, a person should use a frequency count program to get a simple frequency distribution like the one in Table 2.2, which would make the hand calculation of percentile ranks much easier. How to calculate percentile ranks by hand has already been presented. If you are willing to modify the definition of a percentile rank so that it is the percentage of the group that scored at or below a given score (rather than below), you can interpret the Cum. % column values in Table 2.2 as percentile ranks.

For the data in Table 2.1, the SPSS printout of percentiles in units of 5 is presented in Table 2.5. Percentile norms are commonly reported in units of 5. Notice in Table 2.5 that a score is calculated for each percentile. The 70th percentile is 75 (the score with a PR of 70 is 75). Also, notice that in Table 2.5, the 50th percentile is the median score.

TABLE 2.5	SPSS Percentile Output in Units of Five for the Table 2.1 Data
Percentile	Value
95	86.70
90	82.90
85	78.35
80	76.80
75	76.00
70	75.00
65	72.15
60	70.60
55	68.00
50	68.00
45	66.95
40	65.40
35	64.85
30	62.30
25	59.75
20	58.00
15	56.00
10	54.10
5	47.55

Small Score Better

Computer programs usually treat a large score as better than a small score. In situations where a small score is better than a large score (mile run, number of days injured, etc.), how do we obtain percentiles? With the percentile option in the Frequencies program in SPSS, percentiles are calculated treating a large score as better than a small score even though the option selected was to arrange the scores in descending order because a small score is better than a large score. So when a small score is better than a large score, the calculated percentiles are incorrect and must be corrected by this formula:

$$\text{Correct P} = 100 - \text{Calculated P}$$

For example, in Table 2.5 if a small score is better than a large score, the Correct P for the score 58 is 80 (100 − 20).

STANDARD SCORES

Standard scores are used frequently to evaluate individuals based on all the tests administered over a period of time, when the tests differ in unit of measurement. When each student has scores, for example, on sit-ups for abdominal strength, sit-and-reach for flexibility, and mile run for aerobic capacity, how does the teacher determine which student's overall performance is best? A fitness specialist working in a health club or corporate fitness program could face the same problem. The three scores cannot be added together because the unit of measurement differs from test to test (executions, inches, seconds). We eliminate this problem by expressing all test scores in a standard (common) unit of measurement. This involves translating each test score into a standard score and summing the standard scores for each student or participant. The individual with the largest sum is the best overall. One standard score is a z-score.

z-Scores

A **z-score** indicates how many standard deviations above or below the mean a test score lies. We calculate z-scores with the following formula:

$$z = \frac{X - \bar{X}}{s} \tag{2.8}$$

A person who scores at the mean receives a z-score of 0; a person who scores one-half a standard deviation below the mean receives a z-score of −.5. Thus, the mean z-score is 0, and the standard deviation for a distribution of z-scores is 1.

T-Scores

Because z-scores are usually fractional and can be negative, physical educators are more likely to use a standard score called a T-score to combine different tests together. **T-scores** are usually rounded off to the nearest whole number and are rarely negative. The mean T-score is 50, and the standard deviation for a distribution of T-scores is 10. The formula for calculating T-scores is as follows:

$$T = \frac{10(X - \bar{X})}{s} + 50 \tag{2.9}$$

Note that the term $\dfrac{(X - \bar{X})}{s}$ in the T-score formula is the equation for determining the z-score. We could restate the T-score formula, then, as follows:

$$T = 10z + 50$$

Problem 2.10 Given a mean of 87 and a standard deviation of 2.35, determine the T-score for a score of 90.

Solution Where X is 90, $\bar{X}$ is 87, and s is 2.35, T is 63:

$$T = \frac{(10)(90 - 87)}{2.35} + 50 = \frac{(10)(3)}{2.35} + 50$$

$$= \frac{30}{2.35} + 50 = 12.76 + 50 = 62.76$$

$$= 63$$

Notice that z-scores and T-scores rise as performances rise above the mean. When smaller scores are better than larger scores, z-scores and T-scores must rise as performances fall below the mean. Thus, for speed events or any measure where smaller scores are better than larger scores, we use the following formulas to calculate z-scores and T-scores:

$$z = \frac{\bar{X} - X}{s}$$

$$T = \frac{10\,(\bar{X} - X)}{s} + 50 \qquad \textbf{(2.10)}$$

The relationship among test scores, z-scores, and T-scores for a hypothetical test with mean 75 and standard deviation 8 is shown in Table 2.6. From the table we can see that a T-score of 50 is equivalent to a z-score of 0, or a test score equal to the test mean. Also, a test score 2 standard deviations above the mean equals a T-score of 70.

T-scores are easy to interpret if we remember the mean T-score is 50 and the standard deviation for T-scores is 10. For example, a T-score of 65 is 1.5 standard deviations above the mean, a T-score of 40 is 1 standard deviation below the mean, and a T-score of 78 is 2.8 standard deviations above the mean.

The T-scores for 22 students with 3 test scores are listed in Table 2.7, Student 6 is the best overall student because the sum of that student's score (206) is the largest.

Methods of Determining Standard Scores

Obviously, translating test scores to standard scores takes time and effort. Few physical education teachers, exercise specialists, or practitioners, given 5 to 15 scores for each of a hundred or more individuals, have the time to calculate standard scores by hand. However, it would be unfortunate to bypass a good, easy technique for lack of time. There are two methods that allow us to obtain standard scores quickly: calculated conversion tables and computer analysis.

Calculated Conversion Tables   For most tests, each score will be obtained by several people. For example, we can see in Table 2.7 that 10 students did no pull-ups, 6 students did 1 pull-up, and so on. Once the standard score for a test score is determined, it is not necessary to recalculate the standard score every time that test score is repeated. Instead, we develop a test score–standard score conversion table. The method of development is either calculation by hand or calculation by using the computer.

When the number of different scores is small, you can construct the test score–standard score conversion table by hand, calculating the standard score for each existing test score. For example, from the pull-up scores in Table 2.7 we can develop this conversion table for T-scores expressed as a whole number:

X	0	1	2	3	4	5	6	7	8
T	43	48	54	59	64	69	74	80	85

Using the Computer

When the number of different test scores is large, you should use the computer method. From the computer output, you can develop conversion tables.

TABLE 2.6	**Relationships among Test Scores (Mean 75, Standard Deviation 8), z-Scores, and T-Scores**						
	Score Position						
	$\bar{X} - 3s$	$\bar{X} - 2s$	$\bar{X} - s$	$\bar{X}$	$\bar{X} + s$	$\bar{X} + 2s$	$\bar{X} + 3s$
Hypothetical Test Scores	51	59	67	75	83	91	99
z-Scores	−3	−2	−1	0	1	2	3
T-Scores	20	30	40	50	60	70	80

TABLE 2.7			T-Scores Calculated by Formula and Rounded to Whole Numbers				
Student	Mile Run*	Pull-Up†	Sit-Up‡	Mile Run T	Pull-Up T	Sit-Up T	Sum T
1	407	0	43	64	43	52	159
2	511	4	45	51	64	54	169
3	478	2	50	55	54	60	169
4	525	1	51	49	48	61	158
5	480	4	53	55	64	64	183
6	440	8	51	60	85	61	206
7	519	1	39	50	48	47	145
8	488	2	43	54	54	52	160
9	510	0	30	51	43	37	131
10	456	3	47	58	59	57	174
11	603	1	38	40	48	46	134
12	495	0	40	53	43	48	144
13	435	1	45	60	48	54	162
14	588	1	29	42	48	36	126
15	630	0	29	37	43	36	116
16	638	0	42	36	43	51	130
17	511	0	40	51	43	48	142
18	721	0	28	26	43	35	104
19	482	0	52	55	43	62	160
20	630	0	30	37	43	37	117
21	360	1	54	69	48	65	182
22	540	0	30	48	43	37	128

*Mean 520.32; standard deviation 83.47.
†Mean 1.32; standard deviation 1.92.
‡Mean 41.32; standard deviation 8.59.

Computer Analysis   The fastest and easiest way to calculate standard scores is through computer analysis. In fact, with a large amount of data it may be the only feasible method. The standard scores option in the SPSS Descriptive program (see section 15 of the SPSS 14.0 for Windows Statistical Procedures part of Appendix A) calculates z-scores for each score of a person. The z-scores are calculated and attached to the data file as additional variables. To see the z-scores, you must display or print the data file. The z-scores are not saved on the data disk, so if there is a future need for them, it would be best to save the file with the data and z-scores as a new file. In this way you will have one file with the data and a second file with the data and z-

scores. Whether or not the z-scores are saved, after the z-scores are calculated, you probably want the computer to provide you with the sum of the z-scores. See section 16 of the SPSS 14.0 for Windows Statistical Procedures part of Appendix A for how to do this using the transformation feature available in SPSS and in most computer packages of statistical programs.

General database computer programs can also be used to calculate z-scores and T-scores. These programs must be programmed to produce the desired results by using the z-score and T-score equations. Database programs may be used for many different functions other than just z-scores and T-scores.

The Normal Curve

Earlier in this chapter we discussed the normal curve as a model for the graph of a set of scores. Here we discuss the normal curve and its role in making probability statements.

Characteristics

The **normal curve** is a mathematically defined, smooth, bilaterally symmetrical curve, centered around a point that is simultaneously the mode, median, and mean (see Figure 2-8). Because the center point is both the mode and the median, it is both the most frequent score and that score below which half the scores fall. The normal curve, by mathematical definition, has a mean of 0 and a standard deviation of 1. Thus, the normal curve is the graph of an infinite number of z-scores (see Figure 2-9).

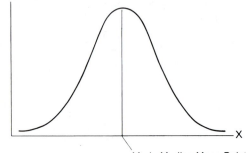

Frequency

Mode-Median-Mean Point

Figure 2-8

Normal curve for test scores.

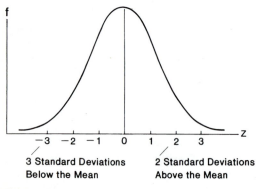

f

−3   −2   −1   0   1   2   3   z

3 Standard Deviations
Below the Mean

2 Standard Deviations
Above the Mean

Figure 2-9

Normal curve for z-scores.

Probability

When you flip a coin, the probability that it will come up heads is $\frac{1}{2}$: there are 2 possible outcomes, and heads (H) represents only 1 of those outcomes, the event or outcome desired. The statement is written $P(H) = \frac{1}{2}$. In general, the probability of an event is the number of possible outcomes that satisfy the event, divided by the total number of possible outcomes.

For example, when you flip two coins, what is the probability of their both coming up tails (TT)? You have 4 possible outcomes: both heads (HH), both tails (TT), the first coin heads and the second tails (HT), and vice versa (TH). The wanted outcome, event TT, is 1 of the 4 possible outcomes, so the probability of TT's occurring is $\frac{1}{4}$:

$$P(TT) = \frac{1}{4}$$

To use the normal curve (see Figure 2-9) to make probability statements, think of the area under the curve as 100 equal portions. If there are 100 possible outcomes under the normal curve, then 50 of these outcomes lie on each side of the mean. Because the curve is symmetrical, the number of outcomes between 0 and −1 equals the number of outcomes between 0 and 1.

Problem 2.11   What is the probability of a z equal to or greater than (≥) 0?

Solution   To begin, we must determine the percentage of the area under the curve that lies to the right of 0. From our definition we know that half of the possible outcomes lie to each side of 0 (the midpoint). Any of the 50 outcomes that lie to the right of 0 would satisfy z > 0. Thus, the probability of z > 0 is $\frac{1}{2}$:

$$P(z \geq 0) = \frac{50}{100} = \frac{1}{2}$$

This problem is simple because we have the answers to it by definition. To answer most probability statements about the normal curve, we have to use a special table, which appears here as Table 2.8. The table allows us to determine the percentage of a given area under the curve, and thus the basis for determining the probability that z will fall

TABLE 2.8	Percentage of Total Area under the Normal Curve between the Mean and Ordinate Points at Any Given Standard Deviation Distance from the Mean								
z	.00	.01	.02	.03	.04	.05	.06	.07	.08	.09
0.0	00.00	00.40	00.80	01.20	01.60	01.99	02.39	02.79	03.19	03.59
0.1	03.98	04.38	04.78	05.17	05.57	05.96	06.36	06.75	07.14	07.53
0.2	07.93	08.32	08.71	09.10	09.48	09.87	10.26	10.64	11.03	11.41
0.3	11.79	12.17	12.55	12.95	13.31	13.68	14.06	14.43	14.80	15.17
0.4	15.54	15.91	16.28	16.64	17.00	17.36	17.72	18.08	18.44	18.79
0.5	19.15	19.50	19.85	20.19	20.54	20.88	21.23	21.57	21.90	22.24
0.6	22.57	22.91	23.24	23.57	23.89	24.22	24.54	24.86	25.17	25.49
0.7	25.80	26.11	26.42	26.73	27.04	27.34	27.64	27.94	28.23	28.52
0.8	28.81	29.10	29.39	29.67	29.95	30.23	30.51	30.78	31.06	31.33
0.9	31.59	31.86	32.12	32.38	32.64	32.90	33.15	33.40	33.65	33.89
1.0	34.13	34.38	34.61	34.85	35.08	35.31	35.54	35.77	35.99	36.21
1.1	36.43	36.65	36.86	37.08	37.29	37.49	37.70	37.90	38.10	38.30
1.2	38.49	38.69	38.88	39.07	39.25	39.44	39.62	39.80	39.97	40.15
1.3	40.32	40.49	40.66	40.82	40.99	41.15	41.31	41.47	41.62	41.77
1.4	41.92	42.07	42.22	42.36	42.51	42.65	42.79	42.92	43.06	43.19
1.5	43.32	43.45	43.57	43.70	43.83	43.94	44.06	44.18	44.29	44.41
1.6	44.52	44.63	44.74	44.84	44.95	45.05	45.15	45.25	45.35	45.45
1.7	45.54	45.64	45.73	45.82	45.91	45.99	46.08	46.16	46.25	46.33
1.8	46.41	46.49	46.56	46.64	46.71	46.78	46.86	46.93	46.99	47.06
1.9	47.13	47.19	47.26	47.32	47.38	47.44	47.50	47.56	47.61	47.67
2.0	47.72	47.78	47.83	47.88	47.93	47.98	48.03	48.08	48.12	48.17
2.1	48.21	48.26	48.30	48.34	48.38	48.42	48.46	48.50	48.54	48.57
2.2	48.61	48.64	48.68	48.71	48.75	48.78	48.81	48.84	48.87	48.90
2.3	48.93	48.96	48.98	49.01	49.04	49.06	49.09	49.11	49.13	49.16
2.4	49.18	49.20	49.22	49.25	49.27	49.29	49.31	49.32	49.34	49.36
2.5	49.38	49.40	49.41	49.43	49.45	49.46	49.48	49.49	49.51	49.52
2.6	49.53	49.55	49.56	49.57	49.59	49.60	49.61	49.62	49.63	49.64
2.7	49.65	49.66	49.67	49.68	49.69	49.70	49.71	49.72	49.73	49.74
2.8	49.74	49.75	49.76	49.77	49.77	49.78	49.79	49.79	49.80	49.81
2.9	49.81	49.82	49.82	49.83	49.84	49.84	49.85	49.85	49.86	49.86
3.0	49.87									
3.5	49.98									
4.0	49.997									
5.0	49.99997									

Source: From Lindquist, E. F., *A First Course in Statistics,* Second Edition. Copyright © 1942 by Houghton Mifflin Company. Used with permission.

within that area. The values along the left side and top of the table are z values, or standard deviation distances from the mean. The values in the body of the table indicate the percentage of the area under the curve between a given z-score and the mean z-score, 0.

Problem 2.12   What percentage of the area under the normal curve lies between 0 (z = 0) and 1.36 (z = 1.36)?

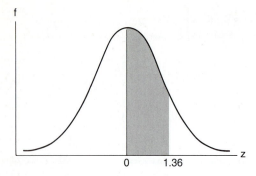

Figure 2-10

Normal curve graph for Problem 2.12.

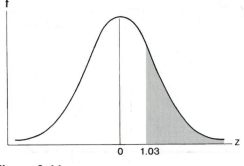

Figure 2-11

Normal curve graph for Problem 2.13.

Solution   Because

$$1.36 = 1.30 + .06$$

we read down the left side of Table 2.8 to 1.3 and across the row to column .06. The value listed there, 41.31, is that percentage of the area under the normal curve that lies between 0 and 1.36 (see Figure 2-10).

Once we know the possible outcomes that satisfy an event, we can determine the probability of that event happening. The probability that z falls between 0 and 1.36 on the normal curve is the satisfactory outcomes (41.31) divided by the possible outcomes (100), or .41:

$$P(z \text{ between } 0 \text{ and } 1.36) = \frac{41.31}{100}$$

$$= .4131 = .41$$

Because the normal curve is symmetrical, the values in Table 2.8 hold true for equivalent distances from the mean to the left of it. That is, the percentage of the area under the normal curve between 0 and −1.36 is still 41.31, and the probability that z falls somewhere between 0 and −1.36 is still .41.

Although the table lists percentages only from the mean, we can extrapolate from it, remembering that 50% of all possible outcomes lie to each side of the mean. To solve any probability statement, make sure the statement is in terms of z, draw a normal curve graph as was done for Problem 2.12, and remember that the normal curve tables provide the percentage of the area under the normal curve between 0 and the z-score

you used in the normal curve table. Thus, the percentage read from the table may not be the answer to the probability statement.

Problem 2.13   What is the probability that z is equal to or greater than 1.03?

Solution   First we determine the overall area between 0 and 1.03. Reading down the left side of Table 2.8 to 1.0 and across to column .03, we see that 34.85% of the total area to the right of the mean lies between 0 and 1.03 (see Figure 2-11). Because we know that the possible outcomes to the right (or left, for that matter) of 0 represent $\frac{50}{100}$, we can subtract the amount we know, $\frac{34.85}{100}$, from $\frac{50}{100}$. The result is our answer. The probability that z is equal to or greater than 1.03 is .15:

$$P(z \geq 1.03) = \frac{50}{100} - \frac{34.85}{100}$$

$$= .50 - .3485 = .1515 = .15$$

Often the probability statement requires a translation from test score X to the equivalent z, or vice versa, as we can see in the following problems.

Problem 2.14   A teacher always administers 100-point tests and always gives A's to scores of 93 and above. On the last test the mean was 72 and the standard deviation was 9. Assuming test scores are normally distributed, what was the probability of receiving an A on that test?

Solution   This is the same as asking what percentage of the class probably received A grades:

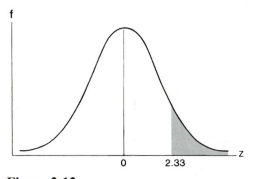

Figure 2-12

Normal curve graph for Problem 2.14.

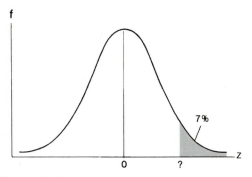

Figure 2-13

Normal curve graph for Problem 2.15.

What is the probability that a score X was greater than or equal to 93? Before we can solve the probability statement, then, we must change score 93 to a z-score. Where X is greater than or equal to 93, $\overline{X}$ is 72, and s is 9, the z-score must be greater than or equal to 2.33:

$$z \geq \frac{93 - 72}{9} \geq \frac{21}{9} \geq 2.33$$

Now, using Figure 2-12 and Table 2.8, it is easy to determine the probability. At the intersection of z row 2.3 and column .03, we see that the percentage under the normal curve between 0 and 2.33 is 49.01. By subtracting that amount from the percentage of possible outcomes above 0, we see that the probability that z is greater than or equal to 2.33 is .01.

$$P(z \geq 2.33) = \frac{50}{100} - \frac{49.01}{100} = \frac{.99}{100}$$
$$= .0099 = .01$$

Problem 2.15 To develop some performance standards, a teacher decides to use the normal curve to determine the test score above which 7% of the scores should fall. First, determine the z-score above which 7% of the area under the normal curve falls (see Figure 2-13).

$$P(z \geq ?) = \frac{7}{100}$$

Solution We know that 43% of the area under the curve lies between 0 and the unknown z-score. If we scan Table 2.8, we see that percentage 43.06 is closest to 43%. Because 43.06 is at the intersection of z row 1.4 and column .08, the unknown z-score (the z-score above which 7% of the area falls) is 1.48. Now, determine the test score (X) above which 7% of the scores should fall, using the following formula to calculate X:

$$X = \overline{X} + z(s)$$
$$X = \overline{X} + 1.48(s)$$
$$\text{and if } \overline{X} = 31.25, s = 5.0 \text{ then}$$
$$X = 31.25 + 1.48(5.0)$$
$$= 31.25 + 7.4 = 38.65$$

DETERMINING RELATIONSHIPS BETWEEN SCORES

There are many situations in which the physical education teacher, exercise specialist, or physical therapist would like to know the relationship between scores on two different tests. For example, if speed and the performance of a sport skill were found to be related, the physical education teacher might try to improve the speed of poor performers. Or, if weight and strength scores were found to be related, the exercise specialist or physical therapist might want to use a different evaluation standard for each weight classification. Knowing the relationship between scores can also lead to greater efficiency in a measurement program. For example, if there are seven tests in a physical fitness battery and two of them are highly related, the battery could be reduced to six tests with no loss of information. We use two different techniques to determine score relationships: a graphing technique and a mathematical technique called correlation.

The Graphing Technique

The graphing technique is quicker than the mathematical technique but not as precise. It requires that each individual have a score on each of the two measures. To graph a relationship, we develop a coordinate system according to those values of one measure listed along the horizontal axis and those of the other measure listed along the vertical axis. We plot a point for each individual above his score on the horizontal axis and opposite his score on the vertical axis, as shown in Figure 2-14. The graph obtained is called a "scattergram."

The point plotted for Person A is at the intersection of push-up score 15 and pull-up score 10,

the scores the person received on the two tests. The straight line—the **line of best fit** or the **regression line**—in Figure 2-14 represents the trend in the data, in this case that individuals with large push-up scores have large pull-up scores, and vice versa. When large scores on one measure are associated with large scores on the other measure, the relationship is *positive*. When large scores on one measure are associated with small scores on the other measure, as shown in Figure 2-15, the relationship is *negative*.

The closer all the plotted points are to the trend line, the higher or larger the relationship. The maximum relationship occurs when all plotted points are on the trend line. When the plotted points resemble a circle, making it impossible to draw a trend line, there is no linear relationship between the two measures being graphed. We can see this in the graph for Figure 2-16.

Desktop computer programs have scattergram graphic programs that facilitate plotting data. In SPSS this program is called Scatterplot. See section 19 of the SPSS 14.0 for Windows Statistical Procedures part of Appendix A for instructions on

Person	Push-Ups	Pull-Ups
A	15	10
B	5	2
C	11	5
D	10	6
E	14	7
F	3	1
G	16	9
H	8	5

Figure 2-14

Graph of a positive relationship.

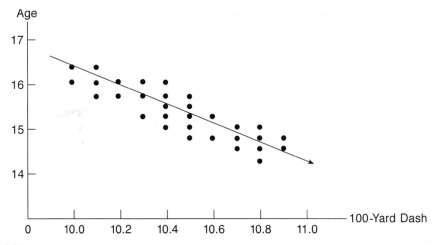

Figure 2-15

Graph of a negative relationship.

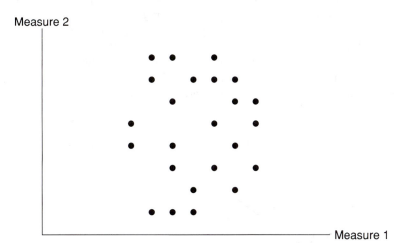

Figure 2-16

Graph of no relationship.

using it. An example of a computer-generated scattergram using the sit-up and pull-up scores from Table 2.9 is presented in Figure 2-17.

The Correlation Technique

Correlation is a mathematical technique for determining the relationship between two sets of scores. The formula was developed by Karl Pearson to determine the degree of relationship between two sets of measures (called X measures and Y measures):

$$r = \frac{n\Sigma XY - (\Sigma X)(\Sigma Y)}{\sqrt{\left[n\Sigma X^2 - (\Sigma X)^2\right]\left[n\Sigma Y^2 - (\Sigma Y)^2\right]}} \quad \textbf{(2.11)}$$

where r is the Pearson product-moment correlation coefficient, n is the number of individuals, ΣXY is the sum of each individual's X times Y value, ΣX is the sum of the scores for one set of measures, ΣY is the sum of the scores for the other set of measures, ΣX^2 is the sum of the squared X scores, and ΣY^2 is the sum of the squared Y scores.

TABLE 2.9	Scores of 45 Students on a Fitness Test				
Student	**Skinfold**	**Mile Run**	**Sit-and-Reach**	**Pull-Up**	**Sit-Up**
1	27.00	407.00	38.00	0.00	43.00
2	24.00	511.00	45.00	4.00	45.00
3	22.00	478.00	22.00	2.00	50.00
4	24.00	525.00	38.00	1.00	51.00
5	23.00	480.00	40.00	4.00	53.00
6	16.00	440.00	41.00	8.00	51.00
7	31.00	519.00	39.00	1.00	39.00
8	33.00	488.00	34.00	2.00	43.00
9	28.00	510.00	40.00	0.00	30.00
10	27.00	456.00	39.00	3.00	47.00
11	28.00	603.00	37.00	1.00	38.00
12	39.00	495.00	31.00	0.00	40.00
13	24.00	435.00	37.00	1.00	45.00
14	22.00	588.00	36.00	1.00	29.00
15	25.00	630.00	34.00	0.00	29.00
16	38.00	638.00	28.00	0.00	42.00
17	43.00	511.00	35.00	0.00	40.00
18	37.00	721.00	28.00	0.00	28.00
19	22.00	482.00	37.00	0.00	52.00
20	25.00	630.00	37.00	0.00	30.00
21	28.00	360.00	36.00	1.00	54.00
22	28.00	540.00	31.00	0.00	30.00
23	30.00	507.00	28.00	2.00	40.00
24	22.00	454.00	33.00	2.00	58.00
25	22.00	472.00	37.00	2.00	54.00
26	34.00	588.00	35.00	1.00	56.00
27	18.00	588.00	28.00	1.00	42.00
28	37.00	524.00	22.00	0.00	48.00
29	38.00	713.00	21.00	0.00	37.00
30	19.00	440.00	28.00	3.00	42.00
31	28.00	417.00	25.00	0.00	30.00
32	40.00	720.00	28.00	0.00	47.00
33	19.00	525.00	21.00	2.00	30.00
34	21.00	400.00	17.00	1.00	25.00
35	20.00	390.00	27.00	5.00	53.00
36	17.00	375.00	33.00	13.00	52.00
37	30.00	390.00	26.00	2.00	49.00
38	18.00	385.00	25.00	4.00	49.00
39	23.00	390.00	34.00	5.00	51.00
40	14.00	342.00	30.00	13.00	45.00
41	42.00	384.00	10.00	1.00	36.00
42	15.00	510.00	31.00	3.00	35.00
43	40.00	592.00	24.00	0.00	43.00
44	19.00	500.00	35.00	5.00	63.00
45	22.00		32.00		47.00

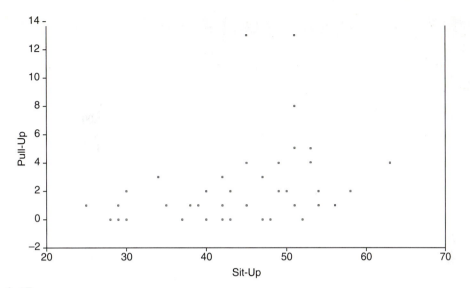

Figure 2-17
Computer-generated scattergram using the Table 2.9 data.

TABLE 2.10	**Scores for Correlation Calculation**				
Individual	**Pull-Up (X)**	**Push-Up (Y)**	**XY**	**X²**	**Y²**
A	10	15	150	100	225
B	2	5	10	4	25
C	5	11	55	25	121
D	6	10	60	36	100
E	7	14	98	49	196
F	1	3	3	1	9
G	9	16	144	81	256
H	5	8	40	25	64
n = 8	ΣX = 45	ΣY = 82	ΣXY = 560	ΣX² = 321	ΣY² = 996

Problem 2.16   Using the scores in Table 2.10, determine the correlation between the pull-up scores (X) and the push-up scores (Y).

Solution   Where n is 8 (the number of individuals), ΣXY is 560 (the sum of column XY), ΣX is 45 (the sum of column X), SY is 82 (the sum of column Y), ΣX² is 321 (the sum of column X²), and ΣY² is 996 (the sum of column Y²), the correlation coefficient, r, is 0.96:

$$r = \frac{(8)\,(560) - (45)\,(82)}{\sqrt{\left[(8)\,(321) - 45^2\right]\left[(8)\,(996) - 82^2\right]}}$$

$$= \frac{4480 - 3690}{\sqrt{(2568 - 2025)\,(7968 - 6724)}}$$

$$= \frac{790}{\sqrt{(543)\,(1244)}}$$

$$= \frac{790}{\sqrt{675492}} = \frac{790}{821.88} = .96$$

TABLE 2.11	Examples of Perfect Relationships				
Individual	Height	Weight	Individual	100-Yard Dash	Pull-Up
A	60	130	A	10.6	14
B	52	122	B	10.6	14
C	75	145	C	11.2	8
D	66	136	D	11.7	3
E	70	140	E	10.5	15
	r = 1			r = −1	

Exact formula: weight = height + 70   Exact formula: dash = 12 − .1 (pull-up)

Correlation coefficients have two characteristics, direction and strength. Direction of the relationship is indicated by whether the correlation coefficient is positive or negative, as indicated under the graphing technique. Strength of the relationship is indicated by how close the r is to 1, the maximum value possible. A correlation of 1 (r = 1) shows a perfect positive relationship, indicating that an increase in scores on one measure is accompanied by an increase in scores on the second measure. A perfect negative relationship (r = −1) indicates that an increase in scores on one measure is accompanied by a decrease in scores on the second. (Notice that a correlation of −1 is just as strong as a correlation of 1.) Perfect relationships are rare, but any such relationship that does exist is exactly described by a mathematical formula. Examples of a perfect positive and a perfect negative relationship are shown in Table 2.11. When the correlation coefficient is 0 (r = 0), there is no linear relationship between the two sets of scores.

Because the relationship between two sets of scores is seldom perfect, the majority of correlation coefficients are fractions (.93, −.85, and the like). The closer the correlation coefficient is to 1 or −1, the stronger the relationship. When the relationship is not perfect, the scores on one measure only tend to change with the scores on the other measure. Look, for example, at Table 2.12. The correlation between height and weight is not perfect: Individual C, whose height is 75 inches, is not heavier than Individual E, whose height is only 70 inches.

TABLE 2.12	Example of an Imperfect Correlation	
Individual	Height (Inches)	Weight (Pounds)
A	60	130
B	52	125
C	75	145
D	66	136
E	70	150
	r = .91	

When the scores for the two sets of scores are ranks, a correlation coefficient called *rho* or *Spearman's rho* or the **rank order correlation coefficient** may be calculated. The formula is just a simplification of the Pearson correlation formula. Since the same value will be obtained by applying the Pearson correlation formula to the two sets of ranks (provided no tied ranks exist), the formula is not presented, but it is commonly included in desktop computer statistical programs.

Interpreting the Correlation Coefficient

A high correlation between two measures does not usually indicate a cause-and-effect relationship. The perfect height and weight relationship in Table 2.11, for example, does not indicate that an increase in weight causes an increase in height. Also, the degree of relationship between two sets of measures does not increase at the same rate as does the correlation coefficient. The true indicator of the degree of relationship is the **coefficient of determination:** the amount of variability in one measure that is explained by the other measure. The coefficient of determination is the square of the correlation coefficient (r^2). For example, the square of the correlation coefficient in Table 2.12 is .83 ($.91^2$), which means that 83% of the variability in height scores is due to the individuals' having different weight scores.

Thus when one correlation coefficient is twice as large as another, the larger coefficient really explains four times the amount of variation that the smaller coefficient explains. For example, when the r between agility and balance is .80 and the r between strength and power is .40, the r^2 for agility and balance is $.80^2$, or 64%, and the r^2 for strength and power is $.40^2$, or 16%.

Remember, when you interpret a correlation coefficient, there are no absolute standards for labeling a given r "good" or "poor"; only the relationship you want or expect determines the quality of a given r. For example, if you or others had obtained a correlation coefficient of .67 between leg strength and standing long jump scores for males, you might expect a similar correlation coefficient in comparing leg strength and long jump scores for females. If the relationship between the females' scores were only .45, you might label that correlation coefficient "poor" because you expected it to be as high as that of the males.

There are two reasons why correlation coefficients can be negative: (1) opposite scoring scales and (2) true negative relationships. When a measure on which a small score is a better score is correlated with a measure on which a larger score is a better score, the correlation coefficient probably will be negative. Consider, for example, the relationship between scores on a speed event like the time it takes to run one mile and a nonspeed event like the number of sit-ups executed in one minute. Usually individuals best on the sit-up test are the best runners, but the correlation is negative because the scoring scales are reversed. Two measures can be negatively related as well. We would expect, for example, a negative correlation between body weight and measures involving support or motion of the body (pull-ups) or between number of risk factors (smoking, drinking, obesity, etc.) and physical health.

The Question of Accuracy

In calculating r, we assume that the relationship between the two sets of scores is basically linear. A **linear relationship** is shown graphically by a straight line, like the trend line in Figure 2-14. However, a relationship between two sets of scores can be represented by a curved line, showing a **curvilinear relationship**. A curvilinear relationship between two measures is best described by a curved line. If a relationship is truly curvilinear, the correlation coefficient will underestimate the relationship. For example, r could equal 0 even when a definite curvilinear relationship exists. More concerning curvilinear relationships is presented later, in the regression section of this chapter.

Although we need not assume when calculating r that the graph of each of the two sets of scores is a normal curve, we do assume that the two graphs resemble each other. If they are dissimilar, the correlation coefficient will underestimate the relationship between the scores. Considerable differences in the two graphs are occasionally found, usually when the number of people tested is small. For this reason, the correlation coefficient ideally should be calculated with the scores of a large group (at least 50).

Other factors also affect the correlation coefficient. One is the reliability of the scores; low reliability reduces the correlation coefficient (see Chapter 3). Another factor is the range in the scores; the correlation coefficient will be smaller for a homogeneous group than for a heterogeneous group. Ferguson and Takane (1989) suggest that generally the range in scores increases as the size of the group tested increases. Certainly small groups exhibit a greater tendency than large groups to be either more homogeneous or more heterogeneous than is typical for the group measured and the test administered. This is another reason to calculate the correlation coefficient only when the group tested is large. Ferguson and Takane (1989) cover this subject in greater detail.

The calculation of the correlation coefficient in Problem 2.16 was easy because the number of scores was small and the values of the scores were small. Usually you will be working with between 25 and 500 scores that may be three- or four-digit numbers. In this case the use of a calculator to speed up the calculations is essential. Many calculators have a correlation key, so only the X and Y scores have to be entered into the calculator and it does the rest.

When the group tested is large or when the physical education teacher and exercise specialist want the correlation between all possible pairings of more than two tests (pull-up and sit-up, pull-up and mile run, sit-up and mile run), using a computer is the most efficient way to obtain the correlation coefficients. Computer programs that calculate correlation coefficients are commonly found in packages of statistical programs for desktop computers. In the SPSS package, the correlation program will calculate the correlation between two variables or among all variables at one time. For example, the correlation between pull-up and push-up scores in Table 2.10 or among all the variables in Table 2.9 could be calculated. See section 10 of the Statistical Procedures part of Appendix A for instructions on using the correlation program in SPSS.

A common printout format is presented in Table 2.13 for the data in Table 2.9. In Table 2.13 the correlation between any two tests is found by finding the value listed in the cell formed by the row and column of the two tests. For example, the correlation between pull-up and sit-up is .40.

PREDICTION-REGRESSION ANALYSIS

The terms *correlation, regression*, and *prediction* are so closely related in statistics that they are often used interchangeably. **Correlation** refers to the relationship between two variables. When two variables are correlated, it becomes possible to make a prediction. **Regression** is the statistical model used to explain variability (variance) in one variable based on one or more other variables. An example is determining the amount of variability in fitness scores based on percent body fat.

Teachers, coaches, exercise specialists, and researchers have long been interested in predicting scores that are either difficult or impossible to obtain at a given moment. **Prediction** is estimating a person's score on one measure based on the person's score on one or more other measures. An example is the prediction of percent body fat from skinfold measurements. This is illustrated in Chapter 12. Although prediction is often imprecise, it is occasionally useful to develop a prediction formula.

Simple Prediction

Simple prediction is predicting an unknown score (Y') for an individual by using that person's performance on a known measure (X). To develop a simple prediction, or regression formula, a large number (at least n = 50, with n > 100 even better) of people must be measured and a score on the **independent**, or predictor, **variable** (X) and the **dependent**, or criterion, **variable** (Y) obtained for each. Based on this data the prediction equation is developed.

TABLE 2.13	**Correlations Among All the Variables for the Data in Table 2.9**				
Label	Skin	Mile	Reach	Pull-up	Sit-up
Skin	1.00	0.45	−0.26	−0.59	−0.20
Mile	0.45	1.00	0.02	−0.52	−0.35
Reach	−0.26	0.02	1.00	0.14	0.28
Pull-up	−0.59	−0.52	0.14	1.00	0.40
Sit-up	−0.20	−0.35	0.28	0.40	1.00

$$Y' = \left[(r) \left(\frac{s_y}{s_x} \right) \right] (X - \bar{X}) + \bar{Y}$$

$$(2.12)$$

where Y' is the predicted Y score for an individual, r is the correlation between X and Y scores, s_y is the standard deviation for the Y scores, s_x is standard deviation for the X scores, X is the individual's known score on measure X, $\bar{X}$ is the mean for the X scores, and $\bar{Y}$ is the mean for the Y scores. Once the formula is developed for any given relationship, only the predictor variable X is needed to predict the performance of an individual on measure Y. Two indexes of the accuracy of a simple prediction equation are r and r^2.

Problem 2.17   A coach found the correlation coefficient between physical fitness and athletic ability to be .88. The mean of the physical fitness test is 12; its standard deviation is 5.15. The mean of the athletic ability test is 9; its standard deviation is 4.30. What is the predicted athletic ability score for an athlete with a physical fitness score of 14?

Solution   Where r is .88, s_y is 4.30, s_x is 5.15, X is 14, $\bar{X}$ is 12, and $\bar{Y}$ is 9, the athlete's predicted athlete ability score, Y', is 10.46:

$$Y' = \left[(.88) \left(\frac{4.30}{5.15} \right) \right] (14 - 12) + 9$$

$$= (.73)(2) + 9 = 1.46 + 9 = 10.46$$

Prediction being a correlational technique, there is a *line of best fit* or *regression line* that can be generated (we have explained the graphing technique in this chapter). In case of simple prediction, this is the regression line for the graph of the X variable on the horizontal axis and the Y variable on the vertical axis.

The general form of the simple prediction equation is

$$Y' = bX + c$$

where b is a constant and termed the slope of the regression line. The slope is the rate at which Y changes with change on X. The constant, c, is called the Y-intercept and is the point at which the line crosses the vertical axis. It is the value of Y

that corresponds to an X of 0. To obtain the slope and Y-intercept, all values except X are put into the prediction formula and then the formula is reduced to simplest form. For the values used in Problem 2.17,

$$Y' = \left[(.88) \left(\frac{4.30}{5.15} \right) \right] (X - 12) + 9$$

$$= (.73)(X - 12) + 9$$

$$= .73X - 8.76 + 9$$

$$= .73X + .24$$

so b = .73 and c = .24. Thus

$$Y' = .73(X) + .24$$

Sometimes calculators and computer programs report the simple prediction equation in terms of slope and Y-intercept. If a calculator or computer is programmed to obtain the simple prediction equation, only the X and Y scores have to be entered.

The Standard Error of Prediction

An individual's predicted score, Y', will not equal the actual score, Y, unless the correlation coefficient used in the formula is perfect—a rare event. Thus, for each individual there is an error of prediction. We estimate the standard deviation of this error, the **standard error of prediction**, using the following formula:

$$\text{estimated } s_{y \cdot x} = s_y \sqrt{1 - r^2}$$

$$(2.13)$$

where $s_{y \cdot x}$ is the standard error of score Y predicted from score X, s_y is the standard deviation for the Y scores, and r^2 is the square of the correlation coefficient (the coefficient of determination) for the X and Y scores. (Notice that the larger the coefficient, the smaller the standard error.) This estimate of $s_{y \cdot x}$ is sufficiently accurate if the number of individuals tested (n) is large (at least n = 50, with n > 100 even better). The standard error of prediction is another index of the accuracy of a simple prediction equation.

The standard error of prediction is not a good index of the error associated with a single prediction. When a Y' is calculated from the X-score of a certain person, the error in it will be smaller when X is near $\bar{X}$ than when X is far from $\bar{X}$.

If the prediction formula and standard error seem acceptable, the physical education teacher or exercise specialist should try to prove the prediction formula on a second group of individuals similar to the first. This process is called **cross-validation**. If the formula works satisfactorily for the second group, it can be used with confidence to predict score Y for any individual who resembles the individuals used to form and cross-validate the equation. If the formula does not work well for the second group, it is unique to the group used to form the equation and has little value in predicting performance.

Multiple Prediction

A prediction formula using a single measure X is usually not very accurate for predicting a person's score on measure Y. *Multiple correlation-regression* techniques allow us to predict score Y using several X scores. For example, a **multiple prediction** formula has been developed to predict arm strength in pounds (Y') using both the number of pull-ups (X_1) and pounds of body weight (X_2):

$$Y' = 3.42(X_1) + 1.77(X_2) - 46$$

A multiple regression equation will have one intercept and several b's, one for each independent variable. The general forms of two- and three-predictor multiple regression equations are

$$Y' = b_1X_1 + b_2X_2 + c$$
$$Y' = b_1X_1 + b_2X_2 + b_3X_3 + c$$

The *multiple correlation coefficient R* is one index of the accuracy of a multiple prediction equation. The minimum and maximum values of R are 0 and 1, respectively. The percentage of variance in the Y scores explained by the multiple prediction equation (R^2) is a second index of the accuracy of a multiple prediction equation. A third index of the accuracy of a multiple prediction equation is the standard error of prediction. Multiple prediction formulas and **multiple correlation** coefficients are presented in later chapters of this book (see Chap-

ter 12, Evaluating Body Composition). More comprehensive coverage of multiple regression can be found in Cohen and Cohen (2003), Ferguson and Takane (1989), and Pedhazur (1997).

Nonlinear Regression

The regression models discussed to this point assume a linear relationship. With some data, this is not the case. For example, when relating age and strength, the relation is linear for the ages of 10 through 17 because the person is growing and gaining muscle mass, but for ages 18 through 65 the relationship is nonlinear. As one starts to reach middle age, aging is associated with a loss of lean body weight, which results in a loss of strength. As explained in the correlation section, if the relationship is not linear, the linear correlation will be lower than the true correlation. Desktop computer programs have what is termed a "polynomial regression" program to compute the curvilinear correlation. Polynomial regression analysis is beyond the scope of this text.

Using the Computer

The simple prediction and multiple prediction equations are both time-consuming and complicated, especially when the number of people being tested is large. (It is suggested that prediction equations be developed using the scores of several hundred people.) Computer programs that do either simple or multiple prediction are commonly available for both the mainframe and the desktop computer.

In the SPSS package, a prediction equation can be obtained by selecting Linear Regression. In this option both a simple and multiple prediction equation can be obtained. See section 11 of the Statistical Procedures part of Appendix A for instructions for using it. The variables to be used must be identified, and then the dependent variable (Y) and the predictor (independent) variables (Xs) must be identified.

Using the data in Table 2.9 with Y equal to the mile run, and X equal to the skinfold, a simple prediction equation was obtained (see Table 2.14). The prediction equation is $Y' = 5.55149(\text{Skin}) +$

TABLE 2.14	**Output from Multiple Regression Using the Data in Table 2.9**	
Dependent Variable	**Mile**	
R = .45081	R-Square = .20323	
Variable	*B*	*Beta*
Skin	5.55149	.45081
Constant	352.32371	
Dependent Variable	**Mile**	
R = .54770	R-Square = .29997	
Variable	*B*	*Beta*
Skin	2.71712	.22064
Pull	−12.53334	−.38694
Constant	455.11206	

352.32371. The R (.45081) and the R-Square (.20323) values for the prediction equation suggest that it is not very accurate. In an effort to obtain a more accurate prediction equation, a multiple prediction equation with Y equal to the mile run, X_1 equal to the skinfold, and X_2 equal to the pull-up was obtained (see Table 2.14). The prediction equation is $Y' = 2.71712(\text{Skin}) - 12.53334(\text{Pull}) + 455.11206$. The R (.54770) and R-Square (.29997) values for the prediction equation suggest that it is not very accurate and not much better than the simple prediction equation. In a multiple prediction equation, a high correlation between the Y-score and each X-score but a low correlation among the X-scores is desirable. Note in Table 2.13 that all three variables used in the multiple prediction equation correlated about the same amount (.45 – .59) with each other.

RELIABILITY OF THE MEAN

Throughout this chapter we have placed considerable emphasis on the usefulness of the mean in describing the performance of a group. The mean is not constant; it can vary from day to day among the same individuals in a retest or from year to year if a new but similar group of individuals is tested. The performance of a group of individuals changes from day to day, even if ability has not changed, simply because people have good days and bad days. And the mean performances of different groups of individuals are seldom identical, even when the individuals are apparently equal in ability. If we can expect little variation in the mean, it is a highly accurate indicator of group ability; if we can expect considerable variation, it is not very accurate. We call the estimated variability of the mean the **standard error of the mean**. It is found using the following formula:

$$S_{\bar{x}} = \frac{s}{\sqrt{n}} \tag{2.14}$$

where $S_{\bar{x}}$ is the standard error of the mean, s is the standard deviation for the scores, and n is the number of individuals in the group.

Statistics books show that when many groups—all members of the same larger group, or population—are tested, the graph of the means is normal, centered around the population mean. The standard error is the standard deviation of the group means. The standard error can be used with the normal curve in the same manner as can the standard deviation; that is, 68% of the group means will be within one standard error of the population mean.

Problem 2.18   The mean for an agility test performed by 81 senior citizens is 12.5; the standard deviation is .81. Determine the standard error of the mean.

Solution   Where s is .81 and n is 81, the standard error of mean 12.5 is .09:

$$S_{\bar{x}} = \frac{.81}{\sqrt{81}} = \frac{.81}{9} = .09$$

If 12.5 is the population mean, 68% of the means for groups belonging to this population (senior citizens) will fall between 12.41 (12.5 − .09) and 12.59 (12.5 + .09). Thus any senior citizen groups with agility test means between 12.41 and 12.59

are probably similar in ability. In fact, if the group with mean 12.5 is tested on another day, the probability is 68% that its mean performance will fall between 12.41 and 12.59.

ADDITIONAL STATISTICAL TECHNIQUES

The statistical techniques presented to this point are those commonly used in measurement situations. The authors recognize that some measurement courses have become statistics courses or some mixture of measurement, statistics, and research courses. A detailed discussion of statistical tests is beyond the scope of this book, but a brief introduction to the logic is presented. If you wish a more detailed coverage of statistical tests, excellent nonmathematical discussions occur in Baumgartner and Hensley (2006) and Huck (2004). Vincent (2005) is a basic statistics book in kinesiology. More complete coverage of statistical tests can be found in any introductory-level statistics book. The presentation by Ferguson and Takane (1989) is easy to follow. Desktop computer packages of statistical programs include most, if not all, of the statistical tests commonly used.

There are times when the goal is to determine if various groups are different, that is, males versus females, or nonathletes versus athletes. Often the goal is to determine if a group has improved in ability due to a treatment like an exercise program. Researchers commonly use **t-tests** (not to be confused with T-scores) and Analysis of Variance (ANOVA) to determine if there is a large enough difference between two or more groups in mean performance to conclude that the groups are not equal in mean performance. Also, the t-tests and ANOVA can be used to determine if a group has improved in ability.

Background to Statistical Tests

Often researchers are interested in the characteristics of a large group. For example, what is the mean percent body fat for the 40,000 males who work for a particular industry, or which of three fitness training techniques is best for the 40,000 workers? To answer the first question, a researcher might measure all 40,000 males for percent body fat and then calculate the mean. This would be very time-consuming and expensive, and likely impossible. Instead of testing all of the large group of interest, called the *population*, the researcher tests some part of the population, called a *sample*. The mean for the sample is calculated, and then the researcher assumes the sample and population mean are equal. In other words, if the sample mean is 17, the researcher infers that the population mean is 17. In the earlier example of which fitness training technique is best, the researchers would obtain three samples and use a different fitness training technique on each sample. After the training technique had been used for a length of time (e.g., 6 weeks or longer) the researcher would test all the participants and determine if the mean performance of the groups was equal. Whatever the outcome, the researcher would infer the sample finding to the population.

In order to make this inference, the sample should be representative of the population and randomly selected. For a sample to be representative it must be taken from an identified population and it must be sufficiently large (i.e., 30 or more) so that all different abilities in the population are represented. Random selection of participants guarantees that all members of the population have an equal chance of being selected. In a research setting, this is done with a special table called a table of random numbers, but in a practical setting it might be accomplished by placing each person's name on a piece of paper, putting all the pieces of paper in a container, drawing out 50 pieces of paper, and designating the people drawn as the sample.

A researcher starts out with a statement concerning what he or she thinks may be the case at the population level. This statement is called the *null hypothesis*. For example, "Eighteen percent is the mean percent body fat for adult males," or "The three fitness training techniques are equally effective, so the means of the three groups are equal." Usually the mean or means obtained from the sample(s) will not equal the values in the null hypothesis. Then the question is whether the difference between what was hypothesized at the population level and found at the sample level is large enough to suggest that the null hypothesis is false or whether the difference is due to sampling error. *Sampling error* is due to the sample(s) not being 100% representative of the population. For example, if the mean percent body fat was hypothesized to be 18 but was 17 in the sample, is the hypothesis false or is this difference due to sampling error? If all three samples do not have the same mean after receiving their respective training technique, does this indicate that the hypothesis is false? To be able to make an objective decision, a statistical test is conducted. This statistical test is much like the probability statements earlier in this chapter. Based on the statistical test, the probability of the sample finding occurring if the null hypothesis is true can be determined. If the probability is quite small, the null hypothesis is rejected and the difference is considered to be real. Otherwise it is accepted and the difference is considered to be due to sampling error. Thus, a researcher must select some probability level that warrants rejection of the null hypothesis. This probability level is called the *alpha level*, and it is usually specified as .05 or .01. What most researchers do is look in the appropriate statistical table to find the value of the statistical test needed to reject the null hypothesis at the alpha level selected. If the value of the statistical test is greater than or equal to the table's value, the researcher rejects the null hypothesis. Many desktop computer programs provide a probability level (p) for the value of the statistical test. In this case the researcher rejects the null hypothesis if the p-value is less than or equal to the alpha level. All of this will become clearer with the examples provided, each with a different research design and statistical test.

t-Test for One Group

Step 1

The researcher's null hypothesis was that the mean percent body fat for the population was 18, so the hypothesized population mean (μ) is 18 (H_0:$\mu = 18$). As alternatives to this hypothesis, the researcher thought it possible that the mean could be less than 18 (H_1:$\mu < 18$) or greater than 18 (H_2:$\mu > 18$).

Step 2

An alpha level of .05 was selected.

Step 3

Knowing that a t-test would be the statistical test and the sample size would be 41, the researcher went to the t-tables and found that to reject the null hypothesis at alpha level .05 the value of the t-test would have to be greater than or equal to 2.021, or less than or equal to –2.021. This step is not needed if a desktop computer program is used, because p-values are calculated.

Step 4

The researcher randomly selected 41 men from the population as the sample, measured their percent body fat, calculated the mean and standard deviation for the body fat measurements, and calculated the t-test.

$$\bar{X} = 16.50 \qquad s = 2.50 \qquad n = 41$$

$$t = \frac{\bar{X} - \mu}{s/\sqrt{n}} = \frac{16.50 - 18}{2.50/\sqrt{41}} = \frac{-1.50}{2.50/6.40}$$

$$= \frac{-1.50}{.39} = -3.85$$

Step 5

Since the calculated value of t (–3.85) at Step 4 is less than the tabled value of t (–2.021) at Step 3, the research concludes that the difference between the null hypothesis valued (18) at Step 1 and the sample value (16.50) at Step 4 is real and not due to sample error. Thus, the researcher rejects the null hypothesis and accepts the most likely alternate hypothesis, which in this case is H_1, "the population mean is less than 18," since the sample mean was less than 18.

Now a few points of information about what was presented in the five-step example. At Step 3 when the researcher went to the t-tables (the tables in Ferguson & Takane were used) to identify the t-value needed for rejecting the null hypothesis, he or she had to line up a value called *degrees of freedom* and the alpha level to find the t-value. The degrees of freedom for this t-test is (n – 1) where n is the sample size. Since there were two alternate hypotheses, the researcher used the alpha level under a *two-tailed test*. For a two-tailed test this value is always interpreted as both plus and minus. If there had been only one alternate hypothesis, the alpha level under a *one-tailed test* would have been used and the value read from the table would have been interpreted as either plus or minus, depending on whether the alternate hypothesis was greater than (table value plus) or less than (table value minus). The table value is sometimes called the *critical value* or *critical region*. At Step 5, if the value of the statistical test at Step 4 is equal to or greater than the table value at Step 3, the difference and the statistical test are called *significant* (the difference is considered to be real), and the null hypothesis is rejected. If the value of the statistical test at Step 4 is not equal to or greater than the table value at Step 3, the difference and statistical test are called *nonsignificant* (the difference is considered to be due to sampling error), and the null hypothesis is accepted.

This t-test is useful in any measurement situation where the mean performance of a group is being compared to an expected mean or a standard or norm expressed as a mean. Does the mean of the group really differ from the expected mean?

Now, this t-test we just studied is one of three t-tests available, and the other two t-tests are not so easy to calculate by hand. Fortunately, most computer packages of statistical programs contain all three t-tests. In SPSS the t-test for one group is called One Sample t-test. See section 3 of the Statistical Procedures part of Appendix A for instructions on using it. The computer will ask for the null hypothesis value.

Presented in Table 2.15 are the scores of three groups on a sit-and-reach test. The scores of Group A were analyzed using the One Sample t-test program to test the null hypothesis that the population mean equals $10 (H_0:\mu = 10)$. The output of this program is presented in Table 2.16. Notice in Table 2.16 that the computer provides a two-tailed significance value (.025 in our example), so that looking up a table value is not necessary.

Dividing in half the two-tailed significance value provided by the computer yields the one-tailed significance value (.0125) if it is needed. In either case, if the significance value is less than or equal to the alpha level selected, the value of the statistical test is significant and the null hypothesis (H_0) is rejected. Otherwise, the null hypothesis is accepted.

t-Test for Two Independent Groups

In the situation of a t-test for two independent groups, either two samples are drawn from the same population and each sample is administered a different treatment or a sample is drawn from each of two populations. In the first case, two samples of size 75 each were drawn from a population of female college freshmen. Each sample received a different fitness program (treatment). Then a fitness test was administered to all the participants in both samples. After the treatments were administered, each sample represented a different population. In the second case, samples of size 40 were

TABLE 2.15	**Scores for Three Groups on a Sit-and-Reach Test**	
Group A	**Group B**	**Group C**
12	7	13
15	10	14
10	11	10
11	8	9
9	9	12
14	10	11
12	12	11
13	9	15

TABLE 2.16	**Output of the One-Sample t-Test of Group A in Table 2.15**
Number of Cases	8
Mean	12.00
Test Value	10.00
Difference	2.00
Standard Deviation	2.00
t-value	2.83
Degrees of Freedom	7
Two-Tailed Significance	.025

drawn from populations of last year's participants in a fitness program and this year's participants in the same fitness program. Then a fitness test was administered to all people in both samples. In either case, in the end the two samples represent different populations, and the question is whether there is a difference between the two samples in mean performance as an indication of whether there is a difference at the population level.

This t-test is useful in any measurement situation where the mean performances of two groups are being compared. For example, is the mean for a group in a fitness program last year equal to the mean for a group in the same fitness program this year, or are two groups in different fitness programs equal in mean performance?

Step 1: $H_0: \mu_1 - \mu_2 = 0$ (hypothesis that population means are equal)

$$H_1: \quad \mu_1 - \mu_2 > 0$$
$$H_2: \quad \mu_1 - \mu_2 < 0$$

Step 2:   Alpha = .05

Step 3:   Find t-test table value with degrees of freedom equal $(n_1 + n_2 - 2)$ where n_1 is the sample size for Group 1 and n_2 is for Group 2.

Step 4:   Conduct the study, collect the data, and calculate the t-test.

Step 5:   Compare the calculated t at Step 4 to the table value t at Step 3 and draw a conclusion to accept or reject H_0.

The Independent Samples t-test in SPSS does this t-test. See section 4 of the Statistical Procedures part of Appendix A for instructions on using it. The data of Groups A and B in Table 2.15 are used for an example analysis with this program. If a data file containing the data of the two groups is developed, each person must have a variable identifying group membership and a second variable that is his score. For example, the researcher might tell the computer that each person has two scores called *group* and *score*. The researcher is using

TABLE 2.17	Output of the t-Test for Independent Samples for Groups A and B in Table 2.15

Item	Group A	Group B
Number of Cases	8	8
Mean	12.00	9.50
Standard Deviation	2.00	1.60
t-value	2.76	
Degrees of Freedom	14	
Two-Tailed Significance	0.015	

group to indicate the group membership and score to indicate the score of the person. Thus, all participants in Group A will have a group score of 1 (always use numbers rather than letters), and all participants in Group B will have a group score of 2. The results of the analysis are presented in Table 2.17, where one can see that there is a significant difference between the two groups in favor of Group A. The two-tailed significance (.015) is less than .05, indicating significance. (The computer program only provides a two-tailed p-value.) (The one-tailed p-value would be .0075, which also indicates significance at .05.) With 14 degrees of freedom (8 + 8 − 2) and alpha .05, the two-tailed tabled t-value is 2.145, which also indicates significance. In either case, significance indicates that the null hypothesis (H_0) is rejected.

t-Test for Two Dependent Groups

One example of a t-test for two dependent groups is a group of people who are measured on two different occasions, usually at the beginning and end of the treatment condition. In this case there is some degree of correlation or dependency between the two columns of scores. This t-test is useful in any measurement situation where you want to determine whether the mean performance of a group changed over time or as the result of an instructional/training program.

Suppose eight people were selected and initially (I) measured for number of mistakes when juggling a ball. Then the people were taught to juggle and finally (F) retested. Let us say that in Table 2.15 the Group A scores are the initial scores and the Group B scores are the retest. To determine if the people improved in juggling ability as a result of the juggling instruction, a t-test for dependent groups is conducted.

Step 1: $H_0: \mu_I - \mu_F = 0$

$\quad\quad\quad H_1: \mu_I - \mu_F < 0$

Step 2:

Alpha = .05

Step 3:

Find t-test table value with degrees of freedom equal to n – 1, where n is the number of people. In this example the degrees of freedom is seven (8 – 1), and the tabled t-value is –1.895 for alpha equals .05 and a one-tailed test.

Step 4:

Conduct the study and calculate the t-test.

The Paired-Samples t-test in SPSS was used to analyze the example data. See section 5 of the Statistical Procedures part of Appendix A for instruc-

tions on using it. The data had to be entered in pairs, so the initial and final scores for Person 1 (12,7) were entered, followed by the initial and final scores for Person 2 (15,10), and so on. The printout of this analysis is presented in Table 2.18.

Step 5:

Since the probability in Table 2.18 is less than the .05 alpha level selected, the difference between the initial and final means is significant, and the null hypothesis is rejected. Notice that the calculated t exceeds the tabled t and the same conclusion would be drawn.

One-Way ANOVA

There are many research situations where there are more than two independent groups. This is just an extension of the two-independent-group situations already discussed. In these situations the statistical analysis is a one-way **analysis of variance** (one-way ANOVA). Actually, one-way ANOVA can be used with two or more independent groups, so it could be used rather than the t-test for two independent groups. The null hypothesis being tested is that the populations represented by the groups (samples) are equal in mean performance. The one alternate hypothesis is that the population means are not equal. One-way ANOVA is presented in Chapter 3 of this book, but with an application to measurement rather than research. However, the calculations are similar or the same with both applications.

One-way ANOVA in SPSS will do the analysis. See section 6 of the Statistical Procedures part of Appendix A for instructions on using it. As in the t-test for two independent groups, when the data are entered there must be a variable identifying group membership and a variable that is the score of a person. One-way ANOVA was applied to the data in Table 2.15. The output from one-way ANOVA for the data in Table 2.15 is presented in Table 2.19.

The statistical test in ANOVA is an F-ratio. From Table 2.19 it can be seen that the probability of the F of 4.45 is .0244. Since this probability is less than an alpha level of .05, a researcher would conclude that there is a significant difference among the means and accept the alternate hypothesis.

TABLE 2.18	Output of the t-Test for Dependent Measures Treating the A and B Groups Data in Table 2.15 as Repeated Measures

Item	Score 1	Score 2
Number of Pairs	*8*	
Mean	12.00	9.50
Std. Dev.	2.00	1.60
Difference in Means	–2.50	
t-value	–2.89	
Degrees of Freedom	7	
Two-Tailed Significance		.028

TABLE 2.19	Output from One-Way ANOVA for the Data in Table 2.15

Source	DF	Sum of Sq.	Mean Sq.	F-Ratio	F Prob.
Between Groups	2	31.75	15.88	4.45	0.0244
Within Groups	21	74.88	3.57		
Total	23	106.63			

Group	Count	Mean	Std. Dev.
A	8	12.00	2.00
B	8	9.50	1.60
C	8	11.88	2.03

TABLE 2.20	Output of the Repeated Measures ANOVA on the Data in Table 2.15, Treating the Three Groups as Repeated Measures

Trial	Mean	Std. Dev.	Cases
A	12.00	2.00	8
B	9.50	1.60	8
C	11.88	2.03	8

Source	Sum of Sq.	DF	Mean Sq.	F	Prob.
Between people	32.63	7	4.66		
Within people	74.00	16	4.63		
Between measures	31.75	2	15.88	5.26	.020
Residual	42.25	14	3.02		
Total	106.63	23	4.64		

Two-Way ANOVA, Repeated Measures

This is just an extension of the t-test for two dependent groups, with people repeatedly measured. In this case each person is measured on two or more occasions. Thus, if there are only two measures for each person, this ANOVA design is an alternative to the t-test for two dependent groups, but if there are more than two measures for each person, this ANOVA design must be used. The null hypothesis being tested is that at the population level the means for the repeated measures are equal. The alternate hypothesis is that the means are not equal. This ANOVA design is presented in Chapter 3 of this book, but with an application to measurement rather than research. However, the calculations are similar or the same with both applications. Using Reliability Analysis, in SPSS with the F-test op-

tion, a repeated measures ANOVA can be obtained. See section 12 of the Statistical Procedures part of Appendix A for instructions on using it. A repeated measures ANOVA was conducted on the data in Table 2.15 as if the first score in each group was the score of Person 1 who was tested under treatments A, B, and C (12,7,13), the second score in each group was the score of Person 2 (15,10,14), and so on. By selecting the option for item (treatment) means, the treatment means were obtained. The output from Reliability Analysis is presented in Table 2.20. The things of interest in Table 2.20 are the between people, between measures, and residual sources plus the F of 5.26, which is significant at the .05 level since the probability is .02. Thus, the alternate hypothesis is accepted and the researcher concludes that the treatment means differ.

SUMMARY

You should be sufficiently familiar with each of the techniques presented in this chapter to determine when it should be used, to calculate its value, and to interpret the results. Among the techniques discussed, means and standard deviations are most widely used. Standard scores, a very useful measure, are being used more frequently every year. The concept of correlation is crucial to the determination of reliability and validity, as we will discuss in Chapters 3 and 4. Also, you will find that percentile-rank norms accompany most physical performance tests.

Some understanding of the additional statistical techniques presented will certainly be helpful in reading the research literature. Good ability to use the desktop computer is an essential outcome of this chapter.

FORMATIVE EVALUATION OF OBJECTIVES

Objective 1   Select the statistical technique that is correct for a given situation.

1. The situations listed below are common to most physical education teachers and exercise specialists. In each case, determine what statistical value(s) is(are) needed.
   a. Determining the typical group performance.
   b. Determining which of two groups is the more heterogeneous in performance.
   c. Determining whether a group has improved in performance during a six-week training unit.
   d. Determining what percentage of the class scores fall below 70 on a 100-point knowledge test.
   e. Determining on which of four fitness tests an individual performed best in reference to the mean performance of his or her peers.
   f. Determining whether a certain test discriminates against heavy individuals.
   g. Determining whether a performance standard for a test is realistic in regard to the mean and standard deviation of the test.
   h. Determining the typical group performance if the scores are ordinal or the distribution of scores is skewed.
2. One reason for calculating various statistical values is to help in describing group performance. What statistics must be calculated to adequately describe the performance of a group?

Objective 2   Calculate accurately with the formulas presented.

1. The ability to calculate accurately using the formulas presented in the text is vital. To check your ability to work with the formulas, use the scores below to calculate.
   a. The three measures of central tendency and the standard deviation for the 50 scores.
   b. The mean and standard deviation for each column of scores.
   c. The percentile rank for scores 66 and 82.

84	82	95	92	83
80	58	82	81	60
79	87	71	90	69
82	75	70	89	85
69	79	80	74	69
84	81	71	90	87
66	79	52	92	72
70	86	87	77	87
90	89	69	68	83
85	92	76	74	89

2. There are many reasons physical education teachers and exercise specialists use standard scores. You should not only realize when standard scores are needed, but you should also be able to calculate them.
   a. Determine the T-score when X is 60 for a 2-minute sit-up test with mean 42 and standard deviation 8.

b. Determine the T-score when X is 11.3 for a 100-yard dash with mean 11.6 and standard deviation .55.

c. Use the information below to determine which individual did best overall when both tests are considered.

	100-yard dash	600-yard run
Tom	10.50	2 minutes
Bill	11.10	1 minute, 35 seconds
Mean	10.74	2 minutes
Standard Deviation	1.12	20 seconds

3. It is possible to solve probability statements using the normal curve, and there are several advantages to doing so. Consider the following probability statements, and solve them using the normal curve.

   a. $P(0 < z < 1.5)$

   b. $P(-.78 < z < 0)$

   c. $P(z < -1.34)$

   d. $P(X > \bar{X} + 2s)$

   e. $P(.5 < z < 1.5)$

   f. $P(z < .53)$

   g. $P(X > 15, \text{if } \bar{X} = 11 \text{ and } s = 2.5)$

   h. $P(z < ?) = (10/100)$

4. The median is sometimes used instead of the mean. Use the counting method to determine the median for each set of scores.

   a. 1,13,12,1,8,4,5,10,2,5,6,8,9

   b. 7,13,2,1,1,9,12,5,6,11,4,10

   c. 5,1,4,8,14,7,1,2,5

5. Correlation coefficients have many uses in physical education, as you will see in the next chapter. A correlation coefficient should be calculated using the scores of a large number of people, but to give you practice, the following are scores of a few people. Calculate the correlation coefficient for the two sets of scores.

Person	Long Jump	Dash
A	67	5.2
B	68	5.4
C	57	6.1
D	60	5.5
E	71	5.1

Objective 3   Interpret the statistical value selected or calculated.

1. In addition to being able to calculate with the formulas presented in the chapter, you should be able to interpret the statistical values you have selected or calculated. For each situation below, indicate how you might explain or describe the statistical value to a group with which you typically work.

   a. Mean 11.67 and standard deviation 2.39 for a pull-up test

   b. Percentile rank 83 for a 100-yard dash score of 11.9

   c. T-score 61 for the test described in (a)

2. In the next chapter, correlation coefficients are used and referenced extensively. It is essential, then, that you understand both the term and its interpretation. In your own words, summarize what a correlation coefficient is and how to interpret either a positive or negative value.

Objective 4   Make decisions based on all available information about a given situation.

1. The text presents several methods for calculating T-scores for the entire class. Identify which formulas you would use if a calculator were used.

Objective 5   Utilize the computer to analyze data.

1. Use the computer to analyze several of the sets of scores in this chapter and check your answers against those in the chapter.

ADDITIONAL LEARNING ACTIVITIES

1. Using the techniques presented for finding T-scores for the entire class, determine the T-score for each score in a set of scores.
2. Select three units you would teach during a semester and decide which tests you would administer after each unit. Now decide which statistical techniques you would apply to the scores collected during the semester.

BIBLIOGRAPHY

Baumgartner, T. A., and L. D. Hensley. 2006. *Conducting and reading research in health and human performance*. 4th ed. New York: McGraw-Hill.

Cohen, J., P. Cohen, S. G. West, and L. S. Aiken. 2003. *Applied multiple regression/correlation analysis for the behavioral sciences.* Mahwah, NJ: Lawrence Erlbaum Associates.

Ferguson, G. A. and Y. Takane. 1989. *Statistical analysis in psychology and education*. 6th ed. New York: McGraw-Hill.

Huck, S. W. 2004. *Reading statistics and research.* 4th ed. Boston: Allyn & Bacon.

Kuzma, J. W. and S. E. Bohnenblust. 2005. *Basic statistics for the health sciences.* 5th ed. New York: McGraw-Hill.

Larose, T. L. 1998. *Ready, Set, Run! A Student Guide to SAS Software for Microsoft Windows*. New York: McGraw-Hill.

Pavkov, T. and K. Pierce. 2007. *Ready, Set, Go! A Student Guide to SPSS 13.0 and 14.0 for Windows*. New York: McGraw-Hill.

Pedhazur, E. J. 1997. *Multiple regression in behavioral research: Explanation and prediction.* 3rd ed. New York: Harcourt Brace College Publishers.

Runyon, R. P. et al. 1996. *Fundamentals of behavioral statistics.* 8th ed. New York: McGraw-Hill.

Sanders, D. H. 1995. *Statistics: A first course.* 5th ed. New York: McGraw-Hill.

SAS. 2004. *JMP, Version 5.1.* Cary, NC: SAS.

SAS. 2005. *SAS Windows Version 9.1.* Cary, NC: SAS.

SPSS. 2005a. *SPSS 14.0.* Chicago, IL: SPSS.

SPSS. 2005b. *SPSS 13.0. Student Version.* Englewood-Cliffs, NJ: Prentice-Hall.

SPSS. 2005c. *SPSS 14.0. Brief Guide.* Englewood-Cliffs, NJ: Prentice-Hall.

Vincent, W. J. 2005. *Statistics in kinesiology.* 3rd ed. Champaign, IL: Human Kinetics.

RELIABILITY AND OBJECTIVITY

C O N T E N T S

K E Y   W O R D S

analysis of variance
confidence limits
criterion score
difference scores
internal-consistency reliability
coefficient
intraclass correlation coefficient
kappa coefficient
objectivity
pilot study
proportion of agreement coefficient
reliability
stability reliability coefficient
standard error of measurement
test-retest method

OBJECTIVES

Discussed in this chapter are the methods used to estimate reliability and objectivity, and the factors that influence the value of both of these characteristics of a test score.

Many physical performance tests can be given several times in the same day. When there are multiple trials of a test, the test administrator must decide how many to administer and what trial(s) to use as the criterion score.

After reading Chapter 3 you should be able to

1. Define and differentiate between reliability and objectivity for norm-referenced test scores, and outline the methods used to estimate these values.
2. Identify those factors that influence reliability and objectivity for norm-referenced test scores.
3. Identify those factors that influence reliability for criterion-referenced test scores.
4. Select a reliable criterion score based on measurement theory.

INTRODUCTION

There are certain characteristics essential to a measurement; without them, little faith can be put in the measurement and little use made of it. These characteristics are discussed in detail in Chapters 3 and 4 and referred to throughout the book. An extensive discussion of these characteristics is presented in Safrit and Wood (1989) and American Educational Research Association (1999).

The most important characteristic of a measurement is validity. Validity is discussed in greater detail in Chapter 4.

The second most important quality of a measurement is **reliability**. A reliable measure is consistently unchanged over a short period of time. That is, if an individual whose ability has not changed is measured twice, within a day or on two days close together, the two scores will be identical. For a measurement to have validity it must be reliable.

Another important characteristic of a measurement is objectivity. **Objectivity** is sometimes called rater reliability, because it is defined in terms of the agreement of competent judges about the value of a measurement. Thus, if two judges scoring the same individual on the same test cannot agree on a score, the measurement lacks objectivity, and neither score has reliability or validity. A lack of objectivity, then, reduces both reliability and validity.

Objectivity is necessary to have reliability, and reliability is necessary to have validity. So, when determining if these three essential characteristics of a measurement exist, objectivity and reliability are determined and then validity is estimated. Thus, objectivity and reliability are discussed in this chapter, and validity is discussed in Chapter 4.

The majority of this chapter deals with reliability and objectivity for norm-referenced tests. Since criterion-referenced tests are becoming quite common, reliability for criterion-referenced tests is presented in the last part of the chapter.

SELECTING A CRITERION SCORE

A **criterion score** is the measure used to indicate a person's ability. Unless a measure has perfect reliability, it is a better indicator when it is developed from more than one trial. Multiple trials are common in physical education with skinfold, flexibility, jumping, throwing, and short running tests—all tests whose performance is not adversely affected by fatigue. Multiple trials with skinfold, flexibility, and strength tests are common in exercise science.

Mean Score versus Best Score

For a multiple-trial test, the criterion score can be either the person's best score or her mean score. The best score is the optimal score a person receives on any one trial; the mean score is the mean of all the person's trial scores.

Much research has been done on the selection of a criterion score (Baumgartner 1974; Berger & Sweney 1965; Disch 1975; Henry 1967; Hetherington 1973; Johnson & Meeter 1977; Whitley & Smith 1963). The choice of best or mean score should be based on the amount of time available to obtain the criterion score and the use to be made of it. It is a much slower process to calculate a mean score than to list a best score for each person. This is probably why standardized instructions for most multiple-trial tests suggest using the best score. Certainly, when the criterion score is to be used as an indicator of maximum possible performance, the best score should be used. Certainly in a track meet where participants are allowed multiple jumps or throws, the best score is the person's score. However, the best score from several trials may not be typical, in that it is unlikely to be achieved again for a long time and may be inflated by measurement error. Reliability of a criterion score increases as the number of measures it is based on increases. Thus, the most reliable criterion score and the best indicator of true ability (typical performance) may be the mean score. In theory, the sum of the errors of measurement is 0 when all of an individual's trial scores are added together. Because in most situations one wants an indication of status or typical performance, the mean score may be the preferred criterion score for a multiple-trial test. So, if multiple skinfold measures were taken at each site, the mean for the measures at a site would be the criterion score for the site. When scores are changing from day to day, as may be true for individuals with disabilities, the mean of the scores collected on several days may well be the only indicator of true ability.

More Considerations

Darracott (1995) believes that for multiple-trial physical performance tests where maximal ability rather than typical ability is desired, and the equipment and scoring procedure are highly accurate (which could be the case with many physiological measurements taken in a laboratory setting), the best score is the best indicator of a person's true ability and it is likely that lower trial scores are due to negative measurement error. Particularly for physiological tests with highly accurate scoring procedures and/or equipment, a person can't score better than his or her physiological capacity. The multiple-trial field-based fitness tests that Darracott analyzed were not physiological capacity type tests, but still the distribution of the trial scores of most of the people were negatively skewed (see Chapter 2) rather than normally distributed. Thus,

the best trial score or maybe the median trial score of a person would seem to be a better criterion score than the mean of the trial scores of a person. Darracott found that the test-retest or stability reliability (discussed in next section) for criterion scores that were the mean trial score and the best trial score were very similar for the several field-based tests she examined.

Further, she found that the trend in the multiple-trial data of individuals did not follow the trend in the multiple-trial data of the group. For example, even though for a four-trial test the mean score for the group was best on trials 2 and 3, with the mean score on trials 1 and 4 much worse, in each trial there were some people who received their best score and some people who received their worst score. This suggests that decisions as to which trial(s) to use in determining the criterion score should be based on individual performance rather than group mean performance. Thus, in the previous four-trial test example, rather than the criterion score being the mean of the scores of trials 2 and 3, it should be the mean of an individual's two best scores. It was suggested at the beginning of this section that the criterion score be based on more than one trial. Also, if the best score of multiple-trial scores is the criterion score, (1) it still follows the suggestion of being based on multiple trials, and (2) it is not the same trial for each person. More on selecting the criterion score based on group mean performance is presented later in this chapter, in the Intraclass R from Two-Way Analysis of Variance section.

Summary

Based on all that has been presented concerning selecting a criterion score, an individual's criterion score for multiple-trial data could be determined in any of the following ways, depending on the situation and what the test administrator believes is most appropriate: (1) mean of all the trial scores, (2) best score of all the trial scores, (3) mean of selected trial scores based on the trials on which the group scored best, or (4) mean of selected trial scores based on the trials on which the individual scored best. In terms of the fourth method (based on the data Darracott [1995] used in her study), if four to six trials are administered, there seems to be a tendency for a person to have one trial score that is markedly worse than the rest of the trial scores. Thus, the worst trial score could be discarded and the mean of the remaining trial scores could be the criterion score. It is interesting to note here that discarding the worst trial score for a person makes the distribution of the remaining trial scores for the person considerably more like a normal distribution (researchers would call the trial score discarded an "outlier"). Thus, the way an individual's criterion score is determined influences the individual's score and is important.

In Chapter 4 you will learn that for a score to have validitity it must be reliable, but reliability does not guarantee validity. Thus, with multiple-trial data the method used to determine the criterion score must be selected by considering what is the criterion score with the most reliability and validity, and not simply what is the score with the most reliability.

TYPES OF RELIABILITY

The reliability of physical performance measures has traditionally been estimated by one of two methods: the test-retest (stability) method, or the internal-consistency method. Because each yields a different reliability coefficient, it is important to use the most appropriate method for a given measuring instrument. It is also important to notice the methods others have used to calculate their reliability coefficients. Remember too that a test may yield reliable scores for one group of individuals and not for another. For example, a test that yields highly reliable scores for college students may yield only moderately reliable scores for high school students or participants in an adult fitness program.

An issue involved in the calculation of a reliability coefficient is whether the reliability coefficient should indicate *stability* or *internal consistency*.

Stability Reliability

When individual scores change little from one day to the next, they are stable. When scores remain stable, we consider them reliable. We use the test-retest method to obtain the **stability reliability coeffi-**

cient. With this method, each person is measured with the same test or instrument on several (usually two) different days. The correlation between these two sets of scores is the stability reliability coefficient. The closer this coefficient is to positive one (+1), the more stable and reliable the scores.

Three factors can contribute to a low stability reliability coefficient:

1. The people tested may perform differently;
2. The measuring instrument may operate or be applied differently; and
3. The person administering the measurement may change.

Lack of sleep, minor injuries, and anxiety all tend to lower one's level of performance. Also, if the instrument is not consistent from day to day—for example, if measuring devices get out of calibration or malfunction—or if the procedures used to collect the measures change, the stability reliability decreases. Finally, if the way in which the administrator scores the people tested or perceives their performance changes, reliability decreases.

Usually, test-retest scores are collected one to three days apart. However, for a maximum-effort test, we advise retesting seven days later, because fatigue and soreness can affect test scores. If the interval between measurements is too long, scores may change because of increased maturation or practice, factors that are generally not considered sources of measurement error.

Some people object to the **test-retest method** because of the time required to administer a measuring instrument at least twice. Also, only the Day 1 scores are used as performance measures; subsequent scores are used solely to determine reliability. Yet the method is probably the most appropriate of the procedures for determining the reliability of physical performance measures. Without test-retest consistency, we lack a true indicator, not only of each participant's ability, but of the faith we can place in the measure.

To save time, a person might calculate the test-retest reliability coefficient by retesting only some of the individuals originally tested. The procedure is to administer the test to all people on Day 1, and then to pick 50 people at random to be retested.

(Draw names from a hat or use any procedure that gives all people an equal chance of being selected.) The test-retest reliability is then calculated using the scores of the randomly selected people. The danger with this procedure is that if the reliability is low, all of the data should be discarded.

Most physical measures are stable from day to day. However, Baumgartner (1969b) found that scores may not be stable if people have not had prior experience and/or practice with the test prior to being measured.

Internal-Consistency Reliability

Many people use an internal-consistency method to estimate the reliability of their measures. The advantage of this method is that all measures are collected in a single day. Internal consistency refers to a consistent rate of scoring by the individuals being tested throughout a test or, when multiple trials are administered, from trial to trial.

Test administrators commonly use multiple trials when measuring physical ability. Examples are multiple measures of the skinfold at a site, multiple measures of the strength of a muscle or muscle group, and multiple trials of a physical performance test.

To obtain an **internal-consistency reliability coefficient**, the evaluator must give at least two trials of the test within a single day. Changes in the scores of the people being tested from trial to trial indicate a lack of test reliability. The correlation among the trial scores is the internal-consistency reliability coefficient. Obviously this technique should not be used with a maximum-performance test (e.g., the mile run) when fatigue would certainly affect the second trial scores.

Stability versus Internal Consistency

The internal-consistency reliability coefficient is not comparable to the stability reliability coefficient. The former is not affected by day-to-day changes in performance, a major source of measurement error in the latter. An internal-consistency reliability coefficient is almost always higher than its corresponding stability reliability coefficient.

Education, psychology, and other disciplines that rely heavily on paper-and-pencil tests seldom, if ever, use the test-retest method, using instead the internal-consistency method. Remember that the stability coefficient assumes that true ability has not changed from one day to the next, an assumption often unjustifiable with paper-and-pencil tests, because cognitive learning usually does occur between administrations. Psychomotor learning is less apt to vary in a one- or two-day span, making the stability coefficient a better indicator of the reliability of physical performance data.

RELIABILITY THEORY

We can better understand reliability for norm-referenced tests if we understand the mathematical theory at its foundation. Reliability can be explained in terms of "observed scores," "true scores," and "error scores." Reliability theory assumes that any measurement on a continuous scale contains an inherent component of error, the measurement error. Any one or more of the following factors can be a source of measurement error:

1. Lack of agreement among scorers (i.e., objectivity);
2. Lack of consistent performance by the individual tested;
3. Failure of an instrument to measure consistently; and
4. Failure of the tester to follow standardized testing procedures.

Assume that we are about to measure the heights of five people, all 68 inches tall. If we report any scores other than 68, an error of measurement has occurred. Thus, the variance for the reported heights is a good indicator of the amount of measurement error. As discussed in Chapter 2, a population is all the people who have a specified set of characteristics; a sample is a subgroup of a population. The variance is the square of the standard deviation and is symbolized as σ^2 for the variance of a population and s^2 for the variance of a sample. If all reported scores are 68, there is no measurement error and the variance is zero. However, if the five people are not all the same height, the variance for the reported heights may be due either to a true difference in height or to an error of measurement. In either case, the variance cannot be used as an indicator of measurement error.

In theory, the observed (recorded) score X is the sum of the true score t and an error of measurement score e:

$$X = t + e$$

For example, if an individual who is 70.25 inches tall (t) has a recorded height of 70.5 (X), the error of measurement (e) is .25:

$$70.5 = 70.25 + .25$$

If that individual is measured again and the recorded score is 69.5, the error of measurement equals $-.75$:

$$69.5 = 70.25 + -.75$$

The variance for a set of observed scores equals the variance of the true scores plus the variance of the error scores:

$$\sigma_x^2 = \sigma_t^2 + \sigma_e^2$$

where σ_x^2 is the variance of the observed scores, σ_t^2 is the variance of the true scores, and σ_e^2 is the variance of the error scores.

Reliability, then, is the ratio of the true-score variance to the observed-score variance:

$$\text{Reliability} = \frac{\sigma_t^2}{\sigma_x^2} = \frac{\sigma_x^2 - \sigma_e^2}{\sigma_x^2} = 1 - \frac{\sigma_e^2}{\sigma_x^2}$$

We can see from this formula that when no measurement error exists—that is, when σ_e^2 equals 0— the reliability is 1. As measurement error increases, σ_e^2 increases and reliability decreases. Thus, reliability is an indicator of the amount of measurement error in a set of scores.

Reliability depends on two basic factors:

1. reducing the variation attributable to measurement error; and
2. detecting individual differences (i.e., variation of the true scores) within the group measured.

The reliability of a set of scores, then, must be viewed in terms of the measurement error (error variance) and how well the scores discriminate among different levels of ability within the group measured (true-score variance).

ESTIMATING RELIABILITY: INTRACLASS CORRELATION

As we have noted, an observed score (X) is theoretically composed of a true score (t) and an error score (e). Furthermore, the variance of the observed scores (σ_x^2) equals the variance of the true scores (σ_t^2) plus the variance of the error scores (σ_e^2). Reliability equals the true-score variance divided by the observed-score variance. Just as observed-score variance can be divided into several parts, the total variability (s^2) for a set of scores can be divided into several parts. To divide, or partition, the variance, we use the technique of **analysis of variance** (ANOVA). We can then use these parts of the total variance to calculate an intraclass reliability coefficient.

Before discussing two analysis of variance models for calculating an intraclass reliability coefficient, there are two things that you need to recognize. First, reliability for a score from a test should be estimated prior to using the test to collect a large amount of data in a measurement program or research study. So, the test is administered to a small group of people similar in characteristics to the group on which the test will ultimately be used, and reliability of the scores is estimated. In research this testing of a small group is called a **pilot study,** so we will use this term. Often the number of test scores collected (multiple-trial or multiple-day scores) for each person in the pilot study is more than in the measurement program or research study. The amount of data collected in the pilot study is necessary in order to be able to calculate an intraclass reliability coefficient. Articles concerned with the reliability of scores from a particular test are found in many research journals. *Measurement in Physical Education and Exercise Science* has many reliability articles.

Second, although the hand calculations for ANOVA are presented, the calculations are difficult and time-consuming. *Most people use the computer to do the ANOVA and use the ANOVA results to quickly and easily calculate an intraclass reliability coeffi-*

cient. Do not allow the hand calculations presented to discourage you from using the ANOVA technique to calculate an intraclass reliability coefficient.

Intraclass R from One-Way Analysis of Variance

To calculate an intraclass correlation coefficient, R, as an estimate of reliability, each person tested in a physical education class, activity or fitness program, or therapy program must have at least two scores. Here we replace the reliability formula

$$\text{Reliability} = \frac{\sigma_t^2}{\sigma_x^2}$$

with

$$R = \frac{MS_A - MS_W}{MS_A} \qquad \textbf{(3.1)}$$

where R is the **intraclass correlation coefficient** (in this formula R is an estimate of the reliability of a criterion score that is the sum or mean test score for each person), MS_A is the mean square among people, and MS_W is the mean square within people. To obtain the two mean squares, a one-way analysis of variance was applied to the data. A mean square value is a variance just like the variance s^2 discussed in Chapter 2.

To calculate MS_A and MS_W, we must first define six values from the sets of scores:

1. The sum of squares total, SS_T (used to check our calculations)
2. The degrees of freedom total, df_T (used to check our calculations)
3. The sum of squares among people, SS_A
4. The sum of squares within people, SS_W
5. The degrees of freedom among people, df_A
6. The degrees of freedom within people, df_W

$$SS_T = \Sigma X^2 - \frac{(\Sigma X)^2}{nk} \qquad df_T = nk - 1$$

$$SS_A = \frac{\Sigma T_i^2}{k} - \frac{(\Sigma X)^2}{nk} \qquad df_A = n - 1$$

$$SS_W = \Sigma X^2 - \frac{\Sigma T_i^2}{k} \qquad df_W = n(k - 1)$$

where ΣX^2 is the sum of the squared scores, ΣX is the sum of the scores of all people, n is the number of people, k is the number of scores for each person, and T_i is the sum of the scores for person i. With these values in hand, it is a simple matter to calculate the mean square among people,

$$MS_A = \frac{SS_A}{df_A} = \frac{SS_A}{n - 1}$$

and the mean square within people,

$$MS_W = \frac{SS_W}{df_W} = \frac{SS_W}{n(k - 1)}$$

In the calculation of MS_A ($MS_A = SS_A/df_A$), SS_A will equal zero if all people have the same score, but will be greater than zero if people differ in score. It is not expected that all people will have the same score, so SS_A and MS_A will be greater than zero and MS_A is used to estimate true score variance (σ_t^2). Further, in the calculation of MS_W ($MS_W = SS_W/df_W$), SS_W will equal zero if for each person all the scores for the person are the same (perfect reliability), but will be greater than zero if scores for any person are not the same. Thus, MS_W is an estimate of error score variance (σ_e^2).

Students in measurement classes of the first author of this book do not calculate the one-way ANOVA values by hand. The students use the computer to get the necessary values to calculate R by hand. Hand calculations of the one-way ANOVA values are presented so that you can see all that is involved and so that if you want to do the hand calculations, you have an example to follow.

Problem 3.1 Using one-way analysis of variance, calculate R for the data in Table 3.1.

Solution To solve for R, we use a nine-step procedure:

TABLE 3.1	**One-Way ANOVA Data**	
Person	**Day 1**	**Day 2**
A	9	9
B	1	2
C	8	7

Step 1

Obtain the sum of the scores, T, for each person:

Person	Day 1	Day 2	T
A	9	9	18
B	1	2	3
C	8	7	15

Step 2

Obtain the sum of the scores, ΣX, and the sum of the squared scores, ΣX^2:

$$\Sigma X = 9 + 9 + 1 + 2 + 8 + 7* = 36$$

$$\Sigma X^2 = 9^2 + 9^2 + 1^2 + 2^2 + 8^2 + 7^2$$
$$= 81 + 81 + 1 + 4 + 64 + 49$$
$$= 280$$

Step 3

Calculate the 3 sum-of-squares values:

$$SS_T = \Sigma X^2 - \frac{(\Sigma X)^2}{nk} = 280 - \frac{36^2}{(3)(2)}$$
$$= 280 - \frac{1296}{6} = 280 - 216 = 64$$

$$SS_A = \frac{\Sigma T_i^2}{k} - \frac{(\Sigma X)^2}{nk}$$
$$= \frac{18^2 + 3^2 + 15^2}{2} - \frac{36^2}{(3)(2)}$$
$$= \frac{558}{2} - \frac{1296}{6} = 279 - 216 = 63$$

$$SS_W = \Sigma X^2 - \frac{\Sigma T_i^2}{k} = 280 - \frac{18^2 + 3^2 + 15^2}{2}$$
$$= 280 - \frac{558}{2} = 280 - 279 = 1$$

Step 4

Check your calculations. The sum of squares among people (SS_A) plus the sum of squares within people (SS_W) should equal the sum of squares total (SS_T):

$$63 + 1 = 64$$

(If your figures here were incorrect, you would go back and recalculate.)

*You could total the T column for this value as well ($18 + 3 + 15 = 36$).

Step 5

Calculate the 3 degrees of freedom values:

$$df_T = nk - 1 = (3)(2) - 1 = 5$$
$$df_A = n - 1 = 3 - 1 = 2$$
$$df_W = n(k - 1) = 3(2 - 1) = 3$$

Step 6

Check your calculations. The degrees of freedom among people (df_A) plus the degrees of freedom within people (df_W) should equal the degrees of freedom total (df_T):

$$2 + 3 = 5$$

Step 7

Calculate MS_A and MS_W. Where SS_A is 63, n is 3, SS_W is 1, and k is 2, the mean square among people, MS_A, is 31.50 and the mean square within people, MS_W, is .33:

$$MS_A = \frac{63}{3 - 1} = \frac{63}{2} = 31.50$$

$$MS_W = \frac{1}{(3)(2 - 1)} = \frac{1}{3} = .33$$

Step 8

Place all your values in an ANOVA summary table to make sure nothing has been left out and everything is correct.

Source	df	SS	MS
Among people	df_A	SS_A	MS_A
Within people	df_W	SS_W	MS_W
Total	df_T		

Source	df	SS	MS
Among people	2	63	31.50
Within people	3	1	.33
Total	5	64	

Step 9

Now we can calculate R. Where MS_A is 31.50 and MS_W is .33, the intraclass reliability coefficient R is .99:

$$R = \frac{MS_A - MS_w}{MS_A}$$

$$= \frac{31.50 - .33}{31.50} = \frac{31.17}{31.50} = .99$$

R is an estimate of the reliability of a criterion score that is the sum or mean test score for each person. When R equals 0 there is no reliability; when R equals 1 there is maximum reliability. Whenever multiple trials are administered on one day or a test is administered on at least two days, we can use R to estimate the reliability of the mean score. if the person's scores change from trial to trial or from day to day, R will be lower.

With the availability of computers, the calculation of R is quite easy. A simple or one-way analysis of variance computer program provides the mean squares needed to calculate R. These computer programs are easily found for any computer. In the SPSS package of statistical programs, the One-Way ANOVA program will do a one-way analysis of variance (see Additional Statistical Techniques in Chapter 2). If a computer program is used, notice that each person is treated as a group. This may be a problem, since the number of people often exceeds the maximum number of groups allowed by a computer program. Further, the data input organization for a one-way ANOVA is not compatible with the data input organization required by other statistical techniques if additional statistical analyses are applied to the data. To avoid these two problems, use a repeated measures ANOVA program for the data analysis (see Computer Use section later in this chapter).

The R formula provided so far and used in Problem 3.1 is for the reliability of a criterion score that is the sum or mean test score for each person. There are other Rs that could be calculated depending on the situation. The data for Problem 3.1 are from each person tested on each of two days. In an actual testing situation, this data would be collected in a pilot study and people would be tested on two days, just so reliability could be estimated. In the actual measurement program the instructor would like to administer the test on one day and be confident that the scores collected were reliable. So, R is calculated for a criterion score that is a single score on one day by this formula:

$$R = \frac{MS_A - MS_W}{MS_A + \left(\frac{k}{k'} - 1\right)(MS_W)} \quad \textbf{(3.2)}$$

where R is an estimate of the reliability for a criterion score composed of k′ scores, k is the number of scores per person in the pilot study, and k′ is the number of scores per person in the actual measurement program.

This is how we would estimate the reliability for a score collected on one day using the data and ANOVA values in Problem 3.1: k = 2 and k′ = 1.

$$R = \frac{31.50 - .33}{31.5 + \left(\frac{2}{1} - 1\right)(.33)} = \frac{31.17}{31.83} = .98$$

If the two scores per person in Problem 3.1 were trials instead of two days, most likely in the pilot study and actual measurement program, two trial scores would be collected for each person, and the criterion score for each person would be the mean or sum of the test scores for each person. So, the R would be as calculated in Step 9 of Problem 3.1 using Formula 3.1. However, if the instructor wanted the criterion score of a person in the actual measurement program to be the better of the two trial scores, in both the pilot study and the actual measurement program two trial scores would be administered, but R would be calculated using Formula 3.2 with k = 2 and k′ = 1. Note that this would be the same formula and the same R value (.98) as earlier for a criterion score composed of a score collected on one day for each person.

This reliability coefficient using a one-way ANOVA is only one of many intraclass reliability coefficients. It is the simplest to determine because it requires the least calculation and decision making. Slightly more advanced procedures may yield a more precise criterion score. Baumgartner (1969a) describes a selection procedure that yields a criterion score minimally influenced by learning or fatigue and the intraclass reliability for that score. Feldt and McKee (1958) present a way to estimate reliability using the intraclass method when multiple trials are administered on each of several days. Safrit and Wood (1989) have several strong chapters on reliability. Wood and Zhu (2006) have an excellent coverage of reliability and other advanced topics in measurement in the physical domain.

TABLE 3.2	Sample ANOVA Summary Table for n People and k Trials		
Source	DF	SS	MS
Among people	$n-1$	SS_p	MS_p
Among trials	$k-1$	SS_t	MS_t
Interaction	$(n-1)(k-1)$	SS_I	MS_I
Total	$nk-1$	SS_T	

Intraclass R from Two-Way Analysis of Variance

Suppose that k scores were collected for each of n people. These scores could have been collected over k trials or k days. For discussion purposes, we will refer to the k scores as trials. If a two-way analysis of variance were applied to the k scores of these n people, a summary table could be developed as shown in Table 3.2.

Most people use the computer to calculate the values in a two-way analysis of variance summary table. Computer use is discussed later in the chapter. However, the formulas and procedures for conducting a two-way analysis of variance are presented for people who are interested.

For two-way ANOVA, the following formulas are used to calculate the various sums of squares:

$$\text{Sum of squares total } (SS_T) = \Sigma X^2 - \frac{(\Sigma X)^2}{nk}$$

Sum of squares among people (SS_P)

$$= \frac{\Sigma(T_i)^2}{k} - \frac{(\Sigma X)^2}{nk}$$

Sum of squares among trials (SS_I)

$$= \frac{\Sigma(T_j)^2}{n} - \frac{(\Sigma X)^2}{nk}$$

Sum of squares interaction (SS_I)

$$= \Sigma X^2 + \frac{(\Sigma X)^2}{nk} - \frac{\Sigma(T_i)^2}{k} - \frac{\Sigma(T_i)^2}{n}$$

$df_T = nk - 1$, $df_p = n - 1$, $df_t = k - 1$

$df_I = (n - 1)(k - 1)$

TABLE 3.3	Two-Way ANOVA Data for Three-Trial Test Administered on One Day		
Person	Trial 1	Trial 2	Trial 3
A	5	6	7
B	3	3	4
C	4	4	5
D	7	6	6
E	6	7	5

where ΣX^2 is the sum of the squared scores, ΣX is the sum of the scores of all people, n is the number of people, k is the number of scores for each person, T_i is the sum of the scores for Person i, and T_j is the sum of the scores for Trial j.

Problem 3.2   Using the two-way analysis of variance formulas, develop a summary table of the data in Table 3.3.

Solution   These first four steps in the procedure are similar to those used in one-way ANOVA.

Step 1

Set up a table to calculate the sum of scores for each person (T_i) and for each trial (T_j):

Person	Trial 1	Trial 2	Trial 3	T_i
A	5	6	7	18
B	3	3	4	10
C	4	4	5	13
D	7	6	6	19
E	6	7	5	18
T_j	25	26	27	78

Step 2

Calculate the values needed to determine the sums of squares: ΣX^2, ΣX, $\dfrac{\Sigma(T_i)^2}{k}$, and $\dfrac{\Sigma(T_j)^2}{n}$.

$$\Sigma X^2 = 5^2 + 6^2 + 7^2 + \ldots + 6^2 + 7^2 + 5^2$$
$$= 432$$
$$\Sigma X = 5 + 6 + 7 + \ldots + 6 + 7 + 5* = 78$$

*Here too, the sum of the T_j column could be used.

$$\frac{\Sigma(T_i)^2}{k} = \frac{18^2 + 10^2 + 13^2 + 19^2 + 18^2}{3}$$

$$= \frac{1278}{3} = 426$$

$$\frac{\Sigma(T_j)^2}{n} = \frac{25^2 + 26^2 + 27^2}{5} = \frac{2030}{5} = 406$$

Step 3

Where ΣX^2 is 432, ΣX is 78, n is 5, k is 3, $\frac{\Sigma(T_i)^2}{k}$ is 426, and $\frac{\Sigma(T_j)^2}{n}$ is 406, SS_T, SS_S, and SS_t, and SS_I are as follows:

$$SS_T = 432 - \frac{78^2}{(5)(3)} = 432 - \frac{6084}{15}$$

$$= 432 - 405.6 = 26.4$$

$$SS_P = 426 - 405.6 = 20.4$$

$$SS_t = 406 - 405.6 = .4$$

$$SS_I = 432 + 405.6 - 426 - 406$$

$$= 837.6 - 832 = 5.6$$

Step 4

Check your calculations. The sum of the sum of squares among people, the sum of squares among trials, and the sum of squares interaction should equal the sum of squares total:

$$20.4 + .4 + 5.6 = 26.4$$

Step 5

Following the procedure in Table 3.2, the summary table for the data in Table 3.3 would look like this:

Source	DF	SS	MS
Among people	4	20.4	5.10
Among trials	2	.4	.20
Interaction	8	5.6	.70
Total	14	26.4	

Selecting the Criterion Score

This section deals with selecting the criterion score and ANOVA model for R, so we recommend that you review the information presented earlier concerning selecting a criterion score. The procedures presented here for selecting the criterion score are usually done with the data in a pilot study, but might be used with the data in the actual measurement program.

Criterion Score Is Mean   If the criterion score will be the mean or sum of the trial scores for a person and not the best score, once the summary table has been developed, we need to determine whether the trial means seem to be different. One way to do this is to visually compare the trial means. For the data used in Problem 3.2, the trial means are 5.0, 5.2, and 5.4; so there does not seem to be a true difference among the trial means. There is nothing wrong with using the visual comparison of the means (and this is what most practitioners will do), but it is approximate. Researchers and people who want to be very precise in making a decision concerning whether the trial means differ will determine whether the trial means differ significantly using the F-test formula $F = MS_t/MS_I$. For example, the F from the summary table in Problem 3.2 is .29 ($F = .20/.70 = .29$). If the F is significant, there is real, or true, difference among the trial means. If the F is nonsignificant, the difference between trial means is not considered a true difference, but rather a chance one. (To review significance versus nonsignificance, see Additional Statistical Techniques in Chapter 2.)

After deciding whether there is a true difference among the trial means, you can proceed with the analysis in one of three potential ways, as shown in Figure 3-1. If there is no true difference among the trial means, the estimated reliability of the criterion score, which is the sum or mean of a person's trial scores, is as follows:

$$R = \frac{MS_P - MS_W}{MS_P} \tag{3.3}$$

$$\text{where } MS_W = \frac{SS_t + SS_I}{df_t + df_I}$$

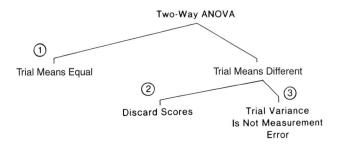

Figure 3-1

Two-way ANOVA decision process.

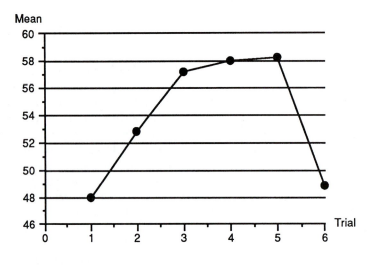

Figure 3-2

Graph of the means for a six-trial test.

Using the data in Problem 3.2, where MS_W is $.6\left(\dfrac{.4 + 5.6}{2 + 8}\right)$, R is .88:

$$R = \frac{5.10 - .6}{5.10} = \frac{4.50}{5.10} = .882 = .88$$

Notice that Formula 3.3 is the same as Formula 3.1 for R presented with a one-way ANOVA since SS_P in a two-way ANOVA is the same as SS_A in a one-way ANOVA. Applying the one-way ANOVA formulas to the data in Table 3.3, we obtain the following:

$$MS_A = \frac{20.4}{5 - 1} = 5.1$$

$$MS_W = \frac{6}{(5)(3 - 1)} = .6$$

$$R = \frac{5.1 - .6}{5.1} = .88$$

The other alternative ways for the analysis to go are possible when the trial means are different. With the first technique (number 2 in Figure 3-1), which can be used when each person is tested several times in one day or on several days, the scores from trials whose means are lower than or not approximately equal to the means of the other trials are discarded (Baumgartner 1969a). A second two-way analysis of variance is then conducted on the retained scores, and a decision made as to whether there is a true difference among the means of the trials retained. If there is no difference among the trial means, Formula 3.3 is used to estimate the reliability of the criterion score, the sum or mean of each person's retained trial scores. For example, suppose the data for a six-trial test were as presented in Figure 3-2. Trials 1, 2, and 6 would be discarded, and another two-way ANOVA would be conducted using the scores from Trials 3, 4, and 5.

The purpose of this technique (number 2 in Figure 3-1) is to find a measurement schedule free of true trial differences and yielding the largest possible criterion score for most people. This criterion score is usually very reliable. Baumgartner and Jackson (1970) used this technique. Trial-to-trial variance is random after finding no true difference among trial means (nonsignificant F), so trial-to-trial variance is considered a measurement error in Formula 3.3. Interaction is also considered a measurement error.

The last alternative (number 3 in Figure 3-1) does not consider a trial-to-trial variance as measurement error. This technique is often used when it is known that people will improve from trial to trial. Also, this technique is often used when estimating objectivity (judges replace trials) and all judges are not expected to use the same standards. The formula for estimating the reliability of the criterion score (the sum or mean of all trials) is as follows:

$$R = \frac{MS_P - MS_I}{MS_P}$$

$$(3.4)$$

For the data in Problem 3.2, using Formula 3.4, R is .86:

$$R = \frac{5.10 - .70}{5.10} = \frac{4.40}{5.10} = .86$$

Measurement error is supposed to be random. True difference among the trial means indicates a lack of randomness. This is often due to people not being ready to be tested or not being sufficiently familiar with the test, so they improve from trial to trial. Thus, when a true difference among the trial means is found, one could argue that the variance for trials should not be combined with the sum of squares interaction to form the mean square within (MS_W) in Formula 3.3. Statistically this position is defensible. However, one could counter that every source of variance not attributable to people is error-score variance. In keeping with this philosophy, you can either conduct a one-way analysis of variance with the test scores or, as Baumgartner (1969a) advocates, discard scores until no significant difference among trial means is found in the data and then use Formula 3.3.

Of the three potential data analyses shown in Figure 3-1, it seems that most people are using al-

ternatives 2 and 3. Only when people must do the data analysis by hand is a one-way ANOVA initially applied to the data.

Criterion Score Is Single Score Earlier in this chapter in the sections on selecting a criterion score and intraclass R from one-way analysis of variance, there was discussion of the criterion score as one score of the multiple-trial or day scores collected. The multiple-trial or day scores might be collected in a pilot study or the actual measurement program. Using a two-way analysis of variance model, the formula used to estimate reliability of a criterion score that is a single score is this:

$$R = \frac{MS_P - MS_I}{MS_P + \left(\dfrac{k}{k'} - 1\right)(MS_I)}$$

$$(3.5)$$

where R is an estimate of the reliability for a criterion score composed of k' scores, k is the number of scores per person in the pilot study, and k' is the number of scores per person in the actual measurement program.

For the data in Problem 3.2, the reliability for the best score of each person for the three trials using Formula 3.5 with k = 3 and k' = 1 is as follows:

$$R = \frac{5.10 - .70}{5.10 + \left(\dfrac{3}{1} - 1\right)(.70)}$$

$$= \frac{4.40}{5.10 + (2)(.70)} = \frac{4.40}{6.50} = .68$$

Computer Use

Most people use the computer to apply a two-way ANOVA to their data. Two-way ANOVA computer programs that will handle repeated measures on each person are commonly available. Some two-way ANOVA programs cannot be used in this situation because they will not handle repeated measures on each person and/or expect the people to be in two or more groups. Unless the amount of data is small, all physical education and exercise science specialists should use the computer to do a two-way ANOVA on their data. The advantage of a two-way ANOVA over a one-way ANOVA is that the computer will give you the mean for each trial, a significance test for difference among trial

TABLE 3.4	Two-Way ANOVA for the Data in Table 3.3 Using the SPSS Reliability Analysis Program					

Source	Sum of Sq.	DF	Mean Sq.	F	Prob.
Between people	20.40	4	5.10		
Within people	6.00	10	0.60		
Between measures	0.40	2	0.20	.29	0.7588
Residual	5.60	8	0.70		
Total	26.40	14	1.89		

Item	Mean	Std. Dev.	Cases
Trial 1	5.00	1.58	5
Trial 2	5.20	1.64	5
Trial 3	5.40	1.14	5

means is possible, and the R can still be calculated as if a one-way ANOVA were used (Formula 3.3) or by using the two-way ANOVA information (Formula 3.4).

In the SPSS version 14.0 package of computer programs, the Reliability Analysis program provides an option to the two-way ANOVA for the analysis of repeated measures on each person. The directions for using the Reliability Analysis program are presented in section 12 of the SPSS 14.0 for Windows Statistical Procedures part of Appendix A. When entering the data in Table 3.3 there must be three variables (Trial 1, Trial 2, Trial 3). The output from the analysis of the data in Table 3.3 is presented in Table 3.4.

In Table 3.4 the "between people" and "within people" are the sources if a one-way ANOVA is applied to the data. The "between people," "between measures," and "residual" are the sources if a two-way ANOVA is applied to the data. Note that within people from the one-way ANOVA is composed of between measures and residual from the two-way ANOVA (check the Sum of Sq. or DF values to see this). In terms of the terminology used up to this point and in Table 3.2, between measures and residual in Table 3.4 are among trials and interaction respectively. There is sufficient information in Table 3.4 to calculate R no matter which formula is selected.

Common Situations for Calculating R

Formulas 3.2 and 3.5 have been presented for estimating reliability for a criterion score that is a single-trial or single-day score of a person where two or more trial or day scores were obtained for each person in a pilot study. Remember, often reliability is estimated in a pilot study with more scores per person collected than will be used in the actual measurement program. Presented below are several common situations and the formulas for calculating R in these situations using Formulas 3.2 and 3.5.

Situation 1   In the pilot study, scores for each person are collected on two days or on two trials within a day.

In the measurement program, the criterion score for a person is the mean day or trial score: $k = 2$, $k' = 2$.

Using Formula 3.2:

$$R = \frac{MS_A - MS_W}{MS_A + \left(\dfrac{k}{k'} - 1\right)(MS_W)}$$

$$= \frac{MS_A - MS_W}{MS_A + \left(\dfrac{2}{2} - 1\right)(MS_W)}$$

$$= \frac{MS_A - MS_W}{MS_A}$$

Using Formula 3.5:

$$R = \frac{MS_P - MS_I}{MS_P + \left(\dfrac{k}{k'} - 1\right)(MS_I)}$$

$$= \frac{MS_P - MS_I}{MS_P + \left(\dfrac{2}{2} - 1\right)(MS_I)}$$

$$= \frac{MS_P - MS_I}{MS_P}$$

In the measurement program, the criterion score for a person is a score from one day or the person's best trial score: $k = 2$, $k' = 1$.

Using Formula 3.2:

$$R = \frac{MS_A - MS_W}{MS_A + \left(\dfrac{k}{k'} - 1\right)(MS_W)}$$

$$= \frac{MS_A - MS_W}{MS_A + \left(\dfrac{2}{1} - 1\right)(MS_W)}$$

$$= \frac{MS_A - MS_W}{MS_A + MS_W}$$

Using Formula 3.5:

$$R = \frac{MS_P - MS_I}{MS_P + \left(\dfrac{k}{k'} - 1\right)(MS_I)}$$

$$= \frac{MS_P - MS_I}{MS_P + \left(\dfrac{2}{1} - 1\right)(MS_I)}$$

$$= \frac{MS_P - MS_I}{MS_P + MS_I}$$

Situation 2   In the pilot study or actual measurement study, scores on five trials within a day are collected for a person.

In the measurement program the criterion score of a person is the mean trial score: $k = 5$, $k' = 5$.

Using Formula 3.2:

$$R = \frac{MS_A - MS_W}{MS_A + \left(\dfrac{k}{k'} - 1\right)(MS_W)}$$

$$= \frac{MS_A - MS_W}{MS_A + \left(\dfrac{5}{5} - 1\right)(MS_W)}$$

$$= \frac{MS_A - MS_W}{MS_A}$$

Using Formula 3.5:

$$R = \frac{MS_P - MS_I}{MS_P + \left(\dfrac{k}{k'} - 1\right)(MS_I)}$$

$$= \frac{MS_P - MS_I}{MS_P + \left(\dfrac{5}{5} - 1\right)(MS_I)}$$

$$= \frac{MS_P - MS_I}{MS_P}$$

In the measurement program the criterion score for a person is the person's best trial score: $k = 5$, $k' = 1$.

Using Formula 3.2:

$$R = \frac{MS_A - MS_W}{MS_A + \left(\dfrac{k}{k'} - 1\right)(MS_W)}$$

$$= \frac{MS_A - MS_W}{MS_A + \left(\dfrac{5}{1} - 1\right)(MS_W)}$$

$$= \frac{MS_A - MS_W}{MS_A + (4)(MS_W)}$$

Using Formula 3.5:

$$R = \frac{MS_P - MS_I}{MS_P + \left(\dfrac{k}{k'} - 1\right)(MS_I)}$$

$$= \frac{MS_P - MS_I}{MS_P + \left(\dfrac{5}{1} - 1\right)(MS_I)}$$

$$= \frac{MS_P - MS_I}{MS_P + (4)(MS_I)}$$

In the measurement program the criterion score for a person is the mean of the three consecutive trials with the highest mean for the group or the mean of the three best trial scores of a person: $k = 5$, $k' = 3$.

Using Formula 3.2:

$$R = \frac{MS_A - MS_W}{MS_A + \left(\dfrac{k}{k'} - 1\right)(MS_W)}$$

$$= \frac{MS_A - MS_W}{MS_A + \left(\dfrac{5}{3} - 1\right)(MS_W)}$$

$$= \frac{MS_A - MS_W}{MS_A + \left(\dfrac{2}{3}\right)(MS_W)}$$

Using Formula 3.5:

$$R = \frac{MS_P - MS_I}{MS_P + \left(\dfrac{k}{k'} - 1\right)(MS_I)}$$

$$= \frac{MS_P - MS_I}{MS_P + \left(\dfrac{5}{3} - 1\right)(MS_I)}$$

$$= \frac{MS_P - MS_I}{MS_P + \left(\dfrac{2}{3}\right)(MS_I)}$$

Sample Size for R

The size of the calculated R is to some degree unique to the scores of the group tested. Thus, some researchers and computer programs report **confidence limits** for the calculated R. For exam-ple, if a person found that R = .80, the person might report that the 90% confidence limits are .72 to .86. The person is indicating that she is 90% confident that the true value (population value) of R is be-tween .72 and .86. It is desirable to have high con-fidence and narrow confidence limits.

Baumgartner and Chung (2001) used the pro-cedures of McGraw and Wong (1996) to calculate 90% confidence limits for three values of R, two sample sizes, and two different criterion scores. They used both a one-way and a two-way ANOVA model with both two and three repeated measures (trials or days) for a person. They found that the confidence limits are the same with a one-way and a two-way ANOVA model when all other factors (e.g., sample size, criterion score) are equal. Fur-ther, as sample size and/or value of R increase, the width of confidence limits decreases. A representa-tive listing of confidence limits for values of R is shown in Table 3.5. Confidence limits are fairly broad in Table 3.5. Also, if the minimum accept-able reliability is .70, a sample size of 50 to 100 and a calculated R of .80 or higher will usually yield 90% confidence limits with a lower limit of .70 or higher. Thus, if R is less than .80, sample size should be greater than 100, but if R is .80 or higher, a sample size of 50 to 100 seems adequate. These suggested sample sizes are larger than those recommended and used in the past.

An option for the Reliability Analysis pro-gram in SPSS is confidence limits for the R calcu-

TABLE 3.5	**Ninety Percent Confidence Limits for Values of R**			
R	**Sample Size**	**Repeated Measures**	**Criterion Score**	**Limits**
.70	100	2	Mean score	.58–.78
.70	100	2	Single score	.61–.77
.80	50	2	Mean score	.68–.88
.80	50	2	Single score	.70–.87
.80	100	2	Mean score	.72–.86
.80	100	2	Single score	.73–.85
.90	50	2	Mean score	.84–.94
.90	50	2	Single score	.84–.94

lated. Selecting this option is recommended, since it yields valuable information for interpreting the calculated R.

Acceptable Reliability

What is an acceptable reliability coefficient is dependent on the test; the age, gender, and experience of the people tested; the size of the reliability coefficients other people typically have obtained; the number of measures (days or trials) included in the criterion score; how much reliability is needed; whether the reliability coefficient is an estimate of stability or internal consistency reliability; and so on. There is not one set of standards for acceptability of reliability coefficients that is appropriate for all situations. Physical performance tests with a defined, easy-to-follow scoring procedure (e.g., laboratory measures, field-based fitness tests) tend to yield scores with reliability in the high .70s to low .90s for healthy youth and adults ages 10 to 30. Maybe .80 and surely .70 should be the minimum acceptable reliability for data obtained with these tests and participants. The very young and very old are not so consistent in their performance, and so perhaps the minimum acceptable reliability coefficient for them should be .70. Sports skills tests, physical activity measures and scales, attitude scales, and questionnaires tend to yield less reliable scores than fitness tests due to less precise scoring procedures and procedures that are not so easy to follow.

The minimum acceptable reliability coefficient may be influenced by the size of the R and the confidence limits for the R. If the confidence limits are so wide that the lower limit is unacceptable reliability but the upper limit is acceptable reliability, probably the reliability coefficient is unacceptable. As we mentioned in the previous section, Sample Size for R, the findings of Baumgartner and Chung (2001) are that the lower the R and the smaller the sample size, the wider the confidence limits.

Many physical performance tests yield scores with stability reliability of .80 to .95. There are others, however, that yield scores with stability reliability less than .70. Internal-consistency reliability coefficients for criterion scores that are the mean of several trial scores are often between .85 and .99 for physical performance tests. As stated at the beginning of this section, there is no one set of standards for evaluating reliability coefficients that is appropriate for all situations. However, it seems that many people use a standard for evaluating reliability coefficients that has these basic guidelines: .70–.79 is below-average acceptable, .80–.89 is average acceptable, and .90–1.0 is above-average acceptable.

Factors Affecting Reliability

Many factors can affect the reliability of measurements. Among them are scoring accuracy, the number of test trials, test difficulty, instructions, and the testing environment, as well as the person's familiarity with the test and present performance level. The range of talent also can affect reliability. The reliability coefficient is larger for scores from a long test than for those from a short one, and for a group with a broad range of abilities than for one with a narrow range of abilities.

Presented in Table 3.6 is a categorization proposed by Zuidema (1969) of the factors that influence test score reliability. We can expect an acceptable degree of reliability when

1. The people are heterogeneous in ability, motivated to do well, ready to be tested, and informed about the nature of the test;
2. The test discriminates among ability groups, and is long enough or repeated sufficiently for each person to show his or her best performance;
3. The testing environment and organization are favorable to good performance; and
4. The person administering the test is competent.

The reliability coefficient should be calculated using the scores of a large group (at least 50 to 100 people), since it is relatively easy to obtain extremely high or low correlation coefficients with a small group.

TABLE 3.6	Factors Influencing Test Reliability
Category of Factors	**Illustrative Sources of Imperfect Reliability**
Characteristics of the performers	Range of talent; motivation; good day vs. bad day; learning; forgetting; fatigue
Characteristics of the test	Length; difficulty; discriminative power; trial homogeneity; number of performers
Characteristics of the testing situation	Instructions; environment; class organization; class management; warm-up opportunity
Characteristics of the measurement process	Nature of measurement instrument; selection of scoring unit; precision; errors in measurement; number of trials; recording errors
Characteristics of the evaluator(s)	Competencies; confidence in test; concentration on task; familiarity with instrument; motivation; number of evaluators
Characteristics of the mode of statistical estimation	Breakdown of observed score variance into true score and error score variance, with retest design: error source is variation within individuals between days. Does not include within-day variance. With split-trial design: variation within individuals between trials. Does not include between-day variance or variance between grouped trials.

Coefficient Alpha

Coefficient alpha is often used to determine the reliability of dichotomous data (see Chapter 16). When the data are ordinal, we may use the coefficient alpha to determine reliability (Ferguson & Takane 1989; Nunnally & Bernstein 1994). In fact, with ordinal or interval data the coefficient alpha is the same as the R using Formula 3.4. Coefficient alpha is an estimate of the reliability of a criterion score that is the sum of the trial scores in one day. There is no reason why the coefficient could not be applied to multiple-day or multiple-judge data to estimate stability reliability or objectivity. We determine coefficient alpha using the following formula:

$$r_\alpha = \left(\frac{k}{k-1} \right) \left(\frac{s_x^2 - s_j^2}{s_x^2} \right)$$

(3.6)

where r_α is coefficient alpha, k is the number of trials, s_x^2 is the variance for the criterion scores, and s_j^2 is the sum of the variances for the trials.

Problem 3.3 Calculate coefficient alpha for the data in Table 3.3.

Solution Here too, the procedure involves multiple steps.

Step 1

The simplest way to do this is to set up a table like the one below:

Person	TRIAL 1 X_1	TRIAL 2 X_2	TRIAL 3 X_3	TOTAL X
A	5	6	7	18
B	3	3	4	10
C	4	4	5	13
D	7	6	6	19
E	6	7	5	18
	25	26	27	78

Step 2

Have the computer calculate the variance for X_1, X_2, X_3, and X. The variances are as follows:

$$s_1^2 = 2.50; \ s_2^2 = 2.70; \ s_3^2 = 1.30; \ s_x^2 = 15.30$$

Step 3

Now we can calculate r_a. Where k is 3, s_x^2 is 15.30, and s_j^2 is 6.50 (the sum of s_1^2, s_2^2, and s_3^2: 2.50 + 2.70 + 1.30), the coefficient alpha r is .86:

$$r_\alpha = \left(\frac{3}{3-1}\right)\left(\frac{15.30 - 6.50}{15.30}\right)$$

$$= \left(\frac{3}{2}\right)\left(\frac{8.80}{15.30}\right) = \frac{26.4}{30.60} = .86$$

Notice that R = .86 with Formula 3.4.

Besides providing the needed variances, the computer can also provide the correlations for the trial scores with the sum of the trial scores, which could be useful in deciding which trials to sum as the criterion score. Only trials that correlate positively at a reasonably high value with the sum of the trial scores should be retained. Normally, with motor performance tests, each trial is correlated with the sum of all trials.

The SPSS program, Reliability Analysis, discussed in this chapter in the section titled Computer Use, calculates coefficient alpha. Coefficient alpha might be calculated by hand, as we did in Problem 3.3, when a repeated measures ANOVA computer program is not available to provide the values needed to calculate an intraclass R. With a large amount of data (persons tested and/or trials), it would be easier to just enter the trial scores and let the computer calculate the criterion score (sum of the trial scores) before calculating the variances. In Problem 3.3 this would require entering the three trial scores for each person, having the computer calculate TOTAL, and finally having the computer calculate the four variances needed to calculate coefficient alpha. The sum of the trial scores can be obtained once the trial scores are entered by using the Transformation program in the SPSS package or any other package of statistical analysis programs. You must indicate to the computer program the name of the variable that is to be the sum of the trial scores (e.g., TOTAL in Problem 3.3) and indicate how the sum of the trial scores is to be formed (e.g., in Problem 3.3, X = X1 + X2 + X3). This procedure is outlined in section 16 of the SPSS 14.0 for Windows Statistical Procedures part of Appendix A.

Intraclass R in Summary

When calculating R, a decision must be made as to whether to calculate R from a one-way or two-way ANOVA. The decision involves how you define

difference among the repeated measure (trials or days) means. If you consider any difference among the repeated measure means to be a lack of reliability, you should use a one-way ANOVA. However, if you consider the difference among the repeated measure means to not be a lack of reliability, you should use a two-way ANOVA.

After calculating a reliability coefficient, it is not enough to just report the value. The following information is needed: whether the reliability coefficient is an intraclass R, the ANOVA design used, the criterion score, whether the reliability coefficient is for internal consistency or stability, and the value of R.

Occasionally, an intraclass correlation coefficient will be lower than wanted even though the test scores seemed reliable (individual scores changed little from trial to trial or day to day). This happens when the sum of squares among people is small, indicating a group homogeneous in ability. In a situation like this, you must understand why the coefficient is low. Or you can try to increase test sensitivity or ability to discriminate among individuals in terms of ability. Remember, though, that you cannot accept something as reliable if the reliability coefficient is low.

Occasionally people want to test intraclass correlation coefficients to determine their value at the population level, to check whether two coefficients are equal, or to develop confidence limits for a coefficient. McGraw and Wong (1996) is an excellent reference for this. Feldt (1990) and Alsawalmeh and Feldt (1992) also address these needs.

SPEARMAN-BROWN PROPHECY FORMULA

This equation is used to estimate the reliability of a measurement when the length of the test is increased. It assumes that the additional length (or new trial), although as difficult as the original, is neither mentally nor physically tiring. This formula estimates the reliability of a criterion score, which is the mean or sum of the trial scores.

$$r_{k,k} = \frac{k(r_{1,1})}{1 + (k-1)(r_{1,1})}$$

where $r_{k,k}$ is the estimated reliability of a measure from a test increased in length k times, k is the number of times the test is increased in length, and $r_{1,1}$ is the reliability of a measurement for the present length of the test.

Problem 3.4   The reliability of a criterion score for a six-trial test was found to be .94. Determine the reliability if 18 trials were administered.

Solution   Where k is 3 and $r_{1,1}$ is .94, the estimated reliability of a criterion score based on 18 trials is .98:

$$r_{k,k} = \frac{(3)(.94)}{1 + (3 - 1)(.94)} = \frac{2.82}{1 + (2)(.94)}$$

$$= \frac{2.82}{1 + 1.88} = \frac{2.82}{2.88} = .979 = .98$$

Baumgartner (1968) investigated the accuracy with which the Spearman-Brown prophecy formula predicts reliability. He compared the predicted reliability coefficients to the reliability coefficients actually obtained when the number of trials of a test was increased. He found that the formula's accuracy increased as the value of k in the formula decreased, concluding, then, that the reliability coefficient predicted by the Spearman-Brown formula is the maximum reliability that can be expected.

STANDARD ERROR OF MEASUREMENT

It is sometimes useful to be able to estimate the measurement error in each test score. If each person is administered multiple trials of a test, a standard deviation for the trial scores could be calculated for each person, and this standard deviation is the measurement error for the individual. If each person is administered only one trial, the average amount of measurement error in the test scores is estimated for the whole group by calculating the standard error of measurement by the following formula:

$$s_e = s_x \sqrt{1 - r_{x,x}}$$

where s_e is the standard error of measurement, s_x is the standard deviation for the test scores, and $r_{x,x}$ is the reliability coefficient for the test scores.

Since the variance of all measurements contains some measurement error, the **standard error of mea-surement** of a test score reflects the degree one may expect a test score to vary due to measurement error.

Problem 3.5   A written test has a standard deviation of 5 and a reliability coefficient for the test scores of .91. Determine the standard error of measurement for the test scores.

Solution   Where s_x is 5 and $r_{x,x}$ is .91, the standard error of measurement s_e is 1.5:

$$s_e = 5\sqrt{1 - .91} = 5\sqrt{.09} = (5)(.3) = 1.5$$

The standard error acts like a test score's standard deviation and can be interpreted in much the same way using the normal curve. From the normal curve table (Table 2.8), we know that approximately 68% of the scores lie within 1 standard deviation of the mean, which in this case is the test score. If a person who scored 73 on the test in Problem 3.5 were to take the test 100 times and his ability did not change, we would expect the person's scores to fall between 71.5 (73 − 1.5) and 74.5 (73 + 1.5) 68 times out of 100. The standard error, then, specifies the limits within which we can expect scores to vary due to measurement error. In fact, there is a growing tendency to report a confidence band—the score, plus and minus the standard error—with test scores. For more lengthy discussion, see Ferguson and Takane (1989) or any other statistics text that includes a chapter on measurement theory. Crocker and Aligna (1986) and Nunnally and Bernstein (1994) are excellent sources on measurement theory.

Be aware that the standard error of measurement is based on the scores of a group, and that not all members of the group will follow the scoring pattern of the group. Darracott (1995) found that the standard deviation for the multiple-trial scores of most individuals is larger than the standard error of measurement.

OBJECTIVITY

Objectivity, or rater reliability, is an important characteristic of a measurement. For a measurement to have validity and reliability, it must have objectivity. We can define objectivity as the close agreement between the scores assigned to each person by two or more judges. Judges in this case could be judges in a sport like gymnastics or scorers of a physical performance test such as a sit-up test.

Factors Affecting Objectivity

Objectivity depends on two related factors: (1) the clarity of the scoring system and (2) the degree to which the judge can assign scores accurately. Certain tests have clearly defined methods of scoring: a mile run is scored with a stopwatch, and a sit-up is scored in executions. In this type of test the rater can easily determine the person's scores. In contrast, an essay test or a dance performance does not offer a well-defined scoring system, relying on the rater's judgment in the assignment of points.

The second factor is more obvious. If a judge does not know how to assign a score, he or she cannot do it accurately. For example, a scorer who is unfamiliar with stopwatches will probably not assign an accurate score on a timed speed event. Of course, it is a simple matter to train a scorer in the use of scoring equipment and scoring procedures.

A high degree of objectivity is essential when two or more people are administering a test. For example, say that a group of 50 people is divided into two groups and each group is tested by a different person. If a high degree of objectivity is lacking because the two scorers of the test use different administrative procedures or scoring standards, a person's score is dependent on the identity of the scorer. If one scorer is more lenient than the other, the people tested by that scorer have an advantage.

A high degree of objectivity is also needed when one person scores on several occasions. For example, a scorer may measure one-third of a group on each of three days, or the entire group at the beginning and end of a teaching or training unit. Certainly, in the first case, it is essential that the same administrative procedures and scoring standards be used each day. This is true in the second case as well, where any variation in a person's scores should represent changed performance, not changed procedures or standards.

Some authors discuss objectivity as being intrajudge or interjudge. Intrajudge objectivity is the degree of agreement between scores assigned to each person by one judge when viewing each person's performance on two different occasions. For example, if people were videotaped as they performed a physical activity or test, a judge could view the videotape and score each person on each of two different days. Interjudge objectivity is the degree of agreement between the scores assigned each person by two or more judges. Objectivity as defined and discussed in this section of the book is interjudge. Intrajudge objectivity is vital to interjudge objectivity, but high intrajudge objectivity does not guarantee high interjudge objectivity. In most measurement situations, high intrajudge objectivity is assumed. Usually intrajudge objectivity will be higher than interjudge objectivity.

Estimation

To estimate the degree of objectivity for a physical performance test score in a pilot study, two or more judges score each person as he or she is tested. Then we calculate an intraclass correlation coefficient on the basis of judges' scores of each person. Probably in the actual measurement program or research study a single judge will be used. Thus the formula for estimating the reliability of a criterion score that is a single score must be used.

To calculate the objectivity coefficient, we think of the judges as trials, inserting their individual scores into the trial terms of our reliability formulas. If all judges are supposed to be using the same standards, we could consider a difference among judges to be measurement error and would estimate objectivity using the one-way ANOVA Formula 3.2.

If all judges are not expected to use the same standards, we would estimate objectivity using the two-way ANOVA Formula 3.5. Very seldom, if ever, would we discard the data of judges, as was suggested by Baumgartner (1969a) with multiple trials. Since objectivity is a type of reliability (rater reliability), information presented earlier in this chapter—sample size for R, acceptable reliability, and so on—generally applies when calculating and interpreting objectivity coefficients.

RELIABILITY OF CRITERION-REFERENCED TEST SCORES

Criterion-referenced standards and the setting of criterion-referenced standards were discussed in Chapter 1. Based on a criterion-referenced standard, a person is classified as either proficient or nonproficient, either pass or fail. In one example, in a Red Cross certification course a person either meets the minimum requirements and is certified or does not meet the minimum requirements and is not certified. In another example, the criterion-referenced standard for an adult fitness course could be the ability to jog continuously for 30 minutes. Based on this standard a person is classified as either proficient or nonproficient. A very nice characteristic of a criterion-referenced standard is that there is no predetermined quota as to how many people are classified as proficient.

Criterion-referenced reliability is defined differently from norm-referenced reliability. In the criterion-referenced case, reliability is defined as consistency of classification. Thus, if a criterion-referenced test score is reliable, a person will be classified the same on each of two occasions. This could be trial-to-trial within a day or day-to-day.

To estimate the reliability of a criterion-referenced test score, form a double classification table as presented in Table 3.7. In the A-box is the number of people who passed on both days and in the D-box is the number of people who failed on both days. Notice the B-box and C-box are the numbers of people who were not classified the same on both occasions. Obviously, larger numbers in the A-box and D-box and smaller numbers in the B-box and C-box are desirable, because reliability is consistency of classification on both occasions. All packages of statistical computer programs have a cross-tabulation program that will provide the double classification table (see Table 3.7) needed to estimate the reliability of a criterion-referenced test.

The most popular way to estimate reliability from this double classification table is to calculate the **proportion of agreement coefficient** (P), where

$$P = \frac{A + D}{A + B + C + D}$$

Problem 3.6 Determine the proportion of agreement (P) for the criterion-referenced test scores using the data in Table 3.8.

Solution Where the sum of the A-box and D-box is 124 and the sum of the four boxes is 150, P = .83:

$$P = \frac{84 + 40}{84 + 21 + 5 + 40} = \frac{124}{150} = .827 = .83$$

The proportion of agreement (P) does not allow for the fact that some same classifications on both occasions may have happened totally by chance. The **kappa coefficient** (k) corrects for chance agreements. The formula for kappa is

$$k = \frac{Pa - Pc}{1 - Pc}$$

where

Pa = proportion of agreement

Pc = proportion of agreement expected by chance

$$= \frac{(A + B)(A + C) + (C + D)(B + D)}{(A + B + C + D)^2}$$

in a 2 × 2 double classification table.

Problem 3.7 Determine the kappa coefficient (k) for the criterion-referenced test scores using the data in Table 3.8.

TABLE 3.7	**Table for Estimating Reliability of a Criterion-Referenced Test**		
		Day 2	
		Pass	*Fail*
Day 1	*Pass*	A	B
	Fail	C	D

TABLE 3.8	**Data for Determining the Reliability of a Criterion-Referenced Test**		
		Trial 2	
		Pass	*Fail*
Trial 1	*Pass*	84	21
	Fail	5	40

Solution   To solve for k, we use a three-step procedure:

Step 1

Calculate Pa:

$$Pa = \frac{A + D}{A + B + C + D} = \frac{84 + 40}{84 + 21 + 5 + 40}$$

$$= \frac{124}{150} = .827 = .83$$

Step 2

Calculate Pc:

$$Pc = \frac{(A + B)(A + C) + (C + D)(B + D)}{(A + B + C + D)^2}$$

$$= \frac{(105)(89) + (45)(61)}{(84 + 21 + 5 + 40)^2} = \frac{9345 + 2745}{150^2}$$

$$= \frac{12090}{22500} = .537 = .54$$

Step 3

Calculate kappa:

$$k = \frac{Pa - Pc}{1 - Pc} = \frac{.83 - .54}{1 - .54} = \frac{.29}{.46} = .63$$

Notice that for the data in Table 3.8 there is a definite difference between the proportion of agreement (P) and the coefficient kappa (k). A more extensive discussion of both coefficients is presented by Looney in Safrit & Wood (1989).

Since P can be affected by classifications by chance, values of P less than .50 are interpreted as unacceptable. Thus, values of P need to be closer to 1.0 than to .50 to be quite acceptable. Values of k also should be closer to 1.0 than 0.00 to be quite acceptable.

RELIABILITY OF DIFFERENCE SCORES

In the first edition of Baumgartner and Jackson (1975) and the next two editions of the book, **difference scores** were discussed. Difference scores are sometimes called change scores or improvement scores. Many people are still using difference scores, and Kane and Lazarus (1999) have presented an improved technique for calculating difference scores. So, difference scores are briefly discussed.

If people start an instructional program or training program with markedly different scores, evaluating people in terms of their scores at the end of the program puts people who start the program with low scores at a disadvantage to people who start the program with high scores. So, difference scores are sometimes calculated to determine the degree to which each person's score has changed over time—from the beginning to the end of an instructional program or training program. A difference score can be quickly and easily calculated as

$$\text{Difference Score} = \text{Final Score} - \text{Initial Score},$$

where initial score is at the beginning and final score is at the end of an instructional program or training program.

Two real problems are posed by the use of difference scores for purposes of comparison among individuals, comparison among groups, and development of performance standards. First, individuals who perform well initially do not have the same opportunity to achieve large difference scores as individuals who begin poorly. For example, the person who initially runs a 6-minute mile has less opportunity for improvement than the person who initially runs a 9-minute mile. Second, difference scores are tremendously unreliable. The formula for estimating the reliability of difference scores $(Y - X)$ is as follows:

$$R_{dd} = \frac{R_{xx}s_x^2 + R_{yy}s_y^2 - 2R_{xy}s_x s_y}{s_x^2 + s_y^2 - 2R_{xy}s_x s_y}$$

where

$$X = \text{the initial score}$$

$$Y = \text{the final score}$$

R_{xx} and R_{yy} = the reliability coefficients for tests X and Y

R_{xy} = the correlation between tests X and Y

R_{dd} = the reliability of difference scores

s_x and s_y = standard deviations for the initial and final scores

The following is an example of estimating the reliability of difference scores. A test with reliability of .90 was administered at the beginning and end of a training program. As is usually the case, the reliability of the test did not change between administrations. The correlation between the two sets of scores was .75. The standard deviation was 2.5 for the initial scores and 2.0 for the final scores.

$$R_{dd}$$
$$= \frac{.90(2.5)^2 + .90(2.0)^2 - 2(.75)(2.5)(2.0)}{(2.5)^2 + (2.0)^2 - 2(.75)(2.5)(2.0)}$$
$$= .63$$

It is apparent from the formula that highly reliable measures between which the correlation is low are necessary if the difference scores are going to be reliable. Since difference scores are usually calculated from scores of a test administered at the beginning and end of an instructional or training program, and the correlation between these two sets of scores is normally .70 or higher, highly reliable difference scores appear impossible.

Other techniques for calculating difference scores have been presented. Kane and Lazarus (1999) discuss the problems in using these techniques and present a difference score technique that does not have the problems. With the Kane and Lazarus technique, (1) each person has an initial (I) and a final (F) score; (2) a change score (C) is calculated for each person where $C = F - I$; (3) using simple prediction as presented in Chapter 2 and available in the SPSS package of computer programs, a change score (C′) is predicted for each person with the independent or predictor variable the initial score (I) so that $C' = (b)(I) + a$; and (4) a difference score (D) is calculated for each person, where $D = C - C'$. A positive difference score is better than a negative difference score, since the change score (C) is greater than was predicted.

SUMMARY

There are three characteristics essential to a good measurement: reliability, objectivity, and validity. Reliability and objectivity were the focus of this chapter. A measurement has reliability when it is consistently the same for each person over a short period of time. There are two types of reliability for norm-referenced tests: stability and internal consistency.

Objectivity, the second vital characteristic of a sound measurement, is the degree to which different judges agree in their scoring of each individual in a group. A fair test is one in which qualified judges rate individuals similarly and/or offer the same conditions of testing to all individuals equally.

Reliability of criterion-referenced test scores was also discussed. The definition of reliability and techniques for estimating reliability differ from those for norm-referenced test scores.

FORMATIVE EVALUATION OF OBJECTIVES

Objective 1   Define and differentiate between reliability and objectivity for norm-referenced test scores, and outline the methods used to estimate these values.

1. Two important characteristics of all measurements are that they be reliable and objective. Describe the basic nature of each of these characteristics.
2. In theory, reliability is the ratio of the true-story variance to the observed-score variance. Observed-score variance consists of both error-score variance and true-score variance. Describe these basic sources of variance and the combination that yields the highest estimate of reliability.
3. Two basic methods are used to estimate the reliability of a measurement: stability reliability and internal-consistency reliability. Briefly describe each method and the procedure it uses to estimate reliability.

4. The standard error of measurement is an estimate of the amount of measurement error in the test score. List the formula for the standard error of measurement and describe the characteristics of the statistic.
5. Objectivity, or rater reliability, is achieved when the scores of two or more different judges closely agree. The correlation between the scores is an objectivity coefficient. Summarize the procedures that yield high objectivity.

Objective 2 Identify those factors that influence reliability and objectivity for norm-referenced test scores.

1. Acceptable reliability is essential for all measurements. Many factors affect the reliability of a measurement, and some of these are listed below. Identify the conditions under which the highest reliability can be expected for the following factors:
   a. People tested
   b. Test length
   c. Testing environment
   d. Test administrator
2. According to measurement theory, if a test is lengthened, the reliability of the test scores is increased. If the reliability of the scores for a standing long jump test composed of two jumps is found to be .83, how reliable might the test scores be if six jumps were scored?
3. A physical performance test administrator can improve test objectivity in several ways. Summarize them.

Objective 3 Identify those factors that influence reliability for criterion-referenced test scores.

1. Acceptable reliability is essential for all measurements. Many factors affect the reliability of a measurement, and some of these are listed below. Identify how each of these factors affects the estimated reliability coefficient obtained:
   a. Reliability coefficient calculated
   b. Chance
   c. Composition of the group

Objective 4 Select a reliable criterion score based on measurement theory.

1. Many psychomotor tests involve several trials. What can a person do to make sure that the criterion score is as reliable as possible?

ADDITIONAL LEARNING ACTIVITIES

1. Many tests suggest two or three trials within a day. The number may have been arbitrarily selected so that the tests can be given quickly. Administer a multiple-trial test with more trials than recommended. By looking at the trial means, determine when the performance of the group reaches its maximum and becomes consistent.
2. There are many tests commonly used in testing programs (runs, jumps, maximum effort). Administer one of these tests and determine the reliability of the scores.
3. Construct a new physical performance test. Administer the test and decide how to calculate the reliability and objectivity of the scores.

BIBLIOGRAPHY

Alsawalmeh, Y. M. and L. S. Feldt. 1992. Test of the hypothesis that the intraclass reliability coefficient is the same for two measurement procedures. *Applied Psychological Measurement* 16(2): 195–205.

American Educational Research Association, American Psychological Association, and National Council on Measurement in Education. 1999. *Standards for educational and psychological testing*. Washington, DC: American Educational Research Association.

Baumgartner, T. A. 1968. The application of the Spearman-Brown prophecy formula when applied to physical performance tests. *Research Quarterly* 39: 847–856.

———. 1969a. Estimating reliability when all test trials are administered on the same day. *Research Quarterly*, 40: 222–225.

———. 1969b. Stability of physical performance test scores. *Research Quarterly*, 40: 257–261.

———. 1974. Criterion score for multiple trial measures. *Research Quarterly* 45: 193–198.

Baumgartner, T. A. and H. Chung. 2001. Confidence limits for intraclass reliability coefficients. *Measurement in Physical Education and Exercise Science* 5: 179–188.

Baumgartner, T. A. and A. S. Jackson. 1970. Measurement schedules for tests of motor performance. *Research Quarterly* 41: 10–17.

Baumgartner, T. A. and A. S. Jackson. 1975. *Measurement for evaluation in physical education.* Boston: Houghton Mifflin.

Berger, R. A. and A. B. Sweney. 1965. Variance and correlation coefficients. *Research Quarterly* 36: 368–370.

Crocker, L. and J. Aligna. 1986. *Introduction to classical and modern test theory.* New York: Holt, Rinehart and Winston.

Darracott, S. H. 1995. Individual differences in variability and pattern of performance as a consideration in the selection of a representative score from multiple trial physical performance data. Ph.D. dissertation, University of Georgia, Athens, GA.

Disch, J. 1975. Considerations for establishing a reliable and valid criterion measure for a multiple trial motor performance test. In T. A. Baumgartner (Ed.). *Proceedings of the C.I.C. symposium on measurement and evaluation in physical education.* Indiana University.

Feldt, L. S. 1990. The sampling theory for the intraclass reliability coefficient. *Applied Measurement in Education* 3: 361–367.

Feldt, L. S. and M. E. McKee. 1958. Estimating the reliability of skill tests. *Research Quarterly* 29: 279–293.

Ferguson, G. A. and Y. Takane. 1989. *Statistical analysis in psychology and education.* 6th ed. New York: McGraw-Hill.

Henry, F. M. 1967. Best versus average individual score. *Research Quarterly* 38: 317–320.

Hetherington, R. 1973. Within subject variation, measurement error, and selection of a criterion score. *Research Quarterly* 44: 113–117.

Johnson, R. and D. Meeter. 1977. Estimation of maximum physical performance. *Research Quarterly* 48: 74–84.

Kane, M. and J. C. Lazarus. 1999. Change scores in physical education and exercise science: Revisiting the Hale and Hale method. *Measurement in Physical Education and Exercise Science* 3: 181–193.

McGraw, K. O. and S. P. Wong. 1996. Forming inferences about some intraclass correlation coefficients. *Psychological Methods* 1: 30–46.

Nunnally, J. C. and I. H. Bernstein. 1994. *Psychometric theory.* 3rd ed. New York: McGraw-Hill.

Safrit, M. J. and T. M. Wood. 1989. *Measurement concepts in physical education and exercise science.* Champaign, IL: Human Kinetics.

Whitley, J. D. and L. E. Smith. 1963. Larger correlations obtained by using average rather than best strength scores. *Research Quarterly* 34: 248–249.

Wood, T. M. and W. Zhu. 2006. *Measurement issues in the physical domain.* Champaign, IL: Human Kinetics.

Zuidema, M. A. 1969. A brief on reliability theory: Theoretical concepts, influencing factors, and empirical estimates of the reliability of measurements especially applied to physical performance tests. Mimeographed. Bloomington: University of Indiana.

VALIDITY

C O N T E N T S

K E Y   W O R D S

concurrent validity
construct validity evidence
content validity evidence
criterion score
criterion validity evidence
decision validity
domain-referenced validity
logical validity evidence
predictive validity
validity

OBJECTIVES

Discussed in this chapter are the methods used to estimate validity with norm-referenced tests, the relationship between reliability and validity, and the factors that influence validity.

Many physical performance tests can be given several times in the same day. When there are multiple trials of a test, the test administrator must decide how many to administer and what trial(s) to use as the criterion score.

Finally, the methods used to estimate validity with criterion-referenced tests are discussed. After reading Chapter 4, you should be able to

1. Define validity, and outline the methods used to estimate it.
2. Describe the influence of test reliability on validity.
3. Identify those factors that influence validity.
4. Select a criterion score based on measurement theory from which valid interpretations can be made.

INTRODUCTION

There are certain characteristics essential to a measurement; without them, little faith can be put in the measurement and little use made of it. Two of these characteristics, reliability and objectivity, were discussed in Chapter 3. A third important characteristic of a measurement is *validity*. The American Educational Research Association (1999) indicates that validity is the most important.

Although a newer definition of validity, used in *Measurement Concepts in Physical Education and Exercise Science* (Safrit & Wood 1989), was presented in 1985, many people in health and human performance have continued to use the older definition. Using the older definition, validity is placed at the test or measuring instrument level; that is, a test or measuring instrument is valid if it measures what it is supposed to measure. For example, using the older definition, push-ups are a valid measure of arm and shoulder girdle strength and endurance, because strength and endurance of the arm and shoulder girdle muscles are necessary to do a push-up.

The newer definition of validity is at the test score interpretation level. Thus, the interpretations based on the test scores are what are valid (correct). So, with the previous example, interpretations as to the amount of arm and shoulder girdle strength based on push-up scores are what are valid. For validity to exist, the test scores must be reliable, but reliability does not guarantee valid interpretations. Obviously, for the interpretations of test scores to be valid, the test or instrument must be measuring consistently. For example, if individuals know they are going to take the mile run test and have had prior experience with the test, the mile run yields reliable scores (stable from day to day) from which valid interpretations of aerobic capacity can be made, but interpretations concerning sprinting speed would not be valid. But what if mile run scores were not reliable (changing from day to day)? On one day a person ran the mile in 13 minutes but two days later ran the mile in 10 minutes. The interpretation of 13 minutes would be markedly different from the interpretation of 10 minutes, and neither interpretation may be correct. Interpretations of mile run scores will not be valid in this situation. If the interpretations based on the data from a test or measuring instrument are invalid, the data are useless. Any decisions made about individuals based on these data will be in error.

Only an overview of validity is presented in this chapter. A more comprehensive coverage of validity is available in sources like Safrit and Wood (1989), Nunnally and Bernstein (1994), Crocker and Algina (1986), and Messick (1989).

VALIDITY AND NORM-REFERENCED TESTS

Validity may be discussed in terms of interpretations based on scores from norm-referenced or criterion-referenced tests. A review of these two types of tests (see Chapter 1) might be helpful. Traditionally, validity has been discussed in terms of interpretations based on scores from norm-referenced tests, so first we will discuss validity from this standpoint.

From what has been presented so far it should be evident that we do not validate tests, but collect *evidence* to validate the interpretations made from test scores. For example, we can interpret the measure of a person's percent body fat in several ways, and depending on the interpretation, we must collect validity evidence to support the particular interpretation. Suppose a woman's sum of skinfold measurements translates to 40% body fat. One interpretation of this percent body fat is that 40% of the woman's body weight is fat tissue. A second interpretation of 40% body fat might be that it is too high and the woman is at risk for future health problems. For the first interpretation, evidence must be collected that there is a high correlation between sum of skinfold measures and percent body fat measured using a criterion, or gold standard, measure such as hydrodensitometry. Interpretation two requires evidence that high sum of skinfold measures as an indication of high percent body fat is associated with certain health problems.

When a test measures what it purports to measure, valid interpretations of the scores are possible. To have validity, then, a test must be both relevant to the trait being measured and the test scores must be reliable.

Types and Estimation

As we will find in this chapter, there are three basic types of validity evidence: **content validity evidence, criterion validity evidence,** and **construct validity evidence** (American Educational Research Association 1999). However, the point is made in numerous sources that there is really only one type of validity: construct validity. That is, all approaches to collecting validity evidence really constitute different ways of investigating construct validity.

Based on the older definition of validity, we used to talk about types of *validity*. Now, using the newer definition of validity, we talk about types of *validity evidence*. Further, it is recommended that several approaches or several types of validity evidence be reported. However, one strong indication is better than several weak indications of validity. Messick (1989) presented what some people consider the state-of-the-art definition and discussion

of validity. He considered content-related evidence alone as weak evidence for validity.

Validity can be estimated either logically or statistically. Recently the trend in education and psychology has been away from the statistical approach, while exercise science depends more on the statistical approach. This does not necessarily mean that physical education and exercise science should abandon the statistical approach. Education and psychology work predominantly with paper-and-pencil tests, while physical education and exercise science work predominantly with physical performance tests. The method of estimating validity must be chosen in terms of the situation, not the trend.

An overview of the commonly used validity approaches and basic issues involved in establishing validity are presented. More comprehensive coverage of validity is presented in the sources referenced in the introduction to this chapter.

Content Validity Evidence

Often this might be called a *logical approach* or *logical* type of evidence. In physical education and exercise science it is usually called **logical validity evidence**. It is established by examining the capacities to be measured and determining whether the test or instrument is, in fact, yielding scores that measure them. For example, a written knowledge test yields scores upon which valid interpretations can be made when its questions are reliable, are based on the material taught, and sample the stated educational objectives of the unit. This is where the term "content validity evidence" originated. This content analysis of the test is a logical approach. Well-trained people in physical education and exercise science use logic like this with physical performance tests and measures. They might state that the 50-yard dash and the 100-yard dash yield scores that allow valid interpretations of running speed because, obviously, the scores indicate the speed a person can run. For a complicated multicomponent skill such as a team sport, a consensus of expert judges (e.g., coaches) may provide the only means of determining the degree of content or logical validity.

It is certainly true that the content validity evidence approach has been both successfully used and badly misused at times. The American Educational Research Association (1999) suggests that, ideally, several different types of validity evidence (content-related, criterion-related, construct-related) be provided with a test, but one solid piece of evidence is better than several weak pieces of evidence. If possible, content validity evidence should be used in conjunction with other validity evidence.

Content validity evidence seems to have been used quite successfully with physical fitness tests and fitness test batteries. For example, sit-up scores yield valid interpretations of abdominal strength and endurance because abdominal strength and endurance are required to do a sit-up. In a second example, the items in the health-related physical fitness tests were logically selected based on what the biggest health problems in the United States are today. However, Jackson and Baker (1986) did not find that sit-and-reach test scores yield valid evidence of hamstring and lower back flexibility. So, sometimes what seems to be content validity evidence really is not.

Content validity evidence seems to have been less successfully used with complex sport skill tests. Some claims of content validity evidence for interpretations of scores from certain sport skill tests and sport skill test batteries have been occasionally questioned. The wall volley test in volleyball is one example. Another example is a comprehensive skill test battery for softball, basketball, or volleyball ability constructed based on the basic components of the sport.

Content validity evidence, then, rests solely on subjective decision making, which has led to criticism of this type of validity evidence. However, this validity evidence is not the only one to rest on subjective decision; criterion-related validity evidence is often determined by using the subjective decisions of an expert judge or judges.

Criterion Validity Evidence

Criterion validity evidence is obtained by determining the correlation between scores for a test and some specified criterion. This is a traditional procedure for obtaining the validity evidence. It involves calculating the Pearson product-moment correlation coefficient or some other similar type of correlation between scores on the test and those achieved on a criterion measure. The resulting correlation coefficient—the validity coefficient—is an estimate of the validity of interpretations based on the test scores. When the validity coefficient is close to 1, the test is measuring similarly to the criterion measure and interpretations based on test scores are thereby considered to be valid; when the coefficient is close to 0, the test and the criterion are measuring in a different manner and interpretations based on test scores have little validity.

A crucial step in obtaining criterion-related validity evidence is the choice of a suitable criterion measure. Expert ratings and tournament standings are commonly used for sport skill tests. Predetermined criteria such as VO_2 max and body composition are commonly used criteria in exercise science.

Expert Ratings   One criterion measure is the subjective rating of one or more experts. Because one judge may overlook certain factors in a person's performance or may have certain biases that affect his ratings, the sum of several qualified judges' ratings is a more reliable criterion measure. Obviously, high objectivity among judges is vital. Scores from the test are correlated (using the Pearson product-moment correlation coefficient or some other appropriate correlation coefficient) with the subjective ratings of the judge or judges.

Subjective ratings usually take the form of either group ranks or a point scale. Using group ranks, the people in the group are ordered from best to worst on the basis of performance. Using a point scale, the people in the group are scored individually on a numbered point scale, as they would be in a gymnastics meet. Group ranks become unworkable as the size of the group increases. Further, a point scale system is preferable, since it does not require that one person be ranked best and another worst. One usually obtains higher validity with a scoring system than with group ranks, provided the scoring system is well defined so that high objectivity is possible.

Expert ratings have been commonly used to estimate the validity of interpretations based on skill test scores. A skill test has certain advantages over tests that must be judged by experts. Provided the judges are qualified, they furnish a good index of skill performance. However, in practice it is hard to find even one expert, let alone several, who has the time to subjectively evaluate a class of students. Additionally, skill tests are usually easier to administer and less time-consuming than are subjective evaluations.

Tournament Standings A second criterion measure is tournament standings. Scores from the test are correlated (using the Pearson product-moment correlation coefficient or some other appropriate correlation coefficient) with the tournament standings of the students being measured. The method assumes that tournament standing is a good indicator of overall ability in the tested skill, usually an individual or dual activity like tennis or badminton. Many teachers are eager to find a test that provides the same information as a tournament. Such a test makes it unnecessary to conduct round-robin tournaments to evaluate the skill levels of the students.

Predetermined Criteria The final criterion measure is a score from a known and well-accepted instrument. Evidence of the validity of interpretations based on test scores is then provided by determining the Pearson product-moment correlation coefficient between scores from the test under examination and scores from the accepted instrument. The method is usually used in developing a test that is quicker and/or easier to administer than is the accepted instrument.

Ideally, the criterion measure is one that everyone recognizes as the "gold standard" (the ultimate or best standard). If there is not a gold standard, and often there isn't, one of the acceptable criterion measures available has to be selected. All people may not agree which criterion measure to use, and the criterion measure selected influences the value of the validity coefficient. This is why it is difficult to conduct a validation using a predetermined criterion, and the validity coefficient may not be high.

For example, the predetermined criterion method has been used to validate interpretations of

body composition based on skinfolds. An accepted measure of percent body fat can be obtained in a laboratory by weighing a person under water (see Chapter 12). A person with a high percentage of body fat weighs less under water because fat tissue is less dense than muscle and bone. Skinfold measurements are easy to obtain and correlate highly (r is at least .80) with the percentage of fat determined by the more complicated underwater weighing method. Further, skinfold measurements can be used on people fearful of being weighed under water. By obtaining selected skinfold measurements, we can estimate the person's percent body fat using a regression equation. In fact, multiple correlation and regression equations (see Chapter 2) are often used to obtain validity coefficients. In these situations, Y is the criterion score (dependent variable), and the several scores used to estimate Y are the X-scores (independent variables). In the earlier example, Y would be the laboratory-determined percent body fat underwater weight, and the X-scores would be the skinfold measures.

The test being examined in the validation process is a practical, or field-based, test. The predetermined criterion is a score from a laboratory instrument or some instrument that is very expensive, difficult, and/or time-consuming to administer and may require considerable training or expertise of the person administering the instrument. There are few gold standards in physical education and exercise science. Often there is not an acceptable predetermined criterion—or, there are several possible predetermined criteria, but people can't agree as to which one to use. Again, this is why it is difficult to conduct a validation using a predetermined criterion. A sit-up test is supposed to measure abdominal strength and endurance. But there is no gold standard criterion measure for abdominal strength and endurance, and it is not likely you could get experts in the field to agree on an acceptable criterion measure.

Look at the literature on measuring physical activity, and you will see many different criterion measures used in collecting criterion validity evidence. There is no agreement as to which criterion measure to use. Maybe this is due to different interpretations of scores from physical activity tests and questionnaires. Scores might be interpreted as to amount of activity, number of calories expended, physical fitness level, and so on. This is what validity is all about: the validity of interpretations based on the test scores.

Construct Validity Evidence

The content validity and criterion-related validity approaches are established procedures for examining validity. The construct validity evidence approach is a newer and more complex validation procedure. It was first introduced in 1954 by the American Psychological Association and has been used extensively in psychological testing since then. Today the procedure is being used more and more in testing in physical education, exercise science, and related fields.

The construct validity approach is used with abstract rather than concrete tests (Nunnally & Bernstein 1994). An abstract test measures something that is not directly observable. Attitudes toward physical activity are abstract human traits that are neither readily apparent nor easily understood by an untrained professional. The number of basketball free throws made out of 100 tries, on the other hand, is a concrete test of free throw shooting skill.

The construct validity approach is based on the scientific method. First, there is a hunch that a test or tests can measure some abstract trait. Second, a theory is developed to explain both the construct and the tests that measure it. Finally, various statistical procedures are applied to confirm or reject the theory.

Construct validity is determined by judging the extent to which theoretical and statistical information supports assumed constructs. The procedure gives physical education teachers and exercise specialists a way to evaluate their tests. For example, consider a test of swimming ability. Is it true that the better your score on the test the more swimming ability you possess? Administer the test to intermediate and advanced swimmers. Because the advanced swimmers are known to be better swimmers, we have construct validity evidence whenever the mean score of the advanced swim-

mers is superior to that of the intermediate swimmers. Probably a statistical test of the significance of the difference between the two means at alpha equal .01 should be conducted (see Additional Statistical Techniques in Chapter 2) to make sure the two swimming groups really do differ.

A second example of this approach is the comparison of the performance of a group before and after instruction or training. This involves testing a group for initial ability, applying some instructional or training technique for multiple weeks, and then retesting the group for final ability. Since the group should have improved in ability as a result of the instruction or training, we have construct validity evidence if the final test mean is significantly better than the initial test mean (see the repeated measures t-test in Chapter 2).

In all cases, validity evidence is collected for a defined population of people. All individuals used in collecting the validity evidence must belong to the population or have abilities similar to those of the individuals who belong to the population. This is particularly true when comparing groups that differ in ability as do the swimmers we have mentioned. If groups vastly different in ability are used for collecting validity evidence, there always will be a significant difference between the groups in mean test scores. For example, if validity evidence were collected for a test to be used on 18-year-old individuals by comparing 6-year-old and 18-year-old individuals in terms of almost any physical ability test, the 18-year-old individuals would be superior. It is hard to believe that any 18-year-old individual would have test scores as poor as those of 6-year-old individuals. Although significant differences between groups would be obtained, the evidence is not generalizable to any intended use of the test.

If, for example, the swimming test given to both intermediate and advanced swimmers is to be used for swimming team selection purposes, useful information would be gained by comparing the performance scores of first-string team members with the scores of second-string team members. Significant differences between groups in mean score would provide validity evidence for this use, or interpretation, of the test scores.

Factor analysis is a statistical procedure that can be used to identify constructs and the tests that yield scores leading to valid interpretations of the ability of individuals in terms of the isolated constructs. In this context, the isolated factor of the analysis is an abstract construct. Factor analysis has often been used to identify the basic components of fitness or of a sport skill (see Chapters 8 and 10).

Validation Procedure Example

We have learned that all types of validity estimation could be considered a construct validation approach, that several indications of validity are recommended, and that all types of validity are not equally strong evidence. When conducting a validity study, you should consider all that has been presented concerning validity. A validity study in a research journal would be a good model to follow in conducting a validity study.

Content validity evidence has been used for the interpretations of push-up and pull-up scores as measures of arm and shoulder-girdle strength and endurance, although criterion-related validity evidence has also been used. Baumgartner, Oh, Chung, and Hales (2002) published an objectivity, reliability, and validity study for a push-up test. Baumgartner and Gaunt (2005) published a validity study that includes references to the objectivity and reliability of a pull-up test.

The Mahar and Rowe (2002) chapter, "Construct Validation in Physical Activity Research," is an excellent source for the procedures to follow in conducting a comprehensive validity study. However, it must be recognized that their procedures may be somewhat unique to physical activity and research situations. Practitioners may have neither the time nor the expertise to use their procedures in total.

Their chapter is organized into the three stages of construct validation and the type of evidence that needs to be collected at each stage. The three stages are the definitional evidence stage, the confirmatory evidence stage, and the theory testing stage.

The definitional evidence stage involves examining the extent to which the operational domain of the test or instrument represents the theoretical domain of the construct. The content or logical approach to collecting validity evidence is used here. Mahar and Rowe point out that definitional evidence of validity differs from other validity evidence approaches in that at this step, properties of the test rather than interpretations of the test scores are being examined. Defining the construct to be measured must be accomplished before any attempt can be made to find or develop a test to measure the construct.

In stage two, the confirmatory evidence stage, the researcher tries to confirm the definition of the construct at stage one. Any of the approaches to collecting validity evidence presented in this chapter under criterion-related or construct validity evidence can be used here.

The third and final stage is the theory testing stage. At this stage in the construct validation procedure, the theory for the construct to be measured is tested using the scientific method. Mahar and Rowe (2002) indicate that Messick (1989) was the first person to introduce the idea that theory testing is an important part of a well-conducted construct validation procedure. In real life, constructs do not exist in isolation. Many factors influence the construct of interest. These factors are called determinants of the construct. The construct of interest in truth influences other constructs. These are called outcomes of the construct. Determinants and outcomes of the construct should be investigated at this stage. In fact, they probably should be investigated simultaneously. Even for a researcher, this is a huge undertaking. At least the practitioner should be aware that some investigation should occur, even though the investigation may be in terms of major determinants and outcomes and not in great depth. Thus, the establishment of validity is an ongoing and never-ending process.

Factors Affecting Validity
Selected Criterion Measure

The magnitude of a validity coefficient, if one is calculated, can be affected by several factors, among them the criterion measure selected. We have suggested several possible criterion measures (expert ratings, tournament standards, predetermined criterion) to use when calculating a validity coefficient. It is reasonable to expect that each measure, when correlated with the same set of test scores, would yield a different validity coefficient. This is particularly true for a test of multicomponent skills.

Characteristics of the Individuals Tested

Characteristics of the individuals tested also play a part in determining validity. A test that yields scores that allow valid interpretations for 6-year-old children may not yield scores that allow valid interpretations for 15-year-olds; a test that yields valid information for males may not do so for females; a test that yields valid information for beginners may not do so for advanced performers. We can assume that a test yields valid information only for individuals similar in age, gender, and experience to those on whom the original validation was conducted. In fact, it is a good idea to determine validity for yourself the first time you use a test, even for like groups, because the individuals you are measuring cannot be exactly like those originally used in the validation study.

Reliability

As we have said, the test scores must be reliable in order to have validity. The validity coefficient is directly related to the reliability of both the test under investigation and the criterion measure. The maximum validity coefficient possible between two tests can be estimated thus:

$$r_{x,y} = \sqrt{(r_{x,x})(r_{y,y})}$$

where $r_{x,y}$ is the correlation between Tests X and Y (e.g., a new test, X, and a "gold standard" test, Y), $r_{x,x}$ is the reliability coefficient for Test X, and $r_{y,y}$ is the reliability coefficient for Test Y (Ferguson & Takane 1989). For example, if the reliability of both Tests X and Y is .90, the maximum validity coefficient possible would be .90:

$$r_{x,y} = \sqrt{(.90)(.90)} = \sqrt{.81} = .90$$

If the reliability of Test X is .90 and that of Test Y is only .40, the maximum validity coefficient is much lower, only .60:

$$r_{x,y} = \sqrt{(.90)(.40)} = \sqrt{.36} = .60$$

Objectivity

Objectivity was defined as the agreement of two or more competent judges or scorers about the value of a measurement. Note that some people call objectivity "rater reliability." If two judges or raters scoring the same individual on the same test cannot agree on a score, the test scores lack objectivity and the score of neither judge contributes to valid interpretations. Thus, a lack of objectivity reduces validity much the way a lack of reliability does.

Lengthened Tests

We know that the validity of the test score interpretations is influenced by the reliability of the test scores. We know, from the Spearman-Brown formula, that reliability increases as the number of test trials or the length of the test increases. Further, the more measures you obtain for each individual, the more valid a conclusion you have concerning his or her true ability. For example, a dribbling test and a shooting test are better indications of basketball-playing ability than just a shooting test, but four measures of basketball-playing ability are preferable to just two. The same thing could be said for skinfold measures in terms of the number of measures taken at each site and the number of sites. Since reliability and validity are related, increasing the length of a test increases not only reliability, but also the validity of test score interpretations.

Size of the Validity Coefficient

What is an acceptable validity coefficient when one is calculated? There are no rigid standards. The American Educational Research Association (1999) does not address the issue. Safrit (1986) suggests that if a test is being used as a substitute for a more sophisticated test, coefficients of .90 and larger are desirable, but values exceeding .80 are acceptable. This recommendation seems to be for validity with a Pearson correlation coefficient. For validity of interpretations based on a prediction equation, she suggests that in some situations values of .50 or .60 may be acceptable. When a predictive test is needed and/or a high validity coefficient is not required in a situation, a test with validity of .50 or .60 is better than nothing, and thus acceptable.

It seems the acceptable value of the validity coefficient must be dependent on many things, such as what the criterion is, whether it is a Pearson correlation coefficient or a multiple correlation coefficient, how good the criterion is, how high a validity coefficient is needed or expected based on what others have obtained in similar situations, how small a standard error (see Chapter 2) is needed, and how much variance must be explained. The fact that the square of the correlation coefficient indicates the amount of variance common to both tests and, thus, the degree to which the two tests measure the same thing should not be overlooked. This might suggest that in most situations a validity coefficient of at least .70 (49% common variance) is required. A review of interpreting correlation coefficients in Chapter 2 might be worthwhile. It is interesting to note the variety of validity values for distance run tests reported in Chapter 9, since many of the values failed the .80 criterion suggested earlier.

VALIDITY AND THE CRITERION SCORE

Selecting the Criterion Score

A **criterion score** is the measure used to indicate a person's ability. Unless a test has perfect reliability, it is a better indicator when it is developed from more than one trial. Multiple-trial tests are common in physical education with skinfold, flexibility, jumping, throwing, and short running—tests whose performance is not adversely affected by fatigue. Multiple trials with skinfold, flexibility, and strength tests are common in exercise science. In Chapter 3 the selection of the criterion score when multiple trials of the test are administered is discussed in detail. A review of this information might be helpful. Remember that reliability is essential for validity but reliability does not guarantee validity. Thus, the criterion score must be selected considering both reliability and validity. Since

1990 a few test developers have found that for multiple-trial sport skill tests the best score and the mean score are similar in reliability; so they have used the best score because it is quicker and easier to obtain. This is a concern if the best score is much less valid than some other criterion score.

The Role of Preparation

Preparation is an important determinant of the validity of interpretations based on a criterion score. A criterion score is a better indicator of true ability if individuals are measured only after they fully understand how to take a test. For example, suppose your instructor announced one day that he or she is going to measure your aerobic capacity by having you run a mile for time. If you had never done any distance running, you would not know how to pace yourself, how to run in a relaxed manner, how to avoid being boxed in by other runners, or how to run near the inside curve. Your score that day would not be a true indication of your aerobic capacity. If you were tested again the next day, your score would improve, not because your aerobic capacity had improved, but because you would have learned how to approach the test. And on a third day you might do better still.

Research indicates that people often need a day of practice before physical performance testing to familiarize themselves with a test, even if they have had experience with it (Baumgartner 1969; Erickson et al. 1946). This practice allows a period of relearning and reinforcement that is necessary because skill retention is never perfect. Researchers have found that a mean trial score for a multiple-trial test will be higher if several practice trials (called practice warm-up trials) are administered just before the test (Baumgartner & Jackson 1970).

VALIDITY AND CRITERION-REFERENCED TESTS

Generally, the same definition of validity for a norm-referenced test applies to a criterion-referenced test. The techniques for estimating validity with a criterion-referenced test are different from the techniques with a norm-referenced test. Remember, a criterion-referenced test is used to classify people as either proficient or nonproficient, either passing or failing.

One technique for estimating validity with a criterion-referenced test is called **domain-referenced validity**. The term *domain* refers to the criterion ability or behavior the test is supposed to measure. Thus, the interpretations based on scores from a criterion-referenced test are logically validated by showing that the test measures the criterion ability or behavior. This technique is basically the same as the content or logical validity technique discussed earlier in this chapter, in the section titled Content Validity Evidence.

Another technique for estimating validity with a criterion-referenced test is called **decision validity**. This deals with the accuracy of the test in classifying people as either proficient or nonproficient. Essential to this technique is the ability to accurately classify people as either proficient or nonproficient, independently of the test. This is often very difficult to do, but for the moment let us say that we have the ability to do it. So, independently of the test and also as a result of the test, we have classified people as either proficient or nonproficient. These classifications enable us to generate a double-entry classification table such as Table 4.1. All packages of statistical computer programs have a cross-tabulation program (see section 9 of the SPSS Statistical Procedures part of Appendix A) that will provide a table like Table 4.1.

From this double-entry classification table, the classification of outcome probabilities (C) can be calculated as an estimate of validity.

$$C = \frac{A + D}{A + B + C + D}$$

Problem 4.1 Calculate C for the data in Table 4.2.

Solution Where the sum of the A-Box and the D-Box is 60 and the sum of the four boxes is 75, C=.80:

$$C = \frac{40 + 20}{40 + 5 + 10 + 20} = \frac{60}{75} = .80$$

If C equals 0.50 it indicates that the classification by the test was no better than chance, and interpretations as to proficiency based on test scores would not be very valid. For this reason a value of C closer to 1.0 than to 0.50 is most desirable.

Another estimate of validity that can be calculated from a double-entry classification table is phi (ϕ).

$$\phi = \frac{(AD) - (BC)}{\sqrt{(A + B)(C + D)(A + C)(B + D)}}$$

Problem 4.2 Calculate ϕ for the data in Table 4.2.

Solution

$$\phi = \frac{(40)(20) - (5)(10)}{\sqrt{(40 + 5)(10 + 20)(40 + 10)(5 + 20)}}$$

$$= \frac{800 - 50}{\sqrt{1687500}} = \frac{750}{1299.04} = .58$$

Phi values can range from - 1.0 to 1.0, so phi coefficients can be interpreted like any other correlation coefficient. However, because phi is the correlation between two dichotomous variables, high values of phi should not be expected (see Chapter 2 on correlation coefficients). A positive value of phi is required for validity. A negative

TABLE 4.1	Table for Estimating Validity with a Criterion-Referenced Test		
		True Classification	
		Proficient	Nonproficient
	Proficient	A	B
Test Classification			
	Nonproficient	C	D

TABLE 4.2	Data for Estimating Validity with a Criterion-Referenced Test		
		True Classification	
		Proficient	Nonproficient
Test Classification	Proficient	40	5
	Nonproficient	10	20

value of phi indicates that the test is classifying individuals opposite to the way the criterion is classifying individuals.

Let us come back to the problem of classifying people as either proficient or nonproficient, independently of the test (the actual classification in the double-entry table). In some instructional situations the proficient classification could be people who had received instruction, and the nonproficient classification could be people who had not received instruction. Also, in an instructional situation the nonproficient could be the classification of people before they received instruction, and the proficient could be the classification of the same people after receiving instruction. In some exercise science situations, an accepted standard or laboratory measure may exist that can be used for classifying people in terms of actual group membership.

The validity of criterion-referenced standards for youth health-related fitness tests could be investigated to determine if the classifications are accurate for the youth. This is **concurrent,** or "for the present," **validity.** However, the validity of criterion-referenced standards for youth health-related fitness tests could be investigated to determine if the classifications are accurate when the youth become adults. Are fit youth fit adults? This is **predictive,** or "for the future," **validity.** So, as we have stated many times, validity applies to the interpretations of the test scores, not to the scores themselves. The predictive validity would be determined by the test classification in the double-entry table being the subject's classification (fit or unfit) as a youth and the true classification in the double-entry table being the subject's classification (fit or unfit) as an adult. Unfortunately, little if any data like this exists.

An excellent discussion of validity with criterion-referenced tests can be found in Safrit and Wood (1989). This source contains other information related to the validity issue, such as setting the cutoff score for proficiency on the criterion-referenced test. An excellent tutorial on standards setting for the mile run test is presented by Cureton and Warren (1990). Safrit and Looney (1992) should be read for their comments on the standards-setting procedures of Cureton and Warren. Shifflett and Schuman (1982) provide a good example of constructing and evaluating a criterion-referenced test for archery. Other examples of evaluating criterion-referenced tests can be found in journals like *Measurement in Physical Education and Exercise Science.*

A discussion of many validity, reliability, and performance standards issues in reference to fitness tests for children is presented by Safrit (1990). She concludes that much has been done, but much more remains to be done to improve fitness tests for children.

SUMMARY

There are three characteristics essential to a good measuring instrument: reliability, objectivity, and validity. Validity evidence with norm-referenced tests may be of three different types: content, criterion, and construct.

Content validity is a logically determined measure: the test score must measure the domain of the construct. With the criterion approach to validity we calculate the correlation between an individual's scores on the test and her scores on an established criterion to determine the degree to which the test and the criterion yield similar information. The construct approach includes a number of different ways of collecting validity information. All approaches to gathering validity information are really construct approaches.

Another major issue in testing is the selection of a criterion score, which can be the person's best score, mean score,

or some other score. A knowledge of how the criterion score is used is essential to intelligent selection and ultimately to the validity of the interpretations based on the criterion score.

Finally, when using criterion-referenced tests, the analyst must estimate the validity of interpretations based on scores from these tests. Two methods for estimating validity were presented.

FORMATIVE EVALUATION OF OBJECTIVES

Objective 1 Define validity, and outline the methods used to estimate it.

1. Important characteristics of all measurements are that they be reliable, objective, and that interpretations based on the measurements be valid. Describe the basic nature of validity.
2. Three types of norm-referenced test validity evidence were discussed. Briefly describe each of these types of evidence and what is found with each type of evidence.
3. Criterion validity evidence involves determining the correlation between a test and a criterion measure. Summarize the criterion measures especially suitable for use in physical education and exercise science.
4. Briefly describe the two methods of estimating validity with criterion-referenced tests following the Mahar and Rowe approach.

Objective 2 Describe the influence of test reliability on validity.

1. A basic principle of measurement theory is that test scores must first be reliable in order for interpretations of test scores to be valid. Why is this so?
2. What effect does objectivity have on validity?

Objective 3 Identify those factors that influence validity.

1. It is well established that test score reliability is an essential factor of validity. What other factors affect validity?

Objective 4 Select a criterion score based on measurement theory from which valid interpretations can be made.

1. Many psychomotor tests involve several trials. What can a person do to make sure that the interpretations of the criterion score are as valid as possible?

ADDITIONAL LEARNING ACTIVITIES

1. There are many tests commonly used in testing programs (runs, lifts, throws). Administer one of these tests and determine the validity of it.
2. Construct a new sport skill test. Administer the test and decide how to calculate its validity.

BIBLIOGRAPHY

American Educational Research Association. 1999. *Standards for educational and psychological testing*. Washington, DC: AERA.

Baumgartner, T. A. 1969. Stability of physical performance test scores. *Research Quarterly* 40: 257–261.

Baumgartner, T. A. and G. J. Gaunt. 2005. Construct related validity for the Baumgartner modified pull-up test. *Measurement in Physical Education and Exercise Science* 9: 51–60.

Baumgartner, T. A. and A. S. Jackson. 1970. Measurement schedules for tests of motor performance. *Research Quarterly* 41: 10–17.

Baumgartner, T. A., S. Oh, H. Chung, and D. Hales. 2002. Objectivity, reliability, and validity for a revised push-up test protocol. *Measurement in Physical Education and Exercise Science* 6: 225–242.

Crocker, L. and J. Algina. 1986. *Introduction to classical and modern test theory*. New York: Holt, Rinehart and Winston.

Cureton, K. J. and G. L. Warren. 1990. Criterion-referenced standards for youth health-related fitness tests: A tutorial. *Research Quarterly for Exercise and Sport* 61: 7–19.

Erickson, L. et al. 1946. The energy cost of horizontal and grade walking on the motor drive treadmill. *American Journal of Physiology* 145: 391–401.

Ferguson, G. A. and Y. Takane. 1989. *Statistical analysis in psychology and education*. 6th ed. New York: McGraw-Hill.

Jackson, A. W. and A. B. Baker. 1986. The relationship of the sit-and-reach test to criterion measures of hamstring and back flexibility in young females.

Research Quarterly for Exercise and Sport 57: 183–186.

Mahar, M. T. and D. A. Rowe. 2002. Construct validity in physical activity research. In G. J. Welk (Ed.). *Physical activity assessment for health-related research*. Champaign, IL: Human Kinetics.

Messick, S. 1989. Validity. In R. Linn (Ed.). *Educational measurement*. 3rd ed., pp. 13–104. Washington, DC: American Council on Education.

Nunnally, J. C. and I. R. Bernstein. 1994. *Psychometric theory*. 3rd ed. New York: McGraw-Hill.

Safrit, M. J. 1986. *Introduction to measurement in physical education and exercise science*. St. Louis: Mosby Year Book.

———. 1990. The validity and reliability of fitness tests for children: A review. *Pediatric Exercise Science* 2: 9–28.

Safrit, M. J. and M. L. Looney. 1992. Should the punishment fit the crime? A measurement dilemma. *Research Quarterly for Exercise and Sport* 63: 124–127.

Safrit, M. J. and T. M. Wood. 1989. *Measurement concepts in physical education and exercise science*. Champaign, IL: Human Kinetics.

Shifflett, B. and B. J. Schuman. 1982. A criterion-referenced test for archery. *Research Quarterly for Exercise and Sport* 53: 330–335.

5

TEST CHARACTERISTICS, ADMINISTRATION, AND INTERPRETATION

CONTENTS

KEY WORDS

mass testability
posttest procedures
pretest planning
useful scores

Forms :
the Rules
of the Game

OBJECTIVES

In the first part of this chapter we will discuss those attributes that make up a sound measuring instrument. These include not only reliability, objectivity, and validity, but also other content-related, person-related, and administration-related characteristics.

Pretest procedures, giving the test, and posttest procedures are also important aspects of testing. Pretest planning, in particular, is the key to a successful measurement procedure, providing the basis for all testing decisions and processes.

Finally, evaluation of the measurements obtained from a testing program is discussed. The differences between formative and summative evaluation are identified.

After reading Chapter 5 you should be able to

1. Identify the important characteristics of a test.
2. Plan the administration of a test.
3. Define and compare the terms *evaluation* and *measurement*.

INTRODUCTION

Many existing measurement programs are neither effective nor efficient, while others produce scores that lead to invalid interpretations because the teacher, researcher, or exercise scientist (fitness specialist, physical therapist, athletic trainer, or program specialist) has been careless in selecting tests or in planning testing procedures. The first level of planning in a good measurement program focuses on the selection or construction of a test. The second level involves the administration of the test. After the test is administered, some evaluation of the scores obtained should occur.

Teachers almost always test a group of students at the same time, with all students going through the test at the same time (the entire group running the mile for time), half the group going through the test while the other students watch or assist in administering the test (half of the students do the sit-up test and the others hold the feet of those being tested and count the number of sit-ups

executed), or one student going through the test while the others in the group watch (the instructor takes skinfold measures). Sometimes researchers and exercise specialists test people in a group, but they are just as likely to test one person at a time, with one person coming to be tested every 30 to 60 minutes. Testing one person at a time is a clinical model common to adult fitness, athletic training, physical therapy, and cardiac rehabilitation programs. Some of the topics discussed in this chapter may not apply to situations where one person is tested at a time. However, many topics apply to all measurement situations.

Testing and evaluating the participants based on their test scores must occur in most classes and programs. Teachers grade their students, but grading is just evaluating the participants in a program that happens to be educational. Exercise scientists such as exercise specialists, athletic trainers, physical therapists, or program instructors must evaluate the participants in their programs. Most of what is presented concerning evaluation applies to all situations.

TEST CHARACTERISTICS

Knowing the important characteristics of a test allows the teacher, researcher, or exercise scientist to construct effective, efficient instruments, and to recognize essential features in tests constructed by others. The characteristics themselves concern the test content, the individuals tested, and the administrative procedures. Most important are reliability, objectivity, and validity issues.

Reliability, Objectivity, and Validity

The three most important characteristics for a test are reliability and objectivity of the test scores and validity of the interpretations of these scores (see Chapters 3 and 4). If a test does not fulfill these requirements, you need not consider it further. Yet there are no rigid standards for acceptable levels of these characteristics. Acceptability is determined by both the testing situation itself and the values others have obtained in their measurement programs. This is not to say that no standards exist. Standards are discussed in Chapter 3 and 4.

Content-Related Attributes

These characteristics relate to the nature of the test content: what it measures and how it does so.

Important Attributes

The authors of this book believe that no more than 10% of the class or program time should involve testing. To meet this goal, only the most important skills and abilities should be measured. These skills and abilities are those listed in the educational objectives for the unit, or are the important components of a program.

Discrimination

A test should discriminate among different ability groups throughout the total range of ability. Ideally, there should be many different scores, and the distribution of the scores should be basically normal, or at least not markedly skewed. Also, it is important to select a test difficult enough so that nobody receives a perfect score, but easy enough so that nobody receives a zero. Consider the problem of two individuals receiving the minimum or maximum score. Although two individuals who receive a zero on a pull-up test are both weak, they are probably not equal in strength per pound of body weight. In a clinical or research situation where individuals are required to curl a weight as many times as possible, you want to select a weight that each person can curl at least once but no one can curl a large (maybe 30 or more) number of times. Remember, however, that the fact that nobody receives a perfect score or a zero is no guarantee that a test discriminates satisfactorily; conversely, the fact that someone does receive a perfect score or a zero is no guarantee that the test is a poor one.

Resemblance to the Activity

When taking a test, particularly a sport skill test, students must be required to use good form, follow the rules of the activity, and perform acts characteristic of the activity. For example, a basketball test in which students are allowed to run with the ball rather than dribble it is neither following the rules of the game nor demanding a performance characteristic of it. The validity of the interpretations of scores from a test is questionable if the test does not resemble the activity.

Specificity

When a test measures a single attribute, it is possible to determine from it why a person is performing poorly; when a test measures an attribute that has several components, it is more difficult to determine why a person is performing at a given level. For example, consider a basketball test of ten shots at the basket. If the student stands three feet away from the basket to shoot and the student misses all ten shots, it is easy to determine that the student is a poor shot. If, however, the student is standing 40 feet away from the basket and misses the ten shots, it is difficult to determine whether the student simply shoots poorly or lacks strength. Likewise, strength tests and flexibility tests should be as specific as possible.

Sometimes it is not possible to measure a single attribute; at other times your reason for testing is to measure how well a person combines several attributes. In either case, the test should be as specific as possible for whatever is being measured.

Unrelated Measures

Often an attribute has several components, so you will measure it using a battery composed of several tests. The tests in a battery should be unrelated—that is, the correlation between the tests should be low—both to save testing time and to be fair to the individuals being tested. Of course, all tests in a battery should correlate highly with the criterion used to determine validity.

When two tests are highly correlated, they are probably measuring the same ability. This wastes time and also gives the measured ability double weight in the battery, a practice unfair to individuals weak in the ability. If two tests in a battery are highly correlated, keep the better of the two and drop the other.

Student and Participant Concerns
Appropriateness to Student and Participants

Performance is influenced by the person's maturity, gender, and experience. For example, older students and boys generally score better on strength tests (push-up, bench press) than do younger students and girls. The strength test scores are usually reliable and the interpretations of these scores valid for a variety of ages and both genders, but performance standards should be based on age and gender. Skill tests, on the other hand, are not universally applicable: they must apply to the age, gender, skill level, strength, and other capacities of the students. Again, the reliability and validity associated with skill tests may be acceptable with junior high students and not acceptable with elementary or high school students; and tests acceptable with females may not be acceptable with males.

Performance is also influenced by the age and disabilities of the person. Physical performance tests (fitness tests in particular) for high school and college students are often not appropriate for adults over 30 years old, and seldom appropriate for adults older than age 60 or for preschool children. Individuals with disabilities often do not score as well as individuals without disabilities on most physical performance tests. Strength and skill tests for individuals without disabilities are usually not acceptable for individuals with disabilities.

Individual Scores

A person's test scores should not be affected by another person's performance. That is, the way a test is administered should not require that several individuals interact and the score of each individual be based on that interaction. For example, consider a basketball lay-up shot test in which Student 1 runs toward the basket and Student 2 throws the ball to him to shoot at the basket. If Student 2 makes a poor or late throw, even the best player is going to miss the basket.

Enjoyable

When individuals enjoy taking a test and understand why they are being tested, they are motivated to do well, and their scores ordinarily represent their maximum capacity. To be enjoyable, a test should be interesting and challenging, within reason. People are more likely to enjoy a test when they have a reasonable chance to achieve an acceptable score. Testing comfort is also an aspect of enjoyment. Although certain aerobic capacity tests and other maximum-effort tests can be uncomfortable, avoid any test so painful that few people can do it well.

Safety

Obviously, you should not use tests that endanger the people being tested. Examine each test's procedures to see whether individuals might overextend themselves or make mistakes that could cause injury. The use of spotters in gymnastic and weight lifting tests, soft, nonbreakable marking devices for obstacle runs or the marking of testing areas, and nonslip surfaces and large areas for running and throwing events are always necessary. The American College of Sports Medicine (ACSM 2000) offers guidelines for administering maximal stress tests. These are summarized in Chapter 11.

Confidentiality and Privacy of Testing

Many students and participants in fitness or rehabilitation programs would prefer that others did not know how well or poorly they score on a test. Often students are embarrassed when they receive a test score that is considerably better or worse than those of their peers. Participants in fitness and rehabilitation programs have similar feelings or just do not think that their score should be known by others. All people conducting measurement programs need to be sensitive to this issue. Testing people one at a time rather than in a group may be the only way to satisfy this concern.

Motivation to Score at Maximum Potential

Students tend to try hard on tests because their grade is affected. Generally, people who are in certification programs or whose job, salary, insurance premium, and so on are affected by their score try hard on tests. Thus, testing can motivate people to learn more and achieve at a higher level. But what motivates people not in these situations to try hard on tests? Poor effort by the person being tested makes scores not reliable and interpretations based on these scores not valid. The tester must motivate participants to do well and constantly watch for lack of effort by participants. Exercise specialists doing testing in therapy programs need to be particularly aware of participant effort.

Administrative Concerns

Mass Testability

When there is a large number of people to test in a short period of time, **mass testability** can be a vital test characteristic. The longer it takes to administer each test, the fewer tests are likely to be administered. With large groups it is essential that people be measured quickly, either successively or simultaneously. A test can be mass testable when a participant performs every 10 to 15 seconds. A sit-up test can be mass testable when half the group is tested while the other half helps with the administration. Remember too that short tests or tests that keep most of the participants active at once help prevent the discipline problems that often result from student inactivity and reduce dissatisfaction of participants in research or fitness programs.

The teacher, researcher, or exercise scientist can become so concerned about mass testing that reliability of the data and, thus, validity of the interpretations based on the data suffer. With careful thought and planning this need not be true.

Minimal Practice

People must be familiar with a test and be allowed to practice before testing. Familiarity, either from previous testing, from the program or class, or from practice sessions prior to the testing day, lessens both explanation and practice time. Even when a test is unfamiliar, if it is easy to understand,

then little time need be spent to explain it. Avoid tests that require elaborate directions or considerable practice.

In research or rehabilitation fitness testing and strength testing situations where participants are tested on treadmill and other equipment with no previous experience on the equipment and with minimum explanation and practice trials of the test, are reliable scores obtained? The equipment may have the potential to provide very reliable scores and interpretations based on these scores that are quite valid, but if poor administrative techniques are used when testing with the equipment, reliable scores and, thus, valid interpretations based on the scores will not be obtained.

Minimal Equipment and Personnel

For teachers, tests that require a lot of equipment and/or administrative personnel are often impractical. Equipment is usually expensive to purchase and maintain and can be time-consuming to assemble. In the same way, when several people are needed to administer a test, time must be spent finding and training them. Even when you plan to use members of the class or program, you must expect to spend time training them.

Insufficient training of all test administrators contributes to lack of test score objectivity (see Chapter 3). In some labs and rehabilitation programs where participants will be tested at regular intervals over a period of time to determine if they are improving, the same person, rather than different people, tests a participant each time to maximize the chances that improvement in the scores of the participant is really an improvement and not due to lack of objectivity.

Ease of Preparation

Select tests that are easy to set up over ones that take more time, provided the first does the job well. Tests that use complex equipment or several pieces of equipment placed at specific spots or that require a large number of boundary or dimension marks on floors and walls are usually neither easily nor quickly set up.

Adequate Directions

When you construct a test, you must develop a set of directions for it. When you use a test constructed by others, you must make sure that complete directions accompany it. Directions should specify how the test is set up, the preparation of individuals to be tested, and administration and scoring procedures.

It seems that the directions for many tests do not adequately address how much a person being tested is allowed to deviate from perfect form yet still receive a test score. For example, the directions for the biceps curl test specify that the weight is to be curled up until the bar touches the chest and then lowered until the arms are straight as many times as possible. Only correctly executed curls are supposed to be counted. An execution of the curl is not supposed to be counted if the bar almost touches the chest in the up position and/or the arms are almost straight in the down position. However, one tester will count a slightly incorrectly executed curl because the form is basically correct, where another tester will not count the execution because it is not perfectly correct. Or, on one day a tester will count a slightly incorrectly executed curl; on another day she will not count it. This lack of sufficient direction as to how to score a slightly incorrect execution curl contributes to low objectivity and reliability for the test scores.

With a push-up test there is an up position (how far a participant must come up for the push-up to be counted), a down position (how far a participant must go down for the push-up to be counted), and a requirement that during the entire time that push-ups are being performed the back be kept straight for a push-up to be counted. Hand placement and other things influences the maximum number of push-ups executed. Directions for many push-up tests are skimpy on details as to when to count or not count a slightly incorrectly executed push-up and what to do about incorrect hand placement. The directions that Baumgartner, Oh, Chung, and Hales (2002) provide with their revised push-up test are an excellent example of complete directions.

Norms

When the norms provided with a test are both recent and appropriate, they can save the time necessary to develop local norms, or at least offer temporary standards until local norms can be developed. Unhappily, norms provided with a test may be so old that they are no longer suitable, or they may be based on a group of different gender, age, or experience, and so not be appropriate to the individuals being tested.

Useful Scores

A test should yield **useful scores.** These are scores that can be used at once or inserted into a formula with little effort. Most physical measures can be used immediately after a measurement session. If scores must be placed in a formula before they can be used, the formula should be sufficiently simple so that calculations can be done quickly. For example,

$$Y = 2X + 5$$

where Y is the calculated score and X is the score collected, is a simple enough formula that a test requiring it could be considered. However, a test that requires the calculation

$$Y = .6754\sqrt{X} + .2156X^2 - 3.14$$

or

$$Y = .4521X_1 + .3334X_2 + 1.2$$

would be very time consuming if a Y score had to be calculated by hand for each of several hundred people. With computer support, the computer program would have the formula for Y in it, and only the X score(s) for each person would have to be entered into the computer. Computer support like this is quite common and should be used more often. In SPSS there is a program called Transform (see section 16 in the Statistical Procedures part of Appendix A) in which calculations can be conducted.

When you are statistically analyzing a set of scores by hand or using the computer, you must express the scores in a single unit of measure. When measuring the height of people, you could record the scores in inches (a useful score) or in feet (Feet) and inches (Inches), and then convert them to a useful score by this formula: Score = (12)(Feet) + Inches. Why would a height score ever be recorded in feet and inches? Because the height-measuring equipment is expressed in feet and inches. Also, when people are asked to indicate their height, they know it in feet and inches. So, in both cases it is more accurate to convert the height scores to inches after the data collection is over.

ADMINISTRATION

The key to good testing is the planning before the test is given and then the follow-up to that planning during and after the test administration.

Pretest Procedures

We plan before giving a test to be sure that our preparation is adequate and that the actual administration will proceed smoothly. **Pretest planning** is all of the preparation that occurs before test administration. It involves a number of tasks: knowing the test, developing test procedures, developing directions, preparing the individuals to be tested, planning warm-up and test trials, securing equipment and preparing the test facility, making scoring sheets, estimating time needed, and giving the test.

Knowing the Test

Whenever you plan to administer a test for the first time, read the directions or test manual several times, thinking about the test as you read. This is the only way to avoid overlooking small details about procedures, dimensions, and the like.

Developing Test Procedures

Once you are familiar with the test, start to develop procedures for administering it. These include selecting the most efficient testing procedure, deciding whether to test all the individuals together or in groups, and determining whether one person will do all the testing or pairs of individuals will test each other.

If you plan to administer several tests on the same day, order them so that fatigue is minimized.

Do not give consecutive tests that tire the same muscle groups. Also, plan to administer very fatiguing events, such as distance runs or other maximum exertion tests, last.

The next step is the identification of exact scoring requirements and units of measurement. For example, in a curl-up test, you could require the person to start in a supine position with both shoulder blades on the floor and the knees flexed, then with the arms crossed and hands placed on opposite shoulders to curl up until both elbows touch the thighs, and finally to return to the starting position, all to score one curl-up. Here too, when necessary, you must select the unit of measurement with which you will score. For example, do you want to express distance in feet or inches or both; time in minutes or seconds or both? To obtain a score that can immediately be analyzed mathematically, you should use only one unit of measurement—usually the smaller one.

At this point you should also decide what to do if an individual makes a mistake during the test. By anticipating possible situations and rulings, you will be able to deal fairly with all individuals. For example, what do you do if an individual fails to go all the way down to the floor on a curl-up? Whether you disregard the mistake, warn the individual and count the curl-up, or discount it, you must follow the same policy for all individuals.

Finally, safety procedures are essential. Always plan to use spotters in tests where people can get injured or when testing the elderly. Consider your marking devices as well. In obstacle runs they should be soft, unbreakable, and tall enough so that participants cannot step over them. Use marking cones instead of chairs or soda bottles when marking testing areas or obstacle courses. Think too about the testing area. Hold running events in a large enough area so that participants do not run into obstacles. Plan for organization of participants waiting to be tested so that participants do not run into them.

If you have never administered a specific test before, try one or two practice administrations before the actual test. This is a good way not only to see what changes and additions to the procedures must be made, but also to train administrative personnel.

Developing Directions

After you have determined procedures, you must develop exact directions. It is perfectly acceptable to read these directions to a group before administering the test to them. The directions should be easy to understand and should specify the following:

1. Administration procedures
2. Instructions on performance
3. Scoring procedure and the policy on incorrect performance
4. Hints on techniques to improve scores

Preparing the Students or Program Participants

Announce the test well in advance so that people can practice if they think it will improve their scores. When the class or group is unfamiliar with a test, spend some time before the day of the test explaining it and the techniques that will improve test scores, and supervising pretest practice.

Even when people have had exposure to a test, they may need some time to relearn the necessary techniques. Girardi (1971) familiarized a group of high school boys with a jump-and-reach test and a 12-minute run test, and then tested them. Eight weeks later, he retested the students without review, and found that a number of them, particularly the poorly skilled, had forgotten the necessary techniques.

With the exception of a few research situations (e.g., learning research), people should know well in advance that they are going to be tested, what the test is, and what it involves. This allows each person to be psychologically and physiologically ready to be tested and score up to his potential. This is vital when important things like grades, admission to or release from programs, or health fitness ratings are involved.

Planning Warm-Up and Test Trials

We saw in Chapter 3 that reliability improves with pretest warm-up. The amount and nature of this warm-up must be planned. Ideally, warm-up should be specific to the skill being tested (i.e, practice rather than calisthenics). It has been shown too that supervised warm-up, in which the tester tells the individuals what to do and ensures that all individuals receive the same amount of practice, is better than unsupervised warm-up. In some situations it is acceptable to administer multiple trials of a test and to consider the first few trials as warm-up, making each individual's score the sum or mean of the latter test trials.

Securing Equipment and Preparing the Testing Facility

You should have all equipment on hand before the day of the test. The equipment should be checked to be sure it works and you know how to use it. Also, before the test, all boundary lines and other markings should be in place. Having all equipment available and all boundary lines and other markings positioned correctly when the people to be tested arrive saves time and avoids the problems that inevitably arise when people are kept waiting while the test is set up.

Making Scoring Sheets

At some point before the test, locate or prepare either a master scoring sheet for the entire group or individual scorecards. Enter each person's name on the sheet or cards before they arrive to be tested.

There are many advantages to using individual scorecards over a master scoring sheet. Scorecards allow people to rotate among testing stations and to quickly record scores when they have tested one another. Even when one person is testing and recording the scores of the entire group, time can be saved by gathering the scorecards in order after the individuals are in line to be tested rather than having the individuals get in line in the same order they are listed on the scoring sheet.

The alternative to using scoring sheets or scorecards is, when you test people, to enter the scores into a PDA for immediate analysis. As with scoring sheets, enter each person's name prior to testing.

Estimating the Time Needed

When a test will not take an entire class or program period, or when half the group will be tested on each day, you must plan some activity to fill the extra time or to occupy the rest of the group. If testing will occur during an agency or corporate fitness program, similar planning is necessary. Estimating the time needed to administer a test both minimizes confusion and maximizes the use of available time.

Giving the Test

If you have planned properly, the testing should go smoothly. Although your primary concern on the day of the test is the administration of the test itself, you should also be concerned with participant preparation, motivation, and safety. If, after you have administered the test, you can say, "The participants were prepared and the test was administered in a way that I would have liked if I were being tested," the testing session undoubtedly will have been a success.

Preparation

The participants should already know what the test is and why it is being given; so your first concern is the warm-up or practice. Next, explain the test instructions and procedures, even demonstrating the test for them if possible. Ask for questions both before and after the demonstration. When the skill or procedures are particularly complicated, let the participants run through a practice trial of the test.

Motivation

Give all participants the same degree of motivation and encouragement. Although we all tend to encourage poor performers and compliment superior ones, in fairness all or none of the participants should receive a comment. Whenever possible, in-

dicate his or her score to a participant immediately after the test trial. This can motivate participants to perform better on a second or third trial. However, the reporting of the score should not embarrass the participant.

Safety

During a testing session, watch for safety problems. Participants often perform unsafely when they are not following instructions. Try to anticipate these or other unsafe situations.

Posttest Procedures

The rationale for testing is to collect information about the participants and, in education, about the instructional program. Only after the test is given can the information be used. Surprisingly, many teachers and exercise scientists fail to do enough, or even any, posttest analysis. The sooner the results of tests are returned to the participants, the more meaningful they will be in the evaluation process. **Posttest procedures** include the analyzing, reporting, and recording of test scores.

Analyzing Test Scores

Shortly after a test, the scores must be analyzed using the appropriate techniques from Chapter 2. This often requires entering the data into the computer so that analysis, record keeping, and/or data retrieval is possible. Analysis serves to reveal characteristics that could influence the teaching procedures or program conduct and to provide information for the group tested and prepare the data for grading or other evaluation purposes. People are usually interested in their scores, their relative standings in the group or class, and their degree of improvement or decline since the last test. Reporting test results to participants is an effective motivational device.

Recording Test Results

The recording of test results is usually nothing more than placing the scoring sheets and your analysis of them in an appropriate file. The information makes possible comparisons between classes or groups within and between years, program evaluation over years, and the development of norms. Notice that these are group or class standards rather than individual standards, based solely on the scores and your analysis. Often it is not even necessary to identify the scores, particularly in situations where a permanent record card for each student or program participant is kept. It is from this card, which follows the student from grade to grade or the program participant from year to year, that you can trace individual improvement over time.

EVALUATION

After administering a test and obtaining a score (measurement), evaluation often follows, taking the form of a judgment about the quality of a performance. Suppose, for example, that each participant in a class or exercise program ran a mile, and their scores were recorded by the teacher or exercise specialist. No matter whether the person classified these measurements "excellent," "good," "average" or "A", "B", "C," she was making an evaluation.

Evaluation can be subjective: the judge uses no set standards for each classification and/or evaluates during the performance without recording any measurements. The objectivity of evaluation increases when it is based on defined standards.

Types of Evaluation

Formative evaluation, as noted in Chapter 1, occurs during instruction or the exercise science program to inform the participant and the teacher or exercise scientist of the participant's status. This information allows the teacher or exercise scientist to judge the effectiveness of the unit in progress and to make future plans. Participants are motivated by knowing the extent to which they are meeting the stated objectives. Thus, for-

mative evaluation is both continuous throughout the teaching unit or program and related to the program's objectives.

Summative evaluation is the final measurement of participant performance at the end of the teaching unit or program. It is often used to assign grades in teaching. This type of evaluation is likely to involve comparisons among students rather than comparisons with a single level of achievement. In an exercise science program the summative evaluation is more likely to be a comparison of the participant's score to a performance goal set earlier or to an ideal standard, but the evaluation may result in the participant's being allowed to discontinue the program or being required to continue the program.

Standards for Evaluation
Criterion-Referenced Standards

Criterion-referenced standards represent the level of achievement that nearly all participants should be able to reach given proper instruction and ample practice. These standards are valuable to the participant because they specify the expected level of performance, and valuable to the teacher or exercise scientist because they clearly define participant status in relation to the standard.

Criterion-referenced standards must be used with explicit objectives—objectives that ordinarily must be accomplished before broader objectives can be achieved. Thus, criterion-referenced standards can be used in formative evaluation to diagnose weaknesses and to determine when participants are ready to progress.

Criterion-referenced standards are used in courses and programs where the objective is certification. For example, criterion-referenced standards are used with the driver's license exam. There is a minimum score that a person must achieve on the knowledge test and the driving test to be issued a driver's license. Achieving at least the minimum score results in passing the exam, but any score less than the minimum score results in failing the exam.

The American Red Cross has developed a hierarchy of swimming skills that reflect criterion-referenced standards:

Beginner Skills

1. Breath holding—10 seconds
2. Rhythmic breathing—10 seconds
3. Prone glide
4. Back glide and recovery
5. Prone glide with kick
6. Back glide with kick
7. Beginner stroke or crawl stroke—15 yards
8. Combined stroke on back—15 yards

Swimming Skills

1. Sidestroke
2. Back crawl
3. Breaststroke
4. Crawl stroke
5. Surface dives—pike, tuck
6. Feet-first surface dive

Obviously, these standards must be met if the participant is to achieve a wanted level of competence in swimming. The inability to meet a specified standard indicates that additional instruction or learning activities are needed. On both the beginner and the swimming skills levels, summative evaluation would focus on combinations of these skills: at the swimming skills level, for example, the distance a person can swim in ten minutes using the breaststroke, sidestroke, crawl, and backstroke.

For an instructional unit on physical fitness, the criterion-referenced standards for ninth-grade boys might be a run of 1½ miles in 12 minutes, 35 bent-knee sit-ups in 2 minutes, and 3 pull-ups. Thus, criterion-referenced standards tend to be pass-fail. In this case, performance on all three tests (the sum of the standard scores; see Chapter 2) could be used to summatively evaluate the broader objective of total fitness.

In some programs there is a move to mastery of program content as the desired outcome. Thus, the evaluation of a participant is in terms of the number of desired outcomes achieved and not in comparison to his peers. This is basically a competency-based criterion-referenced standard situation. In the earlier swimming skills example, each student could be evaluated on how many of the standards were achieved. Passing the course is dependent on reaching a certain outcome if the outcomes are rank ordered or mastering a certain number of outcomes if there is no ordering of outcomes.

Many different procedures are used to develop criterion-referenced standards. One method involves the following steps:

Step 1

Identify the specific behaviors that must be achieved to accomplish a broad objective.

Step 2

Develop clearly defined objectives that correspond to the specific behaviors.

Step 3

Develop standards that give evidence of successful achievement of the objective. These standards may be based on logic, expert opinion, research literature, and/or an analysis of test scores.

Step 4

Try the system and evaluate the standards. Determine whether the standards must be altered and do so if necessary.

The standards set in Step 3 often are arbitrary. If the mastery standard is set too high, it is likely to be obtained by only a few participants, and there will be little positive reinforcement for mastery for very many participants. On the other hand, if the mastery level is too low, then a large number of participants may have the illusion that they have mastered the objective when in fact they have fallen short. Because physical education teachers and exercise scientists use a variety of testing instruments that apply different units of measurement, the importance to them of evaluating and readjusting criterion-referenced standards is evident.

Norm-Referenced Standards

Norm-referenced standards, those that compare the performances of peers, are useful for determining the degree to which participants have achieved a broad objective. In developing norm-referenced standards, levels of performance that distinguish among ability groups are specified; that is, the standards are set so that some participants are classified "high ability" and some "low ability." The traditional grading system (A,B,C,D,F) is based on norm-referenced standards. Grading and the development of norm-referenced standards are discussed in Chapter 6.

In summary, all people do not respond the same way to testing. The same test, test protocol, and performance score expectations cannot be applied to all people. Understanding the characteristics of the people in the population tested and experience in testing people in the population are vital to obtaining test scores upon which you can base valid interpretations.

SUMMARY

Whether you develop your own test or select a pre-constructed test, which is certainly easier, you will require certain attributes in the instrument. It is these characteristics that make the measurement procedure both efficient and meaningful.

Although the successful administration of a test depends on many factors the key to success is good planning in the pretest stage and attention to the details of that planning during and after the testing procedure.

Both physical educators and exercise scientists will be responsible for testing individuals with disabilities. In order to obtain reliable scores and those that lead to valid interpretations, the tests and test procedures must be carefully selected.

FORMATIVE EVALUATION OF OBJECTIVES

Objective 1   Identify the important characteristics of a test.

1. Discussed in the text are many important attributes for a test. In addition to reliability, objectivity, and validity, what are several of these attributes?
2. Certain characteristics listed in the text relate to the individuals taking the tests, while others act simply to make the procedure more efficient. What are the subject-related attributes?

Objective 2   Plan the administration of a test.

1. The success of a testing program depends on how well the pretest planning is carried out. What type of planning and procedures would you use to administer the following tests?
   a. A timed bent-knee sit-up test
   b. A pull-up test
   c. A one-mile run test or some other cardiovascular test

Objective 3   Define and compare the terms *evaluation* and *measurement*.

1. What is the difference between measurement and evaluation?
2. How are formative and summative evaluation different and why should both types of evaluation be used?
3. Why should both criterion-referenced and norm-referenced evaluation standards be used?

ADDITIONAL LEARNING ACTIVITIES

1. From the material in this book and other physical education measurement tests, develop a summary of test characteristics and a checklist of pretest planning procedures.
2. Select a test with which you are unfamiliar and administer it to individuals following the pretest, administrative, and posttest procedures outlined in the text.

BIBLIOGRAPHY

ACSM, 2000. *ACSM's guidelines for exercise testing and prescription*. 6th ed. Philadelphia: Lippincott Williams & Wilkins.

Baumgartner, T. A., S. Oh, H. Chung, and D. Hales. 2002. Objectivity, reliability, and validity for a revised push-up test protocol. *Measurement in Physical Education and Exercise Science* 6: 225–242.

Girardi, G. 1971. A comparison of isokinetic exercises with isometric and isotonic exercises in the development of strength and endurance. P.E.D. dissertation, Indiana University.

Measuring and Evaluating Physical Attributes

SCHOOL-BASED EVALUATION

CONTENTS

KEY WORDS

final grades
natural breaks
program evaluation
rank order
teacher's standards

OBJECTIVES

In this chapter we discuss the development of standards for formative and summative evaluation. The attributes, issues, and techniques of evaluation are such that the process is a complicated and often emotional one. There is no universal agreement among physical education teachers as to which attributes are important or which evaluation system works best. Each issue, each technique, has its supporters; and each has its advantages and disadvantages as well. Finally, we arrive at program evaluation—which should also be part of every teacher's measurement program.

After reading Chapter 6 you should be able to

1. Select the components for inclusion in an evaluation program and determine evaluation standards using several methods.
2. Identify ways to make an evaluation system as quick and efficient as possible.
3. Outline the procedures used for evaluating programs.

INTRODUCTION

This chapter is presented from the standpoint of grading, which is certainly the responsibility of a teacher, but seldom the responsibility of an exercise scientist, such as an exercise specialist, physical therapist, athletic trainer, or program instructor. However, grading is actually just evaluating the participants in a program that happens to be an educational one. Exercise scientists must evaluate the participants in their programs. Thus, think of grading as individual evaluations, and it applies to both teachers and exercise scientists. Just as children do, adults want to know how they compare to others or to a standard, even though grades are not assigned. Much of the process and many of the philosophical issues discussed in terms of grading have implications for exercise scientists in their evaluation programs.

A teacher's primary function is to promote desirable changes in students. The same thing can be said of any exercise scientist in regard to the program participants. The type of change deemed important by the teacher and the exercise scientist depends on two factors: the stated instructional or program objectives and the procedures used to evaluate their achievement. If the instructional or program process is to be meaningful, it is essential that (1) the stated objectives be relevant, (2) the instruction or program be designed to achieve the objectives efficiently, and (3) the evaluation procedures reliably and validly assess student or participant achievement.

We administer tests primarily to facilitate the achievement of instructional and program objectives. As noted in Chapter 1, education tests can be used for placement, diagnosis, evaluation of learning, prediction, program evaluation, and motivation. Every teacher must formally or informally evaluate every student. The evaluation of student achievement is tantamount to the evaluation of the instructional or program process, and so it is a vital part of that process. A student's failure to achieve important objectives can indicate that the program itself has failed and needs revision.

Student evaluation is not a popular issue with some teachers and prospective teachers, primarily because they think of it as synonymous with grading. But evaluation is more than grading. In fact, it need not result in the assignment of grades. This does not mean that grading itself is not necessary. Grading continues to be an integral part of the educational system and thus one of the teacher's responsibilities. A teacher who passes all students without regard to their level of achievement is ignoring a professional responsibility. Grading is too often a system of rewards and punishments, reflecting the teacher's frustrations and biases, rather than a reliable, valid measure of student achievement. Most, if not all, of what has been expressed in this paragraph applies to evaluation situations in exercise science. The exercise specialist, therapist, or program instructor must evaluate participants in a program. If a participant does not perform well, the evaluator does not like having to tell the participant he is not adequate.

Types of evaluation were presented in Chapter 5. Whether the evaluation is formative or summative with criterion-referenced or norm-referenced standards influences how grading standards are developed and used.

GRADING

As indicated in the introduction to this chapter, grading is a responsibility of teachers, but seldom one of exercise scientists. However, much of the grading process and many of the issues discussed in terms of grading have implications for evaluation in all types of programs. The improvement of grading practices has been an educational issue for over 50 years. The grading process is twofold: (1) the selection of the measurements—either subjective or objective—that form the basis of the grade, and (2) the actual calculation. Both steps can be undertaken in many different ways. As described in the systematic model of evaluation (see Chapter 1), the instructional process begins with the instructional objectives and culminates with evaluation. The instructional objectives, then, are the basis on which the factors used to grade students are selected, and the test must be suited to their nature and content. Clearly, using only a written test to grade students in a unit on physical fitness would be illogical and unfair.

Not only must grades be based on important instructional objectives, but the testing instruments must yield reliable scores upon which valid interpretations are based. If the test scores are not reliable, the scores by definition are due entirely to measurement error. Using such a test to calculate a student's grade is much like flipping a coin. Validity is a function of the instructional objectives: a test can yield reliable scores, but scores that are unrelated to the objectives of the unit. Thus, when selecting testing instruments for grading, the teacher must ask these questions: (1) What are the instructional objectives? (2) Were the students taught in accordance with these objectives? (3) Does the test yield reliable scores that reflect achievement of these objectives?

Issues

The relative merits of various attributes for grading have received much attention in professional books and journals. Any suggested attributes should be judged by three criteria:

1. Is it a major objective of the physical education program?
2. Do all students have identical opportunities to demonstrate their ability relative to the attribute?
3. Can the attribute be measured so the test scores are reliable and the interpretations of the scores valid?

A teacher's philosophy on certain issues directly influences the grading system. There is no one correct approach to most of these issues, but you should consider them before developing a grading system. Remember that teachers communicate their values in their grading procedures. Looney (2003), in an excellent article on definitional grading systems, makes this point. It is not uncommon for a grading system to not reflect the teacher's values. She shows how to design a grading system that reflects the teacher's values.

If grades are assigned, it is only fair to explain to the students at the start of the course how grades will be determined. Thus, the teacher should plan the grading system before the course begins. Planning usually works not only to lessen student complaints about assigned grades, but also to make it easier and faster to assign grades.

Grades should be based on a sufficient amount of evidence to be valid. So, a grade should be based on many test scores or pieces of evidence, and each of them must be reliable. One trial where multiple trials of a test were possible or one comprehensive exam at the end of the course is not likely to be sufficient evidence. The worst objective testing situation we can envision for a classroom course is one test at the end of the course composed of one true-false question. If the student answers the question correctly, the student receives a high grade; if not, the student receives a low grade.

The distribution of grades in summative evaluation is a controversial issue. Should physical educators, like teachers of classroom subjects, use A-B-C-D-F grades? Low grades tend to discourage students from continuing with a given subject once basic requirements are fulfilled. In science programs, for example, the grades D and F are assigned to discourage low-ability students from continuing to take science courses. This means that by the senior year in high school, only a select group of students is still in the program. (Of course, because only the better students continue to take courses, a smaller percentage of low grades should be given in advanced courses. For example, more A's and B's should be assigned in a senior-level course than in a junior-level course.) Physical education programs are not developed along these discriminatory lines. In an effort to encourage all students—despite their ability—to continue in the program, many physical educators assign only grades A, B, and C.

Another consideration that relates to the distribution of grades is whether the general quality of the class, or differences among classes, should affect the assignment or distribution of grades. With ability-grouped classes, it seems unfair to assign grades A through F in each class, because every student in a high-ability class would probably have received a C or better if ability grouping were not used. On the other hand, grading A through C in a high-ability class, B through D in a middle-ability class, and C through F in a low-ability class is unfair because it makes no allowance for the misclassification of students. A high-ability student could loaf and still receive a C, while a middle-ability overachiever could never earn an A.

A philosophy endorsed by many experienced teachers and most measurement specialists is that the grade a student receives should not depend on (1) the semester or year in which the class is taken; (2) the instructor (if several instructors teach the course), or (3) the other students in the course. Thus, standards should not change from semester to semester or year to year unless the course itself has been changed or upgraded. For example, if 65 sit-ups represent an A for seventh graders this semester, the same should apply next semester. Likewise, if 65 sit-ups represents an A from one instructor, the same should be true for all instructors. Inherent in this philosophy is the principle that all students should be evaluated by the same standards. Two examples may clarify this point:

1. An instructor teaches five ungrouped eleventh-grade classes, which are combined for grading purposes. The top 20% of the combined group receive A's, the next 30% receive B's, and the remaining students receive C's. If grades had been allotted in the same percentages but assigned by classes, a student's grade would depend on those of the other students in the class. Thus, it would be possible for two students with identical scores to receive different grades if one were in a class with many good performers and the other in a class with many poor performers.

2. An instructor teaches three ability-grouped classes of eighth graders and two ability-grouped classes of ninth graders. The eighth-grade classes are composed of high, middle, and low achievers; the ninth-grade class, of low and middle achievers. Because of the age difference, higher grading standards are applied to the ninth graders than to the eighth graders, but the grading standards for each grade are applied consistently to all classes in that grade.

The teacher must decide whether a grade represents only achievement or student effort as well. The teacher must also decide what type of student achievement (fitness, skill, knowledge) should be considered and how each should be weighted in the grade.

Usually school policy governs certain issues, among them the type of grade assigned (A-B-C-D-F or pass-fail), although the teacher may have a choice. Letter grades (norm-referenced standards) are by far the most prevalent, but pass-fail (criterion-referenced standards) grading is gaining popularity. Pass-fail grading reduces the competitive pressure of letter grading and encourages students to explore new subject areas. However, the system also provides less information about student ability.

If pass-fail grades are assigned, the teacher must decide whether, in reality, anyone will fail. It seems that in many classes, if students attend class regularly, they will not receive a failing grade. Also, the teacher must decide how much information is needed on each student to assign a grade of pass or fail. Possibly less information on each student is needed with a pass-fail system than with a letter-grade system. Finally, the teacher must decide on the standard for a passing grade. Is passing equivalent to a C or a D in a letter grade system?

Other measurement books in physical education and exercise science include discussion of issues and topics concerning grading that are not presented in detail in this chapter. However, these issues and topics might be ones that you should consider, so we present some of them in abbreviated form.

1. Should physical education grades be figured into the overall grade point average? Does whether physical education grades are figured or not figured into the overall grade point average influence your grading procedure or distribution of grades?
2. What percentage of the class should receive each grade assigned if letter grades are assigned, or a passing grade if pass-fail grades are assigned?
3. What should be included in the grade? Should fitness level, attendance, participation, effort, physical skill, knowledge, and so forth be included in the grade?
4. Should grading standards be based on gender, physical size, or other characteristics?
5. Should contract grading be used?
6. Should there be multiple grades with one each for knowledge, skill, improvement, attitude, and so forth?
7. Are grades just for students or are grades also for parents, teachers, administrators, and others?

Methods

Of the four methods that will be discussed, no single method of assigning grades is best for all situations or all teachers. Usually, each method yields a unique distribution of grades. For example, a student who is on the borderline between an A and a B may receive an A with one grading method and a B with another. Thus, it is vital that the teacher understand the advantages and disadvantages of each grading method in order to select the one best suited to the situation. Also, these methods are not restricted to assigning grades.

There are two ways to use several of the following methods. One way is to use the methods on the scores of a group to evaluate individual members of the group. The second way is to use the methods on the scores of a group to develop performance standards (norms) to be used on people who will be participating in the program in the future. Teachers have many participants (students) in a group (class) and often use these methods in both ways.

Further, recognize that these methods can be used for assigning two or more grades. Usually two grades (pass-fail) are a criterion-referenced evaluation, but using data analysis to set criterion-referenced standards is an acceptable technique. Normally these methods are used to develop norm-referenced standards with three or more grades.

Natural Breaks

When scores are listed in order from best to worst, gaps or breaks usually occur in their distribution. The teacher may make each such break a cutoff point between letter grades as shown in Table 6.1. This is a norm-referenced standard.

The other methods to be discussed require that the teacher decide what letter grades are possible (e.g., A to F, or A to C) and usually what percentage of the students should receive each letter grade. This is not required with the **natural breaks** method. In theory, if there were no breaks in the distribution of scores, all students would receive the same grade. For the teacher who does not believe in specifying the possible grades and percentages for these grades, this is a useful method. Thus, the method has some characteristics of a criterion-referenced standard.

Although used by some teachers, this method is the poorest of the four listed here if it is used on the scores of the group to be graded. It provides no semester-to-semester consistency and makes each student's grade dependent on the performance of other students in the class. If, in another year, the

| TABLE 6.1 | | Two Sets of Grades Assigned by Natural Breaks | | | |

First Semester   **Second Semester**

x	f		x	f	
98	1		92	1	
95	1	A	91	2	
93	2		90	1	
92	3		89	2	A
			88	2	
88	4		87	3	
87	5				
85	7	B	82	6	
84	7		80	8	B
83	6		79	7	
			78	11	
77	8				
76	14		73	12	
75	10	C	72	11	
72	5		71	14	C
			70	6	
65	2		68	1	
60	1	D			

breaks in the distribution occur in different places, the cutoff points between letter grades change, as is evident between semesters in Table 6.1. Natural breaks may not be so poor a method if used for developing norms (discussed later in this section) or developing pass-fail standards. For example, in Table 6.1 the passing standard might be a score greater than 65 for the first-semester data and a score greater than 73 for the second-semester data.

Teacher's Standard

Some teachers base grades on their own perceptions of what is fair and appropriate, without analyzing any data. For example, a teacher's standard for a 100-point knowledge test might be A, 93–100; B, 88–92; C, 79–87; D, 70–78; F, 0–69. If the teacher uses the same standard year after year, the grades will be consistent. Furthermore, a student's grade does not depend on the performance of other students in the class: each student who scores 93 points or more receives an A. This is a fine method if the teacher's standards are realistic in terms of the students' abilities, and if measurements are quite reliable and interpretations of the measurements are valid. First-year teachers, and teachers working with students younger than they are familiar with, tend to misuse this method by setting their standards too high.

The **teacher's standards** are norm-referenced, but the procedure used to develop them is very similar to that of criterion-referenced standards, in that standards are set by the teacher with no thought as to what percentage of the class receives a given grade. In theory, the entire class could receive A's or F's.

If the teacher's standards were used in a pass-fail or competent-incompetent system, the standards would be criterion-referenced. Again, in theory the entire class could be judged competent. Many teachers have difficulty selecting the standard for competence; there are no guidelines. The teacher must choose a standard that he or she believes is fair. This standard often becomes one of minimum competence. For example, the teacher might decide that hitting one out of five shots from the free-throw line in basketball or doing one sit-up is minimum competence.

One way minimum competence might be determined is by deciding what grade in a letter system corresponds to "competent" or "pass." The letter grade D is defined as a low pass or minimum competence by some educators; it is defined as a "charity grade" by others who would use the letter grade of C as minimum competence. In most colleges, the instructor does not know which students are taking a graded class on a pass-fail basis. She assigns a letter grade to each student, which is converted to a pass in the records office (for letter grades of D or better).

Rank Order

Rank order is a straightforward, norm-referenced method of grading. The teacher decides what letter grades will be assigned and what percentage of the class should receive each letter grade; the scores are then ordered, and grades are assigned.

For example, assume there are 50 students in a class, and the teacher decides to assign grades as follows: A's to 20% of the class, or 10 students

TABLE 6.2	**Rank-Ordered Scores**								
x	**f**		**x**	**f**		**x**	**f**		**x**	**f**	
78	1		64	4		60	8		51	2	
70	2	A	62	5	B	59	6	C	48	1	D
66	4		61	5		58	5		41	1	
65	4					57	2				

[(.20)(50)]; B's to 30% of the class, or 15 students [(.30)(50)]; C's to 40% of the class, or 20 students [(.40)(50)]; and D's to 10% of the class, or 5 students [(.10)(50)]. Now look at the scores and frequency distribution in Table 6.2. In the table, the first 10 scores were supposed to be A's, but a choice had to be made between 7 and 11 A's. It was decided to use 11 because that number was closer to the desired number of A's. So, A's started at 65 rather than 66. To make up for the extra A, only 14 B's were given. Then a choice had to be made between 19 and 21 C's. The reasons for giving 21 rather than 19 C's are twofold: (1) it is preferable to give the higher grade in borderline cases, and (2) a distinct natural break occurs below score 57.

Among the advantages of the rank-order method are that it is quick and easy to use and that it makes a student's grade dependent on his rank-order position rather than the instructor's feelings about the student. The system also allows grades to be distributed as wanted.

A disadvantage of the method if it is applied to the scores of the group being evaluated is that a student's grade depends on the performance of other students in the class. A student with average ability will receive a higher grade in a class with low-ability students than in a class with high-ability students. Another disadvantage is that no allowance is made for the quality of the class: a certain proportion of students must get high grades and a certain proportion must get low grades. For large, heterogeneous classes, in which all levels of ability are represented, this is probably not a bad method; however, it is not recommended for small or ability-grouped classes unless the teacher adjusts the per-

centages in light of the quality of each class. Teachers who use the rank-order method obtain grade standards that vary from semester to semester and year to year, depending on the quality of their class.

The rank-order method is basically the same as the grading-on-the-curve method. To the extent that the distribution of test scores is not like the normal curve (see Chapter 2), the two methods differ. The grading-on-the-curve method leaves the exact distribution of grades to chance, whereas the rank-order method forces the grades to be distributed as wanted. Thus, the grading-on-the-curve method is not discussed.

Norms

Norms are performance standards based on the analysis of data, not on a subjective standard chosen by a teacher. If norm-referenced standards are being used, norms are the best type of standard. Norms are developed by gathering scores for a large number of individuals of similar age, gender, ability, and other characteristics to the individuals with whom the norms will be used. These data are statistically analyzed, and performance standards are then constructed on the basis of the analysis. Norms have many advantages over other types of standards. First, they are unaffected by the performance of the group or the class being evaluated. For example, if it is considered excellent to run the mile in ten minutes, all the students in the class can excel if they can run the mile within that time. Another advantage is that new performance standards need not be developed each year; once norms are developed, they usually can be used for two to five years. Also, because the same standards are used to evaluate several different groups or classes of students, the grades have a high degree of consistency: a given grade indicates the same degree of ability for each group.

There are many sources for norms. (Examples are given in Chapters 10 through 14.) Statewide tests often provide norms for that state; local norms for an entire school system are not uncommon; and teachers can develop norms using the scores of former students. Although norms should be developed using the scores of students similar to those on whom the norms will be used, this is unlikely to be true of national and state norms. Teacher-developed norms are probably fairest to the students.

The first step in developing norms is the administration of the same test each year under the same conditions as much as is possible for two to five years, until several hundred scores have been collected. These scores are then analyzed and used to develop norms that can be employed for the next two to five years. At the end of this time, several hundred more test scores have been collected, and the test is renormed. The advantages of this procedure are numerous. Because the norms are based on recent student performances, they are applicable to students currently in the class. When combined, scores collected in different years tend to cancel out any differences among years in terms of the quality of the students, and thus represent typical performance. (Norms developed on the scores of students from a single year are not representative if the students are not typical.) Because students and conditions change, norms should be revised every few years. And if major changes are made in the curriculum, norms may need to be revised.

Depending on the needs of the teacher, percentile-rank norms, T-score norms (see Chapter 2), or letter-grade norms may be constructed. Probably because they are easier to explain to students and parents, percentile-rank norms are used more often than T-score norms. In deciding on a type of norm, determine how the norms will be used and then choose the type that best meets your needs. Percentile-rank norms are easily understood and indicate how a student's performance ranks relative to his or her peers. However, you should not add them together to obtain a composite score

based on several measures. If you will eventually need a composite score, choose T-score norms. T-scores are used to add together scores that differ in unit of measurement. Also, T-scores are used to add together scores when tests with the same unit of measurement differ considerably in difficulty or total points possible. For example, T-scores should be used when combining a curl and a bench press score or when combining a 100-yard dash and a mile run score. If students understand T-scores, they can determine their approximate class ranks for a single test. Examples of percentile-rank and T-score norms are shown in Tables 6.3 and 6.4. Using Table 6.3, if a boy executed 45 sit-ups his percentile rank would be 50, whereas a girl with a score of 45 sit-ups would have a percentile rank of 80. Table 6.4 is used in a similar manner.

For grading purposes, letter-grade norms must be developed. The teacher's task is to determine

TABLE 6.3	Sample Percentile-Rank Norms for a One-Minute Sit-Up Test	
Percentile	**Boys**	**Girls**
100th	70	60
95th	61	54
90th	59	52
85th	56	49
80th	54	45
75th	51	42
70th	50	40
65th	48	39
60th	47	36
55th	46	35
50th	45	33
45th	44	33
40th	43	32
35th	41	31
30th	40	30
25th	38	29
20th	36	28
15th	35	27
10th	30	23
5th	28	20
0	20	15

TABLE 6.4	Sample T-Score Norms for a Distance Run		
T-Score	6-Lap Run	T-Score	6-Lap Run
80	287	48	458
78	297	46	468
76	308	44	479
74	319	42	490
72	330	40	500
70	340	38	511
68	351	36	522
66	362	34	532
64	372	32	543
62	383	30	554
60	394	28	564
58	404	26	575
56	415	24	586
54	426	22	597
52	436	20	607
50	447		

the test scores that constitute each letter grade to be assigned. For example, the letter-grade norms for a one-minute sit-up test for boys might be A, 59–70; B, 47–58; C, 35–46; D, 20–34; F, 0–19, using the percentile-rank norms in Table 6.3. These letter-grade norms are developed based on the decision to, over multiple years, assign basically 10% A's, 30% B's, 45% C's, 15% D's, and 0% F's to students evaluated with these standards. The A-grade standard is obtained by observing in Table 6.3 that a score of 59 for boys corresponds to the 90th percentile, so 10% of the scores are 59 or larger. The minimum score to obtain a grade of B is determined by going to the 60th percentile (40% A's & B's; 60% C's & D's) in Table 6.3. This method of developing letter-grade norms is similar to the rank-order method discussed earlier. However, these letter-grade norms could have been developed using any of the other methods previously discussed. No matter what method is used, this grading standard is used each time the one-minute sit-up test is administered. Ideally, these letter-grade norms are developed on the basis of an analysis of the one-minute sit-up scores of students who have taken the test in the past.

A second example of the use of norms involves a physical fitness test with seven items. For each of the seven items, local T-score norms have been developed. When the test is administered, T-scores do not have to be calculated, but can be assigned by using the norms. The sum of the T-scores for the seven items in the test is the student's fitness score. Letter-grade norms corresponding to these fitness scores have been developed:

A, 420 →; B, 385 – 419; C, 315 – 384;

D, 245 – 314; F, ← 244.

Notice that any of the grading methods discussed here can be used to develop letter-grade norms. The teacher's standard is sometimes used, but the rank-order method is more common.

Final Grades

At the end of a grading period a final grade must be assigned on the basis of all the information available on each student. There are many approaches to the assignment of this grade, some very simple, others more complex. The information available, the manner in which it is recorded, and the commitment of the teacher to fairly assign grades influence both the approach chosen and the time required for the procedure.

It is definitely to the teacher's advantage to adopt a simple, quick method of assigning final grades. Some teachers spend countless hours determining grades at the end of each grading period. To be fair to the students and to have a workable system, the teacher should choose a grading system before the course begins. Preplanning allows the teacher to announce the system at the beginning of the course, telling the students on what they will be measured and what standards they must meet. Preplanning is also to the teacher's advantage, allowing many time-consuming problems to be eliminated in advance. Using the Transform program in SPSS (See section 16 of the Statistical Procedures part of Appendix A) or Excel to calculate final grades could improve the accuracy of calculations and save considerable time.

The three common methods of assigning **final grades** are (1) the sum of the letter grades, (2) a point system, and (3) the sum of the T-scores.

Sum of the Letter Grades

This method is used when test scores reflect different units of measure that cannot be summed. The scores on each test are translated into letter grades using one or more of the methods just discussed, and the letter grades, in turn, are translated into points. The sum of these points is used to assign each student a final grade.

Many teachers believe this method is quicker than translating test scores into T-scores, but it is probably at best only slightly faster than calculating T-scores by hand as described in Chapter 2.

If this method is selected, a plus-and-minus system should be used when assigning letter grades to each measure. If an A-B-C-D-F system is used for a given test, only five scores are possible (A is 4, B is 3, C is 2, D is 1, F is 0); a plus-and-minus system allows 15 possible scores (A+ is 14, A is 13, A− is 12, and so on, including F+ and F− values). (The final grades do not have to include pluses and minuses, which are seldom recorded on transcripts.)

To compute the final grade using the plus-and-minus system, we convert the student's letter grade on each test to points, add the points, and divide the sum by the total number of tests. This point value, the mean of the student's scores, is then converted back to a letter grade. For example, in Table 6.5, the student's scores on five tests are changed from letter grades to points and then added. The total, 45, is then divided by the number of tests. The student's mean grade in points, 9, is then converted back into a letter grade, B−.

This process has several drawbacks. In the first place, it is a waste of time to calculate the mean. By multiplying each of the plus-and-minus values by the number of grades per student, we can express the final grade standards in terms of total points: A + is 70 [(5)(14)], A is 65 [(5)(13)], and so on. In the second place, no allowance is made in the final grade for the regression effect—the tendency for individuals who score exceptionally high or low on one measure to score closer to the mean performance of the group on a second. Thus, a student who earns an A or an F on one test is likelier on the next to earn a grade closer to C than to repeat the first performance. The regression effect phenomenon always exists and must be allowed for in assigning final grades. Thus, it would be unusual for a student to receive an A on each of five tests, although a superior student sometimes does. It is much more common to find the best student in the class receiving grades like those in Table 6.6.

Now, according to our standards, a student needs 60 points [(12)(5)] to receive an A− in the course. If the teacher makes no allowance for the regression effect, the best student in the class (grades shown in Table 6.6) will receive a B+, and no one in the class will get an A. In fact, if no allowance is made for the regression effect, very few final grades will be high or low; most students will receive grades in the middle of the possible range.

To allow for the regression effect, the teacher might decide to give the student with 59 points an A− because the student's total is closer to an A− than to a B+. Another procedure is to lower the standards when assigning final grades. For example, the teacher

TABLE 6.5	**Sample Grades and Points for Calculating a Final Grade**	
Test	**Grade**	**Points***
Sit-ups	B+	11
Pull-ups	B	10
Distance run	C+	8
Volleyball	C−	6
Tumbling	B	10
		Sum = 45

*A+ = 14, A = 13, A− = 12, and so on.

TABLE 6.6	**Sample Grades and Points for the Best Student in the Class**	
Test	**Grade**	**Points***
Sit-ups	A	13
Pull-ups	A−	12
Distance run	A−	12
Volleyball	B+	11
Tumbling	B+	11
		Sum = 59

*A+ = 14, A = 13, A− = 12, and so on.

might decide that any student who earns at least 3 A's and 2 B's will receive an A in the course. This means that 58 points are needed to earn an A when the final grade is based on five tests and an A+ is 14 points.

If such an arbitrary adjustment is made, it must be done for each letter grade. In the bottom half of the grading system, the adjustment must be up rather than down to allow for individuals below the mean regressing up toward the mean. But you must be careful in making arbitrary adjustments. If upward adjustments are made in the bottom half of the grading system, it is possible for a student to receive a final grade lower than any grade received on a test.

Rather than make arbitrary adjustments in the total number of points needed for each final grade, it might be better to calculate the total points earned by each student and use the rank-order, or norms, method with the total points scores to assign final grades.

All tests need not be given equal weight in calculating a student's total points. If, using the grades in Table 6.6, the instructor wants 30% of a student's final grade to represent fitness (10% each for scores on sit-ups, pull-ups, and the distance run) and the other two grades to represent 35% each, the following procedure can be used:

Final grade = .10 (sit-ups + pull-ups +

distance run) + .35 (volleyball + tumbling)

$$= (.10)(13 + 12 + 12) + (.35)(11 + 11)$$

$$= (.10)(37) + (.35)(22) = 3.7 + 7.7$$

$$= 11.4 \ (B+ \text{ or } A-)$$

The calculation of final grades with unequally weighted tests is very common, but it can also be time-consuming when there are a large number of tests and/or students to grade. To save time, the teacher can use a calculator or computer.

Problem 6.1   At the end of a tennis unit you have assigned the following weights to the six grades that will make up the final grade: rally test, 20%; serve test, 20%; improvement, 5%; daily work, 10%; game observation, 5%; final exam, 40%. A student's scores on the items were C, B, A+, C+, C+, and C, respectively.

Solution   When using a calculator, you can sum in memory the points from each multiplication as the multiplications take place. Assuming 14 is an A+, 13 is A, and so on, the calculation is as follows:

Step 1

Rally test, 20% of C is .20 times 7 is 1.4.

Step 2

Put 1.4 in the calculator memory.

Step 3

Serve test, 20% of B is .20 times 10 is 2.

Step 4

Add 2 to the calculator memory. (There is now 3.4 [1.4 + 2] in memory.)

The process would continue for each grade and its weight, with the final three steps as follows:

Step 11

Final exam, 40% of C is .40 times 7 is 2.8.

Step 12

Add 2.8 to the calculator memory.

Step 13

Display the sum in memory, which is 8.10 and a C+.

The calculation of final grades with unequally weighted tests using the computer would involve having a program with the letter-grade point values and test weightings already entered into the program so all that would have to be entered for each student would be the letter grades. Then the computer would do the calculations much as we have done in Problem 6.1 and provide an answer. Grading programs like this are presently available commercially or can be easily written or developed on a spreadsheet program.

Point Systems

Point systems are often used by classroom teachers so that all test scores are in the same unit of measure and can be easily combined. In physical education activity classes, point systems require a great deal of planning and the development of

TABLE 6.7	Sample Point System for an Activity Course		
I. Physical ability			70 points
A. Fitness		24 points	
1. sit-ups	8 points		
2. pull-ups	8 points		
3. distance run	8 points		
B. Volleyball		24 points	
1. serving test	8 points		
2. set or spike test	8 points		
3. game play	8 points		
C. Tumbling		22 points	
1. 11 stunts	2 points each		
II. Knowledge			20 points
40 questions	$\frac{1}{2}$ point each		
III. Subjective evaluation			10 points
Instructor's evaluation of effort, improvement, attitude, attendance, and the like			

norms. A sample point system is shown in Table 6.7. To construct this system, the total number of points was chosen, points were allotted to the various activities, and standards were developed for each activity—that is, how many sit-ups earn 8 points, 7 points, and so on.

An instructor using the point system in Table 6.7 would have three fitness scores, three volleyball scores, a tumbling score, a knowledge score, and a subjective score in the record book. Thus, nine scores must be summed before assigning a final grade, a procedure made easier if certain scores are combined before the calculation of final grades. For example, at the end of the fitness unit, the three fitness scores could be combined to form a single score. If the same thing is done at the end of the volleyball unit, only five scores have to be summed to calculate the final grade.

Sum of the T-Scores

When the units of measurement on a series of tests differ, some teachers translate the test scores into letter grades and the letter grades into points, and then sum the points. Another alternative is to change the test scores to T-scores (or some other standard scores) and sum the T-scores, as discussed in Chapter 2. Obviously, it is possible to weight each test differently in sum-

ming the T-scores, by using the procedures outlined for weighting letter-grade points.

Letter Grades versus T-Scores

In deciding between letter grades and T-scores, keep two criteria in mind: precision and speed. The sum of T-scores is more precise than the sum of letter grades because a better score means a higher T-score. For example, 2 students who perform 75 and 85 sit-ups, respectively, might both receive A's with the letter-grade system, while the latter would receive a higher T-score.

Although it is generally believed that the letter-grade system is quicker to use than the T-score system, the time difference is so slight that the loss of precision is not worth the time gain. We can compare the time involved in the two methods with an example.

Assume 40 students are tested on each of 7 items in a fitness test, and a fitness grade is wanted for each student. Assume also that norms or standards applicable to these students are unavailable. To sum the letter grades, a five-step process is used:

1. Develop letter-grade standards for each test.
2. Assign each student a grade on each of the 7 tests, and translate this grade into points.
3. Sum the points for each student.

4. Develop final letter-grade standards based on the sums of the points.
5. Assign final grades.

To sum the T-scores, again five steps are used:

1. Develop T-score norms for each test using the procedures outlined in Chapter 2.
2. Assign each student a T-score for each of the 7 tests.
3. Sum the T-scores for each student.
4. Develop final letter-grade standards.
5. Assign final grades.

Notice that only the first step differs. If the rank-order method is used to develop letter-grade standards for each test, a simple frequency distribution will have to be constructed and standards developed for each test. About one hour per test should be allowed to develop grade standards. The development of T-score standards should also take about one hour per test.

If all five steps must be followed, both the letter-grade and T-score systems are going to take up too much time, assuming you have 200 or more students, each with 7 scores. Even if the first step could be eliminated because standards are available, both systems would still be time-consuming. Of course, we could reduce the number of tests on which the final grade is based, but in this day of accountability it might be hard to explain how 2 or 3 test scores are valid indication of a student's achievement over a semester. Obviously, the solution is to use the computer in assigning final grades. We recommend the use of the Transform program in SPSS (see section 16 in the Statistical Procedures part of Appendix A).

Incomplete Grades

Inevitably, some students do not take all the tests. This can pose a real problem in trying to obtain a total score on which to base a final grade. There is usually a valid reason why students do not take certain tests—injury, disability, or late enrollment, for example—and in such cases it would be unfair to penalize them. One possible solution is to estimate the score the student would have re-

ceived had he or she taken the test. If the teacher feels unqualified to make this decision, the best procedure is to substitute the student's mean performance on the tests taken for each missing score. An estimated total score can thus be obtained, and a final grade assigned. For example, assume a student's scores on 5 of 7 items on a fitness test were as follows:

Item	Score	T-Score
Sit-ups	100.0	56.45
Pull-ups		
Shuttle run	11.3	45.94
Long jump		
Ball throw	135.0	55.13
600-yard run	128.0	44.22
50-yard dash	8.6	41.48

Notice there are no scores for the pull-up and long jump tests. The mean T-score for the 5 tests is 48.64:

$$\frac{243.22}{5} = 48.64$$

The estimated sum of the T-scores for the 7 tests, then, is 340.48:

$$(7)(48.64) = 340.48$$

Grading in Summary

Grading issues and methods have been presented. Other authors of measurement and evaluation books in physical education and exercise science (Lacy & Hastad 2003; Miller 2002; Tritschler 2000) discuss different issues and grading philosophies than those presented in this chapter, but all the authors seem to present about the same grading methods. Grading in classroom courses is often enough different from grading in physical education courses that discussions of grading in the classroom have limited application to physical education. Looney (2003) addressed grading in physical education and mentions some of the issues and methods presented in this chapter. Now that you have read the material on grading in this chapter, you may really understand and appreciate her article. Her presentation of definitional grading systems is excellent. Maybe she casts a little light in dark corners.

OTHER EVALUATION TECHNIQUES

Some standards setting and evaluation situations that commonly occur have not yet been addressed. These situations are not like the grading situations just discussed.

Situation 1

The best five people receive a scholarship or an award/recognition. This is a rank-order situation where the five best people in the present group are rewarded (pass) and the rest of the group get nothing (fail). The important thing in this situation is that the decision is made without personal bias and is based on data or information that allows valid decisions.

Situation 2

The number of people who can be awarded or recognized is not limited. This is a typical criterion-referenced situation. The important thing is that the criterion-referenced standard is as good as possible. Ideally, this standard is like the "gold standard" discussed in Chapter 4. However, it is more likely that there is no gold standard, so that several experts will have to set the standard. In many situations the only expert is you; you must set the standard based on everything you can find in the literature, obtain by talking to people, draw upon based on your training and experience, and so on. The standard can even be set by data analysis. For example, if you believe that 10% of the group do not deserve to be recognized, rewarded, considered proficient, and so on, collect data on the group or a norming group, analyze the data, and set the standard at the score below which 10% (PR = 10) of the group scored (see the sections in this chapter on Rank-Order and Norms grading). No matter how the standard is set, as we have indicated, the standard can be changed at a later time if a better standard is determined.

Situation 3

The athletic trainer must set a standard for releasing people from the therapy program. This is probably a criterion-referenced situation. The standard could be based on the minimum strength or ability needed to function in daily life. With injuries, the standard could be based on the difference between the injured and noninjured limbs, or the difference between the injured limb at the beginning and end of the therapy program, or the difference between the limb before injury and after injury in terms of strength, flexibility, ability, and so on.

PROGRAM EVALUATION

Program evaluation has focused on physical characteristics of the program. Scorecards have been used to determine whether the environment—the facilities, professional staff, curriculum, equipment, and supplies—meets specified criteria. Evaluation specialists, however, view the environment as one of the least important factors in evaluating a program: a program may have excellent facilities and equipment, trained faculty, and so forth, and still meet few of the program objectives.

The success of an instructional program depends less on its physical characteristics than on the manner in which they are used in the instructional process. Thus, student performance offers the most valid index of the success of a program. The most crucial question is this: Are students achieving important instructional objectives? If they are not, there is a need for change. Both formative and summative procedures can be used to judge program effectiveness.

Data Collection for Program Evaluation

Some data must be available in order to do program evaluation. This data may be the result of testing or good daily record keeping. For the teacher it is primarily a result of testing. In both cases some forethought and planning must occur so that data is collected and available to do the program evaluation. The teacher commonly tests students at the beginning and end of a teaching unit or school year.

Barrow, McGee, and Tritschler (1989) have a chapter on program evaluation. They present an excellent discussion of program evaluation issues and several instruments for evaluating physical education, intramural, and athletic programs.

Formative Evaluation

Evaluation is the process of judging performance with reference to an established standard. The qualities and levels of performance that a program is designed to produce are reflected in its stated instructional objectives and criterion-referenced standards. Let us assume that some of the instructional objectives for a fitness unit are the development of (1) muscular strength and endurance of the arms, (2) muscular strength and endurance of the abdominal muscles, and (3) cardiorespiratory endurance. The tests and criterion-referenced standards selected by the teacher are 3 push-ups, 25 bent-knee sit-ups, and a run of 1 mile in 10 minutes.

The formative evaluation of a program is the determination of the extent to which the stated standards are being achieved. The program developers may establish as a criterion that 80% of all students should achieve these goals. Progress toward the goal is easily determined by calculating the percentage of students who achieved the criterion-referenced standard for each fitness test. For example, assume that the percentage of students who achieved these criterion-referenced standards is as listed in Table 6.8.

The program goal of 80% achievement was not reached in 2004 with the one-mile run, which indicates that the instructional program failed in this aspect. The teacher must analyze this failure and make an instructional decision. Several interpretations are possible. First, more aerobic conditioning activities may be needed. Second, it may be that the 10-minute criterion is an unrealistic standard for students; perhaps the time should be changed to 12 minutes. Third, the value of the instructional objective may be questioned, and the objective retained or dropped.

The success of formative program evaluation depends directly on the selection of important,

TABLE 6.8	**Percentage of Students Who Achieved the Criterion-Referenced Standards for Three Fitness Tests**		
Test	2004	2005	2006
Push-up	80	79	83
Bent-knee sit-up	90	93	91
One-mile run	40	75	84

well-defined instructional objectives and the establishment of realistic standards. The failure to achieve a stated standard is thus a good indication that something is wrong. The value of formative program evaluation is that it signals that something is wrong while action can still be taken. In this sense, evaluation is a continuous process.

Summative Evaluation

The success of an instructional program is reflected in the degree of achievement of its broad objectives. Such success can usually be judged by comparing student performance to some norm. For this type of evaluation, published national, statewide, or local norms can serve as the basis for comparison.

It is common to compare a school's performance with national or statewide norms. For example, the mean performance of students from a given school or district might be compared to the norms that accompany a nationally distributed fitness test battery to determine whether the mean is above or below the 50th percentile (P_{50} = Median = Mean in normal curve) (see Chapter 2). Although this procedure does stimulate interest, it also has several disadvantages. First, tests with national or statewide norms may not reflect the true objectives of the school district. For example, if the general objectives of a school were directed primarily toward motor skill development, the national norms for a fitness test would not validly apply. A second disadvantage arises from the geographic and environmental factors that affect performance. Often, the

TABLE 6.9	Summative Evaluation of Weight Training			
Test	**Norm Sample**		**Fall 2005 Sample**	
	Mean	*Standard Deviation*	*Mean*	*Standard Deviation*
1. Dips	17.30	6.65	19.40	6.91
2. Sit-ups	24.71	8.17	25.09	7.70
3. Lat pull	27.33	9.47	34.09	12.70
4. Arm curl	23.45	9.89	28.02	9.77
5. Bench press	17.85	8.34	23.39	8.69

testing conditions used by a school district are not similar to those used to develop national norms.

Local norms offer the most realistic basis for summative program evaluation. Although it is quite likely that all schools in a given system will be above the national norms, several of them may score considerably lower than others, indicating a need for program improvement.

Presented in Table 6.9 are the means and standard deviations for an instructional unit on weight training. The local norm sample represents the performance of over 500 students; the fall 2005 sample represents the performance of a group of students being compared to the established norms. As you can see, the average performance of the fall 2005 group exceeded that of the norm group, indicating that the program is functioning properly in light of these objectives. If a school's means are considerably lower than the local norms, action can be taken to identify and correct the difficulty.

If the means become progressively larger over succeeding years, this may be objective evidence that the program is improving.

Program Improvement

Evaluation is a decision-making process that works toward program improvement. The adoption of appropriate standards is essential for program evaluation and improvement. Formative evaluation leads to higher-level achievement of objectives, evaluated summatively. Furthermore, the use of criterion- and norm-referenced standards helps the students to determine expected levels of performance. People tend to strive to exceed standards. The use of explicit, realistic, and improvement standards, then, is necessary, not only for program evaluation, but also for motivation. A primary objective of program developers should be improved participant performance over time.

SUMMARY

The method and rationale for student evaluation should be determined by the objectives and content of the course or program. It is crucial that evaluation be based on reliable scores and information upon which valid interpretations can be made, and that the process be carefully planned and explained to the participants in the program.

Before evaluating a class, the teacher must decide whether she wants formative or summative evaluation or

both. For summative evaluation, one of the grading methods described in this chapter—or a combination of several—can be used. We cannot stress enough the importance of deciding in advance how final grades will be determined.

Regular measurement and analysis of scores are essential to the ongoing process of evaluating the physical education program. Both formative and summative evaluation should be conducted.

FORMATIVE EVALUATION OF OBJECTIVES

Objective 1   Select the components for inclusion in an evaluation program and determine evaluation standards using several methods.

1. There are certain attributes commonly used for determining grades in physical education. Also, grading programs themselves have desired characteristics. There are several different methods that can be used to assign grades. Considering these three points, outline the grading procedure you would like to use as a teacher.
2. Whatever method you select for assigning grades, it is important that you apply it accurately. Below are three situations to give you practice in using the various grading methods discussed in the text.
   a. Using the rank-order method, assign letter grades for the first-semester scores in Table 6.1, assuming A's, 20%; B's, 30%; C's, 45%; and D's, 5%.
   b. Using the percentages in part (a) and the norms in Table 6.3, what are the scores for an A, B, C, and D for girls on the one-minute sit-up test?
   c. Using a plus-and-minus grading system with A + = 14, A = 13, and so on, what final grade would you assign a student based on the tests and percentages below?

Test	Percentage of Final Grade	Student's Grade
1	15%	C–
2	25%	B–
3	35%	B
4	25%	B+

Objective 2   Identify ways to make an evaluation system as quick and efficient as possible.

1. A common reason for not using an extensive evaluation system in physical education is lack of time. It is true that physical educators have large classes and that it does take time to combine scores from different tests and to grade knowledge tests; but with good planning, the time involved in administering an evaluation system could be minimized. List at least five ways to make an evaluation system as quick and efficient to administer as possible.
2. Which three procedures in question 1 do you think would be easiest to implement? Defend your choices.

Objective 3   Outline the procedures used for evaluating programs.

1. Evaluation of the instructional program is an important part of the total measurement. In your own words, indicate the importance of both formative and summative evaluation.

ADDITIONAL LEARNING ACTIVITIES

1. Interview faculty members at your school and in the local school system. Determine what attributes they consider in their grading systems, what methods they use for assigning grades, and what grading system (A-B-C-D-F, pass-fail) they use.

BIBLIOGRAPHY

Barrow, H. M., R. McGee, and K. A. Tritschler. 1989. *Practical measurement in physical education and sport.* 4th ed. Philadelphia: Lee & Febiger.

Lacy, A. C. and D. N. Hastad. (2003). *Measurement in physical education and exercise science.* 4th ed. New York: Benjamin Cummings.

Looney, M. A. (2003). Facilitate learning with a definitional grading system. *Measurement in Physical Education and Exercise Science* 7: 269–275.

Miller, D. K. (2002). *Measurement by the physical educator: Why and how*. 4th ed. New York: McGraw-Hill.

Tritschler, K. A. (2000). *Barrow & McGee's practical measurement in physical education and sport*. 5th ed. Philadelphia: Lippincott Williams & Wilkins.

AUTHENTIC AND ALTERNATIVE ASSESSMENT

A. Barry Joyner *Georgia Southern University*

Steve Elliott *University of North Carolina at Wilmington*

C O N T E N T S

K E Y   W O R D S

alternative assessment
authentic assessment
rubric

OBJECTIVES

The purpose of this chapter is to introduce the concepts of authentic and alternative assessments in physical education. Although these assessments are being used more often in physical education, reliability and validity issues have not always been addressed.

After reading Chapter 7, you should be able to

1. Differentiate between authentic and alternative assessments.
2. Identify the characteristics of authentic assessments.
3. Define the different types of scoring rubrics.
4. Identify the different types of authentic and alternative assessments.
5. Discuss measurement concerns with authentic and alternative assessments.

INTRODUCTION

The educational reform movement of the 1990s and the passing of the No Child Left Behind Act of 2001 (NCLB; Public Law 107-110) have resulted in assessment and accountability becoming a hot topic in all educational subject areas, including physical education. Traditionally, physical educators have measured student learning through cognitive exams, skill tests, and fitness evaluations. Resulting from dissatisfaction with traditional testing methods and the need for accountability within education, newer **alternative assessment** methods have been incorporated into the teaching and learning process. Alternative assessments are "untraditional" and often involve allowing students to create a product that the teacher will have to grade (e.g., drawing a picture to show correct kicking technique, making a video of a particular skill). Another type of assessment that has become increasingly popular is **authentic assessment**. Authentic assessment can include traditional testing formats (i.e., cognitive tests and qualitative skill tests) and alternative assessments; however, authentic assessments differ in that they are conducted in a "real-life" or authentic context. Authentic assessment requires students to demonstrate meaningful comprehension and application

of essential knowledge and skills in a dynamic and realistic environment.

Proponents of alternative and authentic assessment methods have criticized traditional assessment methods in physical education that place students in a contrived setting for evaluation. For example, some skill tests place the student in situations that do not resemble those in which the skill would actually be used. How often in tennis are players responding to balls thrown to them rather than hit to them? Does hitting volleyball forearm passes against a wall as many times as possible in 30 seconds demonstrate an ability to use the forearm pass in a game? Are these authentic situations?

From a motor-learning perspective, authentic assessment addresses the issue of transfer of learning. Student learning of motor skills is best measured through a transfer test, or retention test (Magill 2004). One of the main goals of physical education is to help develop the "physically educated person" (NASPE 2004) who learns the skills necessary to participate in lifetime activities. Using the volleyball example presented, the physical education teacher should be concerned with whether students can transfer the skill of serving a volleyball to a game situation. An authentic assessment of the volleyball serve would allow the physical educator to assess this transfer of learning.

Characteristics of Authentic Assessments

Lund (1997) has identified the following six characteristics that are present in most authentic assessments.

1. *Authentic assessments present challenges that are representative of real life.* How many times in a real-life situation are students going to be asked to take a multiple-choice test about tennis rules? Wouldn't it be more meaningful for the assessment to mirror what the students will do in real life? Assessing them within a game where they apply the rules, strategies, and skills needed may be more appropriate.
2. *Authentic assessments require students to demonstrate higher-level thinking.* Authentic assessments allow students the opportunity to

apply the concepts they have learned. After testing the students for their knowledge of the rules and strategies, authentic assessment could be used to determine whether the students understand how to apply them in a real-life situation.

3. *Students know the standards for assessment from the beginning.* Authentic assessment involves setting up scoring **rubrics** or standards that serve as the criteria for the assessment. By knowing the criteria in advance, students will constantly be receiving feedback about their progress (Lund 1994). This is not unique to authentic assessment. Many physical educators routinely do this with skill and fitness testing.

4. *Authentic assessments are part of the curriculum.* When using more authentic assessments, teachers essentially teach to the test (Lund 1994). Although some may consider this to be undesirable, a goal of testing should be that the test matches the real-life situation.

5. *Students often present the culmination of the authentic assessment publicly.* This may help to stimulate pride in their work and show the students that the material has meaning. The presentations might be at a PTA meeting, for other classes or other schools, or for the class itself.

6. *There is an emphasis on process and not just product.* How students arrive at the correct answer is just as important as the answer. By focusing solely on the product, students could be rewarded for using poor technique. In a basketball game, a student could have terrible technique yet score a lot of points because he is taller than everyone else.

RUBRICS

Many physical education teachers have used skill tests to qualitatively assess student motor performance. This involves a student performing a skill a predetermined number of times while the teacher uses a checklist to record mastery or nonmastery of

critical elements of the skill. For example, the soccer kick may be broken down into four components (eyes on ball, nonkicking foot placed next to ball, contact with laces, and follow-through), which are assessed during each attempt in the skill test. When students are measured at the beginning and end of a unit, this skill test approach can provide a good indication of student learning that took place during the instructional unit. Teachers have favored this controlled skill test approach because it is relatively objective and can be standardized for all children. In contrast, one early criticism of authentic assessment measures was that motor skill tests were hard to administer and grade when performed in a dynamic gamelike situation due to the lack of standardization. However, most authentic assessments now utilize grading rubrics that allow a teacher to qualitatively assess a student's performance in various contexts.

A rubric is a scoring guide that provides an outline of the guidelines for assessing student performance (Schiemer 2000). Rubrics allow the teacher to compare the student's performance to the criteria specified in various levels of the rubric. Rubrics have various levels for assessing performance, but most range from three (outstanding, acceptable, deficient) to five (excellent, good, satisfactory, fair, poor) levels.

Four main types of rubrics are used in physical education; checklists, point system rubrics, holistic rubrics, and analytical rubrics (Lund & Kirk 2002). *Checklist rubrics* provide a list of characteristics or behaviors that the teacher records as being either present or not present (Lund & Kirk 2002). Checklists are useful for helping students understand the critical elements of a motor skill or for acknowledging completion of certain parts of a performance or activity. Checklist rubrics provide a yes-no rating on a list of characteristics but fail to capture or describe the quality of the characteristics. An example of a checklist rubric designed to assess student performance within an indoor floor hockey unit is shown in Table 7.1.

Point system rubrics are very similar to checklist rubrics in that the teachers are recording the characteristics or behavior as being present or absent. However, they add a point value to each characteristic or behavior that is being assessed. For

TABLE 7.1	A Checklist Rubric to Assess Student Performance within an Indoor Floor Hockey Unit	
Yes	**No**	
X		Follows teacher's directions
X		Follows rules of the game
	X	Plays safely and never raises stick above waist height
	X	Cooperates with teammates
X		Uses correct technique during 5 v 5 games
X		Shows good sportsmanship at end of games

TABLE 7.2	A Point Value Rubric to Assess Student Performance within an Indoor Floor Hockey Unit
1	Follows teacher's directions (1 point)
2	Follows rules of the game (2 points)
0	Plays safely and never raises stick above waist height (1 point)
0	Cooperates with teammates (2 points)
3	Uses correct technique during 5 v 5 games (3 points)
1	Shows good sportsmanship at end of games (1 point)
7	Total

Grading Scale

10	A	Excellent
8–9	B	Good
6–7	C	Satisfactory
4–5	D	Unsatisfactory
0–3	F	Poor

example, perhaps the teacher who designed the checklist for indoor floor hockey in Table 7.1 would like to place more of an assessment emphasis on the items that assess correct technique, following the rules of the game, and cooperation with teammates. To achieve this, the checklist could be converted to a point system rubric whereby the student is awarded a point value instead of a yes-no judgment. A point system rubric does not require the observer to address the quality of a certain aspect of a performance, but it does allow a greater emphasis to be put on certain characteristics. The addition of a point value allows the teacher to easily convert the point value to a grade for the assignment (see Table 7.2).

Holistic rubrics assess the student's motor performance as a whole without breaking the skill down into critical components. This type of rubric requires the teacher to make a judgment about the quality of all criteria simultaneously. The performance levels within a holistic rubric are usually presented in paragraph form. An example of a holistic rubric designed to assess student performance on the skill of ultimate frisbee game play is provided in Table 7.3. Once the holistic rubric has been constructed, the teacher can use a checklist to assess each student's performance in the authentic situation (see Table 7.4). By designing a rubric and a simple checklist, the physical educator can assess students while watching them perform ultimate

frisbee skills in a game situation. This type of assessment is becoming increasingly popular in units taught through the sport education model approach (Siedentop, Hastie & van der Mars 2004).

In contrast to looking at the skill performance as a whole, *analytical rubrics* allow the teacher to assess the student's level of performance on each critical component of a motor skill performance. Although analytical rubrics require more detail and are generally more time-consuming to construct, they allow the teacher to pinpoint areas of weakness within the skill performance, allowing for individualized feedback to the student. Several physical education pedagogy textbooks (e.g., Graham 2001; Lund 2000; Schiemer 2000) and NASPE resources (e.g., *Authentic Assessment of Physical Activity for High School Students* 2002; *Creating Rubrics for Physical Education* 1999) specifically address the issue of rubric creation. For example, to help teachers develop analytical rubrics, Schiemer (2000) has provided specific guidelines that can streamline the rubric development process. First, she recommends creating a grid using either graph paper or a computer software program (e.g., Microsoft

TABLE 7.3	A Holistic Rubric for Assessing Ultimate Frisbee Game Play
3 - Outstanding	Student uses appropriate throws in different situations and consistently executes with proper technique. Throws are accurate and directed toward teammates in advantageous positions. Movement is consistently made to get open and provide passing outlets for teammates. Student provides strong defense within the defensive system of the team and is aware of teammates' positions, opposition runs, and the location of the disk. Student demonstrates a thorough understanding of the rules of the game and calls decisions fairly within the "spirit of ultimate Frisbee."
2 - Satisfactory	Although some incorrect-form performances are evident, throws are usually performed with correct form and technique, and appropriate decision making is usually demonstrated. Participation shows an understanding of rules and strategies of ultimate frisbee. Strong defensive skills are evident in individual situations although the student does not consistently engage in team-oriented defense.
1 - Unsatisfactory	Student performance is characterized by throws made with incorrect form. Decisions are poorly made in terms of shot selection, and minimal movement is made to provide passing opportunities for teammates. Consistent rule infringements demonstrate a lack of understanding of the rules of the game. Defensive skills are weak as demonstrated by poor footwork, anticipation, and individual and team defensive skills.

TABLE 7.4	Checklist to Assess Ultimate Frisbee Skills in Game Play		
	Outstanding	Satisfactory	Unsatisfactory
John	X		
Thomas		X	
Jennifer	X		
Jim			X
Debbie	X		

Excel). Once this template has been constructed, it can be adjusted to score each skill the teacher wishes to assess. Second, the critical components that the teacher plans to assess should be listed down the left-hand column of the grid. Ideally, these critical components are directly related to the cues the teacher provided to the students during the instructional unit. Third, the different levels of performance should be listed across the top row of the grid. Schiemer (2000) recommends that the levels of performance match the reporting system that the teacher uses on the student reporting card, such as percentages, pass/fail, letter grades, or O, S, NI (outstanding, satisfactory, needs improvement). Fourth, each inner cell within the grid should con-

tain a qualitative statement of the criteria necessary to demonstrate competence at each of the designated performance levels. The constructed rubric should be made available to the students who are to be assessed. Finally, the teacher can create a checklist to record student performance while observing the students in a game situation. Tables 7.5 and 7.6 provide examples of an analytical rubric and a student checklist constructed to assess performance on the soccer kick.

Standard Five from the National Standards for Physical Education document urges teachers to design lessons that enable students to "exhibit responsible personal and social behavior that reflects self and others in physical activity settings"

TABLE 7.5	Analytical Rubric for Assessing the Soccer Kick in 5-a-Side Game		
	Achieving (A)	**Developing (D)**	**Not Yet (X)**
Eyes on ball throughout kick	Eyes focused on ball throughout each kick attempt	Eyes focused on ball: (a) for most kicks or (b) for most of the time throughout each kick	Eyes never focused on ball throughout each kick
Nonkicking foot placed next to ball	Nonkicking foot placed next to ball during each kick attempt	Nonkicking foot usually placed beside ball during kicking attempts	Nonkicking foot never placed next to ball during kicking attempts
Contact with laces or instep	Contact always made with the laces or the instep of the foot	Contact sometimes made with the laces or the instep of the foot	Contact rarely or never made with the laces or the instep of the foot
Follow-through with kicking leg in direction of ball	Follow-through always made in the direction of the kick	Follow-through sometimes made in the direction of the kick	Follow-through never made in the direction of the kick

TABLE 7.6	Checklist to Assess Soccer Kick in 5-a-Side Game			
	Eyes	**Foot Placement**	**Contact**	**Follow-through**
Jane	A	A	A	A
Steven	A	A	D	D
Alex	D	D	D	X
Jose	A	X	X	X
Crystal	D	A	D	D

TABLE 7.7	Rubric for Assessing Student Sportsmanship during Basketball Game Play				
Cooperated with teammates	Always	Often	Sometimes	Rarely	Never
Followed referee's decisions	Always	Often	Sometimes	Rarely	Never
Played fairly	Always	Often	Sometimes	Rarely	Never
Reacted appropriately to adversity	Always	Often	Sometimes	Rarely	Never
Played with energy and enthusiasm	Always	Often	Sometimes	Rarely	Never

(NASPE 2004, p. 39). This standard is often reflected in affective objectives such as social behavior, sportsmanship, and cooperation skills. In addition to psychomotor objectives, affective domain objectives can also be evaluated in an authentic situation through the use of a rubric. Tables 7.7 and 7.8 provide examples of a grading rubric and student checklist that could be used either as a self-assessment for students to complete or as an assessment for the teacher to complete while observing students in game play activities.

Today in many school districts, physical educators are responsible not only for assessing students, but also for reporting student scores to a district supervisor or central office. Teachers have had to collect student data using a pencil-and-paper approach in the gymnasium and then return to their office to manually input the scores into a

TABLE 7.8	Checklist for Assessing Student Sportsmanship during Basketball Game Play				
	Cooperated with teammates	Followed referee's decisions	Played fairly	Reacted appropriately to adversity	Played with energy and enthusiasm
Marissa	A	A	O	S	**A**
Juanita	A	A	A	A	A
Mario	O	O	O	O	O
Daniel	R	N	N	N	S
Will	S	S	O	A	A

A = Always
O = Often
S = Sometimes
R = Rarely
N = Never

spreadsheet on their desktop computer. This approach to assessment can be made more efficient through the use of technology, specifically a Pocket PC. A Pocket PC is a handheld computer that has many of the capabilities of modern desktop PCs. The common software bond between the desktop PC and the Pocket PC is the Excel spreadsheet software. Desktop Excel and Pocket Excel share many of the same functions, such as the sorting of data, summing functions, and the arrangement of data in columns. The obvious difference between Excel and Pocket Excel concerns the limited screen real estate on the Pocket PC. Rubrics and checklists are created using the Excel software program on the desktop computer and then saved to the Pocket PC. The teacher then uses the stylus to input data on the Pocket PC while circulating the class and watching students perform skills (see Figure 7-1). The final step in the process requires teachers to transfer their data back to the desktop computer to save in a folder or send to a central location (see Figure 7-2).

TYPES OF AUTHENTIC AND ALTERNATIVE ASSESSMENTS

In 1995, NASPE published the first national document identifying what students should be learning in K–12 physical education classes. A newly revised second edition of *Moving into the Future:*

National Standards for Physical Education was released in 2004 and has been recognized as an essential tool for developing, implementing, and evaluating K–12 physical education programs. The 2004 National Standards clearly identify what students should know and be able to do as a result of a quality physical education program. The National Standards documents present assessment guidelines that encourage physical educators to instructionally align national content standards with clearly defined student expectations and performance outcomes. Furthermore, these documents present various alternative and authentic assessment options to measure student performance outcomes. Examples include student projects, student logs, student journals, peer observation, self-assessment, group projects, portfolios, event tasks, student artwork, video productions, and slide shows, as well as teacher observation (see Table 7.9 on page 149 for a list of alternative assessments). Although these examples are generally considered alternative assessments, they become authentic assessments when applied in real-life situations. Mintah (2003) surveyed 210 public school physical education teachers and found that over 75% of the teachers used authentic assessments. Some of the more commonly used authentic assessments were teacher observations, self-observations, checklists, and peer observations. Also, the teachers perceived a positive impact of the use of authentic

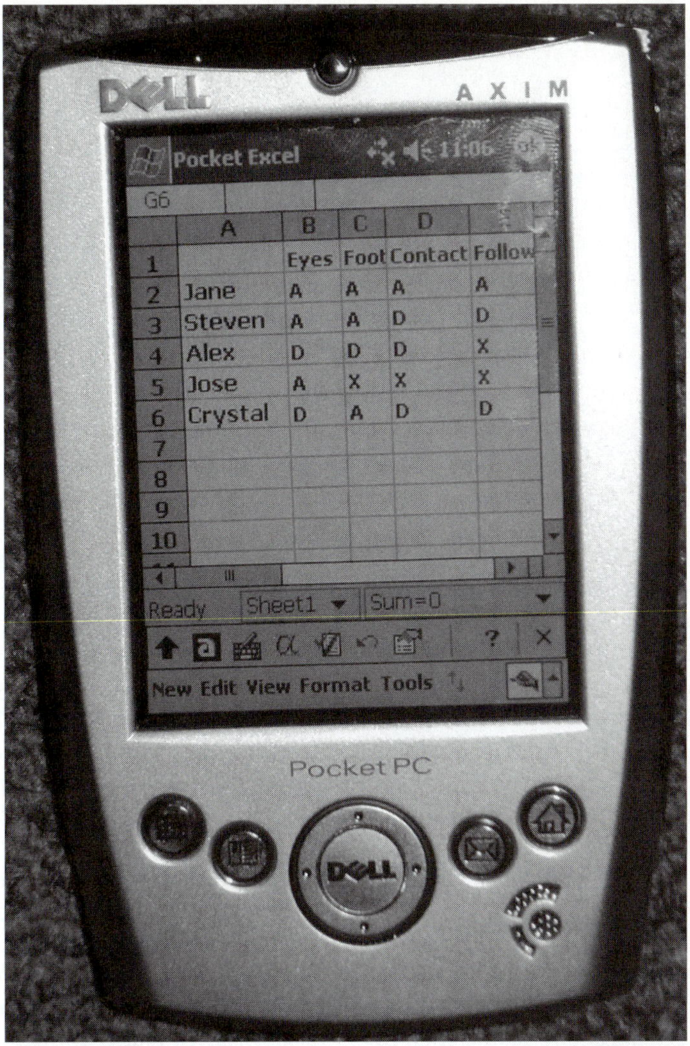

Figure 7-1

Checklist to assess soccer kick using a Pocket PC.

assessments on student self-concept, motivation, and skill achievement.

Portfolios, or collections of student work, have received much recent attention. The increased use of portfolios to assess student performance in physical education has been described by Lund and Kirk (2002) who stated, "With the current widespread emphasis on the use of performance-based, continuous, and authentic assessment of student work to determine their level of achievement of targeted goals and standards, the portfolio has emerged as a new, exciting, and broadly used form of alternative assessment in the middle and secondary schools" (p. 97). NASPE (1995) includes hints for the development and use of portfolios. One suggestion is that the portfolio not include all examples of student work: the teacher specifies a certain number of pieces, and the student selects the pieces to include, submitting a cover letter explaining why those pieces were chosen. A scoring rubric should be included outlining the goals the teacher would like the student to meet

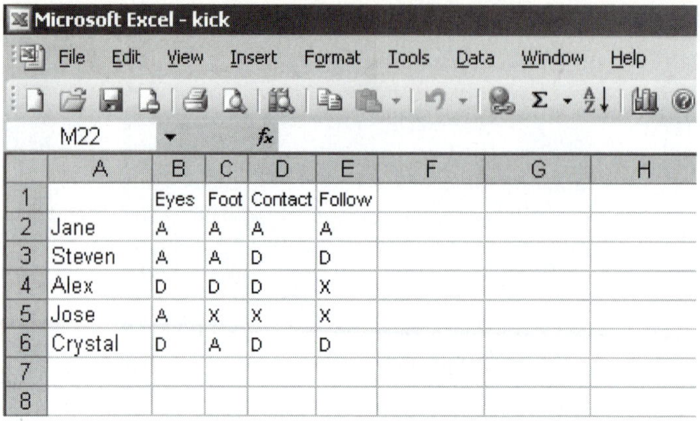

Figure 7-2

Checklist to assess soccer kick saved from Pocket PC to desktop PC.

without limiting the creativity of the student. Kirk (1997) has developed sample portfolio tasks and a sample rubric for use in evaluating portfolios. Having the students include all possible information would make grading the portfolios impractical. Also, in some situations, physical educators may have too many students to make grading portfolios feasible.

Lund and Kirk (2002) and Melagrano (2000) provide examples of different types of portfolios, such as working portfolios (individual student's collections of projects, assignments, and class work), evaluation portfolios (finished portfolios that are submitted for evaluation), thematic portfolios (portfolios based on a specific unit of study), multiyear portfolios (collections of materials to show growth over a number of years), group portfolios (materials from groups within the class), and electronic portfolios (student work collected in an electronic format). Additionally, Lund and Kirk (2002) describe seven guidelines that the teacher should pay attention to when implementing a portfolio grading system in her physical education program (see Table 7.10).

Student portfolios have the advantage of allowing the teacher to triangulate numerous sources of information when engaging in the assessment process. One approach is to instruct the students on what items need to be placed into the student portfolio. Possible items include student essays, stories, drawings, reflections, self-analysis of performance, peer analysis of performance, learning logs, personal fitness logs, activity plans, checklists of cues associated with skills, and opinion pieces (Hopple 1997). Providing a rubric and grade value for each assessment will make the assessing and grading procedure more transparent.

Two excellent examples of the use of portfolios in physical education can be found in *Moving into the Future: National Standards for Physical Education* by NASPE (1995). The first example is a fitness unit involving student assessment of the fitness levels of teachers and staff members at the school, development of individualized exercise programs, instruction for individuals on how to perform the activities, and monitoring of their progress (NASPE 1995). Students develop a portfolio of materials gathered throughout the project and are given feedback continuously. A scoring rubric would have been developed and distributed prior to the assignment so that students would know what criteria they must meet to succeed. The second example is an event task for gymnastics where the students have to develop a routine to perform at a halftime show for local basketball teams. The routine would be based on the gymnastics skills learned in class, and a scoring rubric has

TABLE 7.9	Examples of Alternative and Authentic Assessments	
Assessment	**Description**	**Example**
Slide Shows	Digital photos embedded within a PowerPoint presentation	Images are shown of students using correct technique to perform motor skills.
Video Production	Digital or analog video production of student motor performance	Students could be assigned to groups and asked to make an instructional video explaining and demonstrating the differences between man-to-man defense and zonal defense.
Poster / Banner Creation	An assignment that requires students to create a poster or banner that demonstrates their knowledge of content	Following a health-related physical fitness unit students could be instructed to create a poster illustrating the benefits of being physically fit.
Essays / Reports	A written summary or reflection on an event or concept	During a basketball unit students must watch a basketball game on television and describe and explain the fouls called during a 5-minute span.
Research Papers	An assignment that requires students to actively find information on an issue related to physical education	As part of a multicultural unit, students are assigned a country and are challenged to find one sport / dance / activity that originated in that country.
Personal Fitness Logs	A written personal summary of physical activity over a given time period	As part of a fitness unit, students must complete the Activity Log function of FITNESSGRAM® 8.0.
Opinion Pieces	A written reaction to an issue, concept, or other event	Students enrolled in a team sports class are required to write an opinion piece on different tactical approaches.
Dramatical Performances	Student-designed performances or skits	To develop skills in a cooperative learning unit, students are arranged into groups of five and instructed to create a situation in which a team handles losing well and a situation where the team does not handle losing well.
Officiating Games	Grading students on their knowledge of rules through their ability to officiate a game	In a sport education soccer unit, students take turns officiating the 5-a-side games. Officials are graded by the teacher and their peers through a specifically created rubric.
Oral Reports	Student presentations on an assigned topic	Students are assessed on the oral delivery of their research papers.
Worksheets	Assessing student knowledge of fundamental movement concepts	Images of a girl walking, jumping, and galloping are shown to assess whether a first-grade student can differentiate between these locomotor skills. The student circles the correct response.
Interviews / Focus Groups	Discussions with student(s) to evaluate knowledge	In a team sports unit, the teacher meets with each team to discuss why they implemented certain tactics and strategies.

TABLE 7.10	Guidelines for Portfolio-Based Assessment in Physical Education

1. Identify the learner outcomes that are to be demonstrated through the portfolio assessment.
2. Develop and communicate portfolio guidelines to students.
3. Build flexibility into the class schedule.
4. Provide a variety of performance-based learning and assessment opportunities for students.
5. Guide students in the creation of portfolio ideas.
6. Provide class time for students to work on their portfolios.
7. Provide opportunities for students to share or showcase their portfolios.

Source: Lund and Kirk (2002, p. 105).

TABLE 7.11	Assessment Rubric for Outdoor Education Assignment			
	Excellent (A)	**Good (B)**	**Satisfactory (C)**	**Unsatisfactory (D)**
Use of Compass	Always uses correct technique	Mostly uses correct technique	Sometimes uses correct technique	Rarely uses correct technique
Cooperation Skills	Cooperates and communicates effectively with group all of the time	Cooperates and communicates effectively with group most of the time	Cooperates and communicates effectively with group some of the time	Cooperates and communicates ineffectively with group
Tent Pitching Skills	Uses correct procedure throughout task	Uses correct procedure throughout most of task	Uses correct procedure throughout some of the task	Uses incorrect procedure throughout task
Fire Building Skills	Fire is built safely and efficiently	Fire is built safely and somewhat efficiently	Fire is built safely	Fire is built unsafely
Hot Chocolate Making Skills	Served at perfect temperature, contains no ashes, and is delicious	Served at acceptable temperature, contains no ashes, and is tasty	Served at acceptable temperature, contains some ashes, and is drinkable	Served at incorrect temperature, contains lots of ashes, and is undrinkable

been included for evaluation. This event task could be easily adapted for dance and other activities.

Smith (1997) advocates using a portfolio card for authentic assessment. He points out some of the drawbacks of portfolios previously mentioned and suggests using a portfolio card to document student achievement for each grade level. He has included an example portfolio card and scoring rubric and relates the assessment to national outcomes. This would seem to be a useful way to document student performance and could be adapted to fit different situations.

Event tasks are those the students could complete in one class period, are written so that more than one possible solution can be presented, and are tasks that simulate a real-world experience (NASPE 1995). A good example of an event task comes from Whelan (1997) as a culmination to an outdoor adventure unit. Students are given a compass and directions; using orienteering skills, they have to determine the correct place to pitch their tents. Students must find their way from a beginning point to a predetermined finishing point and pitch their tents within a certain distance of that point. After successfully setting up the tent, the students have to build a fire and make the teacher a cup of hot chocolate without getting ashes in it. These tasks are to be completed within the class period. An example rubric for this assignment is provided in Table 7.11.

Scheimer (2000) published a book of alternative and authentic assessment strategies for elementary physical education. The book includes 58 ready-to-use, reproducible assessment sheets that physical educators can use to assess students' cognitive, psychomotor, and affective learning. All the sheets include teacher tips designed for implementation of the assessment strategies. Hopple (2005) wrote a textbook to help teachers understand, develop, and use alternative methods of assessment to assess program effectiveness and students' progress toward understanding and acquisition of movement and fitness concepts and skills. Additionally, this book addresses the design and use of rubrics for specific assessment tasks. Other examples of alternative assessment are available at the PE Central website (www.pecentral.org/assessment/assessment.html). Alternative assessments for golf, tennis, motor skills, and fitness are available there. Also available are links to other websites containing assessments.

MEASUREMENT CONCERNS WITH AUTHENTIC AND ALTERNATIVE ASSESSMENTS

Although authentic assessment seems attractive as a better way to evaluate students in physical education, it is not without potential problems. Within physical education, little attention has been paid to the psychometric properties (validity, reliability, and objectivity) of these assessments. Also, the question of how teachers can use authentic assessments for grading in physical education needs to addressed.

Concern has been expressed about the quality (i.e., validity, reliability, and objectivity) of authentic assessments. Some authors have conveyed the idea that unless the assessments are used for high-stakes accountability, the quality of the assessments may not be as great a concern (Lund 1994). Grading would seem to involve high-stakes accountability. Many teachers currently use teacher-made tests without regard for reliability and validity; therefore, many may use authentic assessments the same way. However, ignoring validity and reliability in one situation does not justify ignoring it in another situation.

The validity of authentic assessments can be defined as the accuracy of the interpretation of the assessment results. According to Safrit and Wood (1995), validation of authentic assessments has typically been demonstrated through a logical approach or face validity. In other words, does the assessment "look" like it is measuring the desired behavior? However, a logical approach does not provide enough evidence to say that an assessment is valid and would not be acceptable for high-stakes accountability (Burger & Burger 1994).

Elliot (1995) discusses three concerns when considering the validity of authentic assessment. The first deals with how well the test relates to other measures. This is synonymous with a criterion approach. An authentic assessment of volleyball skill should be highly correlated with another measure of volleyball skill. A second concern is the ability of the assessment to predict future performance, which is also a criterion approach for obtaining validity evidence. For example, can an authentic assessment dealing with fitness predict future fitness behaviors? The third issue concerns the assessment covering the content domain. Does the assessment cover all areas of the activity? If you are concerned with overall softball skill, is the assessment reflective of all the components of this domain?

Baker, O'Neill, and Linn (1993) identified several characteristics that good authentic assessments should possess. These include the following: having meaning for both students and teachers, serving as motivation for performance, evaluating attributes that are important to both the teachers and students, requiring demonstration of complex cognition, exemplifying current standards of content quality, minimizing the effects of irrelevant skills, and possessing explicit standards for rating or judgment.

The reliability and objectivity of the authentic assessment are dependent on the scoring rubric developed. A detailed rubric and practice scoring with that rubric can enhance reliability and objectivity by increasing the chances that the scores a teacher assigns the students one day will be similar to the scores that would be assigned on another day or by another teacher. One issue that needs to be addressed within the scope of reliability of authentic assessments is the combination of the tasks. Reliability has usually been established for a single task that was independent of other tasks. With authentic assessments, teachers are usually concerned with a combination of tasks in a real-world setting where various single tasks are part of a set of tasks necessary to achieve a goal. Repeated evidence demonstrating that this combination of tasks is present would help increase the reliability of the assessment.

According to Frisbie (1988), reliability of scores from teacher-made knowledge tests, including alternative assessments, is usually lower than reliability of scores from standardized tests. Frisbie goes on to state that tests with low reliability can be acceptable if they are combined with other information for evaluation and that teachers should be more concerned with the reliability of scores that are a combination of all information rather than individual assessments. If the teacher has only a small number of items on which to evaluate, these must be of high quality. For example, if a teacher is assigning a grade solely on the basis of two skill tests, these must be of high quality. However, if a teacher were to base a grade on two skill tests, two written tests, and two event tasks, the reliability and validity for this combination of items would be of more concern.

Few studies have examined the reliability of authentic assessment scores and the validity of the interpretations of these scores in physical education. Grehaigne, Godbout, and Bouthier (1997) developed an authentic assessment technique for assessing individual performance in a team sport. They found acceptable objectivity, reliability, and criterion validity evidence. Oslin, Mitchell, and Griffin (1998) developed the Game Performance Assessment Instrument (GPAI) to examine tactical understanding and problem solving. The GPAI was field-tested across soccer, basketball, volleyball, and softball games. The results of their study showed that the stability reliability and the objectivity of the scores from the GPAI were acceptable. Also, there was acceptable evidence

for content and construct validity. Cucina (1999) found acceptable objectivity across multiple raters, acceptable stability reliability, and acceptable criterion validity evidence for a badminton game assessment rubric. She correlated the score from the rubric with subjective ratings of playing ability. In 2001, Kulinna and Zhu used Rasch modeling to support the construct validity of fitness portfolios. Williams and Rink (2003) found objectivity was higher when teachers used only a two-level rubric (competent or not competent) compared to four levels that discriminated among levels of competence.

A grade in physical education should reflect whether or not the student has met the objectives of the program. If an objective is for the student to develop skill in a particular activity, teacher observation, event tasks, and student performance logs could be used. To determine if students are meeting cognitive objectives, teacher observation, portfolios, event tasks, group projects, and other authentic assessments could be used. Many different authentic assessments could be used to determine whether affective objectives are being achieved. The use of authentic assessment should not mean the complete elimination of traditional means of evaluation. There may be times when a written test or skill test may be appropriate and should be utilized. Also, when used in conjunction with authentic assessment, more traditional assessments may help to improve the reliability and validity of the final grade given.

Many physical education teachers lament the amount of time needed to grade their students using skill tests or fitness tests. It is unclear whether the use of authentic assessments would result in more or less time spent on grading. Most physical educators spend at least part of each skill unit allowing the students to play the game. By making observations during this time with a rating scale that yields objective and reliable scores and for which the interpretations of the scores are valid, the teacher could grade most, if not all, students in one class period. On the other hand, if a physical educator has 40 students in a class and six classes a day, is it feasible to use portfolios for grading those students? This would seem to work better for classroom teachers who only have 25 to

30 students in a class. In physical education, the number of students may deter the use of portfolios, which could be more time-consuming than traditional methods.

SUMMARY

Authentic and alternative assessments are defined and characteristics of authentic assessments are discussed. Four different types of scoring rubrics—checklists, point system rubrics, holistic rubrics, and analytical rubrics—are discussed in detail, and examples of each are given. Examples of the different types of authentic and alternative assessments are given. Measurement concerns with authentic and alternative assessments are examined.

FORMATIVE EVALUATION OF OBJECTIVES

Objective 1   Differentiate between authentic and alternative assessments.

1. What is the difference between authentic and alternative assessment?
2. When does an alternative assessment become authentic?

Objective 2   Identify the characteristics of authentic assessments.

1. Traditionally, written and skill tests have been used in physical education. Discuss how each of these traditional methods would align with the characteristics in this chapter.

Objective 3   Define the different types of scoring rubrics.

1. How do checklist rubrics and point system rubrics differ?
2. How do holistic rubrics and analytical rubrics differ?
3. How can technology be used to collect student assessment data?

Objective 4   Identify the different types of authentic and alternative assessments.

1. List and describe four different types of alternative assessments in physical education.
2. Provide examples of how different types of alternative assessments can be utilized in authentic settings.

Objective 5   Discuss measurement concerns with authentic and alternative assessments.

1. How could you determine the objectivity of the rubric in Table 7.3?
2. Using the example from Whelan (1997), how could you determine the validity of this assessment?

ADDITIONAL LEARNING ACTIVITIES

1. Using the information provided in this chapter, develop a holistic rubric for an activity of your choice. Have several of your classmates perform the activity and have three of your classmates rate their performance using the rubric. How good is the agreement among the raters? How could you improve the agreement?
2. From the list in Table 7.9, select three different types of alternative assessments and develop assessments of throwing ability.

BIBLIOGRAPHY

Baker, E. L., H. F. O'Neill, Jr., and R. L. Linn. (1993). Policy and validity prospects for performance-based assessments. *American Psychologist* 48: 1210–1218.

Burger, S. E. and D. L. Burger. (1994). Determining the validity of performance-based assessment. *Educational Measurement: Issues and Practice* 13: 9–15.

Cucina, I. M. (1999). *Specificity of feedback using alternative assessment techniques in a secondary physical education badminton class.* Unpublished doctoral dissertation, Springfield College, Springfield, MA.

Elliot, S. N. (1995). *Creating meaningful performance assessments* (Report No. EDO-EC-94-2). Reston, VA: Council for Exceptional Children. (ERIC Document Reproduction Service No. ED 375 566)

Frisbie, D. A. (1988). Reliability of scores from teacher-made tests. *Educational Measurement: Issues and Practices* 79(1): 25–35.

Graham, G. (2001). Teaching children physical education: Becoming a master teacher. 2nd ed. Champaign, IL.: Human Kinetics.

Grehaigne, J. F., P. Godbout, and D. Bouthier. (1997). Performance assessment in team sports. *Journal of Teaching in Physical Education* 16: 500–516.

Hopple, C. J. (1997). Authentic skills assessment in physical education. *Journal of Physical Education, Recreation, and Dance* 68(7): 19–24.

Hopple, C. J. (2005). *Elementary Physical Education Teaching & Assessment.* Champaign, IL.: Human Kinetics.

Kirk, M. F. (1997). Using portfolios to enhance student learning and assessment. *Journal of Physical Education, Recreation, and Dance* 68(7): 29–33.

Kulinna, P. H. and W. Zhu. (2001). Fitness portfolio calibration for first- through sixth-grade children. *Research Quarterly for Exercise and Sport* 72(4): 324–334.

Lund, J. (1994). Authentic assessment: Have we finally found user friendly assessment? *Proceedings of the World Congress for the Association Internationale des Ecoles Superieures d'Education Physique.* Berlin, Germany.

Lund, J. (1997, January). What is authentic assessment? *Measurement News* 2:3.

Lund, J. (2000). *Creating rubrics for physical education.* Reston, VA: American Alliance for Health, Physical Education, Recreation, and Dance.

Lund, J. and M. F. Kirk. (2002). *Performance based assessment for middle and high school physical education.* Champaign, IL: Human Kinetics.

Magill, R. A. (2004). *Motor learning and control: Concepts and applications.* 7th ed. New York: McGraw-Hill.

Melograno, V. J. (2000). *Portfolio Assessment for K–12 Physical Education.* Reston, VA: National Association for Sport and Physical Education.

Mintah, J. K. (2003). Authentic assessment in physical education: Prevalence of use and perceived impact on students' self-concept, motivation, and skill achievement. Measurement in *Physical Education and Exercise Science* 7(3): 161–174.

National Association for Sport and Physical Education. (1995). *Moving into the future: National standards for physical education.* Reston, VA: National Association for Sport and Physical Education.

National Association for Sport and Physical Education. (1999). *Creating rubrics for physical education.* Reston, VA: National Association for Sport and Physical Education.

National Association for Sport and Physical Education. (2002). *Authentic assessment of physical activity for high school students.* Reston, VA: National Association for Sport and Physical Education.

National Association for Sport and Physical Education. (2004). *Moving into the future: National standards for physical education.* 2nd ed. Reston, VA: National Association for Sport and Physical Education.

Oslin, J. L., S. A. Mitchell, and L. L. Griffin. (1998). The Game Performance Assessment Inventory (GPAI): Development and preliminary validation. *Journal of Teaching in Physical Education* 17: 231–243.

Safrit, M. J. and T. M. Wood. (1995). *Introduction to measurement in physical education and exercise science.* 3rd ed. New York: Mosby.

Schiemer, S. (2000). *Assessment strategies for elementary physical education.* Champaign, IL. Human Kinetics.

Siedentop, D., P. A. Hastie, and H. van der Mars. (2004). *Complete guide to sport education.* Champaign, IL.: Human Kinetics.

Smith, T. K. (1997). Authentic assessment: Using a portfolio card in physical education. *Journal of Physical Education, Recreation, and Dance* 68: 46–52.

Whelan, J. (1997, March). *Authentic adventure.* Paper presented at the meeting of the American Alliance for Health, Physical Education, Recreation, and Dance, St. Louis, MO.

Williams, L. and J. Rink. (2003). Teacher competency using observational scoring rubrics. *Journal of Teaching in Physical Education* 22: 552–572.

EVALUATING SKILL ACHIEVEMENT

C O N T E N T S

K E Y   W O R D S

accuracy tests
objective evaluation
rating scales
skill tests
subjective evaluation
wall volley tests

O B J E C T I V E S

The achievement of sport skills can be measured by three general means: skill tests, rating skills, and performance itself. Skill tests are an objective, often-used means of evaluating a variety of psychomotor objectives. These tests can be standardized or developed individually. Rating scales are instruments that standardize and define a performance that will be subjectively evaluated by a teacher. Finally, in some instances the performance itself can be used to evaluate achievement.

After reading Chapter 8, you should be able to

1. Identify the four general types of sport skill tests.
2. Evaluate the four general types of sport skill tests using the criteria of reliability, validity, and feasibility for mass testing.
3. Evaluate the weaknesses and strengths of rating scales.
4. Identify motor skills that are best evaluated by performance.
5. Outline methods that could be used to develop measurement procedures for evaluating motor skill achievement, methods that meet the criteria of reliability, validity, and feasibility for mass testing.

INTRODUCTION

Sport skill testing is seldom conducted outside of physical education programs and athletic programs. For individuals not likely to conduct sport skill testing, this chapter still has value. Most people are going to have measurement situations where they have to develop their own tests and procedures. In this chapter you will encounter a variety of measurement situations, often with measurement problems, and you will see how tests were developed for these situations. The problem solving/test development procedures that were followed in developing sport skill tests are the same procedures used in developing fitness tests, pre-employment screening tests, and other physical performance tests.

A universal goal of physical education programs is to produce permanent, measurable changes in student psychomotor behavior, in skills ranging from touch football to modern dance, from volleyball to scuba diving. For the achievement of psychomotor objectives to be evaluated, the measurement procedures—tests, rating scales, or other instruments—must parallel the instructional objectives. Today the trend is away from standardized evaluation methods, whose objectives often differ from instructional ones (see Authentic Assessment, Chapter 7). Instead, it is the teacher—the person who has developed the instructional objectives—who must develop the procedures for evaluating them.

In developing the evaluation procedures the teacher must remember that age, gender, or experience may influence the skill level of the students. All students don't start a sport skill at the same level of ability. So, the difficulty level and type of evaluation procedures may have to be adjusted to the ability of the students. The evaluation procedure for elementary school students may be markedly different from the evaluation procedure for college students. The evaluation procedures for beginning-, intermediate-, and advanced-level students may differ. For true beginners, it may be impossible to administer a sport skill test at the beginning of a unit, and a short unit on a sport skill does not change the skill level of the students enough to administer a sport skill test at the end of the unit. Thus, a rating scale may have to be used to evaluate sport skill ability.

Sport skill tests are an objective method for evaluating motor skill achievement. Several of these tests are outlined in the chapter. From them, you should be able to develop your own skill tests and document the reliability and validity associated with their use.

Rating scales are a subjective but systematic method for evaluating those skills that do not lend themselves to objective evaluation. The subjectivity of the method presents numerous problems, but there are procedures for constructing scales that can be validly interpreted.

Finally, for certain skills (e.g., golf, bowling, archery) performance can provide an objective score for skill evaluation. The advantages and limitations of performance-derived evaluation are presented here as well.

SPORT SKILL TESTS

Skill tests require an environment similar to the game environment and standardized procedures for administration. The validity associated with skill tests is judged to some extent on the consistency between testing and performing environments. This does not mean you must recreate exactly the playing environment; it does mean that the movements and the activity must correspond to those of the actual sport. For example, you can use repeated volleying of a tennis ball against a wall to measure achievement in the skill of the tennis ground stroke; however, the student must be using the correct form.

The virtue of skill tests is a subject of ongoing debate. Many skill tests offer a method for evaluating motor skill objectives that leads to valid interpretations of ability, while others do not. Do not use a skill test that does not meet your evaluation needs or the important criteria of reliability, validity, and feasibility for mass testing. Also, be sure to adopt tests that were developed on students of the same sex, age, and experience level as your students. You can also modify an existing test to meet your needs. Strand and Wilson (1993) and Collins and Hodges (2001) describe many skill tests that might be adopted or modified for use in your testing program. Chapters in books by Tritschler (2000), Lacy and Hastad (2003), and Miller (2002) may be helpful in identifying sport skill tests. More old than new sport skill tests are available and referenced in these sources.

Although skill tests are most useful for the evaluation of learning, they can also be used for (1) placement, (2) diagnosis, (3) prediction, (4) comparative evaluation, and (5) motivation. The tests used to evaluate achievement can be placed into four groups: (1) accuracy tests, (2) wall volley tests, (3) total bodily movement tests, and (4) throws, kicks, or strokes for power or distance. A few tests have aspects of several groups and so are combination tests. Provided next are sample tests that illustrate each general group of skill tests.

Accuracy Tests

Accuracy tests involve throwing, striking, or kicking an object toward a target for accuracy. Basketball free throws, and badminton or tennis or volleyball serves at a target, are common accuracy tests.

The basic disadvantage of accuracy tests is that the target scoring system (5-4-3-2-1-0 or 3-2-1-0) does not allow discrimination among skill levels. For example, it would be meaningless to use a single tennis serve as an index of serving skill if the score could range from only 0 to 3. This lack of variability reduces reliability. Two general procedures, however, can improve the reliability of accuracy test scores. The first increases the variability of the target. A target with a range from 0 to 1 (hit or miss) provides less reliable scores than a target whose range is from 0 to 2 or 0 to 5. Given 10 serves, the range of scores for a target scored 0 or 1 would be from 0 to 10; on a target scored 0 to 3, the range would be from 0 to 30, a more precise measure. The second procedure increases the number of trials. Obviously, 20 trials yield more reliable results than do five or ten. Ideally, then, 15 to 30 trials should be administered for most accuracy tests. Of course, too many trials can make a test unfeasible for mass testing.

Wall Volley Tests

Wall volley tests require the student to repeatedly stroke, pass, throw, or kick an object at a wall over a specified period of time with the number of successful trials as the unit of measurement, or for a specified number of successful trials with time as the unit of measurement. An example is the number of seconds it takes an individual, using correct form, to pass a basketball against a wall 10 times.

In general, wall volley tests tend to provide reliable scores, but because the testing and playing environments can differ considerably, validity of the score interpretations poses a problem. Does repeatedly passing a ball against a wall truly measure a student's basketball passing skill? Because the wall volley test environment differs from the game environment, it is especially important that students be allowed to practice the test. Then, too, wall volleying can be a useful way to practice a skill, allowing the student both practice in the skill and greater familiarity with the testing environment.

Notice in the example of the basketball passing test that the number of passes against the wall was set (10) and the score was the amount of time it took to complete the 10 passes. An alternative procedure and scoring system for wall volley tests is to count the number of hits on the wall in a set length of time, usually 15 to 60 seconds. The advantage of the alternative procedure is that only one timer is needed and several students may take the test at the same time if sufficient wall space is available. The student's partner counts the number of hits and watches for correct form.

Total Bodily Movement Tests

These tests require the subject to run a standardized test course using movements characteristic of the sport. An example is a basketball dribbling test.

Basketball Control Dribble Test (AAHPERD 1984)

Objective   To measure skill in handling the ball while a player is moving

Equipment   Standard inflated basketballs, a stopwatch, and six obstacles arranged as shown in Figure 8-1

Procedure   The player stands on his nondominant-hand side of Cone A with a ball in hand. At the signal "Go," the player begins dribbling with the nondominant hand to the nondominant-hand side of Cone B and continues to dribble through the course using the preferred hand, changing hands when desired until he crosses the finish line. The ball may be dribbled with either hand, but legal dribbles must be used. Each player is allowed three trials.

Scoring   The score in seconds and tenths of seconds is the time required to dribble the

entire course. The last two trials are timed and recorded, and the sum of the two is the player's score on the test.

Other considerations   In general these tests provide reliable scores. Their value, and thus validity of the score interpretations, is determined by the extent to which they relate to the objectives being taught. Allow students to practice on the test course. They will learn how to travel it more efficiently with each practice or trial. These types of tests, like most skill tests, can also be used as skill practice.

Throws, Kicks, or Strokes for Power or Distance Tests

These tests, among the more common types of skill tests, measure the student's ability to throw, kick, or strike an object forcefully. Obvious examples are the softball throw for distance, the football punt for distance, and the golf drive for distance.

Normally such tests are reliable, because the distance the object travels can be accurately measured. Attention must be paid, however, to each test's relevance to the instructional objectives. Certainly, many variations of this test could be used.

Combination Tests

These tests are a combination of several of the four groupings just mentioned, usually speed and accuracy. An example is a basketball speed shooting test and basketball passing test.

Speed Spot Shooting (AAHPERD 1984)

Objective   To measure skill in rapidly shooting from specified positions

Equipment   Standard inflated basketball, standard goal, stopwatch, marking tape

Procedure   Grades 5 and 6 shoot from 9 feet; grades 7, 8, and 9 shoot from 12 feet; grades 10, 11, 12, and college shoot from 15 feet (Figure 8-2). Three 60-second trials are administered, with the first trial considered practice and the last two scored. Dur-

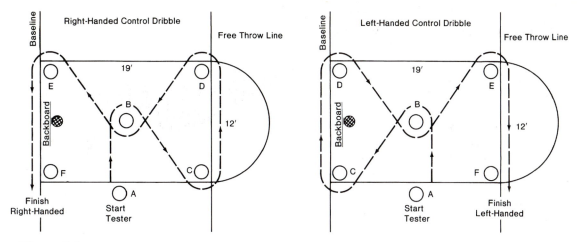

Figure 8-1

AAHPERD Basketball Control Dribble Test as an example of a total bodily movement test.
(Source: Reprinted by permission of the American Alliance for Health, Physical Education, Recreation and Dance, Reston, VA 22091.)

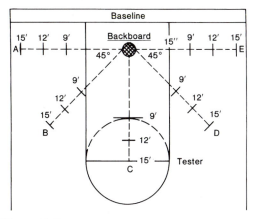

Figure 8-2

Speed Spot Shooting Test.
(Source: AAHPERD, 1984. *Basketball Skills Test Manual for Boys and Girls,* Reston, VA 22091.)

ing each trial a student must shoot at least once from each of the five spots (A–E) and may shoot a maximum of four lay-up shots, but not two in succession.

Scoring   Two points are awarded for each shot made, and one point is awarded for each unsuccessful shot that hits the rim. The final score is the total of the last two trial points.

Passing (AAHPERD 1984)

Objective   To measure skill in passing and recovering the ball while moving

Equipment   Standard inflated basketball, stopwatch, smooth wall surface, marking tape

Procedure   Six squares are marked on the wall, and a restraining line is marked on the floor 8 feet from the wall (Figure 8-3). Three 30-second trials are administered, with the first trial considered practice and the last two timed. The player, holding a ball, stands behind the restraining line and faces target A. On the command "Go," the player chest-passes at target A, recovers the rebound, and moves opposite target B. From behind the restraining line the player chest-passes at target B. This pattern continues until target F, where two chest passes are executed. Then the player moves to the left, passes at target E, and continues to move left, passing at each target in turn.

Scoring   Each pass that hits the desired target counts two points. Each pass hitting the wall but missing the target counts one point. The sum of the last two trial points is the final score.

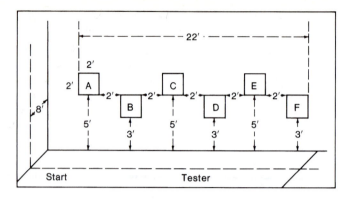

Figure 8-3

Basketball Passing Test.

(Source: From Johnson, B. L. and J. K Nelson, 1979. *Practical Measurements for Evaluation in Physical Education.* Minneapolis, MN: Burgess Publishing Co. and AAHPERD, *Basketball Skills Test Manual for Boys and Girls*, 1984.)

RATING SCALES

Rating scales are useful for evaluating qualities that cannot be measured with a skill test, or at least not easily and efficiently. This section focuses on procedures for constructing and using rating scales, particularly to evaluate skill achievement.

Subjective or Objective Evaluation?

Most of the measurement techniques discussed to this point have had scores with good objectivity for the simple reason that most of the measurements conducted in physical education are objective rather than subjective. With **objective evaluation,** the test has a clearly defined scoring system, so the scorer does not affect the final score. Examples of objective tests are a mile run measured with a stopwatch, a ball throw for distance measured with a tape, a 1-minute sit-up measured in number of executions, or a basketball free throw test. If a student makes seven free throws out of ten shots, two scorers would have little difficulty arriving at the same score. Remember, objectivity is the degree of agreement between the scores of two or more competent scorers. With subjective evaluation, a qualified person or persons judge(s) the quality of a performance and assign(s) a score, so the scorer can and does affect the final score. A subjective evaluation may be based on a defined scoring system, as in the scoring of gymnastics events in competition, or the evaluation may be just

the impressions of each scorer. In the latter case, agreement between the scores of the scorers would probably not be high and objectivity would be low. Rating scales are designed to help objectify subjective evaluation by defining the scoring system, just as a tape measure defines the system of scoring the distance a person throws a ball.

Some people do not think highly of subjective evaluations, but it must be remembered that **subjective evaluations** are often used as the criteria when obtaining validity evidence for objective tests. Judges' ratings are among the most widely used criteria when obtaining validity evidence for skill tests for team sports. Although it is true that anything that exists can be measured, the system for measuring it may not be an objective test. Certainly, wherever feasible, objective evaluation should be used. But many important instructional objectives cannot be measured objectively. In fact, objective skill tests are not even available for gymnastics, folk dancing, fencing, and teamwork. For a number of the more complex team sports, it would be almost impossible to develop a test or test battery that provides scores that may be validly interpreted as total playing ability for two reasons:

1. The difficulty of identifying or measuring in a short period of time all the skill components that make up a given sport, and
2. The difficulty of objectively measuring the interaction among the skill components of a

given sport, making the sum of the measurable components less than descriptive of the whole sport.

Subjective evaluation may also be more efficient than objective testing. Certain subjective scoring can be carried out while the students are practicing or competing, making it unnecessary to set aside special testing periods. Also, the number of trials required in certain tests for objective evaluation can make those tests unfeasible for mass testing. For example, assume that a teacher wants to evaluate student skills in serving and passing a volleyball for a class of 60. If 10 serves and 20 passes are necessary to obtain reliable scores for evaluating these skills, the objective tests could require a total of 600 serves and 1,200 passes. Certainly a more efficient use of time would be to develop a rating scale and evaluate the students while they play the game.

Problems with Subjective Evaluation

Subjective evaluation must not only yield scores with acceptable objectivity and reliability, and interpretation of these scores that is valid, but also be as efficient as possible. We can satisfy these four criteria if the procedure is well planned.

The first stage in the planning process is the determination of which skills are going to be evaluated and how much each skill is going to affect the final score. Consider, for example, a teacher who, at the end of a volleyball unit subjectively evaluates playing ability but has not planned what to evaluate or how to weigh what has been evaluated. This teacher may have neglected not only to observe the same skills in each student, but also to weigh each equally in the final score. Serving skill may account for 35% of one student's final score and only 20% of another's.

The second stage in the planning process is the formulation of performance standards. Suppose that a teacher, having decided which skills to evaluate and their weight, begins to evaluate the students' serves without formulating performance standards. If the teacher expected well-placed, hard-to-return services and the first few students do not serve well, the teacher may unconsciously lower her standards, applying different criteria to the next students. These

sliding standards would give two students of equal ability different scores.

The third stage in the planning process is a system for immediately recording scores. Even when a teacher knows what to evaluate, the weight of each evaluation, and the performance standards, unless the scores are recorded immediately, the scores will probably be not reliable and the interpretations of these scores not valid. Scores are too easily interchanged if the teacher tries to remember the score of each student and record it later.

In a sense, a rating scale reflects the careful planning procedure required to have objectivity, reliability, and validity, with a subjective evaluation. The scale lists the traits to be evaluated, reflects the teacher-determined importance of each trait, describes the performance standards, and provides a format for immediately recording scores.

Constructing a Rating Scale

The process of constructing a rating scale is threefold: (1) determining the purpose of the subjective evaluation, (2) identifying the basic components of the trait being evaluated, and (3) selecting the levels of ability for each component.

Purpose

The purpose of a rating scale determines the degree to which subjective evaluations must discriminate among ability groups. The more they must discriminate, the greater the number of classifications of ability that are needed. If, for example, posture is subjectively evaluated, only two classifications (acceptable-unacceptable) or three classifications (excellent-average-poor) may be needed. For grading purposes, three to five classifications are usually adequate; occasionally, seven to ten are used in competition.

Basic Components

The trait being rated is almost always evaluated in parts or components, which must themselves be identified. The importance of each component and subcomponent must be defined so that points reflecting their relative value can be assigned.

TABLE 8.1	Sample Volleyball Rating Scale

Each of the three components of volleyball-playing ability has a point value of 15, and is scored on a 5-4-3-2-1 basis:

5 points—Exceptional ability, near perfect for the age and sex of the participant.

4 points—Above average ability, not perfect but quite skillful for the age and sex of the participant.

3 points—Average ability, typical for the age and sex of the participant.

2 points—Below average ability, characterized by more mistakes than is typical performance for the age and sex of the participant.

1 point—Inferior ability, far below typical performance for the age and sex of the participant.

For each subheading, circle the appropriate score.

I. Serve

A. *Height above net*	5	4	3	2	1
B. *Accuracy of placement*	5	4	3	2	1
C. *Difficulty of return*	5	4	3	2	1

II. Setting or Spiking—choose one

A. *Setting*

1. Height above net	5	4	3	2	1
2. Accuracy of placement	5	4	3	2	1
3. Coordination with spiker	5	4	3	2	1

B. *Spiking*

1. Accuracy of placement	5	4	3	2	1
2. Difficulty of return	5	4	3	2	1
3. Coordination with setter	5	4	3	2	1

III. General team play

A. *Hustle*	5	4	3	2	1
B. *Alertness—saves and play of difficult shots*	5	4	3	2	1
C. *Teamwork*	5	4	3	2	1

Total Score _____

In Table 8.1, for example, three components are identified and several subcomponents are listed under each. These components and subcomponents reflect the instructional objectives of the activity.

Levels of Ability

The third step in the process is to decide how many levels of ability should be assigned to each component. Two levels—pass-fail—are usually considered too crude an evaluation procedure. When three levels of ability are sufficient, a student can be rated above average, average, or below average on each subcomponent. A five-level scoring system is probably the most common: each student is rated superior, above average, average, below average, or inferior on each subcomponent. Systems beyond five levels require that the teacher be knowledgeable enough about the characteristics being evaluated to identify small differences in ability or status. If a teacher creates more ability levels than he can identify, the reliability of the ratings will be low. Remember that reliability and objectivity are improved when what is looked for in each subcomponent is listed exactly in the rating scale.

Using the Scale

No rating scale, however well prepared, works unless it is used. You should have a copy of the scale for each student and record the ratings on it as you make the evaluation. There are also several ways to improve the effectiveness of a rating scale: increasing the number of qualified raters, retesting on several occasions, allowing sufficient time for doing the rating, preparing the students, and developing your own scale where possible.

Number of Raters

The reliability of subjective evaluation scores and the validity of score interpretations increase as the number of raters increases, as predicted by the Spearman-Brown prophecy formula and the validity prediction formula (Chapters 3 and 4), provided of course that the raters are qualified. One well-qualified rater is preferable to several poorly qualified raters. When there are several raters, objectivity of scores improves if they decide before the rating what they are looking for and what standards to use. For example, assume there are four judges in a gymnastics meet—two college coaches and two high school coaches—and that each rates performers on a 10-point system. The college coaches may expect more of the performers than do the high school coaches. So, the scores of the college coaches will be lower than the scores of the high school coaches. This is lack of objectivity. Thus, if the participants are junior high boys, the judges must decide whether a perfect score indicates perfect performance, or the best that can be expected of this age group.

Number of Trials

Rating each student on several occasions within a short period—three days, for example—and using the average of the ratings as a score usually improves the reliability of scores and the validity of the score interpretations. The justification and advantages of rating each person several times are the same as the reasons for using multiple trials on a physical performance test. By rating each person on several different days, we minimize the chances of a student receiving a poor rating because of an off day, or a high score due to luck.

If you are able to rate a student on several different occasions, do not look at the student's previous ratings, which are likely to influence your evaluation. For example, if you know that a student was rated below average on the first performance, there is little chance that you will rate the student above average on a subsequent performance, even if the student deserves it. This preconceived idea of ability is a problem common to all forms of subjectivity evaluation.

Testing Time

Allow enough time to rate an individual completely and to record the ratings immediately. It is better to rate only ten people each hour and do a good job than to try to rate 30 people in an hour and obtain ratings that are invalidly interpreted.

Student Preparation

As with objective tests, the students should know what is expected of them and what you will be looking for when you evaluate them. Let the students know that you plan to evaluate them in the near future so that they can prepare themselves if they want to. Finally, students should be informed that they are being evaluated the day that ratings are made.

Teacher-Prepared Scales

We believe that teachers should construct their own rating scales. The objectives of the course, the manner in which it is taught, the types of students, and their prior experiences are all variables that affect what is evaluated and how. Only a teacher-made rating scale can meet the evaluation needs of a specific situation. In preparing your own scales, you can look to others, like those shown in Tables 8.2 and 8.3, for help.

Total Score

Throughout the discussion of rating scales, there have been references to obtaining a total score for the rating scale, which is the sum of the points assigned to the parts (basic components) of the rating scale. Notice that for the rating scales in Tables 8.1 through 8.3, there is a place for a total score. Zhu

TABLE 8.2	Badminton Rating Scale

The four areas of badminton-playing ability may all be rated during competition. However, the first two areas may be rated in a noncompetitive situation, if so desired, by asking the student to demonstrate the various serves and strokes.

Each subarea is scored on a 3-2-1 basis:

3 points—Above average ability, considerably more skillful than the performance typical of the student's age and sex.

2 points—Average ability, typical performance for age and sex.

1 point—Below average ability, far inferior to typical performance for age and sex.

For each subarea, circle the appropriate score.

I. Serve

A. Position of shuttlecock upon contact—racket head strikes shuttlecock below waist level.	3	2	1
B. Position of racket at end of serve—if short serve, racket head does not rise above chest; if long serve, racket head stops between shoulders and top of head at end of serve.	3	2	1
C. Placement of serve—well placed relative to type of serve and position of opponent.	3	2	1
D. Height of serve relative to type of serve—short serve is low over net; drive serve is low over net and deep; clear serve is high and deep.	3	2	1

II. Strokes—consider placement and quality of each stroke

A. Clear—high and deep.	3	2	1
B. Smash—hit from position above head and in front of body; path of bird is down.	3	2	1
C. Drive—sharp and low over net; hit from position about shoulder height; can be deep or midcourt, but not short.	3	2	1
D. Drop—hit from position waist to shoulder height; low over net; a hairpin-type shot.	3	2	1

III. Strategy

A. Places shots all over court.	3	2	1
B. Executes a variety of shots at the most opportune moments.	3	2	1
C. Takes advantage of opponent's weaknesses (for example, poor backhand, strength problem in back court, poor net play).	3	2	1
D. Uses own best shots.	3	2	1

IV. Footwork and Position

A. Near center court position, so flexible to play any type of shot.	3	2	1
B. Has control of body at all times during play.	3	2	1
C. Body is in correct position when making each shot (usually determined by the feet).	3	2	1
D. Racket is shoulder-to-head height and ready for use (wrist cocked) at all times; eyes are on the shuttlecock at all times.	3	2	1

Total Score _____

Source: Suggested by Bill Landin, Indiana University.

TABLE 8.3 **Swimming Rating Scale for Elementary Backstroke**

The arm stroke, leg kick, complete stroke, and stroke efficiency are rated on a three-point scale. Complete stroke and stroke efficiency are double-weighted so as to be twice as influential as arm stroke and leg kick in the total rating.

Circle the appropriate score for each area.

A. Arm Stroke

3 points—Arms do not break water or rise above top of head; elbows are kept at sides and fingers move up midline of body; stroke is powerful and smoothly coordinated.

2 points—Arms do not break water or rise above top of head; elbows are usually kept at sides and fingers move up midline to body; stroke is reasonably powerful and reasonably well-coordinated.

1 point—Arms break water and/or rise above top of head; elbows are not kept at sides and fingers do not move up midline of body; stroke is not powerful and/or poorly coordinated.

B. Leg Kick

3 points—Legs drop at knees for whip kick; toes are outside of heels as feet spread; kick is powerful and smoothly coordinated.

2 points—Legs drop at knees for whip kick but some flexation occurs at hips; toes are not outside of heels as feet spread, causing knees to spread; kick is reasonably powerful and reasonably well-coordinated.

1 point—Legs do not drop at knees for whip kick, but are brought toward stomach by flexing at the hips; knees spread too wide; no power in kick; kick is poorly coordinated.

C. Complete Stroke

6 points—Arms and legs are coordinated during stroke; arms are at sides, trunk and legs straight, and toes pointed during glide position.

4 points—Minor deviations from the standard for 6 points occur.

2 points—Arms and legs are not coordinated during stroke; glide position is poor with reference to arm-trunk-leg-toe position.

D. Stroke Efficiency

6 points—Long distance is covered in glide; body is relaxed in water; swims in straight line; hips on surface.

4 points—Average distance is covered in glide; body is relaxed in water; does not swim in straight line; hips slightly below surface.

2 points—Little distance is covered in glide; body is not relaxed in water; does not swim in straight line; hips are well below surface (swimmer is sitting in water rather than lying on top of it).

Total Score _____

(1996) questioned whether a total score for the rating scale in Table 8.2 is appropriate. If the attribute being rated is composed of the parts of the rating scale and the possible scores for the parts are interval scores (see Chapter 2), then a total score is appropriate. If, as Zhu (1996) believes, the possible scores for the parts are ordinal scores (see Chapter 2), then a total score is not appropriate. This is a complex issue that cannot be addressed adequately in a short section of this book. Probably, most rating scales yield ordinal scores. Perhaps a researcher should be more concerned about this than a practitioner. The point values for each rating (e.g., 5 = exceptional) are codes and not measured scores. Thus, any scores could be used as codes. For example, in Table 8.1, rather than using 5-4-3-2-1 codes, we could use 10-6-5-2-1 codes. Usually codes are ordinal scores. In Table 8.1, one could argue that the ability change from "average" to "above average" is the same as the ability change from "average" to "below average," but much smaller than the ability change from "above average" to "exceptional." The codes 5-4-3-2-1 do not reflect this fact, and so these codes are ordinal scores. However, one could argue that in Tables 8.2 and 8.3, the ability change from "average" to "above average" is the same as the ability change from "average" to "below average" so the 3-2-1 scoring system reflects the true situation that there is a common unit of measurement between consecutive scores and the scores are interval scores.

The Performance

For many motor skills, performance is an excellent means of evaluating instructional objectives. It is important to remember that in this context the performance environment is also the evaluation environment. The instructional objectives and the performance may thus be identical, and validity using the logical approach more readily assured. For example, a tumbling objective might be to execute a forward roll; when the student does so, the objective has been evaluated.

When performance is evaluated, it is usually in terms of achievement, but it could be in terms of developmental or biomechanical instructional objectives. Among the skills where performance can serve as a means of evaluation are the following:

Archery. Archery achievement is determined by measuring the student's accuracy in shooting a standardized target from a specified distance.

Bowling. The bowling average achieved under standardized conditions is an objective measure of bowling skill. Subjectively evaluating bowling form would certainly be possible.

Golf. If the school has access to a golf course, the student's score on several rounds can serve as an objective index of golf skill. This criterion is well accepted by touring professionals.

Swimming. The number of breaststrokes required to swim 25 yards is an objective measure of

breaststroke ability. Stroke mechanics and/or form are commonly evaluated.

Procedures for Evaluating Skill Achievement

We recognize that teachers are not researchers. The procedures below for the development of skill test batteries represent the application of scientific test construction principles to the public school teacher's situation. They also represent several years' work. Do not expect high-quality evaluation of psychomotor objectives to be instantly performed.

1. *Define what is to be measured.* This is one of the most important steps in the test construction process; if it is not carried out correctly, subsequent procedures will also be incorrect. Use your instructional objectives as the source of what is to be measured. These objectives describe the skills that should be achieved during an instructional phase, so they also define what needs to be measured.

2. *Select a measuring instrument.* Choose tests or rating scales that measure the achievement of the instructional objectives. In most instances, the process of matching objectives and measuring instruments is based on logic. Remember that the skill learned during instruction must also be the skill used during the test. That is, individual differences in scores on a basketball dribble test must be due to individual differences in dribbling skill, not to unrelated factors.

   In selecting a measuring instrument, you can choose from among published skill tests, construct a rating scale, or use the performance itself. It may be necessary to alter an instrument to fit your instructional objectives. In constructing a skill test battery, skill tests and rating scales can be used together to evaluate the different motor skill components of an activity. For example, you can use a serving test to evaluate the achievement of volleyball serving skill and a rating scale to evaluate spiking skill. When it is impossible to evaluate all the skills you have taught, as it usually is, select those that are most important.

3. *Pretest the instrument.* Before you administer a test or rating scale to a class, try it out on a group of five to fifteen students. No matter how explicit test instructions appear, you will truly understand the test and its procedures only after you have administered it. Several important questions must be answered: Does the test seem to provide test scores that lead to valid interpretations? Does it measure the stated instructional objective? Does it seem to provide test scores that are reliable? Are the directions clear? What is the best way to standardize its administration? How long does it take to test one student? If the test is too long, you may have to set up several test stations and recruit and train additional testing personnel. At this point you should also develop standardized procedures for administering the test.

4. *Revise the test and testing procedures.* On the basis of your findings from the pretest, you may want to revise, delete, or add tests to the battery. If the changes are numerous, you should administer the revised test to another small group.

5. *Administer the instrument.* At the end of the instructional phase, administer the selected test to the class.

6. *Evaluate the administered test.* After you administer the battery, examine the reliability, validity, and feasibility for each test (see Chapters 3 and 4).

   a. *Reliability.* Because testing procedures and the variability of the group can affect reliability, it is important that you estimate the test score reliability for your testing procedures and students. If test scores lack reliability, it may be necessary to use additional trials, to alter your testing procedures, or to search for a better test.

   b. *Validity.* Once you have determined test score reliability, you must obtain validity evidence. In most instances, you can use the logical approach. If the test obviously measures an instructional objective, this is logical evidence of validity. For example, a test that requires a student to swim 25 yards in as few strokes as possible using the sidestroke provides scores that can be validly interpreted in terms of sidestroke skill. If validity cannot be determined using the logical approach, you could compare the scores achieved by the best and poorest students in the class. If the achieved scores do not confirm your observations, the test is suspect. Or, you could compare the test scores with tournament standings. If the tests provide scores that allow valid interpretations, the test scores and tournament standings should be ranking students in a similar manner (i.e., students good on one measure good on the other measure).

   c. *Feasibility.* Tests can provide reliable scores that can be validly interpreted, yet be simply impractical for mass testing. If you cannot revise the testing procedures to make them applicable for mass testing, you must select or develop a new battery.

7. *Revise the final battery.* The final battery should consist of tests for which good reliability and validity documentation exist. These tests must measure important instructional objectives. A battery normally consists of from three to five individual tests. Two criteria for compiling the final battery are (1) that the selected tests be documented in terms of good validity and feasible for mass testing, and (2) that the correlation among the final items be low. If the correlation between two tests in the final battery is high, one should be eliminated.

8. *Develop standards.* Once you have finalized the content of the battery, you must develop norm-referenced or criterion-referenced standards. Standard-score and percentile norms (see Chapters 2 and 6) are especially useful. Standard-score norms have the

advantage of allowing you to sum the test items and calculate a total score for the entire battery. Criterion-referenced standards based on research finds or personal beliefs are useful because they are a minimum proficiency standard. Many published tests provide national norms; however, you should try to develop your own norms, because testing procedures and climatic conditions vary.

ADDITIONAL EVALUATION CONSIDERATIONS

Most of what has been presented in this chapter up to this point has applied to doing a summative evaluation with norm-referenced standards. As presented in Chapter 5, formative evaluation should be conducted and criterion-referenced standards can be used with both formative and summative evaluation. Criterion-referenced standards do not have to be dichotomous (pass-fail, proficient–not proficient), but they tend to be dichotomous. Formative evaluation tends to be conducted with criterion-referenced standards and summative evaluation tends to be conducted with norm-referenced standards, but this does not always have to be the case. Based on the instructional objectives, either type of standard could be used with either type of evaluation. Thus, a sport skill test or rating scale or performance could be used for a formative or summative evaluation. Further, a sport skill test or rating scale or performance could be scored to provide continuous data or dichotomous data with the evaluation standards multiple classifications (like A, B, C, D or above average, average, below average) or two classifications (pass-fail). Earlier in the chapter tests, rating scales, and the performance were presented with a scoring system providing continuous data, but each of these could be scored proficient or not proficient (1 or 0).

In fact, students can be evaluated on form or technique rather than amount of skill if the instructional objectives are in regard to form or technique. This can be a formative or a summative evaluation with dichotomous or multiple classification standards. There is nothing wrong with watching a student shoot from the foul line in basketball and evaluating the form or technique used to make the shot with no regard for whether the shot went through the basket. With middle school boys in a track-and-field unit, it makes sense to evaluate shot put ability based on form rather than how far the shot is thrown. This allows for differences among students in body size. Probably the largest student in the class can throw the shot farther with poor form than the smallest student in the class with good form. But in high school when the two students are about the same size, the student with good form will be able to throw the shot farther.

SAMPLE SPORT SKILL TESTS

AAHPERD Sport Skill Test Series

The Research Council of the AAHPERD (formerly the AAHPER) published several sport skill tests in the late 1960s that were developed from the combined efforts of researchers, city directors of physical education, and public school teachers. The report of a committee that evaluated the 1960s AAHPER series concluded, among other things, that the procedures for the test items are vague and that, although the test items are supposed to measure skill achievement, some of them actually predict potential achievement. This last is of special concern, in that many of the tests include basic ability items (speed, jumping, agility) that predict, rather than indicate, skill ability.

The Measurement and Evaluation Council of the AAHPERD formed a task force in 1979 to revise and expand the AAHPER sport skill test series. The basketball and softball skills tests were revised, and a tennis test was added to the series.

The AAHPERD sport skills tests presently available are not without merit. A brief discussion of each test battery follows, for your reference. Individuals planning to use these tests should obtain the test manuals from AAHPERD in order to have the complete administrative procedures, norms, and recommended drills.

Basketball

The basketball battery consists of four tests recommended for boys and girls in grades 5 through college, with minor changes for sex differences (AAHPERD 1984). The basketball battery test manual presently is not available.

> *Speed Spot Shooting*. This test was presented earlier in the chapter, in the section called "Combination Tests."
>
> *Passing*. This test was presented earlier in the chapter, also as a combination test.
>
> *Control Dribble*. This test was presented earlier in the chapter, under "Total Bodily Movement Tests."
>
> *Defensive Movement*. The purpose of this test is to measure basic defensive movement. A course of six cones is set up on the free throw lane of the court (see Figure 8-4). Three timed trials of side-stepping (slide-step) through the course are administered. The final score is the sum of the last two trial times.

In a factor analysis study of basketball skill tests, 21 items were administered to 70 male students (Hopkins 1977). Four factors were identified: (1) shooting, (2) passing, (3) jumping, and (4) moving with or without the ball. A similar study (Gaunt 1979), using 20 variables administered to 167 female students, also identified four factors: (1) lay-up shooting, (2) passing, (3) explosive leg strength, and (4) dribbling. These findings influenced the selection of tests in this battery.

Softball

The softball battery (AAHPERD 1991) consists of four tests recommended for boys and girls in grades 5 through college.

> *Batting*. The softball outfield is marked off into three power zones (for grades 5–8: 120 feet, 180 feet, and more than 180 feet from home plate) and into three placement areas (left, center, and right field), so there are nine scoring areas. Hit balls that come to rest in the farthest center field scoring area receive the most points. Fewer points are given for hits to right or left field and hits not reaching the farthest scoring area. The test consists of two practice trials and six test trials of hitting a ball off a

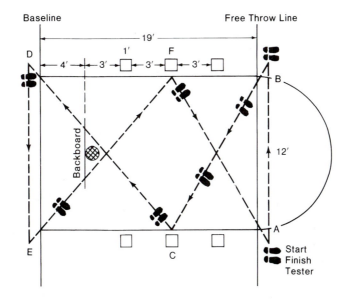

Figure 8-4

AAHPERD Basketball Defensive Movement Test.

(Source: Reprinted by permission of the American Alliance for Health, Physical Education, Recreation and Dance, Reston, VA 22091.)

batting tee for distance and accuracy. The sum of the six test trials is the batter's score.

Fielding Ground Balls. A tester throws a ball on a smooth field and the student tries to field the ball cleanly. Two practice and six test trials are administered. Each test trial is scored based on how cleanly the ball is fielded and where the ball is fielded. The score is the sum of the points for the six test trials. The directions are specific as to dimensions and marking of the test area, ball velocity and placement, and assignment of points.

Overhand Throwing. The test involves throwing a softball for distance and accuracy. Players have 3 to 4 minutes of short-throw warm-up and then have two trials to throw the softball as far and as straight as possible down a throwing line. The trial scored is the ground distance the ball goes before hitting the ground minus the number of feet the ball lands away from the throwing line. The better of the two trials is a player's score. This score is very reliable and more economical than the mean of two trial scores.

Base Running. This test involves running the first two bases for time. One reduced-speed practice trial and two test trials are administered. A trial score is the time it takes to run from home plate to first base to second base. The score is the better of the two trials for the same reason given for the overhand throwing test.

Tennis

The tennis battery (AAHPERD 1989) consists of two tests and an optional test recommended for boys and girls in grades 9 through college. The committee who developed this battery found that tennis is not taught at the junior high school level as much as previously believed. They found three test items that had acceptable reliability, validity, and administrative efficiency documentation.

Ground Stroke: Forehand and Backhand Drive. The test measures the ability to hit ground strokes with both accuracy and power. The score for each trial is based on placement and power. The placement score reflects where the ball lands in a target area, with deep shots on the court receiving more points than shots near the net. The power for each shot landing in the target area is revealed by how deep on the court the second bounce lands. Placement scores are 0 to 4 and power scores are 1 to 3.

Serving. The test measures serving accuracy and power. As with the ground stroke test, the tennis court is marked with scoring areas and power zones. Students are permitted about 5 minutes of warm-up prior to being tested. Sixteen services are scored for placement and power. Accuracy of each serve is scored 0 to 2, and power for each serve landing in the tennis court is scored 1 to 2 depending on how deep the second bounce of the serve lands. The score for the test is the sum of the points for the sixteen trials.

Volley Test (optional). The test measures the ability to volley the ball accurately from a position near the net. The court is divided into seven areas, which are scored 1 to 4 points. The tester hits ten balls to the forehand side and ten balls to the backhand side of the student. The student hits each ball over the net, aiming at the target areas. The first four balls hit from each side are considered practice. The score on the test is the sum of the points for the twelve trials.

Other Sport Skill Tests

Following are numerous other sport skill tests as examples of the types of test that have been used in the past. If these tests meet your needs, use them. However, we hope that many physical education teachers will use these tests as examples to construct their own sport skill tests.

Golf
Green Golf Test (Green, East & Hensley 1987)

Objective   To measure the five basic skill components of golf: putting, chipping, pitching, using middle-distance irons, and driving

Validity and reliability   A group of 146 students were administered each item of the test battery on each of two days near the end of a beginning-level golf class. Reliability coefficients were at least .70, except for the pitch shot for females and the short putt for both males and females.

A group of 66 students completing a beginning-level golf class at the college level were used to estimate validity. Multiple regression was used to estimate validity with the score on 36 holes of golf as the criterion measure, and the predictor variables the golf battery items. The validity coefficient was .72 for a two-item test battery of middle-distance shot and pitch shot, increasing to .77 for a four-item test battery of middle-distance shot, pitch shot, long putt, and chip shot.

Items:

Middle-distance shot   The test was four trials of hitting a ball at a target 140 yards away (males) or 110 yards away (females). The score was the sum of the perpendicular distance in yards each ball came to rest from the target.

Pitch shot   Six trials from 40 yards away from the flagstick were used. A seven through nine iron, pitching wedge, or sand wedge was used for the test. The score for the test was the sum of the distance in feet each of the six pitch shots were from the flagstick.

Long putt   This test was putting from six proportionately spaced positions around the cup. All positions were 25 feet from the cup. The score was the sum of the distance in inches that each putt stopped from the cup.

Chip shot   Six trials from 35 feet away from the flagstick were used. The score for the test was the sum of the distance in feet each of the chip shots stopped from the flagstick.

Gymnastics

Gymnastics Skills Test for College Women (Ellenbrand 1973)

The 16-item battery consists of the following events: balance beam (5 items), floor exercise (4 items), uneven parallel bars (5

items), and vaulting (2 items). The items were selected using the following criteria: contribution to the category in which they were placed, extent to which they were considered basic skills (as opposed to a variation of some skill), progression within the category, and similarity to a gymnastics performance.

Objective   To measure achievement of gymnastics skills

Validity and reliability   Validity was estimated by correlating the sum of the scores of three judges of varied experience (an experienced gymnastics teacher, a college teacher with limited gymnastics teaching experience, a student majoring in physical education with a single basic course in gymnastics) with the sum of the ratings of two experienced gymnastics judges. The correlations were balance beam, .93; floor exercise, .97; uneven parallel bars, .99; vaulting, .88; and total test, .97. The intercorrelations among the four events ranged from .44 to .70, low enough to warrant the inclusion of all four. The reliability for each event and for the total test was investigated again using the three judges of varied experience. In addition, the test was administered on a second day by one teacher. The intraclass reliability estimates were as follows:

Event	Among Teachers	Between Days
Balance beam	.99	.98
Floor exercise	.97	.99
Uneven parallel bars	.99	.94
Vaulting	.97	.99
Total tests	.98	.99

Procedure   The skills for each item were ordered from simple to difficult. The difficulty ratings were logically assigned. The student selects one skill under each item that demonstrates her achievement in that area. She should have an opportunity to practice. Deduct points for falls, but give students the opportunity to repeat stunts.

We present here the test items and difficulty ratings for the floor exercises only (see Table 8.4). For the floor exercise event, skills are performed on the length of mats provided. A return trip can be used if necessary. Connecting skills can be added if needed for preparation of a selected skill (e.g., a round-off to prepare for a back handspring). However, extra steps and runs should be avoided because they detract from the execution rating.

Other considerations   This test is designed to evaluate the instructional objectives of gymnastics for college women only; it should not be used for other students. However, the same logic could be applied to develop a test for any gymnastics or tumbling class.

Racquetball
Racquetball Battery (Poteat 1983)

Objective   To measure basic racquetball-playing ability of beginning players

Validity and reliability   Twelve collegiate and professional racquetball instructors evaluated the skills test battery as to its validity (logical approach) and all agreed that the test battery items measured skills necessary for beginning racquetball players. Further, correlations between test items and expert ratings of the skill involved in the test item varied from .62 to .76.

Stability reliability coefficients for the items varied from .75 to .84. Internal consistency reliability coefficients varied from .85 to .91.

Equipment   A regulation racquetball court with official markings is necessary. Also, a racquetball racquet, stopwatch, measuring tape, four racquetballs, and marking tape are needed.

Procedures   The original battery consisted of forehand and backhand passing shot,

service placement, forehand and backhand wall play, and wall volley tests. Because of high correlations between comparable passing and wall play items, the author suggests dropping the passing shot item but changing the wall play item so it has the same target area and scoring procedure as the passing shot and service placement items. The three suggested test items in their original form are presented here.

1. *Service placement.* The student stands in the center of the service area, bounces the ball, and hits it to the front wall so that it will rebound and hit in or pass through the 10×5 foot target area in the back corner of the court.
2. *Back wall play.* The student stands about 5 feet from the back wall and 20 feet from the side wall. He or she throws the ball to the back wall so that it bounces to the side wall, and then bounces on the floor. The player then returns the ball to the front wall so that the ball does not contact the side wall on the way to the front wall.
3. *Wall volley.* The student, holding two balls, begins the test from the service line 15 feet from the front wall. The student drops one of the balls and hits it to the front wall, then continues to rally the ball for 30 seconds. The ball may bounce any number of times on the return to the subject, or the ball may be volleyed. The student may not cross the service line to contact the ball, but may cross the line to retrieve a ball. Any stroke may be used to rally the ball. If the ball passes the player, he may put the second ball in play.

Other considerations   Poteat (1983) states that all items in his test battery have sufficient range to discriminate among students with varying ability. The test battery takes 15 to 18 minutes to administer to each student. If a single item is administered, it probably should be a wall volley (Hensley, East & Stillwell 1979). Their wall volley test and most tests of this type allow the student to use either a forehand or a backhand stroke. Karpman and Isaacs (1979) maintain there should be one of each.

TABLE 8.4	**Floor Exercise Items from Ellenbrand Gymnastics Test**

Test Item: Tumbling Skills (Rolls)

Difficulty	Skills	Difficulty	Skills
0.5	a. Forward roll to stand	4.5	i. Back extension
0.5	b. Backward roll to knees	5.0	j. Dive forward roll (layout)
1.0	c. Back roll to stand	6.0	k. Back tuck somersault (aerial)
2.0	d. Pike forward or back roll	6.5	l. Back pike somersault
2.0	e. Straddle roll (forward or back)	6.5	m. Forward tuck somersault
3.0	f. Dive forward roll (pike)	7.0	n. Back layout somersault
4.0	g. Handstand forward roll	8.0	o. Somersault with a twist
4.0	h. Back roll to headstand		

Test Item: Tumbling Skills (Springs)

Difficulty	Skills	Difficulty	Skills
1.0	a. Handstand snap-down	5.0	h. Back handspring
2.0	b. Round-off	5.0	i. Front handspring on one hand or with a change of legs
2.5	c. Neck spring (kip)		
3.0	d. Head spring	5.5	j. Series of front handsprings
3.5	e. Front handspring to squat	6.0	k. Series of back handsprings
4.0	f. Front handspring arch to stand	6.5	l. Back handspring to kip (cradle)
4.5	g. Front handspring walk-out	6.5	m. Back handspring with twist

Test Item: Acrobatic Skills

Difficulty	Skills	Difficulty	Skills
1.0	a. Mule kick (three-quarter handstand)	4.0	i. Dive cartwheel
1.0	b. Bridge (back arch position)	4.0	j. Tinsica
2.0	c. Handstand	4.5	k. Dive walk-over
2.0	d. Cartwheel	5.0	l. Handstand with half turn or straddle-down to a sit
2.5	e. Backbend from standing		
3.0	f. Front limber	5.0	m. One-handed walk-over
3.0	g. One-handed cartwheel	6.0	n. Butterfly (side aerial)
4.0	h. Walk-overs (forward and back)	7.0	o. Aerial cartwheel or walk-over

Test Item: Dance Skills

Difficulty	Skills
1.0	a. Half turn (one foot), run, leap
2.0	b. Half turn, step, hitch kick forward, step, leap
3.0	c. Half turn, slide, tour jeté, hitch kick
4.0	d. Full turn (one foot), step, leap, step, leap
5.0	e. Full turn, tour jeté, cabriole (beat kick forward)
6.0	f. One and one-half turns, step, leap, step, leap with a change of legs

Scoring: The score is the product of the skill difficulty and the execution rating. The following scale is used for the execution rating:

3 points: Correct performance; proper mechanics; execution in good form; balance, control, and amplitude in movements.

2 points: Average performance; errors evident in either mechanics or form; some lack of balance, control, or amplitude in movement.

1 point: Poor performance; errors in both mechanics and form; little balance, control, or amplitude in movements.

0 points: Improper or no performance; incorrect mechanics or complete lack of form; no display of balance, control, or amplitude in movements.

Dowd (1990) hypothesized that beginning-level racquetball skill of college students is represented by serve, kill shot, and passing/defense shots. For males, Dowd found that a volley component represented by the long wall volley and a drive serve component represented by the short-drive serve best represented racquetball skill. However, for females, Dowd found that a volley component represented by the long wall volley, a placement component represented by the forehand overhead ceiling shot, and a kill component represented by the forehand kill shot set up with a toss and hit best represented racquetball skill. Lam and Zhang (2002) developed a racquetball test for young adult beginners. Acceptable reliability and validity were documented for a test composed of forehand power drive, backhand power drive, forehand power shot placement, backhand power shot placement, ceiling shot, and wall rally.

Red Cross Swimming Skills

The American Red Cross has identified basic swimming skills for various swimming classification groups. Basic skills for beginners are prone float and prone glide. For more advanced students, the basic skills are crawl stroke and elementary backstroke. The skills are subjectively rated on a pass-fail basis. The ratings can be used for the formative evaluation of swimming achievement. The materials for administering these tests can be obtained from any office of the American Red Cross.

OTHER SKILL TEST REFERENCES

There are physical skills other than sport skills; dance is an example. And there are numerous sport skills. It is impossible in this book to provide example tests for the majority of sport skills, much less for most physical skills. Miller (2002), Tritschler (2000), and Lacy and Hastad (2003) provide more and different test examples than those presented in this book. For example, Tritschler (2000) has a chapter on assessment in dance education written by a dance educator. Miller (2002) and Lacy and Hastad (2003) present many sport skills tests and then, at the end of the chapters, present lists of additional references to sport skills tests.

There has been very little development of sport skill tests since around 1980. No matter which measurement book you consult, you will find many of the same tests—and many of the tests are old. Old is not bad if the conduct of the sport skill and rules for the sport skill have not changed since the test was developed. In addition, many of these tests were developed for a particular age group and/or gender. Thus, most of the tests in any measurement book must be taken as examples, and modified or new tests developed, based on the example test that measures the appropriate skill for a given group of students.

SUMMARY

The achievement of psychomotor objectives is a universal goal of physical education programs. We can measure the achievement of psychomotor skills with three general procedures: skill tests, rating scales, and the performance itself.

Skill tests require the creation of an environment similar to the game environment and the standardization of procedures for administration. The validity of interpretations based on skill test scores can be judged in part by the extent to which the testing environment duplicates the playing environment. There are four general types of skill tests:

1. Accuracy tests. Accuracy tests require the student to throw, strike, or kick an object at a target for accuracy. Examples are the basketball free throw, the badminton short serve, and the volleyball serve.
2. Wall volley tests. Wall volley tests require the student to repeatedly stroke, pass, throw, or kick an object at a wall. The score may be the number

of successful volleys completed during a specified time period or the time required to execute a specified number of volleys.

3. Tests of total bodily movement. These tests require the student to run a standardized test course using movements typical of the sport. Dribbling a basketball through an obstacle course is one example.
4. Throws, kicks, or strokes for power or distance. These tests require the student to throw, kick, or strike an object (a football, a shuttlecock, etc.) for distance.

Rating scales are a device for evaluating skill achievement subjectively. They are used for evaluating qualities that cannot be efficiently measured by objective means. In a sense, these scales add a measure of objectivity to subjective measurements; they can yield reliable measurements of skill achievement that can be validly interpreted if they are properly constructed and used.

For some motor skills, the performance itself is a reliable method of measuring achievement that leads to valid interpretations of ability. This type of evaluation tends to be content-valid because the performance environment is also the evaluation environment. Archery, bowling, golf, and swimming are skills that can be evaluated by performance.

The steps in the development of reliable procedures for validly evaluating skill objectives are as follows:

1. Define what is to be measured.
2. Select a measuring instrument.
3. Pretest the instrument.
4. Revise the test and testing procedures.
5. Administer the instrument.
6. Evaluate the administered test.
7. Revise the final battery.
8. Develop norms.

FORMATIVE EVALUATION OF OBJECTIVES

Objective 1   Identify the four general types of sport skill tests.

1. Skill tests involve creating an environment similar to the game situation and standardizing testing procedures. Numerous skill tests have been published for a variety of sport skills. Skill tests can be categorized under one of four general groups. Summarize the characteristics of each group.
   a. Accuracy tests
   b. Wall volley tests
   c. Tests of total bodily movement
   d. Throws, kicks, or strokes for power or distance

Objective 2   Evaluate the four general types of sport skill tests using the criteria of reliability, validity, and feasibility for mass testing.

1. In order for interpretations of test scores to be valid, the test scores must first be reliable. However, a test for which reliability and validity documentation exist may still not be feasible for mass use. In order to evaluate the achievement of motor skill objectives, the teacher must select skill tests that have documented acceptable levels of reliability and validity and that can be administered in the public school. Each of the four general categories of skill tests has inherent weaknesses and strengths. Identify the basic weakness associated with each category and summarize the actions you could take to improve its effectiveness.
   a. Accuracy tests
   b. Wall volley tests
   c. Tests of total bodily movement
   d. Throws, kicks, or strokes for power or distance

Objective 3   Evaluate the weaknesses and strengths of rating scales.

1. In many evaluation situations it is neither feasible nor possible to measure motor skill achievement with an objective sport skill test. In these situations a rating scale is used. A rating scale is a subjective measurement procedure. Differentiate between the terms *objective* and *subjective* as applied to the evaluation of motor skill achievement.

2. List the weaknesses and strengths of rating scales.
3. Like all forms of measuring instruments, rating scales must provide reliable scores. Certain procedures in the development and use of rating scales help guard against measurement error and ensure objectivity. Outline the procedures you should follow when constructing and using this type of measurement instrument.

Objective 4   Identify motor skills that are best evaluated by performance.

1. For many motor skills the actual performance may be used to evaluate skill achievement. List the basic advantage of using performance as a criterion for skill evaluation.
2. The text offers several illustrations in which skill achievement can be evaluated by performance. Identify an additional motor skill that could be evaluated in this way. Using your example, outline the specific procedures you would follow to evaluate achievement in the skill.

Objective 5   Outline methods that could be used to develop measurement procedures for evaluating motor skill achievement, methods that meet the criteria of reliability, validity, and feasibility for mass testing.

1. The text lists systematic procedures for evaluating skill achievement. Briefly outline these procedures.

ADDITIONAL LEARNING ACTIVITIES

1. Many studies published in research journals deal with attempts to develop sport skill tests. Select three or four articles and review them. Pay close attention to the methods used to establish the reliability and validity associated with these tests and the procedures used to develop the battery. Would you use the tests for your physical education class?
2. Often a published skill test does not fit the specific needs of a teacher, who must either revise the published tests or develop a new one. Select a sport skill and develop a test to evaluate it. You might alter an existing test, develop an alternate scoring system, or develop a new test. Administer the test to a group of students and calculate the reliability for the scores. Is your test feasible for mass use? Do the most highly skilled students achieve the best test scores?
3. Interpretations of test scores can be valid for one group of students but not for another. Select a published sport skill test and obtain criterion validity evidence for the test with a group of students. In order to accomplish this you must select a criterion measure. (You may want to review Chapter 3 before you begin.)
4. Select a skill that cannot be evaluated with an objective skill test and construct a rating scale for it. With a classmate, independently rate the performance of a group of students and then calculate the correlation between your two ratings. How reliable were your ratings? Remember that you can improve reliability by properly training raters.
5. For some skills, performance provides an objective score for evaluating students' achievement. Using a skill such as archery, bowling, or golf, estimate the stability reliability of the performance scores. Remember that for stability reliability, you must have the performance scores of the same group of students for two different days.

BIBLIOGRAPHY

AAHPERD. 1984. *Basketball skills test manual for boys and girls*. Reston, VA.

AAHPERD. 1989. *Tennis skills test manual for boys and girls*. Larry Hensley (Ed.). Reston, VA.

AAHPERD. 1991. *Softball skills test manual for boys and girls*. Roberta Rikli (Ed.). Reston, VA.

Collins, D. R. and P. B Hodges. 2001. *A comprehensive guide to sport skills tests and measurement*. 2nd ed. Lanhan, MD: Scarecrow Press.

Dowd, D. A. 1990. A factor analysis of selected beginning-level racquetball skill tests. Ed.D. dissertation, University of Georgia, Athens, GA.

Ellenbrand, D. A. 1973. Gymnastics skills tests for college women. Master's thesis, Indiana University, Bloomington, IN.

Gaunt, S. 1979. Factor structure of basketball playing ability. P.E.D. dissertation, Indiana University, Bloomington, IN.

Green, K. N., W. B East, and L. D Hensley. 1987. A golf skill test battery for college males and females. *Research Quarterly for Exercise and Sport* 58: 72–76.

Hensley, L., W. East, and J. Stillwell. 1979. A racquetball skills test. *Research Quarterly* 50: 114–118.

Hopkins, D. R. 1977. Factor analysis of selected basketball skill tests. *Research Quarterly* 48: 535–540.

Karpman, M. and L. Isaacs. 1979. An improved racquetball skills test. *Research Quarterly* 50: 526–527.

Lacy, A. C. and D. N. Hastad. 2003. *Measurement and evaluation in physical education and exercise science*. 4th ed. Boston: Benjamin Cummings.

Lam, T. C. and J. J Zhang. 2002. The development and validation of a racquetball skills test battery for young adult beginners. *Measurement in Physical Education and Exercise Science* 6: 95–126.

Miller, D. K. 2002. *Measurement by the physical educator: Why and how*. 4th ed. New York: McGraw-Hill.

Poteat, C. 1983. A skill test battery to measure overall racquetball playing ability. Ed.D. dissertation, University of Georgia, Athens, GA.

Strand, B. N. and R. Wilson. 1993. *Assessing sport skills*. Champaign, IL: Human Kinetics.

Tritschler, K. 2000. *Barrow & McGee's practical measurement and assessment*. 5th ed. Philadelphia: Lippincott Williams & Wilkins.

Zhu, W. 1996. Should total scores from a rating scale be used directly? *Research Quarterly for Exercise and Sport* 67: 363–372.

MEASURING PHYSICAL ACTIVITY

KEY WORDS

exercise
morbidity
mortality
physical activity
reactivity
social desirability

OBJECTIVES

In this chapter, we will present information related to methods of measuring **physical activity**, with particular reference to three stages of the life cycle (childhood-adolescence, adulthood, and older adulthood). There are two sections in this chapter. In the first section, we review the relationship between physical activity and health, and summarize reasons why measuring physical activity is important. This section also describes the most common methods used to measure physical activity, with advantages and limitations. The second section includes information about the physical activity characteristics of three age groups (children and adolescents, young to middle-aged adults, and older adults) and presents reliability and validity evidence for various instruments used with each group.

After reading Chapter 9, you should be able to

1. Recognize and provide examples of many different types of physical activity.
2. Understand the importance of measuring physical activity.
3. Understand some of the unique characteristics of children and adolescents, adults, and older adults that influence their physical activity, and therefore our choice of measurement instrument.
4. Identify the major methods of measuring physical activity.
5. Evaluate example physical activity situations and choose the most appropriate measure of physical activity.

INTRODUCTION

What is physical activity? In perhaps the most commonly cited description, Caspersen (1989) defined physical activity as "any bodily movement produced by skeletal muscle that results in caloric expenditure" (p. 424). Others (e.g., Freedson & Miller 2000) have suggested that physical activity also involves a behavioral component, indicating that physical activity is voluntary. Physical activity therefore has two major components: movement and behavior. Physical activity also encompasses a broad spectrum of behaviors and types of movements (see Figure 9-1). Most physical activity measurement instruments measure only one of these components (movement or behavior), although some measure both. Some do not measure physical activity at all, but instead measure some outcome of physical activity, such as energy expenditure. This does not mean that the terms "physical activity" and "energy expenditure" are synonymous. This means only that for the sake of convenience, the measurement instruments described in this chapter are referred to collectively as methods for measuring physical activity, even though some of them may measure some other, related variable, such as oxygen consumption, heart rate, or energy expenditure. The terms "**exercise**" and "physical activity" also are sometimes used interchangeably, but they represent different constructs. Exercise is any physical activity that is characterized by being planned, involving structure, and having the objective of improving fitness (Pate et al. 1995). As such, all exercise is physical activity, but not all physical activity can be described as exercise.

UNDERSTANDING THE RELATIONSHIP BETWEEN PHYSICAL ACTIVITY AND HEALTH

The study of physical activity increased in importance during the twentieth century, because of its connection to a variety of health outcomes. In the early twentieth century, **morbidity** and **mortality** resulted primarily from infectious diseases such as pneumonia and influenza; today, by contrast, the major causes of morbidity and mortality in modern society are lifestyle-related. Contributory behaviors such as tobacco, alcohol, and drug use, diet, and level of physical activity contribute to health problems such as cardiovascular disease, non-insulin-dependent diabetes mellitus, stroke, cancer, obesity, osteoporosis, and hypertension.

Figure 9-1
Physical activity can take a wide variety of forms.

Although "hypokinetic" diseases, or lifestyle diseases due primarily to inactivity, were recognized earlier in the twentieth century, it is only in recent years that low levels of physical activity or sedentary behavior have been formally recognized at the national and international level as a major contributory factor in many diseases and causes of death. In 2000 David Satcher, then U.S. Surgeon General, unveiled his "Prescription for Health," recommending four lifestyle changes that contribute to a healthier life (Satcher 2000). The first of these four pieces of advice was the recommendation of moderate physical activity on five days per week, for 30 min-

utes a day. The American Heart Association rates the increased risk of coronary heart disease attributable to physical inactivity as comparable with that attributable to high cholesterol, high blood pressure, or cigarette smoking (further information can be found on the American Heart Association website at www.americanheart.org). Additionally, there is an abundance of evidence of the positive association between physical activity and psychological well-being and self-esteem (Seraganian 1993).

The beneficial effects of physical activity on a variety of health outcomes are well accepted, and documented in many well-designed research studies, review texts, and websites associated with organizations such as the National Institutes of Health (www.nih.gov), the Centers for Disease Control and Prevention (www.cdc.gov), and the United States Department of Health and Human Services (www.os.dhhs.gov). In order to understand fully the amount and types of activities we should recommend for the prevention and alleviation of health problems, we must measure physical activity with precision. Studying the relationship between physical activity and health is a complex task. Below are some reasons we still do not fully understand the relationship between physical activity and health:

1. Physical activity is multidimensional and complex in nature. Characteristics such as frequency, intensity, duration, mode, and context may influence acute and chronic responses to physical activity.
2. Our physical activity patterns change throughout our life span. For example, children's physical activity is more short-term and intermittent than such activity for adults; a large part of many adults' physical activity may occur during occupational time; recreational interests and orthopedic problems may influence significantly the physical activity patterns of older adults.
3. The effect of physical activity on health may be different for different health outcomes. For example, physical activity such as yoga may have limited benefit for cardiovascular fitness and obesity, but may have particular benefit for psychological health outcomes and flexibility. Similarly, total physical activity energy expenditure is more relevant to management of body weight, while intensity of physical activity is more relevant to improvement of fitness.

Organizations such as the American College of Sports Medicine and the American Heart Association have published recommendations for the amount and type of physical activity (or exercise) necessary to improve health (or fitness). These recommendations have changed subtly over the years as more is known from research. This ongoing process can only be accomplished if we measure physical activity using the most appropriate (reliable, valid, and practical) instruments available. Questions related to benefits of physical activity and the consequences of inactivity, or sedentary behavior, are complex.

Even within a class of outcomes such as chronic disease prevention or physiological risk factors, the dose-response relationship may be different for, say, coronary heart disease than for non-insulin-dependent diabetes mellitus, or different for high-density lipoprotein levels than for resting blood pressure (Pate 1995). In other words, forms of physical activity that improve one aspect of health (e.g., cardiovascular health) may be different (in terms of frequency, intensity, duration, or mode) from the type of physical activity necessary to improve another aspect of health (e.g., bone health or psychological stress). For example, jogging several miles each week at a high intensity may improve cardiovascular health over the long term, but it will not improve symptoms of osteoarthritis (and may in fact worsen osteoarthritis symptoms).

Physical activity is therefore a multidimensional behavior consisting of psychological and sociological characteristics, which has both short- and long-term physiological and physical outcomes. Unlike structured or planned behaviors such as work, meals, and exercise, physical activity is more likely to be interwoven into the lifestyle, may occur at many time points during the day, in several contexts (home, work, leisure), and may be planned or unplanned, structured or unstructured. This can make recall of physical activity difficult. The outcomes of regular physical activity (or conversely, inactivity) are numerous and vary among health-related (physiological and psychological) and social types of outcome. In any given situation where physical activity is to be measured, we should consider which particular aspects of physical activity we want to measure, and for what purpose. For example, leisure time physical activity questionnaires may not detect large amounts of physical activity in an individual who has a physically demanding occupation, whereas an accelerometer worn all day would do so. Similarly, doubly labeled water is the most accurate method for measuring total energy expenditure over a time period of days, but cannot be used to obtain a profile of patterns of physical activity within the same time period. (These methods are described later in the chapter.)

The Importance of Measuring Physical Activity

The general statement that physical activity has positive health outcomes should be sufficient to justify the importance of measuring physical activity. Physical education and exercise science practitioners who are interested in one of the three major age groups addressed throughout this chapter will have different reasons for wanting to measure physical activity. This may in turn influence how they measure physical activity, or may determine which characteristics of physical activity they decide to measure.

In children and adolescents, it is difficult to determine long-term health outcomes such as mortality, because of the cost of longitudinal research (and because by its nature, this kind of research takes a long time). However, evidence of coronary heart disease risk factors has been found in children as young as seven years of age (Gilliam et al. 1977). Evidence exists that patterns of behavior from childhood and adolescence continue into adulthood. Consequently, physical activity should be encouraged in children and adolescents, in order to increase the likelihood that they will become active adults. Other negative health signs, such as obesity, have risen to epidemic proportions in recent years. The relationship between physical activity participation and psychological indicators such as self-esteem also has been recognized in children and adolescents. In contrast, some forms of physical activity may have negative outcomes in some children and adolescents. There is some research evidence linking competitive sports participation with higher levels of high-risk behaviors, such as smoking, alcohol and drug use, and sexual promiscuity, for example. It is not clear yet whether these behaviors are a consequence of competitive sports participation, or whether they are explained in other ways—for example, by the relationship between personality characteristics of competitiveness and risk-taking.

In older adults, physical activity becomes more important for maintaining functional ability. Levels of strength and flexibility relate to one's ability to perform everyday functions of life, such as bathing, dressing, climbing stairs, and carrying groceries. Physical activity can retard the decline in strength associated with the aging process, thereby delaying the point at which low levels of strength make the older individual functionally dependent. Cardiovascular physical activity habits are perhaps less important in the later years than during young or middle adulthood, as the long-term effect of this type of physical activity has already been seen in premature death. Survivors therefore will require less benefit from physical activity in terms of extended life expectancy and more in terms of independence and general quality of life. Physical activity of an appropriate type may help older adults to maintain balance and motor ability, thereby reducing the risk of falls. Maintenance of bone mass from weight-bearing physical activity above certain thresholds may reduce the risks of bone fractures. Psychosocial outcomes are also important in older adults. Their dependents typically have left home and have families of their own; social interaction through work has ceased following retirement; and, particularly in later years, a spouse may die. Each of these can contribute to an increased risk of depression and loss of self-esteem. Physical activity may alleviate these psychological difficulties, either through direct effects on neurochemicals or through social interaction associated with many physical activity settings.

Types of Instruments for Measuring Physical Activity

Physical activity measurement instruments can be classified according to two important characteristics: amount of participant burden and whether they are subjective or objective. *Participant burden* describes how much effort or inconvenience is

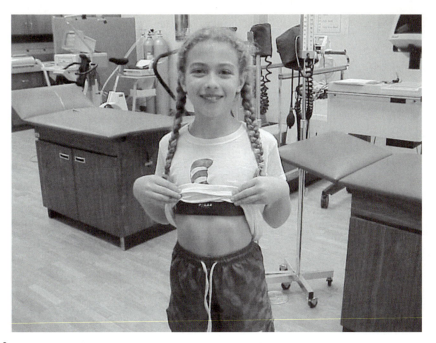

Figure 9-2

A heart rate monitor can be worn unobtrusively.

caused to the person being tested. Heart rate monitors, for example, have a low participant burden because after the heart rate monitor has been put on, it collects data without any extra effort and is fairly unobtrusive (see Figure 9-2). Typically, instruments with a low participant burden have very little effect on the participant's ability to continue with his or her normal daily activities. Physical activity diaries, on the other hand, have a higher participant burden, because they involve ongoing work by the participant to record her behavior throughout the day. Instruments with a high participant burden may interfere with, and change considerably, the participant's typical physical activity behavior.

Classification as either *subjective* or *objective* is based on the procedures leading to allocation of the participant's score(s). Subjective instruments require either the participant or a trained rater to use judgment in determining the score allocated to the participant. This may involve judgment of several characteristics of the physical activity, such as duration, intensity, or mode. Two examples of sub-

jective instruments are direct observation and interview. Direct observation by a rater is used mostly with children, and is conducted in a naturally occurring setting, such as school recess or a physical education lesson. At specific time intervals (e.g., every 15 seconds), the behavior of the participant is recorded using codes to denote the mode of physical activity (e.g., walking, sitting, playing) and intensity. This task requires the rater to be trained in recognizing characteristics of different types of physical activities and subsequently interpreting these by using codes. The interview method requires the subjective interpretation by an interviewer of responses given by a participant, who is asked to recall behaviors over a past time interval. The participant's responses are themselves subjective interpretations of the task she is asked to do.

Data collection using objective instruments does not require interpretation of behaviors by either the participant or a trained rater. These methods involve equipment that objectively registers information relating to movement or some physiological

TABLE 9.1	Major Methods of Measuring Physical Activity, With Characteristics					
Method	Frequency	Intensity	Duration	Mode	Context	Total Physical Activity/ Energy Expenditure
Diary	√	√	√	√	√	x
Questionnaire (self-administered)	√	√	√	√	√	x
Questionnaire (interviewer administered)	√	√	√	√	√	x
Direct observation	√	√	√	√	√	x
HRM	√*	√*	√*	x	x	√*
Accelerometer	√*	√*	√*	x	x	√*
DLW	x	x	x	x	x	√
Pedometer	x	x	x	x	x	√*
Calorimetry	√*	√*	√*	x	x	√

*Denotes that this information is available only from some versions of this type of instrument.

Note: √ = instrument can assess this characteristic of physical activity; x = instrument cannot assess this characteristic of physical activity.

indicator of physical activity. For example, pedometers count the number of steps taken by the participant over a particular time period, and return a total count score.

Following are descriptions of the various methods available for measuring physical activity. Each description begins with the classification of the instrument as requiring either a high or a low participant burden, and as either objective or subjective. The forms of outcome data available from each instrument are then listed. These correspond to the characteristics of physical activity listed earlier—frequency, intensity, duration, mode, and context. Additionally, total physical activity is listed in all cases where this can be obtained. A summary of this information is contained in Table 9.1 for ease of comparison. After presenting the main advantages of each method and also its limitations, detailed description of specific reliability and validity evidence are provided for some of these methods in the later, age-specific sections of the chapter.

Physical Activity Diary
Classification High participant burden, Subjective

Outcome Data Frequency, Intensity, Duration, Mode, Context, Total

Physical activity diaries require the participant to record on an ongoing basis during the period being measured what mode of physical activity he has been engaged in at regular time epochs ranging from one minute to four hours. Data derived from physical activity diaries may be translated into an estimate of energy expenditure. Information recorded about duration, mode, and intensity can be used in conjunction with tables of average energy expenditure associated with a wide variety of common physical activities, such as that compiled by Ainsworth et al. (1993, 2000).

Advantages The physical activity diary involves interpretation of physical activity behavior during the period of the physical activity behavior itself, or shortly afterward. Additionally, time epochs are relatively small. Accuracy of reporting is therefore likely to be better than for recall instruments, particularly those that require the participant to recall over a long time period. Content validity is often better than for some objective measures, because several types of physical activity may be available for selection. All dimensions of physical activity (frequency, duration, etc.) can potentially be measured using the diary method. This method allows measurement of patterns of physical activity as well as total physical activity, enabling differentiation between participants who may be similar in terms of total physical activity (kcals expended), but may achieve this through very different means (e.g., intermittent strength training activity versus sustained steady-state aerobic activity, or structured exercise versus leisure activities). As new modes of physical activity (e.g., in-line skating, skateboarding, Tae-Bo) and sedentary behavior (e.g., use of computers, mobile telephones, electronic games) become relevant, lists can easily be modified, maintaining content validity. Diaries can easily be adapted to meet the needs of measuring a specific sample, although this can also limit generalizability.

Limitations   Unless a participant is particularly motivated, the task of recording data on several occasions over several days may be onerous. This is particularly true for some older adults, who may be restricted by failing eyesight or arthritis in their hands. As with many self-report measures, the possibility of **social desirability** influencing response is an issue that must be considered. Accurate recall (even though it may be over a shorter period in comparison to other types of recall instrument) may be difficult, and interpretation and perception of instructions may be influenced by many cultural factors as well as by reading ability and educational level. This latter point makes physical activity diaries a less viable alternative when measuring physical activity in children. The raw data recorded in a physical activity diary tend to be categorical and ordinal, which may influence the precision of scores and subsequent sensitivity when used to assess changes in physical activity level (for example, as a result of physical activity intervention programs). If lists of activities are provided, they must be population-specific, because preferred mode of physical activity may differ between cultures, between genders, and between ages. Even relatively short time periods within a physical activity diary may be too long for children, who engage in short bursts of physical activity, and some older adults, who may only be able to sustain physical activity for short time periods because of orthopedic limitations and other health problems. **Reactivity** is a potential problem. Because the participant completes the diary during the period being investigated, this may alter her physical activity behavior by, for example, making her more aware of the importance of being active, or by disrupting her typical physical activity routine. In this way, even though recall may be quite accurate (i.e., reliable), it may not represent the participant's typical physical activity behavior (i.e., scores may lack validity as indicators of typical physical activity behavior). Additionally, while the ease of adaptability of questionnaires makes them more versatile, this sometimes poses difficulties in comparing across study populations, or across time, if different versions of a questionnaire, or different questionnaires, have been used.

Recall Questionnaire
Classification   High participant burden, Subjective

Outcome Data   Frequency, Intensity, Duration, Mode, Context, Total

Recall questionnaires may be self-administered, completed by a proxy (e.g., the parent of a child), or administered by a trained interviewer. They have many of the advantages and disadvantages described for physical activity diaries. Similarly, questionnaire data may be used in combination with a physical activity compendium such as that of Ainsworth et al. (1993, 2000) to produce an estimate of physical activity energy expenditure. A wide variety of physical activity recall questionnaires exists, covering many reference periods, such as previous week, previous month, previous year, or "typical" week, month, and so forth.

Advantages   One advantage of the recall questionnaire over the physical activity diary is that reactivity is less of an issue (because the measurement of physical activity does not occur as an ongoing process during the period of time being measured; physical activity occurs before the participant completes the questionnaire). Additionally, if participants can be relied upon to complete the questionnaire correctly without the help of an administrator or interviewer, recall questionnaires enable a relatively inexpensive method of collecting data on a large scale in a relatively short period of time. Presently, questionnaires are perhaps the only practical alternative for large-scale study of physical activity behavior (e.g., in population research, or for surveying activity habits of all the children in a school, or of all employees in a worksite health program).

Limitations   Accuracy of recall is potentially more of an issue for retrospective questionnaires, because participants are asked to recall behaviors over longer periods of time (ranging from previous day to a whole lifetime) than are typical for a physical activity diary. If the questionnaire is interviewer-administered, this makes the measurement process more labor-intensive, requires training, and is more costly.

Motion Sensors
Classification   Low participant burden, Objective

Outcome Data   Frequency, Intensity, Duration, Total

Motion sensors can be divided into two main types, namely, pedometers and accelerometers (which can be classified further depending upon the number of planes measured, e.g., uniaxial, measuring movement in only one plane, or triaxial, measuring movement in three planes). Pedometers are less expensive (generally less than $40), and measure total physical activity (number of steps), whereas accelerometers are more expensive (several hundred dollars), and provide more detailed information regarding intensity and direction of movement. Some accelerometers can be programmed with the participant's age, height, body weight, and gender. From this information, basal metabolic rate can be estimated; then, total and physical activity energy expenditure can be estimated from the accelerometer counts (see Figure 9-3).

Advantages   Most motion sensors are relatively unobtrusive (although some, such as the TriTrac accelerometer, are somewhat heavier and larger than others, such as the Yamax pedometer). This enables them to be used to measure physical activity in naturally occurring settings. They offer a range of costs and complexity, from the Yamax Digi-Walker, costing approximately $20, which measures total steps only and has no memory function, to the Actigraph GT1M, costing under $400, which allows data storage in epochs from one second to one minute. The Actigraph GT1M records activity counts and steps, and can record up to a year of activity data (depending on length of epoch and whether steps and counts are recorded) in its 1 Mb memory. A simple USB connection allows download of data from the GT1M to a computer and also recharging of its lithium ion battery, which can power the GT1M for 14 days without a recharge. Because data are collected using an objective method, they are usually more reliable than subjective methods (such as questionnaires and diaries), particularly subjective methods that are completed by the participant. Most motion sensors are also relatively easy to use. Even accelerometers, which are more sophisticated than pedometers, require fairly straightforward training only. Pedometers in particular are quite inexpensive, and are useful when the predominant mode of physical activity is walking. Additionally, because output is visible, they can be used to motivate participants in walking exercise programs. Most accelerometers enable the storage of data at regular, short epochs (from 1 minute to 15 minutes) over prolonged time periods of several days. The data can subsequently be downloaded to a computer for analysis (see Figure 9-4). This provides information on patterns of time, duration, and intensity dimensions of physical activity, and means that data collection is more convenient for the participant. Because there is no need for the practitioner to monitor or collect the data during the data collection period, the only contact necessary between participant and practitioner is at the beginning and end of the data collection period.

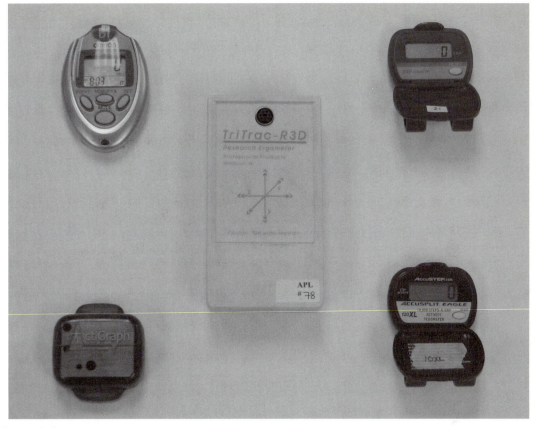

Figure 9-3

Motion sensors come in a variety of shapes, sizes, and functions.

Limitations Despite the sophistication of more technically advanced accelerometers for measuring the time, duration, and intensity of physical activity, they are insensitive to some modes of physical activity. These include static activities such as stationary cycling and weightlifting, and upper body exercise such as swinging weights while walking. They are also not sensitive to changes in energy expenditure due to incline (uphill or downhill). Many models of accelerometers are quite expensive and fragile, and data must be downloaded following the physical activity period (i.e., feedback is not immediately available to the user). This limits their use to small-scale data collection, primarily by researchers. Also, from a purely practical perspective, neither pedometers nor accelerometers are waterproof, and so they must be removed during any water-based physical activity.

Inadequate compliance may adversely affect data collection with motion sensors. During long-term (several days) data collection, participants may forget to put on the motion sensor (although this would be detected in instruments that record day and time data, most pedometers and some accelerometers do not record this information). Placing telephone reminder calls or using other forms of reminder can reduce the likelihood of this. Recently, individual-centered methods have been introduced for replacing missing days of pedometer data when this occurs (Kang et al. 2005), and their effectiveness has been demonstrated in a study of middle school children (Rowe et al. 2004). Some participants, particularly children, may react to the motion sensor either by increasing their level of physical activity (e.g., by jumping up and down)

Figure 9-4
More sophisticated accelerometers such as the Actigraph allow downloading of stored data for further analysis.

or, if the motion sensor is not securely attached, by removing it and shaking it. Pedometers, which have a visual display, may be particularly susceptible to this kind of behavior. However, this phenomenon has not been demonstrated in several recent studies, both with sealed pedometers and unsealed pedometers, over periods of several days (e.g., Rowe et al. 2004; Vincent & Pangrazi 2002a). Similarly, if the reset button is available to children, they may reset the counter, invalidating the results collected at the end of the physical activity period. Some researchers have tried to overcome this problem either by locking the motion sensor in a pouch worn around the waist (see Figure 9-5) or by cutting back the reset button so that it is flush with the surface of the pedometer. In this way, the pedometer can be reset by using the tip of a pen, but is more difficult to reset to zero while being worn, either accidentally or deliberately. The performance of motion sensors can be affected by placement, both in terms of location and in terms of how securely they are attached. If a motion sensor is placed in a waist pouch, it is extremely important that it is sufficiently secure within the pouch (this can be achieved by padding with bubble-wrap) and that the pouch belt is se-

cured tightly enough to prevent extraneous movement. Motion sensors can also be affected by extraneous motion such as vehicle vibrations. Although they offer a relatively inexpensive and reliable alternative, pedometers are generally less sensitive than accelerometers, and measure total physical activity (steps) only. Because pedometers and some less expensive accelerometers (such as the Caltrac) cannot store detailed data related to intensity during discrete time periods, only total physical activity over prolonged time periods can be obtained. An alternative is for the practitioner to monitor and record the output repeatedly over the day (either in person, via telephone, or via e-mail), or the participant may be asked to record the reading at various time points. Again, this means that data collection becomes more inconvenient for the participant. There is evidence also that pedometers are less accurate at slower or faster walking speeds.

Heart Rate Monitors
Classification   Low participant burden, Objective

Outcome Data   Frequency, Intensity, Duration, Total

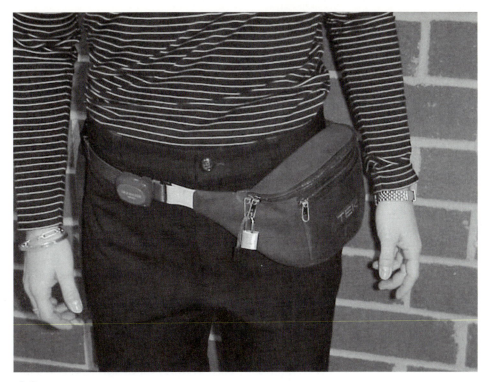

Figure 9-5

A waist pouch allows the use of multiple motion sensors for collecting reliability and validity data—but care must be taken that the motion sensors are held securely within the pouch.

Like motion sensors, heart rate monitors are worn during physical activity, and most models consist of a chest belt transmitter unit and a wrist-worn receiver unit. The simplest models display current heart rate only and are used mainly for immediate feedback on exercise intensity, while more complex models enable the storage and subsequent downloading of heart rate data. Data can be stored from time epochs of a few seconds to a minute, and over several days. Costs of heart rate monitors range from around $50 for the simplest models with no data storage capability to over $500 for those that allow storage and downloading of data to a computer (this includes the cost of the download module, software, and cable).

From stored heart rate data, it is possible to obtain output such as time spent within specific heart rate ranges, or above certain thresholds. If the relationship between the participant's heart rate and oxygen consumption has been determined, this individual calibration can be used to obtain estimates of energy expenditure from heart rate data.

Advantages Heart rate monitors offer a convenient method for measuring a physiological indicator of the amount and intensity of physical work that is being performed. Modern heart rate monitors are sufficiently technologically advanced that small, unobtrusive devices can collect and store heart rate data quite reliably. As with motion sensors, this enables their use for collecting physical activity data in field (i.e., real-life) settings.

The logic of using this method as an indicator of physical activity is based upon the well-established linear relationship between heart rate and $\dot{V}O_2$ in controlled laboratory conditions. This is especially true in the middle of the heart rate range, which is where the average person's heart rate would be during typical physical activity. Where estimates of energy expenditure are required, use of heart rate monitors provides a more objective estimate of this than estimation from subjective measures such as recall questionnaires.

Limitations   Heart rate monitors have few practical limitations. Perhaps the only major practical drawback is their expense, particularly for models with memory and the capacity to download stored data. However, the use of heart rate as an indicator of physical activity is problematic in some situations. The heart rate/$\dot{V}O_2$ relationship is not linear at all levels of physical activity, and is especially weak at lower levels of physical activity (a problem that is particularly relevant for participants, such as older adults, whose physical activity intensity may be quite low). The heart rate/$\dot{V}O_2$ relationship is different between individuals, making tenuous any prediction of energy expenditure for individuals using population-based regression equations. The heart rate response of more fit individuals, for example, is lower for a given physical activity level (making it seem that more fit individuals are less active in comparison to less fit individuals, who are in reality performing at a similar physical activity level). This can be partly overcome by calibrating the heart rate/$\dot{V}O_2$ relationship for an individual in a laboratory setting over a variety of modes of physical activity, or during the individual's typical modes of physical activity, but this adds substantially to the cost of measuring physical activity.

Heart rate is also influenced by factors other than physical activity, such as stress. Additionally, the heart rate/$\dot{V}O_2$ relationship is influenced by several factors—for example, the predominant muscle group being used during physical activity (upper body exercise elicits a higher heart rate than lower body exercise at the same level of oxygen consumption), and environmental factors of temperature and humidity. Following physical activity, heart rate also does not return immediately to baseline, even if the individual is resting. This means that physical activity time may be overestimated from heart rate data.

Doubly Labeled Water

Classification   Low participant burden, Objective

Outcome Data   Total

The doubly labeled water method can be used to measure total energy expenditure over prolonged time periods of several days. Procedures involve ingestion of a small quantity of water containing isotopes of hydrogen and oxygen. Following natural distribution of these isotopes around the body, they are gradually eliminated through urine, sweat, and water vapor, and also, in the case of oxygen isotopes, through exhaled carbon dioxide. By collecting urine, blood, or saliva at regular intervals, elimination levels of the isotopes can be calculated and subsequently used to calculate carbon dioxide production during the intervening period, which then can be used to estimate total energy expenditure.

Advantages   The major advantage of using the doubly labeled water technique is that it is presently the most accurate method (the gold standard) of measuring total energy expenditure. It therefore can serve as a good criterion method for validating the ability of alternative methods to measure total physical activity or energy expenditure. It is unobtrusive, therefore reducing the potential for reactivity to the measurement process. Data collection can be made noninvasively, via urine collection, instead of through blood drawing.

Limitations   Perhaps the major disadvantage of this method is that it is very expensive. The cost of a single administration of DLW is several hundred dollars, although the price may fluctuate in response to market supply and demand. Analysis of a set of urine samples following administration to a single individual costs approximately $100. Prices vary between laboratories, and cost of analysis is recurring (i.e., costs are incurred every time energy expenditure is measured). Results may take several days or weeks, so lack of immediate feedback to either the participant or the practitioner is a problem. Another, initially more costly, alternative is to purchase a spectrometer to enable analysis onsite. Use of doubly labeled water is restricted primarily to institutionally funded research projects. Although it is probably the best method for measuring total energy expenditure, it does not provide information on any other characteristics of physical activity (frequency, intensity, duration, mode, context).

Direct Observation
Classification   Low participant burden, Subjective

Outcome Data   Frequency, Intensity, Duration, Mode, Context, Total

For this method, trained raters conduct direct observation on participants in restricted contexts, such as a school playground, a physical education lesson, or the workplace. Systematic coding methods are used with a prepared form to record at brief, regular intervals (usually of a few seconds) the mode of behavior and some expression of intensity of energy expenditure. By using activity compendia, these records can be converted to estimates of energy expenditure.

Advantages   Probably the biggest advantage of direct observation is that it provides more detailed information than perhaps any other method on all aspects of physical activity. Trained observers are able to evaluate physical activity more objectively than participants themselves (especially in the case of children). Because the physical activity is rated as it occurs, this provides more accurate information than retrospective measures, particularly regarding duration. It is particularly useful for research into the psychosocial characteristics of physical activity, as a trained observer may detect social cues or contexts of physical activity of which the participant is unaware. In physical education contexts, for example, the Systematic Observation of Fitness Instruction Time (SOFIT; McKenzie, Sallis & Nader 1991) can be used to record physical activity behavior concurrently with data regarding lesson context and teacher behaviors.

Limitations   Although information obtained from direct observation is more complete than perhaps any other, the subjective nature of the rating makes accurate measurement highly dependent on the ability and training of the rater. Even for capable raters, the intensive task of rating may be subject to decay as the rater becomes fatigued over time. Direct observation is costly, not only in terms of initial outlay (for training). Costs are incurred during every data collection period. This is unlike other expensive methods such as heart rate monitoring and accelerometers that involve primarily only initial outlay for equipment, followed by relatively cost-effective downloading of data. It is less expensive than the doubly labeled water method, however. Direct observation is more intrusive than most other methods and may cause reactivity, especially in children. It is practical only for some contexts, because the rater must be present to observe the physical activity, which is not possible in the daily lives of most participants. The primary use of this procedure is restricted to individuals in institutional settings, such as children in school or older adults in care facilities or retirement communities. Only relatively short periods of time can be monitored, because of rater fatigue, and because the institutional contexts in which direct observation are used (e.g., school recess and physical education lessons) consist of short periods of time. The data collected during direct observation may consequently be unrepresentative of the participant's physical activity habits in other contexts during a typical day or week. Reliability between and within raters is probably the biggest measurement concern with this method. The data gathered using this method are ordinal, and so may not be sufficiently sensitive to detect changes in behavior. Because the data gathered are only representative to behavior in restricted contexts, the validity of generalizing to behavior outside of these settings is questionable.

Indirect Calorimetry
Classification   Low participant burden, Objective

Outcome Data   Frequency, Intensity, Duration, Total

Indirect calorimetry involves the measurement of gas exchange (oxygen consumption and carbon dioxide production) during a variety of controlled physical activities. This can be accomplished via open-circuit spirometry using relatively small gas analysis equipment. Although portable equipment has become available in recent years, enabling gas analysis in field settings, calorimetry procedures are still usually conducted in laboratory settings. By measuring energy expenditure during specified types of physical activity (e.g., treadmill walking at specific speeds and grades, arm ergometry exercise at specified speeds and resistance), average energy costs of these activities can be obtained.

Advantages   The main advantage of calorimetry is that it provides extremely accurate estimates of energy expenditure associated with specific modes and intensities of exercise. It is therefore useful for compiling compendia of activities and their energy costs. These estimates of energy expenditure can be used to convert ordinal-level questionnaire and diary data into estimates of energy expenditure (although this only helps with interpretation of the data, and does not solve the problems associated with the ordinal nature of the original questionnaire and diary data).

Limitations   Expense is a major limitation of indirect calorimetry. Technical expertise is needed to use this type of equipment correctly. Because these methods are laboratory-based, the modes of physical activities that can be measured are limited. Even though energy cost of activities such as walking, running, and cycling can be reproduced in the laboratory, treadmill and stationary cycle exercise differ from real-life overground walking, running, and cycling. Most recreational sport and leisure activities cannot be reproduced in the laboratory. There is some promise for using portable equipment for calibrating energy expenditure in the field, although the expense and intrusiveness of wearing this equipment makes it unsuitable for long-term measurement of habitual physical activity in real-life settings, or for use in large populations.

MEASURING PHYSICAL ACTIVITY ACROSS THE LIFE SPAN

The nature of physical activity behavior changes across the life span. In order to measure physical activity in one of the three major stages of the life span (childhood to adolescence, young to middle-

aged adulthood, and older adulthood), we should understand the special characteristics of each stage and consider research evidence specific to each age range. In this section, we present some of the most important evidence from recent studies. Because instrumentation in physical activity has changed so much over the past ten years (new models of motion sensors, new questionnaires, etc.), most of the research is from the past ten years. Some earlier research is included if it was well-conducted and the investigated instruments are still in common use today.

The following types of reliability evidence are presented in the remaining tables in this chapter: (a) test-retest reliability; (b) internal consistency (including intertrial reliability, and interday reliability where days are consecutive, with no long-term interval in between days); (c) interrater objectivity; and (d) interinstrument reliability. Interinstrument reliability includes both intermodel reliability (e.g., consistency between two of the same brand and model of pedometer, or a long form and short form of the same questionnaire) and interinstrument reliability (consistency between two models of the same instrument, e.g., two different brands of pedometer or two different questionnaires). Only one reliability study investigated inter- or intrarater objectivity, in any age group.

Validity evidence in the remaining tables includes the following types of evidence: (a) convergent validity evidence (between two different methods of measurement, e.g., questionnaire vs. pedometer); (b) criterion-related validity evidence (where one of the instruments under investigation can reasonably be labeled as a gold standard or reference measure in comparison to the others); (c) known groups evidence; and (d) construct-related validity evidence. Examples of the last two types of evidence were found only for the older-adult age group.

Measuring Physical Activity in Children and Adolescents

Children and adolescents represent a wide variety of cognitive and physical abilities, and of behaviors. Adolescents are more like young adults than young children, especially regarding their ability to read and understand questionnaires, and their attention span. Younger children are very different in this respect. The activity behavior of children is also very different from that of adults. They tend to be active very intermittently, and for much shorter periods of time than adults. Bailey et al. (1995) studied children's activity intensity via direct observation, recording activity level every 3 seconds. The median duration of the children's activity periods was extremely low, for all intensities: low intensity (median duration = 6 seconds), moderate (median duration = 6 seconds), and high (median duration = 3 seconds). Ninety-five percent of vigorous-intensity bouts lasted less than 15 seconds, and almost none (0.1%) of the vigorous-intensity bouts were over 60 seconds. Although rest periods (between activity bouts) were longer than activity periods, almost all rest periods were also relatively short (less than 5 minutes). This has practical implications for measuring physical activity in children. If it is desired to record intensity, data recording periods must occur very frequently (every 5 seconds or so) in order to detect patterns of physical activity within the typical day. In terms of data interpretation, this also means that physical activity recommendations for children should focus on the total amount of physical activity, rather than on periods of continuous physical activity, as with typical adult recommendations.

Welk, Corbin, and Dale (2000) highlighted the danger of using adult-targeted physical activity recommendations with children. They summarized studies in which activity was measured via heart rate monitors and direct observation. Based upon a criterion of sustained (10 or more continuous minutes) aerobic activity, only between 8% and 39% of the children in these studies were classified as physically active. This criterion ignores the intermittent nature of children's physical activity. There should be a move toward recommending an accumulation of physical activity across the day, similar to recent recommendations of the Centers for Disease Control and the American College of Sports Medicine for improvement of health in adults (Pate et al. 1995). When interpreted in terms of total volume of physical activity of at least mod-

erate intensity, the data in the studies reviewed by Welk, Corbin, and Dale indicated that most children accumulate sufficient amounts of moderate-intensity activity.

Questionnaire methods pose other problems when used with children. Children tend to overestimate physical activity when self-report instruments are used, rather than objective measures (McMurray et al. 1998; Pate, Long & Heath, 1994). This may be due to inaccurate estimation of time, or due to the intermittent nature of their activity (e.g., during a self-reported 20-minute bout of activity, a child may be inactive for several periods of time within the 20 minutes).

Because of recall, cognitive, and attention span issues, questionnaires used as the sole measure of physical activity in children should be treated with caution. The most promising are 24-hour (previous day) recall instruments, such as the Previous Day Physical Activity Recall, commonly called the PD-PAR. These types of instruments involve a list of activities, they are quite time-consuming, and repeated administrations are necessary in order to obtain multiday data. Ideally, they should not be administered to large groups of children. In our own research, we have had better success with a trained person leading small groups or individuals through the questionnaire (see Figure 9-6). Computerized surveillance systems are now available, including the ACTIVITYGRAM®, the physical activity portion of the FITNESSGRAM® program (Cooper Institute for Aerobics Research 1999).

Reliability and Validity Evidence— Children and Adolescents

Major details of validity and reliability studies in this age group are presented in Tables 9.2 and 9.3. Most of the research in children has focused on the use of motion sensors (pedometers and accelerometers) and questionnaires. Both are fairly convenient and, in the case of questionnaires and pedometers, low-cost alternatives for use with children. Several studies have investigated the number of days of pedometer data necessary to reliably represent children's physical activity. Generally, from 3 to 4 days of data are needed for reliability > .70,

Figure 9-6
Many of the more detailed questionnaires, such as the PD-PAR, should be administered to children individually or in small groups.

and 5 to 6 days are needed to produce reliability > .80. Similar results have been found for accelerometers, but these types of instruments are usually restricted to research settings because of their excessive cost. Although questionnaires have been shown to be reliable in some child populations, other studies have shown low reliability (e.g., the Activitygram demonstrated low reliability in 8- to 9-year-old girls in a study by Treuth et al. 2003). Questionnaires have correlated lowly with objective measures of physical activity in several studies of children. We found that a 6-day pedometer count was effectively uncorrelated with the Leisure Time Exercise Questionnaire in middle school children, for example. Despite their seeming low criterion and convergent validity as measures of total activity, or minutes of moderate-intensity activity, questionnaires and proxy reports may have utility for providing information on the predominant mode and context of physical activity in children and adolescents.

Measuring Physical Activity in Young to Middle-Aged Adults

Perhaps the most important characteristic distinguishing adults from children, adolescents, and older adults is the amount of time they spend at work each week. Particularly if their occupation is physically demanding, it is important that any measure of physical activity used with working adults be able to detect occupational physical activity. In the case of questionnaires, some questions must address physical activity during work hours. For any objective measure of physical activity to be content relevant, some data must be collected during work hours. In the case of younger adults, a large part of the week will be spent in raising children, and so any physical activity associated with childrearing should be detectable by instruments used with this population. Because this age group has many responsibilities associated with work, raising a family, and home maintenance, less intrusive,

TABLE 9.2	Children — Reliability Evidence				
Authors	**Year**	**Sample**	**Instruments**	**Evidence**	**Results**
Rowe et al.	2004	$N = 299$; grades 5–8	Yamax pedometer	IC	$R = .79$ (6 days); significant difference among days; no evidence of reactivity over 6 days
Barfield et al.	2004	$N = 71$; grades 3–5	Yamax pedometer	II	$R = .92–.98$ (2 Yamax pedometers worn concurrently)
Telford et al.	2004	$N = 169$ ($n = 58$, 5–6 years; $n = 11$, 10–12 years); also one parent per child ($N = 169$)	Children's Leisure Activities Study Survey (CLASS)	TR	$R = .24–.57$ (10–12 years, self-report); $R = .49–.87$ (parents proxy report)
Treuth et al.	2003	$N = 68$; girls 8–9 years	GEMS Activity Questionnaire (GAQ), 3-day computerized Activitygram, Yamax pedometer, MTI accelerometer	IC	$R = .37$ (MTI, 4 days); $R = .08$ (Yamax, 4 days), $R = .24$ (Activitygram, 3 days), $r = .80$ (GAQ yesterday and usual day score)
Vincent & Pangrazi	2002a	$N = 48$, grades 2, 4, and 6	Yamax pedometer (sealed)	IC	No significant differences among 8 weekdays of data, indicating no reactivity. Reliability data indicated 3–4 days necessary for $R \geq .70$, 5 days necessary for $R \geq .80$
Vincent & Pangrazi	2002b	$N = 711$; 6–12 years	Yamax pedometer	IC	$R = .70$ (3 days)

(Continued)

TABLE 9.2	Children — Reliability Evidence *(Continued)*				
Authors	**Year**	**Sample**	**Instruments**	**Evidence**	**Results**
Booth et al.	2001	$N = 226$ ($n = 121$, year 8; $n = 105$, year 10)	World Health Organization health questionnaire physical activity questions	TR	Percent agreement (sufficiently active/ insufficiently active) $= 67\%-85\%$ (2-week interval)
Weston et al.	1997	$N = 119$, grades 7–12	Previous Day Physical Activity Recall	TR IR	$r = .98$ (1-hour interval); $r = .99$ (2 raters)
Ching & Dietz	1995	$N = 69$; preadolescent girls	Recall questionnaire	TR	$R = .81-.84$ (TV/video games); $R < .50$ (other activities); (1-week interval)
Janz et al.	1995	$N = 30$; 7–15 years	CSA accelerometer	IC	$R > .80$ (6 days)

Key: TR = test-retest reliability; IC = internal consistency reliability (including intertrial and interday reliability); IR = interrater reliability; II = interinstrument reliability

TABLE 9.3	Children — Validity Evidence				
Authors	**Year**	**Sample**	**Instruments**	**Evidence**	**Results**
Bender et al.	2005	$N = 65$; 5–12 years, plus one parent per child	Parent proxy 7-day physical activity record (P7-DPAR), CSA accelerometer	CRV	$r = .00-.38$ (P7-DPAR, CSA, various time points)
Treuth et al.	2004	$N = 74$; grade 8 girls	Actigraph accelerometer, Cosmed K4b2 portable indirect calorimeter	CRV	$R^2 = .84$, $SEE = 1.36$ METs (Actigraph counts, Cosmed O_2); 30-second Actigraph count cutoffs developed for moderate (1500 cts/30 secs) and vigorous (> 2600 cts/30 secs) intensity activity

TABLE 9.3	Children — Validity Evidence *(Continued)*				
Authors	**Year**	**Sample**	**Instruments**	**Evidence**	**Results**
Rowe et al.	2004	$N = 299$; grades 5–8	Yamax pedometer and Leisure Time Exercise Questionnaire	CV	$r = .03–.08$ (weekly steps, LTEQ total score)
Cardon & De Bourdeaudhuij	2004	$N = 92$; 6–12 years	Yamax pedometer, activity diary (with parental assistance)	CV	$r = .39$ (steps, self-reported MVPA minutes)
Kelly et al.	2004	$N = 78$; 3–4 years	CSA accelerometer, Actiwatch accelerometer, direct observation	CV CRV	$r = .55$ (CSA, Actiwatch); $r = .72$ (CSA, direct observation); $r = .16$ (Actiwatch, direct observation)
Telford et al.	2004	$N = 169$; ($n = 58$, 5–6 years; $n = 11$, 10–12 years)	Children's Leisure Activities Study Survey (CLASS), MTI accelerometer	CRV	$r = -.06–.24$ (MTI, CLASS, various subscales)
Rowlands et al.	2004	$N = 19$; boys (9.5 ± 0.8 years)	RT3 accelerometer, TriTrac accelerometers, indirect calorimeter	CV CRV	RT3 counts were significantly higher than TriTrac counts across most activities (treadmill walking and running, plus lifestyle activities); $r = .87$ (RT3 counts, VO_2); $r = .87$ (TriTrac counts, VO_2)
Scruggs et al.	2003	$N = 257$; grades 1–4	Yamax pedometer, Computerized System for Observing Fitness Instruction Time (C-SOFIT)	CRV	$r = .82–.89$ (Yamax, C-SOFIT); criterion of 33.3% P.E. time spent in MVPA was equivalent to step rate of 61–63 steps/min (grades 1–2), or 58–61 steps/min (grades 3–4)

(Continued)

TABLE 9.3	Children — Validity Evidence *(Continued)*				

Authors	Year	Sample	Instruments	Evidence	Results
Slinde et al.	2003	$N = 35$; 15-year-old adolescents	Minnesota Leisure Time Physical Activity Questionnaire, doubly labeled water	CRV	$r = .49$ (MLTPAQ kcal, DLW kcal); $r = .73$ when inactivity questions were added to the MLTPAQ; MLTPAQ underestimated DLW kcal in 34 of 35 participants
Pate et al.	2003	$N = 70$; girls in grades 8 and 9	3-Day Physical Activity Recall, CSA accelerometer	CRV	$R = .35–.51$ (3-DPAR, CSA) for METs, MVPA, and VPA over 7 days of monitoring
Scruggs et al.	2003	$N = 369$; validation $n = 246$; cross-validation $n = 123$; grades 1 and 2	Yamax pedometer, Computerized System for Observing Fitness Instruction Time (C-SOFIT)	CRV	$r = .74–.86$ (Yamax, C-SOFIT); criterion of 33.3% P.E. time spent in MVPA was equivalent to step rate of 60–63 steps/min
Treuth et al.	2003	$N = 68$; girls 8–9 years	GEMS Activity Questionnaire (GAQ), 3-day computerized Activitygram, Yamax pedometer, MTI accelerometer	CV	$r = .47$ (MTI, Yamax 4-day); $r = .37$ (MTI, Activitygram 3-day); $r = .27–.29$ (MTI, GAQ yesterday and usual day scores); MTI was not significantly correlated with any single-day score from GAQ or Activitygram
O'Connor et al.	2001	$N = 56$; 7.5 ± 0.8 years	Physical activity questionnaire (PAQ), parent-reported 3-day diary (PRD), TriTrac accelerometer, doubly labeled water (DLW)	CV CRV	$r = .42–.75$ (TriTrac, PRD, various time frames); DLW was not significantly correlated with any other measure

TABLE 9.3		**Children — Validity Evidence** *(Continued)*			
Authors	**Year**	**Sample**	**Instruments**	**Evidence**	**Results**
Mahar et al.	2001	$N = 60$; girls 12–14 years	RT3 accelerometer, indirect calorimetry	CRV	$R^2 = .50–.68$ (RT3, kcal); mean RT3 kcal not significantly different from calorimeter during walking, but significantly overestimated kcal during brisk walking and jogging
Ekelund et al.	2001	$N = 127$; 14.8 ± 0.30 years	Heart rate monitor, indirect calorimeter	CRV	Fitness significantly moderated the HR/$\dot{V}O_2$ relationship during an incremental treadmill test, indicating that absolute heart rates should not be used to assess exercise intensity in adolescents
Eston et al.	1998	$N = 30$; 8–10 years	CSA and TriTrac accelerometers, Yamax pedometer, indirect calorimetry	CRV	$r = .91$ (Tritrac, $\dot{V}O_2$); $r = .78$ (CSA, $\dot{V}O_2$); $r = .81$ (Digi-Walker, $\dot{V}O_2$)
Coleman et al.	1997	$N = 35$; obese children 8–12 years	TriTrac accelerometer, heart rate monitor, questionnaire	CRV	$r = .71$ (Tritrac, HRM); $r = .38$ (Tritrac, questionnaire); $r = .36$ (HRM/ questionnaire)

(Continued)

TABLE 9.3	Children — Validity Evidence *(Continued)*				
Authors	**Year**	**Sample**	**Instruments**	**Evidence**	**Results**
Kowalski, Crocker & Kowalski	1997	$N = 85$; grades 8–12 (16.25 ± 1.51 years)	Physical Activity Questionnaire for Adolescents (PAQ-A); 7-Day Physical Activity Recall (7-DPAR), Leisure Time Exercise Questionnaire (LTEQ), Caltrac accelerometer	CRV	$r = .59$ (PAQ-A, 7-DPAR); $r = .57$ (PAQ-A, LTEQ); $r = .33$ (PAQ-A, Caltrac)
Kowalski, Crocker & Faulkner	1997	$N = 186$; Study 1 $n = 89$, 11.06 ± 1.46 years; Study 2 $n = 97$ (11.30 ± 1.39 years)	Physical Activity Questionnaire for Older Children (PAQ-C); single-item activity self-rating (S-R); 8-item teacher rating (T-R), 7-Day Physical Activity Rating (7-DPAR), Leisure Time Exercise Questionnaire (LTEQ), Caltrac accelerometer	CRV	Study 1: $r = .63$ (PAQ-C, S-R); $r = .45$ (PAQ-C, T-R). Study 2: $r = .57$ (PAQ-C, S-R); $r = .41$ (PAQ-C, LTEQ); $r = .46$ (PAQ-C, 7-DPAR); $r = .39$ (PAQ-C, Caltrac)
Welk & Corbin	1995	$N = 35$; 9–11 years	TriTrac and Caltrac accelerometers, heart rate monitor	CV	$r = .83–.91$ (Tritrac, Caltrac); $r = .44–.70$ (Tritrac, HRM); $r = .47–.57$ (Caltrac, HRM)
Bray et al.	1994	$N = 40$; girls 10–16 years	Caltrac, direct calorimetry	CRV	$r = .80–.85$ (Caltrac, kcal)

Key: CRV = criterion-related validity; CV = convergent validity

more time-efficient methods are probably most practical. Walking is the most common physical activity for adults, as described in the Surgeon General's Report on Physical Activity and Health (United States Department of Health and Human Services 1996). Interestingly, five of the ten most commonly reported physical activities in the Surgeon General's Report (gardening/yard work, stretching, bicycling, weight lifting, and swimming) are not easily measured by motion sensors.

Reliability and Validity Evidence— Young to Middle-Aged Adults

Research evidence for this age group is presented in Tables 9.4 and 9.5. In the past few years, there has been a notable increase in research studies investigating pedometers, reflecting the increased popularity of pedometers for physical activity promotion in adults. Intermodel reliability (consistency between two pedometers of the same brand and model) is generally high for most brands and models of pedometers. For example, Schneider et al. (2003) reported intermodel reliabilities above R = .80 for ten different models, with three models being consistently above the R = .99 level. However, different models of pedometers may disagree quite markedly with each other, especially over extended periods of time spent in lifestyle physical activities. Mean differences of up to several thou-

sand steps were reported by Schneider et al. (2004) between the Yamax SW-200 and 11 other brands and models of pedometers, over a 24-hour period. This study highlights the fact that pedometer scores can be influenced by the sensitivity (threshold amount of movement needed to register one step) and other functions specific to various models. Omron pedometers, for instance, do not count steps unless at least ten steps are registered continuously. This means that incidental, isolated steps associated with standing activities like washing dishes, making beds, and so forth may not register.

Many questionnaires have demonstrated good test-retest and interinstrument reliability in adults, although reliability seems to decrease as the between-administration interval increases. Test-retest reliability was below R = .70 in a study that used a one-year interval (Baranowski et al. 1999),

TABLE 9.4	**Adults—Reliability Evidence**				
Authors	**Year**	**Sample**	**Instruments**	**Evidence**	**Results**
Tudor-Locke et al.	2005	N = 90; (33 men, 49.1 ± 16.2 years; 57 women, 44.8 ± 16.9 years)	Yamax pedometer	IC	Minimum of 3 days needed to obtain R > .80
Schneider et al.	2004	N = 20; (10 men, 39.5 ± 16.6 years; 10 women, 43.3 ± 16.6 years)	12 pedometer models: Accusplit, Freestyle, Colorado on the Move, Kenz, New Lifestyles, Omron, Oregon Scientific, Sportline (2 models), Walk4Life, Yamax (3 models)	II	Over 24-hour period, mean differences ranged from –2,445 (Freestyle) to 3,636 steps (Oregon Scientific), compared to Yamax SW-200; models not significantly different from the Yamax SW-200 were Kenz, New Lifestyles, Yamax SW-701, and Sportline

(Continued)

TABLE 9.4		Adults—Reliability Evidence *(Continued)*			
Authors	**Year**	**Sample**	**Instruments**	**Evidence**	**Results**
Schneider et al.	2003	$N = 20$; (10 men, 34.7 ± 12.6 years; 10 women, 43.1 ± 19.9 years)	10 pedometer models (Freestyle, Kenz, New Lifestyles, Omron, Oregon Scientific, Sportline (2 models), Walk4Life, Yamax (2 models)	II	$R > .80$ between models for all except Sportline; Kenz, Omron, and Yamax Digi-Walker were all $R > .99$
Craig et al.	2003	$N = 3,089$; subsamples from 12 countries ($n = 28$ to $n = 257$)	International Physical Activity Questionnaire (IPAQ), long and short forms, interview and self-administered methods, previous week and typical week reference periods	TR II	$r = .46$–$.96$ (7–10 day interval, different countries); pooled $r = .67$ (short vs. long form, all countries)
Le Masurier & Tudor-Locke	2003	$N = 50$; Study 1 $n = 30$ (13 men 30.0 ± 6.1 years, 17 women 26.4 ± 3.6 years); Study 2 $n = 10$ (12 men 32.8 ± 11.5 years, 8 women 30.4 ± 10.4 years)	Yamax pedometer, CSA accelerometer	II	Yamax detected significantly fewer steps than CSA at treadmill speed of 2.0 mph; no significant differences between Yamax and CSA at 2.5, 3.0, 3.5, and 4.0 mph
Hayden-Wade et al.	2003	$N = 74$; 18–67 years	7-Day Physical Activity Recall (7D-PAR) phone and in-person interview methods	II	$r = .94$–$.97$ (7D-PAR phone administration, 7D-PAR in person administration)
Chasan-Taber et al.	2002	$N = 131$; 39–65 years	Historical Leisure Activity Questionnaire (HLAQ)	TR	$R = .73$–$.86$ (HLAQ total and various subscale scores, 1-year interval)

TABLE 9.4	Adults—Reliability Evidence *(Continued)*				
Authors	**Year**	**Sample**	**Instruments**	**Evidence**	**Results**
Nichols et al.	2000	$N = 20$ of 60 participants; mean age = 23.0 ± 2.9 (men) and 22.9 ± 2.9 years (women)	CSA accelerometer	II	$R = .55–.91$; no significant mean differences
Lowther et al.	1999	$N = 34$; mean age = 33 years	Stanford Seven Day Physical Activity Recall (adapted version)	TR	$R = .998$ (3-day interval); no significant difference between test and retest means
Baranowski et al.	1999	$N = 165$; elementary school teachers	Seven-day recall questionnaire	TR	$R = .66–.69$ (1-year interval)
Nichols et al.	1999	$N = 60$; mean age = 23.8 ± 2.9 years	TriTrac accelerometer	II TR	$R = .73–.87$ (two TriTracs worn simultaneously); $R = .87–.92$ (2-week interval)
Friedenrich et al.	1998	$N = 113$; women (mean age = 61.2 ± 6.4 years)	Lifetime Total Physical Activity Questionnaire	TR	Over 7-week interval: $r = .23$ to $.94$ (Occupational); $r = .22$ to $.83$ (Household); $r = .15$ to $.54$ (Exercise and Sport); $r = .16$ to $.88$ (Total); no significant mean differences
Bassett et al.	1996	$N = 20$; 18–65 years (mean age = 32.6 years)	5 pedometer models (Freestyle, Eddie Bauer, LL Bean, Accusplit, Yamax)	II	Yamax was most consistent (2 pedometers worn simultaneously); mean difference (left vs. right) was .01% (Yamax), 3%–17% (other models)

(Continued)

TABLE 9.4		Adults—Reliability Evidence *(Continued)*			
Authors	**Year**	**Sample**	**Instruments**	**Evidence**	**Results**
Jacobs et al.	1993	$N = 28$ men (mean age = 37.2 ± 10.0 years) and 50 women (mean age = 37.4 ± 9.7 years)	Ten commonly used questionnaires (various subscales)	TR	For 1-month interval: Minnesota Leisure Time Questionnaire ($R = .88–.92$); CARDIA Physical Activity History ($R = .88–.91$); the Baecke Physical Activity Questionnaire ($R = .86–.93$); Minnesota Heart Health Program Questionnaire Work Index score ($.86–.91$); Stanford Seven Day Physical Activity Recall Questionnaire (8 of 9 scales $R < .60$); Godin Leisure Time Index (4 of 5 scales $R < .70$)
Gretebeck & Montoye	1992	$N = 30$; men 24–67 years (mean age = 37 years)	Caltrac accelerometer, Schritte pedometer, HRM	IC	$R = .90$ for 1 day (Caltrac, HRM) or 3 days (Schritte); $R = .95$ for 2 to 5 days.

Key: TR = test-retest reliability; IC = internal consistency reliability (including intertrial and interday reliability); IR = interrater reliability; II = interinstrument reliability

for example. Additionally, reliability is lower for instruments that measure longer time periods. One example is the Lifetime Total Physical Activity Questionnaire, which demonstrated test-retest reliability (over a seven-day interval) as low as $r = .16$ (Friedenrich, Courneya & Bryant 1998).

Validity data for objective instruments are generally good. Accelerometers tend to correlate highly with measured $\dot{V}O_2$ and energy expenditure measured using doubly labeled water. However, absolute validity (mean agreement between kilocalorie estimates from accelerometers and indirect

TABLE 9.5	Adults—Validity Evidence				
Authors	**Year**	**Sample**	**Instruments**	**Evidence**	**Results**
King et al.	2004	$N = 21$ (10 men, 25.2 ± 4.5 years; 11 women, 24.7 ± 5.4 years)	5 physical activity monitors (CSA, TriTrac R3d, RT3, SenseWear armband, Bio-Trainer pro), indirect calorimeter	CV CRV	No significant difference among mean kcal estimated via the 5 monitors; generally, all monitors overestimated kcal compared to indirect calorimetry, except CSA, which underestimated kcal at slowest and fastest treadmill speeds
Rowlands et al.	2004	$N = 15$ men (20.7 ± 1.4 years)	RT3 accelerometer, indirect calorimeter	CRV	$r = .85$ (RT3 counts, $\dot{V}O_2$)
Le Masurier et al.	2003	$N = 59$ women (20–65 years)	Yamax pedometer, CSA accelerometer	CV	Women achieving 10,000+ steps per day were not more likely to accumulate 30+ minutes of CSA-determined moderate PA than women with < 10,000 steps (91% vs. 75%). For continuous bouts of moderate PA, the 10,000+ step group were more likely to achieve 30+ minutes of moderate PA (77% vs. 29% for 5-min bouts, 51% vs. 17% for 10-min bouts)

(Continued)

TABLE 9.5		**Adults—Validity Evidence (*Continued*)**			
Authors	**Year**	**Sample**	**Instruments**	**Evidence**	**Results**
Schneider et al.	2003	$N = 20$; 10 men (34.7 ± 12.6 years), 10 women (43.1 ± 19.9 years)	10 pedometer models: Freestyle, Kenz, New Lifestyles, Omron, Oregon Scientific, Sportline (2 models), Walk4Life, Yamax (2 models), rater-counted steps	CRV	Kenz, New Lifestyles, and Yamax Digi-Walker were most accurate (± 3% of rater-counted steps 95% of the time); Sportline and Omron were least accurate (± 37% of rater-counted steps 95% of the time).
Maiolo et al.	2003	$N = 9$; male soccer players (18.3 ± 2.2 years)	Cosmed K4 RQ portable calorimeter, mass spectrometer	CV	During an incremental maximal treadmill test, mean Cosmed $\dot{V}O_2$ was not significantly different from $\dot{V}O_2$ measured using the mass spectrometer.
Craig et al.	2003	$N = 3,089$; subsamples from 12 countries ($n = 28$ to $n = 257$)	International Physical Activity Questionnaire (IPAQ; long and short forms, interview and self-administered methods, previous week and typical week reference periods), CSA accelerometer	CRV	$r = .30–.33$ (IPAQ, CSA)

calorimetry) is not always good. The TriTrac accelerometer, for example, overestimated kilocalories compared to indirect calorimetry in a young sample (Nichols et al. 1999). Some models of pedometers are highly accurate at measuring steps during walking and running. The Yamax brand has stood out consistently over several studies in this regard. However, only limited published evidence is available on the absolute accuracy of pedometers during lifestyle activities such as household

TABLE 9.5	Adults—Validity Evidence *(Continued)*				
Authors	**Year**	**Sample**	**Instruments**	**Evidence**	**Results**
Washburn et al.	2003	$N = 46$; 17 men (23.9 ± 3.8 years), 29 women (23.3 ± 4.6 years)	7-Day Physical Activity recall (7D-PAR) doubly labeled water	CRV	No significant mean difference between kcal from 7D-PAR and DLW, for total and physical activity, for whole sample and gender subgroups; $R^2 = .86$ for predicting 7D-PAR total kcal from DLW PAEE, gender, BMI, $\dot{V}O_2$ max
Le Masurier & Tudor-Locke	2003	$N = 50$; Study 1 $n = 30$ (13 men 30.0 ± 6.1 years, 17 women 26.4 ± 3.6 years); Study 2 $n = 10$ (12 men 32.8 ± 11.5 years, 8 women 30.4 ± 10.4 years)	Yamax pedometer, CSA accelerometer, rater-counted steps	CRV	Yamax detected significantly fewer steps than counted steps at 2.0 mph, but no significant differences at other speeds between 2.5 mph and 4.0 mph. CSA steps were not significantly different from counted steps at any speed. During a 20.4 mile car ride, Yamax counted 15 steps, CSA counted 250 steps

(Continued)

tasks and work-related physical activity. In a recent study, five motion sensors were compared to the Yamax pedometer over several simulated lifestyle activity protocols (office, grocery, kitchen, sweeping, resistance training, and an interactive video dance game). Two models of Accusplit pedometers (which use a similar internal mechanism to the Yamax) provided scores consistent with the Yamax, but the other three instruments (Actigraph, Omron, and Walk4Life) demonstrated varying bias across

TABLE 9.5	Adults—Validity Evidence *(Continued)*				
Authors	**Year**	**Sample**	**Instruments**	**Evidence**	**Results**
Hayden-Wade et al.	2003	$N = 74$; 18–67 years	7-Day Physical Activity Recall (7D-PAR) phone and in-person interview methods, TriTrac accelerometer	CRV	$r = .26–.78$ (7D-PAR phone administration, TriTrac minutes of total and moderate, hard, and very hard PA); $r = .33–.74$ (7D-PAR in person administration, TriTrac minutes); no significant difference between 7D-PAR and TriTrac minutes of total, moderate, hard, and very hard PA
Chasan-Taber et al.	2002	$N = 131$; 39–65 years	Historical Leisure Activity Questionnaire (HLAQ), activity diary	CV	$r = .15–.52$ (HLAQ, diary records, total and various subscale scores)
Oman	2000	$N = 1,241$; mean age $= 44.4$ years	Leisure Time Exercise Questionnaire, CDC Behavioral Risk Factor Survey (administered via telephone)	CV	$r = .53$ (LTEQ, BRFS, all participants); $r = .68$ (women); $r = .24$ (men)

the lifestyle activities, compared to the Yamax (Kemble et al. 2005).

When compared to objective measures of physical activity, energy expenditure estimates from questionnaires have generally shown weak validity evidence. In a study conducted over 12 countries, the International Physical Activity Questionnaire correlated lowly with the CSA accelerometer ($r = .30$ to $r = .33$). As with children, questionnaires may be more suitable for adding information about the context and mode of physical activity in adults, rather than for estimates of energy expenditure or minutes spent in moderate physical activity.

Measuring Physical Activity in Older Adults

For the purposes of this chapter, older adults are defined as adults over 65 years of age. This corresponds with the typical retirement age, when adults' lifestyles change considerably, including changes

TABLE 9.5	Adults—Validity Evidence *(Continued)*				
Authors	**Year**	**Sample**	**Instruments**	**Evidence**	**Results**
Bassett et al.	2000	$N = 48$ men and 48 women; 25–70 years (mean = 39.9 ± 11.3 years).	Yamax pedometer, Paffenbarger College Alumnus Questionnaire, measuring wheel	CV	$r = .98$ between Yamax counts and measuring wheel distance, and mean distance walked same for pedometer and measuring wheel over 24 hr; $r = .35$ and .48 between College Alumnus Questionnaire distance and Yamax distance (for men andwomen, respectively); participants significantly underreported walking distance on the College Alumnus Questionnaire, compared to Yamax values (1.56 km·day^{-1} vs. 4.02 km·day^{-1} men; 1.30 km·day^{-1} vs. 4.32 km·day^{-1} women)
Nichols et al.	2000	$N = 60$; mean age = 23.0 ± 2.9 years (men), 22.9 ± 2.9 years (women)	CSA accelerometer, indirect calorimeter	CRV	$r = .94$, SEE = 3.72 ml·kg^{-1} min^{-1} (CSA counts and $\dot{V}O_2$)
Sirard et al.	2000	$N = 19$; mean age = 25.0 ± 3.6 years	CSA accelerometer, physical activity diary	CRV	$r = .49$–.65 (CSA counts and diary kcal)
Nichols et al.	1999	$N = 60$; mean age = 23.8 ± 2.9 years	TriTrac accelerometer, indirect calorimeter	CRV	TriTrac kcal overestimated calorimeter kcal

(Continued)

Table 9.5		**Adults—Validity Evidence** *(Continued)*			
Authors	**Year**	**Sample**	**Instruments**	**Evidence**	**Results**
Lowther et al.	1999	$N = 34$ women; mean age = 3 years	Caltrac, Stanford Seven Day Physical Activity Recall (adapted version)	CRV	$r = .13–.52$ (Caltrac counts, recall score)
Matthews et al.	1999	$N = 73$ women; mean age = 49.0 ± 6.8 years	24-hr physical activity report, doubly labeled water	CRV	kcal·day^{-1} significantly lower (611 vs. 732 kcal·day^{-1}) from self-report than DLW
Freedson et al.	1998	$N = 25$ men (mean age = 24.8 ± 4.2 years), and 25 women (mean age = 22.9 ± 3.8 years)	CSA accelerometer, indirect calorimeter	CRV	$r = .88$ (CSA counts and MET); MET cutoffs = 1951 cts/min (3 MET), 1258 cts/min for each MET thereafter
Bassett et al.	1996	$N = 13$ women and 7 men; 18–65 years (mean age = 32.6 years)	Pedometers (Yamax, Eddie Bauer, Pacer)	CRV	During treadmill walking, Yamax measured distance walked significantly more accurately than the other two instruments, but at the fastest speed, there was no significant difference between the distance measured by the three instruments.
Jacobs et al.	1993	$N = 28$ men (mean age = 37.2 ± 10.0 years) and 50 women (mean age = 37.4 ± 9.7 years)	10 commonly used questionnaires, Caltrac accelerometer	CRV	$r = .01–.33$

Table 9.5		Adults—Validity Evidence *(Continued)*			
Authors	**Year**	**Sample**	**Instruments**	**Evidence**	**Results**
Dishman et al.	1992	$N = 44$; mean age = 24 ± 4.8 years	Stanford Seven Day Physical Activity Recall Questionnaire, Caltrac accelerometer	CRV	$r = .35$

Key: CRV = criterion-related validity; CV = convergent validity

that can influence physical activity greatly. The most important of these is the availability of extra leisure time, consequent to giving up full-time employment. This may be positive, in that more time is available for physical activity through leisure pursuits. However, it may be negative for those whose previous occupation involved physical activity. If suitable replacement activities are not pursued, the level of physical activity may decrease considerably during the years immediately following retirement. Clearly, the retired status of most older adults makes occupation classification irrelevant as an indicator of physical activity level in older adults.

Various characteristics of older adults affect the choice of appropriate instruments for measuring physical activity. Impaired memory function and arthritis may limit the ability of some older adults to complete self-recall or diary records of physical activity. Because of changes in efficiency of movement, conversion of questionnaire scores to MET values based on research in younger adults may not be appropriate for use with older adults. Increases in body weight and percent fat in old age may change the meaning of MET value conversions, and extreme levels of body fatness may also affect placement of accelerometers, pedometers, and heart rate monitors. Changes in gait due to orthopedic problems may affect the validity of readings from accelerometers and pedometers. Effects of medications may weaken the validity of the doubly labeled water technique and the use of heart rate monitors. Older adults typically engage

in lower-intensity activities than younger adults (e.g., walking, light recreational activities, household chores, and gardening). It is therefore particularly important that instruments used with older adults are sensitive enough to differentiate between lower levels of physical activity, in order to discriminate between older adults who have different physical activity levels.

The relationship between physical activity and health outcomes is different in older adults, in ways that should be considered when measuring physical activity in this age group. Because the relationship between aerobic physical activity and mortality is weaker in later life, measurement of these types of activities becomes less important. Other outcomes in the complex physical activity/health relationship become more important. Activities that maintain or improve coordination and balance help to reduce the risk of falls, and weight-bearing activities of sufficient intensity to influence bone mineral density help to reduce the risk of bone fractures. So, it is important that instruments used to investigate the health effects of physical activity in the older adult population are designed to measure strengthening exercises and weight-bearing physical activity.

The onset of retirement can influence physical activity greatly, and so measurement of physical activity immediately following this period is especially important. Evenson et al. (2000) measured past-year physical activity using the modified Baecke questionnaire in 2,228 older African American workers and

7,637 older Caucasian workers at baseline and six years later. At the subsequent testing, 28.2% African American women, 24.6% African American men, 29.3% Caucasian women, and 26.7% Caucasian men had retired. Compared to baseline, retirees were more likely to have increased sport participation and also television-watching than those who continued to work. One implication of this is that television-watching may not be a good indicator of leisure time physical activity in retirees, as it may be simply an indicator of increased available leisure time. Retirement status of individuals close to retirement age may determine whether a leisure-time physical activity questionnaire is sufficient, or whether occupational physical activity also needs to be measured.

Five questionnaires have been designed specifically for older adults. The Modified Baecke Questionnaire (Voorrips et al. 1991) is interviewer-administered, and covers a reference point of the previous year. The Zutphen Physical Activity Questionnaire (Caspersen et al. 1991) is a self-administered 17-item questionnaire that requests information on walking, bicycling, gardening, odd jobs, sports, hobbies, and stair climbing over the previous week. Interestingly, it also contains questions on the amount of nighttime and daytime sleeping. The Yale Physical Activity Survey (DiPietro et al. 1993) is interviewer-administered and has 40 items. The reference period for the Yale Physical Activity Survey is a typical week in the past month. The Physical Activity Scale for the Elderly (Washburn et al. 1993) is a self-administered questionnaire covering the previous seven days. The Community Healthy Activity Model Program for Seniors questionnaire assesses weekly frequency and duration of activities typically done by older adults for exercise (e.g., walking, swimming), everyday activities (e.g., gardening), and recreational activities (e.g., tennis, dance).

Reliability and Validity Evidence— Older Adults

Validity and reliability evidence for measurement instruments of physical activity in older adults is limited in comparison to that for children, adolescents, and younger adults. This may be due to the higher safety standards required by ethical proce-

dures committees of researchers conducting physical tests on older adults. Similarly, in comparison to children, who are often readily accessible to researchers via the school system, and younger adults, who are accessible via the higher education system, community-based older adults may be more difficult to recruit and test. However, due to the increasing size of the older adult population and potential consequent responsibility of health care systems for this sector of the population, the quantity of research in this area will likely increase in the near future.

Tables 9.6 and 9.7 present research conducted with this age group. Less physical activity measurement research has been conducted on older adults than on either of the other two age groups described in this chapter. Most of the recent research has focused on questionnaire methods, with a few studies incorporating accelerometers and pedometers. Test-retest reliability has generally been at least minimally acceptable ($R > .70$) for questionnaires over intervals of less than six months, although in one study the Older Adult Exercise Status Inventory was unreliable over a four-week period ($r = .34$). Intervals of six months or longer do not appear to yield reliable data in older adults.

Questionnaires correlated lowly to moderately with objective measures in several older-adult studies. In studies comparing multiple self-report measures, low to moderate correlations were also reported for summary (total) scores, and between subscales measuring similar activity indices (moderate, vigorous, etc.). Cyarto, Myers and Tudor-Locke (2004) reported an important finding on the accuracy of pedometers in older adults. Compared to rater-counted steps, the Yamax pedometer undercounted steps in nursing home residents and recreation center members. This may be a function of the slower walking pace in older adults, as pedometers have been shown to undercount steps at slower walking speeds. Under controlled walking conditions on a treadmill, the TriTrac and Caltrac accelerometers were shown to have poor absolute accuracy in predicting kilocalories from an indirect calorimeter (Fehling et al. 1999). The Caltrac correlated lowly with indirect calorimetry in an earlier study, also.

TABLE 9.6		Older Adults—Reliability Evidence			
Authors	**Year**	**Sample**	**Instruments**	**Evidence**	**Results**
Dinger et al.	2004	$N = 56$ (mean age = 75.7 ± 7.9 years), rural community dwellers	Physical Activity Scale for the Elderly	TR	$R = .91$ (3-day interval)
Stewart et al.	2001	$N = 249$; 173 underactive, 76 active, 65–90 years (74 ± 6 years)	Community Healthy Activity Model Program for Seniors (CHAMPS) questionnaire	TR	$R = .58–.67$ (6-month interval, various subscales, in active cohort)
Sfakianos	1997	$N = 12$ male and 21 female; 70 to 88 years (mean = 78.4 ± 4.89 years)	Physical Activity Scale for the Elderly	TR	$R = .77–.87$ (1-month interval)
Kochersberger et al.	1996	$N = 36$; frail community dwellers (mean age = 77 years)	TriTrac accelerometer	IC	$R = .78–.81$ (3–7 days)
O'Brien-Cousins	1996	$N = 17$ aged 58–80 (Study 1); $N = 29$ aged 65–90 (Study 2)	Older Adult Exercise Status Inventory	TR	$r = .34$ and $r = .77$ (4-week and 1-week intervals, total score); TR for subscale scores ranged from $r = .11–.76$
Bassey et al.	1987	$N = 24$; women over 65 years (mean age = 67 years)	Yamax pedometer	II	$r = .85$ (2 pedometers worn simultaneously)

Key: TR = test-retest reliability; IC = internal consistency reliability (including intertrial and interday reliability); IR = interrater reliability; II = interinstrument reliability

TABLE 9.7		Older Adults—Validity Evidence			
Authors	**Year**	**Sample**	**Instruments**	**Evidence**	**Results**
Dinger et al.	2004	$N = 56$ (mean age = 75.7 ± 7.9 years), rural community dwellers	Physical Activity Scale for the Elderly, CSA accelerometer	CRV	$R = .43$ (PASE total, CSA counts)
Cyarto et al.	2004	$N = 26$ nursing home residents and 28 recreation center members; 79.4 ± 8.2 years and 70.6 ± 5.5 years	Yamax pedometer, observer-counted steps	CRV	Pedometers significantly undercounted steps in nursing home residents by 46%–74% and undercounted 7%–25% of recreation center members; errors were greater at slower speeds

(Continued)

TABLE 9.7		Older Adults—Validity Evidence *(Continued)*			
Authors	**Year**	**Sample**	**Instruments**	**Evidence**	**Results**
Focht et al.	2003	$N = 60$; Study 1 $n = 50$ (45–86 years); Study 2 $n = 10$ (40–78 years)	CSA accelerometer, Yamax pedometer, Cosmed K4 b2 portable calorimeter	CV CRV	$r = .47$ (CSA, Yamax) during 30-minute walk (Study 1); $r = .72$ (CSA, Cosmed $\dot{V}O_2$) during 30-minute rehabilitation exercise (Study 2)
Schuler et al.	2001	$N = 56$; 56–86 years	Yale Physical Activity Survey (YPAS), physical activity diary	CV	$r = .27–.36$ (diary, YPAS total kcal, activity time, and activity summary scores)
Stewart et al.	2001	$N = 249$; 173 underactive, 76 active, 65–90 years (74 ± 6 years)	CHAMPS questionnaire	KG	CHAMPS scores demonstrated significant changes following activity intervention (underactive cohort), reflecting small to moderate effects
Rohm-Young et al.	2001	$N = 59$; 60–80 years	Yale Physical Activity Survey (YPAS), Stanford 7-Day Physical Activity Recall (SPAR)	CV KG	$r = .30–.37$ (SPAR total, YPAS summary indices); $r = .20$ (SPAR moderate, YPAS walking indices); $r = .32$ (SPAR hard/very hard, YPAS vigorous indices); most indices changed significantly following a 12-week aerobic exercise or Tai Chi intervention
Harada et al.	2001	$N = 87$; adults over 65 years from community centers and retirement homes	Physical Activity Scale for the Elderly, Yale Physical Activity Survey, CHAMPS questionnaire, Mini-Logger activity monitor	CV CRV KG	$r = .58–.68$ (among questionnaires); $r = .42–.61$ (between questionnaires and Mini-Logger); significant differences between community-based and retirement home–based participants (all measures)

TABLE 9.7		Older Adults—Validity Evidence *(Continued)*			
Authors	**Year**	**Sample**	**Instruments**	**Evidence**	**Results**
Fehling et al.	1999	N = 44 men and 42 women (mean age = 70.6 ± 3.7 years)	Caltrac accelerometer, TriTrac accelerometer, indirect calorimeter	CRV	Compared to kcal from calorimetry: kcal was significantly over-estimated by Caltrac during treadmill walk-ing and underestimated by Caltrac during bench stepping; TriTrac signif-icantly underestimated kcal during treadmill walking and bench step-ping; neither accelerom-eter detected changes in kcal due to different treadmill grades
Sfakianos	1997	N = 12 male and 21 female; 70 to 88 years (mean = 78.4 ± 4.89 years)	Physical Activity Scale for the Elderly, Caltrac accelerometer	CRV	$r = .48–62$
Kochersberger et al.	1996	N = 30; nursing home residents (mean age = 76 years)	TriTrac accelerometer	KG	TriTrac counts·min^{-1} significantly different for 3 groups classified by nurses as sedentary, moderately active, or active; also significantly different for 3 activity intensities (eating, walking, and a treadmill stress test)
O'Brien-Cousins	1996	N = 327; 70–98 years (mean = 77 years)	Older Adult Exercise Status Inventory	COV	$r = .19–.33$ with several psychosocial determinants of physical activity
Leaf & MacRae	1995	N = 20; (mean age = 71 years, range = 65–81 years)	Caltrac accelerometer, indirect calorimeter	CRV	$r = .32$ (kcal from calorimetry, kcal from Caltrac)
LaPorte et al.	1983	N = 76; postmenopausal women 45–74 years	Paffenbarger/ Harvard Alumni Questionnaire, LSI activity monitor	CRV	$r = .23$

Key: CRV = criterion-related validity; CV = convergent validity; KG = known groups; COV = construct validity

SUMMARY

The measurement of physical activity is important because of the established connection between physical activity and a variety of health outcomes. Much research has been conducted in the past ten years on the measurement of physical activity. Because of this, and rapid improvements in the technology of heart rate monitors, pedometers, and accelerometers, we are in a better situation now than we have ever been. When measuring physical activity, it seems evident that we should choose instruments for which there is strong evidence of reliability and validity for the proposed use. In practice, this does not always happen, however. For example, Foster et al. (2000) found that in a large sample of directors of public health and directors of leisure in England, 71% had developed their own physical activity measures, 23% had modified an existing tool, and only 6% had used an existing instrument with previously determined validity evidence. When selecting an instrument for use with a specific population, we should consider whether the instrument is appropriate for that population. Additionally, because physical activity is complex, and no single instrument measures all aspects of physical activity (i.e., frequency, intensity, duration, mode, context, and energy expenditure), we should be careful that the instrument we choose measures the characteristics of physical activity that we wish to measure.

FORMATIVE EVALUATION OF OBJECTIVES

Objective 1   Recognize and provide examples of many different types of physical activity.

1. List five physical activities that fall into the following categories: (a) recreational, (b) occupational, (c) household.
2. List five physical activities that are most likely to be of a low to moderate intensity, and five that are most likely to be of a high intensity.
3. Are there any physical activities that people in the United States participate in that are not likely to be found in some other countries?

Objective 2   Understand the importance of measuring physical activity.

1. Why has the general recommendation for physical activity changed in recent years from a fitness-based prescription (primarily high-intensity exercise) to more of a moderate-intensity lifestyle activity prescription?
2. What are some common diseases that can occur as a result of physical inactivity?
3. Why is mode of activity important? What modes of activity are likely to improve the following: (a) stress levels, (b) flexibility, (c) balance, (d) cardiovascular health, (e) muscular strength?

Objective 3   Identify the major methods of measuring physical activity.

1. Describe the different types of motion sensors.
2. Which types of measurement methods involve the least burden on the person being measured?
3. Which types of measurement methods require very little training to use and interpret?
4. Which methods measure some physiological indicator of physical activity, rather than physical activity itself?

Objective 4   Understand some of the unique characteristics of children and adolescents, adults, and older adults that influence their physical activity, and therefore our choice of measurement instrument.

1. How do the activity patterns of children differ from those of adults?
2. Why are questionnaires not very reliable when used with young children? How can we improve the reliability of questionnaire administration to children?
3. If you wanted to collect one week of pedometer data from a child, how might you help the child remember to put on the pedometer each morning?

4. How do people's activity habits change after they retire?
5. List five occupations that would involve high levels of physical activity. Why might people in these occupations not be very active during their leisure time?

Objective 5 Be able to evaluate example physical activity situations and choose the most appropriate measure of physical activity.

1. What would be the most appropriate method for large-scale data collection with adults? Why did you select this method?
2. What would be the most appropriate method for accurate measurement of energy expenditure in real-life situations? Why did you select this method?
3. What would be the most appropriate method for recording activity intensity data? Why did you select this method?
4. What would be the most appropriate method for obtaining information on the context and type of physical activity over the course of a day? Why did you select this method?

ADDITIONAL LEARNING ACTIVITIES

1. Wear a pedometer for five successive days, including Saturday and Sunday. Compare your weekday steps with the weekend steps.
2. Choose a child questionnaire and an adult questionnaire, and complete them yourself. Was this easy? Were there any ambiguous or difficult questions? What were the major differences between the two questionnaires?
3. Wear a heart rate monitor during the day, and record your heart rate after two to three minutes of the following activities: (a) while sitting and eating, (b) while walking, (c) while jogging, (d) while raking leaves, and (e) while doing three other activities of your choice. Make sure you allow enough time for your heart rate to be at steady state before you record your heart rate. Were the results what you expected?
4. Administer the PD-PAR to a child you know. How easy was it for the child to answer the questions? Do you feel that the child's responses were accurate?
5. Ask a relative to record his or her activities over the course of a day. Use the Ainsworth et al. compendia (1993; 2000) to assign MET values to each activity. Were there any activities that were difficult to find, or that could be described by more than one of the activity categories in the compendia?

BIBLIOGRAPHY

Ainsworth, B. E. et al. 1993. Compendium of physical activities: Classification of energy costs of human physical activities. *Medicine and Science in Sports and Exercise* 25: 71–80.

Ainsworth, B. E. et al. 2000. Compendium of physical activities: An update of activity codes and MET intensities. *Medicine and Science in Sports and Exercise* 32: S498–S504.

Bailey, R. C. et al. 1995. The level and tempo of children's physical activities: An observation study. *Medicine and Science in Sports and Exercise* 27: 1033–1041.

Baranowski, T. et al. 1999. Intraindividual variability and reliability in a 7-day exercise record. *Medicine and Science in Sports and Exercise* 31: 1619–1622.

Barfield, J. P. et al. 2004. Interinstrument reliability of the Yamax Digi-Walker in elementary school children. *Measurement in Physical Education and Exercise Science* 8: 109–116.

Bassett, D. R., Jr., A. L. Cureton, and B. E. Ainsworth. 2000. Measurement of daily walking distance—questionnaire versus pedometer. *Medicine and Science in Sports and Exercise* 32: 1018–1023.

Bassett, D. R., Jr. et al. 1996. Accuracy of five electronic pedometers for measuring distance walked. *Medicine and Science in Sports and Exercise* 28: 1071–1077.

Bassey, E. J. et al. 1987. Validation of a simple mechanical accelerometer (pedometer) for the estimation of walking activity. *European Journal of Applied Physiology* 56: 323–330.

Bender, J. M. et al. 2005. Children's physical activity: Using accelerometers to validate a parent proxy record. *Medicine and Science in Sports and Exercise* 37: 1409–1413.

Booth, M. L. et al. 2001. The reliability and validity of the physical activity questions in the WHO Health Behaviour in Schoolchildren (HBSC) survey: A population study. *British Journal of Sports Medicine* 35: 263–267.

Bray, M. S. et al. 1994. Caltrac versus calorimeter determination of 24-h energy expenditure in female children. *Medicine and Science in Sports and Exercise* 26: 1524–1530.

Cardon, G. and I. De Bourdeaudhuij. 2004. A pilot study comparing pedometer counts with reported physical activity in elementary schoolchildren. *Pediatric Exercise Science* 16: 355–367.

Caspersen, C. J. 1989. Physical activity epidemiology: concepts, methods, and applications to exercise science. *Exercise and Sports Science Reviews* 17: 423–473.

Caspersen, C. J. et al. 1991. The prevalence of selected physical activities and their relation with coronary heart disease risk factors in elderly men: The Zutphen Study. *American Journal of Epidemiology* 133: 1078–1092.

Chasan-Taber, L. et al. 2002. Validity and reproducibility of a physical activity questionnaire in women. *Medicine and Science in Sports and Exercise* 34: 987–992.

Ching, L. Y. H., and W. H. Dietz Jr. 1995. Reliability and validity of activity measures in preadolescent girls. *Pediatric Exercise Science* 7: 389–399.

Coleman, K. J. et al. 1997. Relationships between TriTrac-R3D vectors, heart rate, and self-report in obese children. *Medicine and Science in Sports and Exercise* 29: 1535–1542.

Cooper Institute for Aerobics Research. 1999. *FITNESSGRAM® test administration manual.* 6th ed. Champaign, IL: Human Kinetics.

Craig, C. L. et al. 2003. International physical activity questionnaire: 12-country reliability and validity. *Medicine and Science in Sports and Exercise* 35: 1381–1395.

Cyarto, E.V., A. M. Myers, and C. Tudor-Locke. 2004. Pedometer accuracy in nursing home and community-dwelling older adults. *Medicine and Science in Sports and Exercise* 36: 205–209.

Dawson, J. et al. 2003. Distant past exercise in women: Measures may be reliable, but are they valid? *Medicine and Science in Sports and Exercise* 35: 862–866.

Dinger, M. K. et al. 2004. Stability and convergent validity of the Physical Activity Scale for the Elderly (PASE). *Journal of Sports Medicine and Physical Fitness* 44: 186–192.

DiPietro, L. et al. 1993. A survey for assessing physical activity among older adults. *Medicine and Science in Sports and Exercise* 25: 628–642.

Dishman, R. K., C. R. Darracott, and L. T. Lambert. 1992. Failure to generalize determinants of self-reported physical activity to a motion sensor. *Medicine and Science in Sports and Exercise* 24: 904–910.

Ekelund, U. et al. 2001. Heart rate as an indicator of the intensity of physical activity in human adolescents. *European Journal of Applied Physiology* 85: 244–249.

Eston, R. G., A. V. Rowlands, and D. K. Ingledew. 1998. Validity of heart rate, pedometry, and accelerometry for predicting the energy cost of children's activity. *Journal of Applied Physiology,* 84: 362–371.

Evenson, K. R. et al. 2000. Measurement implications of retirement on leisure activity. *Measurement in Physical Education and Exercise Science* 4: 254–255.

Fehling, P. C. et al. 1999. Comparison of accelerometers with oxygen consumption in older adults during exercise. *Medicine and Science in Sports and Exercise* 31: 171–175.

Focht, B. C. et al. 2003. Initial validation of the CSA activity monitor during rehabilitative exercise among older adults with chronic disease. *Journal of Aging and Physical Activity* 11: 293–304.

Foster, C. et al. 2000. An evaluation of the types of physical activity measures used to measure behavior change in public health programmes across England. *Measurement in Physical Education and Exercise Science* 4: 193–194.

Freedson, P. S., E. Melanson, and J. Sirard. 1998. Calibration of the Computer Science and

Applications, Inc. accelerometer. *Medicine and Science in Sports and Exercise* 30: 777–781.

Freedson, P. S. and K. Miller. 2000. Objective monitoring of physical activity using motion sensors and heart rate. *Research Quarterly for Exercise and Sport* 71: S21–S29.

Friedenrich, C. M., K. S. Courneya, and H. E. Bryant. 1998. The Lifetime Total Physical Activity Questionnaire: Development and reliability. *Medicine and Science in Sports and Exercise* 30: 266–274.

Gilliam, T. B. et al. 1977. Prevalence of coronary heart disease risk factors in active children 7–12 years of age. *Medicine and Science in Sports* 9: 21–25.

Gretebeck, R. J. and H. J. Montoye. 1992. Variability of some objective measures of physical activity. *Medicine and Science in Sports and Exercise* 24: 1167–1172.

Harada, N. D. et. al. 2001. An evaluation of three self-report physical activity instruments for older adults. *Medicine and Science in Sports and Exercise* 33: 962–970.

Hayden-Wade, H. A. et al. 2003. Validation of the telephone and in-person interview versions of the 7-day PAR. *Medicine and Science in Sports and Exercise* 35: 801–809.

Jacobs, D. R. et al. 1993. A simultaneous evaluation of 10 commonly used physical activity questionnaires. *Medicine and Science in Sports and Exercise* 25: 81–91.

Janz, K. F., J. Witt, and L. T. Mahoney. 1995. The stability of children's physical activity as measured by accelerometry and self-report. *Medicine and Science in Sports and Exercise* 27: 1326–1332.

Kang, M. et al. 2005. Experimental determination of effectiveness of an individual information-centered approach in recovering step-count missing data. *Measurement in Physical Education and Exercise Science* 9: 233–250.

Kelly, L. A. et al. 2004. Comparison of two accelerometers for assessment of physical activity in preschool children. *Pediatric Exercise Science* 16: 324–333.

Kemble, C. et. al. 2005. *Comparison of six brands of activity monitors during free-living physical activities.* Presented at the American College of Sports Medicine and University of Illinois conference on Walking for Health: Measurement

and Research Issues and Challenges, Urbana-Champaign, IL.

King, G. A. et al. 2004. Comparison of activity monitors to estimate energy cost of treadmill exercise. *Medicine and Science in Sports and Exercise* 36: 1244–1251.

Kochersberger, G. et al. 1996. The reliability, validity, and stability of a measure of physical activity in the elderly. *Archives of Physical Medicine and Rehabilitation* 77: 793–795.

Kowalski, K. C., P. R. E. Crocker, and R. A. Faulkner. 1997. Validation of the Physical Activity Questionnaire for Older Children. *Pediatric Exercise Science* 9: 174–186.

Kowalski, K. C., P. R. E. Crocker, and N. P. Kowalski. 1997. Convergent validity of the Physical Activity Questionnaire for Adolescents. *Pediatric Exercise Science* 9: 342–352.

LaPorte, R. E. et al. 1983. The assessment of physical activity in older women: Analysis of the interrelationship and reliability of activity monitoring, activity surveys, and caloric intake. *Journal of Gerontology* 38(4): 394–397.

Leaf, D. A. and H. MacRae. 1995. Validity of two indirect measures of energy expenditure during walking in the elderly. *Journal of Aging and Physical Activity* 3: 97–106.

Le Masurier, G. C. et al. 2003. Accumulating 10,000 steps: Does this meet current physical activity guidelines? *Research Quarterly for Exercise and Sport* 74: 389–394.

Le Masurier, G. C. and C. Tudor-Locke. 2003. Comparison of pedometer and accelerometer accuracy under controlled conditions. *Medicine and Science in Sports and Exercise* 35: 867–871.

Lowther, M. et al. 1999. Development of a Scottish physical activity questionnaire: A tool for use in physical activity interventions. *British Journal of Sports Medicine* 33: 244–249.

Mahar, M. T. et al. 2001. *Prediction of energy expenditure from accelerometry in obese and nonobese girls.* Poster presented at the University of North Carolina Institute of Nutrition Annual Research Symposium, Chapel Hill, NC.

Maiolo, C. et al. 2003. Physical activity energy expenditure measured using a portable telemetric device in comparison with a mass spectrometer. *British Journal of Sports Medicine* 37: 445–447.

Matthews, C. E. et al. 1999. *Physical activity expenditure: Self-report and doubly labeled water comparisons in middle-aged women.* Poster presented at "Measurement of Physical Activity," Cooper Institute Conference Series, Dallas, TX.

McKenzie, T. L., J. F. Sallis, and P. R. Nader. 1991. SOFIT: System for observing fitness instruction time. *Journal of Teaching in Physical Education* 11: 195–205.

McMurray, R. G. et al. 1998. Comparison of a computerized physical activity recall with a triaxial motion sensor in middle school youth. *Medicine and Science in Sports and Exercise* 30: 1238–1245.

Nichols, J. F. et al. 1999. Validity, reliability, and calibration of the TriTrac accelerometer as a measure of physical activity. *Medicine and Science in Sports and Exercise* 31: 908–912.

Nichols, J. F. et al. 2000. Assessment of physical activity with the Computer Science and Applications, Inc. accelerometer: Laboratory versus field validation. *Research Quarterly for Exercise and Sport* 71: 36–43.

O'Brien-Cousins, S. T. 1996. An older adult exercise status inventory: Reliability and validity. *Journal of Sport Behavior* 19: 288–306.

O'Connor, J. et al. 2001. Comparison of total energy expenditure and energy intake in children aged 6–9 years. *American Journal of Clinical Nutrition* 74: 643–649.

Oman, R. F. 2000. A comparison of two established physical activity measures in a survey of inner-city residents. *Measurement in Physical Education and Exercise Science* 4: 192.

Pate, R. R. 1995. Physical activity and health: Dose-response issues. *Research Quarterly for Exercise and Sport* 66: 313–318.

Pate, R. R., B. J. Long, and G. Heath. 1994. Descriptive epidemiology of physical activity in adolescents. *Pediatric Exercise Science* 6: 434–447.

Pate, R. R. et al. 1995. Physical activity and public health: A recommendation from the Centers for Disease Control and Prevention and the American College of Sports Medicine. *Journal of the American Medical Association* 273: 402–407.

Pate, R. R. et al. 2003. Validation of a 3-Day Physical Activity Recall instrument in female youth. *Pediatric Exercise Science* 15: 257–265.

Rohm-Young, D. et al. 2001. A comparison of the Yale Physical Activity Survey with other physical activity measures. *Medicine and Science in Sports and Exercise* 33: 955–961.

Rowe, D. et al. 2004. Measuring physical activity in children with pedometers: Reliability, reactivity, and replacing missing data. *Pediatric Exercise Science* 16: 343–354.

Rowe, P. et al. 2004. Measuring students' physical activity levels: Validating SOFIT for use with high-school students. *Journal of Teaching in Physical Education* 23: 235–251.

Rowlands, A. V. et al. 2004. Validation of the RT3 triaxial accelerometer for the assessment of physical activity. *Medicine and Science in Sports and Exercise* 36: 518–524.

Satcher, D. 2000. *Physical activity in the new millennium.* Presentation at the national convention of the American Alliance for Health, Physical Education, Recreation, and Dance, Orlando, FL.

Schneider, P. L. et al. 2003. Accuracy and reliability of 10 pedometers for measuring steps over a 400-m walk. *Medicine and Science in Sports and Exercise* 35: 1779–1784.

Schneider, P. L. et. al. 2004. Pedometer measures of free-living physical activity: Comparison of 13 models. *Medicine and Science in Sports and Exercise* 36: 331–335.

Schuler, P. B. et al. 2001. Accuracy and repeatability of the Yale Physical Activity Survey in assessing physical activity of older adults. *Perceptual and Motor Skills* 93: 163–177.

Scruggs, P. W. et al. 2003. Quantifying physical activity via pedometry in elementary physical education. *Medicine and Science in Sports and Exercise* 35: 1065–1071.

Seraganian, P. (Ed.). 1993. *Exercise psychology: The influence of physical exercise on psychological processes.* New York: Wiley.

Sfakianos, A. M. 1997. *Validation of the Physical Activity Scale for the Elderly using the Caltrac accelerometer.* Eugene, OR: Microform Publications, International Institute for Sport & Human Performance, University of Oregon.

Sirard, J. R. et al. 2000. Field evaluation of the Computer Science and Applications, Inc. physical activity monitor. *Medicine and Science in Sports and Exercise* 32: 695–700.

Slinde, F. et al. 2003. Minnesota Leisure Time Activity Questionnaire and doubly labeled water in adolescents. *Medicine and Science in Sports and Exercise* 35: 1923–1928.

Stewart, A. L. et al. 2001. CHAMPS physical activity questionnaire for older adults: Outcomes for interventions. *Medicine and Science in Sports and Exercise* 33: 1126–1141.

Telford, A. et al. 2004. Reliability and validity of physical activity questionnaires for children: The Children's Leisure Activities Study Survey (CLASS). *Pediatric Exercise Science* 16: 64–78.

Treuth, M. S. et al. 2003. Validity and reliability of activity measures in African-American girls for GEMS. *Medicine and Science in Sports and Exercise* 35: 532–539.

Treuth, M. S. et al. 2004. Defining accelerometer thresholds for activity intensities in adolescent girls. *Medicine and Science in Sports and Exercise* 36: 1259–1266.

Tudor-Locke, C. et al. 2005. How many days of pedometer monitoring predict weekly physical activity in adults? *Preventive Medicine* 40: 293–298.

United States Department of Health and Human Services. 1996. *Physical activity and health: A report of the Surgeon General.* Atlanta, GA: Author, Centers for Disease Control and Prevention.

Voorrips, L. E. et al. 1991. A physical activity questionnaire for the elderly. *Medicine and Science in Sports and Exercise* 23: 974–979.

Vincent, S. D. and R. P. Pangrazi. 2002a. Does reactivity exist in children when measuring activity levels with pedometers? *Pediatric Exercise Science* 14: 56–63.

Vincent, S. D. and R. P. Pangrazi. 2002b. An examination of the activity patterns of elementary school children. *Pediatric Exercise Science* 14: 432–441.

Washburn, R. A. et al. 1993. The Physical Activity Scale for the Elderly (PASE): Development and evaluation. *Journal of Clinical Epidemiology* 46: 153–162.

Washburn, R. A. et al. 2003. The validity of the Stanford Seven-Day Physical Activity Recall in young adults. *Medicine and Science in Sports and Exercise* 35: 1374–1380.

Welk, G. J. and C. B. Corbin. 1995. The validity of the TriTrac-R3D activity monitor for the assessment of physical activity in children. *Research Quarterly for Exercise and Sport* 66: 202–209.

Welk, G. J., C. B. Corbin, and D. Dale. 2000. Measurement issues in the assessment of physical activity in children. *Research Quarterly for Exercise and Sport* 71: S59–S73.

Weston, A. T., R. Petosa, and R. R. Pate. 1997. Validation of an instrument for measurement of physical activity in youth. *Medicine and Science in Sports and Exercise* 29: 138–143.

10

MEASURING PHYSICAL ABILITIES

C O N T E N T S

K E Y   W O R D S

absolute endurance test
agility
balance
basic physical ability
classification index
closed kinetic chain
flexibility
general motor ability
isokinetic strength
isometric strength
isotonic strength
kinesthesis
motor educability
motor skill
muscular endurance
muscular power
muscular strength
open kinetic chain
power
speed

OBJECTIVES

Physical educators have long accepted the idea of generality; a general test can be used to predict an individual's capacity to perform a wide range of athletic or motor skills. The **classification index** derived from age, height and weight, general motor ability, and motor educability tests was used to measure generality, but it has not proven to be valid. The theory of basic physical abilities does provide a sound model for testing generality. The theory provides the foundation for many different testing programs, the most prominent being adult and youth fitness, testing athletes, and preemployment testing programs for physically demanding jobs. Chapters 13 and 14 cover youth and adult fitness testing, while athletic and preemployment testing is in this chapter. Back injuries are a major problem of industrial workers. One causal factor of industrial back problems is the lack of physical ability to do the work task. This chapter provides data on the role of strength in the risk of back injuries. Finally, this chapter provides common physical ability tests and normative data.

After reading Chapter 10 you should be able to

1. Describe the tests that historically have been used to measure generality.
2. Apply the theory of basic physical abilities to the evaluation of athletes.
3. Identify the methods to develop preemployment tests for physically demanding jobs and the types of tests that compose preemployment batteries.
4. Understand the influence of physical abilities on the risk of back injuries.
5. Identify basic physical abilities and tests that validly measure each ability.

HISTORY OF GENERALITY TESTING

The assumption of the concept of generality is that the performance of many different motor tasks can be predicted from a single test or a limited number of tests. The principle of generality can be traced to the work of Sargent (1921), who first reported a test of generality. The Sargent Physical Test of Man simply measures the height of a vertical jump, on the assumption that a single test is sufficient to measure motor ability. This assumption paralleled the concept of generality once accepted by psychologists, who felt that a g-factor, or general factor of intelligence, was adequate to represent human intellectual ability. While the intellectual g-factor is important, we now understand that there are several different intellectual factors.

The purpose of generality tests was to provide a method by which it would be possible to predict an individual's performance on a wide range of motor activities from a simple test battery. Several types of tests have been used by physical educators to measure generality, but their validity has not been established. Table 10.1 provides a brief overview of these tests.

In the late 1950s, Franklin Henry (1956, 1958) advanced the memory-drum theory of neuromotor reaction, claiming that motor ability is specific to a task rather than general to many tasks. In other words, a student's performance on one **motor skill** is of little or no value in predicting performance on a different task. By his theory, Henry claims that there is no such thing as **general motor ability;** rather, each individual possesses many specific motor abilities. A student who scores well on a general motor test is gifted with several specific abilities, whereas a student who scores poorly has only a few neural patterns stored on his or her memory drum. The theory of specificity casts doubt on the validity of general motor ability and **motor educability** tests, and is largely responsible for the demise of these tests.

Certainly, physical education teachers and exercise specialists must acknowledge the theory of specificity; however, complete acceptance of the theory would signal the need to measure all the specifics that enter the complex domain of motor skills. In fact, the practice of using physical abilities tests is on the rise. Testing programs for athletes are becoming common practice at public school, college, and professional levels. Physical abilities tests are now used to screen applicants for physically demanding occupations such as firefighter or coal miner. Physical abilities tests not only provide a means to evaluate athletic potential and a job applicant's capacity to meet the demands of physically demanding work tasks, but also identify those most

TABLE 10.1 A Historical Overview of Generality Tests Used in Physical Education		
Generality Test	**Type of Tests**	**Comments**
Age-height-weight classification index (McCloy 1932)	Age, height, and weight	The classification index was a multiple regression equation that provided an index of maturity. Most tests are normed on the basis of age and gender. The index does not add any additional information.
Motor educability (McCloy & Young 1954)	Consisted of several gymnastic "stunt-like" tasks	The tests supposedly measured the ability to learn motor skills easily and well. The validity was never established. Motor educability tests have not been shown to correlate with the capacity to learn motor skills.
Motor ability (Barrow 1954; Scott 1939)	Jumping, throwing tests, running tests (speed and agility)	Purported to measure acquired and innate ability to perform motor skills. Lost support with the development of Henry's memory-drum theory.

at risk of injury when performing physically demanding work.

THEORY OF BASIC ABILITIES

The theory of **basic physical abilities** described by Edwin Fleishman (1964) is especially useful for generality testing, because individual performance of a specific motor skill is explained in terms of a relatively small number of psychomotor abilities. His theory is based on research conducted for the U.S. Air Force, in which tests of psychomotor abilities were found valid for predicting the subsequent performance of various air crew members (Fleishman 1956).

Fleishman, a leading industrial/organizational psychologist, distinguishes between psychomotor skills and psychomotor abilities, but considers both essential and complementary. A psychomotor skill is one's level of proficiency on a specific task or limited group of tasks. Dribbling a basketball, catching a softball, swimming the sidestroke, and playing the piano are examples of very different psychomotor skills. Learning a psychomotor skill involves acquiring the sequence of responses that results in a coordinated performance of the task. A psychomotor ability is a more general trait that may be common to many psychomotor tasks. For example, being able to run fast enhances one's abil-

ity to excel in several different specific motor skills athletic events, such as playing football, performing the running long jump, or playing basketball.

Fleishman describes the relationship between basic physical abilities and motor skills as follows:

> The assumption is that the skills involved in complex activities can be described in terms of the more basic physical abilities. For example, the level of performance a man can attain on a turret lathe may depend on his basic physical abilities of manual dexterity and motor coordination. However, these same basic physical abilities may be important to proficiency in other skills as well. Thus, manual dexterity is needed in assembling electrical components, and motor coordination is needed to fly an airplane. Implicit in the previous analysis is the relation between abilities and learning. Thus, individuals with high manual dexterity may more readily learn the specific skill of lathe operation. (1964)

Basic physical abilities are measured with many types of tests, and individuals differ in the extent to which they possess an ability (e.g., some people run faster than others). An individual with many highly developed basic physical abilities can become proficient at a wide variety of specific motor skills. For example, the "all-around" athlete is a person who has many highly developed basic physical abilities important to many different sports. Then, too, certain basic physical abilities are more generalized than others. For example, in our culture, verbal abilities are important in a greater variety of tasks than are many other abilities. Certainly speed, jumping ability, and muscular strength are important basic physical abilities related to athletic success. Both the rate of learning and the final level of skill achieved depend on an individual's level of achievement in the more basic physical abilities.

The development of basic physical abilities is a product of both genetic and environmental influences, with the genetic factor the limiting condition. Consider, for example, muscular strength. By participating in weight-training programs, we can greatly influence the development of muscular strength; but the limit of that development (the maximum strength) depends on our genetics. Basic physical abilities develop during childhood and adolescence, reaching a fairly stable level in adulthood.

Because an ability is a lasting, stable pattern of behavior, individual differences in basic physical abilities make it possible to predict the subsequent performance of specific skills. For example, the SAT measures verbal and quantitative abilities. Using a student's score on the quantitative ability section would be predictive of success in programs such as engineering, where math skills are very important, but not predictive of success in nonmathematical majors such as English. In the same way, running speed is an important factor in the running long jump; on the basis of a student's speed, we could judge better how well he will do on the long jump. Former Olympic champion long jumper Carl Lewis was in a class of his own due to his world-class sprinting speed. He won medals in both the long jump and the 100-meter dash.

Basic abilities are identified with the statistical method called factor analysis. This involves administering several different tests to a large sample of subjects. Typically, some tests are highly correlated with each other, but not correlated with others. Factor analysis identifies the groups of tests that are correlated with each other, and it is assumed that each test measures a common trait termed a factor. In psychology, the factor is termed a "construct." The tests associated with the factor have construct validity—that is, the test is significantly correlated with the factor

or construct. According to the theory, a basic ability is a construct (see Chapter 4). Numerous factor analysis studies have been published that identify basic motor performance abilities (Baumgartner & Zuidema 1972; Bernauer & Bonanno 1975; Considine et al. 1976; Cousins 1955; Cumbee 1954; Disch, Frankiewicz, & Jackson 1975; Fleishman 1964; Harris 1969; Ismail, Falls, & MacLeod 1965; Jackson 1971; Jackson & Frankiewicz 1975; Jackson & Pollock 1976; Larson 1941; Liba 1967; McCloy 1956; Meyers et al. 1984; Safrit 1966; Zuidema & Baumgartner 1974). The interested reader is directed to these sources for detailed coverage of this technique. Table 10.2 provides a summary of these basic abilities.

Basic physical abilities tests have at least two important applications: first, for evaluating athletes, and second, for use as preemployment tests in physically demanding jobs. Additionally, strength and endurance are believed to be associated with the risk of low back injury. These topics are presented next.

Application 1—Testing Athletes

The testing of athletes has become an accepted procedure. Before the 1976 Olympics, sport scientists studied the psychological, physiological, biomechanical, and medical characteristics of 20 world-class distance runners (Pollock et al. 1978). Prior to the unification of Germany, the East German Olympic team, which had been very successful in Olympic competition, conducted an extensive testing program for its athletes. Several years before its 1978 Super Bowl victory, the Dallas Cowboys team had developed a scientific program for evaluating and training its football players.[1] Today, all major university and professional football teams hire a full-time strength coach who is responsible for testing and training athletes. The United States Olympic Committee developed a

---

[1]Presently, draft prospects in football are evaluated at an annual combined workout in Indianapolis. Prospects are measured for height, weight, 225-pound bench press executions, 40-yard run time, vertical jump, standing long jump, 20-yard shuttle run, and 60-yard shuttle run (http://sports.espn.go.com/nfldraft/story?page=combine_dts). More information on sport-specific testing is presented by Brown (2001).

TABLE 10.2	Summary of Basic Gross Motor Basic Abilities
Basic Ability	**Description**
Strength and Power Abilities	
Muscular strength	The maximum force that a muscle group can exert over a brief period. Isometric, isotonic, and isokinetic tests are used to measure strength.
Muscular power	Power is the rate that work is performed. Ergometers are used to measure arm and leg power.
Endurance Abilities	
Muscular endurance	The ability to persist in physical activity or to resist muscular fatigue. Pull-ups and sit-ups are common tests used to measure endurance.
Cardiorespiratory endurance	The capacity to perform exhausting work. This is also termed maximal oxygen uptake, aerobic fitness, and $\dot{V}O_2$ max (see Chapter 11).
Basic Movement Patterns	
Running speed	Capacity to move rapidly. Measured by short runs, 10 to 60 yards in length.
Running agility	The ability to change the direction of the body or body parts rapidly. Measured by standard tests such as the shuttle run.
Jumping ability	The ability to expend maximum energy in one explosive act, projecting the body through space. Traditionally measured with the standing long jump and vertical jump.
Throwing ability	The capacity to throw a relatively light ball (baseball, softball, etc.) overarm for distance.
Neuromuscular Abilities	
Flexibility	The range of movement about a joint. Flexibility tends to be task specific, there being many different types of flexibility. Someone flexible at one joint may not be flexible in others.
Balance	The ability to maintain body position. Traditionally measured with static and dynamic balance tests.
Kinesthetic perception	The ability to perceive the body's position in space and the relationship of its parts. This important ability is very difficult to measure reliably.

central facility for testing athletes in Colorado Springs, Colorado. This facility is fully staffed with exercise scientists who provide comprehensive testing of athletes. These data are given to the athlete and coach and used to improve training and performance.

The important concern is to find the physical abilities that are most relevant to the demands placed on an athlete. The more specific the test is, the more valid it will be. At the U.S. Olympic testing site, for example, different exercise modes are used to measure aerobic capacity ($\dot{V}O_2$ max). For distance runners, a treadmill-running protocol is followed; in contrast, specially devised cycle er-

gometer protocols are used to evaluate cyclists. The physical ability tests that are most appropriate for evaluating athletes are these:

- Aerobic capacity or $\dot{V}O_2$ max (see Chapter 11) Body composition, either percent body fat or weight partitioned into fat weight and fat-free weight (see Chapter 12)
- Muscular strength
- Power
- Running speed, typically 40- or 50-yard dash
- Vertical or standing long jump
- Agility run test that duplicates the athlete's movement patterns

We would suggest following six steps when developing a battery for evaluating athletes:

1. Consider the sport and the basic qualities it demands of the athlete. For example, jumping ability would be especially important for volleyball and basketball players, and $\dot{V}O_2$ max for endurance athletes, such as long-distance runners.
2. Select tests that measure these defined traits. The tests may be found in Chapters 10 through 14.
3. Administer the tests to as many athletes as possible.
4. From their scores, develop percentile-rank norms using the procedures furnished in Chapter 2.
5. Use these norms to evaluate your athletes. The criterion for comparison here also can be earlier data on outstanding athletes, allowing you to evaluate your athletes with both the norm and outstanding players.
6. Reevaluate your selection of tests to be sure you are measuring the abilities most relevant to the sport. You should see a tendency for the best athletes to achieve the highest scores.

Provided in Tables 10.3 and 10.4 are sample test batteries used for female volleyball players and college football players. A profile for an athlete can be obtained by simply plotting her score on the table. In this way the athlete's strengths and weaknesses become apparent. The performance expectations of defined groups of football players are different, so profiles for defined subgroups of players are also provided on the team norms. The subgroup profile is the mean of all players in that subgroup. The subgroups shown in Table 10.4 are backs and linemen. Thus, an athlete's profile can be compared to those of the entire team and any subgroup. The University of Houston players who have gone on to play professional football have all been faster, stronger, and leaner than the average for their respective subgroup. This lends credence to the system.

Percentile-rank norms allow us to plot the athletes' test scores individually in a profile that we can then examine to determine whether an athlete shows a performance level compatible to that needed for a given sport. The profile is more than an evaluative technique that shows variation from the general trend; it provides empirical evidence for designing a training program as well. For example, assume that a profile shows an athlete with a higher level of body fat than average. With this information, the coach can initiate an individualized diet and exercise program for the athlete. The profile provides both the coach and the athlete with an objective means of designing an individualized training program and motivating the athlete. Plotting retests can be used to gauge progress. And finally, the profile may give a coach insight into an athlete's potential.

Application 2—Preemployment Testing

Employers have always used some method to select an employee among potential job applicants. Much of the early preemployment testing focused on cognitive abilities, but with the rise in women seeking jobs that were once male dominated, the need for preemployment physical abilities tests increased. Most major fire and police departments require applicants to pass a physical ability test. Other occupations that use preemployment tests are telephone craft workers who climb poles, steel workers, coal miners, chemical plant workers, electrical transmission lineworkers, military personnel, oil field production workers, and freight handlers.

There are at least three reasons physical ability tests are used as a condition for employment. First, a legal issue: equal employment opportunity legislation resulted in greater numbers of females and individuals with disabilities seeking employment in occupations requiring high levels of physical ability. Second, risk of injury: there was evidence suggesting that physically unfit workers had higher incidences of low back injuries. Third, inadequacy of medical examinations: preemployment medical evaluations used alone are inadequate for personnel selection for physically demanding jobs. With the passage of the Americans with Disabilities Act (July 26, 1992), medical

TABLE 10.3	Percentile-Rank Norms for High School and College Female Volleyball Players								
	High School Players				**College Players**				
Percentile	**Height**	**Vertical Jump**	**20-Yard Dash**	**Basketball Throw†**	**Height**	**Vertical Jump**	**20-Yard Dash**	**Basketball Throw†**	**%Fat***
99	74.0	22.0	2.87	70.8	77.0	24.0	2.83	82.3	11.2
95	71.0	18.5	3.04	64.5	72.0	20.5	3.00	68.5	12.3
90	70.0	17.8	3.12	60.0	71.0	19.8	3.07	66.8	12.6
85	69.0	16.5	3.17	57.0	70.0	19.0	3.12	64.0	13.2
80	68.0	16.0	3.20	55.0	69.5	18.5	3.16	61.2	13.5
75	67.5	15.7	3.23	52.8	69.0	18.0	3.17	59.4	14.0
70	67.0	15.3	3.26	51.5	68.5	17.5	3.20	58.3	14.4
65	66.5	15.0	3.28	50.5	68.5	17.0	3.27	57.6	14.6
60	66.0	14.5	3.32	49.0	68.0	16.8	3.30	56.6	15.1
55	65.5	14.2	3.34	48.4	67.5	16.5	3.33	56.1	15.5
50	65.5	14.0	3.37	47.2	67.5	16.0	3.37	55.0	16.0
45	65.5	13.7	3.42	46.0	67.0	15.8	3.40	53.9	16.5
40	65.0	13.5	3.46	44.5	67.0	15.5	3.42	52.3	17.5
35	65.0	13.3	3.47	43.5	66.0	15.0	3.44	51.1	18.2
30	64.0	13.0	3.50	42.0	66.0	14.7	3.50	51.0	18.8
25	64.0	12.5	3.53	40.8	65.5	14.0	3.53	50.1	20.5
20	63.0	12.3	3.57	39.2	65.0	13.5	3.60	48.7	21.5
15	62.5	12.0	3.60	37.8	64.0	12.7	3.67	46.6	22.9
10	62.0	11.5	3.67	36.4	63.5	11.5	3.73	45.8	26.0
5	61.5	11.0	3.80	33.5	62.5	10.5	3.83	41.2	31.3

Source: Data from Dr. James G. Disch, Associate Professor of Physical Education, Rice University, Houston, TX.

*Percent body fat was not determined for high school players. See Chapter 12 for methods and norms appropriate for high school girls.

†Overhanded basketball throw for distance.

examinations cannot be given until an offer of employment is made. Any medically disqualifying condition must be shown to be job-related. One possible consequence of ADA is that validated physical ability tests will play a greater role in employee selection.

Legal Issues

Preemployment tests face potential legal review because physical ability tests are likely to have an adverse impact on females and ethnic groups such as Asians and Hispanics. Public safety employers (those hiring firefighters, police officers, and correctional officers) have been the target of sex discrimination litigation, and they have not fared well.

In the 1960s and 1970s, height and weight standards were a condition of employment of most public safety workers. Since women and members of some ethnic groups (e.g., Asians and Hispanics) are shorter and lighter, a lower proportion of them met the standard. Arvey and Faley (1988) reported that in 1973, nearly all the nation's large police departments had a minimum height requirement. The average requirement was 68 inches. More than 90% of the women but only 45% of the males failed the 68-inch height requirement. The rationale used to defend the standard was that size was related to physical strength, and the effectiveness of an officer's job performance depended upon strength. The United States Supreme Court ruled that if strength is a real job requirement, then a di-

TABLE 10.4	Percentile-Rank Norms for University Football Players				
Percentile	**0–5 Yards**	**20–40 Yards**	**0–40 Yards**	**% Fat**	**Bench Press**
99	0.985	1.933	4.412	4.1	422
95	1.029	1.995	4.626	6.5	389
90	1.052	2.028	4.737	7.7	376
85	1.067	2.049	4.812	8.7	360
80	1.080	2.067	4.903	9.2	350	LINEMEN
75	1.091	2.083	4.926	9.8	342
70	1.101	2.096	4.973	10.3	335
65	1.109	2.108	5.013	10.7	329
60	1.118	2.121	5.057	11.3	322
55	1.126	2.131	5.094	11.6	316
50	1.134	2.143	5.134	12.0	310
45	1.142	2.155	5.174	12.3	304
40	1.150	2.166	5.212	12.7	298
35	1.159	2.178	5.255	13.2	291	BACKS
30	1.167	2.190	5.295	13.6	285
25	1.177	2.203	5.342	14.1	278
20	1.188	2.219	5.394	14.6	270
15	1.201	2.237	5.456	15.1	260
10	1.216	2.258	5.531	15.9	244
5	1.239	2.291	5.642	16.9	231
1	1.283	2.353	5.856	18.8	198

Source: Data from William F. Yeoman, former Head Football Coach, University of Houston, Houston, TX.

rect measure of strength should have been adopted. The height and weight standards of public safety jobs are being replaced with physical ability tests.

Preemployment Test Methodology

If hiring practices produce adverse impact, as was the case with a height requirement, federal law requires that a validation study must support the selection method. The steps involved in a validation study are (1) complete a task analysis, (2) validate the selected tests, and (3) establish cut scores. Each is briefly reviewed next.

Broadly defined, a job analysis is the collection and analysis of any type of job-related information by any method for any purpose (Gael 1988). The objectives of a job analysis are to find measures of work behavior(s) or performance that are used for the job and to find the extent that they represent critical or important job duties, work behaviors, or work outcomes (EEOC 1978). Task analyses of physically demanding jobs often follow one or more of the following approaches.

Psychophysical Methods These methods involve developing scales that can be used to rate the frequency and intensity of physical demands required by various work tasks. A given scale is administered to several employees who are engaged in these work tasks. This provides data by which work tasks can be compared. For example, employees rated the task of lifting boxes that weigh over 60 pounds to shoulder height more demanding than lifting them to waist height.

Biomechanical Methods The types of data collected include heights, weights of the objects lifted or transported, and forces needed to complete work tasks such as opening and closing valves, or pushing and pulling objects. Biomechanical models provide a means of evaluating the stresses placed on the spine by the tasks of materials handling and lifting.

Physiological Methods   Work tasks such as climbing stairs and fighting fires have a significant aerobic endurance component. Physiological methods document the cardiovascular response of these work tasks. For example, heart rate response when working provides an index of a work task's level of physical demands.

Validation Methods   The failure to conduct a valid task analysis is a major reason preemployment physical ability tests have been ruled by the courts to be illegal. The task analysis becomes the framework for developing and validating a preemployment test. Validating a preemployment test involves determining the accuracy with which a test or other selection device measures the important work behaviors identified with the job analysis.

There are three types of validity evidence that are typically used to support a preemployment test.

Criterion-Related Validity Evidence   This type of evidence requires you to show that the preemployment test predicts, or is significantly correlated with, important elements of job performance. Concurrent validity evidence involves testing current employees, and relating their test scores to current job performance. Predictive validity evidence involves testing people prior to being hired. Job performance is then assessed at a later date, and regression analysis is used to determine whether preemployment test scores accurately predicted subsequent job performance.

Content-Related Validity Evidence   Sometimes called logical validity evidence (see Chapter 4), this type of evidence is gathered as part of a rational process that demonstrates a logical association between the tasks in the preemployment test and important elements of job performance. Key elements are the involvement of expert judges (e.g., ergonomics

experts, employees who are experienced and excellent performers of the job being tested) to determine that the content of the preemployment test adequately represents key elements of performance (tasks) at the job for which people are being selected (EEOC 1978). For example, a task requiring the testee to drag a 150-pound dummy while walking backward is content-relevant to the job of firefighter, but not to the job of mail deliverer.

Construct-Related Validity Evidence   All types of validity evidence could be said to represent construct validity (see Chapter 4). The type of evidence referred to here specifically establishes that a certain construct is necessary to job performance, and subsequently that the preemployment test is measuring that construct. For example, keyboard skills are necessary for many office jobs. To demonstrate that a preemployment task measures this construct appropriately, one might administer the test to a group of master typists and a group of relatively inexperienced typists (students in a community college intermediate-level typing class, for example). If the mean scores of the two groups were significantly different, this would add to the body of evidence supporting the construct validity of the test.

Types of Employment Tests

There are two general types of preemployment tests: (1) work-sample tests and (2) physical ability tests. The advantage of work-sample tests is that they simulate the actual working conditions and are more likely to have content validity. The content validity of the test is judged to the extent that the items or tasks within the test correspond to tasks that are important to performance in the job. Lifting and carrying boxes a specified distance is an example of a materials handling work-sample test. Arvey et al. (1992) reported that many police and firefighter physical ability tests consist of some combination of job sample tests. Figure 10-1 lists work-sample tests commonly included in these public safety preemployment tests.

While work-sample tests have the advantage of appearing to be valid, Ayoub (1982) maintains that they have at least two limitations. The first is safety. Applicants seeking employment are likely to

POLICE OFFICERS

- Scaling a wall, usually 6 feet in height
- Long jumping a set distance
- Crawling through openings at ground level
- Running a set distance, usually a quarter mile
- Dragging a heavy object a set distance
- Running a course consisting of various obstacles

FIREFIGHTERS

- Climbing a ladder
- Pushing and pulling a ceiling hook
- Dragging a dummy a set distance or time period
- Running up stairs carrying hose bundles

Figure 10-1

Common work-sample tests included in police officer and firefighter preemployment tests. (Arvey & Faley 1988).

be highly motivated to pass the work-sample test. A highly motivated applicant who lacks the physical capacity to perform the task is likely to increase the risk of injury. Outdoor telephone craft jobs require employees to climb telephone poles, and accident data showed that this was a dangerous task. Using a pole-climbing test to screen applicants would have content validity but likely would be too dangerous for untrained or physically unfit employees.

A second limitation of job simulation tests is that they do not give any information about the applicant's maximum work capacity. A work-sample test is often scored by pass or fail—for example, lifting a 95-pound jackhammer and carrying it a specified distance. Some can easily complete the test, while others may just pass and be working at their maximum. If it can be assumed that there is a linear relationship between job performance and the preemployment test performance, applicants with the highest test scores can be expected to be the more productive workers. Testing for maximum capacity not only identifies the potentially most productive workers, but also defines a level of reserve that may reduce the risk of musculoskeletal injury.

Physical ability tests are the second type of items used for preemployment tests. The most common include tests of strength, tests of body composition, and aerobic fitness tests. Strength tests are the most common item used. A common strategy has been to relate strength performance to criteria of job success as a validity study (Jackson et al. 1998) or work-sample tests (Jackson, Osborn, & Laughery 1991; Jackson et al. 1992; Jackson et al. 1993). Table 10.5 lists the correlations we have found between isometric strength tests and work-sample test performance. The isometric strength tests are presented in the later section of this chapter. The correlations in Table 10.5 show that isometric strength tests validly estimate an applicant's potential to perform a variety of work tasks. Interestingly, the isometric strength tests are highly correlated with several different types of tasks—not just those

TABLE 10.5	Correlations between the Sum of Isometric Strength* and Simulated Work-Sample Tests		
Reference Work	**Sample Test**	**Type of Test**	**r_{xy}**
Jackson et al. 1991	Shoveling coal	Dynamic, endurance	0.71
Jackson et al. 1991	50-pound bag carry	Dynamic, endurance	0.63
Jackson et al. 1993	Push force	Static, max force	0.78
Jackson et al. 1993	Pull force	Static, max force	0.67
Jackson et al. 1992	Valve-turning	Dynamic, endurance	0.83
Jackson et al. 1993	Box transport	Dynamic, endurance	0.76
Jackson et al. 1993	Moving document bags	Dynamic, endurance	0.70
Jackson et al. 1998	Valve cracking	Static, max force	0.91

*Isometric strength tests provided in this chapter.

involving maximum force output, but also dynamic tasks performed either to exhaustion or at a "comfortable rate" set by the person being tested. A "blue-ribbon" panel suggested that fat-free weight be used to select military personnel for heavy lifting tasks (Marriott & Grumstrup-Scott 1992). Fat-free weight and strength are highly correlated.

Setting Cut Scores

After completing the validation study, the next, difficult step is to set a cut score. The cut score is the test score that an applicant must obtain to be considered for the job. The cut scores should be reasonable and consistent with normal expectations of acceptable proficiency within the workforce. The cut score should be based on a rational process and valid selection system that is flexible and meets the needs of the organization. Based on legal, historical, and professional guidelines, Cascio et al. (1988) offer several recommendations.

- The cut score should be based upon the results of the job analysis. The validity and job-relatedness of the testing procedure are crucial.
- The cut score should be sufficiently high to ensure minimally accepted job performance.
- The performance level associated with a cut score should be consistent with the normal expectations of acceptable proficiency within the workforce.

The strategies used to set cut scores evolved largely from preemployment studies using psychological paper-and-pencil tests. However, in physical testing, the discipline of work physiology is also used. This involves matching the worker to the physiological demands of the task. Maximum oxygen uptake ($\dot{V}O_2$ max) and strength are the physiological variables used to evaluate a worker's capacity to meet the demands of the job.

An important research focus is to define the energy cost needed to fight fires. This research effort can be attributed to litigation leveled at the validity of firefighter preemployment tests and the use of age to terminate employment. Sothmann et al. (1992) published data showing that fire suppression work tasks have a substantial aerobic component. In an excellent study, Sothmann et al. (1990) showed that

the minimum $\dot{V}O_2$ max required to meet the demands of firefighting is 33.5 ml/kg/min. Firefighters with an aerobic capacity below this level were not able to meet basic demands of fire suppression work. Using a $\dot{V}O_2$ max of 33.5 ml/kg/min provides a physiologically sound basis of setting a cut score for firefighters.

Strength is a major determinant of physical capacity to perform physically demanding industrial tasks (Hogan 1991; Jackson 1994). Common work simulation strength tests involve testing one's capacity to complete a lift (e.g., lift 75 pounds from floor to knuckle height) and measuring one's maximum force generation capacity (generating force to move an object). Table 10.5 shows that isometric strength is correlated with these work simulation tasks. This provides a means of determining whether an applicant has sufficient strength to meet the demands of the work task. Provided next are two examples that use regression analysis to define equations that can be used to define the level of strength required by the work task.

Pass-Fail Tests   Lifting and transporting objects (e.g., valves, boxes) is a common physically demanding work task. If a 75-pound load must be lifted and transported, a worker must have sufficient strength to complete the task. The results of the studies summarized in Table 10.5 show that strength is highly correlated with many industrial work-sample tasks. In a study by Jackson et al. (1998), the task analysis documented that a physically demanding task was to lift a valve that weighed 75 pounds from the floor and place it on the back of a truck. This is a basic floor-to-knuckle-height lift. A work-sample test was developed to simulate the lifting task. The work-sample test involved lifting weights that became progressively heavier until the person's physical limit was reached (i.e., they could not lift the weight). As the load got heavier, a higher percentage of individuals were not able to lift the weight.

Continuously Scored Tests   A task analysis showed that cracking industrial valves was a physically demanding task required by oil field production workers (Jackson et al. 1998). One phase of the

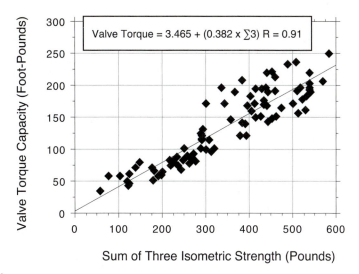

Figure 10-2

Scattergram and simple linear regression equation that defines the relationship between isometric strength and the capacity to generate valve-cracking torque.

(Source: CSI Software Company, Houston, TX. Reprinted by permission.)

task analysis was to go into the oil fields and measure the torque required to crack valves. Work-sample tests were developed to simulate the positions assumed by workers when cracking valves on the job. An electronic torque wrench was used to assess the torque production capacity of both workers and students. Isometric strength was found to be highly correlated ($R = 0.91$) with torque production capacity. Figure 10-2 is a regression plot between the sum of isometric strength and the capacity to generate valve-cracking torque (Jackson et al. 1998). Regression equations define the level of strength needed to generate sufficient torque to crack valves. The regression equation can be used to define the level of strength demanded by the work task. To illustrate, Figure 10-2 shows that the maximum valve-cracking capacity of someone with a strength score of 400 pounds is about 150 foot-pounds of torque. This can also be determined by using the regression equation in Figure 10-2, substituting the strength score of 400 pounds into the equation:

$$\text{Value torque} = 3.465 + (.382 \times 400)$$
$$= 3.465 + 152.8$$
$$= 156.26 \text{ foot-pounds}$$

If the forces required to perform a task are known, the regression equation can be used to select applicants who have the physical capacity to meet the demands of the task. To illustrate, if 150 foot-pounds is the level of valve-cracking torque demanded by the job, 400 pounds of isometric strength would be a valid cut score.

Application 3—Back Injuries

There is evidence that an individual's level of physical fitness is related to the risk of low back injury. The youth and adult fitness health-related fitness batteries (Chapters 13 and 14) include test items designed to detect strong, flexible backs with the hope of reducing the risk of low back injuries. Plowman (1992) published a comprehensive review of the research relating fitness and low back pain. While the medical research is not overwhelming, her review supports the continued use of sit-up and flexibility tests in health-related fitness batteries.

The most convincing research relating physical fitness and back injuries comes from the discipline of ergonomics, the scientific study of work. One conclusion of ergonomic research is the need to match the fitness of the worker with the demands of the job. A goal of preemployment testing is to select workers capable of doing the work without injuring themselves. Reduction of low back injuries is a primary objective of preemployment testing for physically demanding jobs.

Methods of Reducing Industrial Back Injuries

Back injuries sustained by workers are not only costly to the employees in terms of their health, well-being, and lifestyle, but also to the employer in terms of workers' compensation and health care costs. The economic costs absorbed by American industry are in the billions of dollars. About 50% of industrial back injuries are caused by lifting. Other major causes are twisting, bending, pushing, and pulling heavy objects. The ergonomic approaches to reducing the risk of industrial back injuries are these:

- Redesigning the job
- Education, teaching how to lift "correctly"
- Matching the worker to the job design (i.e., preemployment testing)

The goal of job redesign is to engineer the stress out of the task. This is very effective, but it may not be possible or realistic to redesign the job. The educational approach is to teach workers the "correct way to lift." Teaching people the correct way to lift has not proven to be effective. The "correct" lifting technique taught is the bent-leg position pictured in many different texts. Biomechanical research by industrial engineers suggests that the classic bent-knee lifting position taught as the "correct" way to lift *may not* be the safest way and even may be more dangerous than lifting with straight legs (see Waters et al. 1993).

Psychophysical Ratings and Back Injuries

A key causal factor of low back injury is the worker's level of physical ability in relation to the lift load. An acceptable load was psychophysically defined by industrial workers who selected lift weights they could handle "without straining themselves." Lifting injuries could be reduced if workers lifted only loads that they could handle

without undue strain (i.e., within the lifter's physical ability). This psychophysical research is a key element of ergonomic equations (NIOSH 1981; Hidalgo et al. 1997; Waters et al. 1993) designed to define acceptable lift loads for workers. The message from this research is clear and simple: if the lift feels "too heavy," do not attempt it; you are more likely to hurt your back. The major factors that affect "safe lift loads" include not only the weight of the load lifted, but also the type of lift, the rate of work or number of lifts per minute, and whether one is male or female.

Worker Strength and Back Injuries

The initial focus of psychophysically defined "safe lift loads" was on male and female industrial populations, not the individual. Industrial populations are extremely variable in strength. While some individuals may be physically able to lift a load within a margin of safety, others are not. This has motivated researchers (e.g., Chin, Bishu & Halbeck 1995; Hidalgo et al. 1997; Jackson et al. 1997; Karwowski 1996; Resnik 1995) to define acceptable work loads for individuals. This work involves having the lifter rate lift difficulty with Borg's psychophysical rating scales (Borg 1998; Borg 1982; Borg & Ottoson 1986). Chapter 17 provides Borg's psychophysical scales. Research conducted at the University of Houston (Jackson et al. 1997; Jackson et al. 1998) showed that psychophysical lift difficulty was related to strength. Table 10.6 provides the correlations between isometric strength and lift loads ranging from 30 to 85 pounds. The isometric strength tests are described later in this chapter, in the section titled Strength Testing Methods. These data show that psychophysical lift difficulty for these lift loads is correlated with isometric strength level. As one would expect, these lifts are more difficult for weaker individuals. Figure 10-3 graphically illustrates this with floor-to-knuckle-height lift loads ranging from 55 to 85 pounds. Individuals with the lowest levels of strength rate the lifts to be most difficult. There is a growing view that lifts with Borg CR-10 ratings greater than 5 (Heavy) may be unacceptable (Hidalgo et al. 1997; Karwowski 1996). The 55- to

TABLE 10.6	**Correlations between Psychophysical Lift Difficulty and the Sum of Four Isometric Strength Tests**	
Lift Weight	r_{xy}*	r_{xy}†
30	−0.49	−0.52
45	−0.59	−0.55
60	−0.66	−0.62
75	−0.76	−0.65
85	−0.73	−0.52

Sources:*Jackson et al. (1998); †Jackson et al. (1997).

85-pound lifts shown in Figure 10-3 would be too heavy for someone with 200 pounds of isometric strength, but within acceptable levels for individuals with 600 pounds or more of isometric strength.

Ergonomic research showed that workers with strength capacities below that demanded by the work task were at a higher risk of back injury than those with sufficient strength. The risk of injury increased as the workers approached their maximum strength capacity. Borg's psychophysical rating scale measures a person's relative intensity—that is, a percentage of the individual's maximum capacity. Resnik (1995) reported that the CR-10 scale was linearly related ($R^2 = 0.86$) with relative lift load defined as a percentage of the subject's maximum strength. Formula 10.1 defines this relationship.

Relative Strength and CR-10 Rating **(10.1)**

% Max Strength = 10 × CR-10 Rating

To illustrate, a Borg CR-10 rating of 7 would indicate that the subject was lifting a load that was 70% of his maximum. A stronger person would be expected to rate the same lift at a lower rating.

The fitness component associated with low back injury is strength. The link is not with absolute strength, but rather with strength in relation to the physical requirement of the task. The closer the lift demands are to 100% of the individual's maximum strength capacity (CR-10 rating of 10), the higher the risk of injury. This is an important issue of preemployment testing. To reduce the risk of back injury, workers need to be matched to the demands of the task. For example, a 75-pound lift may be within the "safe lift range" for one person, but be too difficult and potentially dangerous for someone with less strength.

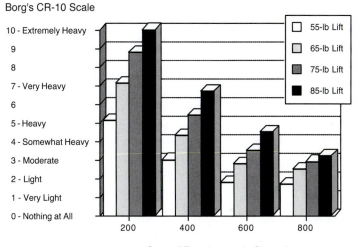

Borg's CR-10 Scale

10 - Extremely Heavy
9
8
7 - Very Heavy
6
5 - Heavy
4 - Somewhat Heavy
3 - Moderate
2 - Light
1 - Very Light
0 - Nothing at All

55-lb Lift
65-lb Lift
75-lb Lift
85-lb Lift

200   400   600   800

Sum of Four Isometric Strength

Figure 10-3

Relationship between psychophysical lift difficulty and strength level.
(Source: CSI Software Company, Houston, TX. Reprinted by permission.)

MUSCULAR STRENGTH

Muscular strength is the maximum force that a muscle group can exert over a brief period. The test methods used to measure muscular strength are discussed later in this chapter. Discussed next are three issues in general strength testing.

Absolute versus Relative Strength

Muscular strength may be evaluated in absolute or relative terms. Absolute strength is the maximum amount of force, measured by the strength test. Absolute strength is correlated with body weight, or more correctly, fat-free weight, which includes the body's force-producing component: muscle. Expressing a strength test score in absolute terms is appropriate when the evaluation decision is related to determining the individual's maximum force generation capacity. This would be relevant when, for example, testing athletes or applicants for physically demanding tasks. In these environments, the goal is to determine an individual's maximum force generation capacity.

Relative strength is expressed in terms of an individual's body weight. Relative strength is more relevant when evaluating the fitness of the individual. There is a positive correlation between body weight and absolute strength; the goal of representing strength in relative terms is to express it independent of body weight. In this context, "independent" means that the correlation between the relative strength measure and weight is zero. A common method is to express strength performance as a ratio of body weight (Gettman 1993). Formula 10.2 shows this.

Relative Strength—Strength/Weight Ratio **(10.2)**

$$\text{Relative Strength Ratio} = \left(\frac{\text{Measured Strength}}{\text{Body weight}} \right)$$

The relative strength ratio is very easy to use, but it does overcorrect for weight. To illustrate, Jackson et al. (1998) found that the correlation between the sum of isometric strength and weight for men was high, 0.61. When expressed as strength per pound of body weight, the correlation was –.17.

The relative strength ratio (Formula 10.2) is slightly biased against heavier individuals.

A second method uses simple linear regression analysis (Chapter 2) to eliminate the influence of body weight. The first step is to estimate the average level of strength for a given body weight. The average strength value would be estimated with a simple linear regression equation (Chapter 2) that uses strength as the dependent variable and body weight as the independent variable. Subtracting from the measured strength score, the estimated strength score provides a residual strength score, a score that has the influence of weight removed. Formula 10.3 shows this.

Relative Strength—Residual Strength Score **(10.3)**

Relative Strength Score = Measured Strength − Average Strength for Body Weight

The residual strength score can be a positive or negative value and represents the degree to which the person is stronger or weaker than others of that body weight. To illustrate, assume that the average arm strength for men weighing 160 pounds is 76 pounds. Further assume that two men were tested and the measured arm strength of the men was 95 pounds and 71 pounds, respectively. Their residual strength scores (Formula 10.3) would be as follows:

Man 1:
Residual Strength Score = 95 – 76 = 19 pounds

Man 2:
Residual Strength Score = 71 – 76 = –5 pounds

One man would be 19 pounds stronger than the average 160-pound man, while the other man would be 5 pounds weaker than the average 160-pound man. A residual strength score of 0 would indicate that the person had average strength for his weight.

The limitation of the residual strength method is that it is somewhat complicated; however, it can be easily accomplished with a computer. The correlation between weight and the residual strength score is 0, the desired goal of expressing strength in relative terms. The standard error of estimate (SEE) is the standard deviation of the residual strength score distribution. Using the estimated score, standard error of estimate, and normal curve (see Chapter 2), it becomes possible to develop normative tables for evaluating a person's strength in relation to her body weight. This is illustrated later in the chapter in Tables 10.11 and 10.12.

Male/Female Differences

Men and women differ in both absolute and relative strength. Much of this difference can be attributed to differences in body weight and body composition. Men not only are heavier than women, but have an average percent body fat about 6% to 7% lower. The differences in body weight and percent body fat produce even larger differences in fat-free weight, which is the primary source of strength differences between males and females.

When strength is expressed in absolute terms, the average strength differences are substantial. A common view is that the average upper-body strength of women is about 50% to 60% that of men, but the difference in leg strength is less. Women reportedly have about 70% of the leg strength of men (McArdle, Katch, & Katch 1991).

Data presented in the strength testing sections of this chapter show that there are also male/female differences in relative strength. This is mainly due to the differences in percent body fat. A higher proportion of women's body weight is fat weight, the weight's non-force-production component. This results in lower strength per pound of body weight.

Closed versus Open Kinetic Chain

Strength testing is closely linked with rehabilitation. The concept of "kinetic chain" is central to rehabilitation and muscle testing (Lephart & Henry 1996; Snyder-Mackler 1996). A kinetic chain can be either *open* or *closed*. An **open kinetic chain** exists when the end of the limb segment is free in space. In contrast, a **closed kinetic chain** exists when the end segment or joint meets with external resistance that prevents or restrains free motion. In a closed kinetic chain, movement at one joint produces movement at the other joints in the chain or system. By contrast, in an open kinetic setting, the distal limb segment can move freely.

The concept of open and closed kinetic chains can be illustrated with common leg strength tests. The leg press test is an example of a closed kinetic chain test. The distal segment of the chain (i.e., feet) meets significant resistance to prevent movement. Movement is produced at all joints in the chain: the ankles, knees, and hips. In contrast, the leg extension test is an open kinetic chain test. In this test, the distal segment (i.e., feet) is able to move freely. The only movement is at the knee joint. The current trend in rehabilitation of muscle injuries is a closed kinetic chain, treating the entire limb rather than an individual joint or muscle. This is one major reason for the current trend to use closed kinetic strength testing.

STRENGTH TESTING METHODS

Muscular strength is the maximum amount of force that a muscle group can exert. Muscle contractions can be either dynamic or static. Static contractions do not involve movement and are called isometric. Dynamic contractions involve movement: either concentric, in which the muscle shortens, or eccentric, in which the muscle lengthens. The dynamic forms include isotonic and isokinetic. Isotonic movement involves moving a weight against gravity. Lifting the weight uses a concentric contraction, while lowering the weight uses an eccentric contraction. Isokinetic movement involves muscle contractions at a fixed speed. Strength testing may involve either an open or a closed kinetic chain. Table 10.7 provides an overview of the strengths and weaknesses of strength testing methods.

Isometric Strength Testing

Isometric strength testing has historically been popular. The equipment is relatively inexpensive. A principle advantage of isometric tests is their flexibility. If a position can be standardized, it is possible to measure isometric strength. Isometric tests have been developed to measure single muscle groups (e.g., elbow flexion or elbow extension) or a combination of muscle groups, such as closed kinetic leg strength.

Isometric strength is the maximum force that a muscle group can exert without movement. Tests of

TABLE 10.7	A Comparison of Strength Testing Methods	
Method	**Strengths**	**Weaknesses**
Isometric	1. Moderately inexpensive. 2. Can be used to test a variety of different muscle groups. 3. Closed kinetic chain. 4. Strong research base for preemployment testing. 5. Normative data are available. 6. Takes very little time to test a subject. 7. Easy to learn how to administer the tests.	1. Only one joint angle is tested. 2. Does not provide a torque strength curve. 3. Cannot measure dynamic contractions.
Isotonic	1. Very inexpensive. 2. Many different types of equipment can be used. 3. Closed kinetic chain. 4. Tests often duplicate strength.development program. 5. Takes very little time to test a subject. 6. Easy to learn how to administer the tests.	1. Never measure "true maximum." 2. Cannot obtain a strength curve. 3. Risk of injury if free weights are used. 4. Different types of equipment affect the score; need equipment-specific norms. 5. Can be difficult to find 1-RM.
Isokinetic	1. Can obtain strength curves for many different speeds. 2. Can obtain both eccentric and concentric contractions. 3. Data can be expressed in many different ways. 4. Valuable for rehabilitation process.	1. Very expensive equipment. 2. Not closed kinetic chain. 3. Velocity of movement affects torque output; need norms for various speeds.

isometric strength are easy to perform, as they require only a single, maximal contraction. In the early days of testing, mechanical devices such as tensiometers and spring dynamometers measured the force applied during an isometric contraction. Electronic load cells are now replacing these mechanical devices, which were somewhat inaccurate and difficult to calibrate.

Isometric testing is a flexible method of evaluating strength. All one needs is to create the equipment to standardize the subject's test position, and place a load cell in such a position that it will record force (e.g., hand grip and cable-chain units). Some expensive back testing equipment uses elaborate chairs to standardize test positions and isolate muscle groups. These systems use load cells to measure strength at several different angles. Provided next are standard isometric strength tests.

Isometric Strength Test Battery

Provided in this section are isometric strength tests that measure major muscle groups. These are common tests that have been used in preemployment test settings (Jackson 1996), and also for general fitness testing (Jackson et al. 1997).

Tests   Arm, Shoulder, Torso, and Leg Strength.

Objective   To measure the maximal force of arm, shoulder, torso, and leg muscle groups using a closed kinetic chain.

Validity   Isometric tests have been recognized as a valid method for measuring strength. The isometric strength tests are highly correlated with simulated work tasks of physically demanding occupations (Jackson 1996). Table 10.5 shows these validity coefficients.

Reliability   The reliability estimates exceed 0.94 for each test.

Equipment   The tests are administered on equipment manufactured by Lafayette Instrument Company, Lafayette, IN (Model 32528). The test equipment consists of a platform with a chain apparatus, and a load cell and digital recorder. The equipment was developed for preemployment testing for physically demanding jobs for the Shell Oil Company, Houston, TX. The equipment is now widely used in medical and rehabilitative settings.

Procedures   Once the subject is in the test position, the tester pushes the "start" button. A "beep" will sound and 3 seconds later a second "beep" will be heard. The subject is instructed to exert force on this first "beep" and stop on the second "beep." The equipment allows you to set the length of the trial. A 3-second trial is used, during which force is recorded only for the last 2 seconds. Typically, subjects will jerk at the start of the trial. By not measuring this first second, you ensure that the jerk is not reflected in the strength score, which is the average force exerted during the final two seconds. A warm-up trial at 50% effort is administered first, followed by two trials for score. External forms of motivation are to be strictly avoided. Do not encourage the subject when he is exerting force. Do not give the subject his score after completing a trial.

1. *Arm Lift.* The arm-lift apparatus is used to measure lifting strength. The load cell is attached and equipment is adjusted so the elbows are at 90° flexion. The cable should be at a right angle to the base. The legs should be straight, and the subject is not allowed to lean back. Maximal lifting force is exerted in this position.
2. *Shoulder Lift.* The bar setting used for the arm-lift test is used for the shoulder lift. To assume the correct position, the subject moves forward until the bar touches his body. The cable should be at a right angle to the base. With the palms facing the rear, the subject grabs the bar so that the inside of his hands are on the inside of the black handle. In this position the elbows are pointing out, away from the body. This test measures the lifting strength of the shoulders. The subject is not allowed to lean back or use his legs (e.g., bending the knees and generating force with the legs). The force is correctly exerted by lifting up with the shoulders while the elbows point outward. These muscle groups are commonly used for lifting tasks.
3. *Torso Strength.* The torso lift test is recommended for preemployment testing. It has been our experience that many are hesitant to be tested in this position. Our research led us to develop the torso pull test, shown in Figure 10-4. With a sample of 246 industrial workers and 204 students, we found a high correlation (r = 0.91) between the two tests. We recommend that the torso pull test be used. The test procedure is described next.

The platform-chain apparatus is placed against the wall with the chain at its lowest point. The bar is set 17 inches from the base of the platform. The subject sits on a mat and places his feet against the platform. The subject uses a reverse grip (palms facing the floor) and keeps the legs straight. The force is correctly exerted by leaning and pulling back. Provided next is a regression equation that can be used to estimate the torso lift strength from that of the torso pull.

TORSO PULL TEST

Figure 10-4

The test position for the torso pull test.

(Source: CSI Software Company, Houston, TX. Reprinted by permission.)

Conversion to Torso Lift Strength   **(10.4)**

$$\text{Torso Lift} = (0.973 \times \text{Torso Pull}) - 18.188$$

4. *Leg-Lift Test.* The following procedures are used to get the subject into the test position to test leg strength. First, the platform is placed on the floor and the lift bar is attached to a chain link that places the bar 17 inches from the base of the platform. The same chain setting is used for all subjects. This is the same setting used for the torso test. The subject stands on the platform with his feet spread a comfortable distance. The bar is rotated 90° so the ends of the bar face the front and back of the platform. The subject grips the bar with the palms facing each other. The hands are as close to the center of the bar as possible. In this position the bar is between the legs with the arms as close to the body as possible. The subject bends his knees, keeping the arms as close to the body as possible. The head is in such a position the subject is forced to look straight ahead, not down. In the test position, force is exerted by the legs. The subject should not jerk, but rather apply force in a consistent, forceful manner.

Scoring   The average of two trials is used for the score. Tables 10.8 and 10.9 give the means, standard deviations, and sample sizes for industrial workers and college students by sex.

Norms   The descriptive statistics in Tables 10.8 and 10.9 provide absolute strength norms for industrial workers and college students. Table 10.10 provides regression equations with functions to estimate strength from body weight. These formulas serve as the basis for the relative strength percentile rank norms (Tables 10.11 and 10.12).

TABLE 10.8	Means, Standard Deviations, and Sample Sizes for Isometric Strength Tests Administered to Male and Female Industrial Workers					
Strength Test	**Males**			**Females**		
	Mean	**SD**	**N**	**Mean**	**SD**	**N**
Arm lift	86.3	16.8	195	49.1	11.8	55
Shoulder lift	118.7	22.6	195	66.8	17.3	55
Torso pull	222.6	57.3	195	119.6	38.9	55
Leg strength	229.7	50.7	195	118.9	38.3	55

TABLE 10.9	Means, Standard Deviations, and Sample Sizes for Isometric Strength Tests Administered to Male and Female College Students					
Strength Test	**Males**			**Females**		
	Mean	**SD**	**N**	**Mean**	**SD**	**N**
Arm lift	74.1	17.4	133	37.9	11.6	249
Shoulder lift	105.1	26.3	133	53.3	17.3	249
Torso pull	222.2	60.0	133	109.5	38.3	249
Leg strength	203.3	58.8	133	103.6	37.0	249

TABLE 10.10	**Regression Equation to Develop Relative Isometric Strength Norms**			
Test	**Gender**	**Equation***	**R**	**SEE**
Arm lift	Female	$Y' = (0.18 \times Wt) + 15.34$	0.37	11.4
Arm lift	Male	$Y' = (0.20 \times Wt) + 44.35$	0.42	16.4
Shoulder lift	Female	$Y' = (0.20 \times Wt) + 28.62$	0.28	17.2
Shoulder lift	Male	$Y' = (0.32 \times Wt) + 54.77$	0.48	22.0
Torso pull	Female	$Y' = (0.46 \times Wt) + 49.84$	0.30	36.6
Torso pull	Male	$Y' = (0.61 \times Wt) + 112.25$	0.38	53.6
Leg strength	Female	$Y' = (0.40 \times Wt) + 54.40$	0.27	35.6
Leg strength	Male	$Y' = (0.70 \times Wt) + 90.14$	0.47	48.4

*The term Y' is the average strength for a given body weight (Wt).

TABLE 10.11	**Percentile-Rank* Norms for Relative Isometric Strength of Women for Four Strength Tests**											
Weight in Pounds	**Arm Lift Percentile**			**Shoulder Lift Percentile**			**Torso Pull Percentile**			**Leg Lift Percentile**		
	25	**50**	**75**	**25**	**50**	**75**	**25**	**50**	**75**	**25**	**50**	**75**
90	24	32	39	35	47	58	67	91	116	67	90	114
100	26	33	41	37	49	60	71	96	120	71	94	118
110	28	35	43	39	51	62	76	100	125	75	98	122
120	29	37	45	41	53	64	81	105	130	79	102	126
130	31	39	46	43	55	66	85	110	134	83	106	130
140	33	41	48	45	57	68	90	114	139	87	110	134
150	35	42	50	47	59	70	94	119	143	91	114	138
160	37	44	52	49	61	72	99	123	148	95	118	142
170	38	46	54	51	63	74	104	128	153	99	122	146
180	40	48	55	53	65	76	108	133	157	103	126	150
190	42	50	57	55	67	78	113	137	162	107	130	154
200	44	51	59	57	69	80	117	142	166	111	134	158

*The 50th percentile is the estimated strength score (Y') from the weight regression equation. The 25th percentile is $Y' - (0.67 \times SEE)$ and the 75th percentile is $Y' + (0.67 \times SEE)$.

Isometric Grip Strength

The grip strength is a common isometric test. Equipment used to measure grip strength includes an electronic load cell, dynamometer, and JAMAR hydraulic unit.

Test   Grip Strength

Objective   To measure the maximal grip strength.

Validity   Grip strength is a standard test used to measure strength.

Reliability   The reliability estimates exceed 0.90 for each test.

| TABLE 10.12 | Percentile-Rank* Norms for Relative Isometric Strength of Men for Four Strength Tests | | | | | | | | | | | |

Weight in Pounds	Arm Lift Percentile			Shoulder Lift Percentile			Torso Pull Percentile			Leg Lift Percentile		
	25	50	75	25	50	75	25	50	75	25	50	75
120	57	68	79	78	93	108	150	185	221	142	174	207
130	59	70	81	82	96	111	156	192	227	149	181	214
140	61	72	83	85	100	114	162	198	234	156	188	221
150	63	74	85	88	103	118	168	204	240	163	195	228
160	65	76	87	91	106	121	174	210	246	170	202	235
170	67	78	89	94	109	124	180	216	252	177	209	242
180	69	80	91	98	112	127	186	222	258	184	216	249
190	71	82	93	101	116	130	192	228	264	191	223	256
200	73	84	95	104	119	134	198	234	270	198	230	263
210	75	86	97	107	122	137	204	240	276	205	237	270
220	77	88	99	110	125	140	211	246	282	212	244	277
230	79	90	101	114	128	143	217	253	288	219	251	284
240	81	92	103	117	132	146	223	259	295	226	258	291
250	83	94	105	120	135	150	229	265	301	233	265	298

*The 50th percentile is the estimated strength score (Y') from the weight regression equation. The 25th percentile is Y' − (0.67 × SEE) and the 75th percentile is Y' + (0.67 × SEE).

Equipment The electronic load cell unit manufactured by Lafayette Instrument Company, Lafayette, IN (Model 32528), and JAMAR hydraulic unit are recommended.

Procedures The procedures for using the electronic load cell unit and JAMAR unit differ.

Load Cell Procedures. The grip strength is tested with the load cell attached to the grip apparatus. The subject is seated at a table with her free hand on the table. The apparatus is gripped with the palm up. Maximal force is exerted in this position.

JAMAR Procedures. The JAMAR hand dynamometer utilizes a hydraulic gauge with a peak-hold needle to record the highest strength effort. The following procedures need to be followed to measure grip strength with the JAMAR unit.

1. The JAMAR displays grip force in pounds and kilograms. Grip strength is measured in pounds.

2. The maximum grip strength is recorded by a special peak-hold needle. After each test trial, reset the needle to "0."

3. The adjustable handle allows for five settings; typically, settings 2 or 3 are used, depending upon hand size.

4. The subject stands comfortably with her shoulder adducted and neutrally rotated. The elbow is flexed to 90° and the forearm and wrist are in neutral position. The subject's right and left grip are tested. In the test position, the subject exerts force by gripping the handle with a single, forceful effort.

Scoring The average of two trials is used for score. Table 10.13 lists the absolute grip strength norms for college students and occupational groups contrasted by sex.

TABLE 10.13	Means, Standard Deviations, and Sample Sizes for Grip Strength Administered to College Students and Different Groups of Industrial Workers					
	Women			**Men**		
Sample	**Mean**	**SD**	**N**	**Mean**	**SD**	**N**
College students	64.1	15.5	207	99.4	27.0	193
Construction workers	80.2	23.3	18	111.1	23.3	234
Gas service workers	70.8	19.0	34	108.8	23.3	212
Police cadets	71.5	16.2 1	7	113.8	25.2	161
Coal miners	*			124.8	17.5	96
Refinery workers	76.8	12.8 1	4	118.1	23.3	75

*Not measured.

TABLE 10.14	Correlations among Isometric Strength Tests and Sums of Tests (n = 632)					
Test	**Arm**	**Shoulder**	**Torso**	**Leg**	**ΣThree***	**ΣFour†**
Arm lift	1.00					
Shoulder lift	0.92	1.00				
Torso pull	0.82	0.80	1.00			
Leg strength	0.85	0.86	0.85	1.00		
ΣThree*	0.93	0.93	0.96	0.90	1.00	
ΣFour†	0.92	0.92	0.95	0.96	0.99	1.00

*Sum of arm, shoulder, and torso.

†Sum of arm, shoulder, torso, and leg.

Sum of Isometric Strength Tests

Table 10.14 provides the correlations among the arm, shoulder, torso, and leg isometric strength tests. The correlations among the four tests are high, ranging from 0.82 to 0.92. The high correlations support the practice of summing the tests for one measure of total strength. The University of Houston preemployment studies have used the sum of all four tests (ΣFour) or the sum of arm, shoulder, and torso (ΣThree). Either sum may be used; the correlation between them is 0.99.

Table 10.15 provides the male and female absolute strength norms for the ΣThree and ΣFour isometric strength tests. Tables 10.16 and 10.17 provide the relative male and female norms for the two sums.

Isotonic Strength Testing

Isotonic strength is measured by determining the maximal force that a muscle group can exert with a single contraction. An isotonic strength test measures the maximum weight that can be lifted with a single repetition. This is the one-repetition maximum test (1-RM). Free-weight or progressive resistance equipment is used to measure 1-RM strength. The most difficult part of the test is to find the subject's maximal load. Several different weights will need to be tried to find the proper 1-RM weight. After an appropriate warm-up, we recommend that you follow a testing procedure similar to that described by the American College of Sports Medicine (2001).

TABLE 10.15	Absolute ΣThree and ΣFour Isometric Strength Norms for Men and Women*						
					Percentile		
Strength Test	Mean	SD	10	25	50	75	90
Men (n = 328)							
ΣThree†	417.0	87.0	302	361	414	479	536
ΣFour‡	635.9	134.0	466	542	632	740	809
Women (n = 304)							
ΣThree†	207.0	61.7	135	165	201	245	284
ΣFour‡	313.3	92.4	202	251	305	371	430

*Data from industrial workers and college students.

†Sum of arm, shoulder, and torso.

‡Sum of arm, shoulder, torso, and leg.

TABLE 10.16	Relative Isometric Strength Norms for Men for the Sum of Three and Four Strength Tests					
Weight in Pounds	Sum of Three* Precentile			Sum of Four† Percentile		
	25	50	75	25	50	75
120	205	347	489	447	523	600
130	217	358	500	465	542	618
140	228	370	511	484	560	637
150	239	381	523	502	579	655
160	251	392	534	520	597	673
170	262	403	545	539	615	692
180	273	415	556	557	634	710
190	284	426	568	576	652	729
200	296	437	579	594	671	747
210	307	449	590	612	689	765
220	318	460	602	631	707	784
230	330	471	613	649	726	802
240	341	483	624	668	744	821
250	352	494	636	686	763	839

Estimated ΣThree = $(1.13 \times Wt) + 211.38$; R = 0.48; SEE = 211.4

Estimated ΣFour = $(1.84 \times Wt) + 302.51$; R = 0.51; SEE = 114.1

*Sum of arm, shoulder, and torso.

†Sum of arm, shoulder, torso, and leg.

1. Begin with a weight that is below the estimated maximum for the participant. For novices, a pretest session is useful for training in correct technique and to gain a rough estimate of the participant's strength level.

2. Allow 2 to 3 minutes of rest between trials, to avoid fatigue.

3. Increase the resistance by 5 to 10 pounds, depending on the difficulty of the previous trial for the participant.

TABLE 10.17	Relative Isometric Strength Norms for Women for the Sum of Three and Four Strength Tests					
Weight in Pounds	**Sum of Three* Precentile**			**Sum of Four† Percentile**		
	25	**50**	**75**	**25**	**50**	**75**
90	132	170	209	202	260	318
100	140	179	217	214	272	330
110	149	187	226	227	285	343
120	157	196	234	239	297	355
130	166	204	243	252	310	368
140	174	213	251	264	322	380
150	183	221	260	277	335	393
160	191	230	268	289	347	405
170	200	238	277	302	360	418
180	208	247	285	314	372	430
190	217	255	294	327	385	443
200	225	264	302	339	397	455

Estimated ΣThree $= (0.85 \times$ Wt$) + 93.80$; R $= 0.34$; SEE $= 57.7$

Estimated ΣFour $= (1.25 \times$ Wt$) + 147.20$; R $= 0.33$; SEE $= 86.5$

*Sum of arm, shoulder, and torso.

†Sum of arm, shoulder, torso, and leg.

4. Repeat the process (with rest between every trial) until the participant either fails an attempt or uses unacceptable form because the lift was so difficult.
5. Record the heaviest weight lifted successfully with acceptable form as the 1-RM score.

Isotonic 1-RM Strength Tests

These tests can be administered with standard barbells, but for safety and convenience we recommend strength development machines common to most facilities. Because equipment varies in design, 1-RM tests need to be specific to the muscle group tested. The maximal weight lifted will be higher for progressive resistance equipment because the resistance changes during the exercise. Because of these differences, it is desirable to establish equipment-specific norms.

Tests   Bench Press and Leg Press

Objective   To measure a closed kinetic chain 1-RM strength.

Validity   Construct validity of muscular strength of the arms and legs.

Equipment   These isotonic tests are especially applicable in facilities that have weight-training machines. Besides serving as a teaching station for weight-training instruction, this type of equipment is excellent for measuring arm strength. Free weights also can be used, with proper spotting.

Procedures   Follow the recommended procedure for finding the person's 1-RM. While it is possible to measure 1-RM many different ways (curls, lat pull, leg extension, etc.), the bench and leg press tests have become standards and are presented next.

1. *Bench Press*. The student can assume any width grasp outside the shoulders. Feet must be on the floor, the back straight. After each repetition the weights must be brought back to the starting position.
2. *Leg Press*. The subject sits in the provided chair, fully extends the legs, and executes a

maximal repetition. The seat should be adjusted to standardize the knee angle at approximately 120°.

Scoring   A student's score is the maximal weight lifted.

Norms   Because of differences in equipment and test procedures, we recommend that you develop situation-specific norms. Tables 10.18 and 10.19 provide relative strength/weight ratio norms for the bench press and leg press 1-RM tests for men and women (Gettman 1993).

TABLE 10.18	**Relative Strength/Weight Ratio, Isotonic 1-RM Standards for Men**				
Age Group	**Evaluation Standard**				
	Excellent	**Good**	**Average**	**Fair**	**Poor**
1-RM Bench Press					
20–29	>1.25	1.17–1.25	0.97–1.16	0.88–0.96	<0.88
30–39	>1.07	1.01–1.07	0.86–1.00	0.79–0.85	<0.79
40–49	>0.96	0.91–0.96	0.78–0.90	0.72–0.77	<0.72
50–59	>0.85	0.81–0.85	0.70–0.80	0.65–0.69	<0.65
≥60	>0.77	0.74–0.77	0.64–0.73	0.60–0.63	<0.60
1-RM Upper Leg Press					
20–29	>2.07	2.00–2.07	1.83–1.99	1.65–1.82	<1.65
30–39	>1.87	1.80–1.87	1.63–1.79	1.55–1.62	<1.55
40–49	>1.75	1.70–1.75	1.56–1.69	1.50–1.55	<1.50
50–59	>1.65	1.60–1.65	1.46–1.59	1.40–1.45	<1.40
≥60	>1.55	1.50–1.55	1.37–1.49	1.31–1.36	<1.31

Source: Used with permission. Norm charts from the *Physical Fitness Specialist Manual*, Cooper Institute, Dallas, TX.

TABLE 10.19	**Relative Strength/Weight Ratio, Isotonic 1-RM Standards for Women**				
Age Group	**Evaluation Standard**				
	Excellent	**Good**	**Average**	**Fair**	**Poor**
1-RM Bench Press					
20–29	>0.77	0.72–0.77	0.59–0.71	0.53–0.58	<0.53
30–39	>0.65	0.62–0.65	0.53–0.61	0.49–0.52	<0.49
40–49	>0.60	0.57–0.60	0.48–0.56	0.44–0.47	<0.44
50–59	>0.53	0.51–0.53	0.43–0.50	0.40–0.42	<0.40
≥60	>0.54	0.51–0.54	0.41–0.50	0.37–0.40	<0.37
1-RM Upper Leg Press					
20–29	>1.62	1.54–1.62	1.35–1.53	1.26–1.34	<1.26
30–39	>1.41	1.35–1.41	1.20–1.34	1.13–1.19	<1.13
40–49	>1.31	1.26–1.31	1.12–1.25	1.06–1.11	<1.06
50–59	>1.25	1.13–1.25	0.99–1.12	0.86–0.98	<0.86
≥60	>1.14	1.08–1.14	0.92–1.07	0.85–0.91	<0.85

Source: Used with permission. Norm charts from the *Physical Fitness Specialist Manual*, Cooper Institute, Dallas, TX.

Isotonic Absolute Endurance

Muscular strength and absolute endurance are highly correlated. In an **absolute endurance test,** a weight load is repeatedly lifted until exhaustion is reached, and the same weight is used for all subjects tested. The correlations between strength and absolute endurance tests are high. The reason for the high relation between strength and absolute endurance is that subjects are lifting at different percentages of maximal strength. For example, assume the maximal bench-press strengths of two people are 120 and 150 pounds. If the weight load for the test is 110 pounds, the weaker person would be lifting at 92% of maximal, while the stronger person would be lifting at 73% of maximal strength. The stronger person would complete more repetitions before becoming exhausted.

The YMCA adult fitness test uses an absolute endurance bench-press test (Golding 2000). A constant weight of 35 pounds is used for testing women, and 80 pounds is used for men. The test is to complete as many repetitions as possible to exhaustion. The test and norms are provided in Chapter 14.

Isokinetic Strength Testing

Tests of **isokinetic strength** measure torque through a defined range of motion while keeping the speed of movement constant. The equipment used to measure isokinetic strength uses a load cell interfaced with a computer. The computer unit controls the speed of movement and measures torque. This yields the muscle group's torque curve for the selected constant velocity. Both muscle strength and the velocity of movement affect the shape and magnitude of the curve (Figure 10-5). As the muscle contracts at a faster rate, it cannot generate as much torque, so a lower curve is obtained. Test results from different test centers are not comparable unless the sites use the same equipment and the same test velocity.

The isokinetic torque curve provides therapists with the capacity to evaluate the muscle group's symmetry. The equipment has the capacity to conduct both eccentric and concentric contractions and compute various ratios of interest—for example, agonist/antagonist, or concentric/eccentric.

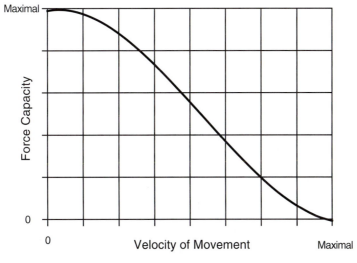

Figure 10-5

Torque curve for velocity of movement and muscular strength.

(Source: Jackson, A.S. and Ross, R.M. *Understanding Exercise for Health and Fitness*, 1997. Reprinted by permission.)

Isokinetic equipment is expensive and so is generally used only at well-equipped testing centers such as NASA, the U.S. Olympic Center, and modern sports medicine and physical therapy facilities. In recent years, isokinetic testing has been losing favor. There are several reasons for this. A major factor is the cost of the equipment coupled with change in our health care systems. Managed health care corporations have dramatically reduced the amount of money they will pay for strength evaluations. Another reason is that isokinetic tests are largely open kinetic chains, whereas the current rehabilitation philosophy is to use a closed kinetic chain.

Correlations among Types of Strength Tests

Strength tests involve dynamic and static contractions. When scored in absolute terms, these two kinds of strength tests are highly correlated. Table 10.5 shows that isometric strength tests are highly correlated with many different types of work-sample strength tests that involve dynamic and static contractions. As previously discussed, the correlations between 1-RM isotonic strength tests and absolute endurance tests are high. Isometric and isotonic 1-RM tests were found to be highly correlated (Russell et al. 1993). Using samples of high school and college students, the correlations between the sum of grip, torso, and arm isometric strength and 1-RM bench press were 0.80 and 0.83, respectively. The correlations between the sum of isometric strength and 1-RM leg strength were slightly lower, 0.73 and 0.74.

Muscular Power

Muscular power has traditionally been defined as maximum force released in the shortest possible time. The vertical jump, standing long jump, and shot put have been the recommended measures of power, but jumping tests are not highly correlated with mechanically measured power. **Power** is the rate that work (product of force and distance) is performed and is defined by Formula 10.5.

Definition of power   **(10.5)**

$$\text{Power} = \left(\frac{\text{Force} \times \text{Distance}}{\text{Time}} \right) = \left(\frac{\text{Work}}{\text{Time}} \right)$$

The trend in power testing has been to use cycle and arm ergometers. An all-out cycling power test was first described in 1973 and called the Katch test (McArdle, Katch, & Katch 1991). This test was refined at the Department of Research and Sport Medicine at the Wingate (Israel) Institute, and is now known as the Wingate anaerobic power test (Inbar, Bar-Or, & Skinner, 1996). This has become the test of choice for measuring power. The Wingate power test involves cycling as fast as possible for 30 seconds at a set resistance.

The Monarch cycle ergometer is one of the most popular testing ergometers. A distance of 6 meters is traveled with each revolution of the flywheel. This ergometer varies flywheel resistance with a weight load. The unit of measurement of the weight load is kiloponds (kp). A kilopond is equal to 2.2 pounds, or 1 kilogram. Both kiloponds and kilograms are used in the literature. Thus, the amount of work performed for each revolution of the flywheel with a resistance of 1 kp would be 6 kilopond meters, or 6 kpm. Increasing resistance to 2 kp increases the work to 12 kpm for each revolution. Power is the ratio of work and time. Power, expressed as kilopond meters per minute (kpm/min), is computed by dividing work by the time required to complete the work.

The time for the Wingate test is constant, 30 seconds (0.5 minutes). For a given kp (kilopond) resistance, differences in Wingate power are a function of the total number of revolutions completed in 30 seconds. Assuming a Monark cycle ergometer, the formula to measure power is

Wingate Power Equation   **(10.6)**

$$\text{Power (kpm/min)} = \left(\frac{6 \times \text{kp} \times \text{R}}{0.5} \right)$$

where 6 is the distance in meters traveled with each revolution of the flywheel, kp is the ergometer resistance, and R is the total number of revolutions completed in 0.5 minutes (30 sec). Power tests are often expressed in watts. The conversion from kpm/min is

Power Expressed in Watts   **(10.7)**

$$\text{Power in Watts} = \left(\frac{\text{Power in kpm/min}}{6.12} \right)$$

Provided next are the test procedures for the Wingate anaerobic power tests.

Test   Wingate Power Test (Bar-Or 1987).

Objective   To measure anaerobic leg power.

Validity   By definition, the test measures leg power.

Reliability   Test-retest reliabilities between 0.89 and 0.98 have been reported for the test.

Equipment   The equipment needed is a calibrated cycle ergometer with the capacity to measure the number of flywheel revolutions completed in 30 seconds. Computerized systems exist that measure the number of revolutions with a photoelectric system that records the revolutions from reflective tape placed on the flywheel. These computer systems also make all calculations.

Procedures   The seat height of the ergometer is set for the subject's best comfort. It is recommended that toe clips be used. A warm-up is recommended. One common warm-up protocol is to have the subject pedal at a low rate at the setting to be used in the test. The warm-up consists of pedaling for about 3 minutes, including two or three all-out 5-second bursts. The subject rests prior to being tested. Test administration involves making choices on resistance setting and starting method. These are discussed next.

Resistance Setting.   The recommended setting is based on a proportion of body weight. The resistance settings (kp) for a Monark ergometer are as follows:

$$\text{Children} = 0.075 \times \text{Body Weight in kg}$$

$$\text{Adult Women} = 0.086 \times \text{Body Weight in kg}$$

$$\text{Adult Men} = 0.087 \times \text{Body Weight in kg}$$

$$\text{Athletes} = 0.10 \times \text{Body Weight in kg}$$

Starting Method. Once the resistance setting is determined, the start method must be selected. The three common start methods are these:

1. *Still Start.* The ergometer is set at the predetermined resistance and the subject starts pedaling as fast as possible on the command of "Go." The test ends after 30 seconds of all-out cycling.
2. *Gradual Start.* The person starts pedaling at a moderate resistance. The resistance is increased as pedaling rate increases. The test starts when the set resistance is reached.
3. *All-Out Start.* The ergometer resistance is set at 0 kp. At the start command, the subject starts to pedal at maximum velocity and the resistance is increased to the predetermined setting. The 30-second test starts when the setting is reached.

Scoring   Power output is determined from the resistance setting and the distance the flywheel traveled in 30 seconds. The test can be scored in absolute or relative terms. Absolute power output is in total watts, and relative power is watts per kilogram of body weight. With computer-controlled equipment, power output can be computed as the average for the 30 seconds or peak power achieved during the 30-second effort. Table 10.20 provides normative data for men and women (Maud & Shultz 1989).

While the Wingate power test has typically measured leg power, the same principles can be used to measure arm power. The same test principles used for leg-power tests are applied to the arm-power test.

MUSCULAR ENDURANCE

Muscular endurance is the ability to persist in physical activity or to resist muscular fatigue. Endurance tests can measure absolute endurance where the weight load moved to exhaustion is the same for all subjects tested, or measure relative endurance where the weight moved varies among the subjects tested. The muscular endurance abilities described here involve moving or maintaining one's own body weight to exhaustion. Since body weights among subjects will vary, these are tests of relative endurance. Three basic endurance abilities have been identified: (1) muscular endurance of the arms and shoulder girdle, (2) muscular endurance

TABLE 10.20	Normative Data for the Wingate Power Test							
	Average Power for 30 Seconds				**Peak Power**			
	Men (n = 60)		**Women (n = 69)**		**Men (n = 60)**		**Women (n = 69)**	
Percentile	Watts	Watts/kg	Watts	Watts/kg	Watts	Watts/kg	Watts	Watts/kg
90	662	8.24	470	7.31	822	10.89	560	9.02
75	604	7.96	413	6.93	768	10.20	518	8.53
50	565	7.44	381	6.39	689	9.22	449	7.65
25	521	6.79	347	5.94	646	8.34	396	6.77
10	471	5.98	306	5.25	570	7.06	353	5.98
Mean	563	7.28	381	6.35	700	9.18	454	7.61
SD	66	0.88	56	0.73	95	1.43	81	1.24

Source: From Maud and Shultz (1989).

of the abdominal muscles, and (3) cardiorespiratory endurance. Tests used to measure these endurance abilities are included in motor fitness and health-related fitness tests (see Chapters 11, 13, and 14).

Arm and Shoulder Girdle Endurance Tests

Tests of arm and shoulder girdle endurance require the subject to move or support the body weight against the pull of gravity and may involve either isometric or isotonic contractions of the muscles executed to exhaustion. It has been claimed that tests of this ability measure both strength and endurance. Dynamic strength, arm and shoulder girdle strength, and muscular endurance are the terms used by physical educators to describe this ability. There is a negative correlation between body weight and this basic physical ability, and the correlation is even higher between percent of body fat and this basic ability.

The tests most often recommended for motor fitness or physical fitness batteries are pull-ups and push-ups. On the pull-up test, the student is required to use the forward grip, palms facing away from the body. The pull-up test can also be administered with the reverse grip, palms facing the body, but then it is usually called a chin-up. Testing procedures for the pull-up and push-up are pro-

vided in Chapter 13. Provided with the test instructions are norms.

When preparing to measure this ability, be sure to select a test of appropriate difficulty for the group being tested. There is a tendency for these test distributions to be positively skewed. Many students have difficulty maintaining or moving their body weight against gravity. A high proportion of students, especially girls, elementary school children, and low-fit students, cannot complete a single pull-up. This has led to increased use of the push-up test and the development of modified pull-up tests. Described next are two modified pull-up tests.

Youth Fitness Modified Pull-Up Test

The FITNESSGRAM® (Cooper Institute for Aerobics Research, 1999) youth fitness test provides an optional test. For this test, the student lies down on her back with the shoulders directly under a bar that has been set 1 to 2 inches above the child's reach. The student grasps the bar with an overhand grip (palms away from the body). From this "down" position with the arms and legs straight, buttocks off the floor, and only the heels touching the floor, the student pulls until the chin reaches an elastic band placed on the pull-up equipment. The band is set 7 inches below the pull-up bar.

Baumgartner Modified Pull-Up Test

Objectivity, reliability, and validity evidence for the test is presented by Baumgartner and Gaunt (2005). The Baumgartner modified pull-up test can also be used for training (Baumgartner & Wood 1984). The equipment can be supported on either a floor stand or a wall bracket. The student lies down on the scooter and grasps the pull-up bar at the top end of the equipment with an overhanded grip, hands about shoulder-width apart (Figure 10-6). The student then assumes a straight-arm hanging position, pulls up the inclined board until the chin is over the bar, and returns to a straight-arm hanging position. This action is repeated as often as possible. The test is scored by the number of completed repetitions. Norms for most ages from six years through college and for both sexes are reported by Baumgartner et al. (1984) and Jackson et al. (1982). Almost without exception, scores range from 3 to 50.

Measuring Abdominal Muscle Endurance

Tests of abdominal muscle endurance require the subject to use the abdominal muscles to move or maintain the body's upper extremity to exhaustion; they may require either isometric or isotonic contractions of these muscles. Tests that measure this ability have been called measures of abdominal muscle strength or endurance. These tests are covered in Chapters 13 and 14.

Measuring Cardiorespiratory Endurance

Cardiorespiratory endurance is another term for aerobic fitness, or $\dot{V}O_2$ max. This topic is fully discussed in Chapter 11.

BASIC MOVEMENT PATTERNS

The importance of basic movement patterns—running, jumping, and throwing—is recognized by physical educators, and tests of these abilities are included in published general motor ability and motor fitness batteries. These abilities are especially important for evaluating athletes.

Measuring Running Speed

Tests of running **speed** require the subject to run at maximum speed in a straight path. The basic physical ability is measured by the elapsed time required to run a specified distance (usually 10 to 60 yards). This basic physical ability is normally represented on motor ability and motor fitness test batteries by a sprinting test ranging from 40 to 60 yards in length. Although sprints as short as 20 yards may reliably measure this basic physical ability, longer sprints, 40 or 50 yards, are more reliable. Most motor ability or motor fitness batteries recommend 50-yard sprints, while 40-yard sprints are universally accepted by football coaches. Testing procedures and norms for the 50-yard dash are provided next.

Test 50-Yard Dash (AAHPER 1976)

Equipment A stopwatch accurate to one-tenth of a second per runner, or a stopwatch accurate to one-tenth of a second with a split timer, and a test course of suitable length to ensure safe stopping after the sprint.

Procedure Have two students run at the same time for competition. The students assume a starting position behind the starting line. The starter uses the commands "Are you ready?" and "Go!" On "Go," the starter makes a downward sweep of the arm, giving a visual signal to the timer to start the watch. The timer, standing at the finish line, stops the watch when the runner crosses the line.

Scoring The participant's score is the elapsed time between the starter's signal and the instant the participant crosses the finish line. Scores are recorded to the nearest tenth of a second. AAHPER (1976) has norms for girls and boys.

Other Considerations Allow students to take one or two warm-up trials before they are timed for score.

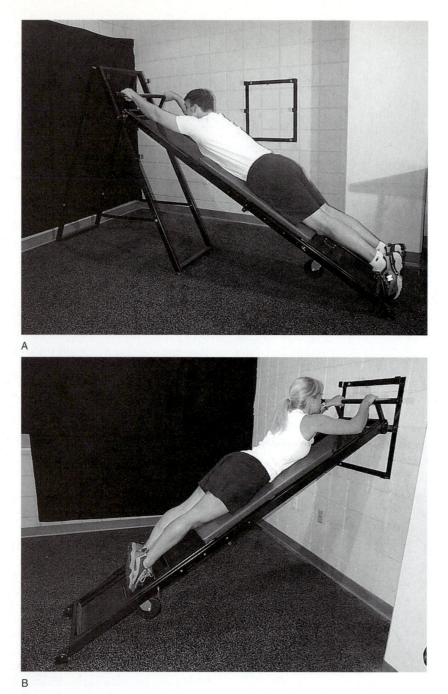

A

B

Figure 10-6

Baumgartner modified pull-up test.

(Equipment pictured from Flaghouse, Hasbrouck Heights, NJ.)

Measuring Running Agility

Agility is the ability to change the direction of the body or body parts rapidly. This ability is measured with running tests that require the subject to turn or start and stop. Such tests appear in most published general motor ability and motor fitness batteries. Running speed tends to be related to agility.

The tests used to measure running agility present a common measurement problem: students learn to perform these tests with practice. When multiple trials are administered, the best scores for the group are achieved on the last trials. These tests are time-consuming, so it would not normally be feasible to allow many trials, but you should give students an opportunity to practice before the test or while other students are being tested. Proper traction is another problem posed by these tests. It is essential that students wear proper shoes and that the test be administered on a suitable surface; a tile floor or a dirty floor may be too slippery.

Many tests of running agility have been published. The shuttle run requires the subject to run back and forth between two parallel lines. A second type of running agility test requires the student to run a test course that calls for constant turning. It would be more appropriate in the athletic setting is to study the types of agility movements made by the athlete and then develop sport-specific agility tests. The shuttle run is presented in Chapter 13.

Test Zigzag Run (Texas Governor's Commission on Physical Fitness 1973)

Objective To run a test course that requires turning as fast and efficiently as possible.

Validity Construct validity of running agility.

Equipment A test course of appropriate size, a stopwatch accurate to one-tenth of a second, and five markers to outline the test course (see Figure 10-7). Although the instructions for several agility tests recommend the use of chairs, volleyball standards, or wooden clubs for outlining the test course, we strongly recommend that you not use these objects because of possible injury to students. Rubber pylons are ideal for safely outlining the course.

Procedure At the signal, the student begins from behind the starting line and runs the outlined course one time as fast as possible.

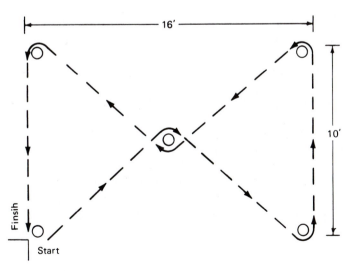

Figure 10-7
Test course for zigzag run.

Scoring   The student's score is the elapsed time accurate to the nearest tenth of a second. Give three trials. The first should be at three-quarter speed to familiarize the student with the procedure and to serve as a specific warm-up. The score is the mean of the last two trials.

Other Considerations   This is an example of an agility run test that involves turning rather than starting and stopping. By studying movements required by various athletes, these tests could be altered to reflect the movements required by the athlete and be more relevant for testing athletes.

Measuring Jumping Ability

Jumping tests measure the ability to expend maximum energy in one explosive act, projecting the body through space. The vertical jump and standing long jump (the easiest to administer) are the most frequently used tests of the ability.

Jumping tests have been described as tests of power and of explosive strength. Although physical educators generally refer to these tests as measures of power, research has reported low correlations between jumping tests and mechanical measures of power.

The need for leg strength in jumping is self-evident; body weight, however, is negatively correlated with jumping ability. The negative relation can be largely attributed to body fatness. More force or greater muscular strength is needed to propel a heavier individual through space. Jumping ability, then, depends on individual differences in leg strength and body composition. If two individuals can generate the same amount of force, all other things being equal, the lighter person will jump highest.

The standing long jump is very easy to administer and is a common test of motor fitness batteries. The vertical jump is used by many coaches to test athletes.

Test   Standing Long Jump (AAHPER 1976)

Equipment   A tape measure at least 10 feet long and masking tape. You can construct the test sta-

tion by attaching the tape measure to the floor with the starting line at 0 inches. We have found the gym floor to be a suitable surface, although mats can also be used.

Procedure   The student should straddle the tape measure, with feet parallel, about shoulder-width apart, and toes behind the starting line. From this position, the student should squat and then jump horizontally as far as possible. The student should land straddling the tape measure.

Scoring   The recommended procedure is to administer three trials and award the student the best of the three trials. The test is scored in feet and inches to the nearest inch. Norms for boys and girls are provided by AAHPER (1976).

Other Considerations   Because the test must be administered individually, it is suggested that several test stations be used. It is important that students be allowed to practice the specific test because a learning effect has been shown to exist.

Test   Vertical Jump (Texas Governor's Commission on Physical Fitness 1973)

Objective   Using a double-foot takeoff, to jump vertically as high as possible with maximum effort.

Validity   Construct validity of jumping ability.

Equipment   A smooth wall of sufficient height, a yardstick, and chalk.

Procedure   Secure the student's standing height by having him stand with heels together on the floor and the side of his dominant hand holding a piece of chalk, next to the wall. From this position the student reaches upward as high as possible and marks on the wall. To execute the jump, the student squats next to the wall, jumps as high as possible, and marks the wall. Once in the starting position, the student should not walk in or step into the jump.

Scoring   The height of the jump is the measured distance between the standing and jumping heights. Measurements accurate to the nearest inch are precise enough for reliable results. Give three trials, the first at three-quarter speed to familiarize the student with the procedure and to serve as a specific warm-up. The score is the mean of the last two trials to the nearest half-inch.

Other Considerations Vertical jump scoring equipment is available. The vertical jump is more relevant for testing athletes such as volleyball and basketball players, because jumping is an important part of the game. We are not aware of good normative data for this test. You are encouraged to develop norms relevant for your group.

Measuring Throwing Ability

Tests of throwing ability require the subject to throw a relatively light ball (baseball, softball, or basketball) overarm for distance. These tests have been reported to measure arm and shoulder girdle strength and/or coordination. There is a high correlation between muscular strength and speed of movement when the mass of the ball is high relative to the strength of the muscle groups involved. Obviously, strength is necessary to throw a ball for distance; however, the weight of the ball relative to the strength of the thrower must be considered. For example, if young and relatively weak children are required to throw a basketball, muscular arm strength or power may be the dominant factor measured; if a Little League baseball is used, throwing ability is more likely to be measured. Given adequate strength, the basic physical ability measured is the execution of a coordinated overarm pattern with maximal speed.

Orthopedic surgeons have questioned the advisability of having children throw with maximal effort. "Little League elbow" is a common injury among preteen athletes. The softball throw for distance, once an item in the AAHPER Youth Fitness battery, was dropped with the 1975 revision. For any throw for distance, it is recommended that the students be conditioned and warmed up before testing. Do not allow students who complain of sore arms to take the test.

The throws are made with both feet parallel to the restraining line. The subject may not take a step to throw, but may follow through by stepping over the line after the throw, minimizing the action of the lower body. In this way the throw more closely represents the overarm pattern used in volleyball and similar sports. Each subject is awarded five throws.

The student's score is the distance thrown to the nearest half-foot. Often, there is a practice/warm-up effect with this test; thus, the best score achieved is the recommended score. Norms for female volleyball players are listed in Table 10.3.

FLEXIBILITY

Flexibility is the range of movement about a joint. Individual differences in flexibility depend on physiological characteristics that influence the extensibility of the muscles and ligaments surrounding a joint. Physical educators agree that certain levels and types of flexibility are wanted, but the degree of flexibility desired is yet to be determined.

Physical therapists use a protractor-like instrument called a goniometer to measure joint flexibility; in research laboratories, electronic and slow-motion photographic methods are used to measure flexibility. Although these are reliable methods for measuring flexibility, the investment of time and money prohibits their use out of the laboratory setting.

Flexibility is often regarded as a single general factor or ability. However, there are tests that measure the movement of a limb involving only one joint action and composite measures of movements that require more than one joint or more than one type of action within a single joint. There is no evidence that flexibility is a single general factor.

We must think in terms of several types of flexibilities. We can easily recognize the importance of different types of flexibility in different motor skills. The type of flexibility needed by the modern dancer or gymnast is not the same as for a football player. Specific types of flexibility are developed over time with special stretching exercises and practice in the given skills. The specificity of flexibility, then, means that we cannot use a single test to measure the various types of flexibility necessary to the execution of different motor skills.

A degree of flexibility in the back and hamstring muscle groups is essential for the prevention of lower back disorders. The value of flexibility for a healthy lower back is recognized by physicians, physical therapists, and physical educators. It is for this reason that the sit-and-reach test is a recommended test of health-related youth fitness tests reviewed in Chapter 13. Test procedures and norms for these tests are provided in Chapter 13.

BALANCE

Balance is the ability to maintain body position, which is obviously essential to the successful execution of motor skills. Two general types of balance are commonly recognized: static balance is the ability to maintain total body equilibrium while standing in one spot, and dynamic balance is the ability to maintain equilibrium while moving from one point to another. Static balance depends on the ability to coordinate stimuli from three sources: the three semicircular canals; the proprioceptive receptors located in the muscles, tendons, and joints; and visual perception. Dynamic balance depends on similar but more complex stimuli.

Different motor skills require different types of balance. The balance needed by the tennis player differs from that needed by the swimmer. Probably there are several factors in balance. In static balance, one factor is measured with the eyes closed and another factor is measured with the eyes open. Because dynamic balance is more complex, it is likely to be composed of several more factors.

Due to the specificity of balance, the value of balance tests in the instructional process is yet to be determined. Balance tasks are often used by researchers of motor learning because significant improvements can be noted in a relatively short time. This learning effect, inherent in balance tests, indicates that they are not reliable in terms of stability. Thus, the tests do not offer stable measure-

ments for purposes of placement, diagnosis, or prediction. By contrast, many gymnastic and tumbling stunts, including the headstand, involve learning a specific type of balance. Because the performance of balance stunts is an instructional objective of a tumbling or gymnastics unit, the value of measuring these specific types of balance is easily defended. Described next are common tests of static balance (eyes open or shut) and a test of dynamic balance commonly used to study skill acquisition.

Static Balance

Wooden sticks (1 inch by 1 inch by 12 or more inches) are taped to the floor. At the word "Ready," the subject places the supporting foot lengthwise on the stick. At the command "Go," the subject raises the free foot and holds this position as long as possible for a maximum of 60 seconds. The test is terminated if (1) either foot touches the floor or (2) balance is maintained for 60 seconds. The subject is given three practice trials, and the subject's score is the sum of six trials of the test. This test can be administered with the eyes open and closed.

Dynamic Balance

Dynamic balance can be measured with a stability platform (Figure 10-8). The objective is to keep the balancing platform as level as possible during a regulated time period. Electronic clocks and interval timers are used to measure the subject's capacity to maintain balance for a given time period, often 30 seconds in duration.

KINESTHETIC PERCEPTION

Kinesthesis, or kinesthetic perception, is the ability to perceive the body's position in space and the relationship of its parts. The proprioceptors, highly developed sense organs located in the muscles, tendons, and joints, compose a highly sensitive system of kinesthetic perception. They provide the brain with information about what the parts of the body are doing when executing a skill.

Figure 10-8
A stability platform is used to measure dynamic balance.
(Photo courtesy of Lafayette Instrument Company, Lafayette, IN.)

The need for and importance of kinesthesis for skill learning is universally acknowledged, and several physical educators (Roloff 1953; Scott 1955; Wiebe 1954; Young 1954) have tried to develop kinesthesis tests. These tests tend to have very low reliabilities, and their value for general testing is questionable. Kinesthesis is central to the execution of motor skill, but it cannot be measured with accuracy.

FINE PSYCHOMOTOR ABILITIES

Fine motor abilities are those that do not involve total body movement. Some more common abilities are simple and complex forms of hand-eye coordination, reaction time, and movement time. These psychomotor abilities are usually measured in the laboratory. Fine psychomotor abilities are often used to study psychomotor skill acquisition.

SUMMARY

Physical educators have traditionally accepted the notion of generality and believe that a test or group of tests is predictive of a wide range of motor skills. The theory of specificity of motor skill acquisition was largely responsible for showing that motor ability and motor educability tests lacked validity. The theory of basic physical abilities does provide a theoretically sound base for generality testing. This theory is especially useful for testing athletes, for preemployment testing for physically demanding jobs, and for estimating a worker's capacity to be able to complete physically demanding work tasks. Adequate levels of physical ability are important for reducing the risk of back injuries associated with lifting.

Researchers have identified three basic motor performance abilities—muscular strength, muscular power, and endurance—and three basic movement patterns—running, jumping, and throwing. Several different tests are available to measure each ability. Although tests can be used for general evaluation, they are especially useful for identifying students with athletic potential.

The assessment of flexibility, balance, and kinesthesis is a difficult problem. Flexibility is not a general factor; rather, it is task-specific, and different types are needed to perform different motor tasks.

There were thought to be two basic types of balance: dynamic and static. However, research suggests that several additional types of balance also exist. Kinesthesis is the ability to perceive the body's position in space and the relationship of its parts. The reliability of kinesthetic tests tends to be low, making this trait difficult to measure.

FORMATIVE EVALUATION OF OBJECTIVES

Objective 1   Describe the tests that historically have been used to measure generality.

1. Summarize the traditional procedures used to measure the generality of motor performance.
2. Describe the differences between motor educability and general motor ability.
3. What effect did Henry's memory-drum theory have on the generality concept?
4. The terms *ability* and *skill* are often used interchangeably. Describe the essential difference between the two.
5. Could a basic ability be considered a measure of generality?

Objective 2   Apply the theory of basic physical abilities to the evaluation of athletes.

1. In evaluating different groups of athletes (e.g., gymnasts and basketball players), would you test the same basic abilities?
2. Outline the steps a teacher or coach could follow to develop a test for athletes.

Objective 3   Identify the methods to develop preemployment tests for physically demanding jobs and the types of tests that make up preemployment batteries.

1. What are the steps used to develop a preemployment physical test?
2. What kinds of tests are used for a preemployment test?
3. What types of physical ability tests are most often used for preemployment testing?

Objective 4   Understand the relation of physical ability to the risk of back injuries.
1. What are the primary reasons workers suffer low back problems?
2. What is the relationship between psychophysical ratings of lift difficulty and the risk of injury?
3. What is the relationship between strength and lift difficulty?

Objective 5   Identify basic physical abilities and tests that validly measure each ability.

1. The text provides a system for classifying basic abilities and describes tests that measure each ability. Summarize the general characteristics of each basic ability and list one test that measures each.
2. Develop a five-item motor performance battery that includes tests of different basic abilities. Use tests that are feasible for mass testing.

ADDITIONAL LEARNING ACTIVITIES

1. Summarize the research supporting the specificity of motor-skill learning. Pay close attention to the procedures used by the researcher to conclude specificity or generality.
2. Select a sport and identify the basic abilities demanded by it. Develop a test battery that could be used to evaluate athletes.
3. Examine the effect of lift weight on psychophysical ratings of the lift. Put different weight loads (e.g., 25 to 95 pounds) in several different boxes. Starting with the lightest load, have a person lift the box and place it on a

table. After completing the lift, have the person rate the lift difficulty with Borg's CR-10 scale. Move on to the next heaviest box and repeat the task until all boxes have been lifted and rated. Do not let the person know the weight in each box until he has completed the lifts. You can use this data to help the person determine his acceptable lift weight.

4. A test can be made more reliable, valid, and feasible for mass use by improving the procedures used to administer it. For example, some have constructed inexpensive devices to measure balance, vertical jumping, and push-ups. Try to develop equipment that would improve the testing of some basic ability.

5. Are absolute endurance and 1-RM really highly correlated? If you have access to weight-lifting equipment, devise tests that measure both. Administer the tests to a group of students and determine if the 1-RM score is correlated with the absolute endurance score.

6. Gain testing experience by using some of the tests listed in this chapter and administer the tests to a group of students. Determine how reliable your testing methods are.

BIBLIOGRAPHY

AAHPER. 1976. *Youth fitness test manual.* Washington, DC: AAHPER.

American College of Sports Medicine. (2001). *ACSM's resource manual for guidelines for exercise testing and prescription.* 4th ed. Philadelphia: Lippincott Williams & Wilkins.

Arvey, R. D. and R. H. Faley. 1988. *Fairness in selecting employees.* 2nd ed. Reading, MA: Addison-Wesley.

Arvey, R. D., S. M. Nutting, and T. E. Landon. 1992. Validation strategies for physical ability testing in police and fire settings. *Public Personnel Management* 21: 301–312.

Ayoub, M. A. 1982. Control of manual lifting hazards: II. Job redesign. *Journal of Occupational Medicine* 24: 676–688.

Bar-Or, O. 1987. The Wingate anaerobic test: An update on methodology, reliability and validity. *Sports Medicine* 4: 381–394.

Barrow, H. M. (1954). Test of motor ability for college men. *Research Quarterly* 25: 253–260.

Baumgartner, T. A. and S. J. Gaunt. 2005. Construct related validity for the Baumgartner modified pull-up test. *Measurement in Physical Education and Exercise Science* 9: 51–60.

Baumgartner, T. A. and S. Wood. 1984. Development of shoulder-girdle strength-endurance in elementary children. *Research Quarterly for Exercise and Sport* 55: 169–171.

Baumgartner, T. A. and M. A. Zuidema. 1972. Factor analysis of physical fitness tests. *Research Quarterly* 43: 443–450.

Baumgartner, T. A. et al. 1984. Equipment improvements and additional norms for the modified pull-up test. *Research Quarterly for Exercise and Sport* 55: 64–68.

Bernauer, E. M. and J. Bonanno. 1975. Development of physical profiles for specific jobs. *Journal of Occupational Medicine* 17: 22–33.

Borg, G. 1982. A category scale with ratio properties for intermodal and interindividual comparisons. In H. G. Geissler, and P. Petzold (Eds.). *Psychophysical judgment and the process of perception.* Berlin: VEB Deutscher Verlag der Wissenschaften.

———.1998. *Borg's perceived exertion and pain scaling method.* Champaign: Human Kinetics.

Borg, G. and D. Ottoson. 1986. *The perception of exertion and physical work.* Stockholm: Wenner-Gren Center.

Brown, J. 2001. *Sports talent.* Champaign, IL: Human Kinetics.

Cascio, W. F., R. A. Alexander, and G. V. Barrett. 1988. Setting cutoff scores: Legal, psychometric, and professional issues and guidelines. *Personnel Psychology* 41: 1–24.

Chin, A., R. R. Bishu, and S. Halbeck. 1995. Psychophysical measures of exertion. Are they muscle group dependent. *Proceedings of the Human Factors Society* 39: 694–698.

Considine, W. et al. 1976. Developing a physical performance test battery for screening Chicago fire fighting applicants. *Public Personnel Management* 5: 7–14.

Cooper Institute for Aerobics Research. 1999. *FITNESSGRAM® test administration manual.* 2nd ed. Champaign, IL: Human Kinetics.

Cousins, G. F. 1955. A factor analysis of selected wartime fitness tests. *Research Quarterly* 26: 277–288.

Cumbee, F. 1954. A factorial analysis of motor coordination. *Research Quarterly* 25: 412–420.

Disch, J., R. Frankiewicz, and A. S. Jackson. 1975. Construct validation of distance run tests. *Research Quarterly* 46: 169–176.

EEOC. 1978. Uniform guidelines on employment selection procedures. *Federal Register 43* (38289 28309).

Fleishman, E. A. 1956. Psychomotor selection tests: Research and application in the U.S. Air Force. *Personnel Psychology* 9: 449–467.

Fleishman, E. A. 1964. *The structure and measurement of physical fitness.* Englewood Cliffs, NJ: Prentice-Hall.

Gael, S. 1988. *The job analysis handbook for business, industry, and government.* Vol. I. New York: John Wiley. & Sons.

Gettman, L. R. 1993. Fitness testing. Chapter 19 in *Resource manual for guidelines for exercise testing and prescription.* Philadelphia: Lea & Febiger.

Golding, L. A. 2000. *The Y's way to physical fitness.* 4th ed. Champaign, IL: YMCA of the USA.

Harris, M. 1969. A factor analytic study of flexibility. *Research Quarterly* 40: 62–70.

Henry, F. M. 1956. Coordination and motor learning. In *59th Annual Proceedings College Physical Education Association* 59: 68–75.

Henry, F. M. 1958. Specificity vs. generality in learning motor skills. In *61st Annual Proceedings College Physical Education Association* 61: 126–128.

Hidalgo, J. et al. 1997. A comprehensive lifting model: Beyond the NIOSH lifting equation. *Ergonomics* 40(9): 916–927.

Hogan, J. C. 1991. Chapter 11. Physical abilities. In M. D. Dunette and L. M. Hough (Eds.). *Handbook of industrial and organizational psychology.* 2nd ed. Vol. 2 (pp. 743–831). Palo Alto, CA: Consulting Psychologist Press.

Inbar, O., O. Bar-Or, and J. Skinner. (1996). *The Wingate Anaerobic Test.* Champaign, IL: Human Kinetics.

Ismail, A., H. Falls, and D. MacLeod. 1965. Development of a criterion for physical fitness tests from factor analysis results. *Journal of Applied Physiology* 20: 991–999.

Jackson, A. S. 1971. Factor analysis of selected muscular strength and motor performance test. *Research Quarterly* 42: 164–172.

———.1994. Chapter 3. Preemployment physical evaluation. *Exercise and Sport Science Review* 22: 53–90.

——— .1996. *Physical work capacity pre-employment evaluation system.* Lafayette, IN: Lafayette Instrument Co.

Jackson, A. S. and R. J. Frankiewicz. 1975. Factorial expressions of muscular strength. *Research Quarterly* 46: 206–217.

Jackson, A. S., H. G. Osburn, and K. R. Laughery. 1991. Validity of isometric strength tests for predicting endurance work tasks of coal miners. *Proceedings of the Human Factors Society 35th Annual Meeting* 1: 763–767.

Jackson, A. S. and M. L. Pollock. 1976. Factor analysis and multivariate scaling of anthropometric variables for the assessment of body composition. *Medicine and Science in Sports* 8: 196–203.

Jackson, A. S. and R. M. Ross. 1997. *Understanding exercise for health and fitness.* 3rd ed. Dubuque, IA: Kendall/Hunt.

Jackson, A. S. et al. 1991. Strength demands of chemical plant work tasks. *Proceedings of the Human Factors Society 35th Annual Meeting* 1: 758–762.

Jackson, A. S. et al. 1992. Validity of isometric strength tests for predicting the capacity to crack, open and close industrial valves. *Proceedings of the Human Factors Society 36th Annual Meeting* 1: 688–691.

Jackson, A. S. et al. 1993. *Validation of physical strength tests for the Federal Express Corporation.* Center of Applied Psychological Services, Rice University, Houston, TX.

Jackson, A. S. et al. 1997. Role of physical work capacity and load weight on psychophysical lift ratings. *International Journal of Industrial Ergonomics* 20: 181–190.

Jackson, A. S. et al. 1998. *Revalidation of methods for pre-employment assessment of physical abilities at Shell Western Exploration and Production, Inc., and CalResources LLC.* Houston, TX: Departments of HHP and Psychology, University of Houston, and Department of Psychology, Rice University.

Jackson, A. W. et al. 1982. Baumgartner's modified pull-up test for male and female elementary school-aged children. *Research Quarterly for Exercise and Sport* 53: 163–164.

Karwowski, W. 1996. Maximum safe weight of lift: A new paradigm for setting design limits in manual lifting tasks based on the psychophysical approach. *Proceedings of the Human Factors Society*, 40: 614–618.

Larson, L. A. 1941. A factor analysis of motor ability variables and tests for college men. *Research Quarterly* 12: 499–517.

Lephart, S. M. and T. J. Henry. 1996. The physiological basis for open and closed kinetic chain rehabilitation for the upper extremity. *Journal of Sport Rehabilitation* 5(1): 71–87.

Liba, M. R. 1967. Factor analysis of strength variables. *Research Quarterly* 38: 649–662.

Marriott, B. M. and J. Grumstrup-Scott (Eds.). 1992. *Body composition and physical performance: Application for the military services*. Washington, DC: National Academy Press.

Maud, P. J. and B. B. Shultz. 1989. Norms for the Wingate anaerobic test with comparison to another similar test. *Research Quarterly for Exercise and Sport* 60(2): 144–150.

McArdle, W. D., F. I. Katch, and V. L. Katch. 1991. *Exercise physiology: Energy, nutrition, and human performance*. 3rd ed. Philadelphia: Lea & Febiger.

McCloy, C. H. 1932. *The measurement of athletic power*. New York: Barnes.

McCloy, C. H. 1956. A factor analysis of tests of endurance. *Research Quarterly* 27: 213–216.

McCloy, C. H. and N. D. Young. 1954. *Test and measurements in health and physical education*. New York: Appleton-Century-Crofts.

Meyers, D. C. et al. 1984. Factor analysis of strength, cardiovascular endurance, flexibility, and body composition measures (Tech. Rep. R83-9). Bethesda, MD: Advanced Research Resources Organization.

NIOSH. 1981. *Work practices guide for manual lifting*. Washington, DC: U.S. Department of Health and Human Services.

Plowman, S. A. 1992. Chapter 8. Physical activity, physical fitness, and low back pain. In J. O. Holloszy, (Ed.). *Exercise and Sport Sciences Reviews*. Baltimore, MD: Williams & Wilkins.

Pollock, M. L. et al. 1978. Characteristics of elite class distance runners. *Annals of New York Academy of Sciences* 301: 278–410.

Resnik, M. L. 1995. The generalizability of psychophysical ratings in predicting the perception of lift difficulty. *Proceedings of the Human Factors Society* 39: 679–682.

Roloff, L. L. 1953. Kinesthesis in relation to the learning of selected motor skills. *Research Quarterly* 24: 210–217.

Russell, J. A. et al. 1993. Can isometric strength measures be used to predict isotonic strength? *Research Quarterly for Exercise and Sport* 64: A-45.

Safrit, M. J. 1966. *The structure of gross motor skill patterns*. Washington, DC: U.S. Department of Health, Education, and Welfare. Office of Education Cooperative Research Project No. S 397.

Sargent, D. A. 1921. The physical test of man. *American Physical Education Review* 26: 188–194.

Scott, M. G. (1939). The assessment of motor abilities of college women through objective tests. *Research Quarterly* 10: 63–83.

Scott, M. G. 1955. Test of kinesthesis. *Research Quarterly* 26: 324–341.

Snyder-Mackler, L. 1996. Scientific rationale and physiological basis for the use of closed kinetic chain exercise in the lower extremity. *Journal of Sport Rehabilitation* 5(1): 2–12.

Sothmann, M. S. et al. 1990. Advancing age and the cardiorespiratory stress of fire suppression: Determining a minimum standard for aerobic fitness. *Human Performance* 3: 217–236.

Sothmann, M. S. et al. 1992. Heart rate response of firefighters to actual emergencies. *Journal of Occupational Medicine* 34: 797–800.

Texas Governor's Commission on Physical Fitness. 1973. *Physical fitness–motor ability test*. Austin, TX.

Waters, T. R. et al. 1993. Revised NIOSH equation for the design and evaluation of manual lifting tasks. *Ergonomics* 7: 749–766.

Wiebe, V. R. 1954. A study of test of kinesthesis. *Research Quarterly* 25: 222–227.

Young, O. G. 1954. A study of kinesthesis in relation to selected movements. *Research Quarterly* 16: 277–287.

Zuidema, M. A. and T. A. Baumgartner. 1974. Second factor analysis of physical fitness tests. *Research Quarterly* 45: 247–256.

11

EVALUATING AEROBIC FITNESS

C O N T E N T S

K E Y   W O R D S

aerobic fitness
cycle ergometer
distance run tests
maximal exercise test
MET (metabolic equivalent)
moderate exercise
multi-stage exercise test
nonexercise models
open-circuit spirometry
oxygen consumption
Physical Activity Readiness
  Questionnaire (PAR-Q)
power output
rating of perceived exertion (RPE)
single-stage exercise test
steady state exercise
submaximal exercise test
submaximal $\dot{V}O_2$
treadmill
vigorous exercise
$\dot{V}O_2$ max
watts

OBJECTIVES

Aerobic fitness, like body composition, is a major component of both adult and youth fitness. Epidemiological research has demonstrated that low levels of aerobic fitness are associated with an increased risk of mortality. The most widely accepted index of aerobic fitness is measured maximal oxygen consumption ($\dot{V}O_2$ max), and most tests of aerobic fitness attempt to estimate this index. Treadmill and cycle ergometer tests are typically used to estimate aerobic fitness in adults, whereas field tests, such as distance runs, are more often used to estimate aerobic fitness in youth. Chapter 13 covers field tests used to measure aerobic fitness, and other health-related fitness components, in youth. Evaluation of aerobic fitness in adults is most likely to be done by an exercise specialist. The purpose of this chapter is to outline the tests used to measure aerobic fitness. This involves integration of measurement theory with exercise physiology.

After reading Chapter 11 you should be able to

1. Define aerobic fitness.
2. Explain the relationship between aerobic fitness and health.
3. Explain the idea of risk stratification prior to exercise testing.
4. Define the methods used to determine power output from cycle ergometer and treadmill tests.
5. Identify laboratory-based methods used to assess $\dot{V}O_2$ max during maximal exercise testing.
6. Identify laboratory-based methods used to assess $\dot{V}O_2$ max during submaximal exercise testing.
7. Identify the various field tests of aerobic fitness used with adults.

INTRODUCTION

Aerobic fitness is the ability of the heart, lungs, and blood vessels to supply oxygen to the working muscles and the ability of the muscles to use the available oxygen to continue work or exercise. The public health reports (U.S. Public Health Service, 1990, 1996) reviewed in Chapter 1 place special importance on aerobic exercise and fitness for health promotion. Aerobic exercise is the most efficient form of exercise for developing aerobic fitness and expending a sufficient amount of energy (i.e., calories). Caloric expenditure is important not only for weight control and reducing the prevalence of overweight, but also for protection from heart disease. In this chapter, we briefly review the role of aerobic fitness in health, and the screening, risk stratification, and safety precautions that exercise specialists need to consider when testing adults. In addition, we fully present laboratory and field tests that are available to measure and evaluate aerobic fitness.

ESSENTIAL DEFINITIONS

Oxygen consumption ($\dot{V}O_2$) is the volume of oxygen used by the body under given conditions. $\dot{V}O_2$ may be measured at rest, during submaximal exercise, or during maximal exercise. When $\dot{V}O_2$ is measured during maximal exercise, it is called **$\dot{V}O_2$ max.** $\dot{V}O_2$ max is the maximal volume of oxygen one can consume during exhausting exercise, and is considered the best index of aerobic fitness (American College of Sports Medicine [ACSM] 2006; Åstrand & Rodahl 1986; Mitchell & Blomqvist 1971; Mitchell, Sproule & Chapman 1958; Rowell, Taylor & Wang 1964).

$\dot{V}O_2$ is expressed either in absolute terms or relative to body mass. In absolute terms, $\dot{V}O_2$ is expressed as the total volume of oxygen used for a standard length of time. For example, $\dot{V}O_2$ can be expressed in milliliters of oxygen per minute ($ml \cdot min^{-1}$) or in liters of oxygen per minute ($L \cdot min^{-1}$). The total volume of oxygen used is a function of one's muscle mass. The more muscle mass, the greater the volume of oxygen used.

To control for differences in body size, $\dot{V}O_2$ in milliliters per minute is often divided by body mass in kilograms. Thus, relative $\dot{V}O_2$ is expressed as milliliters of oxygen per kilogram of body mass per minute ($ml \cdot kg^{-1} \cdot min^{-1}$). The following equation demonstrates the calculation of $\dot{V}O_2$ per kilogram of body mass.

$$\dot{V}O_2 \ (ml \cdot kg^{-1} \cdot min^{-1}) = (\dot{V}O_2 \ L \cdot min^{-1}$$
$$\times 1000 \ ml \cdot L^{-1}) \div (weight \ in \ kg) \qquad \textbf{(11.1)}$$

Computation Example Assume a 65-kilogram woman exercises on a cycle ergometer at an absolute $\dot{V}O_2$ of 1.5 L·min⁻¹. Her relative $\dot{V}O_2$ expressed as ml·kg⁻¹·min⁻¹ (Formula 11.1) would be

$$\dot{V}O_2 \ (ml \cdot kg^{-1} \cdot min^{-1})$$
$$= (1.5 \ L \cdot min^{-1} \times 1{,}000 \ ml \cdot L^{-1}) \div (65 \ kg)$$
$$= (1500 \ ml \cdot min^{-1} \div 65 \ kg) = 23.1$$

Oxygen consumption is also expressed in **metabolic equivalents (METs)**. One MET is a $\dot{V}O_2$ of 3.5 ml·kg⁻¹·min⁻¹ and is the amount of oxygen used at rest. The unit of METs quantifies oxygen uptake in multiples above resting. For example, a person working at an 8-MET intensity $(8 \times 3.5 = 28 \ ml \cdot kg^{-1} \cdot min^{-1})$ is working at an intensity 8 times that of resting. The following equation is used to convert $\dot{V}O_2$ to METs.

$$METs = \dot{V}O_2 \ ml \cdot kg^{-1} \cdot min^{-1} \div 3.5 \ ml$$
$$\cdot kg^{-1} \cdot min^{-1} \qquad \textbf{(11.2)}$$

Computation Example Assume that the $\dot{V}O_2$ a person uses to jog 6 miles per hour is 35 ml·kg⁻¹·min⁻¹. Formula 11.2 can be used to demonstrate that this level of exercise is 10 METs, or 10 times above the resting state.

$$METs = 35 \ ml \cdot kg^{-1} \cdot min^{-1} \div 3.5 \ ml$$
$$\cdot kg^{-1} \cdot min^{-1} = 10$$

During a maximal exercise test, $\dot{V}O_2$ max is the point at which an increase in power output of the treadmill or cycle ergometer does not produce an increase in oxygen consumption. Figure 11-1 shows computer-generated graphs of two $\dot{V}O_2$ max tests. The graphs demonstrate that as power output increased (i.e., with increased speed and/or elevation of the treadmill), $\dot{V}O_2$ steadily increased and then flattened out (i.e., reached a plateau) dur-

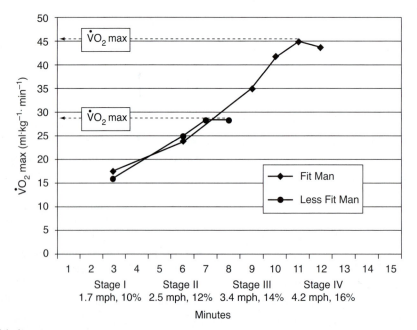

Figure 11-1

$\dot{V}O_2$ max tests of a fit person and a less fit person. The fit person exercised for 12 minutes on the Bruce protocol and had a measured $\dot{V}O_2$ max of 45 ml·kg⁻¹·min⁻¹. The less fit person exercised for 8 minutes on the Bruce protocol and had a measured $\dot{V}O_2$ max of 28.5 ml·kg⁻¹·min⁻¹.

ing the last two minutes of the test, when each person reached $\dot{V}O_2$ max.

Criteria often used to document that maximal effort was achieved during the exercise test include (a) a plateau in oxygen consumption with increased power output (this plateau is often operationally defined as failure of $\dot{V}O_2$ to increase by 150 ml·min^{-1} with increased workload); (b) a respiratory exchange ratio ≥ 1.15 (some investigators use 1.10 instead of 1.15); (c) exercising to voluntary exhaustion documented by a rating of perceived exertion > 17 (on the 6–20 scale); and (d) failure of heart rate to increase with an increase in power output. Use of age-predicted maximal heart rate alone should not be used as an indication of maximal effort, because of the large interindividual variability associated with age-predicted maximal heart rate (ACSM 2006).

AEROBIC FITNESS AND HEALTH

The relationship between aerobic fitness and health has been well documented. A classic study from the Cooper Institute for Aerobics Research in Dallas, Texas, showed that a low level of aerobic fitness was associated with higher mortality rates (Blair et al. 1989). Study participants were healthy people who were free of diseases such as high blood pressure or diabetes. After a maximal exercise test, participants were divided into five groups based upon aerobic fitness (adjusted for age) and followed for several years. Figure 11-2 provides a graphic summary of the study. The greatest drop in mortality was between the lowest fitness group (lowest quintile, or lowest 20%) and the next quintile. Both men and women in the lowest fitness group were over three times more likely

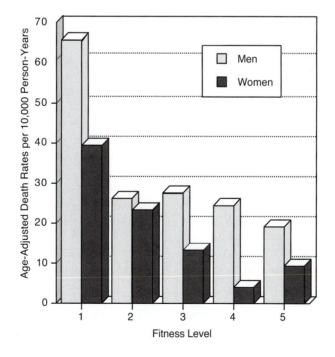

Figure 11-2

Age-adjusted all-cause death rates by fitness in men and women. Participants in the lowest fitness group had the highest death rates. Death rates drop dramatically as you move from the lowest fitness group to higher fitness groups. The greatest public health benefit would result by moving people out of the lowest fitness group. The graph was developed from published data.

(Blair et al. 1989).

to die than participants in the other groups. The risk of mortality for the highest fitness group was not much lower than the risk for the moderate fitness group, but moving out of the lowest fitness group was associated with a significant reduction in risk.

The level of aerobic fitness needed to move out of the lowest fitness group and reduce mortality risk is within reach of most people who are moderately physically active. These values are 10 METs (35 ml·kg^{-1}·min^{-1}) for men and 9 METs (31.5 ml·kg^{-1}·min^{-1}) for women. For most people, the physical activity needed to reach this level of fitness can be accomplished with a brisk walk each day of 30 to 60 minutes.

In a second study, these researchers discovered that changes in fitness were related to changes in mortality risk (Blair et al. 1995). Participants who improved their aerobic fitness by moving from the low to the moderate or high categories reduced their future risk of death. Moderate fitness levels can be attained by most people who engage in regular aerobic exercise, by doing the equivalent of walking about three miles a day.

EVALUATION OF AEROBIC FITNESS

Measurement or estimation of $\dot{V}O_2$ max is common for many fitness evaluations and medical examinations. Exercise specialists can use the results of these tests to help them provide a safe and effective exercise prescription, and physicians can use them to indicate mortality risk and the need for increased physical activity for their patients. Because of the importance of aerobic fitness on one's health, it is important to become familiar with $\dot{V}O_2$ max values. The standards used for athletes would not be suitable for evaluating the fitness level of nonathletic adults. Figure 11-3 provides average $\dot{V}O_2$ max values for elite runners and average men and women. High-level endurance athletes (e.g., cross-country skiers and long-distance runners) have the highest aerobic fitness, nearly double the value of the fitness of the typical person. As a group, women have an aerobic fitness about 20% lower than that of men of a similar age. This

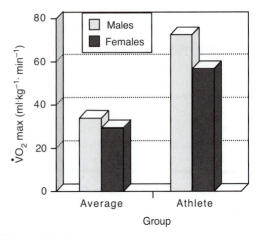

Figure 11-3

Average aerobic fitness values for normal adults and elite endurance athletes. The aerobic fitness level of the average man or woman is about 50% that of highly trained endurance athletes. The average aerobic fitness of women is about 80% that of men.

is primarily due to hormonal differences that cause women to have lower concentrations of hemoglobin in their blood and higher percentages of body fat.

Although most people have neither the ability nor the motivation to become world-class endurance athletes, everyone needs a suitable level of aerobic fitness for health and fitness. Aerobic fitness is age-dependent, steadily increasing during childhood and reaching a peak at about age 25, after which it slowly declines (Buskirk & Hodgson 1987). Table 11.1 provides aerobic fitness standards by age and sex (ACSM 2006). The values in Table 11.1 were provided by the Cooper Institute for Aerobics Research and correspond closely to research published by Blair et al. (1989), which suggest levels of aerobic fitness suitable for health promotion. Table 11.2 lists aerobic fitness levels suitable for health promotion that account for the age-related decline in aerobic fitness. The values in Table 11.2 were developed to account for the expected decline in aerobic fitness with age. These values suggest the fitness level needed at each age

TABLE 11.1	American College of Sports Medicine Standards for $\dot{V}O_2$ max (ml·kg^{-1}·min^{-1})				
	Age in Years				
Standard	**20–29**	**30–39**	**40–49**	**50–59**	**60+**
Men					
Excellent (top 20%)	≥ 48.3	≥ 46.9	≥ 44.2	≥ 41.1	≥ 38.2
Good (next 20%)	44.3–48.2	42.5–46.8	40.0–44.1	36.8–41.0	33.7–38.1
Average (middle 20%)	41.1–44.2	39.0–42.4	36.8–39.9	33.9–36.7	30.3–33.6
Fair (next 20%)	37.2–41.0	35.5–38.9	33.1–36.7	30.3–33.8	26.6–30.2
Poor (lowest 20%)	≤ 37.1	≤ 35.4	≤ 33.0	≤ 30.2	≤ 26.5
Women					
Excellent (top 20%)	≥ 41.1	≥ 38.7	≥ 36.4	≥ 32.4	≥ 31.3
Good (next 20%)	36.8–41.0	34.7–38.6	32.4–36.3	29.5–32.3	27.3–31.2
Average (middle 20%)	33.9–36.7	32.4–34.6	29.6–32.3	27.0–29.4	24.6–27.2
Fair (next 20%)	30.7–33.8	28.8–32.3	26.6–29.5	24.4–26.9	22.9–24.5
Poor (lowest 20%)	≤ 30.6	≤ 28.7	≤ 26.5	≤ 24.3	≤ 22.8

TABLE 11.2	Age-Adjusted Aerobic Fitness Standards for Health Promotion in Adults. Values represent $\dot{V}O_2$ max (ml·kg^{-1}·min^{-1}) needed for decreased risk of mortality	
Age Group	**Men**	**Women**
≤ 45	35	32
50	34	31
55	32	29
60	31	28
≥ 65	30	27

Note: Standards developed from data (Jackson et al. 1995, 1996) and personal communication with S. Blair, September 30, 1993.

listed that would be associated with an aerobic fitness of 35 ml·kg^{-1}·min^{-1} for men and 32 ml·kg^{-1}·min^{-1} for women at age 45 years, assuming one maintains his or her current level of exercise and percent body fat. Research has demonstrated that changing exercise habits and percent body fat dra-matically affect the rate that aerobic fitness changes with age (Jackson et al. 1995, 1996).

RISK STRATIFICATION FOR EXERCISE TESTING

Several studies have documented the risk associated with exercise testing. According to the American College of Sports Medicine (2006), the risk of a cardiac event (e.g., heart attack or sudden death) from exercise testing is as low as 0.06%. The risk is much lower for submaximal tests than for maximal exercise tests. Although this risk of exercise testing is low, the safety of exercise testing depends to a great extent on knowing when a test should not be performed and when a physician should be present during the test. ACSM (2006) provides recommendations for (a) whether a medical examination and exercise test should be conducted prior to participation in an exercise program, and (b) whether physician supervision is needed for exercise tests. To follow these ACSM recommendations, clients are first categorized as "low risk," "moderate risk," or "high risk" for an untoward event during exercise. Age and health status relative to

TABLE 11.3	**Signs and Symptoms of Cardiovascular and Pulmonary Disease**

- Pain or discomfort in the chest, neck, jaw, or arms that may be due to ischemia
- Shortness of breath
- Dizziness or syncope
- Orthopnea or dyspnea
- Ankle edema
- Palpitations or tachycardia
- Intermittent claudication
- Known heart murmur
- Unusual fatigue or shortness of breath

Note: See ACSM (2006) for further clarification.

risk factors and symptoms are used to classify clients into one of these strata. Signs and symptoms of cardiovascular and pulmonary disease, as identified by ACSM (2006), are presented in Table 11.3. Coronary artery disease risk factors,

as identified by ACSM are presented in Table 11.4.

ACSM suggests the following risk stratification:

- *Low-risk* clients are younger than age 45 for men and 55 for women who do not have any symptoms and have no more than one of the listed risk factors.
- *Moderate-risk* clients are aged 45 and older for men and 55 and older for women, or are those who have two or more of the listed risk factors.
- *High-risk* clients are those with any signs or symptoms, or those with known cardiovascular, pulmonary, or metabolic disease.

After clients are classified as to their risk strata, recommendations regarding exercise testing are made. A medical examination and exercise test prior to participation in an exercise program is recommended for all high-risk clients and for moderate-risk clients who plan to participate in vigorous-intensity exercise. **Vigorous exercise** is defined as activities performed at an intensity greater than

TABLE 11.4	**Coronary Artery Disease Risk Factors**
Risk Factor	**Defining Criteria**
Positive	
Family history	Heart attack or sudden death before age 55 in father, brother, or son; or before age 65 in mother, sister, or daughter
Cigarette smoking	Current cigarette smoker or quit within 6 months
Hypertension	Systolic blood pressure ≥ 140 mm Hg or diastolic ≥ 90 mm Hg, or on antihypertensive medication
Dyslipidemia	Total cholesterol > 200 mg/dL or high-density lipoprotein (HDL) cholesterol < 40 mg/dL, or on lipid-lowering medication. If low-density lipoprotein (LDL) is available, use LDL > 130 mg/dL rather than total cholesterol > 200 mg/dL
Impaired fasting glucose	Fasting blood glucose of ≥100 mg/dL
Obesity	Body mass index ≥ 30 kg/m² or waist girth > 102 cm for men, > 88 cm for women; or waist/hip ratio ≥ 0.95 for men and ≥ 0.86 for women
Sedentary lifestyle	Persons not participating in a regular exercise program or not meeting the minimal physical activity recommendations from the U.S. Surgeon General's Report (U.S. Public Health Service 1996)*
Negative	
High HDL cholesterol	HDL > 60 mg/dL

*The U.S. Surgeon General's Report recommends accumulating 30 minutes or more of moderate physical activity on most days of the week.

Note: It is common to sum risk factors in making clinical judgments. If HDL cholesterol is high, subtract one risk factor from the sum of positive risk factors, because high HDL decreases CAD risk.

6 METs (21 ml·kg^{-1}·min^{-1}), with an intensity greater than 60% of $\dot{V}O_2$ max, or as exercise intense enough to represent a substantial cardiorespiratory challenge. **Moderate exercise** is defined as activities performed at an intensity between 3 and 6 METs (10.5–21 ml·kg^{-1}·min^{-1}), an intensity 40 to 60% of $\dot{V}O_2$ max, or as exercise with an intensity that can be sustained comfortably for approximately 45 minutes. A medical examination and exercise test are not necessary for low-risk clients or moderate-risk clients who want to participate in moderate-intensity exercise.

Physician supervision is recommended during an exercise test for all high-risk clients and for moderate-risk clients during a maximal exercise test. We will elaborate upon differences between maximal and submaximal exercise tests later in this chapter. A **maximal exercise test** is one in which the client is asked to exercise to exhaustion. During a **submaximal exercise test**, the client is asked to exercise at some level less than maximal (i.e., submaximal) that is often defined by the heart rate response to the exercise. Physician supervision during an exercise test is not necessary for low-risk clients or for moderate-risk clients during a submaximal exercise test.

In your attempts to decide if physician supervision is necessary, various resources are available. One widely accepted method for making a decision on whether or not a person is ready to begin an exercise program is the Physical Activity Readiness Questionnaire.

The **Physical Activity Readiness Questionnaire (PAR-Q)** is a screening method that has been used extensively in Canada to determine if individuals should not exercise or should not take an exercise test (ACSM 2006). Almost all individuals for whom it might be dangerous to start a moderate exercise program or take an exercise test can be identified with the PAR-Q. Answering "Yes" to any of the seven questions would mean that a client should talk with his or her physician before becoming more active and before exercise testing. Questions included in the PAR-Q are presented in Table 11.5. Another method for screening participants prior to exercise testing is the AHA/ACSM Health/Fitness Facility Preparticipation Screening Questionnaire (ACSM 2006).

LABORATORY-BASED AEROBIC FITNESS TESTS

Aerobic fitness can be measured in the laboratory with either a maximal or a submaximal test. At maximal exercise, $\dot{V}O_2$ can be measured from expired gases, estimated from maximal treadmill time, or estimated from power output. For submaximal tests, the heart rate response to a given power output on a treadmill or cycle ergometer is used to estimate aerobic fitness. Laboratory tests,

---

TABLE 11.5	**Physical Activity Readiness Questionnaire (PAR-Q)**

Instructions: Please read the questions carefully and answer each one honestly: yes or no.

1. Has your doctor ever said you have a heart condition *and* that you should only do physical activity recommended by a doctor?
2. Do you feel pain in your chest when you do physical activity?
3. In the past month, have you had chest pain when you were not doing physical activity?
4. Do you lose your balance because of dizziness or do you ever lose consciousness?
5. Do you have a bone or joint problem that could be made worse by a change in your physical activity?
6. Is your doctor currently prescribing drugs (for example, water pills) for your blood pressure or heart condition?
7. Do you know of *any other reason* why you should not do physical activity?

Note: If clients answer "yes" to any of the questions, they should talk with their doctor *before* becoming much more physically active and *before* they have a fitness appraisal.

as used in this text, involve using a standard method of regulating power output, typically from a cycle ergometer or treadmill. Quantification of power output from treadmill and cycle ergometer exercise is discussed next.

Regulating Power Output

Power output is the rate of work used to define exercise. Oxygen consumption increases linearly with power output (Åstrand & Rodahl 1986). As power output increases, the exercising muscles require more oxygen. This can be easily seen as one walks up a hill. As the hill gets steeper (increased power output), heart rate and breathing rates increase as the body needs and uses more oxygen (increased oxygen consumption). In a laboratory setting, cycle ergometers and treadmills are usually used to regulate power output for an exercise test.

Cycle Ergometer Power Output

Power output on a **cycle ergometer** is changed by altering the resistance placed on the flywheel, and/or altering the pedaling rate. A kilopond (kp) is the force placed on the cycle ergometer flywheel. A kilopond is equal to 1 kilogram (kg) at unit gravitational pull. Both kp and kg have been used to identify the resistance placed on the flywheel. For consistency, the term kg will be used in this book. The number of revolutions the flywheel completes per minute (rev·min^{-1}) is the second factor used to calculate cycle ergometer power output. The final factor necessary to calculate power output is the distance the flywheel travels with each revolution. The Monark cycle ergometer is one of the most popular testing ergometers. The distance a Monark cycle ergometer flywheel travels in one revolution is 6 meters. A Monark arm ergometer travels 2.4 meters per revolution.

 Power output of a cycle ergometer is expressed as kilogram meters of work per minute (kg·m·min^{-1}) and is computed from resistance (kg), distance traveled per revolution (m·rev^{-1}), and speed of movement (rev·min^{-1}). The basic formula to calculate power output from a cycle ergometer is presented in the following equation.

$$kg \cdot m \cdot min^{-1} = kg \times m \cdot rev^{-1} \times rev \cdot min^{-1} \quad \textbf{(11.3)}$$

 Other units used to quantify cycle ergometer power output are **watts** and $\dot{V}O_2$ (ml·kg^{-1}·min^{-1}). One watt is equal to 6.12 kg·m·min^{-1} (Åstrand & Rodahl 1986). This value is typically rounded to 6 kg·m·min^{-1} for ease of calculation (ACSM 2006). Thus, the following formula is used to calculate power output in watts.

$$Watts = kg \cdot m \cdot min^{-1} \div 6 \quad \textbf{(11.4)}$$

 To estimate $\dot{V}O_2$ during cycle ergometry, one must consider the oxygen demand of unloaded cycling, the oxygen cost of the external load placed on the cycle, and resting oxygen consumption (ACSM 2006). The cost of unloaded cycling (i.e., movement of the legs) is approximately 3.5 ml·kg^{-1}·min^{-1} above rest. The cost of the external load placed on the ergometer is approximately 1.8 ml·kg^{-1}·m^{-1}. Resting $\dot{V}O_2$ is estimated to be 3.5 ml·kg^{-1}·min^{-1}. The following formula is used to estimate power output $\dot{V}O_2$ (ml·kg^{-1}·min^{-1}).

ACSM Cycling Equation

$$\dot{V}O_2 \ (ml \cdot kg^{-1} \cdot min^{-1})$$
$$= (1.8 \ ml \cdot kg^{-1} \cdot m^{-1} \times kg \cdot m \cdot min^{-1})$$
$$\div \ body \ weight \ in \ kg)$$
$$+ \ 7 \ ml \cdot kg^{-1} \cdot min^{-1} \quad \textbf{(11.5)}$$

where 1.8 is a constant, kg·m·min^{-1} is the work performed on the cycle ergometer, body weight is the participant's weight in kilograms, and 7 represents the cost of unloaded cycling plus resting $\dot{V}O_2$ (3.5 + 3.5).

Computation Example Assume a person who weighs 70 kg is tested on a Monark cycle ergometer (i.e., the distance traveled with each revolution of the flywheel is 6 meters). If the pedal rate is 50 rev·min^{-1} at a resistance of 3 kg, the power output

TABLE 11.6	Cycle Ergometer Energy Expenditure Estimates for Selected Resistance Settings, Pedaling at a Rate of 50 rev·min^{-1}			
Resistance Kg	Power Output kg·m·min^{-1}	$\dot{V}O_2$ (ml·kg^{-1}·min^{-1}) for Selected Body Masses		
		50 kg	60 kg	70 kg	80 kg
0.5	150	12.4	11.5	10.9	10.4
1.0	300	17.8	16.0	14.7	13.8
1.5	450	23.2	20.5	18.6	17.1
2.0	600	28.6	25.0	22.4	20.5
2.5	750	34.0	29.5	26.3	23.9
3.0	900	39.4	34.0	30.1	27.3
3.5	1050	44.8	38.5	34.0	30.6
4.0	1200	50.2	43.0	37.9	34.0
4.5	1350	55.6	47.5	41.7	37.4
5.0	1500	61.0	52.0	45.6	40.8
5.5	1650	66.4	56.5	49.4	44.1
6.0	1800	71.8	61.0	53.3	47.5
6.5	1950	77.2	65.5	57.1	50.9
7.0	2100	82.6	70.0	61.0	54.3

Note: These estimates are for cycle ergometers with a flywheel that covers 6 m·rev^{-1} (e.g., Monark cycle ergometers).

in kg·m·min^{-1}, watts, and $\dot{V}O_2$ (ml·kg^{-1}·min^{-1}) would be

$$\text{kg·m·min}^{-1} = 3 \times 6 \times 50 = 900$$

$$\text{Watts} = 900 \div 6 = 150$$

$$\dot{V}O_2 \text{ (ml·kg}^{-1}\text{·min}^{-1}) = (1.8 \times 900 \div 70) + 7 = 30.14$$

The common method for increasing power output during an exercise test on a cycle ergometer is to have the participant pedal at a constant rate (e.g., 50 or 60 rev·min^{-1}) and to systematically adjust the resistance placed on the flywheel. The approximate energy costs (i.e., $\dot{V}O_2$ in ml·kg^{-1}·min^{-1}) during cycle ergometry calculated with the ACSM equations are presented in Table 11.6.

Treadmill Power Output

The power output of a **treadmill** is regulated by changing treadmill speed and/or elevation. For a maximal test, $\dot{V}O_2$ max can be estimated from the maximal time to exhaustion on a standardized treadmill protocol or from the maximal power output attained. Maximal treadmill time equations are presented in the next section.

Standard equations (ACSM 2006) have been published to convert treadmill speed and elevation into $\dot{V}O_2$ (ml·kg^{-1}·min^{-1}). The oxygen demand of walking and running is composed of the cost of horizontal movement, vertical movement, and resting energy expenditure. The ACSM walking equation is presented next.

ACSM Walking Equation

$$\dot{V}O_2 \text{ (ml·kg}^{-1}\text{·min}^{-1}) = 0.1(\text{speed})$$
$$+1.8(\text{speed})(\text{fractional grade}) + 3.5 \quad \textbf{(11.6)}$$

where speed is in m·min^{-1} (1 mph = 26.8 m·min^{-1}) and fractional grade is the treadmill grade expressed as a fraction. The constants in the equation of 0.1 and 1.8 come from previous research (Balke & Ware 1959; Dill 1965; Nagle et al. 1971; Nagle, Balke & Naughton 1965). The constant of 0.1 represents the oxygen cost of transporting 1 kg of body mass 1 meter of horizontal distance (ml·kg^{-1}·m^{-1}). For vertical movement, the oxygen cost of moving 1 kg of body mass 1 meter vertically is approximately 1.8 $ml \cdot kg^{-1} \cdot m^{-1}$. The oxygen cost of rest is approximately 3.5 $ml \cdot kg^{-1} \cdot min^{-1}$. The ACSM walking equation is appropriate for speeds of 1.9 to 3.7 mph (50 to 100 $m \cdot min^{-1}$).

The ACSM running equation is presented below.

ACSM Running Equation

$$\dot{V}O_2 \ (ml \cdot kg^{-1} \cdot min^{-1}) = 0.2(speed)$$
$$+ 0.9(speed)(fractional\ grade) + 3.5 \quad \textbf{(11.7)}$$

where speed is in $m \cdot min^{-1}$ and fractional grade is the treadmill grade expressed as a fraction. The constant of 0.2 represents the oxygen cost of moving 1 kilogram 1 meter of horizontal distance. Thus, the oxygen demand for running is about twice as great as that for walking for the horizontal component (Balke 1963; Margaria et al. 1963). This is not the case for the vertical component of the oxygen cost of running. Because some of the vertical work of running is accomplished during the horizontal movement of running, the coefficient that represents the vertical component in the running equation is reduced to 0.9 $ml \cdot kg^{-1} \cdot m^{-1}$. The oxygen cost of rest is the same (3.5 $ml \cdot kg^{-1} \cdot min^{-1}$). The ACSM running equation is appropriate for speeds over 5 mph (134 $m \cdot min^{-1}$) or for speeds as low as 3 mph (80 $m \cdot min^{-1}$) if the person is running and not walking.

Computation Example   Assume we test a person on a treadmill at two levels: (a) walking at 3.4 mph at 0% elevation, and (b) running at 6 mph at 8% elevation. The $\dot{V}O_2$ for treadmill exercise at these levels would be as follows:

Speed ($m \cdot min^{-1}$) = mph × 26.8 = 3.4 × 26.8

$$= 91.12$$

$\dot{V}O_2$ ($ml \cdot kg^{-1} \cdot min^{-1}$) = 0.1(91.12)

$$+ 1.8(91.12)(0) + 3.5$$

$$= 9.112 + 0 + 3.5 = 12.6$$

Speed ($m \cdot min^{-1}$) = mph × 26.8

$$= 6 × 26.8 = 160.8$$

$\dot{V}O_2$ ($ml \cdot kg^{-1} \cdot min^{-1}$) = 0.2(160.8)

$$+ 0.9(160.8)(.08) + 3.5$$

$$= 32.16 + 11.5776 + 3.5 = 47.2$$

Table 11.7 provides estimates of the oxygen cost of the stages of three submaximal treadmill protocols that can be used for submaximal testing.

LABORATORY-BASED MAXIMAL TESTS OF AEROBIC FITNESS

The objective of a maximal exercise test is to systematically increase exercise intensity until the participant reaches exhaustion. Measurement of oxygen consumption is done by open-circuit spirometry (see Figure 11-4). $\dot{V}O_2$ max can be estimated from maximal treadmill time or from maximal power output attained during a maximal test by using the appropriate ACSM equations.

Open-Circuit Spirometry

$\dot{V}O_2$ max is most accurately determined by measuring expired gases during maximal exercise. The measurement of expired gases is called **open-circuit spirometry**. Measurement of $\dot{V}O_2$ max through open-circuit spirometry is relatively expensive and requires highly trained personnel. The subject is required to exercise to exhaustion (usually on a treadmill or cycle ergometer). The exercise protocol usually requires that the intensity of exercise be slowly and systematically increased until the subject reaches exhaustion. During this exercise, a computer-controlled metabolic system is used to assess the oxygen and carbon dioxide concentrations and the volume of expired air (see Figure 11-4).

This method is conceptually simple, but requires trained technicians and expensive equipment. The objective of a maximal test is to increase power output at a linear rate throughout the test (e.g., increase treadmill elevation by 4% every 3 minutes, or increase cycle ergometer resistance by 150 $kg \cdot m \cdot min^{-1}$ every 3 minutes) until the individual reaches exhaustion. Expired gases are collected throughout the exercise test and at a person's maximal level of exertion. The volume of oxygen consumed at the exhausting level of exercise (i.e., maximal exercise capacity) is $\dot{V}O_2$ max (see Figure 11-1). The parameters needed to calculate $\dot{V}O_2$ max are oxygen and carbon dioxide concentrations and

Stage	Minutes	mph	% Grade	$\dot{V}O_2$ (ml·kg⁻¹·min⁻¹)	METs
TABLE 11.7 Estimated $\dot{V}O_2$ and MET Levels for Stages of Submaximal Treadmill Test Protocols					
Bruce Protocol					
I	1–3	1.7	10	16.257	4.6
II	4–6	2.5	12	24.672	7.0
III	7–9	3.4	14	35.574	10.2
Ross Submaximal Protocol—Women					
I	1–3	3.4	0	12.612	3.6
II	4–6	3.4	3	17.532	5.0
III	7–9	3.4	6	22.453	6.4
IV	10–12	3.4	9	27.373	7.8
V	13–15	3.4	12	32.294	9.2
Ross Submaximal Protocol—Men					
I	1–3	3.4	0	12.612	3.6
II	4–6	3.4	4	19.173	5.5
III	7–9	3.4	8	25.733	7.4
IV	10–12	3.4	12	32.294	9.2
V	13–15	3.4	16	38.855	11.1

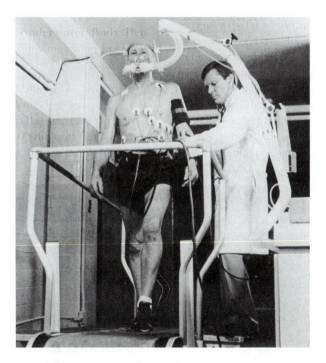

Figure 11-4

Dr. Michael Pollock monitoring an exercise test designed to measure $\dot{V}O_2$ max by analyzing expired gases. Electrodes placed on the chest provides a means of monitoring the heart's rhythm and produces an electrocardiogram (EKG).

Figure 11-5

Portable metabolic systems enable measurement of $\dot{V}O_2$ max outside of laboratory settings.

volume of expired air. Standard methods are available for calculating oxygen consumption (Consolazio, Johnson & Pecora 1963; Jones & Campbell 1982).

Although the measurement of $\dot{V}O_2$ max is relatively difficult, several computer-driven commercial systems are available to speed these measurements. $\dot{V}O_2$ max is assessed at professional, clinical, and research institutions. At NASA/Johnson Space Center in Houston, Texas, the aerobic fitness of astronauts is measured yearly and is even measured in space. Many colleges and universities have the capacity to evaluate $\dot{V}O_2$ max by open-circuit spirometry. Some of the newer metabolic systems are even portable, which means that the measurements can be made outside of a laboratory setting (see Figure 11-5).

Actual measurement of $\dot{V}O_2$ max through open-circuit spirometry is not necessary except in certain circumstances (e.g., research studies). Because oxygen consumption is linearly related with external work and with heart rate, $\dot{V}O_2$ max can be estimated relatively accurately.

Maximal Treadmill Tests

A maximal treadmill test is performed to voluntary exhaustion. The potential for a cardiac event during a maximal test is low (ACSM 2006). Even with this low risk, caution needs to be exercised when testing adults, especially those at risk for cardiovascular disease. Exercise test administrators should always consider the American College of Sports Medicine guidelines presented in the section in this chapter titled "Risk Stratification for Exercise Testing" regarding physician supervision during exercise tests.

Measures commonly taken during maximal exercise tests include heart rate, blood pressure, and **rating of perceived exertion (RPE)**. Borg's RPE scale is used during exercise tests to gain additional insight to the level of exertion and to help determine if a person is reaching her maximal level of exertion (Borg 1977; Pollock, Jackson & Foster 1986). Additional information about RPE scales can be found in Chapter 17.

Aerobic fitness can be measured during many forms of exercise, most commonly maximal treadmill or cycle ergometer exercise. It is generally recommended that people be tested on the mode of exercise that they commonly employ. For example, highly trained cyclists should be tested with cycle tests. However, many people are not accustomed to riding a cycle ergometer and find it difficult to reach their maximum exercise capacity on a cycle because of

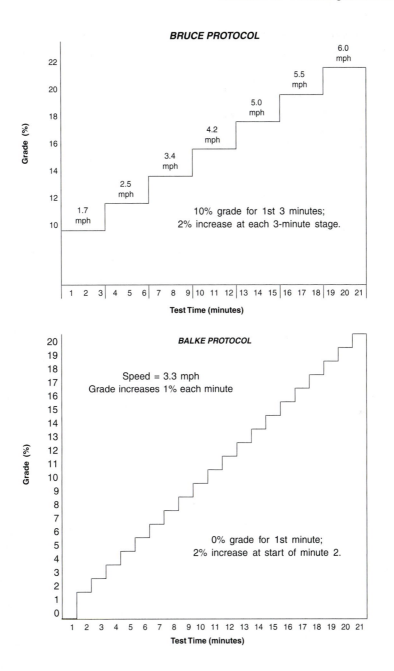

Figure 11-6

Bruce and Balke treadmill protocols are most often used during maximal exercise tests.

leg fatigue. For this reason, most maximal exercise tests are performed on a treadmill. Standard treadmill protocols include the Bruce protocol and the Balke protocol. For the Bruce and Balke protocols, power output is systematically increased with treadmill time. The elapsed time to reach exhaustion on these protocols can be used to estimate aerobic fitness. A graphic representation of the Bruce and Balke protocols is provided in Figure 11-6.

Several valid regression equations have been published to estimate $\dot{V}O_2$ max from maximal treadmill time (Bruce, Kusumi & Hosmer 1973; Foster et al. 1984; Pollock et al. 1976). Since each treadmill protocol increases power output at different rates, unique equations are needed for each protocol. The reported correlations between directly measured $\dot{V}O_2$ max and maximal treadmill time are high, ranging from .88 to .97. The standard error of estimate is about 3 $ml \cdot kg^{-1} \cdot min^{-1}$ from maximal treadmill time for the Bruce ($R = .97$) and Balke ($R = .88$) protocols.

The equation to estimate $\dot{V}O_2$ max from the Bruce protocol is nonlinear and was developed on both healthy persons and cardiac patients (Foster et al. 1984). The $\dot{V}O_2$ max of cardiac patients is 4.2 $ml \cdot kg^{-1} \cdot min^{-1}$ lower than that of healthy persons for each maximal treadmill time. The following formula is used to estimate $\dot{V}O_2$ max ($ml \cdot kg^{-1} \cdot min^{-1}$) from maximal treadmill time on the Bruce protocol for persons free from cardiovascular disease.

Bruce Protocol Equation

$$\dot{V}O_2 \text{ max } (ml \cdot kg^{-1} \cdot min^{-1}) = 17.50$$
$$-(0.30 \times TT) + (0.297 \times TT^2)$$
$$-(0.0077 \times TT^3) \qquad \textbf{(11.8)}$$

where TT is maximal treadmill time in minutes, TT^2 is maximal treadmill time squared, and TT^3 is maximal treadmill time cubed.

The formula to estimate $\dot{V}O_2$ max from maximal treadmill time on the Balke protocol is presented next.

Balke Protocol Equation

$$\dot{V}O_2 \text{ max } (ml \cdot kg^{-1} \cdot min^{-1}) = 14.99$$
$$+ (1.44 \times TT) \qquad \textbf{(11.9)}$$

where TT is maximal treadmill time.

Computation Example $\dot{V}O_2$ max estimates for a person who has a maximal treadmill time of 12 minutes and 35 seconds (12.58 minutes) would differ depending on which treadmill protocol was used. The estimates for the Bruce and Balke protocols for this maximal treadmill time would be as follows:

Bruce Protocol Equation

$$\dot{V}O_2 \text{ max } (ml \cdot kg^{-1} \cdot min^{-1}) = 17.50$$
$$- (0.30 \times 12.58) + (0.297 \times 12.58^2)$$
$$- (0.0077 \times 12.58^3) = 17.50 - (3.774)$$
$$+ (47.002) - (15.330) = 45.4$$

Balke Protocol Equation

$$\dot{V}O_2 \text{ max } (ml \cdot kg^{-1} \cdot min^{-1}) = 14.99$$
$$+ (1.44 \times 12.58) = 14.99 + 18.12 = 33.1$$

Figure 11-7 graphically shows $\dot{V}O_2$ max estimated from treadmill time for the Bruce and Balke protocols. After the first three minutes of treadmill performance, the estimated $\dot{V}O_2$ max on the Bruce protocol is higher than the corresponding time for the Balke protocol.

LABORATORY-BASED SUBMAXIMAL TESTS OF AEROBIC FITNESS

Exercising to $\dot{V}O_2$ max is physically exhausting, is time-consuming, and requires medical supervision when testing high-risk subjects. In addition, participant motivation is important for maximal testing because the participant is asked to exercise to exhaustion, something that one rarely does. Submaximal exercise tests provide a less accurate but more practical method for estimating aerobic fitness than maximal tests. The measurement objective of a submaximal exercise test is to define the slope of the individual's heart rate response to exercise and then to use the slope to estimate $\dot{V}O_2$ max from submaximal heart rate and power output. Submaximal exercise tests are based on the following physiological principles.

1. Heart rate increases in direct proportion to the oxygen used during aerobic exercise.
2. $\dot{V}O_2$ max is reached at maximal heart rate.
3. A less fit person will have a higher heart rate at any submaximal exercise intensity than someone who is more aerobically fit.

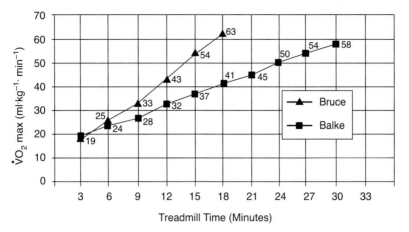

Figure 11-7

Estimated $\dot{V}O_2$ max (ml·kg^{-1}·min^{-1}) from maximal treadmill time for the Bruce and Balke treadmill protocols.

Oxygen consumption ($\dot{V}O_2$) at any level of exercise is the product of cardiac output and the difference in the oxygen content between arterial blood and venous blood (i.e., a-v O_2 difference). Cardiac output is the product of heart rate and stroke volume (i.e., the volume of blood pumped with each heartbeat). Stroke volume increases early in exercise, stabilizing at about 45% of $\dot{V}O_2$ max (see Figure 11-8). Thus, any further change in cardiac output during exercise is due to an increase in heart rate. To estimate $\dot{V}O_2$ max from submaximal parameters, one should exercise at an intensity that raises heart rate to between 45% and 70% of $\dot{V}O_2$ max. This usually corresponds with heart rates between 110 and 150 beats per minute. For younger individuals the submaximal heart rate response may be higher than 150 beats per minute, because maximal heart rate is inversely related to age. Both single-stage and multi-stage submaximal models can be used to estimate $\dot{V}O_2$ max from submaximal power output and exercise heart rates between 45% and 70% of $\dot{V}O_2$ max. Single-stage and multi-stage models are presented in the next section.

Single-Stage Model

The **single-stage exercise test** model is easier to use and slightly more accurate than the multi-stage

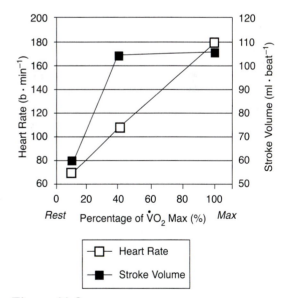

Figure 11-8

Response of heart rate and stroke volume to exercise intensity. Cardiac output is the product of heart rate and stroke volume. Stroke volume reaches maximum at about 40–45% of $\dot{V}O_2$ max. The increase in cardiac output after this exercise intensity is due to an increase in heart rate.

model presented next (Mahar et al. 1985). The single-stage model was initially popularized by the Åstrand-Ryhming nomogram (Åstrand & Ryhming 1954; Åstrand & Rodahl 1986). The single-stage model to estimate $\dot{V}O_2$ max is presented next.

Single-Stage $\dot{V}O_2$ max Equation

$$\dot{V}O_2 \text{ max (ml·kg}^{-1}\text{·min}^{-1}) = SM\dot{V}O_2$$
$$\times (220 - \text{age} - k) \div (SMHR - k) \quad \textbf{(11.10)}$$

where $SM\dot{V}O_2$ is the $\dot{V}O_2$ in ml·kg^{-1}·min^{-1} at the submaximal exercise intensity, $220 - \text{age}$ is the estimate of maximal heart rate, SMHR is the submaximal heart rate at $SM\dot{V}O_2$, and k is a constant of 63 for males and 73 for females. The constants for k were solved from the original data published by Åstrand and Ryhming (Mahar 1987). These values represent the intercepts of the regression lines.

Either a cycle ergometer or a treadmill can be used to regulate power output. The submaximal exercise at which a person is tested should be **steady state exercise**. Steady state heart rate is defined as two successive heart rates within 5 beats·min^{-1} (ACSM 2006). A person will typically reach steady state in the first three minutes of exercise at a given submaximal intensity. For this reason, most submaximal test protocols have three-minute stages.

Recommended procedures for a cycle ergometer protocol are listed next.

1. The pedaling position should be comfortable for the participant. Seat height should be adjusted so that the knee has a slight bend (approximately 5°) on the downward stroke.
2. A suitable pedaling rate should be chosen (often this is 50 rev·min^{-1}). A metronome is commonly used to standardize the pedaling rate.
3. Recommended starting loads are 300 to 600 kg·m·min^{-1} for women, and 300 to 900 kg·m·min^{-1} for men. Lower starting loads would be used for women and less fit participants.

4. Heart rate should be monitored at the end of each minute of exercise. The goal is to reach a steady state heart rate greater than 110 beats·min^{-1}. The single-stage model (Equation 11.10) can be used with one steady state heart rate greater than 110 beats·min^{-1}, but greater prediction accuracy can be expected as the steady state heart rates represent a higher percentage of $\dot{V}O_2$ max. ACSM recommends that the submaximal test be terminated when the participant reaches 85% of age-predicted maximal heart rate. Many submaximal protocols use three-minute stages. If exercise heart rate after three minutes is not steady state, then the exercise should be continued at the same stage for another minute or until steady state heart rate is reached.

Computation Example   Assume a 35-year-old man who weighs 70 kg was administered a submaximal exercise test on a cycle ergometer. Submaximal heart rate was 144 beats·min^{-1} at a power output of 750 kg·m·min^{-1}. $\dot{V}O_2$ max would be estimated from the single-stage model as follows:
Submaximal $\dot{V}O_2$ ($SM\dot{V}O_2$) must first be estimated from Equation 11.5, the ACSM Cycling Equation.

ACSM Cycling Equation

$$\dot{V}O_2 \text{ (ml·kg}^{-1}\text{·min}^{-1}) =$$
$$(1.8 \text{ ml·kg}^{-1}\text{·m}^{-1} \times \text{kg·m·min}^{-1}$$
$$\div \text{ body mass in kg}) + 7 \text{ ml·kg}^{-1}\text{·min}^{-1}$$

$$\dot{V}O_2 \text{ (ml·kg}^{-1}\text{·min}^{-1}) =$$
$$(1.8 \times 750 \div 70) + 7 = 26.29$$

Then the submaximal $\dot{V}O_2$ from the ACSM Cycling Equation is substituted into the Single-Stage $\dot{V}O_2$ max Equation as shown below.

Single-Stage $\dot{V}O_2$ max Equation

$$\dot{V}O_2 \text{ max (ml·kg}^{-1}\text{·min}^{-1}) = 26.29$$
$$\times (220 - 35 - 63) \div (144 - 63) = 39.6$$

Åstrand-Ryhming Single-Stage Test

The Åstrand-Ryhming single-stage test can be administered on a cycle ergometer, treadmill, or step. The cycle ergometer protocol lasts 6 minutes (Åstrand & Ryhming 1954). The pedal rate is 50 rev·min^{-1}. Åstrand and Ryhming recommended that submaximal heart rates between 125 and 170 beats·min^{-1} be used for prediction. The average of the heart rate of minutes 5 and 6 of the test is used in the prediction equation. If after 6 minutes the submaximal heart rate is between 125 and 170 beats·min^{-1}, then the test is ended. If heart rate is below 125 beats·min^{-1}, then 150 to 300 kg·m·min^{-1} is added to the power output and the test is continued for an additional 4 to 6 minutes. An age-correction factor was added to the Åstrand-Ryhming prediction model (Åstrand 1960) to account for the decrease in maximal heart rate with an increase in age. We recommend the use of the formula 220 − age as an estimate of maximal heart rate rather than application of a correction factor to the predicted value of $\dot{V}O_2$ max.

Multi-Stage Model

The **multi-stage exercise test** model requires that heart rate and power output be measured at two or more submaximal levels (Golding, Myers & Sinning, 1989). The regression line developed from the heart rate and power output data points is extrapolated to age-predicted maximal heart rate, and then used to estimate $\dot{V}O_2$ max. The multi-stage model is the procedure used for the YMCA Adult Fitness Test (Golding et al. 1989). The YMCA test is administered on a cycle ergometer and follows the protocol in Figure 11-9 to regulate power output for each three-minute stage. The goal of the YMCA test is to obtain two submaximal heart rates between 110 and 150 beats·min^{-1}. $\dot{V}O_2$ max is estimated by plotting the linear increase in exercise heart rate associated with the increases in power output with each exercise stage. Connecting the two points defines the slope of heart rate and power output relationship. Using this slope, the line is extended to age-predicted maximal heart rate. A perpendicular line is then drawn down to the power output scale as demonstrated in Figure 11-10. The point where this line crosses the power output scale on the x-axis represents the maximal power output that would be expected if the person had exercised to her maximal capacity. $\dot{V}O_2$ max can then be estimated by using Equation 11.5 and the predicted maximal power output.

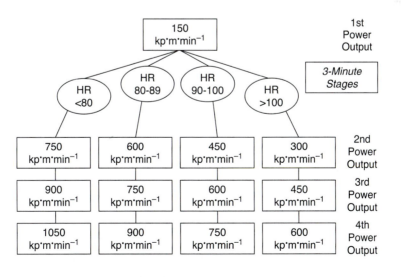

Figure 11-9

Cycle ergometer protocol used for the YMCA adult fitness test (Golding et al. 1989). The test starts at a low power output, and the heart rate response to the first stage determines the next power output level. Each stage is three minutes in length.

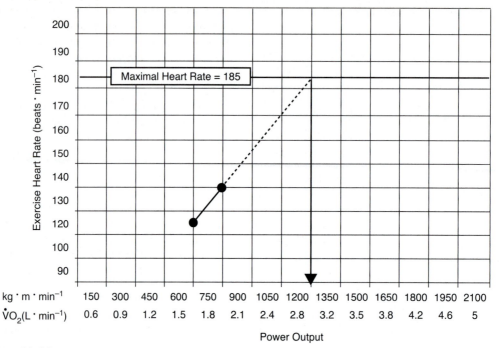

Figure 11-10

Illustration of method to estimate $\dot{V}O_2$ max with the multi-stage model following the YMCA test (Golding et al. 1989).

Ross and Jackson (1990) presented the multi-stage model as a regression equation that aids in computer calculation of $\dot{V}O_2$ max and eliminates any graphing errors that might occur from plotting points by hand. The multi-stage model prediction equation is presented below.

Multi-Stage $\dot{V}O_2$ max Equation

$$\dot{V}O_2 \text{ max } (ml \cdot kg^{-1} \cdot min^{-1}) =$$
$$\dot{V}O_{2.2} + b(220 - age - HR_2) \quad \textbf{(11.11)}$$

$$b = (\dot{V}O_{2.2} - \dot{V}O_{2.1}) \div (HR_2 - HR_1) \quad \textbf{(11.12)}$$

where $\dot{V}O_{2.2}$ is $\dot{V}O_2$ at stage II, $\dot{V}O_{2.1}$ is $\dot{V}O_2$ at stage I, HR[2] is heart rate at stage II, and HR[1] is heart rate at stage I. The slope (b) between heart rate and $\dot{V}O_2$ must first be calculated with Formula 11.12.

Computation Example   Assume a 52-year-old woman who weighs 60 kg was administered a multi-stage test on a cycle ergometer. At a power

output of 450 $kg \cdot m \cdot min^{-1}$, her heart rate was 130 $beats \cdot min^{-1}$ (stage I), and at a power output of 600 $kg \cdot m \cdot min^{-1}$, her heart rate was 149 $beats \cdot min^{-1}$ (stage II). $\dot{V}O_2$ at stage I and stage II can be estimated using Equation 11.5.

ACSM Cycling Equation

Stage I:

$$\dot{V}O_2 \ (ml \cdot kg^{-1} \cdot min^{-1}) =$$
$$(1.8 \times 450 \div 60) + 7 = 20.5$$

Stage II:

$$\dot{V}O_2 \ (ml \cdot kg^{-1} \cdot min^{-1})$$
$$= (1.8 \times 600 \div 60) + 7 = 25.0$$

Slope for Multi-Stage $\dot{V}O_2$ max Equation

$$b = (25.0 - 20.5) \div (149 - 137) = 0.375$$

Multi-Stage $\dot{V}O_2$ max Equation

$$\dot{V}O_2 \text{ max } (ml \cdot kg^{-1} \cdot min^{-1}) =$$
$$25.0 + 0.375(220 - 52 - 149) = 32.1$$

The YMCA model is one of the most widely used submaximal tests to estimate $\dot{V}O_2$ max (ACSM 2006). The multi-stage model takes longer to administer than the single-stage model because steady state heart rate must be obtained at two stages instead of just one stage. In addition, multi-stage models have been shown to be less accurate than single-stage models (Mahar et al. 1985). Thus, single-stage models appear to be more accurate and more practical than multi-stage models.

Submaximal Treadmill Protocols

Submaximal treadmill protocols are provided in Table 11.7. For the Bruce protocol, a heart rate between 135 and 150 beats·min^{-1} will be reached during the first 6 minutes of the test for most people. For the Ross submaximal protocol, stages IV and V should be used only for individuals under age 50 years. The Ross submaximal protocol is a modification of the Balke protocol. The Ross submaximal protocol is a better choice for the multi-stage model than the Bruce protocol, because power output is increased at a slower rate. Electronic equipment should be used to measure heart rate during treadmill tests, because the movement produced by walking on a treadmill makes it difficult to measure heart rate by palpation.

Computation Example Assume a 28-year-old woman's exercise heart rate is 145 beats·min^{-1} at stage III of the Ross submaximal treadmill protocol. The $\dot{V}O_2$ for stage III is 22.453 ml·kg^{-1}·min^{-1}. This value can be looked up in Table 11.7 or calculated from the ACSM walking equation (Equation 11.6). Estimated $\dot{V}O_2$ max from the single-stage model would be as follows:

$$\dot{V}O_2 \text{ max (ml·kg}^{-1}\text{·min}^{-1}) = 22.453$$
$$\times (220 - 28 - 73) \div (145 - 73) = 37.1$$

Several $\dot{V}O_2$ max prediction models have been developed for treadmill testing. The three presented below are both easy to use and relatively accurate.

Single-Stage 4-Minute Treadmill Walking Test

The 4-minute treadmill walking test (Ebbeling et al. 1991) consists of walking at either 2, 3, 4, or 4.5 mph at a 5% grade. The speed for each subject

should be established at a brisk but comfortable pace with a 4-minute warm-up prior to the test. The following model was developed on 117 men and women ages 20 to 59 years.

$$\dot{V}O_2 \text{ max (ml·kg}^{-1}\text{·min}^{-1})$$
$$= 15.1 + 21.8(\text{speed})$$
$$- 0.327(\text{submaximal HR})$$
$$- 0.263(\text{speed} \times \text{age})$$
$$+ 0.00504(\text{submaximal heart rate} \times \text{age})$$
$$+ 5.98(\text{gender})$$
$$(R = .93, \, SEE = 4.85 \text{ ml·kg}^{-1}\text{·min}^{-1}) \quad \textbf{(11.13)}$$

where speed is in mph, submaximal HR is submaximal heart rate at the submaximal exercise level used in the test, age is in years, and gender is coded as 1 for male and 0 for female.

Computation Example Assume a 36-year-old woman had a heart rate of 141 beats·min^{-1} while walking at 4 mph (5% grade). Her estimated $\dot{V}O_2$ max would be calculated thus:

$$\dot{V}O_2 \text{ max (ml·kg}^{-1}\text{·min}^{-1}) = 15.1$$
$$+ 21.8(4) - 0.327(141)$$
$$- 0.263(4 \times 36) + 0.00504(141 \times 36)$$
$$+ 5.98(0) = 43.9$$

Single-Stage Treadmill Walking Test

A practical and accurate single-stage treadmill walking test was developed and validated by DiNallo, Jackson, and Mahar (2000). The regression models were developed and cross-validated on a large sample of men that varied in age and fitness level. The prediction equations are among the most accurate and stable equations available to estimate $\dot{V}O_2$ max from submaximal exercise. The models to predict $\dot{V}O_2$ max use the following predictors: submaximal heart rate, submaximal $\dot{V}O_2$, age, self-reported physical activity, and a measure of body composition (percent fat for equation 1 and body mass index (BMI) for equation 2). Submaximal data were taken from one of the first three stages of the Bruce protocol. The following models were developed on 1,320 men aged 17 to 70 years. Single-stage treadmill walking models for women were developed on 209 women aged 21 to 66 years, using the same predictor variable.

Single-Stage Treadmill Walking Test Percent Fat Model (MEN)

$\dot{V}O_2$ max (ml·kg^{-1}·min^{-1}; model 1)

$$= 42.338 - 0.252(\text{age}) + 1.018(\text{PAR})$$
$$- 0.06702(\text{submaximal HR})$$
$$+ 0.708(\text{submaximal } \dot{V}O_2)$$
$$- 0.316(\text{percent fat})$$

$(R = .87, SEE = 4.0 \text{ ml·kg}^{-1}\text{·min}^{-1})$ **(11.14)**

Single-Stage Treadmill Walking Test BMI Model (MEN)

$\dot{V}O_2$ max (ml·kg^{-1}·min^{-1}; model 2)

$$= 47.34 - 0.306(\text{age}) + 1.117(\text{PAR})$$
$$- 0.08166(\text{submaximal HR})$$
$$+ 0.793(\text{submaximal } \dot{V}O_2)$$
$$- 0.381(\text{BMI})$$

$(R = .86, SEE = 4.1 \text{ ml·kg}^{-1}\text{·min}^{-1})$ **(11.15)**

where age is in years, PAR is self-reported physical activity on the 0–7 scale presented in Table 11.10, submaximal HR is submaximal heart rate at the submaximal exercise level used in the test, submaximal $\dot{V}O_2$ is estimated from the ACSM models (see Table 11.7), percent fat is estimated from skinfolds, and BMI is calculated from height and weight.

Computation Example Assume a 30-year-old man was 6 feet tall (71 inches or 1.8034 meters), weighed 80 kg (BMI = 80 ÷ 1.8034^2 = 24.6), and had a heart rate of 141 beats·min^{-1} while walking at stage III of the Bruce protocol. His self-reported physical activity from Table 11.10 was 4. His estimated $\dot{V}O_2$ max would be as follows:

$\dot{V}O_2$ max (ml·kg^{-1}·min^{-1}) = 47.34
$$- 0.306(30) + 1.117(4)$$
$$- 0.08166(141) + 0.793(35.574)$$
$$- 0.381(24.6) = 50.0$$

Single-Stage Treadmill Walking Test Percent Fat Model (WOMEN)

$\dot{V}O_2$ max (ml·kg^{-1}·min^{-1}; model 1)

$$= 54.801 - 0.270(\text{age}) + 1.088(\text{PAR})$$
$$- 0.081(\text{submaximal HR})$$
$$+ 0.185(\text{submaximal } \dot{V}O_2)$$
$$- 0.386(\text{percent fat})$$

$(R = .85, SEE = 4.2 \text{ ml·kg}^{-1}\text{·min}^{-1})$ **(11.16)**

Single-Stage Treadmill Walking Test BMI Model (WOMEN)

$\dot{V}O_2$ max (ml·kg^{-1}·min^{-1}; model 2)

$$= 59.808 - 0.323(\text{age}) + 1.284(\text{PAR})$$
$$- 0.093(\text{submaximal HR})$$
$$+ 0.265(\text{submaximal } \dot{V}O_2)$$
$$- 0.589(\text{BMI})$$

$(R = .84, SEE = 4.4 \text{ ml·kg}^{-1}\text{·min}^{-1})$ **(11.17)**

where age is in years, PAR is self-reported physical activity on the 0–7 scale presented in Table 11.10, submaximal HR is submaximal heart rate at the submaximal exercise level used in the test, submaximal $\dot{V}O_2$ is estimated from the ACSM models (see Table 11.7), percent fat is estimated from skinfolds, and BMI is calculated from height and weight.

Computation Example Assume a 21-year-old woman was 5 feet 4 inches tall (64 inches or 1.6256 meters), weighed 60 kg (BMI = 60 ÷ 1.6256^2 = 22.7), and had a heart rate of 137 beats·min^{-1} while walking at stage II of the Bruce protocol. Her self-reported physical activity from Table 11.10 was 5. Her estimated $\dot{V}O_2$ max would be as follows:

$\dot{V}O_2$ max (ml·kg^{-1}·min^{-1}) =
$$= 59.808 - 0.323(21) + 1.284(5)$$
$$- 0.093(137) + 0.265(24.672)$$
$$- 0.589(22.7) = 39.9$$

FIELD TESTS OF AEROBIC FITNESS

Field tests are useful for testing large numbers of people. Field tests available to estimate aerobic fitness include distance run/walk tests and 1-mile walking and running tests. The 12-minute run/walk (Cooper 1968, 1970), the 1.5-mile run/walk test (ACSM 2006), the generalized 1-mile run test (Cureton et al. 1995), and the 20-meter shuttle run test (Leger & Gadoury 1989) are presented in this section. The Rockport 1-mile walk test and the BYU jog test, which use the heart rate response to movement time to assess aerobic capacity, are also presented.

Maximal Distance Run Tests

Running performance is highly related to aerobic fitness. When maximal **distance run tests** are performed properly they provide valid assessments of aerobic fitness, but are less accurate than the regression equations derived for treadmill protocols in which the speed and elevation are regulated. The 12-minute run/walk requires participants to run or walk as far as possible in 12 minutes. The 1-mile and 1.5-mile run/walk tests are used to assess how quickly a participant covers that particular distance. The 20-meter shuttle run, commonly called the PACER, requires individuals to run back and forth across a 20-meter distance to a given pace, which increases every stage. It is important to remember that distance run tests are maximal exercise tests with all of the attendant risks of maximal testing. Unsupervised maximal distance run tests are not appropriate for older people or for those at an increased risk for heart disease.

12-Minute Run/Walk Test

Dr. Kenneth Cooper was one of the first to popularize distance run/walk tests. The goal of his research (Cooper 1968) was to provide a field test to assess the aerobic fitness of United States Air Force personnel. His sample consisted of 115 men who ranged from 17 to 52 years of age. The participants first completed the 12-minute distance run/walk test. The distance in miles covered in 12 minutes was recorded. On the next day the participants completed a maximal treadmill test in which $\dot{V}O_2$ max was measured. A very high correlation ($r = .90$) between distance covered in 12 minutes and measured $\dot{V}O_2$ max was found. Cooper published a regression equation to estimate distance traveled in miles from $\dot{V}O_2$ max ($ml \cdot kg^{-1} \cdot min^{-1}$). This equation can be rearranged to estimate $\dot{V}O_2$ max from distance covered in 12 minutes and is presented below.

Cooper 12-Minute Run/Walk Test

$$\dot{V}O_2 \text{ max } (ml \cdot kg^{-1} \cdot min^{-1})$$
$$= (\text{Distance} - 0.3138) \div 0.0278 \quad \textbf{(11.18)}$$
where distance is in miles.

Computation Example Assume a person covers 1.43 miles during the 12-minute run/walk. Estimated $\dot{V}O_2$ max would be as follows:

$$\dot{V}O_2 \text{ max } (ml \cdot kg^{-1} \cdot min^{-1}) =$$
$$(1.43 - 0.3138) \div 0.0278 = 40.2$$

Table 11.8 provides $\dot{V}O_2$ max estimates for various distances covered during the 12-minute run/walk test computed from Formula 11.18.

1.5-Mile Run Test

The 1.5-mile run test has become more popular than the 12-minute run as an adult field test of aerobic fitness because it is easier to measure time required to complete 1.5 miles than distance covered in 12 minutes. For the 1.5-mile run test all participants start and finish at the same point, so the tester needs to record only the time when the participant crosses the point that indicates he has covered 1.5 miles. ACSM (2006) guidelines suggest the following equation to estimate $\dot{V}O_2$ max from 1.5-mile run time.

1.5-Mile Run Test

$$\dot{V}O_2 \text{ max } (ml \cdot kg^{-1} \cdot min^{-1}) =$$
$$3.5 + (438 \div \text{time in minutes}) \quad \textbf{(11.19)}$$

where time in minutes represents the time it takes the participant to cover 1.5 miles. This formula was developed by rearranging the ACSM running equation. Table 11.8 provides $\dot{V}O_2$ max estimates for various 1.5-mile run times computed from Formula 11.19.

TABLE 11.8 $\dot{V}O_2$ **max Estimated from the 12-minute Run/Walk Test Performance and 1.5 Mile Run Time**

$\dot{V}O_2$ max (ml·kg^{-1}·min^{-1})	Miles in 12 Minutes	1.5-Mile Run Time (min:sec)
66	2.15	7:44
64	2.10	7:59
62	2.04	8:15
60	1.98	8:33
58	1.93	8:52
56	1.87	9:12
54	1.82	9:34
52	1.76	9:58
50	1.70	10:23
48	1.65	10:51
46	1.59	11:22
44	1.54	11:56
42	1.48	12:33
40	1.43	13:14
38	1.37	14:00
36	1.31	14:52
34	1.26	15:50
32	1.20	16:57
30	1.15	18:14
28	1.09	19:43
26	1.04	21:28
24	0.98	23:34

Computation Example   Assume that a person ran 1.5 miles in 12 minutes and 30 seconds (i.e., 12.5 minutes). Estimated $\dot{V}O_2$ max would be as follows:

$$\dot{V}O_2 \text{ max (ml·kg}^{-1}\text{·min}^{-1})$$
$$= 3.5 + (483 \div 12.5) = 42.1$$

Generalized 1-Mile Run/Walk Test

Cureton et al. (1995) published a comprehensive study relating 1-mile run/walk performance with $\dot{V}O_2$ max. Their sample consisted of over 750 males and females who ranged in age from 8 to 25 years. The goal was to develop a generalized regression equation that provided valid estimates of aerobic fitness for youth and adults of both sexes. This classic study provides an excellent example of a concurrent validation study.

These researchers found that the relationship between 1-mile run time and $\dot{V}O_2$ max was not linear and that sex, age, and body mass index (BMI) ac-counted for a significant proportion of the variance in aerobic fitness. The generalized 1-mile run/walk equation to estimate $\dot{V}O_2$ max is presented below.

Cureton et al. 1-Mile Run/Walk Equation

$$\dot{V}O_2 \text{ max (ml·kg}^{-1}\text{·min}^{-1}) = 108.94$$
$$- 8.41(\text{time}) + 0.34(\text{time}^2)$$
$$+ 0.21(\text{age} \times \text{gender}) - 0.84(\text{BMI})$$
$(R = .72, \; SEE = 4.8 \text{ ml·kg}^{-1}\text{·min}^{-1})$ **(11.20)**

where time is mile run/walk time in minutes, age is in years, gender is coded as 1 for male and 0 for female, and BMI is body mass index.

Computation Example   Assume a 17-year-old male weighed 76 kg and was 69 inches (1.7526 meters) tall (BMI = 24.7 kg·m^{-2}). If he ran the 1-mile run/walk in 8 minutes and 10 seconds (i.e., 8.17 minutes), then his estimated $\dot{V}O_2$ max would be this:

TABLE 11.9	Estimates of $\dot{V}O_2$ max (ml·kg⁻¹·min⁻¹) from 1-Mile Run/Walk Performance for Selected Age and BMI Levels							

Mile Run/Walk Time (min)	Male BMI Level				Female BMI Level			
	15	20	25	30	15	20	25	30
Age 10 Years								
6	60	56	52	48	58	54	50	46
8	53	49	44	40	51	47	42	38
10	46	42	38	34	44	40	36	32
12	46	42	38	34	44	40	36	32
Age 15 Years								
6	61	57	53	49	58	54	50	46
8	54	50	46	41	51	47	42	39
10	49	45	41	37	46	42	38	34
12	48	43	39	35	44	40	36	32
Age 20 Years								
6	62	58	54	50	58	54	50	46
8	55	51	47	42	51	47	42	38
10	50	46	42	38	46	42	38	34
12	49	44	40	36	44	40	36	32

$$\dot{V}O_2 \text{ max (ml·kg}^{-1}\text{·min}^{-1}) = 108.94$$
$$- 8.41(8.17) + 0.34(8.17^2)$$
$$+ 0.21(17 \times 1) - 0.84(24.7) = 45.7$$

One limitation of the generalized 1-mile run/walk equation is that it becomes inaccurate for very slow mile run/walk times. The equation should not be used if the mile run/walk time is more than 12 minutes. Table 11.9 provides $\dot{V}O_2$ max estimates for selected values of mile run/walk time, BMI, and age for both males and females.

20-Meter Shuttle Run (PACER)

Leger and Gadoury (1989) validated a 20-meter shuttle run test to estimate aerobic fitness in adults. This test has come to be known as the PACER in the U.S. The goal of this test is to complete as many laps as possible back and forth across a 20-meter distance at a specified pace. All participants run at the same pace throughout the test and run from one side of the course to the other side (20 meters away) while maintaining the specified pace. The pace, set by a prerecorded audio file, starts out at 8.5 km·hour⁻¹ and increases by 1 km·hour⁻¹ each minute so that eventually less fit participants cannot maintain the pace and stop the test. The design of this test is characteristic of a progressive maximal exercise test on a treadmill, in which power output is increased systematically as test time increases. The equation to estimate $\dot{V}O_2$ max from the 20-meter shuttle run was developed on 77 males and females ages 20 to 47 years, and is presented next.

20-Meter Shuttle Run Test

$$\dot{V}O_2 \text{ max (ml} \cdot \text{kg}^{-1} \cdot \text{min}^{-1}) =$$
$$-32.678 + 6.592(\text{maximal speed})$$
$$(R = .90, \; SEE = 4.4 \text{ ml·kg}^{-1}\text{·min}^{-1}) \quad \textbf{(11.21)}$$

where maximal speed is the maximal speed in km·hour⁻¹ attained during the 20-meter shuttle run test.

Computation Example   If a person's maximal speed attained during the 20-meter shuttle run was 12 km·hour^{-1}, the estimated $\dot{V}O_2$ max would be the following:

$$\dot{V}O_2 \text{ max (ml·kg}^{-1}\text{·min}^{-1}) =$$
$$-32.678 + 6.592(12) = 50.7$$

Distance Run Test Procedures

Following are the general steps to follow when administering distance run tests:

1. Select the appropriate test.
2. Try to ensure that the participant is motivated to achieve her best score. Ideally, the participant should be reasonably exhausted at the end of the test.
3. Give the participant time to practice and learn her walking/running pace prior to taking the test. Traveling too fast will lead to exhaustion prior to completing the distance, and traveling too slowly will not fully tax maximal aerobic capacity.
4. Convert the distance run performance to $\dot{V}O_2$ max to evaluate aerobic fitness.

Safety Considerations   A distance run test should be considered a maximal exercise test, with all of the attendant risks of a maximal test. In addition, it has the added risk of being less supervised. Maximal distance run tests are suitable only for young people in good physical condition without significant cardiovascular disease risk factors.

Walking and Jogging Tests

Laboratory tests require use of a treadmill or cycle ergometer to regulate power output. Walking and jogging on level ground is another way to regulate power output. The walking and jogging tests described next allow a person to walk or jog at a self-determined pace. $\dot{V}O_2$ max is estimated from movement time and the heart rate response to the exercise.

Rockport 1-Mile Walk Test

The Rockport 1-mile walk test (Kline et al. 1987) provides a means of estimating $\dot{V}O_2$ max from the heart rate response to walking speed. Age, body weight, and gender are also used as predictor variables. The distance of the walk and the heart rate response to the walk must be accurately measured. The test involves walking as fast as possible for one mile, and then measuring the exercise heart rate immediately after the walk. In the original study, heart rate was monitored electronically.

Participants should be allowed to practice walking one mile at a brisk but constant pace. Participants should walk fast enough to get their heart rate above 120 beats·min^{-1}. If a person is too fit to increase his heart rate to this level while walking, then he is probably too fit to get an accurate estimate of aerobic fitness from this test. In addition, individuals who are taking medications that affect heart rate (e.g., hypertensive medications) should not use a prediction model that depends on the heart rate response to exercise.

Multiple regression equations were developed from data on 343 males and females aged 30 to 69 years to estimate $\dot{V}O_2$ max. The Rockport 1-mile walk test equation is presented below.

Rockport 1-Mile Walk Test

$$\dot{V}O_2 \text{ max (ml·kg}^{-1}\text{·min}^{-1}) = 132.853$$
$$- 0.3877(\text{age}) - 0.0769(\text{weight})$$
$$- 3.2649(\text{walk time}) - 0.1565(\text{heart rate})$$
$$+ 6.315(\text{gender})$$

$(R = .88, \; SEE = 5.0 \text{ ml·kg}^{-1}\text{·min}^{-1})$ **(11.22)**

where age is in years, weight is body weight in pounds, walk time is the time it takes to walk the 1-mile course in minutes, heart rate is measured immediately at the conclusion of the walk, and gender is coded as 1 for male and 0 for female.

Computation Example   Assume a 40-year-old man who weighs 166 pounds completed the test. After walking the 1-mile course in 13 minutes and 54 seconds (13.9 minutes), his heart rate was 145 beats·min^{-1}. His $\dot{V}O_2$ max estimated from the Rockport 1-mile walk test equation would be this:

$$\dot{V}O_2 \text{ max (ml·kg}^{-1}\cdot\text{min}^{-1}) = 132.853$$
$$- 0.3877(40) - 0.0769(166)$$
$$- 3.2649(13.9) - 0.1565(145)$$
$$+ 6.315(1) = 42.8$$

BYU Jog Test

A limitation of the Rockport 1-mile walk test is that highly fit individuals may not be able to walk fast enough to elevate their heart rate above 45% of $\dot{V}O_2$ max ($\approx$ 120 beats·min^{-1}). Researchers at Brigham Young University (BYU) developed a similar test that replaces walking with jogging (George et al. 1993). The test protocol requires the participant to jog at a steady pace for one mile. Exercise heart rate is measured immediately after the run.

Participants should be allowed to warm up with a 2- to 3-minute jog. They should jog the mile at a steady and suitable pace. Many subjects tend to run an "all out" race. However, this should be a submaximal test. Average heart rates during the jog in the original publication were about 170 beats·min^{-1}. To ensure that the jog represents a submaximal effort, run time limits of $\geq$ 8 minutes per mile for males and $\geq$ 9 minutes per mile for females are set. In addition, exercise heart rate should be $\leq$ 180 beats·min^{-1}.

A multiple regression equation to estimate $\dot{V}O_2$ max was developed on 54 males and females aged 18 to 29 years. The BYU jog test equation is presented below.

$$\dot{V}O_2 \text{ max (ml·kg}^{-1}\cdot\text{min}^{-1}) = 100.5$$
$$-0.1636(\text{weight}) - 1.438(\text{jog time})$$
$$-0.1928(\text{heart rate}) + 8.344(\text{gender})$$
$$(R = .87, \; SEE = 3.0 \text{ ml·kg}^{-1}\cdot\text{min}^{-1}) \qquad \textbf{(11.23)}$$

where weight is body weight in kg, jog time is the time required to jog 1 mile in minutes, heart rate is exercise heart rate measured immediately after the test, and gender is coded as 1 for male and 0 for female.

Computation Example Assume a woman who weighs 154 pounds (70 kg) jogged 1 mile in 10 minutes and 20 seconds (10.33 minutes), and had

an exercise heart rate of 174 beats·min^{-1}. Her estimated $\dot{V}O_2$ max from the BYU jog test equation would be as follows:

$$\dot{V}O_2 \text{ max (ml·kg}^{-1}\cdot\text{min}^{-1}) = 100.5$$
$$-0.1636(70) - 1.438(10.33)$$
$$-0.1928(174) + 8.344(0) = 40.6$$

The BYU jog test was developed from a homogeneous sample of young, fit college students. The test is probably not suitable for less fit people. The Rockport 1-mile walk test would probably be more suitable for less fit subjects.

NONEXERCISE ESTIMATES OF AEROBIC FITNESS

$\dot{V}O_2$ max can be accurately estimated without exercise testing. Jackson et al. (1990) developed multiple regression equations to estimate $\dot{V}O_2$ max from participant data that can be easily collected without exercise testing. The predictor variables used in these **nonexercise models** include age, sex, body composition, and self-reported physical activity. Two prediction models were developed and they differed by the measure of body composition used. One model used percent fat estimated from skinfolds and the other model used body mass index (BMI), which is calculated from height and weight. Use of self-reported physical activity is a unique aspect of these models. Because regular physical activity often results in increased aerobic capacity, self-reported physical activity was a significant predictor of $\dot{V}O_2$ max in the models. The scale used to measure self-reported physical activity for the previous 30 days is presented in Table 11.10. The only variable in the prediction model more highly correlated with $\dot{V}O_2$ max than self-reported physical activity was percent fat.

As can be seen in Table 11.10, participants are asked to self-report their physical activity for the previous month on a 0 to 7 scale.

Jackson et al. (1995, 1996) updated the original nonexercise models by including an interaction term in the equation. The percent fat nonexercise

TABLE 11.10	**Self-Reported Physical Activity for the Previous 30 Days**

Use the Appropriate Number (0 to 7) That Best Describes Your General Activity Level for the Previous Month

Do not participate regularly in programmed recreation, sport, or heavy physical activity.

0 - Avoid walking or exertion, e.g., always use elevator, ride whenever possible instead of walking.

1 - Walk for pleasure, routinely use stairs, occasionally exercise sufficiently to cause heavy breathing or perspiration.

Participate regularly in recreation or work requiring modest physical activity, such as gymnastics, horseback riding, calisthenics, table tennis, softball, baseball, weight lifting, yard work.

2 - Spend 10 to 60 minutes per week in these types of physical activity.

3 - Spend over 1 hour per week in these types of physical activity.

Participate regularly in heavy physical exercise, e.g., running or jogging, swimming, cycling, rowing, jumping rope, or engaging in vigorous aerobic activity type exercise such as tennis, basketball, soccer, or other similar sports activities.

4 - Run less than 1 mile per week or spend less than 30 minutes per week in comparable physical activity.

5 - Run 1 to 5 miles per week or spend 30 to 60 minutes per week in comparable physical activity.

6 - Run 5 to 10 miles per week or spend 1 to 3 hours per week in comparable physical activity.

7 - Run over 10 miles per week or spend over 3 hours per week in comparable physical activity.

Note: This scale was developed for use in the Cardio-Pulmonary Laboratory, NASA/Johnson Space Center, Houston, TX.

model and the BMI nonexercise model are presented below.

University of Houston Nonexercise Percent Fat Equation for Men

$$\dot{V}O_2 \text{ max (ml·kg}^{-1}\text{·min}^{-1}) = 47.820$$
$$-0.259(\text{age}) - 0.216(\%\text{fat}) + 3.275(\text{SRPA})$$
$$-0.082(\%\text{fat} \times \text{SRPA})$$
$$(R = .79, SEE = 4.9 \text{ ml·kg}^{-1}\text{·min}^{-1}) \qquad \textbf{(11.24)}$$

University of Houston Nonexercise Percent Fat Equation for Women

$$\dot{V}O_2 \text{ max (ml·kg}^{-1}\text{·min}^{-1}) = 45.628$$
$$-0.265(\text{age}) - 0.309(\%\text{fat}) + 2.175(\text{SRPA})$$
$$-0.044(\%\text{fat} \times \text{SRPA})$$
$$(R = .85, SEE = 4.4 \text{ ml·kg}^{-1}\text{·min}^{-1}) \qquad \textbf{(11.25)}$$

where age is in years, %fat is percent fat assessed from skinfolds, SRPA is self-reported physical ac-

tivity from the 0–7 scale in Table 11.10, and %fat × SRPA is an interaction term that improves prediction accuracy.

Computation Example Assume a 28-year-old man with a percent fat of 27.4% had a self-reported physical activity rating of 3 from Table 11.10. His estimated $\dot{V}O_2$ max from the University of Houston nonexercise percent fat model would be this:

$$\dot{V}O_2 \text{ max (ml·kg}^{-1}\text{·min}^{-1}) = 47.820$$
$$- 0.259(28) - 0.216(27.4)$$
$$+ 3.275(3) - 0.082(27.4 \times 3) = 37.7$$

These equations require measurement of skinfolds to estimate percent fat. In some situations, such as in epidemiological research in which large samples of subjects are followed, the BMI models presented next are more feasible, because only height and weight need be assessed to calculate BMI.

University of Houston Nonexercise BMI Equation for Men

$$\dot{V}O_2 \text{ max } (ml \cdot kg^{-1} \cdot min^{-1}) = 55.688$$
$$- 0.362(age) - 0.331(BMI) + 4.310(SRPA)$$
$$- 0.096(BMI \times SRPA)$$

$(R = .74, SEE = 5.4 \text{ ml} \cdot kg^{-1} \cdot min^{-1})$ **(11.26)**

University of Houston Nonexercise BMI Equation for Women

$$\dot{V}O_2 \text{ max } (ml \cdot kg^{-1} \cdot min^{-1}) = 44.310$$
$$- 0.326(age) - 0.227(BMI) + 4.471(SRPA)$$
$$- 0.135(BMI \times SRPA)$$

$(R = .82, SEE = 4.7 \text{ ml} \cdot kg^{-1} \cdot min^{-1})$ **(11.27)**

where age is in years, BMI is body mass index calculated as weight (kg) ÷ height (m²), SRPA is self-reported physical activity from the 0–7 scale in Table 11.10, and BMI × SRPA is an interaction term that improves prediction accuracy.

Computation Example Assume a 32-year-old woman with a BMI of 21.3 had a self-reported physical activity rating of 7 from Table 11.10. Her estimated $\dot{V}O_2$ max from the University of Houston nonexercise BMI model would be as follows:

$$\dot{V}O_2 \text{ max } (ml \cdot kg^{-1} \cdot min^{-1}) = 44.310$$
$$- 0.326(32) - 0.227(21.3)$$
$$+ 4.471(7) - 0.135(21.3 \times 7) = 40.2$$

Tables 11.11 and 11.12 present estimates of $\dot{V}O_2$ max for selected ages and BMI levels for the nonexercise BMI prediction model for men and women, respectively. These tables greatly ease the application of the nonexercise models.

The nonexercise equations are especially feasible for mass testing. Because heart rate is not a factor in the nonexercise model, the nonexercise estimates of $\dot{V}O_2$ max can be validly used with individuals who take medications that affect heart rate. The nonexercise models provide surprisingly accurate estimates of aerobic fitness, given that no exercise testing is needed. However, it should be noted that the nonexercise models are less accurate for highly fit individuals. For men with a $\dot{V}O_2$ max ≥ 55 ml·kg^{-1}·min^{-1} and women with a $\dot{V}O_2$ max ≥ 45 ml·kg^{-1}·min^{-1} the standard errors of estimate of the nonexercise models increase. This level of aerobic fitness represents only about 5% of men and women. For these participants a maximal exercise model should be used to estimate aerobic fitness.

SUMMARY

Aerobic fitness is a major component of adult fitness tests and is important for health promotion. Many universities, YMCAs, private corporations, and commercial organizations provide adult health-related fitness programs. Potential participants should be screened for cardiovascular disease risk factors and symptoms of heart disease. American College of Sports Medicine recommendations should be followed regarding a medical examination prior to participation and physician supervision during exercise testing.

Many different methods are available to evaluate aerobic fitness. In research settings, $\dot{V}O_2$ max may be measured using open-circuit spirometry. $\dot{V}O_2$ max can be estimated from maximal tests, submaximal tests, and nonexercise models. In addition, both maximal and submaximal laboratory and field tests of aerobic capacity are available. Laboratory-based maximal exercise tests include estimation of $\dot{V}O_2$ max from maximal treadmill time on specified exercise protocols, like the Bruce and Balke protocols. Laboratory-based submaximal exercise tests include single-stage and multi-stage models in which the heart rate response to a specific submaximal exercise intensity is used to estimate $\dot{V}O_2$ max. Several choices of laboratory-based submaximal tests are available, with single-stage treadmill tests providing perhaps the most accurate alternative for tests of this type. ACSM metabolic equations are important for estimation of submaximal power output for many of the laboratory-based prediction models.

Field tests of aerobic fitness provide an alternative to laboratory-based tests that are more feasible for mass testing. Maximal distance run tests (e.g., 12-minute run/walk, 1.5-mile run, 1-mile run/walk, and 20-m shuttle run tests) generally provide accurate estimates of aerobic fitness; however, they are maximal tests, and care must be taken to minimize risk of an untoward event during these tests.

TABLE 11.11	Estimated $\dot{V}O_2$ max $(ml \cdot kg^{-1} \cdot min^{-1})$ from the Nonexercise BMI Model for Men for Selected Ages and Levels of Body Composition

Activity Level	Body Mass Index								
	16	18	20	22	24	26	28	30	32
Age 20 years									
7	61.1	59.6	58.1	56.6	55.1	53.6	52.1	50.6	49.0
6	59.2	57.7	56.2	54.7	53.2	51.7	50.1	48.6	47.1
5	57.3	55.8	54.3	52.7	51.2	49.7	48.2	46.7	45.2
4	55.4	53.8	52.3	50.8	49.3	47.8	46.3	44.8	43.3
3	53.4	51.9	50.4	48.9	47.4	45.9	44.4	42.9	41.4
2	51.5	50.0	48.5	47.0	45.5	44.0	42.5	41.0	39.4
1	49.6	48.1	46.6	45.1	43.6	42.0	40.5	39.0	37.5
0	47.7	46.2	44.7	43.1	41.6	40.1	38.6	37.1	35.6
Age 25 years									
7	59.2	57.7	56.2	54.7	53.2	51.7	50.2	48.7	47.1
6	57.3	55.8	54.3	52.8	51.3	49.7	48.2	46.7	45.2
5	55.4	53.9	52.4	50.8	49.3	47.8	46.3	44.8	43.3
4	53.4	51.9	50.4	48.9	47.4	45.9	44.4	42.9	41.4
3	51.5	50.0	48.5	47.0	45.5	44.0	42.5	41.0	39.5
2	49.6	48.1	46.6	45.1	43.6	42.1	40.6	39.0	37.5
1	47.7	46.2	44.7	43.2	41.7	40.1	38.6	37.1	35.6
0	45.8	44.3	42.7	41.2	39.7	38.2	36.7	35.2	33.7
Age 30 years									
7	57.3	55.8	54.3	52.8	51.3	49.8	48.3	46.7	45.2
6	55.4	53.9	52.4	50.9	49.4	47.8	46.3	44.8	43.3
5	53.5	52.0	50.4	48.9	47.4	45.9	44.4	42.9	41.4
4	51.5	50.0	48.5	47.0	45.5	44.0	42.5	41.0	39.5
3	49.6	48.1	46.6	45.1	43.6	42.1	40.6	39.1	37.6
2	47.7	46.2	44.7	43.2	41.7	40.2	38.7	37.1	35.6
1	45.8	44.3	42.8	41.3	39.7	38.2	36.7	35.2	33.7
0	43.9	42.3	40.8	39.3	37.8	36.3	34.8	33.3	31.8
Age 35 years									
7	55.4	53.9	52.4	50.9	49.4	47.9	46.4	44.8	43.3
6	53.5	52.0	50.5	49.0	47.4	45.9	44.4	42.9	41.4
5	51.6	50.0	48.5	47.0	45.5	44.0	42.5	41.0	39.5
4	49.6	48.1	46.6	45.1	43.6	42.1	40.6	39.1	37.6
3	47.7	46.2	44.7	43.2	41.7	40.2	38.7	37.2	35.7
2	45.8	44.3	42.8	41.3	39.8	38.3	36.7	35.2	33.7
1	43.9	42.4	40.9	39.3	37.8	36.3	34.8	33.3	31.8
0	42.0	40.4	38.9	37.4	35.9	34.4	32.9	31.4	29.9

TABLE 11.12	Estimated $\dot{V}O_2$ max (ml·kg^{-1}·min^{-1}) from the Nonexercise BMI Model for Men for Selected Ages and Levels of BMI

Activity Level	Body Mass Index							
	16	18	20	22	24	26	28	30
Age 20 years								
7	50.1	48.6	47.1	45.6	44.1	42.6	41.1	39.6
6	48.2	46.7	45.2	43.7	42.2	40.7	39.2	37.7
5	46.3	44.8	43.3	41.8	40.3	38.8	37.3	35.8
4	44.4	42.9	41.4	39.9	38.4	36.9	35.4	33.9
3	42.4	41.0	39.4	37.9	36.4	34.9	33.4	31.9
2	40.5	39.0	37.5	36.0	34.5	33.0	31.5	30.0
1	38.6	37.1	35.6	34.1	32.6	31.1	29.6	28.1
0	36.7	35.2	33.7	32.2	30.7	29.2	27.7	26.2
Age 25 years								
7	48.2	46.7	45.2	43.7	42.2	40.7	39.2	37.7
6	46.3	44.8	43.3	41.8	40.3	38.8	37.3	35.8
5	44.4	42.9	41.4	39.9	38.4	36.9	35.4	33.9
4	42.5	41.0	39.4	38.0	36.5	35.0	33.5	32.0
3	40.5	39.0	37.5	36.0	34.5	33.0	31.5	30.0
2	38.6	37.1	35.6	34.1	32.6	31.1	29.6	28.1
1	36.7	35.2	33.7	32.2	30.7	29.2	27.7	26.2
0	34.8	33.3	31.8	30.3	28.8	27.3	25.8	24.3
Age 30 years								
7	46.3	44.8	43.3	41.8	40.3	38.8	37.3	35.7
6	44.4	42.9	41.4	39.9	38.4	36.9	35.4	33.8
5	42.5	41.0	39.5	38.0	36.5	35.0	33.5	31.9
4	40.6	39.1	37.6	36.1	34.6	33.1	31.6	30.0
3	38.6	37.1	35.6	34.1	32.6	31.1	29.6	28.0
2	36.7	35.2	33.7	32.2	30.7	29.2	27.7	26.1
1	34.8	33.3	31.8	30.3	28.8	27.3	25.8	24.2
0	32.9	31.4	29.9	28.4	26.9	25.4	23.9	22.3
Age 35 years								
7	44.4	42.9	41.4	39.9	38.4	36.9	35.4	33.8
6	42.5	41.0	39.5	38.0	36.5	35.0	33.5	31.9
5	40.6	39.1	37.6	36.1	34.6	33.1	31.6	30.0
4	38.7	37.2	35.7	34.2	32.7	31.2	29.7	28.1
3	36.7	35.2	33.7	32.2	30.7	29.2	27.7	26.1
2	34.8	33.3	31.8	30.3	28.8	27.3	25.8	24.2
1	32.9	31.4	29.9	28.4	26.9	25.4	23.9	22.3
0	31.0	29.5	28.0	26.5	25.0	23.5	22.0	20.4

For this reason, maximal distance run tests are generally administered only to young, healthy people.

Another category of tests includes the walking and jogging field tests. The Rockport 1-mile walk test and the BYU jogging test allow participants to move at self-selected speeds and use the heart rate response to exercise to estimate $\dot{V}O_2$ max. An attractive alternative for epidemiological studies, or other situations in which exercise testing is difficult, is the University of Houston nonexercise model, in which $\dot{V}O_2$ max can be estimated by parameters collected without exercise testing. The various methods to estimate aerobic fitness are presented in Table 11.13.

TABLE 11.13	Comparison of Methods Used to Estimate Aerobic Fitness		
Method	**Strengths**	**Limitations**	**Comments and Cautions**
Maximal Tests			
Open-Circuit Spirometry	Most accurate	Maximal effort required; expensive equipment and trained personnel needed	High-risk subjects need to be monitored by physician
Maximal Treadmill Time	Highly accurate	Maximal effort required; expensive equipment and trained personnel needed	High-risk subjects need to be monitored by physician
Distance Run Tests	Feasible for mass testing	Maximal effort required; motivation affects results	Appropriate for young, healthy subjects
Submaximal Tests			
Single-Stage	Submaximal effort required	Expensive equipment needed; variability in heart rate limits accuracy; use of estimated maximal heart rate limits accuracy	Not suitable for subjects on medications that alter heart rate
Multi-Stage	Submaximal effort required	Expensive equipment needed; variability in heart rate limits accuracy; use of estimated maximal heart rate limits accuracy; difficult to measure multiple stages	Not suitable for subjects on medications that alter heart rate; least accurate
Walk or Jog Field Tests			
Rockport 1-mile Walk Test	Less dependent on participant effort than maximal tests	May be too easy for highly fit subjects	Not suitable for subjects on medications that alter heart rate
BYU Jog Test	Submaximal effort required	May be too difficult for less fit subjects	Not suitable for subjects on medications that alter heart rate; developed on young, fit subjects
Nonexercise Models			
Percent Fat Model	Variables easily measured	Subjective rating of activity	Not appropriate for highly fit subjects
BMI Model	Variables easily measured	Subjective rating of activity	Not appropriate for highly fit subjects

FORMATIVE EVALUATION OF OBJECTIVES

Objective 1   Define aerobic fitness.

1. How are $\dot{V}O_2$ and METs related?
2. Differentiate between absolute and relative $\dot{V}O_2$.
3. What criteria are used to determine whether a maximal effort was given during a maximal exercise test?

Objective 2   Explain the relationship between aerobic fitness and health.

1. Define the levels of aerobic fitness needed for health promotion.
2. What level of regular exercise is needed in order for people to reach the level of fitness necessary for health benefits?

Objective 3   Explain the idea of risk stratification prior to exercise testing.

1. What are the signs and symptoms of cardiovascular and pulmonary disease identified by the American College of Sports Medicine?
2. What are the coronary artery disease risk factors identified by the American College of Sports Medicine?
3. Differentiate between low-risk, moderate-risk, and high-risk clients.
4. Differentiate between moderate intensity and vigorous intensity exercise.
5. Identify individuals who should have an exercise test prior to participation in moderate or vigorous exercise programs.
6. Identify individuals who should have physician supervision during an exercise test.

Objective 4   Define the methods used to determine power output from cycle ergometer and treadmill tests.

1. What is the power output (in $kg \cdot m \cdot min^{-1}$ and watts) on a Monark cycle ergometer if a person pedals at 50 $rev \cdot min^{-1}$ with a resistance of 2 kg?
2. Using the ACSM cycling equation, what is the estimated $\dot{V}O_2$ if a person who weighs 65 kg cycles at 450 $kg \cdot m \cdot min^{-1}$?
3. Using the ACSM walking equation, what would be the estimated $\dot{V}O_2$ for a person who walked at 3 mph at a 10% elevation?
4. Using the ACSM running equation, what would be the estimated $\dot{V}O_2$ for a person who ran at 6.5 mph at a 4% elevation?

Objective 5   Identify laboratory-based methods used to assess $\dot{V}O_2$ max during maximal exercise testing.

1. What is the most accurate method to determine $\dot{V}O_2$ max?
2. What are the limitations to the direct measurement of $\dot{V}O_2$ max through open-circuit spirometry?
3. How can $\dot{V}O_2$ max be estimated from maximal exercise?
4. What is the standard error of estimate for estimating $\dot{V}O_2$ max from maximal treadmill time, and how does this compare to the error in other estimation methods?
5. If a person exercises to exhaustion in 10 minutes, what would the estimated $\dot{V}O_2$ max be if the Bruce protocol were used? If the Balke protocol were used?
6. Is the Bruce protocol or Balke protocol more intense?

Objective 6   Identify laboratory-based methods used to assess $\dot{V}O_2$ max during submaximal exercise testing.

1. What parameters are used to estimate $\dot{V}O_2$ max from submaximal tests?
2. What are the physiological principles upon which submaximal exercise tests are based?
3. Differentiate between single-stage and multi-stage models to estimate $\dot{V}O_2$ max.
4. What would be the estimated $\dot{V}O_2$ max from the single-stage model for a 28-year-old woman with a submaximal heart rate of 132 $beats \cdot min^{-1}$ at power output of 600 $kg \cdot m \cdot min^{-1}$ on a cycle ergometer?

5. What would be the estimated $\dot{V}O_2$ max for a female with a maximal heart rate of 187, and submaximal values of 6 METs and a heart rate of 145 beats·min^{-1}?

6. What would be the estimated $\dot{V}O_2$ max for a 37-year-old man who had a heart rate of 140 beats·min^{-1} at a power output of 900 kg·m·min^{-1} on a cycle ergometer?

7. What would be the estimated $\dot{V}O_2$ max for a 28-year-old woman who had a heart rate of 146 beats·min^{-1} while walking at 3.4 mph at a 9% grade on a treadmill?

8. Why might one choose the single-stage submaximal model over the multi-stage submaximal model to estimate aerobic fitness?

9. Estimate $\dot{V}O_2$ max from the single-stage 4-minute walking test and from the single-stage treadmill walking test from the following data: age = 25 years, gender = female, submaximal heart rate = 136 beats·min^{-1}, treadmill walking speed = 3.4 mph, percent fat = 22%, and BMI = 25.5 kg·m^{-2}.

10. What procedures would you need to follow to estimate $\dot{V}O_2$ max with the multi-stage model?

Objective 7   Identify the various field tests of aerobic fitness used with adults.

1. How do the 12-minute run/walk and 1.5-mile run tests differ?

2. What would be the estimated $\dot{V}O_2$ max for a 15-year-old boy with a BMI of 19 kg·m^{-2} who ran 1 mile in 7 minutes and 20 seconds?

3. What variables are needed to estimate aerobic capacity from the Rockport 1-mile walk test and the BYU jog test? How are these tests similar to laboratory-based submaximal tests?

4. How does the 20-m shuttle run differ from traditional distance run tests of aerobic capacity?

5. Explain the idea that distance runs are maximal exercise tests and state which individuals distance run tests are appropriate for, and the precautions that should be taken for such tests.

6. What advantages do nonexercise models to estimate aerobic fitness have over other estimation methods?

7. What variables are needed to estimate aerobic fitness from nonexercise models? Explain why we can expect these predictor variables to be related to $\dot{V}O_2$ max.

ADDITIONAL LEARNING ACTIVITIES

You can best obtain a true understanding of $\dot{V}O_2$ max by measuring it.

1. With a partner or in a small group, estimate your $\dot{V}O_2$ max with the following models: (a) single-stage model, (b) multi-stage model, (c) Rockport 1-mile walk test, and (d) BYU jog test. If your college or university has a metabolic system to measure $\dot{V}O_2$ max directly, have your $\dot{V}O_2$ max measured, and compare the results with the estimates from the models listed in this question.

2. Complete either the maximal Bruce treadmill protocol or the maximal Balke treadmill protocol, and estimate your $\dot{V}O_2$ max from maximal treadmill time. Compare this estimate to $\dot{V}O_2$ max estimated from a single-stage treadmill test. Highly fit subjects should choose the Bruce rather than the Balke protocol.

3. It may be difficult to complete some $\dot{V}O_2$ max tests, but this is not true for the nonexercise models. Evaluate your aerobic fitness with the nonexercise models and compare the results.

4. Maximal distance run tests can be used to evaluate aerobic fitness. Have a group of students complete the 1.5-mile run/walk test. Then have the same students estimate their aerobic fitness with the nonexercise BMI model. Calculate the correlation between these estimates of $\dot{V}O_2$ max.

5. Develop a computer program to complete the calculations presented in this chapter. You can do this on spreadsheet or database programs (e.g., Excel).

BIBLIOGRAPHY

American College of Sports Medicine. 2006. *ACSM's guidelines for exercise testing and prescription.* 7th ed. Philadelphia: Lippincott Williams & Wilkins.

Åstrand, I. 1960. Aerobic work capacity in men and women with special reference to age. *Acta Physiologica Scandinavica* 49(Suppl. 169): 45–60.

Åstrand, P.-O. and I. Ryhming. 1954. A nomogram for assessment of aerobic capacity (physical fitness) from pulse rate during submaximal work. *Journal of Applied Physiology* 7: 218–221.

Åstrand, P.-O. and K. Rodahl. 1986. *Textbook of work physiology.* 3rd ed. New York: McGraw-Hill.

Balke, B. 1963. A simple field test for assessment of physical fitness. *Civil Aeromedical Research Institute Report,* 63–66.

Balke, B. and R. W. Ware. 1959. An experimental study of "physical fitness" of Air Force personnel. *US Armed Forces Medical Journal* 10: 675–688.

Blair, S. N. et al. 1989. Physical fitness and all-cause mortality: A prospective study of healthy men and women. *Journal of the American Medical Association* 262: 2395–2401.

Blair, S. N. et al. 1995. Changes in physical fitness and all-cause mortality: A prospective study of healthy and unhealthy men. *Journal of the American Medical Association* 273: 1093–1098.

Borg, G. 1977. Physical work and effort. *Proceedings of the First International Symposium.* Wenner-Gren Center, Stockholm, Sweden. Oxford, England: Pergamon Press.

Bruce, R. A., A. Kusumi, and D. Hosmer. 1973. Maximal oxygen intake and nomographic assessment of functional aerobic impairment in cardiovascular disease. *American Heart Journal* 85: 546–562.

Buskirk, E. R. and J. L. Hodgson. 1987. Age and aerobic power: The rate of change in men and women. *Federation Proceedings* 46: 1824–1829.

Consolazio, L. J., R. F. Johnson, and L. J. Pecora. 1963. *Physiologic measurements of metabolic functions in man.* New York: McGraw-Hill.

Cooper, K. H. 1968. A means of assessing maximal oxygen intake. *Journal of the American Medical Association* 203: 201–204.

Cooper, K. H. 1970. *The new aerobics.* New York: Bantam Books.

Cureton, K. J. et al. 1995. A generalized equation for prediction of $\dot{V}O_2$ peak from 1-mile run/walk performance. *Medicine and Science in Sports and Exercise* 27: 445–451.

Dill, D. B. 1965. Oxygen cost of horizontal and grade walking and running on the treadmill. *Journal of Applied Physiology* 20: 19–22.

DiNallo, J. M., A. S. Jackson, and M. T. Mahar. 2000. A submaximal treadmill test for prediction of aerobic capacity. *Medicine and Science in Sports and Exercise* 32(Suppl.): S318.

Ebbeling, C. B. et al. 1991. Development of a single-stage submaximal treadmill walking test. *Medicine and Science in Sports and Exercise* 23: 966–973.

Foster, C. et al. 1984. Generalized equations for predicting functional capacity from treadmill performance. *American Heart Journal* 107: 1229–1234.

George, J. D. et al. 1993. $\dot{V}O_2$ max estimation from a submaximal 1-mile track jog for fit college-age individuals. *Medicine and Science in Sports and Exercise* 25: 401–406.

Golding, L. A., C. R. Myers, and W. E. Sinning. 1989. *The Y's way to physical fitness.* 3rd ed. Champaign, IL: Human Kinetics for the National Council of YMCA.

Jackson, A. S. et al. 1990. Prediction of functional aerobic capacity without exercise testing. *Medicine and Science in Sports and Exercise* 22: 863–870.

Jackson, A. S. et al. 1995. Changes in aerobic power of men ages 25–70 years. *Medicine and Science in Sports and Exercise* 27: 113–120.

Jackson, A. S. et al. 1996. Changes in aerobic power of women, ages 20–64 years. *Medicine and Science in Sports and Exercise* 28: 884–891.

Jones, N. L. and E. J. M. Campbell. 1982. *Clinical exercise testing.* Philadelphia: W. B. Saunders.

Kline, G. M. et al. 1987. Estimation of $\dot{V}O_2$ max from a one-mile track walk, gender, age, and body weight. *Medicine and Science in Sports and Exercise* 19: 253–259.

Leger, L. and C. Gadoury. 1989. Validity of the 20 m shuttle run test with 1 min stages to predict $\dot{V}O_2$ max in adults. *Canadian Journal of Sport Science* 14: 21–26.

Mahar, M. T. 1987. Accuracy of estimating $\dot{V}O_2$ max from submaximal treadmill exercise. Unpublished master's thesis, University of Houston, TX.

Mahar, M. T. et al. 1985. Predictive accuracy of single stage and double stage submax treadmill work for estimating aerobic capacity. *Medicine and Science in Sports and Exercise* 17(Suppl.): 206–207.

Margaria, R., P. Cerretelli, and P. Aghemo. 1963. Energy cost of running. *Journal of Applied Physiology* 18: 367–370.

Mitchell, J. H. and G. Blomqvist. 1971. Maximal oxygen uptake. *The New England Journal of Medicine* 284: 1018–1022.

Mitchell, J. H., B. J. Sproule, and C. B. Chapman. 1958. The physiological meaning of the maximal oxygen intake test. *Journal of Clinical Investigation* 37: 538–547.

Nagle, F. J. et al. 1971. Compatibility of progressive treadmill, cycle, and step tests based on oxygen uptake responses. *Medicine and Science in Sports and Exercise* 3: 149–154.

Nagle, F. J., B. Balke, and J. P. Naughton. 1965. Gradational step tests for assessing work capacity. *Journal of Applied Physiology* 20: 745–748.

Pollock, M. L., A. S. Jackson, and C. Foster. 1986. The use of the perception scale for exercise prescription. In G. Borg and D. Ottoson (Eds.). The perception of exertion in physical work. *Proceedings of an International Symposium.* Stockholm, Sweden: Wiener-Glenn.

Pollock, M. L. et al. 1976. A comparative analysis of four protocols for maximal treadmill stress testing. *American Heart Journal* 92: 39–42.

Ross, R. M. and A. S. Jackson. 1990. *Exercise concepts, calculations, and computer applications.* Carmel, IN: Benchmark Press.

Rowell, L. B., H. L. Taylor, and Y. Wang. 1964. Limitations to prediction of maximal oxygen intake. *Journal of Applied Physiology* 19: 919–927.

U.S. Public Health Service. 1990. *Healthy People 2000: National health promotion and disease prevention objectives.* Washington, DC: U.S. Department of Health and Human Services.

U.S. Public Health Service. 1996. *Physical activity and health: A report of the Surgeon General.* Washington, DC: U.S. Department of Health and Human Services.

EVALUATING BODY COMPOSITION

C O N T E N T S

K E Y   W O R D S

android obesity
anorexia nervosa
bioelectrical impedance analysis (BIA)
body composition
body density
body mass index (BMI)
circumferences
fat-free weight
fat weight
generalized equations
gynoid obesity
healthy weight
hydrostatic weighing
multicomponent model
obesity
overweight
percent body fat
plethysmograph
residual lung volume
two-component model

OBJECTIVES

With the growing body of literature supporting the value of regular physical activity for health and fitness, the evaluation of body composition has become an important aspect of both youth and adult fitness. Additionally, suitable body composition levels are important for athletic performance. The purposes of this chapter are to (1) provide an understanding of public health problems associated with body composition, (2) outline the methods used to evaluate body composition, and (3) evaluate the validity of common field methods.

After reading Chapter 12, you should be able to

1. Identify the public health problems associated with body composition.
2. Identify the methods used to measure body composition of youth and adults.
3. Identify the limitations of the two-component percent body fat model when applied to children, older adults, and members of various racial groups.
4. Calculate percent body fat of youth and adults from skinfold equations.
5. Evaluate body composition of youth and adults.
6. Calculate weight goals for selected levels of desired percent body fat.
7. Evaluate the accuracy of the various methods used to measure body composition.

INTRODUCTION

Health-related fitness and athletic training programs are designed to control body weight and body composition. This is accomplished through regular exercise and proper nutrition. Suitable levels of **body composition** are also important for athletic competition. Excess body fat lowers aerobic fitness and reduces the ability to perform many activities that require jumping and moving quickly. However, being too thin is not desirable either. Suitable body composition is important for general health and appearance and for maximizing athletic performance. For these reasons, accurate measurements of body composition are needed to develop sound preventive health programs and athletic programs.

A growing body of medical research documents that undesirable levels of body composition are associated with public health problems. Unfortunately, data also show that the proportion of Americans who are overweight and obese is growing. The World Health Organization (WHO) and Centers for Disease Control and Prevention (CDC) define **overweight** as a body mass index (BMI) of 25–29.9 $kg \cdot m^{-2}$, and **obesity** as a BMI 30 $kg \cdot m^{-2}$ and higher (WHO 1998). BMI is a measure of weight adjusted for height. Table 12.1 gives the percentage of Americans who were listed as overweight, as defined by WHO/CDC criteria since 1960. These data show that the percentage of American men and women who were overweight or obese has steadily grown. In the last National Health and Nutrition Examination Survey (NHANES 1999–2002), over 68% of men and nearly 62% of women were overweight (Hedley et al. 2004).

PUBLIC HEALTH RISKS

The relationship between weight and mortality is J-shaped (Lew & Garfinkel 1979). This means that being significantly under or over healthy weight can have serious health consequences. Figure 12-1 illustrates this relationship. A certain degree of musculature and body fat not only provides protection from injury and thermal stress, but also enhances good health. Although much of the high mortality associated with being too thin is due to underlying diseases such as cancer, even when this is taken into consideration, being too thin is still not healthy. Excessive weight loss caused by severe diet restriction can be a health hazard and should be avoided. Eating disorders associated with being too thin are a serious health problem.

Cardiovascular Diseases

Being overweight is associated with many medical problems, such as hypertension, diabetes, and heart disease. These illnesses lead to increased morbidity and reduced longevity. Between the ages of 25 and 50 years, an average American

TABLE 12.1	Age-Adjusted Percentages of U.S. Men and Women Who Are Overweight (Body Mass Index (BMI) > 25) or Obese (BMI > 30), 1960–2004			
Survey	**Years**	**Men**	**Women**	**Total**
NHES	1960–1962	48.2%	38.7%	43.3%
NHANES I	1971–1974	52.9%	39.7%	46.1%
NHANES II	1976–1980	51.4%	40.8%	46.0%
NHANES III	1988–1994	59.3%	49.6%	54.4%
NHANES	1999–2000	67.2%	61.9%	64.5%
NHANES	2001–2002	70.0%	61.4%	65.7%
NHANES	2003–2004	70.8%	61.8%	66.3%

Note: NHES National Health Examination Survey: NHANES: National Health and Nutrition Examination Survey; Data from NHES (1973); Hedley et al. (2004); Ogden et al. (2006).

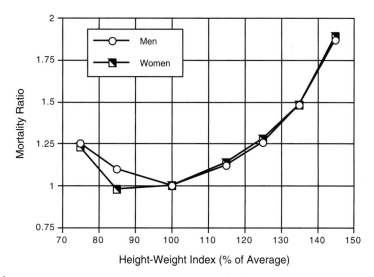

Figure 12-1

All-cause mortality ratio for various percentages of average weight. For both men and women, when compared to average weight, the underweight and overweight individuals had the higher mortality ratios. Graph made from published data (Lew & Garfinkel 1979).

(Source: Graph from Jackson & Ross 1997. Used with permission.)

gains about 50 pounds of body weight—about 2 pounds per year. Almost all of this weight gain is body fat. The success rate for the treatment of adulthood obesity is only 25%, lower than the cure rate for most cancers. Overweight people are more likely to lead a sedentary life, and if they decide to start an exercise program, are less likely to be successful (Dishman 1988). Early intervention with proper diet, exercise, and education are key factors for maintaining a healthy weight.

Many overweight people become diabetic during adulthood. Adult-onset diabetes is a disease primarily of the obese, and a major cardiovascular disease risk factor. Not all obese people are diabetic, but a subgroup of the obese are particularly at risk. Adults who have "apple-shaped" bodies are particularly prone to develop diabetes mellitus. The "apple shape" is due to the accumulation of body fat around the abdomen. This pattern of fat accumulation has more serious health consequences than general adiposity. Just as being overweight can cause diabetes, losing weight can reverse the condition. Often, when people with diabetes lose weight, they are no longer diabetic. This adult form of diabetes is a true "lifestyle" disease.

Overweight people are more likely to be diabetic, hypertensive, and have higher cholesterol levels. Since these are major, independent risk factors in cardiovascular disease, some believe that the increased incidence of cardiovascular disease associated with being overweight is due just to these risk factors. This is not true. Hubert and colleagues (1983) found that being overweight puts you at a higher risk of heart disease and stroke. Figure 12-2 graphically shows that being overweight increases the risk of cardiovascular disease. These researchers also discovered that changes in weight affected risk. Overweight people who lost weight reduced their risk of cardiovascular disease (Figure 12-3).

The results of a major epidemiological study showed that the negative health effects of being obese were lessened if an individual was aerobically fit. Studying nearly 22,000 men, researchers discovered that the risk of both all-cause and cardiovascular disease mortality of obese men who were aerobically fit did not differ from the risk for lean, aerobically fit men (Lee, Blair & Jackson, 1999). Being fit was defined as having a treadmill-determined $\dot{V}O_2$ max above the 20th percentile for one's age. This represents a $\dot{V}O_2$ max above 35 $ml \cdot kg^{-1} \cdot min^{-1}$ for men aged 45 years. The lean men had a measured percent body fat below 16.7%, while the percent body fat of obese men was 25% and higher. Interestingly, the all-cause and cardiovascular disease mortality rates of lean men who were not aerobically fit were over two times higher than those of the obese, aerobically fit men. In other words, the health risks were higher for lean, unfit men than for overweight men who were aerobically fit. These data led the authors to this conclusion: "The health benefits of leanness are limited to fit men, and being fit may reduce the hazards of obesity."

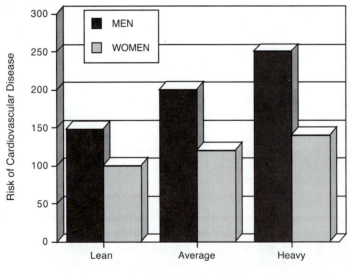

Figure 12-2

The 26-year incidence of cardiovascular disease (per 100,000) based upon weight for a given height for the men and women in the Framingham heart study. The subjects were nonsmokers who were under 50 years of age, and had normal cholesterol and blood pressure levels. Graph made from published data (Hubert et al. 1983).

(Source: Graph from Jackson & Ross 1997. Used with permission.)

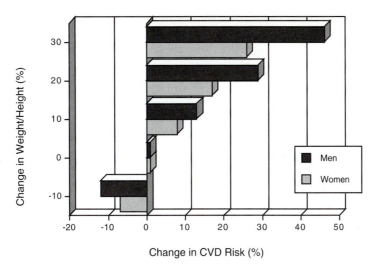

Figure 12-3

Losing weight decreases the risk of cardiovascular disease (CVD), while gaining weight increases the risk. This provides evidence that the relationship between obesity and cardiovascular disease may be causal. Graph developed from published data (Hubert et al. 1983).

(Source: Graph from Jackson & Ross 1997. Used with permission.)

Breast Cancer

Breast cancer is the most common cancer among women. And it is second only to lung cancer as a cause of death from cancer among women. The causes of breast cancer are very complex, but recent research showed that weight gain is associated with the risk of breast cancer.

Medical researchers (Huang 1997) studied over 95,000 U.S. female nurses aged 30 to 55 years who were followed for 16 years. They discovered that weight gain after the age of 18 years was unrelated to breast cancer incidence before menopause, but was associated with the incidence after menopause. Postmenopausal weight gain increased both the risk of breast cancer incidence and the mortality. About 16% of the breast cancers were attributed to excessive weight gain ($\geq$ 44 pounds). While the medical complexities of breast cancer go well beyond the intent of this text, this important public health study does highlight the importance of body composition and weight control on women's health. Breast cancer is one of the most dreaded diseases of women. Avoiding excessive weight gain during adult life appears to be an important factor in reducing the risk of this cancer.

Eating Disorders

While medical problems associated with body composition are most often related to being overweight, being seriously underweight also is associated with health problems, namely, eating disorders. Anorexia nervosa and bulimia nervosa are eating disorders that are on the rise and correspond to societal pressure for women to be thin. It is estimated that about 90% of individuals with eating disorders are women. **Anorexia nervosa** most often begins in early to late adolescence, with the greatest risk for onset between the ages of 14 and 18 years. The average age of onset for bulimia is 17 to 19 years. It is estimated that about 1% of young women are anorexic. The prevalence of bulimia nervosa is approximately 1% to 3%, but it has been estimated that 4% to 19% of young women engage in significant levels of bulimic behavior.

The causes of anorexia nervosa and bulimia nervosa are complex and not well understood. In American society, beauty is often associated with thinness. Advertisements in the mass media constantly reinforce this notion. The intelligent application of body composition assessment and education can help people establish desirable, intelligent weight goals. The healthy body weight for a well-muscled woman is often higher than what is the social norm. Percent body fat evaluation offers a sound method of establishing a person's desirable weight. Body composition methods and standards, and methods of determining one's healthy weight (Formula 12.17), are fully presented in this chapter. A serious problem is that many believe that their percent body fat should be as low as possible. This is not true; a body fat percentage that is too low carries serious health risks (see Figure 12-1). Chapter 7 discusses eating disorder scales.

SOURCES OF ADULTHOOD OBESITY

The prevalence of obesity is going up for both children and adults (Kuczmarski et al. 1994; Troiano et al. 1995). The scientific reason for weight gain is that the person consumes more calories than she expends. While the principle of caloric balance is well understood, it is not clear why some persons gain while others do not. The difference may be due to genetic, environmental, and psychological influences.

The medical problems associated with obesity usually occur in adulthood, but the success of adult weight-reduction programs is poor (Panel 1993; Skender et al. 1996). Medical researchers (Whitaker et al. 1997) studied medical records of parents and children in an effort to determine the factors that lead to obesity in young adulthood (ages 21 to 29 years).[1] The factors considered were the person's obesity status in childhood and their parents' obesity status. Figure 12-4 summarizes the results of this study.

For a child younger than 5 years, the primary predictor of obesity in young adulthood is the obesity of his parents. If both parents are obese, the child's chances of being obese in adulthood are 14 to 15 times higher than for a child with nonobese parents. From the ages of 6 to 9 years, both childhood and parental obesity are related to adulthood obesity. For ages 10 to 17 years, the obesity status of the child becomes a dramatic determinate of adult-

hood obesity. A 10- to 17-year-old obese child is about 20 times more likely to be obese as an adult.

The association between parental obesity and adulthood obesity is likely due to both genetic and environmental factors within families. The high risk of adulthood obesity associated with adolescent obesity is much more likely to be due to environmental factors. These data signal the need for sound adolescent weight-control programs. The methods for evaluating body composition presented in this chapter can be useful to identify youth at risk of becoming obese adults.

Laboratory Body Composition Methods

In simple terms, body weight consists of fat weight and fat-free weight. **Percent body fat** is simply the proportion of total weight that is fat weight. One laboratory method of measuring percent body fat is to measure **body density**, the ratio of body weight and body volume. The most common laboratory method used to measure body volume is underwater weighing. A newer method that is growing in popularity is to measure the body's volume by measuring the air the body displaces in a special body box. Once body density is known, equations are available to estimate percent body fat from body density. A new X-ray, computer-controlled, method called dual energy X-ray absorptiometry (DXA), is becoming a popular, accepted laboratory body composition measurement method. DXA is also used to measure bone density, an important medical concern of aging adults. The DXA units currently can be found largely in medical facilities.

Measuring Body Density by Underwater Weighing

The **hydrostatic** (or underwater) **weighing** method (see Figure 12-5) is the most common laboratory method used to measure body composition. Numerous laboratories located at universities and medical centers have the equipment for underwater weighing determinations. The measurement objective of the hydrostatic weighing is to measure body volume, which is then used with body weight

---

[1] Obesity was defined as a body mass index (Formula 12.10) at or above the 85th percentile for the person's age and sex.

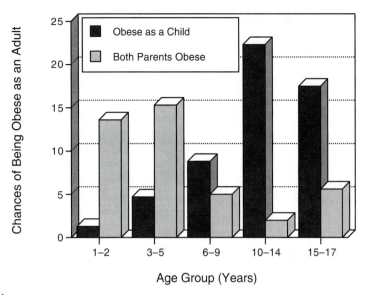

Figure 12-4

Odds ratios for obesity in young adulthood according to the subject's obesity status in childhood and parents' obesity status. Graph made from published data (Whitaker et al. 1997).

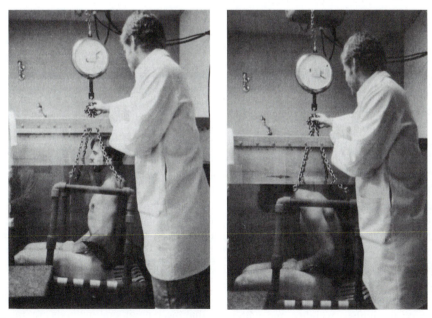

Figure 12-5

Method of determining body density by underwater weighing.

(Photos courtesy of Dr. M. L. Pollock, University of Florida.)

to calculate body density. Percent fat is calculated from body density.

Underwater Weighing

The underwater weighing method is based on the Archimedes principle for measuring the density of an object. When an object, in this case a person, is submerged under water, the difference between the weight in air and the weight under water equals the weight of water displaced. The weight of water displaced divided by the density of water is the volume of water displaced, or the volume of the object (i.e., the person). The objective of underwater weighing is to measure body volume. Body density is the ratio of weight in air and body volume. Dry land weight, underwater weight, residual lung volume, and water density are needed to calculate body density. We summarize the basic steps needed to measure hydrostatically determined body density next.

Determining Underwater Weight   Body density is typically measured in the laboratory in a specially constructed tank (see Figure 12-5), but it can be measured in a swimming pool if there is no turbulence. The subject sits on a specially devised chair that is attached to a scale, leans forward, and submerges the head while performing a maximal expiration. Since many subjects are too buoyant, it may be difficult to submerge them. In these instances, a scuba weight belt is placed on the subject's lap. Figure 12-5 shows that the subject is typically sitting on a chair. Both the weight of the chair and the scuba weight belt must be subtracted from the obtained weight to calculate true underwater weight.

Underwater weight is measured to the nearest 0.01 kg with a calibrated scale. The Chatillon 15-kilogram scale shown is commonly used; however, electronic scales that use load cells are also commercially available. A minimum of seven to ten trials should be administered. The average of the three trials with the highest weights, and within 0.025 kg, is used. It has been shown that underwater weight will systematically increase. The person must practice to reach true underwater weight, which is typically reached after three to five trials. The underwater weight is greatly dependent on the

amount of air in the lungs when submerged. The subject must be weighed while holding her breath after a complete expiration.

Determining Land Weight   Body weight can be easily and accurately determined by weighing. However, it is important to be weighed under standard conditions, because total body water, which is a major determinant of body weight, can vary considerably from day to day. The body is composed of approximately 60% water. That is, a 70-kg individual has over 40 kg of body water. Heavy exercise may result in a water loss as high as 2 to 3 kg per hour.

Determining Air in the Body   The volume of the body that is air can introduce the largest source of error in the underwater weighing method. This is primarily because the density of air and other gases in the body is so close to zero that even a small error in volume measurement makes a significant change in total body density. The major potential sources of measurement error are (1) the volume of air left in the lungs after expiration (residual volume) and (2) air elsewhere, particularly in the gastrointestinal tract. The most common method used to measure the body's air component is to measure **residual lung volume** and add a value of 100 ml to residual volume to account for air in the gastrointestinal tract. Air bubbles in the hair, in bathing caps, in bathing suits, and on the body also can introduce errors. The methods used to estimate residual volume are based on dilution or wash-out techniques. Wilmore (1969) describes these methods in detail.

Residual lung volume is often difficult to measure and some have suggested it be estimated. The suggested prediction methods (Going 1996) are estimating it (1) with a regression equation using age, height, and sex, or (2) as a constant fraction of vital capacity (0.24 in males and 0.28 in females). Research (Morrow et al. 1986) has shown that these prediction methods are not suitable and can introduce considerable measurement error.

Determining the Density of Water   The density of water is a function of its temperature and can be calculated thus:

Density of water   **(12.1)**

$$Dw = 1.005932 - (0.0003394 \times TW)$$

where Dw is water density and TW is the temperature of water measured in centigrade.

Computing Body Volume The values needed to calculate body volume (BV) are body weight on land (Wt), body weight in water (Ww), the density of water (Dw), and the body's air component (Ba) (e.g., residual lung volume + 100 ml). Body volume (BV) is calculated thus:

Body Volume   **(12.2)**

$$BV = \left(\frac{Wt - Ww}{Dw}\right) - Ba$$

Computing Body Density The values needed to compute body density are body volume (BV) and body weight on land (Wt).

Body Density   **(12.3)**

$$BD = \left(\frac{Wt}{BV}\right)$$

Calculation Example: Underwater Body Density Assume that the following values were obtained on an individual.

- Body weight (Wt): 70.15 kg
- Underwater weight (Ww): 3.36 kg
- Body's air component (Ba): 1.2 L (RV = 1.1, gastrointestinal tract 100 ml, or 0.1L)
- Density of water (Dw): 0.995678 (30°C)

Formula 12.2 is used to measure body volume (BV), and Formula 12.3 determines body density (BD). The calculations are as follows:

Computing Body Volume

$$BV = \left(\frac{70.15 - 3.36}{0.995678}\right) - 12 = 65.88$$

Computing Body Density (g/cc)

$$BD = \left(\frac{70.15}{65.88}\right) = 1.065$$

Accuracy of Underwater Weighing Method

The underwater weighing method is considered the "gold standard" of measuring body density. While many believe that measuring underwater weight is the biggest source of inaccuracy, this is not the case. The air component is the most error-prone variable. Table 12.2 provides the potential errors associated with realistic measurement errors of the variables used to measure underwater percent body fat. Provided is the degree that actual percent body fat would vary for three different error conditions. Typically, the measurement error of underwater weight is less than 0.1 kg. Body weight and water temperature can be measured very accurately. Residual lung volume can be difficult to measure, and the air in the gastrointestinal tract is estimated at 100 ml (0.1 L). Air component errors of ±0.1 L translate to percent body fat errors of ±0.7% fat, but air component errors of ±1 L result

TABLE 12.2 **Effects of Component Errors on Underwater-Determined Percent Body Fat**

Underwater Weight Variable	Actual Value	Error Conditions		
		1	2	3
Air component (L)	1.2	1.3	1.6	2.2
% fat	15.0	14.3	12.2	8.0
Underwater weight (kg)	3.36	3.38	3.41	3.46
%fat	15.0	14.9	14.6	14.3
Body weight (kg)	70.0	70.1	70.5	71.0
%fat	15.0	15.1	15.3	15.5
Water temp (°C)	36.0	36.1	36.5	37.0
%fat	15.0	15.1	15.1	15.2

Note: Constructed from published data in Going (1996).

Figure 12-6

The BOD POD "body box" uses plethysmography technology to measure body volume using the pressure/volume relationship explained by Boyle's law. (Courtesy of LMi Measurement, Inc. For more information, go to www.bodpod.com.)

in huge percent body fat errors of ±8.0% fat. Estimating residual volume from age, height, and sex yields air component errors in this magnitude (Morrow et al. 1986). If the underwater weighing method is to be used, the air component must be measured accurately.

Measuring Body Density with a Body Box
Plethysmography

Body volume can also be measured in a "body box," or body **plethysmograph** (see Figure 12-6). This technique is based on Boyle's law, which states that the pressure of a gas varies inversely with its volume. Since the air volume of the box can be determined, adding the person changes the pressure and makes it possible to measure the new volume in the box. The major advantage of the body box over underwater weighing is ease in testing. It can be very difficult to measure the underwater body weight of someone who is not comfortable in the water. A commercial "body box" is now available to measure body composition. Figure 12-6 shows the BOD POD. In a well-designed study, Fields et al. (2001) tested 42 adult

women with both underwater weighing and the BOD POD. They found that the mean body density for both methods was 1.035 kg/L and the standard deviations were nearly identical, 0.019 kg/L and 0.021 kg/L for underwater weighing and the BOD POD body box. The correlation between body density determined by the two methods was very high: 0.97.

Converting Body Density to Percent Body Fat

Variation in body density can be due to air, fat weight, and fat-free weight. The density of air is zero, and the density of fat weight (tissue) is about 0.90 g/cc. The density of fat-free weight varies from about 1.0 g/cc to as high as 3.0 g/cc, with an average assumed to be 1.10 g/cc. Fat-free weight consists of muscle, blood, bone, and organs. The two-component models for computing percent body fat from body density are based on the assumption that the density of fat tissue is 0.90 g/cc, and that of fat-free weight is 1.10 g/cc. This assumption does not apply universally when computing the percent body fat of youth, older adults, and ethnic groups. This has led to the development of four component models.

Two-Component Models

The first equations developed for converting body density to percent body fat were published by Siri (1961) and Brožek et al. (1963). The equations provide nearly identical percent body fat values throughout the human range of body fatness. The formulas are based on the **two-component model,** which assumes that the density of fat tissue is 0.9 g/cc and the density of fat-free weight is 1.10 g/cc.

Siri Percent Body Fat   **(12.4)**

$$\%\text{fat} = \left(\frac{495}{\text{BD}}\right) - 450$$

Brožek Percent Body Fat   **(12.5)**

$$\%\text{fat} = \left(\frac{457}{\text{BD}}\right) - 414$$

There is growing evidence that the Siri and Brožek equations may not be appropriate when applied to ethnic groups other than whites. Published research suggests that the body composition race effect is complex. Wagner and Heyward (2000) published an excellent review article comparing body composition differences between black and white individuals. They reported that blacks have a greater bone density and body protein content than whites, which produced a higher density in FFM in blacks. Cross-sectional data (Vickery et al. 1988) show that the mean body density of black men (1.075 kg/L) was significantly higher than that of white men (1.065 kg/L), while the mean of the sum of seven skinfolds did differ. This suggested that "the difference in the relationship of skinfolds to body density in African-American and white men is due to variation in the composition of "fat-free weight."

African Americans have higher bone mineral content and total body potassium than Caucasians, which results in a fat-free density higher than the value of 1.1 g/cc assumed by the Brožek and Siri equations. Schutte et al. (1984) developed an equation to convert body density to percent fat for African American men. The Schutte equation was developed on 15 African American men and assumes a fat-free body density of 1.113 g/cc using a two-component model. The Schutte formula for African American men is this:

$$\%\text{fat} = \left(\frac{437.4}{\text{BD}}\right) - 392.8 \qquad (12.6)$$

Wagner and Heyward (2001) also developed an equation to estimate percent fat from body density for African American men. Their equation was derived from a multicomponent model and a sample of 30 African American men and assumes a fat-free body density of 1.106 g/cc. The Wagner and Heyward formula for African American men is this:

$$\%\text{fat} = \left(\frac{486}{\text{BD}}\right) - 439 \qquad (12.7)$$

Ortiz et al. (1992) developed an equation to estimate percent fat from body density for African American women. Ortiz et al. developed their equation on 28 African American women and also

found a fat-free body density of 1.106. The Ortiz et al. equation for African American women is this:

$$\%\text{fat} = \left(\frac{485}{\text{BD}}\right) - 439 \qquad (12.8)$$

Figure 12-7 compares the Siri, Brožek, Schutte, Wagner, and Ortiz equations for computing percent body fat from body density. The Siri and Brožek equations yield almost identical estimates through the body density range. The Schutte, Wagner, and Ortiz equations give higher percent body fat estimates than the Brožek and Siri equations through the range, with the largest differences under 25%. The Schutte equation yields higher estimates of percent fat for the same body density below about 20% fat. Because the Schutte equation was developed on young and fit participants, it may be appropriate for lean African American athletes.

Calculation Example: Determining Percent Body Fat from Body Density Given next is percent body fat computed with the two-component models for a body density of 1.065 g/cc. Provided are estimates with the Siri (Formula 12.4), Brožek (Formula 12.5), Schutte (Formula 12.6), Wagner (Formula 12.7), and Ortiz (Formula 12.8) equations.

Siri Percent Body Fat

$$\%\text{fat} = \left(\frac{495}{1.065}\right) - 450 = 14.8\%$$

Brožek Percent Body Fat

$$\%\text{fat} = \left(\frac{457}{1.065}\right) - 414 = 15.1\%$$

Schutte Formula for
African American Males

$$\%\text{fat} = \left(\frac{437.4}{1.065}\right) - 392.8 = 17.9\%$$

Wagner Formula for
African American Males

$$\%\text{fat} = \left(\frac{486}{1.065}\right) - 439 = 17.3\%$$

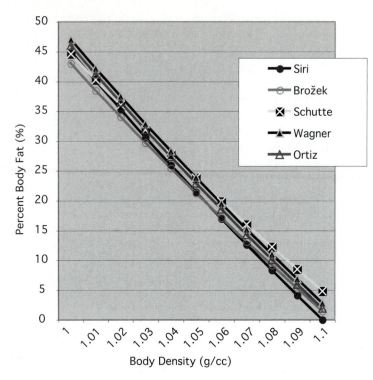

Figure 12-7

Comparison of body density equations to estimate percent fat.

Ortiz Formula for
African American Females

$$\%\text{fat} = \left(\frac{485}{1.065}\right) - 439 = 16.4\%$$

Multicomponent Model

The Siri, Brožek, and Schutte methods of estimating percent body fat from body density are based on the two-component model. The Siri and Brožek equations assume the density of fat tissue to be 0.9 g/cc and the density of fat-free weight to be 1.10 g/cc. This is likely true for adults between the ages of 20 and 50 years. Lohman (1992) argues convincingly that the two-component model has serious limitations when measuring the body composition of older adults, children, and possibly members of nonwhite ethnic groups, because the total body water and bone mineral content of these extreme groups vary from the values of the 20- to 50-year-old subjects. The Wagner and Ortiz equa-

tions should improve the accuracy of prediction for African American participants.

During childhood and the older years, the body is changing more dramatically. Changes in body water and bone mineral content alter the density of the fat-free component. As these values increase over reference values, there is a linear increase in percent body fat errors obtained with the two-component method. Lohman (1992) provides an excellent discussion on the effect of bone mineral differences on the accuracy of percent body fat determinations. Changes in the body's bone mineral content alter the density of fat-free weight. The two major sources of differences among individuals in bone mineral content can be traced to genetics and environmental conditions. Some inherit a higher bone mineral content than others. Due to lifestyle, some will develop a higher mineral content. For example, it has been shown that the bone diameter of the playing arm of tennis players is larger than that of their other arm.

Because differences in water and bone mineral content affect body density, the equations for converting body density of adults to percent body fat cannot be validly used with children. The development of multicomponent formulas for use with children and youth is described in a series of reports (Boileau et al. 1985; Lohman 1992; Lohman 1986; Lohman et al. 1984). The **multicomponent model** includes not only body density (BD) but also water (w) and mineral (m) content. A multicomponent formula (Lohman 1992) that can be used for children or adults of any age and any ethnicity is this:

Four-Component Percent Fat Model   **(12.9)**

$$\%\text{fat} = \left(\frac{2.749}{\text{BD}} \right) - (0.727 \times \text{w}) - (1.146 \times \text{m}) - 2.053$$

With the development of dual energy X-ray absorptiometry (DXA), technology is becoming available to estimate bone mineral content and bone density. This presents the possibility of developing a multicomponent model that adjusts for water and bone mineral content variance in fat-free weight. A detailed discussion of this topic is beyond the scope of this text, and the interested reader is directed to the work of Lohman (1992) and Heymsfield et al. (1996). The multicomponent model is typically used in body composition laboratories found in medical settings.

Comparison of Two- and Four-Component Models

The four-component method is now viewed as the most accurate method to measure percent body fat. This is largely based on the assumption that fat-free weight does not have a constant density of 1.1 kg/L for all racial groups. An important study with large samples of black and white American men and women suggests that the differences in accuracy between two- and four-component determinations of percent body fat are not large. Using a sample of 668 black and white men and women researchers, Visser et al. (1997) showed that the mineral fraction of fat-free mass of black men and women was significantly higher than that in whites. This fact is

well known (Wagner & Heyward 2000). They also found that the water fraction of fat-free mass of blacks was higher than that in the white subjects. The bone density and water fraction differences offset each other, producing nonsignificant race and gender differences in the density of fat-free mass. The mean density of fat-free mass of the gender and race groups ranged from 1.098 kg/L for white men to 1.101 kg/L for white women. None of these means were different from 1.100 kg/L. This led the authors to conclude that the two-compartment model was valid for black and white men and women at a group level, but that the four-compartment model should be used when making fine percent fat distinctions among individuals.

While much of the comparison of methods have involved black and white individuals, research suggests that the greatest errors associated with the two-compartment method may be with Asians. Using height and weight equations developed on whites to estimate two-component percent body fat, Deurenberg and colleagues discovered that the errors in estimating four-component percent fat of Chinese, Malays, and Indians in Singapore were substantial (Deurenberg, Yap & vamStaveren 1998; Deurenberg et al. 2000). What is not known is the accuracy of the two-component model for determining the percent fat of Americans of Asian descent, who constitute a growing population of Americans.

DXA

Dual energy X-ray absorptiometry, DXA, is a radionuclide method that is becoming a more prominent laboratory body composition method. DXA has an X-ray source and detector. Figure 12-8 shows the Lunar® DXA unit. The method requires the subject to assume a position on a table and complete a total body scan. A major advantage of DXA is that it can be used where it is difficult or impossible to measure people by the underwater weighing method. This would include people not comfortable in water, children, older people, or those who are ill.

The initial application of DXA was the measurement of bone mineral density to assess risk for osteoporosis. The DXA body composition method assumes that humans consist of three components

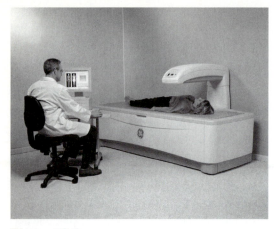

Figure 12-8

The DXA system for measuring body composition. Shown is the system manufactured by the LUNAR® Corporation (Madison, WI).

(Photo courtesy of the LUNAR® Corporation.)

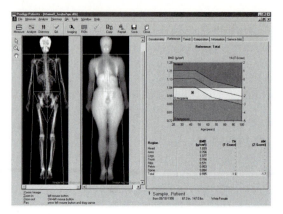

Figure 12-9

The DXA sample computer-generated body composition report. Shown is the report of the LUNAR® system.

(Report courtesy of the LUNAR® Corporation, Madison, WI.)

that are distinguishable by their X-ray attenuation properties. The method divides soft tissue, or non-bone tissue, into fat and lean components. This provides the three components, consisting of total body bone mineral mass, bone-free lean tissue, and fat mass. The sum of these components equals total body weight. Percent body fat is computed as the ratio of fat mass and total body weight. Fat-free mass is the sum of total body bone mineral mass and bone-free lean tissue. An assumption of the method is that water is a constant fraction of lean tissue mass. Unlike the four-component model, DXA does not measure total body water (Kohrt 1995; Pietrobelli et al. 1996).

Figure 12-9 is a sample computer-generated DXA report. The report shows the sample fat, bone-free lean tissue, and bone mineral mass values. Where the underwater weighing and BOD POD methods measure total body composition, the DXA method has the capacity to measure not only total body composition, but also, as the report shows, regional body composition. The ease of administration, scientific validity, and capacity to measure regional body composition suggests that DXA will become a more prominent laboratory method used to measure body composition. A limitation of DXA is that the equipment is expensive.

ANTHROPOMETRIC ASSESSMENT OF BODY COMPOSITION

Due to the need for highly trained technicians and expensive equipment, laboratory methods are rarely used in field settings. The most common alternative is to use some form of anthropometric method. This includes weight-height ratios, body circumferences, and skinfold measurements.

Body Mass Index

Body mass index (BMI) is the weight-height ratio often used in field settings. It is the measure of body composition typically used in large-scale public health studies, but it also is an alternative item on the FITNESSGRAM® youth fitness battery. BMI is computed thus:

$$\text{Body Mass Index} \qquad \textbf{(12.10)}$$

$$\text{BMI} = \left(\frac{\text{Weight}}{\text{Height} \times \text{Height}} \right)$$

where weight is in kilograms and height is in meters.

Calculation Example: Computing BMI   Assume that a person's weight is 142 pounds (64.61 kg) and her height is 5 feet 4 inches, or 64 inches (1.63 meters). The person's BMI (Formula 12.10) is 24.3 kg/m².

$$\text{BMI} = \left(\frac{64.61}{1.63 \times 1.63} \right) = \frac{64.61}{2.6569} = 24.3$$

While various types of weight and height indices have been used to evaluate body composition, the most recent trend has been to use BMI. An important document published in 1998 was a World Health Organization (WHO) report signaling a worldwide obesity epidemic (WHO 1998). An important part of the report was a body composition classification system based on BMI. Table 12.3 gives the WHO BMI classification of overweight and obesity. The merits of the system are that it is simple, it is based on a large body of epidemiological and clinical data, and it provides a useful evaluation tool.

Laboratory-measured percent body fat is viewed as the body composition "gold standard" for defining obesity. The WHO recommendation of using a single value to define overweight (BMI = 25) and obesity (BMI = 30) implies that other variables such as age, sex, and ethnicity do not influence the BMI and percent body fat relationship. There is a growing body of scientific research showing that the relationship between BMI and

TABLE 12.3	The World Health Organization (WHO) Criteria for Overweight and Obesity by BMI
Category	**BMI**
Underweight	<18.5
Normal Weight	18.5–24.9
Overweight	25.0–29.9
Obesity Class I	30.0–34.9
Obesity Class II	35–39.9
Obesity Class III	>40

percent body fat is indeed influenced by gender, age and ethnicity. Gallagher et al. (1996) published a prediction equation to estimate four-component laboratory-determined percent body fat from age, sex, and race. Their sample included over 700 black and white men and women who varied greatly in age and body composition. They found that age and gender, but not race, affected the relationship between BMI and percent body fat. They published an equation to estimate percent body fat from BMI, age, and gender coded 0 for women and 1 for men. In an effort to confirm the accuracy of the Gallagher et al. equation, the Jackson-Pollock body composition data were reanalyzed (Jackson et al. 2002) to examine this relationship. The Jackson-Pollock data consisted of 679 men and women who were predominately white. Percent body fat was determined with the two-component method. These equations are given next.

Gallagher et al. (1996)   **(12.11)**

$$R = 0.81, \; SEE = 5.7\%\text{fat}$$

$$\%\text{fat} = (1.46 \times \text{BMI}) + (0.14 \times \text{Age}) - (11.61 \times \text{Sex}) - 10.02$$

Jackson-Pollock (Jackson & Pollock 1978; Jackson et al. 1980; Jackson et al. 2002)

(12.12)

$$R = 0.75, \; SEE = 5.5\%\text{fat}$$

$$\%\text{fat} = (1.61 \times \text{BMI}) + (0.13 \times \text{Age}) - (12.11 \times \text{Sex}) - 13.91$$

Table 12.4 gives the male and female percent body fat estimates for the WHO overweight and obese standards for ages 20, 40, and 60 years of age. These data show that even with the major race and methodological differences of these two databases, the equations for these two samples provide very similar percent body fat estimates. The table also shows the male and female percent body fat values associated with the WHO overweight and obese BMI standards of 25 and 30 kg/m². The percent body fat level for the WHO BMI overweight standard is about 20% for men and 30% for women. The percent fat level for the WHO obese standard is about 27% for men and

	TABLE 12.4	Percent Body Fat Estimates for WHO BMI Overweight and Obese Values for Men and Women of Different Ages						

	BMI = 25 (Overweight)				BMI = 30 (Obese)			
Age	Men		Women		Men		Women	
	G*	J*	G	J	G	J	G	J
20	17.7	16.8	29.3	28.9	25.0	24.9	36.6	37.0
40	20.5	19.4	32.1	31.5	27.8	27.5	39.4	39.6
60	23.3	22.0	34.9	34.1	30.6	30.1	42.2	42.2

*Key: G = percent body fat estimated with the Gallagher et al. (1996) equation; J = percent body fat estimated with the Jackson et al. (2002) equation.

nearly 40% for women. The percent body fat of men and women age 60 years can be expected to be about 6% higher than that at age 20 years for the same BMI.

The BMI is most useful for defining the body composition of groups of individuals. It lacks accuracy when evaluating the body composition of individuals. In many cases, it is individual estimates that are of interest. The major limitation of BMI is that the weight factor is not partitioned into fat-free weight and fat weight. The BMI of two individuals may be the same, even though they may differ substantially in percent body fat. Physically fit, well-muscled individuals may exceed the WHO overweight and obese standards, but have a very low percent body fat. When evaluating the body composition of individuals, you should use the most accurate method available. If it is not possible to use a laboratory method to determine percent body fat, the methods of choice are body circumferences, skinfolds, or bioelectrical impedance.

Body Circumferences

Body **circumferences** have also been used to assess body composition. The approaches followed include estimating body density from combinations of body circumference measurements, and using the ratio of waist and hip circumference measurements.

Body circumferences are correlated with hydrostatically determined body density. The circumferences that tend to be most highly correlated are

in the abdominal and hip regions. In 1981, the United States Navy changed from using height and weight standards to percent body fat estimated from body circumferences (Hodgdon & Beckett 1984a; Hodgdon & Beckett 1984b). The variables used for the Navy equations are height, abdomen circumference, hip circumference, and neck circumference (Hodgdon & Beckett 1984c). Tran and associates (1989, 1988) published generalized equations for estimating hydrostatically determined body density from various combinations of circumference measurements. The subjects used varied considerably in age and body composition. Table 12.5 gives the generalized equations developed on the general population. The procedures for measuring body circumferences are given in other sources (American College of Sports Medicine 2006; Behnke & Wilmore 1974; Hodgdon & Beckett 1984c).

Waist-Hip Ratio (WHR)

Medical research has shown that people with central, visceral types of obesity are particularly at risk for developing cardiovascular disease, stroke, and non-insulin-dependent diabetes mellitus. This central visceral obesity is measured by the waist-hip ratio. The measurements used in the waist-hip ratio equation are as follows:

- Waist circumference (waist-C) is measured at the narrowest point between the umbilicus and xiphoid process.

TABLE 12.5	Generalized Regression Equations for Predicting Body Density of Men and Women from Body Circumference Measurements		
	Regression Equation	**R**	**SEE g/cc**
Males	$BD = 1.21142 + (0.00085 \times V_1) - (0.00050 \times V_2) - (0.00061 \times V_3) - (0.00138 \times V_4)$	0.84	0.009
Females	$BD = 1.168297 - (0.002824 \times V_4) + (0.000012 \times V_1)^2 - (0.000733 \times V_3) + (0.000510 \times V_5) - (0.00216 \times V_6)$	0.89	0.009

Key: V_1 = weight (kg); V_2 = iliac circumference (cm); V_3 = hip circumference (cm); V_4 = abdominal circumference (cm); V_5 = height (cm); V_6 = age (years).

• Hip circumference (hip-C) is measured at the largest horizontal circumference around the buttocks.

$$\text{Waist-Hip Ratio (WHR)} \qquad \textbf{(12.13)}$$

$$\text{WHR} = \left(\frac{\text{Waist–C}}{\text{Hip–C}} \right)$$

The development of central, visceral obesity is believed to be caused by an alteration in the body's metabolic system. Several of these endocrine abnormalities are associated with insulin resistance that is believed to be the cause of the increased disease risk. Obesity and overweight have traditionally been defined by body mass index. Accumulated evidence, however, suggests that waist-to-hip ratio may be a better index of obesity. Yusuf et al. (2005) reported results from an important study of over 27,000 people from 52 countries that represented several major ethnic groups. Waist-to-hip ratio was the obesity measure most highly associated with heart attacks, more strongly associated than was BMI. These researchers noted that the previous estimates of the impact of obesity as a cardiovascular disease risk factor would be higher if waist-to-hip ratio were used to document obesity, rather than BMI. If waist-to-hip ratio were used to assess cardiovascular disease risk, these data suggest that a larger proportion of people worldwide would be classified as obese. Other investigators have suggested that the practice of determining obesity with BMI is obsolete and that the preferred

simple assessment of obesity should be with waist-to-hip ratio (Kragelund & Omland 2005). As values of waist-to-hip ratio increase, the risk of heart attack increases progressively, with no evidence of a threshold value. This means that the risk gets worse as the ratio increases. In the Yusuf et al. study, participants of all ages and ethnic groups had a significantly increased risk of heart attack when waist-to-hip ratio was 0.90 or greater in men and 0.83 or greater in women.

The term **android obesity** is used to describe central or upper body adiposity and has been referred to as apple-shaped. Increased waist-to-hip ratios are indicative of android obesity and a higher risk of heart attack. Lower-body obesity is known as **gynoid obesity** and results when excess fat is deposited in the hips and thighs. Gynoid obesity is also referred to as pear-shaped and is associated with a lower risk of heart attack.

Skinfolds

Skinfold measurements are highly correlated with hydrostatically determined body density. Skinfold measurements involve measuring a double thickness of subcutaneous fat with a specially designed caliper (Figure 12-10). Several acceptable calipers are available for measuring skinfold fat. A skinfold caliper that conforms to specifications established by the committee of the Food and Nutrition Board of the National Research Council of the United States should be used. The Lange, Harpenden, and

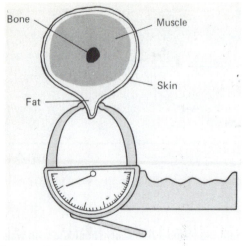

Figure 12-10
Measurement of skinfold fat.

Lafayette calipers meet these criteria.[2] The Harpenden caliper gives measurements about 1 to 4 mm lower than the Lange and Lafayette calipers (Lohman 1981).

Skinfold Sites

Many are concerned about the accuracy of skinfolds. Accuracy is ensured by using a suitable caliper and having a trained technician measure skinfold fat at the proper locations. Improper site selection is probably the most common reason for error in measuring skinfold fat. The skinfold sites and methods are listed here. All measurements are taken on the right side of the body. Figures 12-11 through 12-18 illustrate the measurement methods and site locations.

1. **Chest:** a diagonal fold taken half the distance between the anterior axillary line and the nipple for men and one-third of the distance from the anterior axillary line to the nipple for women (Figure 12-11).

2. **Axillary:** a vertical fold on the midaxillary line at the level of the xiphoid process of the sternum (Figure 12-12).
3. **Triceps:** a vertical fold on the posterior midline of the upper arm (over the triceps muscle), halfway between the acromion and olecranon processes; the elbow should be extended and relaxed (Figure 12-13).
4. **Subscapula:** a fold taken on a diagonal line coming from the vertebral border to 1–2 cm from the inferior angle of the scapula (Figure 12-14).
5. **Abdomen:** a vertical fold taken at a lateral distance of approximately 2 cm from the umbilicus (Figure 12-15).
6. **Suprailium:** a diagonal fold above the crest of the ilium at the spot where an imaginary line would come down from the anterior axillary line (Figure 12-16).
7. **Thigh:** a vertical fold on the anterior aspect of the thigh midway between hip and knee joints (Figure 12-17).
8. **Medial calf:** The right leg is placed on a bench with the knee flexed at 90°. The level of the greatest calf girth is marked on the medial border. A vertical skinfold is raised on the medial side of the right calf 1 cm above the mark, and the fold is measured at the maximal girth (see Figure 12-18).

Skinfold Test Methods

When taking a skinfold measurement, pinch and pull the skin with your left hand, and hold the caliper in your right hand. Grasp the skinfold firmly by the thumb and index finger. The caliper is perpendicular to the fold at approximately 1 cm (0.25 in) from the thumb and forefinger. Then release the caliper grip so that full tension is exerted on the skinfold. Use the pads at the tip of thumb and finger to grasp the skinfold. (Testers may need to trim their nails.) Read the dial to the nearest 0.5 mm approximately one to two seconds after the grip has been released. You should take a minimum of two measurements. If they vary by more than 1 mm, take a third.

[2]The Lange caliper is manufactured by Cambridge Scientific Industries, Cambridge, MD. The Harpenden caliper is manufactured by British Indicators LTD., St. Albans, Herts, England, and distributed in the United States by Quinton Equipment, Seattle, WA. Lafayette Instrument Company, Lafayette, IN, manufactures the Lafayette caliper.

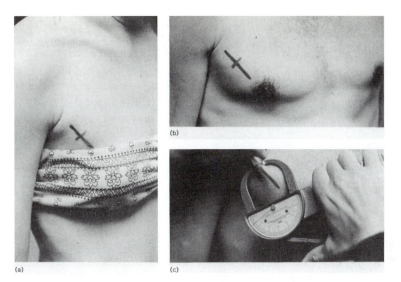

Figure 12-11

(a) and (b) Skinfold test sites for women and men; (c) placement of calipers for chest skinfold test.

(Photos courtesy of Pollock, M. L., D. H. Schmidt, & A. S. Jackson, *Measurement of Cardiorespiratory Fitness and Body Composition in the Clinical Setting, Comprehensive Therapy*, Vol. 6(9), pgs. 12–27, 1980. Published with permission of the Laux Company, Inc., Harvard, MA.)

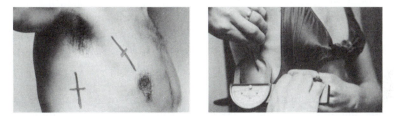

Figure 12-12

Test site and placement of calipers for axilla skinfold. The axilla skinfold site is shown in relation to the man's chest site.

(Photos courtesy of Pollock, M. L., D. H. Schmidt, & A. S. Jackson, *Measurement of Cardiorespiratory Fitness and Body Composition in the Clinical Setting, Comprehensive Therapy*, Vol. 6(9), pgs. 12–27, 1980. Published with permission of the Laux Company, Inc., Harvard, MA.)

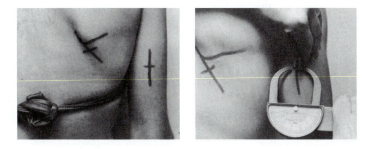

Figure 12-13

Test site and placement of calipers for triceps skinfold. The triceps skinfold site is shown in relation to the subscapular skinfold site.

(Photos courtesy of Pollock, M. L., D. H. Schmidt, & A. S. Jackson, *Measurement of Cardiorespiratory Fitness and Body Composition in the Clinical Setting, Comprehensive Therapy*, Vol. 6(9), pgs. 12–27, 1980. Published with permission of the Laux Company, Inc., Harvard, MA.)

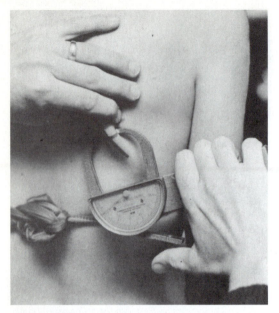

Figure 12-14

Placement of calipers for subscapular skinfold. The proper site location is shown in Figure 12-13.

(Photos courtesy of Pollock, M. L., D. H. Schmidt, & A. S. Jackson, *Measurement of Cardiorespiratory Fitness and Body Composition in the Clinical Setting, Comprehensive Therapy*, Vol. 6(9), pgs. 12–27, 1980. Published with permission of the Laux Company, Inc., Harvard, MA.)

If consecutive fat measurements become smaller and smaller, the fat is being compressed; this occurs mainly with "fleshy" people. The tester should go on to the next site and return to the trouble spot after finishing the other measure-

ments; the final value will be the average of the two that seem to best represent the skinfold fat site. Typically, the tester should complete a measurement at one site before moving to another. It is better to make measurements when the skin is dry, because when the skin is moist or wet the tester may grasp extra skin (fat) and get larger values. Measurements should not be taken immediately after exercise or when a subject is overheated, because the shift of body fluid to the skin will increase skinfold size. Practice is necessary to grasp the same size of skinfold consistently at the same location every time. Consistency can be ensured by having several technicians take the same measurements and comparing results. Proficiency in measuring skinfolds may take practice sessions with up to 50 to 100 subjects.

Skinfold Assessment of Percent Body Fat of Adults

Many people have published regression equations with functions to predict hydrostatically measured body density from various combinations of anthropometric variables. More than one hundred equations appear in the literature.

Early researchers developed equations for relatively homogeneous populations, termed population-specific equations. Because population-specific equations were developed on homogeneous samples, their application is limited to those specific samples. **Generalized equations**

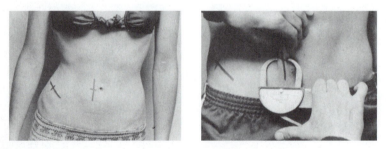

Figure 12-15

Test site and placement of calipers for abdominal skinfold. The abdominal site is shown in relation to the suprailium site.

(Photos courtesy of Pollock, M. L., D. H. Schmidt, & A. S. Jackson, *Measurement of Cardiorespiratory Fitness and Body Composition in the Clinical Setting, Comprehensive Therapy*, Vol. 6(9), pgs. 12–27, 1980. Published with permission of the Laux Company, Inc., Harvard, MA.)

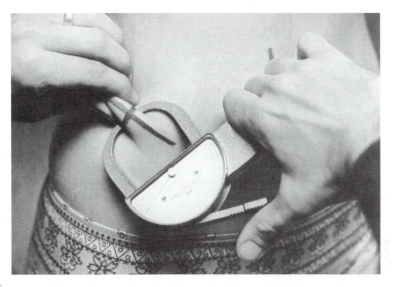

Figure 12-16

Caliper placement for suprailium skinfold. The proper site location is shown in Figure 12-15.

(Photos courtesy of Pollock, M. L., D. H. Schmidt, & A. S. Jackson, *Measurement of Cardiorespiratory Fitness and Body Composition in the Clinical Setting, Comprehensive Therapy*, Vol. 6(9), pgs. 12–27, 1980. Published with permission of the Laux Company, Inc., Harvard, MA.)

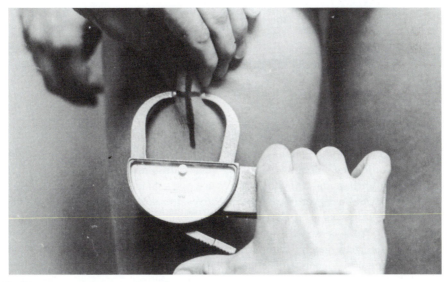

Figure 12-17

Caliper placement for thigh skinfold.

(Photos courtesy of Pollock, M. L., D. H. Schmidt, & A. S. Jackson, *Measurement of Cardiorespiratory Fitness and Body Composition in the Clinical Setting, Comprehensive Therapy*, Vol. 6(9), pgs. 12–27, 1980. Published with permission of the Laux Company, Inc., Harvard, MA.)

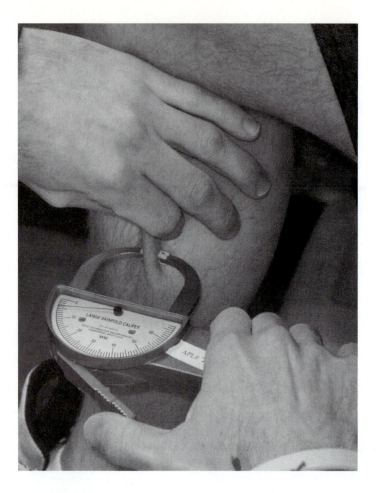

Figure 12-18

Caliper placement for the calf skinfold.

were developed on large heterogeneous samples using models that accounted for the nonlinear relationship between skinfold fat and body density. Age was found to be an important variable for generalized equations (Durnin & Wormsley 1974; Jackson & Pollock 1978; Jackson et al. 1980). The main advantage of the generalized approach is that one equation replaces several without a loss in prediction accuracy. Generalized equations can be validly used to estimate percent fat in men and women of various ages and body composition levels. A detailed discussion of population-specific and generalized equations can be found in other sources (Cureton et al. 1975; Jackson 1984; Lohman 1992).

Generalized Skinfold Equations

Separate skinfold equations are needed for men and women. Men and women differ in both storage and essential fat content (Figure 12-19). Table 12.6 gives the descriptive statistics for the variables used to develop generalized equations for men and women. When all seven skinfolds were summed, the mean of the men's and women's distribution was nearly the same, but men and women differed considerably at the various sites. The women's means for the limb skinfold, triceps, and thigh were substantially higher than the men's values, while the men's means on the remaining five sites, mainly in the region of the trunk, tended to be higher.

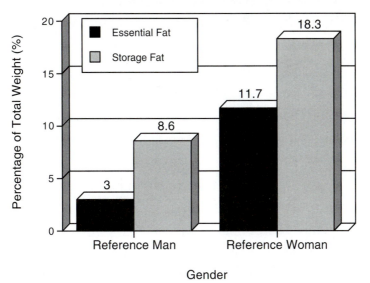

Figure 12-19

Not only do women have a higher percentage of their weight in storage fat, but also in essential fat consisting of lipids of the bone marrow, central nervous system, mammary glands, and other organs. Graph made from published data (Lohman 1992) of the fat distribution in reference to man and woman with the following characteristics: reference man, body weight 70 kg, 14.7% body fat; reference woman, body weight 56.8 kg, 26.9% body fat.

Multiple regression models were used to develop generalized skinfold equations for men (Jackson & Pollock 1978) and women (Jackson et al. 1980). Figure 12-20 gives the scattergram between the sum of seven skinfolds and hydrostatically measured body density. The male and female bivariate distributions are similar, except that the distribution of women is "shifted" downward. For the same sum of seven skinfold values, women tend to have a lower body density. This is due to their higher percent body fat, which is due largely to the women's higher level of essential fat. Table 12.7 gives generalized skinfold equations for the sum of seven skinfolds for men and women. A quadratic component is used to adjust for the nonlinearity, and age is an independent variable to account for aging.

Equations that use the sum of three skinfolds (Σ3) were highly correlated (R = 0.97) with the sum of seven skinfolds (Jackson & Pollock 1978; Jackson et al. 1980). This showed that the sum of three skinfolds can be used without loss of accuracy. The sum of three skinfolds equations has become the standard. To enhance testing, different sites are used for men and women. The female and male sites and equations are as follows:

Female: Σ3 = Triceps, Suprailium,
and Thigh ($R = 0.84$, *SEE* = 0.009) **(12.14)**

$$BD = 1.099421 - (0.0009928 \times \Sigma3) + (0.00000023 \times \Sigma3^2) - (0.0001382 \times Age)$$

Males: Σ3 = Chest, Abdomen,
and Thigh ($R = 0.91$, *SEE* = 0.008) **(12.15)**

$$BD = 1.10938 - (0.0008267 \times \Sigma3) + (0.0000016 \times \Sigma3^2) - (0.0002574 \times Age)$$

Calculation Example: Estimating Percent Body Fat from Sum of Skinfolds   Assume the following measurements for a man and a woman.

- Woman: age 29 years, skinfolds: triceps = 18 mm, suprailium = 14 mm, thigh = 30 mm; Σ3 = 62 mm. Using Formula 12.14 to estimate body density and the Siri equation (Formula 12.4), percent body fat is 24.5%.

TABLE 12.6	Descriptive Statistics of Samples Used to Develop Generalized Body Density Equations for Men and Women			
	Men (n = 402)		**Women (n = 283)**	
Variables	**Mean**	**SD**	**Mean**	**SD**
GENERAL CHARACTERISTICS				
Age (yr)	32.8	11.0	31.8	11.5
Height (cm)	179.0	6.4	168.6	5.8
Weight (kg)	78.2	11.7	57.5	7.4
Body mass index	24.4	3.2	20.2	2.2
LABORATORY DETERMINED				
Body density (g/cc)	1.058	0.018	1.044	0.016
Percent fat (%)	17.9	8.0	24.4	7.2
Lean weight (kg)	63.5	7.3	43.1	4.2
Fat weight (kg)	14.6	7.9	14.3	5.7
SKINFOLDS (mm)				
Chest	15.2	8.0	12.6	4.8
Axilla	17.3	8.7	13.0	6.1
Triceps	14.2	6.1	18.2	5.9
Subscapula	16.0	7.0	14.2	6.4
Abdomen	25.1	10.8	24.2	9.6
Suprailium	16.2	8.9	14.0	7.1
Thigh	18.9	7.7	29.5	8.0
SUM OF SKINFOLDS (mm)				
All seven	122.9	52.0	125.6	42.0
Chest, abdomen, thigh ($\Sigma 3$) (men)	59.2	24.5		
Triceps, suprailium, thigh ($\Sigma 3$) (women)			61.6	19.0

$$BD = 1.099994921 - (0.0009929 \times 62) +$$
$$[0.0000023 \times (62 \times 62)] - (0.0001392 \times 29)$$
$$= 1.099994921 - 0.0615598 + 0.0088412 -$$
$$0.0040368 = 1.0431$$

$$\%\text{fat} = \left(\frac{495}{1.0431}\right) - 450 = 24.5\%$$

- Man: age 40 years, skinfolds: chest = 15 mm, abdomen = 26 mm, thigh = 20 mm; $\Sigma 3$ = 61 mm. Using Formula 12.15 to estimate body density and the Siri equation (Formula 12.4), percent body fat is 19.9%.

$$BD = 1.10938 - (0.0008267 \times 61) +$$
$$(0.0000016 \times (61 \times 61) - (0.0002574 \times 40)$$
$$= 1.10938 - 0.0504287 + 0.0059536 -$$
$$0.010296 = 1.0533$$

$$\%\text{fat} = \left(\frac{495}{1.0533}\right) - 450 = 19.95\%$$

Tables 12.8 and 12.9 provide percent body fat estimates from the sum of three skinfolds and age. The YMCA adult fitness test (Golding et al. 1989) includes a similar table for a different combination of skinfolds. To use these tables, first select the appropriate skinfold sites

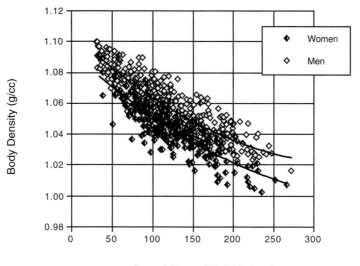

Figure 12-20

The nonlinear relationship between the sum of seven skinfolds of men and women and body density measured by the underwater weighing method. For the same level of skinfold fat, women have a lower body density. This is due to the difference in essential fat that is measured by the underwater weighing method, but not the skinfold method. Graph developed from published data (Jackson & Pollock 1978; Jackson, Pollock & Ward 1980).

TABLE 12.7	**Generalized Regression Equations for Predicting Body Density of Men and Women from the Sum of Skinfold Fat and Age**			
			Standard Error of Estimate	
	Regression Equation	**R**	**g/cc**	**% fat**
Males	$BD = 1.11200000 - (0.00043499 \times V_1) + (0.00000055 \times V_1)^2 - (0.00028826 \times V_2)$	0.90	0.008	3.4
Females	$BD = 1.0970 - (0.0004697 \times V_1) + (0.00000562 \times V_1)^2 - (0.00012828 \times V_2)$	0.85	0.008	3.8

Key: V_1 = sum of seven skinfolds; V_2 = age in years.

and measure them following the recommended measurement procedures. Using the sum of three skinfolds and age, find the percentage that is closest to the subject's age and sum of skinfolds. For example, if the sum of the triceps, suprailium, and thigh skinfolds for a 29-year-old woman is 62 millimeters, the closest age category is 30 years and the closest sum of skinfolds is 61 millimeters. Her estimated percent body fat would be approximately 24.2%, as

| TABLE 12.8 | Estimates of Percentage of Fat for Men; Sum of Chest, Abdomen, and Thigh Skinfolds | | | | | | | |

Sum of Skinfolds (mm)	Age in Years							
	20	25	30	35	40	45	50	55
16	3.5	4.1	4.6	5.2	5.7	6.2	6.8	7.3
19	4.5	5.0	5.6	6.1	6.7	7.2	7.7	8.3
22	5.5	6.0	6.5	7.1	7.6	8.2	8.7	9.3
25	6.4	6.9	7.5	8.0	8.6	9.1	9.7	10.2
28	7.3	7.9	8.4	9.0	9.5	10.1	10.6	11.2
31	8.3	8.8	9.4	9.9	10.5	11.0	11.6	12.1
34	9.2	9.7	10.3	10.8	11.4	12.0	12.5	13.1
37	10.1	10.7	11.2	11.8	12.3	12.9	13.4	14.0
40	11.0	11.6	12.1	12.7	13.2	13.8	14.4	14.9
43	11.9	12.5	13.0	13.6	14.1	14.7	15.3	15.8
46	12.8	13.4	13.9	14.5	15.0	15.6	16.2	16.7
49	13.7	14.2	14.8	15.4	15.9	16.5	17.1	17.6
52	14.5	15.1	15.7	16.2	16.8	17.4	17.9	18.5
55	15.4	16.0	16.5	17.1	17.7	18.2	18.8	19.4
58	16.2	16.8	17.4	18.0	18.5	19.1	19.7	20.2
61	17.1	17.7	18.2	18.8	19.4	19.9	20.5	21.1
64	17.9	18.5	19.1	19.6	20.2	20.8	21.4	21.9
67	18.7	19.3	19.9	20.5	21.0	21.6	22.2	22.8
70	19.5	20.1	20.7	21.3	21.9	22.4	23.0	23.6
73	20.3	20.9	21.5	22.1	22.7	23.2	23.8	24.4
76	21.1	21.7	22.3	22.9	23.5	24.0	24.6	25.2
79	21.9	22.5	23.1	23.7	24.2	24.8	25.4	26.0
82	22.7	23.3	23.9	24.4	25.0	25.6	26.2	26.8
85	23.4	24.0	24.6	25.2	25.8	26.4	27.0	27.6
88	24.2	24.8	25.4	26.0	26.5	27.1	27.7	28.3
91	24.9	25.5	26.1	26.7	27.3	27.9	28.5	29.1
94	25.7	26.2	26.8	27.4	28.0	28.6	29.2	29.8
97	26.4	27.0	27.6	28.2	28.7	29.3	29.9	30.5
100	27.1	27.7	28.3	28.9	29.5	30.1	30.7	31.3
103	27.8	28.4	29.0	29.6	30.2	30.8	31.4	32.0
106	28.5	29.1	29.6	30.2	30.8	31.4	32.1	32.7
109	29.1	29.7	30.3	30.9	31.5	32.1	32.7	33.3
112	29.8	30.4	31.0	31.6	32.2	32.8	33.4	34.0
115	30.4	31.0	31.6	32.2	32.8	33.5	34.1	34.7

Source: From Jackson and Pollock (1978).

compared to the calculated value of 24.5%. The generalized equations can be difficult to use without computational help. You can solve them easily with a PC and common spreadsheets and relational database computer programs.

The multiple correlations and standard errors of measurement for the generalized equations are well within the range reported for population-specific equations. These findings show that a generalized equation can be used to replace several

TABLE 12.9	Estimates of Percentage of Fat for Women; Sum of Triceps, Suprailium, and Thigh Skinfolds							
Sum of Skinfolds (mm)	Age in Years							
	20	**25**	**30**	**35**	**40**	**45**	**50**	**55**
22	9.8	10.1	10.4	10.7	11.0	11.3	11.6	11.9
25	11.0	11.3	11.6	11.9	12.2	12.5	12.8	13.1
28	12.1	12.4	12.7	13.0	13.3	13.6	13.9	14.2
31	13.2	13.5	13.8	14.1	14.4	14.7	15.0	15.3
34	14.3	14.6	14.9	15.2	15.5	15.8	16.1	16.4
37	15.4	15.7	16.0	16.3	16.6	16.9	17.2	17.5
40	16.5	16.8	17.1	17.4	17.7	18.0	18.3	18.6
43	17.5	17.8	18.1	18.4	18.8	19.1	19.4	19.7
46	18.6	18.9	19.2	19.5	19.8	20.1	20.4	20.7
49	19.6	19.9	20.2	20.5	20.8	21.2	21.5	21.8
52	20.6	20.9	21.2	21.6	21.9	22.2	22.5	22.8
55	21.6	21.9	22.3	22.6	22.9	23.2	23.5	23.8
58	22.6	22.9	23.2	23.6	23.9	24.2	24.5	24.8
61	23.6	23.9	24.2	24.5	24.9	25.2	25.5	25.8
64	24.6	24.9	25.2	25.5	25.8	26.1	26.5	26.8
67	25.5	25.8	26.1	26.5	26.8	27.1	27.4	27.7
70	26.4	26.7	27.1	27.4	27.7	28.0	28.4	28.7
73	27.3	27.7	28.0	28.3	28.6	29.0	29.3	29.6
76	28.2	28.6	28.9	29.2	29.5	29.9	30.2	30.5
79	29.1	29.5	29.8	30.1	30.4	30.7	31.1	31.4
82	30.0	30.3	30.6	31.0	31.3	31.6	31.9	32.3
85	30.8	31.2	31.5	31.8	32.2	32.5	32.8	33.1
88	31.7	32.0	32.3	32.7	33.0	33.3	33.6	34.0
91	32.5	32.8	33.2	33.5	33.8	34.1	34.5	34.8
94	33.3	33.6	34.0	34.3	34.6	35.0	35.3	35.6
97	34.1	34.4	34.7	35.1	35.4	35.7	36.1	36.4
100	34.9	35.2	35.5	35.9	36.2	36.5	36.8	37.2
103	35.6	35.9	36.3	36.6	36.9	37.3	37.6	37.9
106	36.3	36.7	37.0	37.3	37.7	38.0	38.3	38.7
109	37.1	37.4	37.7	38.1	38.4	38.7	39.1	39.4
112	37.8	38.1	38.4	38.8	39.1	39.4	39.8	40.1
115	38.4	38.8	39.1	39.4	39.8	40.1	40.5	40.8

Source: From Jackson, Pollock, and Ward (1980).

different population-specific equations and are valid for adults varying greatly in age and body fatness. Still, an important caution should be raised about the generalized equations. They were developed on men and women ranging from 18 to 61 years of age and using the two-component model, which does not consider body water and mineral content. These equations should not be applied to children, and may lose accuracy with older adults (Lohman 1992). We should also note that the Jackson-Pollock equations were published over 20 years ago, and the American adult population has become heavier (see Table 12.1). It is likely that the equations will not be so accurate with extremely obese individuals. A final limitation is that the Jackson-Pollock equations were developed on mainly white individuals.

Bioelectrical Impedance Analysis (BIA)

Bioelectrical Impedance Analysis (BIA) is another technique that can be used to estimate body composition. BIA is based on the principle that the resistance to the flow of a low-level electrical current is related to total body water. Total body water and fat-free weight are highly related. The resistance to flow of the electrical current is greater in people with a higher percentage of body fat. The traditional BIA method is called a tetrapolar configuration because it requires attachment of four electrodes (two near the wrist and two near the ankle), and thus involves whole-body measurement (from wrist to ankle). Newer methods that do not require attachment of electrodes, such as the hand-to-hand and foot-to-foot analyzers, are now available. Pressure contact electrodes are part of these analyzers. These newer methods provide an estimate of percent fat, but do not provide the resistance reading that is used to estimate percent fat. In addition, the equations built into the hand-to-hand and foot-to-foot analyzers to estimate percent fat are proprietary equations of the manufacturers and are not supplied to the user. For these reasons, the accuracy of these equations has not been as well documented as for the traditional, whole-body analyzers. Currently, the accuracy of the foot-to-foot and hand-to-hand analyzers is lower than the accuracy for the whole-body (wrist to ankle) analyzers. When the appropriate equations are used, the accuracy of whole-body BIA analyzers (in particular for RJL and Valhalla systems) is similar to the accuracy of skinfolds (Lohman 1992). It is recommended that BIA analyzers should provide the user with resistance, reactance (another measure of the opposition to the flow of the electrical current), the prediction equations used to derive estimates of body composition, and the estimated body composition values (Ellis et al. 1999).

With BIA, a nondetectable electrical current is transmitted into the participant, and the resistance in ohms is measured. Some combination of resistance, height, body mass, age, and sex is then typically used in a regression equation to estimate fat-free mass. Population-specific equations have been developed for African Americans, American Indians, Asians, Caucasians, Hispanics, athletes, children, obese individuals, and older adults. More research is needed to develop generalized BIA equations. Proficiency in using BIA requires less training than with skinfolds, and BIA may be better accepted by participants who desire more privacy than can be afforded with skinfolds. Several factors affect BIA output, including dehydration, exercise, eating, drinking, alcohol consumption, diuretic medications, and menstrual cycle stage. The following guidelines should be followed to help clients prepare for BIA assessment:

1. Do not take diuretic medications within a week of the test.
2. Avoid alcohol within 2 days of the test.
3. Avoid exercise within 12 hours of the test.
4. Avoid eating or drinking within 4 hours of the test.
5. Urinate within 30 minutes of the test.

EVALUATING BODY COMPOSITION OF ADULTS

It is important to assess both body weight and percent body fat because they provide two related pieces of information about a person's body composition. Body weight is easy to measure, and once someone has an understanding of a desirable body weight for his frame, he can use weight to monitor changes in body composition. The shortcoming of using only body weight is that the fat-free weight component, frame size, and muscle development are not accurately considered. Two individuals of the same height, sex, and age may weigh the same but have different levels of fat-free weight and body fat.

Percent Body Fat Standards

What is a desirable percent body fat standard for adults? Being seriously overweight clearly increases one's risk of heart disease, hypertension, and diabetes, and results in a shorter life expectancy. Still, too many Americans, especially young women, are overly concerned about being thin. Being underweight, too, can result in serious health problems. Athletes generally have a lower percent body fat than the total population. The percent body fat level depends on the athlete's sex and event performed. Table 12.10 presents data published by Wilmore and Costill (1994) of percent body fat ranges of elite athletic groups. Highly trained endurance athletes (e.g., distance runners) will normally have very low levels of body fat. The average percent body fat of world-class distance runners is very low, averaging about 5% for men and ranging from 12% to 15% for women. This is an unrealistically low level for most people who are not exercising to the level of these athletes. Most world-class runners run from 10 to 15 miles each day of the week. At this mileage, they expend over 1,000 kilocalories a day just from exercise.

Table 12.11 gives standards for evaluating body composition of adults considering these limitations. These standards were developed from major published normative databases that consider both sex and age characteristics. The interpretation

TABLE 12.10	Ranges of Percent Body Fat for Male and Female Athletes	
	Percent Fat Range	
Sport	**Men**	**Women**
Baseball/softball	8–14	12–18
Basketball	6–12	10–16
Cycling	5–11	8–15
Football	6–18	
Golf	10–16	12–20
Gymnastics	5–12	8–16
Ice/field hockey	8–16	12–18
Racquetball	6–14	10–18
Rowing	6–14	8–16
Rugby	6–16	
Skating	5–12	8–16
Skiing	7–15	10–18
Swimming	6–12	10–18
Tennis	6–14	10–20
Track—running events	5–12	8–15
Track—field events	8–18	12–20
Triathlon	5–12	8–15
Volleyball	7–15	10–18

Source: From published data in Wilmore and Costill (1994).

TABLE 12.11	Standards for Evaluating Body Composition of Adults			
Body Composition Standard	**Age Groups In Years**			
	Under 30	**30–39**	**40–49**	**Over 49**
MEN				
High	>28%	>29%	>30%	>31%
Moderately high	22–28%	23–29%	24–30%	25–31%
Optimal range	11–21%	12–22%	13–23%	14–24%
Low	6–10%	7–11%	8–12%	9–13%
Very low	≥5%	≥6%	≥7%	≥8%
WOMEN				
High	>32%	>33%	>34%	>35%
Moderately high	26–32%	27–33%	28–34%	29–35%
Optimal range	15–25%	16–26%	17–27%	18–28%
Low	12–14%	13–15%	14–16%	15–17%
Very low	≥11%	≥12%	≥13%	≥14%

TABLE 12.12	**Standards for the Interpretation of Adult Percent Body Fat Standards**
High	Percent fat at this level indicates the person is seriously overweight to a degree that this can have adverse health consequences. The person should be encouraged to lose weight through diet and exercise. Maintaining weight at this level for a long period of time places the person at risk of hypertension, heart disease, and diabetes. A long-term weight loss and exercise program should be initiated.
Moderately High	It is likely that the person is significantly overweight, but the level could be high due in part to measurement inaccuracies. It would be wise to carefully monitor people in this category and encourage them not to gain additional weight. People in this category may want to have their body composition assessed by the underwater weighing method.
Optimal Range	It would be highly desirable to maintain body composition at this level.
Low	This is an acceptable body composition level, but there is no reason to seek a lower percent body fat level. Loss of additional body weight could have health consequences.
Very Low	Percent fat level at this range should be reached only by high-level endurance athletes who are in training. Being this thin may carry its own additional mortality. Individuals, especially females, this low are at risk of having an eating disorder such as anorexia nervosa.

of the standards is furnished in Table 12.12. These standards consider not only the problems associated with obesity, but also the problem of being underweight. The relation between weight and all-cause mortality is J-shaped; the highest and lowest death rates are associated with being too light as well as being too heavy (Lew & Garfinkel 1979). This was shown at the beginning of this chapter. It has also been shown that failing to gain weight is associated with a shorter life expectancy, compared to individuals who are at the optimal weight range for their age, sex, and height (Paffenbarger et al. 1986). It is likely that the J-shaped weight and mortality rates found in epidemiological studies can be traced partly to wasting diseases such as cancer, but there is morbidity associated with diet restrictions and/or high levels of exercise. For example, anorexia nervosa is characterized by excessive diet and exercise, resulting in extreme weight loss. This is most prevalent in young women and, for too many, is a fatal disease.

Defining Weight-Reduction Goals

It is possible for two individuals of the same height and body weight to differ substantially in percent body fat, which is why we use percent body fat as the standard for evaluating body composition. If percent body fat (%fat) and body weight are known, it becomes possible to calculate **fat weight** and **fat-free weight**. Once these are known, it becomes possible to estimate a sound weight goal, or **healthy weight**. For many adults, the goal is weight reduction. If percent body fat is known, an estimate of a realistic goal can be easily obtained. The weight-reduction goal is the estimated body weight for a desired percent body fat level. It is estimated from fat-free weight and desired percent fat level. The formulas for making these calculations are as follows:

$$\text{Fat Weight} \quad \textbf{(12.16)}$$

$$\text{Fat Weight} = \left[\text{Weight} \times \left(\frac{\%\text{fat}}{100} \right) \right]$$

$$\text{Fat-Free Weight} \quad \textbf{(12.17)}$$

$$\text{Fat-Free Weight} = (\text{Weight} - \text{Fat Weight})$$

$$\text{Determination of Weight Goal} \quad \textbf{(12.18)}$$

$$\text{Weight Goal} = \frac{\text{Fat-Free Weight}}{\left[1 - \left(\frac{\text{Desired }\%\text{Fat}}{100} \right) \right]}$$

Calculation Example   The formula can be easily illustrated. Assume that the body composition characteristics of a man are the following: weight, 187 pounds, and percent body fat, 26.3%. We must first calculate fat weight (Formula 12.16) and fat-free weight (Formula 12.17).

$$\text{Fat Weight} = \left[187 \times \left(\frac{26.3}{100} \right) \right] = 49.2 \text{ pounds}$$

$$\text{Fat-Free Weight} = 187 - 49.2 = 137.8 \text{ pounds}$$

The weight goal for 20%fat (Formula 12.18) would be determined thus:

$$\text{Weight Goal (20\%fat)} = \frac{137.8}{\left[1 - \left(\frac{20}{100} \right) \right]}$$

$$= \frac{137.8}{0.80} = 172.25 \text{ pounds}$$

The weight goal provides an estimate of what the person's weight would be if her fat-free weight component remained the same, but her body fat changed to the weight goal. Sedentary adults who start an exercise program tend to increase muscle mass and lose fat weight. This results in a decrease in percent fat, but sometimes without the projected weight loss. When a program uses only diet, both fat and fat-free weight are lost, often leaving percent fat relatively unchanged or even slightly increased, while total weight is reduced. It is important to monitor both body weight and percent body fat during an adult weight-reduction program to be sure that the participant's body composition is being altered in the desired direction.

Screening Tool for Steroid Abuse—FFMI

As previously documented in this chapter, BMI has become the accepted public health method of defining overweight (BMI = 25.0 to 29.9) and obesity (BMI ≥ 30). Harvard Medical researchers (Kouri et al. 1995) introduced and validated the fat-free mass index (FFMI) as a method to providing medical professionals with a screening method to assess for steriod abuse. Steroids are controlled substances in the United States. These medical researchers note that it is widely acknowledged that steroids increase muscle mass and strength well beyond the upper limits developed naturally. They reported that the tool is important not just to help diagnose medical and psychiatric effects, but also for forensic applications because steroid abuse may cause violent criminal behavior.

Computing FFMI

The variables needed to calculate FFMI are body weight in kilograms, height in meters and percent body fat. Kouri et al. (1995) used the skinfold equation provided in this chapter to measure percent body fat. The first step is to use body weight and percent body fat to calculate fat-free mass. Equations 12.16 and 12.17 give the method to compute fat-free weight.

The FFMI equation is similar to BMI with the exception that body weight is replaced with fat-free mass.

$$\text{FFMI} = \left[\text{fat-free mass/(height} \times \text{height)} \right] \textbf{(12.19)}$$

Where fat-free mass is in kilograms and height is in meters.

Kouri et al. (1995) found that FFMI and height were correlated. They added a normalized model to control for height. The model normalizes height to a 1.8–m athlete. The normalized equation is:

$$\text{Normalized FFMI} = \text{FFMI} + \left[6.3 \times (1.8 - \text{height in meters}) \right] \textbf{(12.20)}$$

Validity of FFMI

The FFMI was validated by comparing the FFMI of 134 dedicated body builders—74 who had never used steroids and 83 who were steroid users. The athlete's history of steroid use was obtained by urine testing and a detailed personal interview. Kouri et al. (1995) showed that the normalized FFMI of steroid users (mean = 24.9 ± 2.2) was significantly higher than the nonusers (mean = 21.8 ± 1.8). A plot of each athlete's data showed that the nonusers FFMI maximum value was 25.0, whereas many steroid users extend well beyond this limit. These data suggest that a FFMI above 25 is a level that an athlete cannot be expected to attain without pharmacological assistance. Kouri et al. (1995) concluded that "it appears that FFMI may represent a useful initial measure to screen for possible steroid abuse, especially in athletic, medical, or forensic situations in which individuals may attempt to deny such behavior." (p. 223)

SKINFOLD ASSESSMENTS OF PERCENT BODY FAT OF CHILDREN AND YOUTH

Body composition of American youth is changing in an unfavorable direction: children are fatter than they were 20 years ago. Several investigations (Table 12.13) have used the two-component model to estimate body density of children from anthropometric variables. Children vary considerably in growth and developmental characteristics during their school years. In comparison to adults, children have a higher water and lower bone mineral content, and these values change during their developmental years. Figure 12-21 shows this age-dependent decrease in body water for boys and girls. Chemical maturity is not reached until late adolescence. Due to chemical immaturity, the two-component model overestimates the percent body fat of children (Lohman 1992).

Many laboratories have the capacity to conduct underwater weighing studies, but very few have the capacity to measure body water and mineral content. Slaughter et al. (1988) developed several skinfold equations for estimating the percent body fat of youth. These equations use the sums of two different skinfold combinations: (1) sum of triceps and calf skinfolds and (2) sum of triceps and subscapula skinfolds. The sex-specific triceps and calf skinfold equations were developed with the multicomponent model and are recommended for use with children and youth of any age or ethnicity. These formulas are as follows:

$$\text{Percent Body Fat Equation for}$$
$$\text{Children and Youth—Males} \quad \textbf{(12.21)}$$
$$\%\text{fat} = \left[(0.735 \times \text{Triceps} + \text{Calf})\right] + 1.0$$

$$\text{Percent Body Fat Equation for}$$
$$\text{Children and Youth—Females} \quad \textbf{(12.22)}$$
$$\%\text{fat} = \left[(0.610 \times \text{Triceps} + \text{Calf}) + 5.0\right]$$

Calculation Example: Estimating Percent Body Fat of Youth   Assume that the sums of triceps and calf skinfolds for a boy and girl are both 20 mm. Formula 12.21 is used to estimate percent body fat for the boy, and Formula 12.22 is used for the girl. The percent body fat estimates are 15.7% and 17.2% for the boy and girl, respectively.

TABLE 12.13	**Means and Standard Deviations of Hydrostatically Determined Body Density and Concurrent Validity of Regression Equations for Youth**					
	Sample		**Body Density**		**Regression Analysis**	
Source	**Age**	**n**	**Mean**	**SD**	**R**	**SE**
MALES						
Cureton et al. (1975)	8–11	49	1.053	.013	.77	.008
Durnin and Rahaman (1967)	12–15	48	1.063	.012	.76	.008
Harsha et al. (1978)	6–16	79	1.046	.018	.84	.010
Harsha et al. (1978)	6–16	49	1.055	.020	.90	.009
Parizkova (1961)	9–12	57	–	–	.92	.011
FEMALES						
Durnin and Rahaman (1967)	13–16	38	1.045	.011	.78	.008
Harsha et al. (1978)	6–16	52	1.033	.016	.85	.008
Harsha et al. (1978)	6–16	39	1.041	.019	.90	.008
Parizkova (1961)	9–12	56	–	–	.81	.012
Parizkova (1961)	13–16	62	–	–	.82	.010

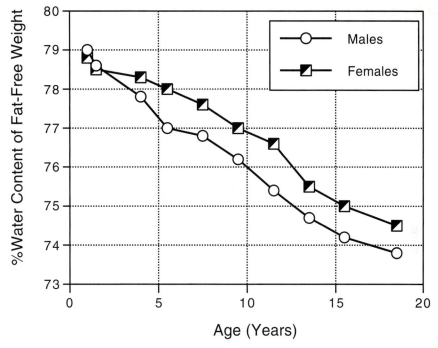

Figure 12-21

The percentage of body water content of fat-free weight of children declines with age. Not correcting for these differences in body water results in an overestimate of a child's true percent body fat. Graph made from published data (Lohman 1992).

TABLE 12.14	Sum of Triceps and Calf Skinfolds, Estimated Percent Body Fat, and Standard for Evaluating Body Composition of Children and Youth			
	Males		**Females**	
Standard	**Σ Triceps and Calf**	**%Fat**	**Σ Triceps and Calf**	**%Fat**
Very low	≤5	≤4.7%	≤11	≤12%
Low	6–10	5.2– 9.0%	12–16	12.1–15.0%
Optimal	11–25	9.1–20.0%	17–32	15.1–25.0%
Moderately high	26–32	20.1–25.0%	33–40	25.1–29.9%
High	33–40	25.1–31.0%	41–50	30–36.0%
Very high	>40	>31.0%	>50	>36.0%

Source: Constructed from data published by Lohman (1992).

Boy Sum of 2 = 20

$$\%\text{fat} = (0.735 \times 20) + 1.0 = 15.7\%$$

Girl Sum of 2 = 20

$$\%\text{fat} = (0.610 \times 20) + 5.0 = 17.2\%$$

Table 12.14 gives the standards suggested by Lohman (1992) to evaluate the body composition of children and youth. Provided are the sums of triceps and calf skinfolds and the equivalent percent body fat values. These standards are consistent with the adult standards previously presented.

TABLE 12.15	Comparison of Methods Available to Evaluate Body Composition of Humans		
Method	**Strengths**	**Limitations**	**Accuracy— %Fat**
Body density— Multicomponent	Most accurate; can be used for all age groups	Need expensive equipment; very few labs have the capacity to measure body water and mineral content; must measure residual lung volume	1%fat, >3% if residual volume is not measured
Body density— Two-component	Accurate with mature adults; many labs have the capacity	Need expensive equipment; cannot be used with children and older adults; must measure residual lung volume	1%fat, >3% if residual volume is not measured
DXA	Feasible to test a wide variety of subjects, measures three components, and measures regional body composition	Need expensive equipment; typically done at Medical Center	1–2%fat
Skinfolds— Generalized equations	Inexpensive; feasible for mass testing; appropriate for most adults (ages 20–50)	Tester errors measuring skinfolds; does not measure essential fat; developed with two-component model	3.5–4%fat
Skinfolds— Population-specific equations	Inexpensive; feasible for mass testing	Does not measure essential fat; developed with two-component model; suitable for limited populations (e.g., young adult males)	3.5–4.0%fat for the limited population
Skinfolds— Lohman's children's equations	Inexpensive; feasible for mass testing; based on multicomponent model	Tester errors measuring skinfolds; does not measure essential fat	3.6–3.9%fat
Bioelectrical impedance	Feasible for mass testing; just need to attach four electrodes; potential method of measuring body water	Validated on two-component model; standard equations are not readily available; lacks accuracy with very lean and obese; whole-body analyzers are expensive	3.5–4.5%fat
Body circumferences	Very inexpensive; feasible for mass testing	Tester errors measuring circumferences; does not measure essential fat; developed on two-component model; not very popular	3.7–4.5%fat
Body mass index (BMI)	Most feasible for mass testing (just need height and weight); large normative databases available; overweight standards are defined	Does not differentiate between fat and fat-free weight; does not estimate %fat; least accurate	≥4.5%fat
Waist-hip ratio	Feasible for mass testing; measures body fat that appears to increase the risk of diabetes and cardiovascular diseases	Does not provide an estimate of percent body fat	Not known

COMPARISON OF BODY COMPOSITION METHODS

Table 12.15 provides an evaluation and comparison of the methods available to assess body composition. If accuracy is a major concern, body density assessed with a laboratory technique or DXA needs to be used. The disadvantage of these methods is that they are expensive and require specialized equipment and trained testers. In addition, many do not enjoy the underwater weighing experience, and it is impossible to measure underwater weight accurately if the subject has a fear of water and cannot sit still fully submerged after an expiration. The BOD POD or DXA can be used with such individuals. Using predicted residual lung volume rather than measuring it makes the underwater weighing method much less accurate. With increased interest in assessing the body composition of children, older adults, and various ethnic groups, more researchers will move to the multicomponent model.

A common problem associated with skinfold measurements is the measurement error among testers. With properly trained testers, percent body fat estimated from skinfolds can be reliably measured. Using three testers who varied in experience, but practiced together, the reliability was found to exceed 0.99 for the sum of seven and three skinfolds. The standard error of measurement was about 1% body fat (Jackson, Pollock & Gettman 1978). In a more comprehensive study

(Jackson et al. 1988), both day-to-day and tester-to-tester measurement error of the skinfold, BIA, and hydrostatic estimates of percent body fat were examined. Table 12.16 lists these results. All reliability estimates were high, with standard errors of measurement about 1% body fat. The skinfold method is likely the most feasible option for general use and offers several advantages over the other field methods:

1. **Accuracy and reproducibility**. When testers are properly trained, it is reliable—results are reproducible from day to day and tester to tester.
2. **Simplicity and cost**. The skinfold method is simple to perform, not embarrassing, and easy to teach to others, and the equipment required is not expensive. While the BIA method may have similar accuracy, the wrist-to-ankle analyzers are much more expensive. The BMI method is most practical but less accurate.
3. **Fat deposits**. Not only is total body fat related to health, but also the location of the fat deposits is important (Larsson et al. 1984; Yusef et al. 2005). Fat around the abdomen seems to be a greater risk factor for heart disease than total body fat. The waist-hip ratio provides a good measure of this body fat. DXA does provide the capacity to measure body fat in the abdominal region.

TABLE 12.16	Reliability Estimates and Standard Errors of Measurement (%Fat) for Hydrostatically Determined Percent Body Fat, for Estimated Percent Body Fat from the Sum of Skinfolds, and for Bioelectrical Impedance				
	Males (n = 24)		**Females (n = 44)**		
Variable	**R_{xx}***	**SEM**	**R_{xx}***	**SEM**	
Measured percent body fat	.97	1.1	.97	1.2	
Skinfold estimated percent body fat	.98	1.0	.99	0.9	
BIA estimated percent body fat	.96	1.4	.97	1.5	

Source: From Jackson et al. (1988).

*Indicating reliability.

4. **Education**. Individuals can gain better understanding of the concept of excess body fat by actually measuring body fat. They may then use subjective assessments such as "pinch an inch" to gauge their progress.

5. **Measuring fat**. Gaining body fat results in the accumulation of subcutaneous fat, which is the fat that can be pinched. Thus, even if there is an error in estimating percent body fat, a reduction in the sum of skinfolds means a reduction in fat.

SUMMARY

Overweight is excessive body weight for an individual's height, while obesity is the excessive accumulation of body fat. Both have a negative influence on health. Cardiovascular diseases, diabetes, and breast cancer are associated with the excessive accumulation of body fat. In contrast, being too lean can suggest the presence of an eating disorder. Adulthood obesity is related to both one's genetic makeup and the level of one's body composition as a youth. While the body mass index (BMI) is often used to assess overweight and obesity from height and weight, its limitation is that it does not differentiate between fat and fat-free weight. Body density is the ratio of body volume and dry land weight. Body density can be validly assessed by underwater weighing and by the BOD POD body box. Once density is known, standard equations are available to convert body density to percent body fat. These calculations are based on assumptions about the density of fat weight and the density of lean weight. These estimates of density may vary somewhat among individuals, which introduces biological errors in calculating percent body fat, especially for children, older adults, and various racial groups. The four-component model, which uses total body water and bone mineral content, corrects for these biological errors. The major source of measurement error of the underwater weighing method is the failure to measure residual lung volume. DXA is another laboratory method that is growing in use. Advantages of DXA include ease in use and the capacity to evaluate regional body composition. The most common field methods are skinfolds, bioelectrical impedance analysis (BIA), circumferences, and BMI. These methods are less accurate but more feasible for mass testing. Skinfolds are likely the most common field method used to estimate percent body fat, but with the development of more generalized equations, the BIA methods will become an attractive alternative. Body mass index is suitable for defining overweight in populations of individuals, but lacks the accuracy to assess an individual's body composition.

FORMATIVE EVALUATION OF OBJECTIVES

Objective 1   Identify the public health problems associated with body composition.
  1. Identify the medical problems associated with high levels of percent body fat.
  2. What problems are associated with being too lean?

Objective 2   Identify the methods used to measure body composition of youth and adults.

  1. Outline the steps you would follow to measure percent body fat by the hydrostatic weighing method.
  2. Outline the steps you would follow to measure percent body fat using the generalized skinfold equations.
  3. For whom are the generalized skinfold equations suitable?
  4. How do you estimate the percent body fat of children?

Objective 3   Identify the limitations of the two-component model for computing percent body fat when applied to children, older adults, and members of various racial groups.

  1. What is the limitation of the two-component model for computing percent body fat?
  2. How does the multicomponent model adjust for the limitation?

Objective 4   Calculate percent body fat of youth and adults from skinfold equations.

1. A 42-year-old woman has a sum of seven skinfolds of 130 mm. What is her body density and percent body fat? What would these values be if she had a sum of three skinfolds of 64 mm?
2. A 38-year-old man has the following skinfold values: sum of seven of 142 mm and sum of three of 65 mm. What would be his estimated body density and percent body fat?
3. What is the percent body fat for a 15-year-old boy with a sum of 25 mm for calf and triceps skinfold?
4. Evaluate the body composition of a 12-year-old girl with a sum of 32 mm for calf and triceps skinfolds.

Objective 5   Be able to evaluate body composition of youth and adults.

1. What is the percent body fat level used to define level of obesity in children?
2. Why are adult body composition standards adjusted for age?
3. What is the danger in having a percent body fat that is too low?

Objective 6   Calculate weight goals for selected levels of desired percent body fat.

1. Assume a 165-pound woman's percent body fat is 35%. What would her weight goal be if her desired percent fat were 23%? How about 28%?
2. Assume a football player's body weight is 245 pounds and his measured percent body fat is 23%. If the coach would like the player's body composition to be between 10% and 15%, what would his weight goal range between?

Objective 7   Evaluate the accuracy of the various methods used to measure body composition.

1. What is the major source of measurement error for measuring percent body fat by the hydrostatic weighing method?
2. The standard error of estimate for estimating percent body fat from skinfolds ranges from about 3.5% to 4.0% body fat. What does this mean?
3. What is the limitation of using BMI to evaluate percent body fat?

ADDITIONAL LEARNING ACTIVITIES

1. Measure the skinfold thickness on several individuals. The secret to obtaining accurate percent body fat estimates from the generalized skinfold equations is to measure skinfold thickness correctly. Work with a partner and compare your results. Follow the instructions and pictures provided in this chapter.
2. Have your body composition determined by the underwater weighing method, Bod Pod, or DXA. These are the most valid methods of measuring body composition. Be certain your residual lung volume is measured if underwater weighing is used.
3. Many commercial fitness centers use electronic machines to estimate the percent body fat of members; a common method is the BIA method. Go to a center to have your body composition measured, and if you have also had it done by the hydrostatic method, compare the results. Ask the person taking the measurements to explain to you how the machine works and how accurate the equations are.
4. Help a college, high school, middle school, or elementary physical education teacher assess body composition of his or her class. The more experience you obtain now, the more understanding and confidence you will gain.

BIBLIOGRAPHY

American College of Sports Medicine. 2006. *ACSM's guidelines for exercise testing and prescription*. 7th ed. Philadelphia: Lippincott Williams & Wilkins.

Behnke, A. R. and J. H. Wilmore. 1974. *Evaluation and regulation of body build and composition*. Englewood Cliffs, NJ: Prentice-Hall.

Boileau, R. A., T. G. Lohman, and M. H. Slaughter. 1985. Exercise and body composition in children and youth. *Scandinavian Journal of Sport Sciences* 7: 17–27.

Brožek, J., F. Grande, and J. T. Anderson. 1963. Densitometric analysis of body composition: Revision of some quantitive assumptions. *Annals of New York Academy of Science* 110: 113–140.

Cureton, K. J., R. A. Boileau, and T. G. Lohman. 1975. A comparison of densitometric, Potassium-40, and skinfold estimates of body composition in prepubescent boys. *Human Biology* 47: 321–336.

Deurenberg, P., M. Yap, and W. A. vamStaveren. 1998. Body mass index and percent body fat: A meta analysis among different ethnic groups. *International Journal of Obesity* 22: 1164–1171.

Deurenberg, P. et al. 2000. The paradox of low body mass index and high body fat percentage among Chinese, Malays and Indians in Singapore. *International Journal of Obesity* 24: 1011–1017.

Dishman, R. K. (Ed.). 1988. *Exercise adherence: Its impact on public health*. Champaign, IL: Human Kinetics.

Durnin, J. V. G. A. and J. Wormsley. 1974. Body fat assessed from total body density and its estimation from skinfold thickness: Measurements on 481 men and women aged from 16 to 72 years. *British Journal of Nutrition* 32: 77–92.

Ellis, K. J. et al. 1999. Bioelectrical impedance methods in clinical research: A follow-up to the NIH technology assessment conference. *Nutrition* 15: 874–880.

Fields, D. A. et al. 2001. Comparison of the Bod Pod with the four-compartment model in adult females. 2001. *Medicine and Science in Sports and Exercise* 33: 1605–1610.

Gallagher, D. et al. 1996. How useful is body mass index for comparison of body fatness across age, sex, and ethnic groups? *American Journal of Epidemiology* 143: 228–239.

Going, S. B. 1996. Chapter 1. Densitometry. In A. F. Roche, S. B. Heymsfield, and T. G. Lohman (Eds.). *Human body composition*. Champaign, IL: Human Kinetics.

Golding, L. A., C. R. Meyers, and W. E. Sinning. 1989. *The Y's way to physical fitness*. 3rd ed. Chicago: National Board of YMCA.

Hedley, A. A. et al. 2004. Prevalence of overweight and obesity among U.S. children, adolescents, and adults: 1999–2002. *JAMA* 291: 2847–2850.

Heymsfield, S. B., Z. Wang, and R. T. Withers. 1996. Chapter 7. Multicomponent molecular level models of body composition analysis. In A. F. Roche, S. B. Heymsfield, and T. G. Lohman (Eds.). *Human body composition*. Champaign, IL: Human Kinetics.

Hodgdon, J. A. and M. B. Beckett. 1984a. *Prediction of percent body fat for U.S. Navy men from body circumferences and height*. Report No. 8411, Naval Health Research Center, San Diego, CA.

Hodgdon, J. A. and M. B. Beckett. 1984b. *Prediction of percent body fat for U.S. Navy women from body circumferences and height*. Report No. 8429, Naval Health Research Center, San Diego, CA.

Hodgdon, J. A. and M. B. Beckett. 1984c. *Technique for measuring body circumferences and skinfold thickness*. Report No. 84 39, Naval Health Research Center, San Diego, CA.

Huang, Z. et al. 1997. Dual effects of weight and weight gain on breast cancer risk. *Journal of the American Medical Association* 278: 1407–1411.

Hubert, H. B. et al. 1983. Obesity as an independent risk factor for cardiovascular diseases: A 26-year follow-up of participants in the Framingham heart study. *Circulation* 67: 968–977.

Jackson, A. S. 1984. Research progress in research design and analysis of data procedures for predicting body density. *Medicine and Science in Sports and Exercise* 16: 616–620.

Jackson, A. S. and M. L. Pollock. 1978. Generalized equations for predicting body density of men. *British Journal of Nutrition* 40: 497–504.

Jackson, A. S., M. L. Pollock, and L. R. Gettman. 1978. Intertester reliability of selected skinfold and circumference measurements and percent fat estimates. *Research Quarterly* 49: 546–551.

Jackson, A. S., M. L. Pollock, and A. Ward. 1980. Generalized equations for predicting body density of women. *Medicine and Science in Sports and Exercise* 12: 175–182.

Jackson, A. S. and, R. M. Ross. 1997. *Understanding exercise for health and fitness*. 3rd ed. Dubugue, IA: Kendall/Hunt.

Jackson, A. S. et al. 1988. Reliability and validity of bioelectrical impedance in determining body composition. *Journal of Applied Physiology* 64: 529–534.

Jackson, A. S. et al. 2002. The effect of sex, age, and race on estimating percent body fat from body mass index: The Heritage Family Study. *International Journal of Obesity* 26: 789–796.

Kohrt, W. M. 1995. Body composition by DXA: Tried and true? *Medicine and Science in Sports and Exercise* 27: 1349–1353.

Kouri, E. M., Pope, H. G., Katz, D. L., and Oliva, P. 1995. Fat-free mass index in users and nonusers of anabolic–androgenic steroids. *Clinical Journal of Sport Medicine.* 5(4): 223–228.

Kragelund, C. and T. Omland. 2005. A farewell to body-mass index? *Lancet* 366: 1589–1591.

Kuczmarski, R. J. and K. M. Flegal. 2000. Criteria for definition of overweight in transition: Background and recommendations for the United States. *American Journal of Clinical Nutrition* 72: 1075–1081.

Kuczmarski, R. J. et al. 1994. Increasing prevalence of overweight among US adults: The National Health and Nutrition Examination Surveys, 1960 to 1991. *Journal of the American Medical Association* 272: 205–211.

Larsson, B. et al. 1984. Abdominal adipose tissue distribution, obesity, and risk of cardiovascular disease and death: 13-year follow-up of participants in the study of men born in 1913. *British Medical Journal* 288: 1401–1404.

Lee, C. D., S. N. Blair, and A. S. Jackson. 1990. Cardiorespiratory fitness, body composition, and all-cause and cardiovascular disease mortality in men. *American Journal of Clinical Nutrition* 69: 373–380.

Lew, E. A. and L. Garfinkel. 1979. Variations in mortality by weight among 750,000 men and women. *Journal of Chronic Diseases* 32: 181–225.

Lohman, T. G. 1981. Skinfolds and body density and their relation to body fatness: A review. *Human Biology* 53: 181–225.

Lohman, T. G. 1986. Application of body composition techniques and constants for children and youth. *Exercise and Sport Sciences Reviews* 14: 325–357.

Lohman, T. G. 1992. *Advances in body composition assessment.* Champaign IL: Human Kinetics.

Lohman, T. G. et al. 1984. Bone mineral measurements and their relation to body density relationship in children, youth and adults. *Human Biology* 56: 667–679.

Morrow, J. R. et al. 1986. Accuracy of measured and predicted residual lung volume on body density measurement. *Medicine and Science in Sports and Exercise* 18: 647–652.

NHES. 1973. *Sample design and estimation procedures for a national health examination survey of children* (National Center for Health Statistics Publication No. HRA 74 1005). Rockville, MD: Health Resources Administration.

Ogden, C. L.., M. D. Carroll, L. R. Curtain, M. A. McDowell, C. J. Tabak, and K. M. Flegal. 2006. Prevalence of Overweight and Obesity in the United States, 1994–2004. *JAMA* 295: 1549–1555.

Ortiz, O. et al. 1992. Differences in skeletal muscle and bone mineral mass between black and white females and their relevance to estimates of body composition. *American Journal of Clinical Nutrition* 55: 8–13.

Paffenbarger, R. J. et al. 1986. Physical activity, all cause mortality, and longevity of college alumni. *New England Journal of Medicine* 314: 605–613.

Panel NIH Technology Assessment Conference. 1993. Methods for voluntary weight loss and control. *Annals of Internal Medicine* 199: 764–770.

Pietrobelli, A. et al. 1996. Dual-energy X-ray absorptiometry body composition model: Review of physical concepts. *American Journal of Physiology* (Endocrinol. Metab 34) 271: E941–E951.

Schutte, J. E. et al. 1984. Density of lean body mass is greater in blacks than in whites. *Journal of Applied Physiology: Respiratory, Environmental and Exercise Physiology* 56: 1647–1649.

Siri, W. E. 1961. Body composition from fluid space and density. In J. Brožek, and A. Henschel (Eds.). *Techniques for measuring body composition.* Washington, DC: National Academy of Science.

Skender, M. L. et al. 1996. Comparison of 2-year weight loss trends in behavioral treatments of obesity: Diet, exercise, and combination interventions. *Journal of the American Dietetic Association* 96: 342–346.

Slaughter, M. H. et al. 1988. Skinfold equations for estimating of body fatness in children and youth. *Human Biology* 60: 709–723.

Tran, Z. and A. Weltman. 1989. Generalized equation for predicting body density of women from girth measurements. *Medicine and Science in Sports and Exercise* 21: 101–104.

Tran, Z. V., A. Weltman, and R. L. Seip. 1988. Predicting body composition of men from girth measurements. *Human Biology* 60: 167–176.

Troiano, R. P. et al. 1995. Overweight prevalence and trends for children and adolescents: The National

Health and Nutrition Examination Surveys, 1963 to 1991. *Archives of Pediatric and Adolescent Medicine* 149: 1085–1091.

Vickery, S. R., K. J. Cureton, and M. A. Collins. 1988. Prediction of body density from skinfolds in black and white young men. *Human Biology* 60: 135–149.

Visser, M. et al. 1997. Density of fat-free body mass: Relationship with race, age, and level of body fatness. *American Journal of Physiology* (Endocrinol. Metab 35): E781–E787.

Wagner, D. R. and V. H. Heyward. 2000. Measures of body composition in blacks and whites: A comparative review. *American Journal of Clinical Nutrition* 71: 1392–1402.

Wagner, D. R. and V. H. Heyward. 2001. Validity of two-component models of estimating body fat of black men. *Journal of Applied Physiology* 90: 649–656.

Whitaker, R. C. et al. 1997. Predicting obesity in young adulthood from childhood and parental obesity. *The New England Journal of Medicine* 337: 869–873.

WHO. 1998. *Obesity: Preventing and managing the global epidemic*. Report of a WHO Consultation on Obesity. Geneva: World Health Organization.

Wilmore, J. H. 1969. A simplified method for determination of residual lung volumes. *Journal of Applied Physiology* 27: 96–100.

Wilmore, J. H. and D. L. Costill. 1994. *Physiology of sport and exercise*. Champaign, IL.: Human Kinetics.

Yusuf, S. et al. 2005. Obesity and the risk of myocardial infarction in 27,000 participants from 52 countries: A case-control study. *Lancet* 366: 1640–1649.

EVALUATING YOUTH FITNESS AND PHYSICAL ACTIVITY

C O N T E N T S

K E Y   W O R D S

OBJECTIVES

One important goal of school physical education programs is to develop physical fitness. The two methods used to evaluate youth fitness are motor fitness tests and health-related fitness tests. Here we describe the historical shift in youth fitness testing. The first youth fitness tests were motor fitness tests that placed emphasis on athletic excellence. The athletic fitness orientation has been replaced with health-related tests that reflect a public health concern. The public health information in Chapter 1 provides the academic foundation for the move from an athletic orientation to one with emphasis on health promotion. Presently, there are two national youth fitness programs: (1) FITNESSGRAM®/ ACTIVITYGRAM® and (2) President's Challenge. These two programs are described, compared, and evaluated. After reading Chapter 13, you should be able to

1. Identify the general tests that compose a motor fitness battery.
2. Identify the general tests that compose a health-related fitness battery.
3. Differentiate between motor fitness and health-related fitness batteries.
4. Identify and evaluate the national health-related fitness programs.
5. Understand how to administer the FITNESSGRAM®/ACTIVITYGRAM® and President's Challenge test batteries to evaluate youth fitness and physical activity.

INTRODUCTION

The concern for positive health extends to all ages. Periodic fitness testing emphasizes an active lifestyle to achieve and maintain low amounts of fat, high levels of aerobic fitness, and sufficient muscular strength, muscular endurance, and flexibility in the lower trunk and posterior thigh areas for healthy low back function (AAHPERD 1980; AAHPERD 1984). In the past, physical fitness has been defined in broad terms, and tests have measured either an aspect of physiological function or selected aspects of motor performance. This type of test has been termed "motor fitness" and includes not only strength and endurance components, but also factors of speed, power, and agility (Clarke 1971). Motor fitness tests represent potential for athletic excellence more than fitness for health promotion. As the concept of physical fitness moved away from athletic participation toward health, the components changed to include cardiorespiratory function, body composition (leanness/fatness), strength, endurance, and low back flexibility, traits shown by medical and exercise scientists to promote health and reduce the risk of disease. The most recent change in youth fitness testing involves an attempt to assess physical activity, in addition to physical fitness.

In the text both motor fitness and health-related batteries are discussed. A review of these tests and health-related fitness programs provides you with an understanding of the essential difference between motor fitness and health-related fitness and of the programs available for use in the public schools.

HISTORICAL VIEW OF YOUTH FITNESS TESTING

Americans have always valued physical fitness. Sometimes a specific event has stimulated interest in promoting youth physical fitness. For example, early interest in physical fitness can be traced to the number of men who failed physical examinations for induction into the military during World War II. Even though most of the medical examination failures were not related to physical fitness, they still heightened the concern for youth fitness. In the middle 1950s, publication of the Kraus and Hirschland study (1954) showed that European children scored higher than American children on the Kraus-Weber minimum muscular fitness test. While the Kraus-Weber test was not a true fitness test, it was the motivating force behind our first national youth fitness test, the American Association for Health, Physical Education, and Recreation (AAHPER) Youth Fitness Test (1958). The most recent event motivating an emphasis on youth fitness is the growing body of medical research relating physical activity and obesity to health and degenerative diseases. This is discussed in Chapter 1.

These historical events led to the development of youth fitness programs.

What Is Physical Fitness?

In order to measure something, we must first operationally define it. While there has always been a general acceptance of the value of physical fitness, it is difficult to find a precise definition of physical fitness. This can be seen in one of the initial definitions of physical fitness advanced by the President's Council on Physical Fitness and Sports (Clarke 1971). Physical fitness was defined as

> the ability to carry out daily tasks with vigor and alertness, without undue fatigue, and with ample energy to enjoy leisure time pursuits and to meet unforeseen emergencies. Thus, physical fitness is the ability to last, to bear up, to withstand stress, and to persevere under difficult circumstances where an unfit person would quit. It is the opposite to becoming fatigued from ordinary efforts, to lacking energy to enter zestfully into life's activities, and to becoming exhausted from unexpected, demanding physical exertion.
>
> The definition given implies that physical fitness is more than "not being sick" or merely "being well." It is different from immunity to disease. It is a positive quality, extending on a scale from death to abundant life. All living individuals, thus, have some degree of physical fitness, which is minimal in the severely ill and maximal in the highly trained athlete; it varies considerably in different people and in the same person from time to time.

This broad definition of physical fitness did not give test makers much direction. In fact, the actual tests used to evaluate this elusive construct have provided the operational definitions of physical fitness. The initial youth fitness tests placed an emphasis on athletic excellence, while the most current youth fitness tests focus on health. Provided next is a brief overview of this historical movement.

Motor Fitness

The initial physical fitness tests were what Clarke (1971) termed **motor fitness** tests. Six components composed motor fitness. Table 13.1 provides these six motor fitness components and items that were

TABLE 13.1	Motor Fitness Components and Common Youth Fitness Test Items
Component	**Common Test Item**
Muscular strength	Pull-ups
	Flexed arm hangs
	Push-ups
Muscular endurance	Bent-knee sit-ups
Circulatory-respiratory endurance	600-yard run
Muscular power	Standing long jump
Agility	Shuttle run test
Speed	50-yard dash

commonly included on youth fitness tests to measure each component. The **AAHPER Youth Fitness Test (YFT)** was the first national fitness test and was used extensively in the public schools. The original AAHPER YFT was published in 1958 and revised in 1975 and 1976. The initial items of the AAHPER YFT were these:

1. 50-yard dash
2. Pull-ups (boys) and flexed arm hang (girls)
3. Sit-ups (straight leg)
4. Shuttle run
5. Standing broad jump
6. Softball throw for distance
7. 600-yard run/walk

The AAHPER YFT was developed by a group of physical educators who met and selected tests based on logic; it was not developed through test validation research. The running, jumping, and throwing test items were included in the original battery to encourage athletic excellence. This has led some to refer to these types of tests as "athletic fitness" rather than "motor" or "physical fitness" tests.

Health-Related Physical Fitness

The development of **health-related physical fitness** tests represented a major shift away from an athletic emphasis to promotion of health. These tests were developed in response to both the growing dissatisfaction with traditional motor fitness batteries and the growing body of evidence supporting the value of regular, vigorous exercise for health promotion. In 1975 a group of exercise physiologists and measurement specialists met at Indiana University to discuss the growing medical evidence supporting the role of fitness and physical activity in health. This meeting led to the development of the term "health-related fitness" and the publication of a position paper on the role of fitness in health (Jackson et al. 1976). The position paper defined health-related fitness, criteria for test selection, and health-related fitness components. These are provided next.

Definition. Physical fitness testing, and programs for development of fitness, should emphasize the relationship between health and physical activity. Physical fitness is a multifaceted continuum that is affected by physical activity. . . .

Criteria for Test Selection. Since physical fitness can be operationally defined by the tests used for its evaluation, specific criteria were needed for choosing the tests. The criteria selected were as follows:

1. A physical fitness test should measure an area that extends from severely limited dysfunction to high levels of functional capacity.
2. It should measure capacities that can be improved with appropriate physical activity.
3. It should accurately reflect an individual's physical fitness status as well as changes in functional capacity by corresponding test scores and changes in these scores.

Health-Related Components. The areas of physiological function that are related to positive health, are a national concern, and appear to meet the above criteria are the following:

1. Cardiorespiratory function
2. Body composition (leanness/fatness)
3. Abdominal and low back/hamstring musculoskeletal function

Table 13.2 provides a historical summary of health-related fitness tests. These tests are the ba-

sis of the current youth fitness tests presented at the end of this chapter. Listed are the test items and comments relating to each test.

NATIONAL HEALTH-RELATED YOUTH FITNESS TESTS

In the early stages of development, youth fitness programs consisted of just a test battery. The public school fitness programs consisted of just testing students. The Texas Youth Fitness Test and the American Alliance for Health, Physical Education, Recreation, and Dance **(AAHPERD) Health-Related Fitness Test (HRFT)** programs changed this by developing educational programs that integrated a health and fitness curriculum with testing. The two current national youth fitness programs are (1) the FITNESSGRAM®[1], and (2) the President's Challenge.[2] In January 1994, AAHPERD adopted the FITNESSGRAM® in an effort to help create a single youth fitness program for all of the nation's schools; however, both the FITNESSGRAM® and the President's Challenge continue to be widely used. Provided next is a review of the FITNESSGRAM® and the President's Challenge. This will be followed by a comparison of the criterion-referenced standards for these two programs.

It may be useful to view training videos when learning to administer health-related fitness tests. Training videos can be viewed at the following website: www.ecu.edu/cs-hhp/exss/apl.cfm. Click on Youth Fitness Assessment Training Videos. Enter the password exss4804. Then choose one of the tests of health-related physical fitness to view.

FITNESSGRAM®

The **FITNESSGRAM®** is a comprehensive and academically sound health-related fitness program. This program was developed by a team of professionals working with personnel from the Cooper Institute for Aerobics Research. The FITNESSGRAM® test items and criterion-referenced standards have been

---

[1]For information on the FITNESSGRAM®/ACTIVITYGRAM® visit www.fitnessgram.net.
[2]For information on the President's Challenge visit www.presidentschallenge.org.

TABLE 13.2	Health-Related Fitness Tests That Led to the Development of Contemporary Tests	
Test	**Test Items**	**Comments**
Texas Youth Fitness Test (1973)	***Physical Fitness Components*** 1. Pull-ups, dips, and flexed-arm hangs 2. Bent-leg sit-ups (2 min) 3. 1. 5 mile and 12-minute run/walk for distance (grades 7–12); 9-minute run/walk for time, 1-mile run/walk for time (grades 4–6) ***Motor Ability Components*** 1. 50-yard timed sprint 2. Shuttle run 3. Standing long jump	1. Split test items into physical fitness and motor ability (athletic) components 2. First test to use distance-run tests longer than 600 yards 3. Provided award for just the fitness components 4. Was a motivating influence on developing the health-related movement
Manitoba Physical Performance Test (1977)	1. Cardiovascular endurance: 800-meter run (ages 5–9); 1600-meter run (ages 10–12); 2400-meter run (ages 13–19) 2. Flexibility: sit-and-reach 3. Muscular endurance: 1-minute speed bent-knee sit-ups and flexed-arm hangs 4. Body composition: percentage fat estimated from biceps, triceps, subscapular, and suprailium skinfolds	1. Developed by the Manitoba (Canada) Department of Education (1977) for boys and girls ages 5 to 19 2. Broadened the geographic scope of the health-related fitness movement
South Carolina Test (Pate 1978)	1. Cardiorespiratory function: 1-mile run/walk or 9-minute run for distance 2. Body composition: the sum of triceps and abdominal skinfolds 3. Abdominal and low back musculoskeletal function: bent-knee sit-ups in 1 minute, and sit-and-reach	1. Followed guidelines of the health-related position paper 2. Used criterion-referenced standards
AAHPERD HRFT (1980, 1984)	1. Cardiorespiratory function: 1-mile run/walk or 9-minute run for all students. The 1. 5-mile or 12-minute run/walk tests are optional for students 13 years or older 2. Body composition (leanness/fatness): sum of triceps and subscapular skinfolds or triceps skinfold if only one site is used 3. Abdominal and low back/hamstring musculoskeletal function. Modified, timed (60 sec), bent-knee sit-ups and sit-and-reach tests	1. Developed by a joint committee representing the Measurement and Evaluation, Physical Fitness, and Research Councils of AAHPERD 2. First national health-related fitness test, but did not develop into a popular test 3. Included not only test items and norms, but also information on the general principles of exercise prescription

(Continued)

TABLE 13.2	**Health-Related Fitness Tests That Led to the Development of Contemporary Tests** *(Continued)*	
Test	**Test Items**	**Comments**
Fit Youth Today (1986)	1. 20-minute steady state run 2. Bent-knee curl-ups 3. Sit-and-reach 4. Body composition: percent body fat estimated from the sum of triceps and medial calf skinfolds	1. Used criterion-referenced standards 2. Endorsed by the ACSM 3. The FYT curriculum emphasized student understanding of key health-related fitness concepts
Physical Best	1. 1-mile run/walk 2. Body composition by skinfolds and optional body mass index 3. Sit-and-reach 4. Bent-knee sit-ups 5. Pull-ups	1. National test program with good educational component and award system 2. Did not prove to be successful and merged with the FITNESSGRAM® in January 1994

consistently revised in light of new scientific evidence.

This popular youth fitness program includes an excellent health-related fitness test with sound criterion-referenced standards and well-developed educational materials, as well as a computerized reporting system. The program is designed not only to enhance physical fitness, but also to develop affective, cognitive, and behavioral components that enhance participation in regular physical activity. The FITNESSGRAM® provides a recommended test for each component, along with alternative test items that the user may choose instead of the recommended test item. The **ACTIVITYGRAM**® is a physical activity assessment tool that was added to the FITNESSGRAM® in 1999. The ACTIVITYGRAM® was the first attempt within a comprehensive youth fitness program to assess **physical activity,** in addition to physical fitness.

Criterion-Referenced Standards

The goal of the criterion-referenced standard is to define a level of fitness suitable for health promotion. The FITNESSGRAM® program provides standards for "upper and lower" limits of healthy fitness. Figure 13-1 provides an example of the computer output used to score the test and shows the **Healthy Fitness**

Zone. The computer scoring system is an important aspect of the FITNESSGRAM®. It clearly communicates a student's fitness status. The lower level ("good") reflects a "minimally acceptable level of health," and the upper standard ("better") represents a level designed to motivate students and provide a fitness challenge.

With adequate levels of physical activity, all students should be able to achieve the "good" level. The "Healthy Fitness Zone" was developed with the use of the best available public health and exercise physiology data. Cureton and Warren (1990) provide an excellent discussion of the methods used to develop the aerobic capacity healthy fitness zone.

Test Items

The FITNESSGRAM® test items measure three components: (1) **aerobic capacity;** (2) **body composition;** and (3) **muscular strength, muscular endurance,** and **flexibility.** There are five recommended tests and several alternative tests that can be used.

The FITNESSGRAM® test items are listed next.

1. Aerobic Capacity:
   - PACER (recommended test)
   - 1-mile run (alternative test)
   - Walk test (alternative test)

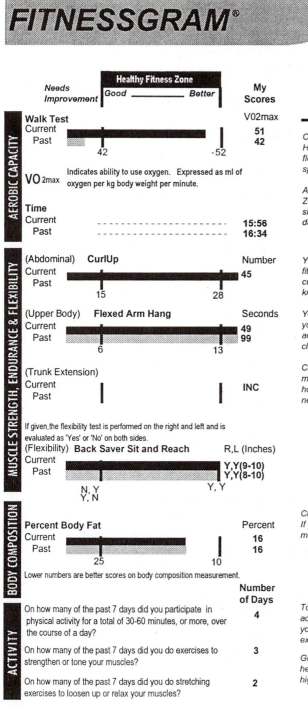

FITNESSGRAM®

Charlie Brown
Grade: 5   Age: 11
Madison County Elementary School
Instructor: Kathy Read

	Test Date	Height	Weight
Past	07/15/99	5'1"	105
Current	07/13/00	5'3"	122

AEROBIC CAPACITY

Healthy Fitness Zone
Needs Improvement | Good — Better | My Scores

Walk Test
Current
Past
42   ·52
My Scores: VO2max 51 / 42

VO 2max Indicates ability to use oxygen. Expressed as ml of oxygen per kg body weight per minute.

Time
Current — 15:56
Past — 16:34

MUSCLE STRENGTH, ENDURANCE & FLEXIBILITY

(Abdominal) CurlUp
Current
Past
15   28
Number 45

(Upper Body) Flexed Arm Hang
Current
Past
6   13
Seconds 49 / 99

(Trunk Extension)
Current
Past
INC

If given, the flexibility test is performed on the right and left and is evaluated as 'Yes' or 'No' on both sides.
(Flexibility) Back Saver Sit and Reach
Current
Past
N, Y / Y, N   Y, Y
R,L (Inches) Y,Y(9-10) / Y,Y(8-10)

BODY COMPOSITION

Percent Body Fat
Current
Past
25   10
Percent 16 / 16

Lower numbers are better scores on body composition measurement.

ACTIVITY

	Number of Days
On how many of the past 7 days did you participate in physical activity for a total of 30-60 minutes, or more, over the course of a day?	4
On how many of the past 7 days did you do exercises to strengthen or tone your muscles?	3
On how many of the past 7 days did you do stretching exercises to loosen up or relax your muscles?	2

MESSAGES

Charlie, your scores on all test items were in or above the Healthy Fitness Zone. You are also doing strength and flexibility exercises. However, you need to play active games, sports or other activities at least 5 days each week.

Although your aerobic capacity score is in the Healthy Fitness Zone now, you are not doing enough physical activity. You should try to play very actively at least 60 minutes at least five days each week to look and feel good.

Your abdominal strength was very good. To maintain your fitness level be sure that your strength activities include curl-ups 3 to 5 days each week. Remember to keep your knees bent. Avoid having someone hold your feet.

Your upper body strength was very good, Charlie. To maintain your fitness level be sure that your strength activities include arm exercises such as push-ups, modified push-ups or climbing activities 2 to 3 days each week.

Charlie, your flexibility is in the Healthy Fitness Zone. To maintain your fitness, stretch slowly 3 or 4 days each week, holding the stretch 20 - 30 seconds. Don't forget that you need to stretch all areas of the body.

Charlie, your body composition is in the Healthy Fitness Zone. If you will be active most days each week, it may help to maintain your level of body composition.

To be healthy and fit it is important to do some physical activity almost every day. Aerobic exercise is good for your heart and body composition. Strength and flexibilty exercises are good for your muscles and joints.

Good job, you are doing enough physical activity for your health. Additional vigorous activity would help to promote higher levels of fitness.

©The Cooper Institute for Aerobics Research

Figure 13-1

Computer printout for the FITNESSGRAM® Youth Fitness Program.
(Source: Reprinted with permission. The Cooper Institute, Dallas, TX.)

2. Body Composition:
   - Percent body fat from sum of triceps and calf skinfolds (recommended test)
   - Body mass index (alternative test)
3. Muscle Strength, Endurance, and Flexibility:
   - Abdominal strength and endurance: curl-up (recommended test)
   - Trunk extensor strength and flexibility: trunk lift (recommended test)
   - Upper body strength and endurance:
     - 90° push-up (recommended test)
     - modified pull-up (alternative test)
     - pull-up (alternative test)
     - flexed arm hang (alternative test)
   - Flexibility (optional):
     - back-saver sit and reach
     - shoulder stretch

Aerobic Capacity

Aerobic capacity may be evaluated with the PACER, 1-mile run, or walk test (secondary students only).

Test PACER 20-Meter Multi-Stage Shuttle Run

Description The PACER 20-meter multi-stage shuttle run is the newest addition to the measures of aerobic capacity used with youth. Leger et al. (1988) presented a regression equation to estimate $\dot{V}O_2$ max from the maximal speed attained during the PACER and age. The PACER starts out slowly and gets faster each minute. This is somewhat similar to a graded exercise test on a treadmill that increases in speed and/or grade at each stage. Students must maintain the pace throughout the test. The pace is controlled by a CD or cassette tape and is set to music. Students continue running back and forth across the 20-meter distance until they are unable to maintain the pace. Thus, the less fit students will end the test first, while the more fit students will continue for a longer period. Students in grades K–3 are encouraged to run as long as they wish, but it is not necessary to make them run to exhaustion. No criterion-referenced standards are provided for students aged 9 years and younger for any of the aerobic capacity tests. The FITNESSGRAM®

computer report simply acknowledges that the younger students have completed the test.

Objective To run as long as possible back and forth across a 20-meter distance while following the specified pace. The pace gets faster each minute and is controlled by an audio recording.

Validity and Reliability Limited evidence of the validity and reliability of the PACER is available in the literature. The equation used for young children in the FITNESSGRAM® to estimate $\dot{V}O_2$ max from PACER performance is this:

$$\dot{V}O_2 \text{ max} = 31.025 + 3.238(\text{speed}) - 3.248(\text{age})$$
$$+ 0.1536(\text{speed} \times \text{age}),$$

where speed is maximal shuttle running speed in $k \cdot hr^{-1}$ attained during the PACER run (Leger et al. 1988). The authors developed this equation on 188 boys and girls aged 8 to 19 years. This equation had a multiple $R = .71$ and *standard error of estimate* $= 5.9$ ml·kg^{-1}·min^{-1}. Small sample sizes of boys and girls were thus used at some or all of the age categories. This suggests that more work needs to be done on the norm-referenced validity evidence of the PACER in children. Norm-referenced reliability estimates for the PACER have generally been high ($R > .80$). Mahar et al. (1997) reported intraclass reliability estimates for one trial of the PACER of $R = .80$ for boys and $R = .79$ for girls.

Criterion-referenced validity and reliability may be of greater interest because the FITNESSGRAM® is a criterion-referenced test; however, little work of this type has been done, especially in young children. Criterion-referenced stability reliability coefficients were reported by Mahar et al. (1997) on 147 boys and 119 girls aged 10 and 11 years. The proportion of agreement for boys was $P = .82$ (modified kappa $= .65$). The proportion of agreement for girls was $P = .97$ (modified kappa $= .94$). The extremely high reliability estimates for girls were due to the very low criterion-referenced standards for girls in this age group (i.e., nearly everyone passed both trials). The FITNESSGRAM® standards for 10- and 11-year-old girls have since been increased.

Of even greater interest might be the criterion-referenced equivalence reliability estimates between the PACER and the 1-mile run. This evidence would suggest the agreement, in terms of categorizing participants as passing or failing, between these two different tests of aerobic capacity. That is, it would suggest whether the standards for these tests are really set equivalently, so that regardless of which test the teacher chooses, the same students will pass or fail. Mahar et al. (1997) reported acceptable criterion-referenced equivalence reliability estimates for boys ($P = .83$, modified kappa $= .65$), but poor agreement between these tests for girls ($P = .66$, modified kappa $= .33$). Higher classification agreement between alternate tests of the same construct (e.g., PACER and 1-mile run) should be expected as criterion-referenced standards are adjusted. Little work on criterion-referenced equivalence reliability estimates has been done. These are the types of measurement studies that physical education teachers can conduct at their own school.

Equipment A flat surface at least 20 meters long with a little room at each end for safety considerations is needed. Because the pace is set by an audio recording, the PACER CD or cassette tape, along with a CD or cassette player that has adequate volume, is needed. The 20-meter distance should be measured with a measuring tape or wheel and the distance marked in some fashion, often with marker cones. The PACER score sheets and pencils are needed to keep track of the lap number and to record the number of laps completed.

Procedures The 20-meter distance (21 yards and 32 inches) should be measured accurately and marked with cones at each side. Instructing the students to run back and forth to the same cone will help them to run in a straight line. Each runner should have an adequate distance (e.g., 40–60 inches wide) for running safely and not running into other runners. Typically, only half the class can run at one time. The other half of the class can participate in other fitness testing stations, or be kept busy by keeping track of the number of laps each one's partner has completed by marking each lap off on the PACER scoresheet.

Students should be allowed at least two practice sessions so that they know how to follow the pace appropriately and know what to expect before they are tested. The teacher can choose either a music version of the PACER or a version with beeps only. The audio recording beeps at the end of each lap to let the runners know that they should continue back to the other side of the 20-meter course.

When the test begins, students run from one side of the 20-meter course to the other side and go around a cone or touch the boundary line with their foot by the time the beep sounds. When runners hear the beep, they return to the original start location. The test continues in this manner until the student can no longer maintain the pace for two laps. The goal is to complete as many laps as possible.

The pace starts out slowly and increases each minute. The PACER allows the runner 9 seconds to cover the 20-meter distance at the start. The time allowed to complete each lap is then decreased by one-half second every minute. By allowing practice before testing, students will learn that they should not start out the test running too fast.

Scoring The score on the PACER is the number of laps completed. A lap is one 20-meter distance. The first time that a student does not reach the line by the time the beep sounds, he or she should reverse direction immediately and try to catch up with the pace. When a student fails to reach the line by the time of the beep a second time, his or her test is ended. The first lap in which the student does not reach the beep is counted as a lap completed for scoring purposes. An alternative scoring procedure is available that allows students to continue running for as long as they want until the leader stops, whereby only the number of laps successfully completed as described above is recorded. For this alternative scoring procedure, no student is forced to stop running; however, his or her score for the number of laps successfully completed is consistent with the traditional scoring procedure.

TABLE 13.3	FITNESSGRAM® Criterion-Referenced Standards for the PACER, 1-Mile Run, and Walk Tests for Boys		
Age	PACER (# laps)	1-Mile Run (min:sec)	Walk Test ($\dot{V}O_2$ max in mL·kg⁻¹·min⁻¹)
5			
6	Participation	Participation	Recommended
7	only	only	for secondary
8	No standards	No standards	students only
9	recommended	recommended	
10	23 61	11:30 9:00	
11	23 72	11:00 8:30	
12	32 72	10:30 8:00	
13	41 72	10:00 7:30	42 52
14	41 83	9:30 7:00	42 52
15	51 94	9:00 7:00	42 52
16	61 94	8:30 7:00	42 52
17	61 94	8:30 7:00	42 52
17+	61 94	8:30 7:00	42 52

Note: The number on the left is the lower end of the Healthy Fitness Zone that the student must reach to pass the test. This value is labeled as "Good" on the computer printout and represents a level thought to decrease one's risk of diseases related to a sedentary lifestyle. The number on the right is the upper end of the Healthy Fitness Zone and is labeled as "Better" on the computer printout.

Standards   The number of laps successfully completed on the PACER is compared to the criterion-referenced standards that are presented in Table 13.3 for boys and in Table 13.4 for girls. The FITNESSGRAM® provides standards for the Healthy Fitness Zone. If a student's performance is within the Healthy Fitness Zone, then his or her performance is considered adequate for health promotion purposes. If a student's score is worse than the Healthy Fitness Zone, then he or she is categorized as "Needs Improvement." Performance standards have not been established for students in grades K–3. Concerns exist regarding the reliability and validity of aerobic capacity tests for very young children. The goals for these students are participation in the PACER, learning how to take the test and pace oneself, and enjoying the activity.

Comment   The PACER is unique as a test of aerobic fitness. For the traditional distance run test of the 1-mile run/walk, the least-fit participants will finish the mile distance last (i.e., it takes them longer to run a mile). For the PACER, the least-fit participants will

finish first, because they will not be able to keep up with the pace as long as the more fit participants. The alternative scoring system may allow for the less fit children to feel better about their performance, because they can try until they choose to stop.

Test   1-Mile Run

Description   The 1-mile run is an alternative test of aerobic capacity. Students are encouraged to run 1 mile as fast as possible. Walking is permitted for students who cannot run the entire mile.

Objective   To cover the 1-mile distance as fast as possible. This is a maximal test and depends to a great extent on the participant providing his or her best effort.

Validity and Reliability   Cureton et al. (1995) provided the best evidence of the accuracy of the 1-mile run in youth. They developed a regression equation to estimate $\dot{V}O_2$ max from 1-mile run performance, age, gender, and body mass index (BMI)

TABLE 13.4	FITNESSGRAM® Criterion-Referenced Standards for the PACER, 1-Mile Run, and Walk Tests for Girls					
Age	PACER (# laps)		1-Mile Run (min:sec)		Walk Test ($\dot{V}O_2$ max in mL·kg^{-1}·min^{-1})	
5						
6	Participation		Participation		Recommended	
7	only		only		for secondary	
8	No Standards		No Standards		students only	
9	recomended		recomended			
10	15	41	12:30	9:30		
11	15	41	12:00	9:00		
12	23	41	12:00	9:00		
13	23	51	11:30	9:00	37	45
14	23	51	11:00	8:30	36	44
15	23	51	10:30	8:00	35	43
16	32	61	10:00	8:00	35	43
17	41	61	10:00	8:00	35	43
17+	41	61	10:00	8:00	35	43

Note: The number on the left is the lower end of the Healthy Fitness Zone that the student must reach to pass the test. This value is labeled as "Good" on the computer printout and represents a level thought to decrease one's risk of diseases related to a sedentary lifestyle. The number on the right is the upper end of the Healthy Fitness Zone and is labeled as "Better" on the computer printout.

that provides reasonable accuracy. The equation used in the FITNESSGRAM® is as follows:

$$\dot{V}O_2 \text{ max} = 108.94 + 0.21(\text{age} \times \text{gender})$$
$$- 0.84(\text{BMI}) - 8.41(1\text{-mile time})$$
$$+ 0.34(1\text{-mile time}^2)$$

where gender is coded as 1 = male and 0 = female, and 1-mile run time is in minutes. The authors developed this equation on over 750 males and females 8 to 25 years old. This equation has a multiple $R = .72$ and a standard error of estimate $=4.84$ ml·kg^{-1}·min^{-1}. This paper provides an excellent example of a study that provides concurrent evidence of validity. Rikli et al. (1992) examined the norm-referenced and criterion-referenced reliability of the 1-mile run and several tests of shorter distance for K–4 students. They reported acceptable intraclass reliability estimates ($R > .80$) for children in grades 3 and 4, but lower estimates for younger children.

Cureton and Warren (1990) evaluated the validity of the FITNESSGRAM® standards on over 500 children aged 7 to 14 years old and reported that 85% of the children were correctly classified. Rikli et al. (1992) reported consistently acceptable criterion-referenced reliability estimates ($P > .80$) for 8- and 9-year-old children, but less consistent results for 5- through 7-year-old children (.45 $< P <$ .85).

Equipment The 1-mile run can be administered on any track or other flat measured area (e.g., 100-meter straight-away, outside fields, indoor courts). Sample courses are shown in Figure 13-2. If the course is too short, the large number of turns required may affect mile run performance. A stopwatch to time the run and recording forms are needed.

Procedures Students should run on a clearly marked course for 1 mile. The time for each lap is typically called out by the teacher and recorded by the runner's partner. The time to complete the mile is recorded. For this test it is important that students are properly prepared. This means that they should have adequate practice running distances and know

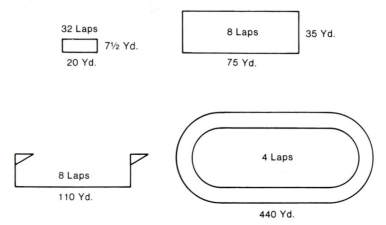

Figure 13-2
Test courses for administering distance run tests.

how to properly pace themselves. Students who must walk should be encouraged to walk at a fast pace and to start running again when they are able. Proper warm-up and cool-down procedures should be followed.

Scoring   A lower time is better for the 1-mile run test. No performance standards were established for children 9 years old and younger due to concerns with reliability and validity of distance run tests in young children.

Standards   FITNESSGRAM® criterion-referenced standards for the 1-mile run are presented in Table 13.3 for boys and Table 13.4 for girls. The interpretation of the results is similar to that for the PACER. If participants are within the Healthy Fitness Zone, then their aerobic fitness level is probably adequate for health purposes. If the participant does not meet the standard, then he or she is classified as Needs Improvement and is encouraged to participate in activities that can improve aerobic capacity. Because of concerns with reliability and validity of distance run tests with young children, no standards are provided for children aged 9 years or younger.

Comment   The 1-mile run has been a popular field test of aerobic capacity, but has been criticized

because many students are not highly motivated to perform at their maximum effort. Factors other than motivation, such as body fatness, running economy, and maturity, also affect distance run performance.

Test   Walk Test

Description   The walk test is an alternative test of aerobic capacity that can be used with participants ages 13 years and older. Participants are instructed to walk 1 mile at the fastest possible pace that they can maintain for the entire test. Less motivation is required of participants to walk one mile than to run one mile; however, participants still need to walk the distance as quickly as possible. Heart rate during the final 15 seconds of the test should be recorded. $\dot{V}O_2$ max is estimated from walk time, heart rate, body weight, and gender.

Objective   To walk 1 mile as quickly as possible at a constant pace.

Validity and Reliability   Kline et al. (1987) published a formula commonly called the Rockport Fitness Walking Test to estimate $\dot{V}O_2$ max $(mL \cdot kg^{-1} \cdot min^{-1})$ from the walk test. The regression formula is this:

$$\dot{V}O_2 \text{ max} = 132.853 - 0.0769(\text{weight})$$
$$- 0.3877(\text{age}) + 6.315(\text{gender})$$
$$- 3.2649(\text{walk time}) - 0.1565(\text{heart rate})$$

where weight is in pounds, gender is coded as 1 = male and 0 = female, walk time is in minutes, and heart rate is measured during the last 15 seconds of the walk. This equation was developed on 343 males and females aged 30 to 69 years. This formula had a multiple $R = .88$ and $SEE = 5.0$ mL·kg^{-1}·min^{-1}.

McSwegin et al. (1998) cross-validated the walk test on male and female high school students. They reported a multiple $R = .80$ and $SEE = 4.99$ mL·kg^{-1}·min^{-1}. Norm-referenced reliability estimates for the walk test were calculated on 21 males and females. A high intraclass reliability estimate was reported for estimated $\dot{V}O_2$ max ($R > .90$), although lower reliability estimates were found for walk time ($R = .67$) and heart rate ($R = .60$).

Criterion-referenced validity of the walk test was also reported by McSwegin et al. (1998). They found that 88% of the 24 females and 95% of the 20 males were correctly classified using the FITNESSGRAM® criterion-referenced standards of 35 mL·kg^{-1}·min^{-1} for females and 42 mL·kg^{-1}·min^{-1} for males. Criterion-referenced stability reliability was estimated on 21 participants. All students were consistently classified ($P = 1.0$).

Equipment The walk test can be administered on any track or other flat measured area (similar to the space required for the 1-mile run). Sample courses are shown in Figure 13-2. A stopwatch to time the walk and recording forms are needed. Use of heart rate monitors makes administration of the test much easier. If heart rate monitors are not available, then accurate measurement of heart rate at the conclusion of the walk is essential for accurate estimates of $\dot{V}O_2$ max.

Procedures Participants should walk the 1-mile distance at the fastest possible pace. They should maintain the same pace throughout the test. At the completion of the test, the elapsed time is recorded and heart rate must be measured. Recording of the elapsed time is often accomplished by having a partner record the number of laps and finish times on a recording form. If heart rate monitors are used, then the heart rate at the end of the walk is recorded. If heart rate monitors are unavailable, the participant should count his or her heart rate for 15 seconds immediately after completing the test. The 15-second heart rate is multiplied by 4 to get heart rate in beats per minute.

Scoring The variables needed to estimate $\dot{V}O_2$ max from the walk test include body weight, age, gender, walk time, and heart rate response to the walk. The estimated $\dot{V}O_2$ max is compared to the FITNESSGRAM® criterion-referenced standards. Thus, it is the value estimated from the walk test that is compared to criterion-referenced standards, rather than the value measured during the test itself.

Standards The estimated $\dot{V}O_2$ max from the walk test is compared to the criterion-referenced standards that are presented in Table 13.3 for boys and in Table 13.4 for girls. The criterion-referenced standard for boys is 42 mL·kg^{-1}·min^{-1} to pass the test. For girls, the criterion-referenced standard for passing the test varies with age, but is 35 mL·kg^{-1}·min^{-1} for girls ages 15 years and older.

Comment It is important to emphasize to the students that they should walk at a constant pace for the entire test. Walking faster at the end of the test will increase heart rate, and that will affect the estimated $\dot{V}O_2$ max. Practice in pacing the walk will improve the accuracy of test results. An accurate measure of heart rate is important. Therefore, if students are to measure their own heart rate at the end of the walk, they should have adequate practice in this skill. If high school students learn to administer this test, it is one that they can self-administer throughout their life to monitor their levels of aerobic capacity.

Body Composition

Body composition can be measured by percent body fat estimated from the sum of triceps and calf skinfolds, or by body mass index. The equations developed by Slaughter et al. (1988) are used to estimate percent body fat. The body mass index (BMI) is an alternative body composition test.

Test   Skinfold Measurements to Estimate Percent Body Fat

Description   The triceps and calf **skinfolds** are measured and used to estimate **percent body fat.** A double layer of skin and fat is pinched at these sites with skinfold calipers. Skinfold calipers can cost over $200, but even inexpensive plastic calipers (approximately $5), when used appropriately, provide accurate measurements of skinfolds. The triceps and calf skinfolds are both easy to measure and do not require that a student remove any clothing. Skinfold measures should always be taken in a setting that provides privacy and reduces potential embarrassment.

Objective   To measure triceps and calf skinfolds and to use these measurements to estimate percent body fat.

Validity and Reliability   Skinfolds can be measured with a high degree of reliability among trained testers. Testers can be trained in a measurement class as long as adequate practice taking skinfolds is provided. Use of videotapes is an effective way to learn proper skinfold testing procedures (Shaw 1986). More detailed information regarding skinfold assessment is presented in Chapter 12. Slaughter et al. (1988) published the regression equations used in the FITNESSGRAM® to estimate percent body fat from the sum of triceps and calf skinfolds. The separate regression equations for boys and girls are provided next.

Boys: Percent body fat = (Sum of triceps and calf skinfolds × 0.735) + 1

Girls: Percent body fat = (Sum of triceps and calf skinfolds × 0.61) + 5.1

These equations were developed on 310 subjects aged 8 to 29 years. The multiple $R = .88$ and $SEE = 3.8\%$ fat.

An abundance of evidence exists for the accurate measurement of body composition through skinfolds. Physical educators should make it a pri-ority to learn to take skinfolds and then to measure their students and provide appropriate feedback. This information is important for students in terms of monitoring their health, and may even help extremely thin students who have eating disorders to understand that they are in or below the Healthy Fitness Zone.

Equipment   A skinfold caliper is needed. Either expensive or inexpensive plastic calipers have been shown to provide accurate measures of skinfolds. A privacy barrier should be used when measuring skinfolds in order to protect students' confidentiality.

Procedures   The triceps skinfold is measured on the back of the right arm over the triceps muscle. The site is located midway between the shoulder (acromion process) and the elbow. The pinch is made slightly above the midway point so that the skinfold calipers can be placed directly on the site. For the calf skinfold, students place their right foot on a stool so that the knee is at a 90° angle. The calf skinfold site is located on the right leg, medially at the largest calf girth. The pinch is made slightly above the largest girth so that the skinfold calipers can be placed directly on the site. Pictures of these skinfold sites can be seen in Figure 13-3.

For college students, the FITNESSGRAM® also uses the abdominal skinfold to estimate percent body fat. The abdominal skinfold site is located 3 cm to the side of the umbilicus on the right side of the body. This skinfold is horizontal, which differs from the vertical abdominal skinfold described in Chapter 12. Proper skinfold measurement procedures are detailed in Chapter 12.

Scoring   Each skinfold is measured three times and the median value is recorded to the nearest 0.5 mm. Percent body fat is then estimated from the formulas of Slaughter et al. (1988) already presented in this section.

Standards   The estimated percent body fat from skinfolds is compared to the criterion-referenced standards. The Healthy Fitness Zone for boys is 10% to 25% fat. Thus, boys with less than 25% fat

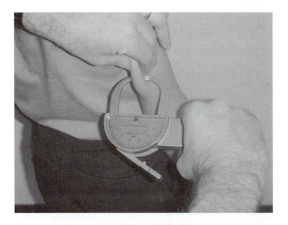

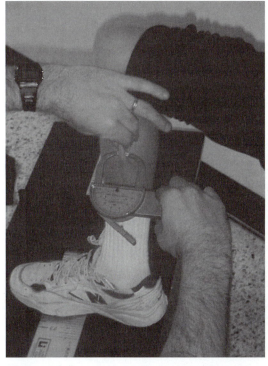

Figure 13-3
Caliper placement for the triceps and calf skinfolds.

are considered lean enough for reducing the risk of inactivity-related diseases. The FITNESSGRAM® presents an "Optimal Range" within the Healthy Fitness Zone of percent body fat for boys of 10% to 20% fat. For girls, the Healthy Fitness Zone is 17% to 32% fat. The Optimal Range for girls is 15% to 25% fat.

Comment Remember to consider the child's feelings when taking skinfold measures and to provide privacy. If skinfold measures are to be repeated on the same students later in the year or on subsequent years, we recommend that the same tester take the measures. In addition, teachers should measure the same gender student whenever possible. Once you measure about 75 to 100 participants and your measures compare closely with those of an experienced tester, you can consider yourself trained in taking skinfolds. When interpreting results, keep in mind that although skinfolds provide an accurate estimate of percent body fat, a 3% to 5% measurement error exists.

Test Body Mass Index

Description The body mass index (BMI) is an alternative to the skinfold test. BMI is calculated from height and weight, but does not provide a measure of body fatness. BMI provides a measure of weight relative to height. BMI can misclassify individuals who are lean, but muscular, as overfat. In addition, a person who does not weigh much, but has a high percent fat with little muscular development, may be misclassified into the Healthy Fitness Zone. Because of the potential for misclassification by BMI on this important component of health, we recommend that all physical education teachers learn to measure skinfolds accurately. The FITNESSGRAM® computer program only calculates BMI when skinfold measurements are not entered.

Objective To measure height and weight and calculate a measure of weight relative to height.

Validity and Reliability Because height and weight can be measured accurately and consistently on calibrated scales, BMI can be measured with a high degree of reliability. For most people, health problems associated with obesity increase when BMI is greater than 25 $kg \cdot m^{-2}$. However, percent body fat cannot be estimated accurately from BMI.

Equipment Scales to accurately measure height and weight are needed.

Procedures   Height and weight should be measured accurately. Height can be measured by having students stand against a tape measure attached to a wall. Weight should be measured with an accurate scale, and students should be afforded privacy during the measurement.

Scoring   BMI is calculated as weight in kilograms divided by the square of height in meters with the following formula:

$$BMI = Weight\ (kilograms) \div Height^2 (meters)$$

Weight in pounds and height in inches can be converted to the metric units with the following formulas:

$$Kilograms = pounds \div 2.2$$
$$Meters = inches \times 0.0254$$

Standards   The BMI is compared to the criterion-referenced standards presented in Table 13.5.

The Healthy Fitness Zone increases slightly with age for both boys and girls.

Comment   Although BMI is probably easier to measure than skinfolds, it does not provide a measure of body fatness. A high BMI is related to increased health problems in the general population; however, some individuals have a high BMI because of their musculature rather than because of an excessive accumulation of fat. In adults, a BMI of 25 to 29.9 $kg \cdot m^{-2}$ is categorized as overweight and a BMI $\geq$ 30 $kg \cdot m^{-2}$ is categorized as obese (Expert Panel 1998).

Muscle Strength, Endurance, and Flexibility

The FITNESSGRAM® includes strength, endurance, and flexibility test items of the upper body and abdominal/trunk region. It is hypothesized that scoring in the Healthy Fitness Zone on these items will promote functional health and correct posture.

TABLE 13.5	**FITNESSGRAM® and President's Challenge Health Fitness Test Criterion-Referenced Standards for Body Mass Index ($kg \cdot m^{-2}$)**						
	Boys				**Girls**		
Age	**FITNESSGRAM®**		**President's Challenge**		**FITNESSGRAM®**		**President's Challenge**
5	20	14.7			21	16.2		
6	20	14.7	19.5	13.3	21	16.2	19.5	13.3
7	20	14.9	19.5	13.3	22	16.2	19.5	13.3
8	20	15.1	20.5	13.4	22	16.2	20.5	13.4
9	20	15.2	21.4	13.7	23	16.2	21.4	13.7
10	21	15.3	22.5	14.0	23.5	16.6	22.5	14.0
11	21	15.8	23.7	14.0	24	16.9	23.7	14.0
12	22	16.0	24.1	14.8	24.5	16.9	24.1	14.8
13	23	16.6	24.7	15.4	24.5	17.5	24.7	15.4
14	24.5	17.5	25.4	16.1	25	17.5	25.4	16.1
15	25	18.1	26.4	16.6	25	17.5	26.4	16.6
16	26.5	18.5	26.8	17.2	25	17.5	26.8	17.2
17	27	18.8	27.5	17.7	26	17.5	27.5	17.7
17+	27.8	19.0			27.3	18.0		

Note: For the FITNESSGRAM®, the number on the left is the lower end of the Healthy Fitness Zone that the student must reach to pass the test. This value is labeled "Good" on the computer printout and represents a level thought to decrease one's risk of diseases related to a sedentary lifestyle. The number on the right is the upper end of the Healthy Fitness Zone and is labeled "Better" on the computer printout. For the President's Challenge Health Fitness Test, the desirable range is presented and can be interpreted in a similar fashion.

Test Curl-Up

Description The curl-up is a test of abdominal strength and endurance. The curl-up is a modification of the traditional sit-up test, whereby the feet are not held and only the initial phase of the sit-up is completed. These procedures were implemented to isolate the abdominal muscles and minimize the involvement of the hip flexor muscles. The test is completed at a specified cadence of 20 curl-ups per minute.

Objective To complete as many curl-ups as possible at a specified cadence of 20 curl-ups per minute. If a student is able to do 75 curl-ups, the test is stopped.

Validity and Reliability The curl-up test possesses evidence of logical validity. Research supported by electromyography has demonstrated that abdominal muscles are being used during the curl-up (Godfrey et al. 1977; Noble 1981). Little research has been conducted on the reliability of the curl-up for young children. Because the proper form is necessary for a correctly completed curl-up, more research also needs to be done on the objectivity of curl-ups in youth. Validity and reliability can be improved by providing sufficient instruction and practice before testing.

Equipment Mats or other comfortable surfaces and measuring strips are needed. The measuring strip is used to help participants know how far to curl up. A 3-inch-wide measuring strip is used for children aged 5 to 9 years. Older participants use a 4.5-inch-wide measuring strip. An audio recording, to maintain the cadence of the curl-up at 20 curl-ups per minute, and a CD or cassette player are needed.

Procedures The cadence of 1 curl-up every 3 seconds is regulated with the CD or tape or by the teacher until a maximum of 75 is reached. The student being tested assumes a supine position on a mat with the knees bent at about 140° and feet flat on the floor. The arms are straight and parallel to the trunk with the palms resting on the mat.

The measuring strip is placed under the knees with the fingers touching the nearest edge. The student slowly curls up while keeping his or her heels in contact with the mat. A completed repetition involves curling up so that the fingers slide to the other side of the strip.

Scoring The score is the number of curl-ups completed. The student is stopped when 75 curl-ups are completed or after the second curl-up performed with incorrect form.

Standards The number of curl-ups completed is compared to the criterion-referenced standards that are presented in Table 13.6 for boys and Table 13.7 for girls.

Comment It is important to allow students time to practice and learn the skill of the curl-up. If testing is done before students have adequate practice, many procedural errors can be expected, and it will be more difficult to count the correctly completed curl-ups.

Test Trunk Lift

Description The trunk lift test measures the student's trunk extensor strength and flexibility. The test requires the student to lift the upper body to a maximum of 12 inches off the floor using the back muscles.

Objective To lift the upper body off the floor from a prone position.

Validity and Reliability The trunk lift test possesses evidence of logical validity. This test is a measure of trunk extension strength and flexibility, and the trunk lift movement requires these attributes for successful completion. Most students will easily pass this test. The fact that trunk extension strength and flexibility is being measured emphasizes to the students the importance of this area of the body to low back health.

Equipment Mats and a measuring stick (yardstick or 15-inch ruler) are required. The measuring stick should be marked at 6, 9, and 12 inches.

TABLE 13.6	Criterion-Referenced Standards for the FITNESSGRAM® for Boys										
Age	Curl-Up (Number)		Trunk Lift (Inches)		90° Push-Up (Number)		Modified Pull-Up (Number)		Pull-Up (Number)		Flexed Arm Hang (Seconds)	
5	2	10	6	12	3	8	2	7	1	2	2	8
6	2	10	6	12	3	8	2	7	1	2	2	8
7	4	14	6	12	4	10	3	9	1	2	3	8
8	6	20	6	12	5	13	4	11	1	2	3	8
9	9	24	6	12	6	15	5	11	1	2	4	10
10	12	24	9	12	7	20	5	15	1	2	4	10
11	15	28	9	12	8	20	6	17	1	3	6	13
12	18	36	9	12	10	20	7	20	1	3	6	13
13	21	40	9	12	12	25	8	22	1	4	12	17
14	24	45	9	12	14	30	9	25	2	5	15	20
15	24	47	9	12	16	35	10	27	3	7	15	20
16	24	47	9	12	18	35	12	30	5	8	15	20
17	24	47	9	12	18	35	14	30	5	8	15	20
>17	24	47	9	12	18	35	14	30	5	8	15	20

Note: The number on the left is the minimum score needed to pass for each test and the number on the right is the more desirable standard for each test.

TABLE 13.7	Criterion-Referenced Standards for the FITNESSGRAM® for Girls										
Age	Curl-Up (Number)		Trunk Lift (Inches)		90° Push-Up (Number)		Modified Pull-Up (Number)		Pull-Up (Number)		Flexed Arm Hang (Seconds)	
5	2	10	6	12	3	8	2	7	1	2	2	8
6	2	10	6	12	3	8	2	7	1	2	2	8
7	4	14	6	12	4	10	3	9	1	2	3	8
8	6	20	6	12	5	13	4	11	1	2	3	10
9	9	22	6	12	6	15	4	11	1	2	4	10
10	12	26	9	12	7	15	4	13	1	2	4	10
11	15	29	9	12	7	15	4	13	1	2	6	12
12	18	32	9	12	7	15	4	13	1	2	7	12
13	18	32	9	12	7	15	4	13	1	2	8	12
14	18	32	9	12	7	15	4	13	1	2	8	12
15	18	35	9	12	7	15	4	13	1	2	8	12
16	18	35	9	12	7	15	4	13	1	2	8	12
17	18	35	9	12	7	15	4	13	1	2	8	12
>17	18	35	9	12	7	15	4	13	1	2	8	12

Note: The number on the left is the minimum score needed to pass for each test and the number on the right is the more desirable standard for each test.

Procedures   The student starts the test lying face down on a mat with his or her hands under the thighs. The test involves lifting the upper body up to a maximum height of 12 inches. The student holds the position until the height of the lift can be measured with a ruler. The height is measured from the floor to the chin.

Scoring   Each student is given two trials. The score is the height the chin is held off the floor, measured to the nearest inch. Students are encouraged not to exceed 12 inches, because excessive arching can cause compression of the discs in the back.

Standards   FITNESSGRAM® criterion-referenced standards for the trunk lift are presented in Table 13.6 for boys and Table 13.7 for girls.

Comment   Health-related fitness tests often note that lower back problems affect the majority of people at some time in their life; however, this is the first youth fitness program to actually include a measure of lower back strength and flexibility. The measures of abdominal strength and flexibility (e.g., curl-up or sit-up) and lower back and hamstring flexibility (e.g., sit and reach test) have been included in health-related fitness testing batteries because of their perceived relationship with lower back health. The inclusion of this test on the FITNESSGRAM® provides a good opportunity for teaching students about specificity of training and about the importance of adequate strength and flexibility of the lower back. Safety must be guarded carefully on this test. Students should be instructed to lift the upper body in a slow and controlled manner and not to raise it higher than 12 inches from the floor. The maximum value the FITNESSGRAM® software will accept for this test is 12 inches.

Test   90° Push-Up

Description   The test involves completing as many push-ups as possible at a set cadence of 1 push-up every 3 seconds.

Objective   To complete as many push-ups as possible at a specific cadence of 20 push-ups per minute.

Validity and Reliability   Few studies have been conducted on the psychometric properties of the push-up test. Saint Romain and Mahar (2001) reported high intraclass reliability estimates for one trial of the push-up for boys ($R = .99$) and girls ($R = .94$) in grades 5 and 6. However, contradictory results were reported by McManis, Baumgartner,

and Wuest (2000). In their study, intraclass reliability estimates for one trial were variable ($R = .87$ for high school girls, $R = .50$ for high school boys, $R = .64$ for elementary school girls, and $R = .71$ for elementary school boys). Scores were higher when students counted the push-ups than when trained testers counted the push-ups. McManis et al. concluded that elementary students were not capable of counting push-ups accurately. The higher reliability in the Saint Romain and Mahar study, compared to the McManis et al. study, may be explained by the amount of practice provided to the students. Saint Romain and Mahar had students participate once a week for four weeks at a push-up station as part of a fitness training unit, where students received feedback on correct form. Participants in the McManis et al. study practiced for only one day. Even when judges trained together, objectivity estimates on college-age students' push-up scores ranged from low ($R = .16$) to high ($R = .91$; McManis et al. 2000). Potential problems with judging the push-up arise from determining correct body position (e.g., elbow angle at the down position, acceptable degree of back arch). Other difficulties arise from the slow cadence, which makes the test particularly difficult for young children, and variable interpretation of correct hand placement. More research is needed to examine the reliability and objectivity of the push-up used in the FITNESSGRAM®. Evidence of concurrent validity of the push-up has been examined in several studies. Correlations with criterion tests of upper body strength have been low to moderate. The tests that have been selected as criteria by various authors include the bench press, latissimus pull-down, and arm curl. The low concurrent validity evidence of the push-up may be related to questions regarding the appropriate criterion measure, as well as to the confounding effect of body weight on the test and criterion. That is, for the push-up test body weight is moved, but for the criterion measures that have been used in previous research, body weight is not moved. Much more research on the validity of the FITNESSGRAM® push-up needs to be conducted. Validity and reliability can be improved by providing sufficient instruction and practice before testing.

Equipment   Mats or other comfortable surfaces are needed, as well as an audio recording with the correct cadence and a CD or cassette player.

Procedures   Students work in pairs, one taking the test while the other counts the number of completed push-ups. The test taker starts face down with hands under the shoulders and body straight. From this position, the student pushes his or her body up, while keeping the body straight, until the arms are straight. Then the student lowers his or her body, while keeping the body straight, until the arms bend to a 90° angle and the upper arms are parallel to the floor. The student then pushes up to the straight-arm position. This is repeated at a cadence of 20 repetitions per minute (1 push-up every 3 seconds). The test is continued until the student cannot maintain the pace or demonstrates poor form.

Scoring   The score is the number of push-ups completed.

Standards   The number of push-ups completed is compared to the criterion-referenced standards that are presented in Table 13.6 for boys and Table 13.7 for girls.

Comment   It is important to allow students time to practice and learn the 90° push-up. Adequate practice will allow students to know how much they should bend their arms for each push-up. Also, young students especially need instruction on keeping the body straight during the push-up. With the push-up, half of the class can be tested at one time. This is not true for the modified pull-up, where one student at a time is tested. In addition, most students can do one or more push-ups, so few scores of zero are seen. This is not always the case for the traditional pull-up and flexed arm hang. The push-up is also an activity that can be done throughout one's life. However, it is often difficult to get students to perform this test using the proper form. For example, the arms may not bend to the correct angle on each push-up, the body may not be kept straight throughout the push-up, and many children let their thighs touch the ground on each

push-up. These problems are easier to control on the modified pull-up, but administration of the modified pull-up takes more time because the modified pull-up stand can be used by only one person at a time.

Test   Modified Pull-Up

Description   A modified pull-up stand is used for this test. Participants take a position at the stand with their hands on the bar and heels on the floor (see Figure 13-4). The back is just a few inches from the floor. While keeping the heels on the floor, the student pulls his or her chin above an elastic band suspended 7 to 8 inches below the bar and then lowers the body until the arms are straight. This is modified from the traditional pull-up, in that the heels are kept on the ground at all times. Thus, this test is easier than the traditional pull-up and few zero scores result.

Objective   To complete as many modified pull-ups as possible.

Validity and Reliability   Saint Romain and Mahar (2001) examined the norm-referenced and criterion-referenced reliability of the modified pull-up in 30 boys and 32 girls aged 10 to 13 years. Very high intraclass reliability estimates were found for one trial of the modified pull-up in both boys and

Figure 13-4
FITNESSGRAM® modified pull-up test.

girls ($R \geq .94$). Engelman and Morrow (1991) reported lower two-way intraclass reliability estimates for children in grades 3 through 5 ($R = .77$ for boys; $R = .81$ for girls). Criterion-referenced reliability estimates were also high for boys ($P = .93$, modified kappa $= .87$) and girls ($P = .97$, modified kappa $= .94$).

The equivalence reliability estimates between the FITNESSGRAM® push-up and modified pull-up provide an indication of whether the standards for the two upper body strength tests are set equivalently so that students are categorized in the same way (either passing or failing) by both tests. Criterion-referenced equivalence reliability estimates were moderate, with only about 70% of both boys and girls being classified similarly by the modified pull-up and the push-up. The correlation (i.e., norm-referenced equivalence reliability) between the two tests was .64 for boys and .70 for girls (Saint Romain & Mahar 2001). Engelman and Morrow (1991) reported correlations between the modified pull-up and traditional pull-up of .63 for 242 boys in grades 3 through 5. The correlation for 228 girls in grades 3 through 5 was .60.

Equipment   A modified pull-up stand is needed. This can be made out of wood or PVC pipe, but should be sturdy, because of the type of use it will probably get.

Procedures   The student assumes a position under the modified pull-up bar on his or her back. The bar should be set about 1 to 2 inches above the person's reach. An elastic band is placed 7 to 8 inches below the bar using an overhand grasp. The student then pulls up until the chin is above the elastic band. The body is kept straight throughout the motion and the heels remain in contact with the floor. The body is then lowered until the arms are straight. This pull-up motion is performed continuously until no more modified pull-ups can be completed or until the student starts to use incorrect form.

Scoring   The score is the number of modified pull-ups performed.

Standards   The number of modified pull-ups completed is compared to the criterion-referenced standards that are presented in Table 13.6 for boys and Table 13.7 for girls.

Comment   The modified pull-up may be the best field test of upper body strength available to teachers. There is some expense in obtaining a modified pull-up stand, but the stand can be made inexpensively with PVC pipe. One drawback to the modified pull-up is that only one student can be tested at a time. However, it is much easier to administer the modified pull-up so that the correct form is used than to do so for other tests of upper body strength. It is very difficult to get all students to adhere to the proper form during the push-up test. The problem of zero scores for the traditional pull-up and flexed arm hang does not exist for the modified pull-up, because most students can do one or more. Teaching the proper procedure and then using the modified pull-up as one of several fitness testing stations can ease the burden of having to test one student at a time and make it easier to use the modified pull-up.

Test   Pull-Up

Description   The pull-up test is the traditional test that was used to test the upper body strength of boys in the AAHPER Youth Fitness Test, which was first published in 1958. The participant pulls his or her body weight from a straight-armed free-hanging position to a position with the chin above the bar. The pull-up test has fallen out of favor and is not often used in physical education classes because many students are unable to perform even one pull-up, and body weight has a large effect on test performance (Cotten 1990; Pate et al. 1987). Also, this test does not appear to be sensitive to changes in upper body strength.

Objective   To complete as many pull-ups as possible.

Validity and Reliability   Engelman and Morrow (1991) reported high ($R \geq .83$ for boys; $R \geq .91$ for girls) two-way intraclass reliability estimates for one trial of the pull-up for students in grades 3 through 5. Cotten (1990) reported comparable results. Several researchers have examined evidence of concurrent validity of the pull-up with various criterion measures. Correlations between the pull-up and 1-repetition maximum (1-RM) bench press scores have been low ($R = .27$) to moderate ($R = .56$). Even lower correlations were found when pull-up scores were correlated with latissimus pull-down 1-RM scores (Ball 1993; Pate et al. 1993; Rutherford & Corbin 1994).

Equipment   A horizontal bar positioned at a height that allows the student to hang freely above the floor is needed.

Procedures   The bar should be adjusted to a height that allows students to hang freely above the floor with their arms extended. Using an overhand grasp (palms forward), the body is pulled upward until the chin is above the bar and then lowered until the arms are straight. This movement is repeated as many times as possible. The student is not allowed to kick or use a kip movement. The teacher can help to keep the student from swinging by placing an arm in front of the student's thighs.

Scoring   The score is the number of pull-ups performed. The FITNESSGRAM® software will not accept a score of zero for the pull-up. If students cannot do 1 pull-up, you should choose another test of upper body strength.

Standards   The number of pull-ups completed is compared to the criterion-referenced standards that are presented in Table 13.6 for boys and in Table 13.7 for girls. The passing standard for girls and for boys up through age 13 years is 1 pull-up.

Comment   The pull-up test is generally not chosen by teachers as the measure of upper body strength. The large number of students who score zero on the pull-up may present a motivational problem. For this reason, the modified pull-up is probably a better choice than the pull-up for physical education teachers.

Test   Flexed Arm Hang

Description   The flexed arm hang test was used to test the upper body strength of girls in the AAHPER Youth Fitness Test. The student holds his or her chin above a horizontal bar with arms in a flexed position.

Objective   To hang with the chin above the bar for as long as possible.

Validity and Reliability   Pate et al. (1993) reported high intraclass reliability estimates ($R \geq .85$) for 9- to 10-year-old boys and girls for one trial of the flexed arm hang. The flexed arm hang has also been shown to be a reliable measure in college students (DiNucci, McCune, & Shows, 1990). When evidence of concurrent validity was examined in 9- to 10-year-old children, low correlations of $R = -.23$ for boys and $R = -.12$ for girls with the criterion of the arm curl were found.

Equipment   A horizontal bar positioned at a height that allows the student to hang without touching the ground and a stopwatch are needed.

Procedures   Using an overhand grasp (palms forward), the student lifts his or her body upward until the chin is above the bar. The student can be assisted into this position by the teacher. The elbows should be flexed and the chest held close to the bar. The stopwatch is started when the student is in position. The student attempts to hold this position as long as possible. The stopwatch is stopped when (a) the student's chin touches the bar, (b) the student's head tilts backward to keep the chin above the bar, or (c) the student's chin falls below the level of the bar.

Scoring   The score is the number of seconds that the student maintained the hanging position.

Standards   The number of seconds the student is able to hang in the correct position is compared to the criterion-referenced standards that are presented in Table 13.6 for boys and Table 13.7 for girls.

Comment   Little research has been conducted on the flexed arm hang criterion-referenced standards, and this test does not appear to be as popular a choice of physical educators as the modified pull-up.

Test   Back-Saver Sit and Reach

Description   The sit and reach test has been used in most health-related fitness test batteries as a measure of low back/hamstring flexibility. The FIT-NESSGRAM® uses a modified version called the back-saver sit and reach. The modification is to test only one leg at a time. The student sits on the floor with one leg straight and extended toward the sit and reach box and the other leg bent. Then the student slowly reaches forward along the sit and reach box and holds the farthest stretched position.

Objective   To reach forward the specified distance on each side of the body to allow assessment of hamstring flexibility.

Validity and Reliability   Jackson and Baker (1986) reported an intraclass reliability estimate of $R = .99$ for 100 girls aged 13 to 15 years on the traditional sit and reach test. Other researchers also reported high reliability estimates for the sit and reach test across various age groups. Validation studies have demonstrated that the sit and reach test is moderately correlated with criterion tests of hamstring flexibility, but has low correlations with criterion tests of low back flexibility. For example, Jackson and Baker reported a correlation between the sit and reach and the criterion measure of hamstring flexibility of $r = .64$, but a correlation of only $r = .28$ with a criterion measure of lower back flexibility. The sit and reach test has evidence of logical validity because the student must have good flexibility in the hamstring muscles to score well.

Validity and reliability are improved by providing sufficient instruction and warm-up. Warm-up should include slow, sustained, static stretching of the hamstring muscles (posterior thighs) and lower back.

Equipment   The sit and reach box is about 12 inches high, with a measuring scale attached to the top. The zero marker on the measuring scale is nearest the student, and the 9-inch mark is parallel to the spot where the student's foot will be set. Specially constructed sit and reach boxes can be purchased, or a wooden box with a yardstick can be used.

Procedures   The student should remove his or her shoes for testing. One leg is fully extended with the foot resting against the sit and reach box (parallel to the 9-inch mark on the scale). The knee of the other leg is bent, with the foot resting on the floor to the side of the extended knee. With hands placed one on top of the other and the arms straight, the student reaches forward along the scale in a slow and controlled manner four times and holds the position of the last reach for at least 1 second. The other side is then measured in a similar manner.

Scoring   The score is the farthest distance reached on the scale and is recorded to the nearest half inch. The maximum score recorded is 12 inches. The hands should reach forward evenly and the extended knee should remain straight. The teacher can help keep the knee from bending by placing one hand on the knee as a reminder to the student to keep the knee straight.

Standards   The distance reached for each leg is compared to the criterion-referenced standards. For boys, the passing standard is 8 inches for all ages. For girls, the standard is 9 inches up to age 10 years, increases to 10 inches for ages 11 to 14 years, and is 12 inches for ages 15 years and older.

Comment   This is an optional test in the FITNESSGRAM®. The flexibility measures in the FITNESSGRAM® can be used to teach that flexibility is joint specific and that flexibility is important to functional health, especially as individuals age.

Test   Shoulder Stretch

Description   The shoulder stretch is an enjoyable test of upper body flexibility in which the student tries to touch his or her fingers behind the back while reaching one arm over the shoulder and the other arm under the elbow.

Objective   To touch the fingertips together behind the back while reaching over the shoulder and under the elbow.

Validity and Reliability   The shoulder stretch has evidence of logical validity, because shoulder flexibility is necessary in order for one to touch his or her hands behind the back. No other reliability or validity evidence is available.

Equipment   No equipment is necessary.

Procedures   The student reaches the right hand over the shoulder and the left hand under the elbow in order to test the flexibility in the right shoulder. The student then tries to touch the fingertips of his or her hands together. The opposite is done to test the left shoulder flexibility.

Scoring   A passing score or "Yes" is recorded for each side if the student is able to touch the fingertips together behind the back. If the student is not able to touch the fingertips behind the back, a "No" or failing score is recorded.

Standards   The standard is touching the fingertips behind the back.

Comment   The importance of this test is in educating the students that flexibility is joint specific. For example, the students may pass on one side and not the other, emphasizing the need to stretch all joints of the body.

THE PRESIDENT'S CHALLENGE

The President's Challenge is sponsored by the President's Council on Physical Fitness and Sports (PCPFS). The President's Challenge offers two different fitness tests: the **President's Challenge Physical Fitness Test** and the **President's Chal-**lenge Health Fitness Test.** Many similarities exist between the FITNESSGRAM® and the President's Challenge Health Fitness Test. They both offer measures of aerobic capacity, body composition (only BMI for President's Challenge), abdominal strength and endurance, upper body strength, and flexibility. The FITNESSGRAM® offers a test of trunk extensor strength and flexibility and a measure of percent body fat through skinfolds that are not offered by the President's Challenge. The President's Challenge now offers a physical activity assessment, continuing the important trend of recognizing active lifestyles that was started by the FITNESSGRAM® in 1999. The President's Challenge Physical Fitness Test includes a measure of agility (a motor fitness component), but does not include a measure of body composition.

Physical Fitness Test Items

The President's Challenge Physical Fitness Test items measure (1) aerobic capacity; (2) muscular strength, muscular endurance, and flexibility; and (3) agility. The President's Challenge test items are listed next.

1. Aerobic Capacity:
   - 1-mile run (for 10- to 17-year-olds)
   - ½-mile run (for 8- to 9-year-olds)
   - ¼-mile run (for 6- to 7-year-olds)
2. Muscular Strength, Endurance, and Flexibility:
   - Abdominal Strength and Endurance:
     - partial curl-ups (recommended)
     - curl-ups
   - Upper Body Strength and Endurance:
     - right angle push-ups (recommended)
     - pull-ups
     - flexed arm hang (cannot be used for Presidential Physical Fitness Award)
   - Flexibility:
     - V-sit reach
     - sit and reach
3. Agility: Shuttle Run

Health Fitness Test Items

The President's Challenge Health Fitness Test items measure (1) aerobic capacity; (2) body composition; and (3) muscular strength, muscular endurance, and flexibility.

1. Aerobic Capacity:
   - 1-mile run (for 10- to 17-year-olds)
   - ½-mile run (for 8- to 9-year-olds)
   - ¼-mile run (for 6- to 7-year-olds)
2. Body Composition: Body mass index
3. Muscular Strength, Endurance, and Flexibility:
   - Abdominal Strength and Endurance: partial curl-ups
   - Upper Body Strength and Endurance:
     - right angle push-ups (recommended)
     - pull-ups
   - Flexibility:
     - V-sit reach
     - sit and reach

Aerobic Capacity

The test for aerobic capacity depends upon the age of the participant. Participants 10 years old and older are evaluated with the mile run. This is an alternative item for the FITNESSGRAM® assessment. Participants aged 8 to 9 years run ½ mile. Participants aged 6 to 7 years run ¼ mile.

Test 1-Mile Run or ½-Mile Run or ¼-Mile Run

Description This is the same as the description used for the 1-mile run in the FITNESSGRAM®. Students are instructed to cover the 1-mile, ½-mile, or ¼-mile distance in the fastest possible time.

Objective To cover the 1-mile, ½-mile, or ¼-mile distance as fast as possible.

Equipment A track or other flat measured distance, stopwatch, and recording forms are needed. The President's Challenge recommends that the area be large enough so that no more than 8 laps are necessary to complete the mile. If using a 400-meter track, the conversions for the 1-mile, ½-mile, and ¼-mile distances are as follows: 1 mile = 4 laps + 9 meters; ½ mile = 2 laps + 4.5 meters; and ¼ mile = 1 lap + 2.25 meters.

Procedures These are the same as the procedures used for the 1-mile run in the FITNESSGRAM®. Students run for 1 mile, ½ mile, or ¼ mile depending on their age. The teacher calls out the time for each lap, which is typically recorded on a recording form by the runner's partner. The time to complete the distance is recorded.

Scoring Times to complete the distance are recorded in minutes and seconds.

Standards The President's Challenge has standards for the Presidential Physical Fitness Award, the National Physical Fitness Award, and the Health Fitness Award. For the Presidential Physical Fitness Award the standard is set at the 85th percentile. For the National Physical Fitness Award the standard is set at the 50th percentile. Health Fitness Award standards were adapted from several sources. The norms from which the 1-mile run standards were derived are from the 1985 PCPFS National School Population Fitness Survey. The ¼-mile run and ½-mile run standards are from the Amateur Athletic Union Physical Fitness Program. The President's Challenge Standards for the aerobic capacity component are listed in Table 13.8.

Comment The President's Challenge provides the 85th and 50th percentiles for the ½-mile and ¼-mile distances, but states that time standards are not recommended for younger children. The goal for the younger children is to learn to run at a consistent pace and to develop a positive attitude toward the run.

Muscle Strength, Endurance, and Flexibility
Test Partial Curl-Up

Description This test is similar to the curl-up test of the FITNESSGRAM®. The partial curl-up was designed to be a better measure of the strength and endurance of the abdominal muscles than the traditional curl-up, because the feet are not held. This allows the participant to isolate the abdominal muscles and not use the hip flexor muscles during the slow movement of the curl-up.

| TABLE 13.8 | Qualifying Standards for the President's Challenge Awards Program for the Aerobic Capacity Tests (1-Mile, ½-Mile, or ¼-Mile Run) | | | | | |

| | Boys | | | Girls | | |
Age	Presidential Award (min:sec)	National Award (min:sec)	Health Fitness Award (min:sec)	Presidential Award (min:sec)	National Award (min:sec)	Health Fitness Award (min:sec)
6	1:55	2:21	2:30	2:00	2:26	2:50
7	1:48	2:10	2:20	1:55	2:21	2:40
8	3:30	4:22	4:45	3:58	4:56	5:35
9	3:30	4:14	4:35	3:53	4:50	5:25
10	7:57	9:48	9:30	9:19	11:22	10:00
11	7:32	9:20	9:00	9:02	11:17	10:00
12	7:11	8:40	9:00	8:23	11:05	10:30
13	6:50	8:06	8:00	8:13	10:23	10:30
14	6:26	7:44	8:00	7:59	10:06	10:30
15	6:20	7:30	7:30	8:08	9:58	10:00
16	6:08	7:10	7:30	8:23	10:31	10:00
17	6:06	7:04	7:30	8:15	10:22	10:00

Note: 6- and 7-year-olds run ¼ mile; 8- and 9-year-olds run ½ mile; 10- to 17-year-olds run 1 mile. Presidential Award standards are set at the 85th percentile. National Award standards are set at the 50th percentile. Health Fitness Award standards are adapted from the AAU Physical Fitness Program; AAHPERD Physical Best (1989); FITNESSGRAM® (Cooper Institute 1999); Corbin and Lindsey (1997); and the YMCA Youth Fitness Test.

Objective   To measure abdominal strength and endurance by completing as many partial curl-ups as possible to a cadence of 20 curl-ups per minute.

Equipment   A mat or other comfortable surface and a metronome to pace the movement are needed.

Procedures   In the starting position the student lies on his or her back with the knees bent and the feet about 12 inches from the buttocks. The arms are extended with the fingers resting on the front of the thighs. The knees are not held or anchored. The student curls up slowly until the fingertips touch the knees. Then the student slowly curls back down to the starting position. The pace is controlled by a metronome or some other technique (e.g., audio tape, clapping) and is set at a cadence of 1 partial curl-up every 3 seconds. The test continues until the student is unable to maintain the pace or has reached the target number of partial curl-ups.

Scoring   The score is the number of partial curl-ups completed. This score is then compared to the standards for the Presidential Physical Fitness Award, National Physical Fitness Award, or Health Fitness Award.

Standards   Standards for the Presidential Physical Fitness Award, National Physical Fitness Award, and Health Fitness Award are presented in Table 13.9 for boys and in Table 13.10 for girls. For the Presidential Physical Fitness Award the standard is set at the 85th percentile. For the National Physical Fitness Award the standard is set at the 50th percentile. Health Fitness Award standards were adapted from several sources. The norms from which the partial curl-up standards were derived are from the Canada Fitness Award Program.

Comment   The traditional curl-up test with the feet held is no longer recommended as a measure of abdominal strength and endurance, because the

TABLE 13.9	Qualifying Standards for the President's Challenge Awards Program for Muscular Strength, Endurance, and Flexibility Components for Boys

	Partial Curl-Up			Curl-Up	
Age	Presidential Award (#)	National Award (#)	Health Fitness Award (#)	Presidential Award (# in 1 minute)	National Award (# in 1 minute)
6	22	10	12	33	22
7	24	13	12	36	28
8	30	17	15	40	31
9	37	20	15	41	32
10	35	24	20	45	35
11	43	26	20	47	37
12	64	32	20	50	40
13	59	39	25	53	42
14	62	40	25	56	45
15	75	45	30	57	45
16	73	37	30	56	45
17	66	42	30	55	44

Note: Partial curl-up standards are from the Canada Fitness Award Program. Curl-up standards are from the 1985 PCPFS National School Population Fitness Survey. Presidential Award standards are set at the 85th percentile. National Award standards are set at the 50th percentile. Health Fitness Award standards are adapted from the AAU Physical Fitness Program; AAHPERD Physical Best (1989); FITNESSGRAM® (Cooper Institute 1999); Corbin and Lindsey (1997); and the YMCA Youth Fitness Test.

TABLE 13.10	Qualifying Standards for the President's Challenge Awards Program for Muscular Strength, Endurance, and Flexibility Components for Girls

	Partial Curl-Up			Curl-Up	
Age	Presidential Award (#)	National Award (#)	Health Fitness Award (#)	Presidential Award (# in 1 minute)	National Award (# in 1 minute)
6	22	10	12	32	23
7	24	13	12	34	25
8	30	17	15	38	29
9	37	20	15	39	30
10	33	24	20	40	30
11	43	27	20	42	32
12	50	30	20	45	35
13	59	40	25	46	37
14	48	30	25	47	37
15	38	26	30	48	36
16	49	26	30	45	35
17	58	40	30	44	34

Note: Partial curl-up standards are from the Canada Fitness Award Program. Curl-up standards are from the 1985 PCPFS National School Population Fitness Survey. Presidential Award standards are set at the 85th percentile. National Award standards are set at the 50th percentile. Health Fitness Award standards are adapted from the AAU Physical Fitness Program; AAHPERD Physical Best (1989); FITNESSGRAM® (Cooper Institute 1999); Corbin and Lindsey (1997); and the YMCA Youth Fitness Test.

hip flexor muscles (iliopsoas) are used to a great extent when the feet are held.

Test Curl-Up

Description This is the traditional curl-up test, in which the student's feet are held and the student completes as many curl-ups as possible in 1 minute.

Objective To measure abdominal strength and endurance by completing as many curl-ups as possible in 1 minute.

Equipment A mat or other comfortable surface and a stopwatch are needed.

Procedures In the starting position the student lies on his or her back with the knees bent and the feet about 12 inches from the buttocks. The arms are placed across the chest with the hands placed on the opposite shoulders. The knees are held by a partner. While the arms are held close to the chest, the student curls up so that the elbows touch the thighs. Then the student lowers his shoulder blades back to the floor. The student tries to complete as many curl-ups as possible in 1 minute.

Scoring The score is the number of curl-ups completed in 1 minute. This score is then compared to the standards for the Presidential Physical Fitness Award and the National Physical Fitness Award.

Standards The standards for the Presidential Physical Fitness Award and the National Physical Fitness Award are presented in Table 13.9 for boys and in Table 13.10 for girls. For the Presidential Physical Fitness Award the standard is set at the 85th percentile. For the National Physical Fitness Award the standard is set at the 50th percentile. The norms from which the curl-up standards were derived are from the 1985 PCPFS National School Population Fitness Survey.

Comment The President's Challenge states that the traditional curl-ups (i.e., with the feet held) are for testing only and not for training. A test should also be appropriate for training or practice; there-

fore, it is unclear why the traditional curl-ups are still included in this test battery.

Test Right Angle Push-Up

Description This test is similar to the 90° push-up test of the FITNESSGRAM®. The student completes as many push-ups as possible to a set cadence of 1 push-up every 3 seconds.

Objective To complete as many right angle push-ups as possible at a specified cadence of 20 push-ups per minute (1 push-up every 3 seconds).

Equipment A mat or other comfortable surface and a metronome to pace the push-ups are needed.

Procedures Each student works with a partner. In the starting position, the student lies face down on the mat with his or her hands under the shoulders and the body straight. From this position, the student pushes the body up by straightening the arms, while keeping the body straight. Then the student lowers the body until the elbows are bent at a 90° angle, with the upper arms parallel to the floor. The body (legs and back) is kept straight throughout the movement. The partner is positioned at the participant's head and places his or her hands at the position of the 90° angle to provide the person being tested with a stopping point at the proper down position. This movement is completed as many times as possible to a cadence of 1 push-up every 3 seconds or 20 push-ups per minute. The pace is controlled by a metronome or some other technique (e.g., audio tape, clapping). The test continues until the student is unable to maintain the pace or has reached the target number of push-ups.

Scoring The score is the number of right angle push-ups completed. Only push-ups done with the proper form to the cadence are counted. This score is then compared to the standards for the Presidential Physical Fitness Award, National Physical Fitness Award, and Health Fitness Award.

Standards Standards for the Presidential Physical Fitness Award, National Physical Fitness

Award, and Health Fitness Award are presented in Table 13.11 for boys and in Table 13.12 for girls. For the Presidential Physical Fitness Award the standard is set at the 85th percentile. For the National Physical Fitness Award the standard is set at the 50th percentile. Health Fitness Award standards were adapted from several sources. The norms from which the right angle push-up standards were derived are from the Canada Fitness Award Program.

Comment   The President's Challenge recommends the right angle push-up as the test of upper body strength and endurance, because many children are unable to do even one pull-up. However, the President's Challenge states that pull-ups are an option for students with higher levels of upper body strength and endurance.

Test   Pull-Up

Description   The pull-up test requires the participant to pull his or her body weight upward while the arms and body are fully extended from a bar. This test was originally used for boys in the AAHPER Youth Fitness Test in 1958, while the modified pull-up was originally used for girls.

Objective   To complete as many pull-ups as possible.

Equipment   A horizontal bar positioned at a height that allows the student to hang without touching the ground is needed.

Procedures   The student hangs from a horizontal bar with arms fully extended. Either an overhand grip (palms forward) or an underhand grip (palms facing toward body) can be used. The body is pulled upward until the chin clears the bar and then lowered until the arms are straight. This movement is repeated as many times as possible. The student is not allowed to use a kick or "kip" movement, and the body should not swing during the movement.

Scoring   The score is the number of correctly performed pull-ups. This score is then compared to the standards for the Presidential Physical Fitness Award, National Physical Fitness Award, and Health Fitness Award.

Standards   Standards for the Presidential Physical Fitness Award, National Physical Fitness Award, and Health Fitness Award are presented in Table 13.11 for boys and in Table 13.12 for girls. For the Presidential Physical Fitness Award the standard is set at the 85th percentile. For the National Physical Fitness Award the standard is set at the 50th percentile. Health Fitness Award standards were adapted from several sources. The norms from which the pull-up standards were derived are from the 1985 PCPFS National School Population Fitness Survey.

Comment   The pull-up is still included as an alternative test on both the FITNESSGRAM® and the President's Challenge, but is not the recommended test for either youth fitness program, because many children cannot perform any pull-ups. Thus, for many children, pull-ups are not sensitive enough to differentiate among variations in upper body strength.

Test   Flexed Arm Hang

Description   The student tries to remain in a position similar to the up position of a pull-up (arms flexed and chin above the bar) for as long as possible. This test was used for girls in the 1976 revision of the AAHPER Youth Fitness Test.

Objective   To maintain the flexed arm hang position for as long as possible.

Equipment   A horizontal bar positioned at a height that allows the student to hang without touching the ground and a stopwatch to time the hang time.

Procedures   The student can use either an overhand or an underhand grasp. The student takes the flexed arm hang position with the chin above the bar, elbows flexed, and chest close to the bar. The student

TABLE 13.11	Qualifying Standards for the President's Challenge Awards Program for Upper Body Strength and Endurance Components for Boys						

| | Right Angle Push-Up | | | Pull-Up | | | Flexed Arm Hang |
Age	Presidential Award (#)	National Award (#)	Health Fitness Award (#)	Presidential Award (#)	National Award (#)	Health Fitness Award (#)	National Award (sec)
6	9	7	3	2	1	1	6
7	14	8	4	4	1	1	8
8	17	9	5	5	1	1	10
9	18	12	6	5	2	1	10
10	22	14	7	6	2	1	12
11	27	15	8	6	2	2	11
12	31	18	9	7	2	2	12
13	39	24	10	7	3	2	14
14	40	24	12	10	5	3	20
15	42	30	14	11	6	4	30
16	44	30	16	11	7	5	28
17	53	37	18	13	8	6	30

Note: Right angle push-up standards are from the Canada Fitness Award Program. Pull-up and flexed arm hang standards are from the 1985 PCPFS National School Population Fitness Survey. Health Fitness Award standards are adapted from other sources. Presidential Award standards are set at the 85th percentile. National Award standards are set at the 50th percentile.

TABLE 13.12	Qualifying Standards for the President's Challenge Awards Program for Upper Body Strength and Endurance Components for Girls						

| | Right Angle Push-Up | | | Pull-Up | | | Flexed Arm Hang |
Age	Presidential Award (#)	National Award (#)	Health Fitness Award (#)	Presidential Award (#)	National Award (#)	Health Fitness Award (#)	National Award (sec)
6	9	6	3	2	1	1	6
7	14	8	4	2	1	1	6
8	17	9	5	2	1	1	8
9	18	12	6	2	1	1	8
10	20	13	7	3	1	1	8
11	19	11	7	3	1	1	7
12	20	10	8	2	1	1	7
13	21	11	7	2	1	1	8
14	20	10	7	2	1	1	9
15	20	15	7	2	1	1	7
16	24	12	7	1	1	1	7
17	25	16	7	1	1	1	7

Note: Right angle push-up standards are from the Canada Fitness Award Program. Pull-up and flexed arm hang standards are from the 1985 PCPFS National School Population Fitness Survey. Health Fitness Award standards are adapted from other sources. Presidential Award standards are set at the 85th percentile. National Award standards are set at the 50th percentile.

may be lifted to the bar by a spotter. The stopwatch is started when the student takes the proper position and stopped when the chin touches or falls below the level of the bar.

Scoring The score is the number of seconds the student maintains the flexed arm hang position. The score is then compared to the standards for the National Physical Fitness Award. The flexed arm hang cannot be used for the Presidential Physical Fitness Award or the Health Fitness Award.

Standards The standards for the National Physical Fitness Award are presented in Table 13.11 for boys and in Table 13.12 for girls. For the National Physical Fitness Award, the standard is set at the 50th percentile. The norms from which the flexed arm hang standards were derived are from the 1985 PCPFS National School Population Fitness Survey.

Comment The flexed arm hang is an alternative test of upper body strength for both the FITNESSGRAM® and the President's Challenge. In the President's Challenge, the flexed arm hang can be used only for the National Physical Fitness Award.

Test V-Sit Reach

Description This test is designed to measure lower back and hamstring flexibility, but like the sit and reach test, is probably a better measure of hamstring flexibility than of lower back flexibility. The student sits with the legs in a "V" position, about 8 to 12 inches apart, and slowly reaches forward as far as possible along a measuring stick.

Objective To reach forward from the correct V-sit position as far as possible to allow measurement of the flexibility of the hamstring muscles (posterior thighs).

Equipment Tape to mark a baseline and a measuring line. A yardstick or other measuring device is needed to mark the measuring line.

Procedures A straight line is marked on the floor as the baseline. The student sits on the floor (without shoes) and places his or her heels just behind the baseline 8 to 12 inches apart. This places the legs in a "V" position. The measuring line is drawn perpendicular to the baseline and is midway between the participant's feet. The measuring line should extend 2 feet on each side of the baseline and intersect at the "0" point. Thus, if a participant reaches to the baseline, his or her score is zero inches. The measuring line is marked off in half inches. Points beyond the baseline are positive (e.g., + 1.0 inches) and points behind the baseline are negative (e.g., −1.5 inches). The participant clasps the thumbs together and places the palms down on the measuring line. The legs are kept straight by a partner as the participant slowly reaches forward as far as possible along the measuring line. The student slowly reaches forward four times and then holds the fourth reach for 3 seconds as the score is recorded.

Scoring The score is the farthest point reached to the nearest half inch and held for 3 seconds.

Standards Standards for the Presidential Physical Fitness Award, National Physical Fitness Award, and Health Fitness Award are presented in Table 13.13 for boys and in Table 13.14 for girls. For the Presidential Physical Fitness Award the standard is set at the 85th percentile. For the National Physical Fitness Award the standard is set at the 50th percentile. Health Fitness Award standards were adapted from several sources. The norms from which the V-sit reach standards were derived are from the 1985 PCPFS National School Population Fitness Survey.

Comment Sufficient instruction and warm-up should be provided to improve the reliability and validity of this test. Warm-up should include static stretching of the lower back and hamstring muscles. Little equipment is needed for this test, while a specially designed measuring box is needed for the sit and reach test.

TABLE 13.13	Qualifying Standards for the President's Challenge Awards Program for Flexibility and Agility Components for Boys							
	V-Sit Reach			Sit and Reach			Shuttle Run	
Age	Presidential Award (inches)	National Award (inches)	Health Fitness Award (inches)	Presidential Award (cm)	National Award (cm)	Health Fitness Award (cm)	Presidential Award (sec)	National Award (sec)
6	+3.5	+1.0	+1	31	26	21	12.1	13.3
7	+3.5	+1.0	+1	30	25	21	11.5	12.8
8	+3.0	+0.5	+1	31	25	21	11.1	12.2
9	+3.0	+1.0	+1	31	25	21	10.9	11.9
10	+4.0	+1.0	+1	30	25	21	10.3	11.5
11	+4.0	+1.0	+1	31	25	21	10.0	11.1
12	+4.0	+1.0	+1	31	26	21	9.8	10.6
13	+3.5	+0.5	+1	33	26	21	9.5	10.2
14	+4.5	+1.0	+1	36	28	21	9.1	9.9
15	+5.0	+2.0	+1	37	30	21	9.0	9.7
16	+6.0	+3.0	+1	38	30	21	8.7	9.4
17	+7.0	+3.0	+1	41	34	21	8.7	9.4

Note: V-sit reach, sit and reach, and shuttle run standards are from the 1985 PCPFS National School Population Fitness Survey. Health Fitness Award standards are adapted from other sources. Presidential Award standards are set at the 85th percentile. National Award standards are set at the 50th percentile.

TABLE 13.14	Qualifying Standards for the President's Challenge Awards Program for Flexibility and Agility Components for Girls							
	V-Sit Reach			Sit and Reach			Shuttle Run	
Age	Presidential Award (inches)	National Award (inches)	Health Fitness Award (inches)	Presidential Award (cm)	National Award (cm)	Health Fitness Award (cm)	Presidential Award (sec)	National Award (sec)
6	+5.5	+2.5	+2	32	27	23	12.4	13.8
7	+5.0	+2.0	+2	32	22	23	12.1	13.2
8	+4.5	+2.0	+2	33	28	23	11.8	12.9
9	+5.5	+2.0	+2	33	28	23	11.1	12.5
10	+6.0	+3.0	+2	33	28	23	10.8	12.1
11	+6.5	+3.0	+2	34	29	23	10.5	11.5
12	+7.0	+3.5	+2	36	30	23	10.4	11.3
13	+7.0	+3.5	+3	38	31	25	10.2	11.1
14	+8.0	+4.5	+3	40	33	25	10.1	11.2
15	+8.0	+5.0	+3	43	36	25	10.0	11.0
16	+9.0	+5.5	+3	42	34	25	10.1	10.9
17	+8.0	+4.5	+3	42	35	25	10.0	11.0

Note: V-sit reach, sit and reach, and shuttle run standards are from the 1985 PCPFS National School Population Fitness Survey. Health Fitness Award standards are adapted from other sources. Presidential Award standards are set at the 85th percentile. National Award standards are set at the 50th percentile.

Test   Sit and Reach

Description   This is the traditional sit and reach test that is proposed to measure lower back and hamstring flexibility, but is a better measure of hamstring flexibility than lower back flexibility. A student sits with feet placed at the side of the sit and reach box. With the hands together (one on top of the other) and knees straight, the student slowly reaches forward as far as possible.

Objective   To reach forward along the sit and reach box as far possible to allow measurement of the flexibility of the hamstring muscles (posterior thighs).

Equipment   The test apparatus is a specially constructed box (12″ × 12″ × 12″ with a 21″ long scale attached to the top). The level of the feet should be at the 23 cm mark on the scale.

Procedures   The student sits on the floor (without shoes) and places his or her feet flat on the side of the sit and reach box where the scale is set at 23 cm. The feet are placed shoulder-width apart and one hand is placed on top of the other so that the fingertips of each hand are even. The student slowly reaches forward four times along the scale keeping the palms down and legs straight. The fourth reach is held while the distance is recorded. The test administrator can place a hand lightly on the knees to remind the participant to keep the knees straight.

Scoring   The score is the farthest point reached on the scale measured to the nearest centimeter.

Standards   Standards for the Presidential Physical Fitness Award, National Physical Fitness Award, and Health Fitness Award are presented in Table 13.13 for boys and in Table 13.14 for girls. For the Presidential Physical Fitness Award the standard is set at the 85th percentile. For the National Physical Fitness Award the standard is set at the 50th percentile. Health Fitness Award standards were adapted from several sources. The norms from which the sit and reach standards were derived are from the 1985 PCPFS National School Population Fitness Survey.

Comment   This test is similar to the FITNESSGRAM® back-saver sit and reach test, except that only one leg is measured at a time for the FITNESSGRAM® test. The sit and reach test was used in the 1980 AAHPERD Health-Related Fitness Test. Proper instruction and warm-up should be given before administering the test.

Agility
Test   Shuttle Run

Description   This is the only test included in the President's Challenge that is not a health-related fitness test. The Shuttle Run is a measure of agility that is a component of motor fitness or athletic fitness. The student runs a total of 40 yards by running back and forth across a 10-yard course and picking up a block from one side and carrying it to the other side.

Objective   To allow a measure of agility by completing the shuttle run as fast as possible.

Equipment   Two parallel lines are marked 30 feet apart. Two blocks of wood or other similar object (2″ × 2″ × 4″) and a stopwatch are needed.

Procedures   The student starts behind one of the lines and runs to the other line, picks up one of the blocks, and returns it to the starting line. The first block should be placed on the starting line, not thrown across the line. Then the student runs back, picks up the second block, and runs back across the starting line.

Scoring   The score is the time it takes to complete the shuttle run to the nearest tenth of a second.

Standards   The standards for the Presidential Physical Fitness Award and the National Physical Fitness Award are presented in Table 13.13 for boys and in Table 13.14 for girls. For the Presidential Physical Fitness Award the standard is set at the 85th percentile. For the National Physical Fitness Award the standard is set at the 50th percentile. The norms from which the shuttle run standards were derived are from the 1985 PCPFS National School Population Fitness Survey.

Comment The shuttle run performance may be related to athletic performance in some sports, but is probably not related to health.

Body Composition
Test Body Mass Index (BMI)

Description The measure of body composition used for the President's Challenge Health Fitness Test is BMI. BMI is calculated from height and weight. Thus, BMI is a measure of weight relative to height, but does not provide a measure of percent body fat. BMI is an alternate test on the FITNESSGRAM®; skinfold measurement to estimate percent body fat is the recommended test for the FITNESSGRAM®.

Objective To measure height and weight and calculate a measure of weight relative to height.

Equipment Scales to accurately measure height and weight are needed.

Procedures Height and weight should be measured accurately and students should be afforded privacy during the measurement.

Scoring BMI is calculated as weight in kilograms divided by the square of height in meters with the following formula:

$$BMI = Weight (kilograms) \div Height^2 (meters)$$

Standards The standards for the President's Challenge Health Fitness Award are presented in Table 13.5.

Comment The values of BMI for the desirable range for the President's Challenge Health Fitness Test and the FITNESSGRAM® Healthy Fitness Zone are relatively similar. However, for boys

aged 9–13 and 15 years and for girls aged 6–10 and 15–17 years the criterion-referenced standards differ by ≥ 1 kg·m^{-2}.

COMPARISON OF YOUTH FITNESS TESTS

Test Items
Table 13.15 lists the fitness components and test items of the FITNESSGRAM® and President's Challenge youth fitness tests. The President's Challenge is composed of the President's Challenge Physical Fitness Test and the President's Challenge Health Fitness Test. All three tests use the 1-mile run to evaluate aerobic fitness and offer the pull-up test as a measure of upper body strength and endurance. The FITNESSGRAM® and the Health Fitness Test both have body mass index as a measure of body composition. The President's Challenge Physical Fitness Test does not evaluate body composition. The Physical Fitness Test includes a motor fitness item, while the FITNESSGRAM® and Health Fitness Test do not include a motor fitness item.

Criterion-Referenced Standards
The FITNESSGRAM® and the President's Challenge Health Fitness Test appear to have similar goals. The criterion-referenced standards for the 1-mile run for these two tests, however, are quite different. For boys, the Health Fitness Test passing standards are between 1 minute and 2 minutes faster than the corresponding FITNESSGRAM® passing standards. The two tests have similar standards for the 1-mile run for 16- and 17-year-old girls, but the Health Fitness passing standards are between 30 seconds and 2.5 minutes faster than the corresponding FITNESSGRAM® passing standards for the younger girls.

The FITNESSGRAM® criterion-referenced standards most closely represent minimal values needed for adequate health. Cureton and Warren (1990) provide a detailed discussion of the process followed to develop the FITNESSGRAM® passing standard for the 1-mile run. They make convincing arguments based on scientific evidence that the FITNESSGRAM® standards represent the minimal value of aerobic capacity needed for health promotion.

TABLE 13.15	National Youth Fitness Programs Contrasted by Fitness Component and Test Item		
Fitness Component	**President's Challenge Physical Fitness Test**	**President's Challenge Health Fitness Test**	**FITNESSGRAM®**
Aerobic Fitness	1-mile, ½-mile, or ¼-mile run	1-mile, ½-mile, or ¼-mile run	PACER 1-mile run Walk Test
Body Composition	None	Body mass index	Skinfolds or body mass index
Strength and Endurance Components			
Abdominal	Partial curl-up, curl-up	Partial curl-up	Curl-up
Upper Body	Right angle push-up Pull-up Flexed arm hang	Right angle push-up Pull-up	90° Push-up Pull-up Flexed arm hang Modified pull-up
Trunk and Lower Body Flexibility	V-sit reach Sit and reach	V-sit reach Sit and reach	Trunk lift Back-saver sit and reach Shoulder stretch
Motor Fitness Components	Shuttle run	None	None

FITNESSGRAM® PHYSICAL ACTIVITY ASSESSMENT

The FITNESSGRAM® was the first youth fitness program that attempted to measure physical activity, in addition to physical fitness. Physical activity and physical fitness, while interrelated, are different constructs. By measuring physical activity, the FITNESSGRAM® emphasizes to the students the importance of being physically active. Based on the wealth of research evidence that relates physically active lifestyles to improved health, it is clear that this trend to assess physical activity should be encouraged.

The FITNESSGRAM® offers two opportunities to assess physical activity: (a) the FITNESSGRAM® physical activity questionnaire, and (b) the ACTIVITYGRAM® Physical Activity Recall. For both of the physical activity assessment programs, children enter their own information into the computer.

FITNESSGRAM® Physical Activity Questionnaire

The three questions that were added to the FITNESSGRAM® to assess physical activity are listed below.

1. **Aerobic Activity Question:** "On how many of the past 7 days did you participate in physical activity for a total of 30–60 minutes or more over the course of the day? This includes moderate activities (walking, slow bicycling, or outdoor play) as well as vigorous activities (jogging, active games, or active sports such as basketball, tennis, or soccer)."

   0   1   2   3   4   5   6   7 (circle one)

2. **Strength Activity Question:** "On how many of the past 7 days did you do exercise to strengthen your muscles? This includes exercises such as push-ups, sit-ups, or weight lifting."

   0   1   2   3   4   5   6   7 (circle one)

3. **Flexibility Activity Question:** "On how many of the past 7 days did you do stretching exercises to loosen up or relax your muscles? This includes exercises such as toe touches, knee bending, or leg stretching."

0   1   2   3   4   5   6   7 (circle one)

It is difficult for young children to accurately recall behavior for the previous week. Validity of the activity recall may be improved by preparing children for this assessment. Preparation may take the form of educating them about different types of activity (e.g., aerobic, strength, flexibility) and about how to estimate the amount of time they were physically active. Note that the aerobic activity question refers to a "total of 30–60 minutes" so the idea that activity accumulates can be emphasized. That is, the aerobic activity does not have to occur all at once to count on the FITNESSGRAM® or to be beneficial. Three 10-minute bouts of aerobic activity equals 30 minutes for this assessment.

The inclusion of this activity assessment will provide additional individualized feedback on the FITNESSGRAM® report. In particular, children who report being physically active who do not reach the Healthy Fitness Zone will receive a motivational message to maintain their efforts to be physically active. Conversely, children who do score in the Healthy Fitness Zone but do not report being physically active will receive a message that it is important to participate in regular physical activity in order to keep fit.

ACTIVITYGRAM® Physical Activity Recall

The ACTIVITYGRAM® requires children to recall their level of physical activity for the previous day. The assessment was designed based on the Previous Day Physical Activity Recall (PDPAR) (Weston, Petosa & Pate 1997). The child is asked to record from a list of activities the primary activity he or she was doing for each 30-minute block of time from 7:00 A.M. to 11:00 P.M. The activities are divided into categories by type of activity as follows: (a) rest, (b) lifestyle activity, (c) aerobic activity, (d) aerobic sports, (e) muscular activity, and (f) flexibility.

For each activity recorded other than rest, the child is asked to rate the intensity of that activity as (a) light, (b) moderate, or (c) vigorous. Clearly, in order to use the ACTIVITYGRAM®, teachers need to educate students about type and intensity of activity. *Light activity* is categorized as activity with "little or no movement, no increase in breathing rate, easy." *Moderate activity* is categorized as "movement equal in intensity to a brisk walk, some increase in breathing rate, not too difficult." *Vigorous activity* is categorized as "moving quickly, breathing hard, hard effort level" (Meredith & Welk 2004).

It is recommended that the ACTIVITYGRAM® take place over a two-week period and be conducted as an event that involves the whole school. It is helpful to get classroom teachers involved, because the children need to be given time to complete two or three days of assessments.

At least two days of assessment are needed in order to receive a printed ACTIVITYGRAM® report. An example of the computer printout for the ACTIVITYGRAM® report is presented in Figure 13-5. It is recommended that activity data be collected on both school days and nonschool days. The **Healthy Activity Zone** is set at three bouts of activity per day for children and two bouts of activity per day for adolescents. The ACTIVITYGRAM® report also provides a time profile that can indicate to students and parents when the student could be more active. An activity profile indicates the types of activities that each child has reported, including the amount of time spent watching television and playing computer games. Research has shown that decreasing sedentary behaviors may be an effective way to improve health (Robinson 1999).

Although the validity of using questionnaires to assess physical activity in young children is questionable, the benefit of assessing physical activity on these children may be great. Physical educators emphasize to children what is important by what they assess. If we assess physical activity in addition to physical fitness, we will emphasize that it is important to be physically active. One of the main goals of many physical education programs is to promote physically active lifestyles in the students. Assessment of physical activity is an important tool to use to help reach this goal.

ACTIVITYGRAM

ADAM BODENSTEIN
ACTIVITYGRAM - 4/13/99
Madison County Elementary School

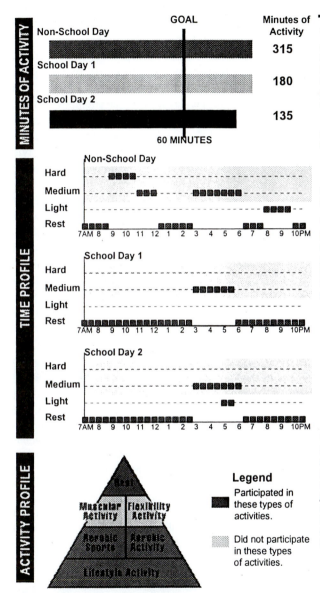

MINUTES OF ACTIVITY

	GOAL	Minutes of Activity
Non-School Day		315
School Day 1		180
School Day 2		135

60 MINUTES

TIME PROFILE

Non-School Day
- Hard
- Medium
- Light
- Rest

7AM 8 9 10 11 12 1 2 3 4 5 6 7 8 9 10PM

School Day 1
- Hard
- Medium
- Light
- Rest

7AM 8 9 10 11 12 1 2 3 4 5 6 7 8 9 10PM

School Day 2
- Hard
- Medium
- Light
- Rest

7AM 8 9 10 11 12 1 2 3 4 5 6 7 8 9 10PM

ACTIVITY PROFILE

Activity pyramid: Rest / Muscular Activity / Flexibility Activity / Aerobic Sports / Aerobic Activity / Lifestyle Activity

Legend

Participated in these types of activities.

Did not participate in these types of activities.

MESSAGES

The chart shows the number of minutes that you reported doing moderate (medium) or vigorous (hard) activity on each day. Congratulations, your log indicates that you are doing at least 60 minutes of activity on most every day. This will help to promote good fitness and wellness. For fun and variety, try some new activities that you have never done before.

The minutes of activity reported may be higher than what was actually accomplished, because there are always minutes of rest during an activity.

The goal in ACTIVITYGRAM is to find ways to include activity in levels medium and hard each day (shaded areas are medium to hard).

The time profile shows the activity level you reported for each 30 minute period of the day. Your results show that you were not active during school but that you were active after school and on weekends. If it is not possible to be active during school in PE or recess then try to be more active after school. Keep up the good work.

The activity pyramid reveals the different types of activity that you reported doing over a few days. Your results indicate that you participated in regular lifestyle activity and some aerobic activity. This is great! Try to add some additional activity from the 3rd level of the pyramid. Your results indicate that you spend an average of 2 hours per day watching TV or working on the computer. While some time on these activities is okay, you should try to limit the total time to less than 2 hours.

ACTIVITYGRAM provides information about your normal levels of physical activity. The report shows what types of activity you do and how often you do them. It includes information that you reported for two or three days during one week.

ACTIVITYGRAM is a module within FITNESSGRAM 6.0 software. FITNESSGRAM materials are distributed by the American Fitness Alliance, a division of Human Kinetics. www.americanfitness.net

©The Cooper Institute for Aerobics Research

Figure 13-5

Computer printout for the ACTIVITYGRAM®.

(Source: Reprinted with permission. The Cooper Institute, Dallas, TX.)

PRESIDENT'S CHALLENGE PHYSICAL ACTIVITY ASSESSMENT

The newest addition to the President's Challenge is the assessment of physical activity and the recognition of active lifestyles with the **Presidential Active Lifestyle Award.** The idea behind this award is to encourage all children to adopt physically active lifestyles by recognizing individuals who are physically active nearly every day.

The requirements for the Presidential Active Lifestyle Award are that children be physically active a minimum of five days a week for six weeks. Physical activities must be recorded for each day on a log sheet. Students can accumulate 60 minutes of physical activity per day. Students can log their activities online or record their activity on a log sheet that can be downloaded from the President's Challenge website. Alternately, students can use pedometers to assess physical activity. The activity goal for girls 6 to 17 years of age is at least 11,000 steps per day. The activity goal for boys 6 to 17

years of age is at least 13,000 steps per day. The values of 11,000 steps a day for girls and 13,000 steps a day for boys should not be viewed as a health standard or a threshold. Those values were set as award criteria because boys average about 2,000 steps per day more than girls. By setting the standards at 11,000 steps per day for girls and 13,000 steps per day for boys, an attempt was made to give girls and boys the same chance of receiving the Active Lifestyle Award. Students are encouraged to earn additional Presidential Active Lifestyle Awards by repeating the requirements for other six-week periods.

The trend to measure and recognize physically active lifestyles by the FITNESSGRAM® and by the President's Challenge demonstrates that these youth fitness programs continually change based on research about the relationship of physical activity, fitness, and health. Physical education teachers are encouraged to keep current by incorporating the assessment of physical activity, in addition to physical fitness, into their curriculums.

SUMMARY

The evaluation of youth fitness has evolved from an emphasis on motor fitness to one on health-related fitness. Motor fitness tests include tests not only of strength and endurance, but also of speed, power, and agility. Motor fitness tests reflect an athletic orientation and endorse the philosophy of awarding the athletically gifted. With the growing body of medical evidence supporting the role of exercise, weight control, and aerobic fitness in health, the trend in youth fitness testing has shifted away from this athletic orientation to one of health promotion. The components of health-related batteries are aerobic fitness, body composition, muscular strength

and endurance, and flexibility. There are two national youth fitness test programs available. The philosophy of fitness test award programs is moving from one that rewards only a high level of performance to one that encourages regular exercise designed to achieve fitness levels suitable for health promotion. Criterion-referenced standards are being refined to define the level of fitness needed for health. The most recent change in youth fitness programs is the inclusion of the assessment and recognition of physical activity. This is an important trend that has evolved from research that has clearly demonstrated the health benefits of physically active lifestyles.

FORMATIVE EVALUATION OF OBJECTIVES

Objective 1   Identify the general tests that compose a motor fitness battery.

1. The most popular motor fitness test is the AAHPER YFT. List the tests that compose this battery.
2. What is the general nature of motor fitness test items?

Objective 2   Identify the general tests that compose a health-related battery.

1. What is the general nature of health-related fitness test items?
2. What are the test items of the FITNESSGRAM® and President's Challenge Health Fitness test batteries?

Objective 3 Differentiate between motor fitness and health-related fitness batteries.

1. Motor fitness and health-related fitness batteries evolved from different philosophies of fitness. Explain these philosophies.
2. What is the major difference between the test items included on motor fitness batteries and those on health-related fitness batteries?

Objective 4 Identify and evaluate the national youth fitness programs.

1. List and describe the FITNESSGRAM® and President's Challenge youth fitness programs.
2. What is the difference between the two youth fitness programs?

Objective 5 Understand how to administer the FITNESSGRAM® test battery to evaluate youth fitness and physical activity.

1. Describe the test items of the FITNESSGRAM®.
2. Describe how you would evaluate the fitness of a person who has been tested with the FITNESSGRAM®.
3. Describe the physical activity assessment portion of the FITNESSGRAM®/ACTIVITYGRAM®.

Objective 6 Understand how to administer the President's Challenge test batteries to evaluate youth fitness and physical activity.

1. Describe the test items of the President's Challenge Physical Fitness Test and Health Fitness Test.
2. Describe the award system used by the President's Challenge.
3. Thoroughly read the information available online for the FITNESSGRAM®/ACTIVITYGRAM® (www.fitnessgram.net) and the President's Challenge (www.presidentschallenge.org).
4. Describe the physical activity assessment portion of the President's Challenge.

ADDITIONAL LEARNING ACTIVITIES

1. Gain experience in youth fitness testing. Go to the public schools and help a teacher administer fitness tests.
2. Learn how to take skinfold measurements accurately. With one or more of your classmates, take triceps and calf skinfolds on a group of students. Compare your results with your classmates. If your scores do not agree, figure out what you are doing differently. Check the procedures and pictures in Chapter 12 to standardize your testing methods. Repeat the procedure and check your results again.
3. Order a health-related youth fitness test package. You will be surprised by how comprehensive they are.

BIBLIOGRAPHY

American Association for Health, Physical Education, and Recreation (AAHPER). 1958. *Youth fitness test manual.* Washington, DC: Author.

American Alliance for Health, Physical Education, and Recreation (AAHPER). 1976. *Youth fitness test manual.* Reston, VA: Author.

American Alliance for Health, Physical Education, Recreation, and Dance (AAHPERD). 1980. *Health-related physical fitness test manual.* Reston, VA: Author.

American Alliance for Health, Physical Education, Recreation, and Dance (AAHPERD). 1984. *Technical manual: Health-related physical fitness test.* Reston, VA: Author.

American Alliance for Health, Physical Education, Recreation, and Dance (AAHPERD). 1989. *Physical Best: Instructor's guide.* Reston, VA: Author.

American Health and Fitness Foundation. 1987. *Fit youth today.* Austin, TX: Author.

Ball, T. E. 1993. The predictability of muscular strength and endurance from calisthenics. *Research Quarterly for Exercise and Sport* 64(Suppl.): A-39.

Clarke, H. H. (Ed.). 1971. Basic understanding of physical fitness. In *Physical fitness research digest.* Washington, DC: President's Council on Physical Fitness and Sport.

Cooper Institute for Aerobics Research. 1999. *FITNESSGRAM® test administration manual.* 2nd ed. Champaign, IL: Human Kinetics.

Cotten, D. J. 1990. An analysis of the NCYFS II modified pull-up test. *Research Quarterly for Exercise and Sport* 61: 272–274.

Corbin, C. B., and R. Lindsey. 1997. *Fitness for life.* 4th ed. Globe Fearon.

Cureton, K. J. and G. L. Warren. 1990. Criterion-referenced standards for youth health-related fitness tests: A tutorial. *Research Quarterly for Exercise and Sport* 61: 7–19.

Cureton K. J. et al. 1995. A generalized equation for prediction of $\dot{V}O_2$ peak from 1-mile run/walk performance. *Medicine and Science in Sport and Exercise* 27: 445–451.

DiNucci, J., D. McCune, and D. Shows. 1990. Reliability of a modification of the health-related fitness test for use with physical education majors. *Research Quarterly for Exercise and Sport* 61: 20–25.

Engelman, M. E. and J. R. Morrow Jr. 1991. Reliability and skinfold correlates for traditional and modified pull-ups in children grades 3–5. *Research Quarterly for Exercise and Sport* 62: 88–91.

Expert Panel on the Identification, Evaluation, and Treatment of Overweight and Obesity in Adults. 1998. Executive summary of the clinical guidelines on the identification, evaluation, and treatment of overweight and obesity in adults. *Archives of Internal Medicine* 158: 1855–1867.

Godfrey, K. E., L. E. Kindig, and E. J. Windell. 1977. Electromyographic study of duration of muscle activity in sit-up variations. *Archives of Physical Medicine and Rehabilitation* 58: 132–135.

Jackson, A. W. and A. Baker. 1986. The relationship of the sit and reach test to criterion measures of hamstring and back flexibility in young females. *Research Quarterly for Exercise and Sport* 57: 183–186.

Jackson, A. S. et al. 1976. A position paper on physical fitness. Position paper of a joint committee representing the Measurement and Evaluation, Physical Fitness, and Research councils of the AAHPER. Washington, DC: AAHPER.

Kline, G. M. et al. 1987. Estimation of $\dot{V}O_2$ max from a one-mile track walk, gender, age, and body weight. *Medicine and Science in Sports and Exercise* 19: 253–259.

Kraus, H. and R. P. Hirschland. 1954. Minimum muscular fitness test in school children. *Research Quarterly* 25: 177–188.

Leger, L. A. et al. 1988. The multistage 20 metre shuttle run test for aerobic fitness. *Journal of Sports Science* 6: 93–101.

Mahar, M. T. et al. 1997. Criterion-referenced and norm-referenced agreement between the one mile run/walk and PACER. *Measurement in Physical Education and Exercise Science* 1: 245–258.

Manitoba Department of Education. 1977. *Manitoba physical fitness performance test manual and fitness objectives.* Manitoba, Canada.

McManis, B. G., T. A. Baumgartner, and D. A.Wuest, 2000. Objectivity and reliability of the 90° push-up. *Measurement in Physical Education and Exercise Science,* 4: 57–67.

McSwegin, P. J. et al. 1998. The validity of a one-mile walk test for high school age individuals. *Measurement in Physical Education and Exercise Science* 2: 47–63.

Meredith, M. D. and G. J. Welk. (Eds). 2004. *FITNESSGRAM®/ACTIVITYGRAM® test administration manual* (3rd ed.). Champaign, IL: Human Kinetics.

Noble, L. 1981. Effects of various types of sit-ups on iEMG of the abdominal musculature. *Journal of Human Movement Studies* 7: 124–130.

Pate, R. R. (Ed.). 1978. *South Carolina physical fitness test manual.* Columbia, SC: Governor's Council on Physical Fitness.

Pate, R. R. et al. 1987. The modified pull-up test. *Journal of Physical Education, Recreation and Dance* 58(9): 71–73.

Pate, R. R. et al. 1993. Validity of field tests of upper body muscular strength. *Research Quarterly for Exercise and Sport* 64: 17–24.

Rikli, R. E., C. Petray, and T. A. Baumgartner. 1992. The reliability of distance run tests for children in grades K–4. *Research Quarterly for Exercise and Sport* 63: 270–276.

Robinson, T. N. 1999. Reducing children's television viewing to prevent obesity: A randomized controlled trial. *Journal of the American Medical Association* 282: 1561–1567.

Rutherford, W. J. and C. B. Corbin. 1994. Validation of criterion-referenced standards for tests of arm and shoulder girdle strength and endurance. *Research Quarterly for Exercise and Sport* 65: 110–119.

Saint Romain, B. and M. T. Mahar. 2001. Norm-referenced and criterion-referenced reliability of the push-up and modified pull-up.

Measurement in Physical Education and Exercise Science 5: 67–80.

Shaw, V. W. 1986. The accuracy of two training methods of skinfold assessment. *Research Quarterly for Exercise and Sport* 57: 85–90.

Slaughter, M. et al. 1988. Skinfold equations for the estimation of body fatness in children and youth. *Human Biology* 60: 709–723.

Texas Governor's Commission on Physical Fitness, 1973. *Physical fitness-motor ability test.* Austin, TX.

Weston, A. T., R. Petosa, and R. R. Pate. 1997. Validation of an instrument for measurement of physical activity in youth. *Medicine and Science in Sports and Exercise* 29: 138–143.

14

ADULT AND OLDER ADULT FITNESS

CONTENTS

KEY WORDS

OBJECTIVES

As America's older population increases, the fitness of older adults is becoming an important priority. Public health research clearly documents that a sedentary lifestyle is a risk of all-cause mortality and many degenerative diseases. Not only is fitness an important determinant of health; it is also a key factor of "quality of life." An adequate level of fitness is needed for independent living for older adults. Many older individuals do not have the level of fitness needed to live independently. As our older adult population grows, this will become more of a problem. The low fitness exhibited by many older Americans is due not just to aging but also to lifestyle. This chapter will help you understand the effect of aging and lifestyle on fitness and health. The methods used to evaluate adult and older adult fitness are presented. After reading Chapter 14 you should be able to

1. Identify the methods used to study the decline in fitness associated with aging.
2. Understand the general age-related decline in health-related fitness.
3. Identify the types of tests used to evaluate adult fitness.
4. Identify the types of tests used to evaluate functional adult fitness.

AGING AND FITNESS

In the year 2000, the population of the United States had grown to over 281 million people.[1] The population as a whole was also older than it had been in 1990, when the previous national census was taken. In the intervening ten years, the median age increased from 32.9 years to 35.3 years. The number of people 65 years of age and over increased from a little over 32 million to almost 35 million. This corresponds to 12.5% of the total population (in comparison, in 1950, only 8% of the population were 65 years of age or older). A period of even greater increase is expected from 2011 on-

ward. This is when the baby boom generation, born in the years immediately after World War II, will pass retirement age.

Older Americans have more health problems and are more inactive than middle-aged and younger adults. Over 40% of people over age 65 report no leisure-time physical activity. Less than one-third participate in regular moderate physical activity, such as walking and gardening, and less than 10% engage routinely in vigorous physical activity. In the National Health Interview Survey (Kovar 1986), nearly 40% of men and women over age 65 reported activity-dependent limitations. The National Institute on Aging found that many adults over age 65 cannot perform common physical tasks (Cornoni-Huntley et al. 1986). Over half could not do heavy housework, and up to one-third could not walk one-half mile. Although some of this disability is due to chronic health problems such as arthritis, emphysema, and cardiovascular disease, it is also due, in part, to low levels of physical fitness.

Research Methods

To understand the effect of aging on fitness, a discussion of the research methods used to study aging is helpful. The two methods used to study the rate at which fitness declines with age are cross-sectional and longitudinal. A brief discussion of each follows.

Cross-Sectional Method

The **cross-sectional method** is used more than the longitudinal method because cross-sectional data are easier to obtain. Cross-sectional data collection involves testing a large sample at one time, with various age groups (e.g., young, middle-aged, and older adults) represented within the sample. All that is needed is a large sample of subjects who were tested once and vary greatly in age. For example, the Y's Way to Fitness test has a large normative database ($N \approx 35,000$) of men and women who vary from age 18 to over age 65 (Golding 2000). This would be suitable for a cross-sectional study.

There are two general ways to examine the cross-sectional change in fitness with age. The first method is quite simply to plot a measure of central

---

[1]For this and other national census statistics, visit the U.S. government census website at www.census.gov.

tendency (i.e., mean or median) with age. This provides a "graphic picture" of the general trend. A second method is to define the rate of decline. Regression is the statistical technique used to define the rate of decline. Typically, simple linear regression is used, but if the relationship is not linear, a nonlinear equation can be used. These statistical methods are presented in Chapter 2. The basic formula for a simple linear model is

Cross-Sectional Aging Equation   **(14.1)**

$$Y = bX + a$$

where Y is the fitness variable, b is the regression weight, X is age, and a is the intercept of the simple linear regression equation. The regression weight (b) defines the cross-sectional, age-related rate of decline.

Figure 14-1 illustrates this method. Provided are data to define the cross-sectional rate at which $\dot{V}O_2$ max declines with the age of women. The bivariate plot and the simple regression line define the change in the X variable, age, associated with the Y variable, measured $\dot{V}O_2$ max

$(ml \cdot kg^{-1} \cdot min^{-1})$. These data come from a study (Jackson et al. 1996) designed to define the rate at which aerobic fitness of women declines with age. While regression equations are often used to predict one variable from another (e.g., to estimate $\dot{V}O_2$ max from mile run time), the purpose of the regression analysis in a cross-sectional aging study is to define the age–$\dot{V}O_2$ max slope, or the rate at which aerobic fitness declines with age. The slope, in this context, is the regression weight (b). Figure 14-1 shows that the regression slope is −0.537. Based on these data, the cross-sectional rate at which the aerobic fitness of women declines with age was defined as 0.537 $ml \cdot kg^{-1} min^{-1} \cdot year^{-1}$.

While cross-sectional methods are often used to define the aging rate, the method suffers from at least two major problems. First, the sample is not completely representative of the total population. It is well known that mortality rates are related to age. As we age, our chances for survival decrease. The older subjects of cross-sectional samples tend to be the healthiest subjects of the sample. The least healthy do not live to the oldest age group.

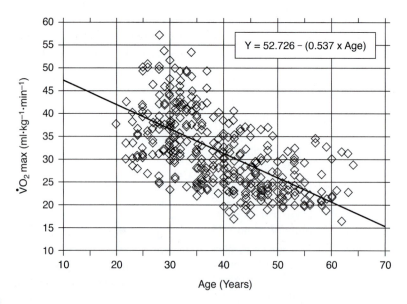

Figure 14-1

A bivariate plot showing the cross-sectional rate at which aerobic fitness of women declines with age. The graph was made from data from over 400 women, who were each tested just once.

(Data from Jackson et al. 1996 and graph from CSI Software Company, Houston, TX.)

This is especially true for aerobic fitness, where low fitness levels increase the risk for all-cause mortality (Blair et al. 1989). A second problem is that cross-sectional slopes define the general trend, not the true aging effect. For example, it is well known that lifestyle affects the rate at which aerobic fitness declines with age (Buskirk & Hodgson 1987; Jackson et al. 1995; Jackson et al. 1996). Cross-sectional methods can assess only age differences, not age changes (Spirduso et al. 2005).

Longitudinal Method

The **longitudinal method** is the other method used to examine the age-related change of fitness. Longitudinal data collection involves testing a group, waiting several years, and then testing the same sample again. This method is used less because two measures are needed over two periods of time. The objective is to evaluate age changes. The basic formula is

Longitudinal Aging Equation   **(14.2)**

$$\text{Rate of Decline} = \left(\frac{T1 - T2}{\text{Age } 2 - \text{Age } 1} \right)$$

where T2 is the variable measured at Age 2 and T1 is the variable measured at Age 1. This can easily be shown with published data (Jackson et al. 1996). The aerobic fitness of NASA female employees was measured on two occasions. The mean ages and levels of aerobic fitness were as follows: T1, Age 1 = 44.1 years, $\dot{V}O_2$ max = 30.1 $ml \cdot kg^{-1} \cdot min^{-1}$ and T2, Age 2 = 47.9 years, $\dot{V}O_2$ max = 27.8 $ml \cdot kg^{-1} \cdot min^{-1}$. Using Formula 14.2, the longitudinal rate was defined as -0.61 $ml \cdot kg^{-1} \cdot min^{-1} \cdot year^{-1}$.

While the longitudinal method provides the actual rate at which the person declined with age, the method also has limitations. First, two measures at two different points in time are needed. This tends to be expensive and sometimes impossible to achieve. Second, while a longitudinal change reflects the actual change of the individual, the change is not likely due to the biological effects of aging alone. A summary of longitudinal aerobic fitness studies shows that age-related longitudinal changes in aerobic fitness ranged from no change to declines of nearly 1.5

$ml \cdot kg^{-1} \cdot min^{-1} \cdot year^{-1}$ (Buskirk & Hodgson 1987). This large difference can be traced to both the biological effects of aging and the effects of lifestyle behavior such as exercise.

Defining the Age Decline of Fitness

Cross-sectional and longitudinal research clearly show that adult fitness declines with age. Provided next is a brief discussion of the trends associated with aerobic fitness, body composition, and strength. In the discussion of the YMCA adult fitness tests, additional cross-sectional changes are provided.

Aerobic Fitness

It is well established that the aerobic fitness of men and women declines with age. The Fick equation (McArdle, Katch & Katch 2001) provides the physiological logic for the aging effect associated with aerobic fitness. The Fick equation defines $\dot{V}O_2$ max as the product of three variables:

- **Maximum heart rate**. The number of times per minute that the heart beats, during maximal work
- **Stroke volume**. The volume of oxygenated blood that is ejected with each heartbeat
- **Arterial-venous oxygen difference**. The difference in the oxygen concentration between arterial blood (when it leaves the left ventricle) and venous blood (when the blood returns to the right atrium). The arterial-venous oxygen difference represents the volume of oxygen extracted by the body to produce energy.

It is well established that maximum heart rate declines with age and that maximum heart rate is unaffected by exercise training. If stroke volume and the arterial-venous components were unaffected, the decline in maximum heart rate would explain the age-related decline in aerobic fitness. Exercise habits have been shown to increase stroke volume and enhance the body's capacity to extract oxygen from the blood (Hagberg et al. 1985). The cross-sectional estimates of the age-related decline in aerobic fitness are consistently reported to be in the range of 0.4–0.5 $ml \cdot kg^{-1} \cdot min^{-1} \cdot year^{-1}$. In contrast, the longitudinal estimates range from 0.04 to 1.43 $ml \cdot kg^{-1} \cdot min^{-1} \cdot year^{-1}$ (Buskirk & Hodgson 1987). The results of two large studies (Jackson et al. 1995; Jackson et al. 1996) conducted with NASA/Johnson Space Center employees showed that the difference in results found with cross-sectional and longitudinal studies is largely due to lifestyle.

As men and women age, they not only put on fat weight and lose fat-free weight but also become less active. The NASA studies showed that about 50% of the cross-sectional decline in aerobic fitness associated with age was due to differences in percent body fat and exercise habits. Figure 14-2 shows the results of the study. The average rate of decline was 0.46 $ml \cdot kg^{-1} \cdot min^{-1} \cdot year^{-1}$ and 0.54 $ml \cdot kg^{-1} \cdot min^{-1} \cdot year^{-1}$ for men and women, respectively. However, when percent body fat and self-reported level of physical activity were statistically controlled, the rate of decline in $\dot{V}O_2$ max was cut nearly in half to 0.26 $ml \cdot kg^{-1} \cdot min^{-1} \cdot year^{-1}$. This means that if individuals do not change their percent body fat and exercise habits, the rate of decline can be expected to be 0.26 $ml \cdot kg^{-1} \cdot min^{-1} \cdot year^{-1}$.

This illustrates the importance of maintaining a healthy body composition and physical activity habits as we age.

A cross-sectional rate of decline in aerobic fitness of 0.26 $ml \cdot kg^{-1} \cdot min^{-1} \cdot year^{-1}$ does have support from longitudinal research. Kasch and associates (1985, 1990) compared 25-year longitudinal changes of physically active and inactive men. The rate of decline in aerobic power of their active men was 0.25 $ml \cdot kg^{-1} \cdot min^{-1} \cdot year^{-1}$, nearly identical to the NASA data. In contrast, the aerobic fitness of inactive men declined at a rate of 0.77 $ml \cdot kg^{-1} \cdot min^{-1} \cdot year^{-1}$. Over the 25 years, the active subjects lost an average of 7.5 pounds of weight, while the inactive subjects gained about 7 pounds. At the start of the study, the percent body fat levels of the men were similar, but at the conclusion of the 25-year study, the body fat levels were 17% and 26% for the active and inactive men, respectively. The inactive men became less active and increased their percent body fat, and their aerobic fitness declined at a steeper rate.

The NASA aging studies (Jackson et al. 1995; Jackson et al. 1996) also included longitudinal data.

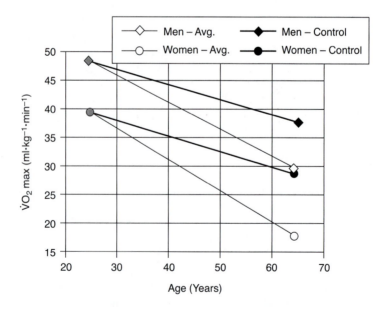

Figure 14-2

The average (Avg.) and controlled (Control) decline in aerobic fitness from age 25 to 65 years. The controlled rate of decline is the rate of decline if activities, habits, and percent body fat remain unchanged.

(Data from Jackson et al. 1995, 1996 and graph from CSI Software Company, Houston, TX.)

While the average aerobic fitness of the men did not change between tests, the women's aerobic fitness declined at a rate of 0.6 ml·kg^{-1}·min^{-1}·year^{-1}. The primary reason the men did not show a longitudinal decline was that many had enrolled in a health-related fitness program and increased their fitness. Closer analysis showed that lifestyle dramatically influenced the rate at which aerobic fitness longitudinally changed. Figure 14-3 graphically illustrates this. Those men and women who decreased their exercise level and increased their percent body fat showed the steepest yearly decrease in aerobic fitness. In contrast, those men and women who increased their exercise level and decreased their percent body fat actually increased their $\dot{V}O_2$ max between the two tests.

These data show that the change in aerobic fitness over the adult life span varies considerably, and is due not only to aging but to lifestyle.

Figure 14-4 illustrates the change in aerobic fitness as it relates to aging. The average aerobic fitness of the NASA men (Jackson et al. 1995) at age 30 was 45 ml·kg^{-1}·min^{-1}, and represents men who were moderately active (30–60 minutes of aerobic exercise per week), and somewhat lean (15–20%fat). Figure 14-4 shows the theoretical decline from the average fitness level for a 30-year old man of 45 ml·kg^{-1}·min^{-1} to projected levels at age 70 for three different lifestyles. If men maintained a physically active lifestyle (i.e., aerobically exercised 3 or more hours per week) and remained lean ($\approx$15%fat), their projected aerobic capacity at age 70 would be 42 ml·kg^{-1}·min^{-1}, only 3 ml·kg^{-1}·min^{-1} below that of the average 30-year old man. This would be just a 7% decline in aerobic capacity. The figure also shows the projected change from average for men who became sedentary and increased their percent body fat to about

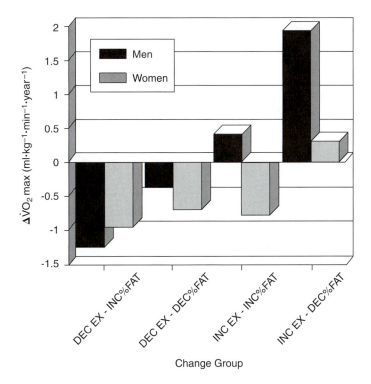

Figure 14-3

Longitudinal changes in aerobic fitness of men and women who changed their lifestyle. The rate at which aerobic fitness declines is directly related with changes in lifestyle. (DEC EX-INC%FAT = decreased exercise and increased % fat)

(Data from Jackson et al. 1995, 1996 and graph from CSI Software Company, Houston, TX.)

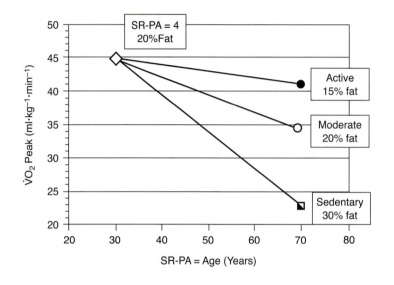

Figure 14-4

Projected changes in aerobic fitness from age 30 to 70 years for different exercise and body composition conditions. (Graph from CSI Software Company, Houston, TX.)

30%. The estimated aerobic capacity at age 70 for these sedentary men would be in the low 20s, representing a loss of nearly 50% of their aerobic capacity. Many of these men are at risk of losing their capacity to function independently. The third example represents men at about 20% fat who remained moderately active by exercising aerobically for 30 to 60 minutes a week. A 70-year-old man with this profile would be expected to have an aerobic capacity of 34 ml·kg^{-1}·min^{-1}, a 40-year decline of less than 25% in his aerobic fitness, about half the decline projected for the sedentary man.

The importance of aerobic fitness has been demonstrated by Blair and associates, who showed that low levels of aerobic fitness increase the risk of mortality (Blair et al. 1989; Blair et al. 1995). For many older adults, living an active lifestyle is more important than longevity (Larson & Bruce 1987). A goal of aging is not just living longer and dying later, but also what Shephard (1986) terms a "quality-adjusted lifespan." For many older adults, the goal is the level of aerobic fitness needed to function independently. The cross-sectional and longitudinal data show that lifestyle, exercise, and body composition are major determinants of this.

The levels of aerobic fitness defined by the American Medical Association for independent living are

- Severe impairment—15 ml·kg^{-1}·min^{-1}
- Moderate impairment—20 ml·kg^{-1}·min^{-1}

Body Composition

The weight and percent body fat of American adults increase with age. Figure 14-5 shows the average change in body mass index (BMI) of American men and women for different age groups (Frisancho 1990). These data are a representative sample of American men and women and show that the BMI of both men and women increases steadily to about age 45 years. At that point, the BMI of men levels off, while the women's continues to increase and levels off about 10 years later.

Figure 14-6 gives the cross-sectional trend for age and percent body fat. These data came from the medical database at the Cooper Clinic in Dallas (Pollock & Wilmore 1990). These cross-sectional data show that percent body fat of both men and women systematically increases from the early 20s to the 50s, where there is a tendency to level off.

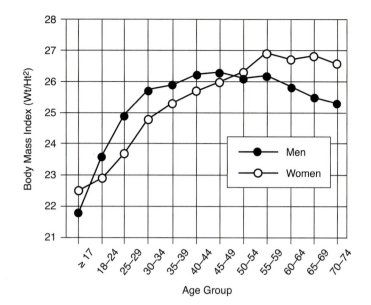

Figure 14-5

Average cross-sectional change in body mass index of American men and women.

(NHANES data published by Frisancho 1990 and graph from CSI Software Company, Houston, TX.)

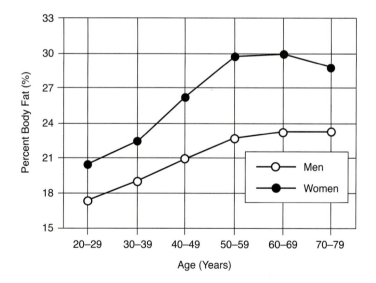

Figure 14-6

Average cross-sectional change in percent body fat of men and women.

(Data from the Cooper Clinic Coronary Risk Profile Charts, Dallas, TX [Pollock & Wilmore 1990] and graph from CSI Software Company, Houston, TX.)

The increase for women is at a steeper rate than that for men. This systematic increase in percent body fat is likely due to increases in fat weight and decreases in fat-free weight. After age 30, a general decrease in fat-free mass and muscle mass has been observed (Wilmore & Costill 1994). How much of the decrease in fat-free mass is due to aging and how much is due to exercise habits is difficult to determine. However, research published on master runners suggests that some loss of fat-free mass is due to aging. Pollock et al. (1987) reported that the master runners who average running over 22 miles a week still showed a loss of fat-free weight at a rate of about 0.25 pounds per year.

Longitudinal research shows that lifestyle is a major determinant of changes in body composition. Research (Skender 1996) from the Behavioral Medicine Research Center at Baylor College of Medicine (Houston, TX) provides a comprehensive view of the longitudinal effect of weight changes associated with diet and exercise. In a two-year experimental study, Baylor scientists compared the weight loss of three groups: (1) diet only, (2) exercise only, and (3) diet and exercise. The 127 men and women who participated in the study were at least 30 pounds overweight when they started. Figure 14-7 gives the results of the study. During the first three months, the exercise group lost very little, while the two diet groups showed dramatic weight losses. Between 3 and 12 months the diet-only group leveled off, and then during the next 12 months gained all their weight back and even exceeded their start point. The exercise-only group progressively lost weight over the first 12 months and maintained the weight loss for the next 12 months. The diet-and-exercise group lost the most weight during the first 12 months, but their weight rebounded in the final 12 months to the level reached by the exercise-only group. These data not only demonstrate the importance of exercise on weight control, but also the influence of lifestyle on the age-related changes in body composition. Aging is responsible for part of the adult changes in body composition, but lifestyle plays a major role.

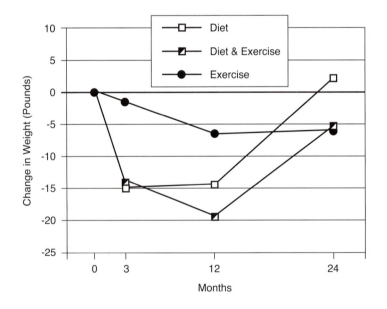

Figure 14-7

Longitudinal two-year changes in body weight associated with diet and exercise programs. Lifestyle greatly influences weight change and body composition.

(Data from Skender 1996 and graph from Jackson and Ross, *Understanding Exercise for Health and Fitness,* 1997.)

Muscular Strength

In youth, muscular strength increases with age. The maximum strength of men and women generally is reached between the ages of 20 and 30 years. After this age, there tends to be a gradual decrease in strength (McArdle, Katch & Katch 2001; Montoye & Lamphiear 1977). Figure 14-8 shows this general trend.

While a general age-related decrease in strength has consistently been shown with the general adult population, those who work at jobs that require strength above the levels essential for a sedentary lifestyle do not show a decline in strength with age (Blakley 1994; Petrofsky & Lind 1975). Figure 14-9 shows the cross-sectional strength trends of over 12,000 construction workers. Included are data on over 900 men aged 50 and older (Blakley 1994). The strength tests are the isometric tests presented in Chapter 10. The graphs show very little change in grip, arm, and back strength. The mean differences between the strongest age group and workers in the 60- to 70-year-old group were quite small. These data suggest that physically de-

manding jobs provide a training effect that helps workers maintain strength as they age. These data suggest that much of the age-related decline in strength found in the general population is due to the lack of activities that overload the major muscle groups.

While the general trend for adults is to lose strength as they age, research shows that strength training can increase strength substantially in adults at any age. Strength development programs for older adults are gaining in popularity. Muscular strength is related to functional mobility. Leg strength is important in maintaining balance, in walking, and in preventing falls in older adults (Spirduso, Francis & MacRae 2005). Strength training studies show that older adults can have the same rate of strength gain as the young, but they start and end at lower levels. The strength training results achieved with the elderly are summarized in another source (Spirduso et al. 2005). As the population of the United States ages, the need to maintain strength while we age is becoming more recognized.

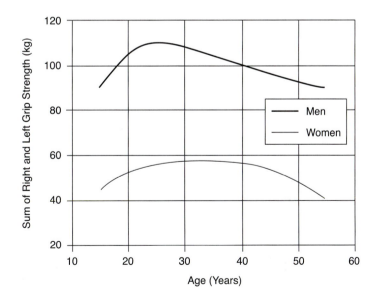

Figure 14-8

Cross-sectional age-related change in grip strength of men and women. Strength levels increase in youth, reaching peak strength in the 30s and 40s, and then systematically declines.

(Data from Montoye & Lamphiear 1977 and graph from CSI Software Company, Houston, TX.)

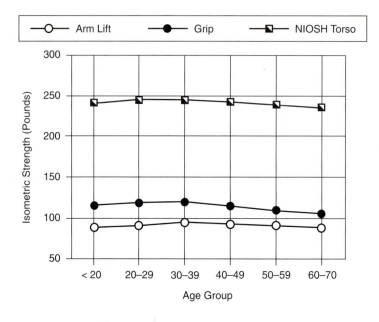

Figure 14-9

Cross-sectional change in isometric strength of construction workers.

(Data from Blakley et al. 1994 and graph from CSI Software Company, Houston, TX.)

EVALUATING ADULT FITNESS

This section presents adult fitness tests. The first is the test developed by the YMCA, which is the central component of the YMCA's adult fitness program. It is likely the most popular adult fitness test. The second test is the United States Army Physical Fitness Test (APFT). While the APFT is not used with civilians, it illustrates a philosophy on adult physical fitness testing.

Y's Way to Fitness

The Y's Way to Physical Fitness program is one of the most comprehensive, popular adult fitness programs (Golding 2000). It is more than just a fitness test; it is a complete adult fitness program. Leading exercise science and medical professionals helped develop the program. In addition to test procedures and norms, the test includes basic exercise physiology; program administration recommendations; medical guidelines; and fitness programming. Provided next are the Y's adult fitness tests and normative standards. The included tests tend to be

standard adult health-related fitness tests that have been supported by good reliability and validity evidence. The norms are extensive. They were developed on data from approximately 35,000 men and women of various ages. The cross-sectional age-related changes in fitness are also provided.

Aerobic Fitness

Either a cycle ergometer or a step test can be used to evaluate aerobic fitness. The cycle ergometer test is a submaximal test consisting of several workloads. The Y's $\dot{V}O_2$ max norms are given in Table 14.1. Figure 14-10 shows the cross-sectional decline in aerobic fitness with age. These data show the familiar linear decline in fitness with age. The average rate of decline was about 0.43 ml·kg^{-1}·min^{-1}·year^{-1} for men and about 0.40 ml·kg^{-1}·min^{-1}·year^{-1} for women.

Test   YMCA 3-Minute Step Test

Purpose   To measure exercise heart rate after 3 minutes of exercise. The step test is provided to replace the cycle test in environments where a cycle ergometer test is not suitable.

TABLE 14.1	YMCA Adult Norms for $\dot{V}O_2$ max (ml·kg^{-1}·min^{-1})				
Age	95th	75th	50th	25th	5th
Men					
18–25	75	53	44	36	26
26–35	66	50	40	33	24
36–45	61	45	37	30	21
46–55	55	40	37	27	20
56–65	50	37	31	25	18
over 65	42	32	27	22	16
Women					
18–25	69	50	40	33	24
26–35	65	48	40	32	22
36–45	56	42	34	28	20
46–55	51	36	30	25	18
56–65	44	33	27	22	15
over 65	48	29	24	19	14

Source: Adapted from Golding, L. A., *YMCA Fitness Testing and Assessment Manual,* 2000.

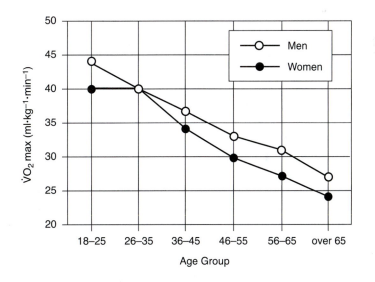

Figure 14-10

Cross-sectional change in aerobic fitness of men and women.

(Data from Golding 2000.)

Equipment   A 12-inch-high sturdy bench; a metronome set at 96 beats per minute; a timer to measure the 3-minute test period and recovery heart rate; and a stethoscope or heart rate monitor to count recovery heart rate.

Test Procedures   The step test is first demonstrated to the subject. The step rate is 24 steps per minute. The metronome is set at 96 beats per minute, four clicks per step—that is, up, up, down, down (4 × 24 = 96). The subject faces the bench and steps in place to pick up the beat of the metronome. Once the subject is stepping at the correct pace, the test can begin. When the subject starts the first step, the timer is started. The subject continues bench stepping at 24 steps per minute for 3 minutes. At the end of the last step, the subject sits down immediately. The test administrator places the stethoscope on the person's chest, picks up the heart rhythm, and counts the heart rate for 1 minute. The count begins on a beat, counting that beat as "zero one." In many settings, a heart rate

monitor is available and appropriate for use to measure heart rate. However, for the YMCA step test, a heart rate monitor should be used to count heart beats for one minute (not to obtain a posttest heart rate reading).

Score   The subject's score is the 1-minute post-exercise heart rate. Table 14.2 provides normative data to evaluate performance.

Body Composition

Body composition is evaluated from the sum of skinfold fat. The YMCA test uses the same sites for men and women. Either the sum of three (Σ3) or the sum of four (Σ4) skinfold measurements may be used. The recommended sites are

Σ3	Σ4
1. Abdomen	1. Abdomen
2. Ilium	2. Ilium
3. Triceps	3. Triceps
	4. Thigh

TABLE 14.2	YMCA Norms for the 3-Minute Step Test (Heart Rate Beats per Minute)				
Age	95th	75th	50th	25th	5th
Men					
18–25	71	84	97	111	132
26–35	70	85	100	114	134
36–45	70	88	101	116	138
46–55	77	93	107	121	139
56–65	71	94	105	119	136
over 65	74	92	106	121	136
Women					
18–25	75	93	108	122	143
26–35	74	92	107	122	141
36–45	77	96	109	124	142
46–55	85	101	115	126	143
56–65	83	103	116	129	147
over 65	85	101	120	128	145

Source: Adapted from Golding, L. A., *YMCA Fitness Testing and Assessment Manual,* 2000.

The methods used to measure skinfold fat are fully presented in Chapter 12. Published data (Jackson & Pollock 1978; Jackson, Pollock & Ward 1980) were used to develop sex-specific regression equations to estimate percent body fat from the sum of skinfolds. The YMCA test manual provides "look-up" tables to expedite the calculations. Table 14.3 gives the Y's percent body fat normative standards. Figure 14-11 shows the age-related change in percent body fat for the YMCA database. Percent body fat for both men and women increases with age, then levels off and declines slightly.

Muscular Strength

The bench press is used to measure strength and endurance. Rather than using a 1-RM test, The Y's bench press test is an absolute endurance test. Absolute endurance is measured by using the same load for everyone. A 35-pound barbell is used with women and an 80-pound barbell for men. For some older adults and unfit adults, who may only be able to perform 1 or 2 repetitions, it would of course be more a measure of muscular strength. The correla-

tion between absolute endurance and maximum strength is high, ranging from 0.75 to 0.97 (deVries & Housh 1994). Figure 14-12 gives the cross-sectional decline in bench press performance of men and women tested with the Y's Way to Fitness test (Golding 2000). These data show that bench press absolute endurance of men and women declines with age at a linear rate.

Test　Bench Press

Purpose　To measure muscular strength and absolute muscular endurance.

Equipment　A 35-pound barbell for women and an 80-pound barbell for men; a metronome set at 60 beats per minute; and a bench that is commonly used for the bench press exercise.

Test Procedures　The subject assumes a supine position on the bench with the knees bent and feet on the floor. Hand the barbell to the subject in the "down" position. From this position, the subject

TABLE 14.3	**YMCA Adult Norms for Percent Body Fat (%fat)**				
Age	95th	75th	50th	25th	5th
		Men			
18–25	5	10	14	19	27
26–35	8	13	18	23	29
36–45	11	17	21	26	31
46–55	14	19	23	28	33
56–65	16	21	25	28	33
over 65	16	20	24	27	32
		Women			
18–25	15	19	23	27	35
26–35	15	20	24	29	37
36–45	16	22	27	32	40
46–55	19	25	30	34	41
56–65	19	26	31	36	41
over 65	18	25	30	35	40

Source: Adapted from Golding, L. A., *YMCA Fitness Testing and Assessment Manual*, 2000.

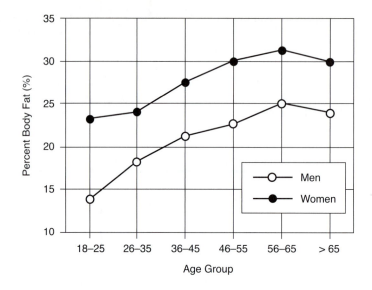

Figure 14-11

Cross-sectional change in percent body fat of men and women.
(Data from Golding 2000.)

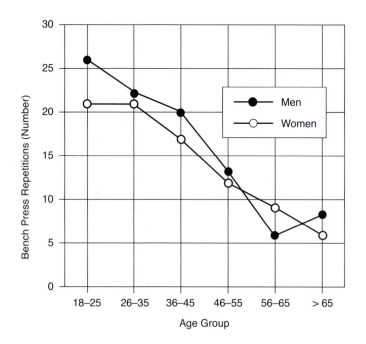

Figure 14-12

Cross-sectional change in bench press strength of men and women.
(Data from Golding 2000.)

TABLE 14.4	YMCA Norms for the Bench Press Test (Number of Repetitions)				
Age	95th	75th	50th	25th	5th
Men					
18–25	49	34	26	17	5
26–35	48	30	22	16	4
36–45	41	26	20	12	2
46–55	33	21	13	8	1
56–65	28	17	10	4	0
over 65	22	12	8	3	0
Women					
18–25	49	30	21	13	2
26–35	46	29	21	13	2
36–45	41	26	17	10	1
46–55	33	20	12	6	0
56–65	29	17	9	4	0
over 65	22	12	6	2	0

Source: Adapted from Golding, L. A., *YMCA Fitness Testing and Assessment Manual,* 2000.

presses the barbell upward to extend the elbows fully and then returns to the "down" position. The rhythm is kept by the metronome, with each click representing a movement up or down. The subject exercises at a rate of 30 repetitions per minute ($2 \times 30 = 60$). The subject is encouraged to breathe regularly and not strain during the test, so as to avoid the Valsalva maneuver.

Score The subject's score is the number of repetitions completed to exhaustion. Table 14.4 provides bench press norms for age and sex.

Muscular Endurance

A 1-minute half sit-up test is used to measure muscular endurance. Figure 14-13 shows the cross-sectional change in the half sit-up test. Aging and sit-up performance has not been a topic of research in aging research, so it has not been determined how much of the loss is due to aging and how much is due to lack of training.

Test 1-Minute Half Sit-Up

Purpose To measure muscular endurance of the abdominal muscles.

Equipment A stopwatch; a soft mat; and four 6-inch strips of self-adhesive Velcro placed rough side up, 3.5 inches apart. The strips should be perpendicular to the participant's body, at approximately hip level.

Test Procedures The participant should lie supine on the mat, with his knees at right angles and the soles of his feet flat on the floor. Before starting the test, the participant should adjust his position so that with his arms held straight down, his fingertips touch the nearest Velcro strips. At the start signal, the participant curls his trunk upward and reaches downward to touch the second set of Velcro strips. He then returns to the start position and continues for 1 minute. After starting, the

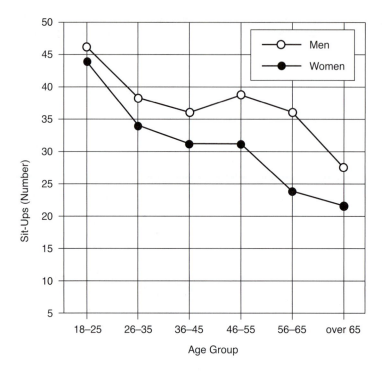

Figure 14-13

Cross-sectional change in half sit-up performance of men and women.
(Data from Golding 2000.)

participant's shoulders should touch the mat with each repetition. The head does not have to touch the mat.

Score   The subject's score is the number of correct half sit-ups completed in 1 minute. Table 14.5 provides normative data to evaluate performance.

Flexibility

Trunk flexibility is a common component of both youth and adult fitness tests. Trunk flexibility is believed to be important for the prevention of low back problems, but the link has not been clearly defined (Plowman 1992). Figure 14-14 shows the cross-sectional change in flexibility found in the YMCA normative database (Golding 2000). These data show that women are more flexible than men over all age groups. This sex difference is consistent with youth fitness results (Cooper Institute for Aerobics Research 1999). With age, both men and

women lose flexibility. The rate of loss for men is greater than that for women.

Test   Trunk Flexion

Purpose   To measure trunk flexion.

Equipment   While commercial equipment is available for this test, measurement can also be done with just a yardstick. The yardstick is taped to the floor at the 15-inch mark of the yardstick. The 15-inch mark is where the feet are placed.

Test Procedures   The subject sits on the floor straddling the yardstick with the 0 mark toward her body. The legs are extended and the feet are at the 15-inch tape. The feet are about 10 to 12 inches apart. The participant slowly reaches forward with both hands as far as possible on the yardstick and holds the position momentarily. The subject is

TABLE 14.5	\multicolumn{5}{l}{YMCA Norms for the Half Sit-Up Test (Number of Repetitions)}
Age	95th	75th	50th	25th	5th
\multicolumn{6}{c}{**Men**}
18–25	83	61	46	35	23
26–35	68	53	38	32	17
36–45	65	48	36	28	13
46–55	68	52	39	25	11
56–65	63	48	36	25	17
over 65	65	38	27	21	10
\multicolumn{6}{c}{**Women**}
18–25	76	58	44	33	24
26–35	60	44	34	26	17
36–45	60	42	31	22	14
46–55	57	37	31	23	9
56–65	55	35	24	15	7
over 65	41	31	22	13	8

Source: Adapted from Golding, L. A., *YMCA Fitness Testing and Assessment Manual,* 2000.

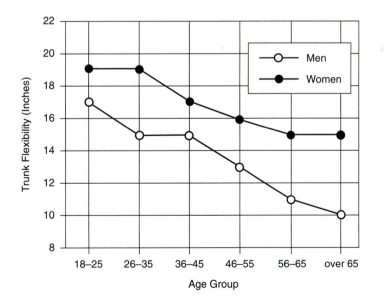

Figure 14-14

Cross-sectional change in flexibility of men and women.

(Data from Golding 2000.)

TABLE 14.6		YMCA Norms for the Flexibility Test (Distance Reached in Inches)			
Age	95th	75th	50th	25th	5th
		Men			
18–25	22	18	16	12	9
26–35	22	18	15	12	7
36–45	21	17	14	11	5
46–55	20	16	12	9	4
56–65	19	15	11	7	3
over 65	18	13	10	7	3
		Women			
18–25	25	21	19	16	12
26–35	24	20	18	15	11
36–45	23	19	16	13	9
46–55	22	18	16	13	8
56–65	21	18	15	12	7
over 65	21	18	15	11	6

Source: Adapted from Golding, L. A., *YMCA Fitness Testing aned Assessment Manual,* 2000.

encouraged to exhale and drop her head between her arms. The fingertips together are in contact with the yardstick.

Score   The best of three trials measured to the nearest 0.25 of an inch is the subject's score. Norms for men and women of selected age groups are provided in Table 14.6.

U.S. Army Fitness Test

The United States Army requires soldiers to maintain a level of physical fitness. The Army Physical Fitness Test (APFT) consists of three items designed to assess muscular endurance and cardiorespiratory endurance. The test items are push-ups, sit-ups, and the 2-mile run. The fitness program provides alternate tests for soldiers who cannot take the APFT for medical reasons. Soldiers over age 40 must be cleared through a cardiovascular screening program before taking the APFT. Details of the test standards and a three-month program for training

for the test can be found at the Army health and wellness website (www.hooah4health.com).

APFT Test Items

Provided next is a brief description of the three-item APFT. A complete discussion of the APFT is provided in the U.S. Army physical fitness manual (U.S. Army 1992).

Push-Up Test   The push-up test is the number of correct push-ups that can be completed in 2 minutes. At the start of the test, the soldier assumes the front-leaning rest position in which, when viewed from the side, the body should form a generally straight line from the shoulders to the ankles. On the command "Go," the soldier begins the push-up by bending the elbows and lowering the entire body as a single unit until the upper arms are at least parallel to the ground. The soldier may rest in the front-leaning rest position, but cannot rest on the ground. The soldier completes as many push-ups as possible in 2 minutes at his own cadence.

TABLE 14.7	Level of Performance Required to Pass the Army Physical Fitness Test (APFT) for Men and Women, Contrasted by Age Groups					
	Push-Ups (Number)		Sit-Ups (Number)		2-Mile Run (min:sec)	
Age Group	**Men**	**Women**	**Men**	**Women**	**Men**	**Women**
17–21	42	19	53	53	15:54	18:54
22–26	40	17	50	50	16:36	19:36
27–31	39	17	45	45	17:00	20:30
32–36	36	15	42	42	17:42	21:42
37–41	34	13	38	38	18:18	22:42
42–46	30	12	32	32	18:42	23:42
47–51	25	10	30	30	19:30	24:00
≥ 52	20	9	28	28	19:48	24:24

Source: Taken from www.hooah4health.com.

Sit-Up Test   The objective of the sit-up test is to do as many sit-ups as possible within a 2-minute test period. The starting position is lying on the back with the knees bent at a 90° angle. Another person holds the soldier's ankles with just the hands. The soldier's fingers are interlocked behind the head, and the backs of the hands must be touching the ground. At the command "Go," the upper body is raised forward to, or beyond, the vertical position; that is, the base of the neck is beyond the base of the spine. After reaching the vertical position, the upper body is lowered to the ground until the bottom of the shoulder blades touches the ground. The head, hands, arms, and elbows are not required to touch the ground. The test is terminated if the soldier stops and rests in the down (starting) position. The person maintains her own cadence.

2-Mile Run Test   The 2-mile run test is used to measure aerobic fitness. The soldiers are instructed to complete the run without any physical help—for example, by being pulled, pushed, or carried. Walking is permitted, but discouraged. The goal is to complete the 2-mile distance as fast as possible.

APFT Performance Standards

Age-adjusted performance standards are provided for men and women. Test performance is converted to a score scale that ranges from 0 to 100. While the top score is 100 points, a score of 60 is required to pass a test. The 0- to 100-point score scale is adjusted to account for sex and age differences. The scoring standards are comprehensive and can be found on the Army health and wellness website (www.hooah4health.com). Provided in Table 14.7 are levels of performance required to pass the APFT for the selected age groups.

Alternate APFT Events

The APFT alternate events are provided for soldiers who, for medical reasons, cannot take the three-item test. The alternate tests are timed endurance tests. Table 14.8 provides the alternate test standards by event, sex, and age. The alternate aerobic events are

- 800-yard swim test
- 6.2-mile stationary cycle ergometer test with a resistance setting of 2 kiloponds (see Chapter 11)
- 6.2-mile bicycle test on a conventional bicycle using one speed
- 2.5-mile walk test

U.S. Army Body Composition

Although the test is not part of the APFT, the body composition of soldiers is evaluated. Soldiers who

TABLE 14.8	Army Physical Fitness Test (APFT) Alternate Test Standards (min:sec) by Event, Sex, and Age					
	800-Yard Swim		**6.2-Mile Bike**		**2.5-Mile Walk**	
Age Group	**Men**	**Women**	**Men**	**Women**	**Men**	**Women**
17–21	20:00	21:00	24:00	25:00	34:00	37:00
22–26	20:30	21:30	24:30	25:30	34:30	37:30
27–31	21:00	22:00	25:00	26:00	35:00	38:00
32–36	21:30	22:30	25:30	26:30	35:30	38:30
37–41	22:00	23:00	26:00	27:00	36:00	39:00
42–46	22:30	23:30	27:00	28:00	36:30	39:30
47–51	23:00	24:00	28:00	30:00	37:00	40:00
≥ 52	24:00	25:00	30:00	32:00	37:30	40:30

Source: www.hooah4health.com.

do not meet weight standards for their height or whose appearance suggests that they have excessive body fat are required to have their body composition measured. Age and sex standards are used to evaluate a soldier's percent body fat. Those who do not meet the standards are placed on a formal, supervised weight-loss program that includes diet and exercise components. Provided next are the United States Army percent body fat standards for men and women adjusted for age.

Percent Body Fat Standards

Age	Men	Women
17–20	20%	30%
21–27	22%	32%
28–39	24%	34%
≥40	26%	36%

EVALUATING FUNCTIONAL ADULT FITNESS

While the YMCA and U.S. Army tests are similar to youth fitness tests, the "graying of America" has led to a new concept in adult fitness testing: functional adult fitness tests. The need for **functional adult fitness** testing and exercise training programs for older adults can be traced to the increasing number of older Americans and escalating health care costs.

The U.S. House of Representatives Select Committee on Aging estimated in 1992 that the annual cost of physical frailty was $54–80 billion and would likely be over $132 billion by the year 2030. There is good evidence to suggest that increasing the functional fitness of older adults can reduce these costs (Rikli & Jones 1997; Spirduso et al. 2005).

Functional adult fitness tests are designed to measure basic fitness components such as strength, endurance, and motor ability (Rikli & Jones 1997). Spirduso et al. (2005) identified five hierarchical categories of the functional ability of older adults.

1. *Physically Dependent.* The **physically dependent** are individuals who cannot execute basic activities of daily living, such as dressing and bathing. These individuals require full-time help.
2. *Physically Frail.* The **physically frail** are individuals who can meet their basic needs, but cannot perform many activities of daily living, such as preparing meals or shopping.
3. *Physically Independent.* The **physically independent** are fully independent individuals who are quite sedentary. They are likely borderline frail and close to losing their capacity to function independently.
4. *Physically Fit.* The **physically fit** are individuals who exercise regularly and are

TABLE 14.9	Functional Adult Fitness Components and Corresponding Test Items		
Fitness Component	**AAHPERD Test**	**Senior Fitness Test**	**Groningen Test**
Aerobic fitness	880-yard walk	6-minute walk, or 2-min step-in-place	Walking endurance
Upper body strength	Arm curl	Arm curl	Grip strength
Lower body strength	None	Chair stand	None
Upper body flexibility	None	Scratch test	Shoulder flexibility
Lower body flexibility	Sit- and- reach	Chair sit- and- reach	Sit- and- reach
Agility and/or balance	Agility/dynamic balance	8-foot up-and-go	Balance test
Body composition	Ponderal index	Body mass index	None
Fine motor abilities	"Soda pop" coordination test	None	Manual dexterity reaction time

typically well above average in functional ability. They likely engage regularly in strenuous activities such as jogging, rowing, tennis, and other forms of aerobic exercise.

5. *Physically Elite*. The **physically elite** are a very small proportion of men and women who train regularly and compete in master athletic events. These are master athletes who are very fit (see Pollock et al. 1987 for an example of master athletes).

The primary target group of functional fitness tests are the individuals in the physically independent group. The test items of functional adult fitness tests reflect the person's ability to perform common activities of daily living, such as rising from a chair, walking, stair climbing, lifting, reaching, and bending (Rikli & Jones 1997). Provided next are three adult functional fitness tests. The first is the AAHPERD test, the second is the Senior Fitness Test, and the final test is the Groningen test developed in The Netherlands. Table 14.9 provides a comparison of the fitness components and test items of these three functional fitness tests.

AAHPERD Test

The American Alliance for Health, Physical Education, Recreation and Dance (AAHPERD) test (Osness et al. 1996) was developed by a committee appointed by AAHPERD's Council on Aging and Adult Development. The definition used to define functional fitness by the AAHPERD Committee was "the physical capacity of the individual to meet ordinary and unexpected demands of daily life safely and effectively." The general purposes of the AAHPERD functional fitness test are to

- assess the individual's current condition to be able to determine the appropriate exercise prescription that will reduce risk and enhance physiological and psychological change.
- be able to quantify change that may have taken place during an exercise program.

Provided next is a basic description of each test. Table 14.10 provides the normative data for men and women of various age groups. The sample sizes used to develop these statistics ranged from 11 to over 300 individuals for each age group. These norms were used to develop three functional fitness levels: below average, average, and above average. The test methods and evaluation standards are fully presented in the test manual (Osness et al. 1996).

Body Composition Component
Test   Ponderal Index

Procedure   The ponderal index is a height-weight ratio. The manual provides a nomogram to make this calculation. Unlike the more commonly used body mass index (see Chapter 12), a low ponderal index reflects a high body weight for a given height, that is, a high level of body fatness.

		Age Group					
TABLE 14.10	**Means and Standard Deviations for the AAHPERD Functional Fitness Test Contrasted by Gender and Age Groups**						
Gender	**Test Statistic**	**60–64**	**65–69**	**70–74**	**75–79**	**80–84**	**85–90**
PONDERAL INDEX (RATIO OF HEIGHT IN INCHES BY CUBE ROOT OF WEIGHT IN POUNDS)							
Men	Mean	11.92	11.89	12.03	11.93	11.61	11.88
Men	SD	0.44	0.48	0.64	0.64	0.55	0.68
Women	Mean	11.69	11.82	11.83	11.92	11.64	12.01
Women	SD	0.80	0.81	0.77	0.69	0.95	0.80
FLEXIBILITY—MEN (INCHES)							
Men	Mean	19.9	19.8	17.9	18.5	18.4	16.2
Women	SD	5.0	5.0	6.1	5.6	3.9	2.8
Women	Mean	23.2	23.6	22.6	22.9	20.9	19.5
Women	SD	5.0	6.2	5.7	6.3	5.9	6.2
AGILITY/BALANCE—MEN (ELAPSED TIME, SEC)							
Men	Mean	25.4	26.5	28.2	31.7	32.6	33.6
Men	SD	6.1	8.0	13.1	8.3	9.2	16.5
Women	Mean	25.0	27.4	29.0	34.0	37.1	42.2
Women	SD	5.4	6.2	7.0	10.6	15.1	15.7
COORDINATION—MEN (ELAPSED TIME, SEC)							
Men	Mean	11.7	12.5	13.0	13.4	14.2	13.6
Men	SD	2.7	2.3	3.5	2.4	3.1	3.4
Women	Mean	12.1	12.6	12.9	13.6	14.5	15.7
Women	SD	3.2	3.4	3.7	4.6	3.8	3.3
STRENGTH/ENDURANCE—MEN (REPETITIONS)							
Men	Mean	23.7	21.5	21.1	20.1	20.5	17.8
Men	SD	5.5	6.9	5.8	4.1	2.6	5.1
Women	Mean	21.8	21.2	20.8	17.7	17.6	16.2
Women	SD	6.2	6.7	6.1	5.2	4.9	4.8
880-YARD WALK—MEN (MINUTES)							
Men	Mean	7.1	7.8	8.3	9.7	8.1	9.5
Men	SD	1.3	1.5	1.3	3.7	1.4	1.4
Women	Mean	8.4	9.0	9.1	10.0	10.7	10.4
Women	SD	1.6	2.1	2.4	1.9	2.3	2.1

Source: From Osness, W. H. et al. *Functional Fitness Assessment for Adults Over 60 Years.* Dubuque, IA: Kendall/Hunt, 1996, pp 28–33.

Lower Body Flexibility Component

Test   Trunk/Leg Flexibility

Procedure   The test equipment is similar to that used for the YMCA test. A yardstick is taped to the floor with a line at the 25-inch mark (the YMCA test uses the 15-inch mark). The subject sits with the legs flat on the floor and heels at the 25-inch line. The feet are spread about 12 inches. The test requires the subject to reach forward, keeping both hands together. The object is to reach the farthest point possible on the yardstick. The person is first given two warm-up trials, followed by two trials for score.

Scoring The person's score is the best score of the two trials. The test is scored to the nearest 0.5 inch.

Agility and/or Balance Component
Test Agility/Dynamic Balance

Procedure The test station consists of a chair with arms and two cones that are located 6 feet to the side of the chair and 5 feet behind the chair. On command, the subject stands, moves to the right, goes around the cone, returns to the chair, sits down, lifts the feet off the ground, and without hesitating, immediately stands and repeats the move (with the exception of going around the left cone), and then returns to the chair. This is the first circuit. The entire circuit is then immediately repeated. The test consists of the two circuits. After a 30-second rest, the second trial (consisting of two circuits) is administered. A warm-up trial is administered first to be certain the subject understands the test.

Scoring The time for each trial (two circuits) is measured to the nearest 0.1 second. The subject's score is the time for the best trial.

Fine Motor Abilities Component
Test "Soda Pop" Coordination Test

Procedure The test is administered with the person sitting on a chair facing a table. The general tasks involve lifting an unopened (12-oz) soda can, turning the can, and placing it on a target taped on the table. The test target is made from masking tape. A 30-inch strip is placed on the table, with 6 crosses (numbered 1 to 6) placed across the 30-inch strip. The crosses are 5 inches apart. The test starts with a soda can on every other cross, that is, numbers 1, 3, and 5. On a starting command, the subject lifts the first can, turns it over and places it on the next cross (i.e., number 2), moves can 2 from cross 3 to cross 4, and moves the third can from cross 5 to cross 6. Once the third can is placed, the subject immediately returns the cans to the original spot, that is, from cross 6 to 5, 4 to 3, and 2 to 1. This com-

pletes the first trip. Without hesitation, the same six moves are repeated. The test trial involves lifting, turning, and moving the cans a total of 12 times.

Scoring The subject is given two practice trials, followed by two trials for score. The trial is scored to the nearest 0.1 seconds required to complete the 12 moves. The best score of the two trials is the subject's score.

Upper Body Strength Component
Test Strength/Endurance

Procedure The test is an absolute endurance test in which the subject repeatedly lifts a weight with his arm. A 4-pound weight is used with women and a 8-pound weight with men. If 4- and 8-pound dumbbells are not available, it is recommended that half-gallon plastic milk bottles filled with sand to the proper weight be used. The subject sits in a chair with his back straight against the chair and the nondominant hand at rest in his lap. The dominant arm is hanging to the side. Using his dominant arm, the subject repeatedly lifts the weight through the biceps' full range of motion for 30 seconds.

Scoring The subject's score is the number of repetitions completed in 30 seconds.

Aerobic Fitness Component
Test 880-Yard Walk

Procedure A suitable test course is needed. The test involves walking as fast as possible for 880 yards. Running is not allowed. Care needs to be taken to screen for orthopedic and cardiovascular conditions (Osness et al. 1996, p. 20), including the following:

- Significant orthopedic problems that may be aggravated by prolonged continuous walking (8–10 min)
- History of cardiac problems (i.e., recent heart attack, frequent arrhythmia, valvular defects) that can be negatively influenced by exertion
- Lightheadedness upon activity
- History of uncontrolled hypertension (high blood pressure)

Scoring One trial is given, with time recorded in minutes and seconds. The test is scored to the nearest second.

Senior Fitness Test

The Senior Fitness Test was developed over several years as part of the LifeSpan Project at the California State University, Fullerton. This battery of tests was developed to provide easily administered measures of functional fitness in older adults. An extensive amount of data was collected in order to develop age-specific norms and to provide validity and reliability evidence for the tests. Detailed results of the test development, norming, and reliability and validity process are available in a series of published research articles (Jones, Rikli & Beam 1999; Jones et al. 1998; Rikli & Jones 1998; Rikli & Jones 1999a; Rikli & Jones 1999b). This information is also summarized in a user-friendly test manual (Rikli & Jones 2001). The test manual is recommended to anyone who is interested in the development of fitness tests, especially functional fitness tests, for use with older adults. The authors provide clear directions and photographs to support administration of the tests, and present sound conceptual information linking functional fitness testing to theories of physical decline in older age, along with scientifically relevant evidence of validity and reliability.

The LifeSpan Project involved a national scientific review panel consisting of leading professionals in medicine, exercise science, and gerontology. Because of the scientific rigor involved in the development and assessment process, the Senior Fitness Test should be considered as the standard against which all other tests of older adult functional fitness should be compared. The test developers established ground rules prior to developing the test battery. These included requiring that each test meet suitable criteria in at least two of three types of validity evidence (content-related, criterion-related, and construct-related), and that test-retest reliability coefficients be .80 or above.

Eleven criteria were established to guide the test development process. Briefly, these criteria required the test to

1. represent the major functional fitness components;
2. have acceptable test-retest reliability;
3. have acceptable, documented validity evidence;
4. reflect age-related changes in functional fitness;
5. detect changes in functional fitness due to training or exercise;
6. assess a wide range of functional abilities, so that all, or most, participants would receive a score;
7. be easy to administer;
8. be reasonably quick to administer;
9. require minimum equipment and space;
10. be safe to perform without medical release for most older adults; and
11. be socially acceptable, meaningful, and motivational.

Senior Fitness Test Items

The Senior Fitness Test includes eight tests that measure five broad fitness components. Strength is measured with the chair stand test (lower body) and the arm curl test (upper body). Flexibility is measured with the chair sit-and-reach test (lower body) and the scratch test (upper body). Aerobic fitness can be tested with either the 6-minute walk test or the 2-minute step-in-place test. Agility and dynamic balance are measured with the 8-foot up-and-go test. Finally, body composition is measured with the body mass index.

Although there is similarity between some of the Senior Fitness Test items and items on the AAHPERD functional fitness test, there are important differences. First, the Senior Fitness Test battery includes a lower body strength component. This is related to mobility, and therefore potential for falling, in older adults. Falling is a major health hazard for older adults, and can result in bone fracture, disability, and death. Second, unlike the AAHPERD 880-yard walk test of aerobic endurance, the two aerobic endurance tests in the Senior Fitness Test battery can be performed easily by most older adults and require much less space.

Basic descriptions of the eight items in the Senior Fitness Test battery are provided next. Besides the instructions for standardized administration of the tests, the test manual includes methods for adapting the test, and guidance on safety precautions. Adaptations are recommended for situations in which an older adult's fitness level prevents her from achieving a minimal score (e.g., one repetition in the arm curl test). In this situation, scores from an adapted administration process should not be compared to the large normative database, but can be used to assess individual progress. Safety precautions are provided in recognition of the dangers of overexertion and the loss of dynamic balance capabilities in this age group. Anyone intending to administer the Senior Fitness Test battery to older adults should first consult the test manual for these adaptations and safety precautions.

Lower Body Strength Component
Test Chair Stand Test

Equipment A stopwatch, and a straight-backed or folding chair with a seat height of 17 inches

Procedures The chair should be placed against a wall for stability, or someone should hold the chair steady. The test begins with the participant seated in the middle of the chair, back straight, and feet approximately shoulder-width apart and flat on the floor. The arms are crossed at the wrist and held flat against the chest. The purpose of the test is to stand up and sit down as many times as possible in 30 seconds. Following a demonstration by the tester, a practice trial of one or two repetitions is given, to ensure correct form. One test trial is performed.

Scoring The score is the total number of stands performed within 30 seconds. If the participant is more than halfway up when 30 seconds has elapsed, he is credited with a full stand.

Upper Body Strength Component
Test Arm Curl Test

Equipment A stopwatch, a straight-backed or folding chair with no arm rests, and a 5-pound dumbbell (women) or 8-pound dumbbell (men)

Procedures The participant sits on the chair, with back straight and feet flat on the floor, and the dominant side of the body close to the edge of the chair. The purpose of the test is to complete as many arm curls as possible in 30 seconds. Correct form is with the upper arm held close to the side of the body, and ranges from a full extension of the elbow to a full flexion. Starting with the arm extended, and perpendicular to the floor, the participant lifts the dumbbell through a full range of motion, and then returns it to the start position. Following a demonstration by the tester, a practice trial of two or three repetitions without the dumbbell is given, to ensure correct form. One test trial is performed.

Scoring The score is the number of complete arm curls performed in 30 seconds. If the dumbbell is more than halfway up when 30 seconds has elapsed, the participant is credited with a complete arm curl.

Lower Body Flexibility
Test Chair Sit-and-Reach Test

Equipment A chair with a seat height of 17 inches, and an 18-inch ruler. The chair should have forward-angled front legs (as a folding chair has) to prevent tipping over.

Procedures The starting position is sitting on the front edge of the chair with one leg extended and the other bent with the foot flat on the floor. The test involves bending forward and reaching down toward the extended leg, as if to touch the toes of that leg. One hand is on top of the other, with the middle fingers aligned. Following a demonstration by the tester, the participant is asked to determine the preferred leg. This should be determined by a practice trial with each leg, to see which leg would result in a higher score. Two further practice trials are then given, followed by two test trials. The outstretched position should be held for 2 seconds during the test trials.

Scoring   Using the 18-inch ruler, the scorer records the number of inches (to the nearest .5 inch) between the tips of the toes and the end of the middle fingers. If the participant does not reach the toe, the score will be a numerically negative (−) score, and if the participant reaches past the toe, the score will be a numerically positive (+) score. The better score from the two test trials is used.

Upper Body Flexibility
Test   Scratch Test

Equipment   An 18-inch ruler

Procedures   In a standing position, the participant places the preferred hand over the same shoulder, reaching down toward the middle of the back, with the elbow pointing upward, the palm facing toward the back, and the fingers extended downward. The hand of the other arm is reached behind the back, with the elbow pointing downward, the palm facing away from the back, and the fingers extended upward. The participant should try to touch or overlap the middle fingers of both hands. Following a demonstration by the tester, the participant is asked to determine arm preference. This should be determined by a practice trial with each arm, to see which arm combination (left arm up, right arm down, or left arm down, right arm up) would result in a higher score. Two further practice trials are then given, followed by two test trials. The outstretched position should be held for 2 seconds during the test trials.

Scoring   The participant's score is the distance (to the nearest .5 inch) of overlap (resulting in a + score), or distance between the tips of the middle fingers (resulting in a − score). The better of the two test trial scores is used.

Aerobic Fitness Component
Test   6-Minute Walk Test or 2-Minute Step-in-Place Test

Equipment (6-Minute Walk Test)   A long measuring tape, a stopwatch (or, if possible, 2 stopwatches, in case one stops working), 4 cones, masking tape, a magic marker (to mark distances on the masking tape), and 12–15 popsicle sticks per participant (or some other convenient method for recording number of laps completed). Chairs (for resting participants) are also recommended.

Procedures (6-Minute Walk Test)   The test station consists of a rectangle 20 yards long and 5 yards wide, marked off in 5-yard sections from the starting corner. One complete circuit of the course is therefore 50 yards. Cones should be placed at the inside of each corner. The purpose of the test is to walk as quickly as possible around the course for 6 minutes. The test manual recommends that at least two participants should be tested at a time, to provide motivation, that 6 participants can be tested manageably, and that a skilled tester can test up to 12 participants at the same time. Start and stop times should be staggered by 10 seconds, to spread participants apart. A running lap count can be maintained by giving out a popsicle stick every time a participant passes the start line. At the end of the test, each participant's distance is calculated by multiplying the number of popsicle sticks by 50, then adding the elapsed distance between the start point and finishing point (using the distance-marked masking tape). For purposes of pacing, the tester should call out the time elapsed at the halfway point, and also when about 2 minutes are left. In order to keep track of each participant's finishing point, the participants should step aside when finished, and pace on the spot to cool down. A practice trial is recommended, to improve pacing, but should be administered on a separate day from the test trial.

Scoring (6-Minute Walk Test)   The score is the total number of yards completed in 6 minutes, to the nearest 5 yards.

Equipment (2-Minute Step-in-Place Test)   A stopwatch, a piece of string 30 inches long, masking tape, and a tally counter

Procedures (2-Minute Step-in-Place Test)   The test station is set up by first marking the step height on a wall. The step height is halfway between the middle of the participant's kneecap and her iliac crest. The midpoint is determined by stretching the string between these two points, then folding it in two from either the top or the bottom. This point can be marked on a wall with masking tape by asking the participant to stand next to the wall while the correct height is measured, then attaching a small piece of tape on the corresponding point on the wall. Alternatively, books can be stacked on a desk or chair to indicate the correct step height. The purpose of the test is to step as many times as possible in 2 minutes. At the start signal, the participant steps on the spot (using a walking, not running, action), raising each knee level with the wall marking on every step. One practice trial can be given on a separate day from the test day, to improve pacing and correct form.

Scoring (2-Minute Step-in-Place Test)   The score is the number of full steps completed in 2 minutes. A full step is counted for every two-step beat (i.e., a left-right combination is equal to one full step).

Agility and Dynamic Balance Components
Test   8-Foot Up-and-Go Test

Equipment   A chair with seat height of 17 inches, a tape measure, and a cone

Procedures   The test station is set up with the chair against a wall (or alternatively, with someone holding the chair steady from behind), and the cone 8 feet in front (the distance should be measured from the front of the chair seat to the back of the cone). The participant starts in a seated position on the chair, with the torso leaning slightly forward, hands on the thighs, and feet flat on the floor (one foot should be slightly in front of the other). At the start signal, the participant stands up as quickly as possible, walks quickly around the cone, and returns to the chair. Following a demonstration by the tester, one practice trial should be given, followed by two test trials.

Scoring   The score is the time elapsed from the start signal to when the participant is re-seated on the chair, recorded to the nearest .1 second. The faster score from the two test trials is used.

Body Composition Component
Test   Body Mass Index

Equipment   A weighing scale, a tape measure, masking tape, and a ruler (or other straight edge)

Procedures   The testing station should be set up so that the weighing station is close to the height station. The tape measure is taped to the wall, with the zero at the bottom. Heavy clothing (coats, sweatshirts, shoes, etc.) should be removed prior to weighing, and shoes should be removed prior to measuring height. During weight measurement, participants should stand still close to the center of the base of the scale. During height measurement, participants should stand upright, with feet together, eyes looking straight ahead, with the back against the wall. A ruler or similar straight edge is placed flat on the top of the head, extending back to the measuring tape, and height is read off the measuring tape.

Scoring   Weight is measured to the nearest pound, and height is measured to the nearest .5 inch. Body mass index is calculated using the following formula:

$$BMI = \frac{WTKG}{HTM^2}$$

where WTKG is weight in kilograms and HTM^2 is height in meters, squared. Factors for converting imperial measures to metric are these: meters = inches × .0254; and kilograms = pounds/2.2046. Users of the body mass index should be careful not to interpret BMI as being equivalent to percent fat; a BMI of 27, for example, is not equivalent to 27% fat.

Groningen Fitness Test for the Elderly

The Groningen test (Lemmink 1996; VanHeuvelen et al. 1998) was developed in The Netherlands and

TABLE 14.11	Means, Standard Deviations, Stability Reliability, and Concurrent Validity Coefficients of the Groningen Fitness Test for the Elderly							
	Men				**Women**			
Test	**Mean**	**SD**	r_{xx}	r_{xy}	**Mean**	**SD**	r_{xx}	r_{xy}
Walking (# of 16.67-m int.)	44.1	18.4	0.94	0.49	34.2	17.5	0.95	0.72
Grip strength (kg)	43.0	8.6	0.94	*	26.7	5.6	0.91	*
Hip flexibility (cm)	21.9	5.9	0.98	0.74	29.6	8.8	0.96	0.63
Shoulder flexibility(°)	47.9	50.5	0.88	0.51	50.5	6.9	0.86	0.54
Balance (time)	73.8	12.2	0.87	0.80	71.6	13.7	0.85	0.15
Manual dexterity (sec)	51.9	12.9	0.92	0.67	48.6	9.0	0.88	0.46
Reaction time (msec)	245	57	0.83	0.52	262	62	0.87	0.75

*Assumed face validity.

Source: Data from VanHeuvelen (1998).

is being used in longitudinal research designed to study the health-related fitness of older people. The test measures the quality of life. The test consists of seven items that were supported by reliability and validity evidence. The items were correlated with laboratory items to establish concurrent validity. Table 14.11 provides a summary of the test statistics. Provided are the means, standard deviations, stability reliability coefficients, and concurrent validity coefficients. The participants tested included over 600 men and women who ranged in age from 57 to 91 years. Each of the test items was found to negatively correlate with age, showing that performance decreases with age. Provided next is an abridged description of the test items (VanHeuvelen et al. 1998). You are encouraged to contact the authors for a complete copy of the test.

Aerobic Fitness Component
Test   Walking Endurance

Test Description   This test is administered on a rectangular course divided into three 16.7-meter (≈18-yard) intervals. The test starts by having the subject walk at a pace of 4 kilometers per hour (2.5 miles per hour). Every 3 minutes, walking speed is increased by 1 kilometer per hour (0.625 miles per hour). The top speed is 7 kilometers per hour (≈ 4.4 miles per hour). The objective is

to keep up the effort as long as possible. The score is the number of 16.7-meter intervals completed.

Upper Body Strength Component
Test   Grip Strength

Test Description   Grip strength is measured on a hand dynamometer (see Chapter 10) with the preferred hand, arm held at the side. The subject is given three trials and the best of the three trials is used for the subject's score.

Lower Body Flexibility Component
Test   Hip Flexibility

Test Description   The test is the common sit-and-reach test. The subject is given three trials, and the best of the three trials is used for the subject's score.

Upper Body Flexibility Component
Test   Shoulder Flexibility

Test Description   The subject holds both handles of a cord. One handle is fixed, and the other is a sliding handle. The subject passes the cord over the head from the front of the body to behind the body. The arms are kept straight and as close together as possible. The shaft of the sliding handle combined with the length of the arm is used to determine the score. The subject is given three trials, and the best of the three trials is used for the subject's score.

Agility and/or Balance Component
Test   Balance

Test Description   The subject stands on a platform that can tilt sideways. For 30 seconds the subject attempts to keep the platform in equilibrium, that is, so that the base does not touch the floor. The total time in equilibrium is the score. The subject is given three trials, and the best of the three trials is used for the subject's score.

Fine Motor Abilities Component
Tests   Manual Dexterity and Reaction Time

Test Description—Manual Dexterity   The manual dexterity task requires the subject to replace 40 blocks from a full board to an empty board as quickly as possible. The subject uses the preferred hand. The score is the time taken to complete the task.

Test Description—Reaction Time   This is a standard simple reaction time test (Rudisill & Jackson 1992). A visual stimulus is presented to the subject, who responds by pushing a button as quickly as possible. The reaction time is the elapsed time between signal and reaction. The subject's score is the median of 15 trials.

ADULT FITNESS COMPUTER APPLICATIONS

The use of computer technology in adult fitness and the health promotion industry has grown at an accelerated pace. This trend was started in the late 1960s by Dr. Kenneth Cooper when the Institute for Aerobics Research developed a computer system for the quantification of exercise with aerobics points (Cooper 1970). This computer system was designed to develop a database for studying the effects of exercise on health. This database was used to document that low aerobic fitness is a risk factor of all-cause mortality (Blair et al. 1989; Blair et al. 1995).

When the Tenneco Corporation of Houston, Texas, developed its employee health and fitness program, a computerized system was developed to quantify exercise by caloric expenditure (Baun & Baun 1985). The Tenneco system was especially important because it signaled that the trend in the corporate fitness industry was a commitment to computerization. Tenneco's development of its own customized computer software was a very expensive venture. Now, more affordable commercial software is available for evaluating adult fitness.

Provided next is a brief discussion of commercial software available for adult fitness programs. There are many different types of programs with adult fitness applications, such as health risk appraisals, nutritional analyses, fitness assessments, exercise prescription, and quantification of energy expenditure (i.e., exercise logging). We have limited the presentation to just fitness assessment, exercise prescription, and monitoring energy expenditure. An excellent recent summary of computer technology for personal trainers is Vogel (2004).

Assessing Fitness—General Fitness Assessment (GFA)

Evaluation of fitness is an essential component of an individualized exercise program. Figure 14-15 is the three-page computerized report of a sample fitness evaluation. The report includes all the major components of fitness, an individualized interpretation of the person's fitness, and training parameters for developing physical fitness. The bar graph is a display of the person's fitness in comparison to others of a similar age and the same sex. Below the bar graph is a complete listing of the person's data. The value next to the score is the average score for a person of a similar age and the same sex, that is, norm. The next two pages of the report provide the person with an individualized interpretation of his fitness and scientifically sound training suggestions. The final section of the report describes training parameters. The training parameters for all forms of aerobic exercise are standard output of the GFA. The training parameters come from the person's $\dot{V}O_2$ max, and parameters are provided for various forms of exercise.

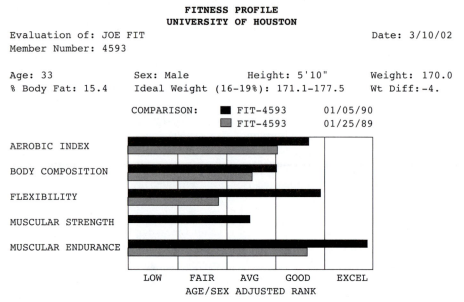

Figure 14-15a

Sample printout of a General Fitness Assessment showing the person's fitness level, an interpretation of his fitness, and training parameters for improving fitness.

(Modified from CSI Software Company, Houston, TX.)

The field of personal training has become a new career option for graduates of programs in physical education and exercise science. A major responsibility of a personal trainer is to design an individualized exercise program. Commercial software like this can be valuable to the personal trainer. Once a client's fitness data are in the computer and the fitness profile developed, the CSI software has the capacity to develop a sound individualized exercise program, as illustrated in Figure 14-16. Using the training parameters from the fitness evaluation, the computer can generate a weekly workout sheet consisting of

- Warm-up and cool-down activities
- Appropriate aerobic exercise
- Strength development activities

Strength training may be prescribed by sets and repetitions of certain weights. Aerobic intensity can be prescribed by units such as miles traveled or by percentage of $\dot{V}O_2$ max, training heart rate zone (THRZ), or RPE. The trainer can then use these values to document a well-balanced exercise program as well as to determine energy expended by calories expended and aerobic minutes.

Monitoring Aerobic Exercise— Exercise Logging

Paffenbarger's classic studies (Paffenbarger et al. 1986; Paffenbarger et al. 1984) have shown that exercise caloric expenditure is related to health. Logging exercise caloric expenditure by hand is difficult and cumbersome; the computer simplifies the task. In addition, it provides instantaneous feedback of various key aspects of exercise, such as energy expenditure and training intensity. With a computer logging program, body weight, activities done, calories, and aerobic minutes of exercise can be tracked. The CSI Exerlog program is very user-friendly and can calculate the energy expenditure for many different exercise modes. Figure 14-17 shows an example of an exercise logging computer report.

Member Name: **Date: 3/12/02**

INTERPRETATION

The General Fitness Assessment (GFA) evaluates the key elements of fitness; Aerobic Capacity, Body Composition, Flexibility, Muscular Strength and Endurance. If you are fit your body functions well. You work, play and exercise with minimal risk of injury or fatigue. You have the energy you need. You are trim and you reduce the risk of serious health problems including cardiovascular disease, the leading cause of death. In short, you look good, and are taking good care of yourself. Let's review some of your specific needs.

AEROBIC CAPACITY

Adequate Aerobic Capacity is the heart of good fitness. Aerobic exercise conditions your cardiovascular system (heart, muscles and lungs), consumes calories (reducing body fat) and protects you from cardiovascular disease. Maximum aerobic capacity or the maximum amount of oxygen you can consume per minute is also known as $\dot{V}O_2$max. It is much like maximum horsepower for an automobile. Your $\dot{V}O_2$max is 35.3 ml/kg/min. Normal for you is 31. Your aerobic fitness is AVERAGE.

Aerobic exercise consists of activities such as walking, jogging, swimming, running, stairclimbing, cycling and aerobic dance. In order to exercise at a sufficient intensity to improve your fitness but not too strenuously, so as not to cause injury and burnout, follow your heart rate. Your training heart rate should be approximately 144 to 156 beats per minute. These are the heart rates at 65% to 74% of your $\dot{V}O_2$max. At the present level of fitness this will burn approximately 430 to 490 calories per hour.

BODY COMPOSITION

Proper body composition is important in order to look good, feel good and also reduce your risk of heart disease. It is determined by assessing body weight and the relative proportion of fat-free weight and body fat. Body composition is affected by both diet and exercise.

Your weight is 137 lbs. and your percent body fat is 20.8%. This represents 28 pounds of fat. Normal percent body fat range for a person of your age and sex is 23 to 32. In order to achieve this goal you should lose about 0 pounds of fat while maintaining the same fat-free weight.

Your fat-free weight, consisting primarily of muscle, bone and vital organs is 108 pounds. The ideal weight range for you, based upon normal body fat is 130 to 142 pounds.

Figure 14-15b   *(Continued)*

SUMMARY

The average age of the population of the United States is increasing. In 1975, the median age for Americans was 29 years; by 2000, this had increased to 35 years. Public health research confirms the importance of adults maintaining an appropriate level of functional fitness. Cross-sectional and longitudinal research evidence has documented that fitness decreases during the later adult years. We are less sure of the extent to which this decline is due to the biological process of aging and the extent to which it is due to changes in behavior (e.g., decreased activity levels) that often accompany older adulthood. There is ample research to show that suitable types of exercise slow down the age-related decline in fitness. Current methods used to test adult fitness can be divided into two main types. The first involves tests that are similar to those used to test youth fitness. The YMCA's adult fitness program is a popular, scientifically sound test with normative standards. The YMCA

Based upon these results your Body Composition category is GOOD. As you change your body weight, periodically check your percent body fat to make sure you are maintaining adequate muscle mass.

MUSCULAR FLEXIBILITY
Flexibility refers to the ability of the muscles, tendons and ligaments around a joint to provide support while allowing movement throughout the full range of motion. In order to prevent injury, it is important that a joint has sufficient range of motion and is strong enough to withstand the stress and strain of exercise. Your flexibility measurements are FAIR. Stretch after warming up to increase or maintain flexibility.

MUSCULAR STRENGTH
Your muscular strength score compared to other women in your age group is FAIR. Muscular Strength is the maximum force that a muscle group can exert under various conditions. Resistance training using relatively low repetitions and higher intensity will maximize strength gains. Be sure to adequately warm up before resistance training.

MUSCULAR ENDURANCE
Muscular endurance allows you to work or exercise for a long period of time without fatigue. Generally, a lower intensity, higher repetition, muscle resistance program will produce optimal improvements. Your muscular endurance assessment is AVERAGE.

SUMMARY
Megan, your overall fitness score is 48.4, which is AVERAGE.

TRAINING PARAMETERS
Train at least 30 minutes per session and 4 sessions per week.

Watts	95 to 110	$\dot{V}O_2$ml	1430 to 1650
KPM	560 to 670	$\dot{V}O_2$ml/kg/min	23 to 26.5
KCal/hour	430 to 490	METs	6.6 to 7.6
Walk/Jog (min/mile)	11.4 to 9.9	Heart Rate	144 to 156

Figure 14-15b *Continued*

Trainee: **Trainer:** I.M. Fit

WarmUP: **Cool:**
Side Stretches - Stretch slowly (5 minutes)   Cool Down - 5 minutes
Warm-up All Muscle Groups
STEP 4-6 PLTFRM - Easy does it

EXERCISES	DESCRIPTION	3/18/06 SAT	3/19/06 SUN	3/20/06 MON	3/21/06 TUE	3/22/06 WED	3/23/06 THU	3/24/06 FRI
Aerobics	45 min 70-85% THRZ			*		*		*
Cycling (Road)	60 min 10 Miles Hard	*	*					
Step Aerobics	55 min 70-85% THRZ				*		*	
Walk/Jog/Run	25 min 2 Miles		*		*		*	
Strength Training	15 reps 45 lbs			*		*		*

Figure 14-16
Sample computer-generated individualized training program. The symbol * indicates the exercise to be done on the given day.
(Modified from CSI Software Company, Houston, TX.)

Page 1

	MOST RECENT	(LOSS) or GAIN
BODY WEIGHT	124.0	0

	AVERAGE MILE (MIN)	8.7	BEST MILE (MIN)	7.7

DATE: 05/05/06   **MEMBER #** 2222A

FREDA A FITNESS
2345 FRED STREET
HOUSTON, TX 77001-1111

MESSAGE:

BE A PART OF IT! JOIN OUR
SUMMER SOFTBALL TEAM. SEE
PATTI IN ATHLETICS.

THIS MONTH'S ACTIVITIES

DATE	ACTIVITY	UNITS	DURATION	AEROBIC POINTS	CALORIES	AEROBIC MINUTES
04/05/06	WALK/JOG/RUN	5.8 MI	45:00	33.5	566	43.0
04/06/06	TREADMILL		45:00	32.7	554	41.0
04/06/06	STAIRMASTER		55:00	55.2	560	50.0
04/06/06	SWIMMING	1.2 MI	45:00	25.1	354	35.0
04/07/06	CYCLING (ROAD)	25.0 MI	120:00	23.5	985	100.0
04/08/06	CYCLE ERGOMETER		55:00	55.2	560	50.0
04/09/06	AEROBIC DANCE		55:00	11.0	411	35.0
04/09/06	PROG RESISTANCE		30:00	6.0	189	10.0
04/10/06	SUPER CIRCUIT		25:00	6.5	187	10.0
04/10/06	TENNIS DOUBLES	3.0 SET	75:00	1.2	391	30.0
04/11/06	WALK/JOG/RUN	3.0 MI	30:00	14.0	295	
04/11/06	SCHWINN AIRDYNE		45:00	17.5	458	30.0
04/12/06	WALK/JOG/RUN	6.2 MI	48:00	36.2	610	48.0

TOTALS

ACTIVITY	PREVIOUS TOTAL	THIS MONTH'S TOTAL	CUMULATIVE YEAR'S TOTAL
WALK/JOG/RUN (MI)	38.30	15.00	53.30
STAIRMASTER (HRS)	4.00	0.92	4.92
CYCLE ERGOMETER (HRS)	3.82	0.92	4.74
SWIMMING (MI)	3.30	1.20	4.50
CYCLING (ROAD) (MI)	127.00	25.00	152.00
TOTAL CALORIES (1.7 lbs)	46194	6120	52314
TOTAL AEROBIC MINUTES	2993	482	3475
TOTAL AEROBIC POINTS	1507	317	1825

AEROBIC POINTS: ONE POINT EQUALS APPROXIMATELY 7.0 ML/KG/MIN OF OXYGEN UPTAKE ABOVE RESTING. TRY TO OBTAIN AT LEAST 30 POINTS PER WEEK.
AEROBIC MINUTES: THE NUMBER OF MINUTES YOUR HEART IS PERFORMING IN ITS TRAINING ZONE . TRY TO OBTAIN AT LEAST 60 PER WEEK.
CALORIES: 3500 CALORIES REPRESENTS THE ENERGY DERIVED FROM LOSING APPROXIMATELY 1 LB. OF WEIGHT.

Figure 14-17

Sample output from the Exerlog program. After receiving information, the program provides instantaneous feedback in kilocalories, the number of minutes that exercise was done at a suitable intensity (aerobic minutes), and aerobic points, which are numerical descriptions of exercise intensity and duration.

(Modified from CSI Software Company, Houston, TX.)

test battery includes the same fitness components measured in youth fitness tests, i.e., aerobic fitness, body composition, flexibility, and muscular strength and endurance. The second type consists of functional fitness tests. These relatively recently developed tests are designed specifically for older adults, and are designed to test whether older adults can function independently. The Senior Fitness Test battery was developed most recently, and can be administered fairly easily without specialized or expensive equipment or facilities. The tests are suitable for older adults with a wide range of functional fitness levels, and norm tables are provided to interpret the results. Functional fitness is extremely important to older individuals and to the general society of the United States. Older adults do not want to be dependent on others, and the public health care costs for functionally dependent older adults is higher than for those who can function independently. As the baby boom generation reaches retirement age, these issues will become increasingly important.

FORMATIVE EVALUATION OF OBJECTIVES

Objective 1   Identify the methods used to study the decline in fitness associated with aging.

1. How is the rate at which fitness declines with age determined with a cross-sectional research study?
2. How is the rate at which fitness declines with age determined with a longitudinal research study?
3. What are the limitations of the cross-sectional and longitudinal methods?

Objective 2   Understand the general age-related decline in health-related fitness.

1. Describe the expected change in fitness associated with aging.
2. What is the influence of exercise and body composition on the decline in fitness with aging?

Objective 3   Identify the types of tests used to evaluate adult fitness.

1. What are the tests of the YMCA battery?
2. How do the adult fitness test items compare to youth fitness test items?

Objective 4   Identify the types of tests used to evaluate functional adult fitness.

1. What is the general philosophy of functional fitness tests?
2. What are the tests of the Senior Fitness Test battery?

Objective 5   Identify the computer programs available to use in adult fitness programs.

1. What types of computer programs are available for adult fitness evaluation?
2. Describe how an exercise specialist or personal trainer could use computer programs to individualize an adult fitness program.

ADDITIONAL LEARNING ACTIVITIES

1. Visit a YMCA and gain an understanding of the Y's Way to Fitness program. If you have the opportunity, become involved in the testing phase of the program. It is the most widely used adult health-related fitness test.
2. There are many different adult fitness programs—at corporations, hospitals, or even at your college or university. Volunteer to work in a program. You learn through experience, and the experience can help you find a job.
3. Investigate fitness programs for older adults. These can be found in community centers or retirement homes. You may be surprised to find that they are becoming very popular. Volunteer to work in this setting. This experience could become very valuable in the future.

4. If you can find the opportunity, work with someone to administer a functional adult fitness test.
5. Visit an adult fitness facility and ask if you can examine its computer applications.

BIBLIOGRAPHY

Baun, W. B. and M. Baun. 1985. A corporate health and fitness program: Motivation and management by computers. *JOPERD* 55: 43–45.

Blair, S. N. et al. 1989. Physical fitness and all-cause mortality: A prospective study of healthy men and women. *Journal of the American Medical Association* 262: 2395–2401.

Blair, S. N. et al. 1995. Changes in physical fitness and all-cause mortality: A prospective study of healthy and unhealthy men. *Journal of the American Medical Association* 273(14): 1093–1098.

Blakley, B. R. et al. 1994. The validity of isometric strength tests. *Personnel Psychology* 37: 247–274.

Buskirk, E. R. and J. L. Hodgson. 1987. Age and aerobic power: The rate of change in men and women. *Federation Proceedings* 46: 1824–1829.

Cooper, K. H. 1970. *The new aerobics*. New York: Bantam Books.

Cooper Institute for Aerobics Research. 1999. *FITNESSGRAM® Test Administration Manual*. 2nd ed. Champaign, IL: Human Kinetics.

Cornoni-Huntley et al. 1986. *Populations for epidemiologic studies of the elderly: Resource data book*. Government Printing Office, NIH Pub. No. 86-2443.

deVries, H. A. and T. J. Housh. 1994. *Physiology of exercise for physical education, athletics and exercise science*. 5th ed. Dubuque, IA: Wm. C. Brown.

Frisancho, A. R. 1990. *Anthropometric standards for assessment of growth and nutritional status*. Ann Arbor: University of Michigan Press.

Golding, L. A. (Ed.). 2000. YMCA fitness testing and assessment manual. 4th ed. Champaign, IL: Human Kinetics.

Hagberg, J. M. et al. 1985. A hemodynamic comparison of young and older endurance athletes during exercise. *Journal of Applied Physiology* 58(6): 2041–2046.

Jackson, A. S. and M. L. Pollock. 1978. Generalized equations for predicting body density of men. *British Journal of Nutrition* 40: 497–504.

Jackson, A. S., M. L. Pollock, and A. Ward. 1980. Generalized equations for predicting body density of women. *Medicine and Science in Sports and Exercise* 12: 175–182.

Jackson, A. S. and R. M. Ross. 1997. *Understanding exercise for health and fitness*. 3rd ed. Dubuque, IA: Kendall/Hunt.

Jackson, A. S. et al. 1995. Changes in aerobic power of men ages 25–70 years. *Medicine and Science in Sports and Exercise* 27: 113–120.

Jackson, A. S. et al. 1996. Changes in aerobic power of women, ages 20 to 64 years. *Medicine and Science in Sports and Exercise* 28: 884–891.

Jones, C. J., R. E. Rikli, and W. C. Beam. 1999. A 30-s chair-stand test as a measure of lower body strength in community-residing older adults. *Research Quarterly for Exercise and Sport* 70: 113–119.

Jones, C. J. et al. 1998. The reliability and validity of a chair sit-and-reach test as a measure of hamstring flexibility in older adults. *Research Quarterly for Exercise and Sport* 69: 338–343.

Kasch, F. W., J. P. Wallace, and S. P. VanCamp. 1985. Effects of 18 years of endurance exercise on the physical work capacity of older men. *Journal of Cardiopulmonary Rehabilitation* 5: 308–312.

Kasch, F. W. et al. 1990. The effect of physical activity and inactivity on aerobic power in older men (a longitudinal study). *The Physician and Sportsmedicine* 18: 73–81.

Kovar, M. G. 1986. National Center for Health Statistics, *Aging in the eighties, preliminary data from the supplement on aging to the national health interview survey, United States, January–June 1984. Advanced data from vital and health statistics*. No. 115. DHHS Pub. No. 86-1250. Public Health Service, Hyattsville, MD.

Larson, E. B. and R. A. Bruce. 1987. Health benefits of exercise in an aging society. *Archives of Internal Medicine* 147: 353–356.

Lemmink, K. 1996. The Groningen Fitness Test for the Elderly: Development of a measurement instrument.

Ph.D Dissertation, Department of Human Movement Sciences, University of Groningen, Groningen, The Netherlands.

McArdle, W., F. Katch, and V. Katch. 2001. *Exercise physiology–energy, nutrition, and human performance*. 5th ed. Philadelphia: Lippincott Williams & Wilkins.

Montoye, H. J. and Lamphiear, D. E. 1977. Grip and arm strength in males and females, age 10 to 69. *Research Quarterly* 48: 109–120.

Osness, W. H. et al. 1996. *Functional fitness assessment for adults over 60 years: A field based assessment*. 2nd ed. Dubuque, IA: Kendall/Hunt.

Paffenbarger, R. S. Jr. et al. 1984. A natural history of athleticism and cardiovascular health. *Journal of the American Medical Association* 252: 491–495.

Paffenbarger, R. S. Jr. et al. 1986. Physical activity, all cause mortality, and longevity of college alumni. *New England Journal of Medicine* 314: 605–613.

Petrofsky, J. S. and A. R. Lind. 1975. Aging, isometric strength and endurance and cardiovascular responses to static effort. *Journal of Applied Physiology* 38: 91–95.

Plowman, S. A. 1992. Chapter 8. Physical activity, physical fitness, and low back pain. In J. O. Holloszy, (Ed.). *Exercise and sport sciences reviews*. Baltimore: Williams & Wilkins.

Pollock, M. L. and J. H. Wilmore. 1990. *Exercise in health and disease*. 2nd ed. Philadelphia: W. B. Saunders.

Pollock, M. L. et al. 1987. Effect of age and training on aerobic capacity and body composition of master athletes. *Journal of Applied Physiology* 62(2): 725–731.

Rikli, R. E. and C. J. Jones. 1997. Assessing physical performance in independent older adults: Issues and guidelines. *Journal of Aging and Physical Activity* 5: 244–261.

Rikli, R. E. and C. J. Jones. 1998. The reliability and validity of a 6-minute walk test as a measure of physical endurance in older adults. *Journal of Aging and Physical Activity* 6: 363–375.

Rikli, R. E. and C. J. Jones. 1999a. Development and validation of a functional fitness test for community-residing older adults. *Journal of Aging and Physical Activity* 7: 127–159.

Rikli, R. E. and C. J. Jones. 1999b. Functional fitness normative scores for community-residing adults, age 60–94. *Journal of Aging and Physical Activity* 7: 162–181.

Rikli, R. E. and C. J. Jones. 2001. *Senior Fitness Test Manual*. Champaign, IL Human Kinetics.

Rudisill, M. E. and A. S. Jackson. 1992. *Theory and application of motor learning*. Onalaska, TX: MacJ-R Publishing.

Shephard, R. J. 1986. Physical training for the elderly. *Clinical Sports Medicine* 5: 515–533.

Skender, M. L. et al. 1996. Comparison of 2-year weight loss trends in behavioral treatments of obesity: Diet, exercise, and combination interventions. *Journal of the American Dietetic Association* 96: 342–346.

Spirduso, W. W., K. L. Francis, and P. G. MacRae. 2005. *Physical dimensions of aging*. 2nd ed. Champaign, IL: Human Kinetics.

U.S. Army. 1992. *FM 21–20 physical fitness training*. Washington DC: Department of the Army.

VanHeuvelen, M. et al. 1998. Physical fitness related to age and physical activity in older persons. *Medicine and Science in Sports and Exercise* 30(3): 434–441.

Vogel, A. (2004). Fitness goes hi-tech: How today's electronic gadgets are changing the face of fitness. *IDEA Fitness Journal*, July/August, 116–118, 121.

Wilmore, J. H. and D. L. Costill. 1994. *Physiology of sport and exercise*. Champaign, IL: Human Kinetics.

APPLICATIONS TO PERSONS WITH DISABILITIES

J. P. Barfield   *Tennessee Tech University*

C O N T E N T S

K E Y   W O R D S

Brockport Physical Fitness Test
disability sport
ecological validity
functional classification
medical classification
step activity monitor
task analysis

OBJECTIVES

The Individuals with Disabilities Education Act (IDEA; Public Law 108-446) identifies appropriate educational services for persons with disabilities. This legislation documents specific disability categories that qualify for services and is one example of how to classify varying disability types (Table 15.1). The listing is not exhaustive but is a good reference for the population that will be described in this chapter, namely individuals with varying levels of sensory, physical, and cognitive abilities (Table 15.2). Test administration and evaluation are given additional attention when applied to persons with disabilities because tests and evaluation standards can be quite distinct from standards used with the general population. To further complicate decisions regarding assessment, ability levels can vary dramatically within each disability type. For instance, a test for an individual with a low-level spinal cord injury may not be appropriate for an individual with a high-level injury. However, with a general awareness of testing considerations specific to individuals with disabilities, you should be able to make appropriate test choices for individuals with a wide range of ability levels. After reading Chapter 15, you should be able to

1. Select appropriate physical activity assessments for persons with disabilities.
2. Recognize the appropriateness of standardized physical fitness test items for persons with disabilities.
3. Select motor assessments appropriate for various ages and ability levels.
4. Distinguish between medical and functional sport classification models.
5. Develop authentic assessments appropriate for particular outcomes.
6. Identify environmental factors that impact test scores and interpretation.

TABLE 15.1	**Individuals with Disabilities Education Act Disability Categories**

Mental Retardation
Hearing Impairment (including deafness)
Speech or Language Impairment
Visual Impairment (including blindness)
Serious Emotional Disturbance
Orthopedic Impairment (e.g., cerebral palsy)
Autism
Traumatic Brain Injury
Other Health Impairments (e.g., asthma)
Specific Learning Disabilities
Developmental Delay* (for children ages 3 through 9)

*Developmental Delay indicates atypical progress in physical development (as well as other areas).

INTRODUCTION

The National Center on Physical Activity and Disability (2005) reported that 20 to 30% of the population has a disability that interferes with activities of daily living. Measurement and evaluation are important practices within this population, and

TABLE 15.2	**Disability Types Stratified by General Category**
Category	**Examples of Disability Types**
Sensory	Blindness, deafness, hearing impairments, and visual impairments
Cognitive	Developmental delays, emotional disturbance, learning disabilities, mental retardation
Physical	Cerebral palsy, traumatic brain injury, spinal cord injury, stroke
Health	Asthma, cystic fibrosis, muscular dystrophy, sickle cell anemia, spinal muscular atrophy

Note: Autism may result in cognitive deficits but is classically defined as a communication disorder.

school-age children with disabilities have a multitude of assessment requirements compared to the general population. In addition to sport performance and health improvement outcomes studied in the general population, prevention of secondary health problems and improved functional ability are priority outcomes among individuals with disabilities (Durstine et al. 2000; Rimmer et al. 2004). Function, in this sense, is a broad term used to describe the ability to complete a variety of everyday tasks, including activity, sport, leisure, self-care, and independent living (Figure 15-1). Function reflects the extent that an individual can or cannot complete intended tasks; therefore, tests employing criterion-referenced standards (see Chapter 2) receive greater priority than in the able-bodied population.

PHYSICAL ACTIVITY

Regular physical activity is a beneficial lifetime behavior. Benefits of regular activity among individuals with disabilities include reduced risk of secondary disease associated with disability and improved func-

tional capacity (Davis 1993; Kosma, Cardinal & Rintala 2002; McDonald 2002). However, fewer individuals with disabilities engage in regular activity compared to the predominantly sedentary general population (Rimmer et al. 2004). Physical activity is a priority outcome for individuals with disabilities because inactivity leads to dependence upon others and reduced social opportunities (Durstine et al. 2000). Selection of a physical activity measurement instrument for this population requires more consideration than in the able-bodied population, and test administrators must select instruments that can accurately assess and detect changes in physical activity in specific populations. This section addresses six commonly reported physical activity measurement instruments/methods and the reliability, validity, and practicality of each relative to disability-specific populations.

Instrument Pedometers

Description Pedometers are reliable activity monitors that measure step counts. Although they are a practical instrument for the assessment of

Figure 15-1
A child using a racing wheelchair for sport.
(Photo © 2005 Brian Love.)

activity in the general population, practitioners must consider the validity of step scores among individuals with physical disabilities.

Validity and Reliability   Among individuals with atypical physical function (e.g., cerebral palsy, spinal cord injury), inconsistent stride length, atypical gait, and wheelchair use affect the suitability of pedometers. Although reliability within this population is not the primary measurement concern, the validity of scores intended to assess daily physical activity is essential to address prior to use. Any ambulatory variation from the able-bodied population will alter the measurement and therefore evaluation of physical activity within this population. Pedometers are least accurate at low walking speeds (Bassett 2000; McDonald 2002), and many individuals with disabilities demonstrate slow walking compared to the general population.

These instruments are appropriate for many individuals with cognitive or alternative sensory disabilities. Pedometers are suitable instruments for deaf individuals, individuals with asthma, or individuals with mild mental retardation. Gait affects pedometer validity, but the use of pedometers is suitable for a variety of individuals without gait difficulties. Neurological difficulty itself should not deter the use of pedometers, and pedometers provided greater sensitivity to changes in activity levels than seven-day recall instruments among individuals with multiple sclerosis (Ng & Kent-Braun 1997). Additionally, age and cognitive function of the person being measured may require the tester to tape the pedometer shut (prevent accidental resetting) or record scores within controlled settings (e.g., during the school day).

Comment   Disability status alone does not prevent use of a pedometer, but one must be certain step counts are an appropriate measure of activity level.

Instrument   Activity Monitors

Description   An alternative to pedometers that is suitable for a broad range of individuals with disabilities is the **step activity monitor** (SAM;

Coleman et al. 1999). The SAM attaches just above the ankle and quantitatively records step frequency, duration, and intensity (steps per minute).

Objective   The device stores patterns of activity and inactivity in adjustable time intervals and identifies a "peak activity index," which is the 30-minute time period with the greatest number of step counts each one-minute interval. The benefit of this device in disability populations is its sensitivity to cadence and gait speed, which can be adjusted for individual participants during practice sessions (Busse et al. 2005; McDonald 2002).

Reliability and Validity   Whereas pedometers may not be valid assessment tools for individuals with atypical gaits (e.g., stroke), step activity monitors provide a good measurement option in disability populations. Busse and colleagues documented a test-retest intraclass correlation coefficient (ICC) of .86 on seven-day mean step count among ten individuals with neurological impairments (2005). This reliability estimate is consistent with an error rate of less than 1% during outdoor walking and less than 4% during stair stepping among individuals with alternative disability types (Coleman et al. 1999).

Comment   The advantage of the step activity monitor over three-dimensional activity monitors (e.g., Caltrac, Tritrac) is the usefulness of the measurement unit. McDonald (2002) has documented the need for an objective and meaningful "real-world" activity unit for disability populations. Unlike activity monitors that are appropriate for the general population, the step activity monitor is easy to administer and accounts for variations due to physical impairment within a meaningful unit of activity, such as walking. McDonald has also provided step rate per minute criteria for low (1–15), medium (16–30), and high (>30) intensity activity.

Method   Direct Observation

Description   Direct observation is a precise and valid measurement of physical activity within disability populations but is not practical in many instances. Direct observation enables a researcher or practitioner to monitor duration, frequency, intensity, and mode of exercise across various lengths of time, and software currently exists to code actions into activity bouts (McKenzie 2002).

Reliability and Validity Two obstacles exist with this assessment method within disability populations. First, the time necessary to record individual scores of a participant must be observed continuously by a data collector. Time constraints prevent this option from being utilized in large-scale research studies despite the validity of evaluation. Time constraints also limit the ability of an adapted physical educator, consultant, or teacher aid to track individual students across a school day. However, for small-scale research studies, direct observation would provide strong internal and external validity relative to physical activity. Second, direct observation systems were developed for able-bodied students with heart rate (HR), in many cases, being the validation variable to estimate energy expenditure. The linear relationship between HR and intensity documented in the general population does not necessarily apply to wheelchair users or other individuals with physical disabilities, thereby limiting the validity of scoring within this population. In essence, energy expenditure within this population cannot be predicted based on direct observation prediction equations.

Instrument Self-Report

Test Physical Activity and Disability Survey (PADS)

Description The PADS is a structured self-report survey specifically designed for individuals with disabilities and chronic disease (Rimmer, Riley & Rubin 2001). The scale consists of 28 items grouped into the following subscales: (a) exercise, (b) household activity, (c) time indoors, and (d) leisure time.

Reliability and Validity Rimmer and colleagues (2001) reported moderately high internal consistency (Chronbach's α = .67 to .77) and acceptable

test-retest reliability (ICC > .78) across subscales and total activity score. Interrater reliability (ICC) was high for all subscales (>.92). However, predictive criterion-related validity evidence is lacking from the current instrument, as a weak relationship was documented between PADS and peak $\dot{V}O_2$ (r = .23).

Test Physical Activity Scale for Individuals with Disabilities (PASID)

Description This instrument is intended to assess physical activity bouts of individuals with physical disabilities over the previous seven days. Thirteen questions are divided among leisure-time, household, and work-related activities (Washburn et al. 2002). Questions are applicable to wheelchair users, unlike questions in instruments typically used with able-bodied persons (Figure 15-2).

Reliability and Validity Scores distinguish between active individuals and completely inactive individuals, but additional reliability and validity evidence of the instrument is needed.

In general, activity recall is the least effective physical activity assessment for persons with disabilities. Reliability and validity of recall instruments are lowest among young people, and school-age participants comprise the majority of individuals with disabilities that are regularly assessed. Recall is not suitable for individuals with cognitive deficits because single-day and multiple-day processing of events may be unrealistic. Additionally, the majority of self-report instruments document activities for the able-bodied and are therefore nonapplicable to individuals with motor impairments.

Comment Although easy to administer, standardized recall instruments that are suitable for the able-bodied population require too many adaptations, thereby reducing their suitability for use with individuals with disabilities. Survey instruments should be validated on an intended population before use.

Instrument Heart Rate Monitors

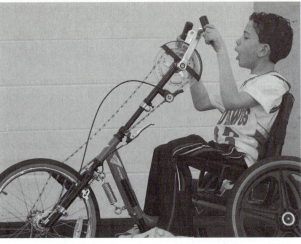

Figure 15-2

Hand cycle in motion. Mode of ambulation may dictate the choice of physical activity assessment. (Photo © 2005 Brian Love.)

Objective   Estimate energy expenditure from activity heart rate

Reliability and Validity   Prediction of energy expenditure has been validated among both children (Rose et al. 1989) and adults (Tobimatsu et al. 1998) with cerebral palsy. Heart rate monitoring is not a valid estimate of energy expenditure among many individuals with spinal cord injuries due to the possibility of blunted heart rate responses to exercise. Test-retest estimates of resting and submaximal HR have not proven to be highly reliable in this population (ICC ≤ .70; Stewart et al. 2000).

Method   Doubly Labeled Water

Description   This technique provides an estimate of daily energy expenditure and has proven accurate in some disability populations. Unfortunately, the cost of this method delimits its use to well-funded research studies. Documentation of its use in persons with disabilities is beyond the scope of this chapter.

Table 15.3 provides a summary of the physical activity instruments for persons with disabilities.

PHYSICAL FITNESS

Physical fitness is an essential outcome to many individuals with disabilities, especially physical disabilities, because improved fitness can result in greater independence (Rimmer 2001). The ability of an individual to transfer himself or herself from a wheelchair to the bed or toilet is influenced by the strength of shoulder girdle muscles. The ability of an individual to push his or her wheelchair without assistance and therefore travel independently is influenced by aerobic capacity. Unfortunately, fitness assessment is not mandated by all states and insufficient testing exists within the school or recreation setting due, in part, to tester anxiety. When first exposed to children receiving special education or adapted physical education services, readers of this text may be more apprehensive than within regular education environments and fear that a child with a disability will "break" due to simple play activity. It is common for undergraduate students to feel apprehensive when testing individuals with disabilities. Fortunately, disease and disability are not exacerbated by physical contact, and interaction with individuals of various abilities will alleviate anxiety.

TABLE 15.3	**Physical Activity Instruments and Appropriate Applications for Persons with Disabilities**
Instrument	Appropriate Applications/Comments
Pedometer	Cognitive, health, and sensory impairments
Activity Monitor	Cognitive, health, physical, and sensory impairments with the exception being wheelchair users
Direct Observation	Cognitive, health, physical, and sensory impairments; impractical
Self-Report	Health, physical, and sensory impairments; tester should use disability-specific instrument
Heart Rate Monitoring	Cognitive and sensory impairments
Doubly Labeled Water	Cognitive, health, physical, and sensory impairments; expensive and impractical

Youth Fitness Assessments

Test   Brockport Physical Fitness Test (BPFT)

Description   The **Brockport Physical Fitness Test** (Table 15.4) is a comprehensive physical fitness battery that identifies minimum levels of function and fitness necessary for good health among youth with disabilities ages 10 to 17 (Winnick & Short 1999).

Objective   This battery is an outgrowth of Project Target, a federally funded program intended to document criterion-referenced fitness standards for children and youth with disabilities. It is similar to the FITNESSGRAM® battery used with able-bodied populations. The battery contains 27 test items addressing aerobic functioning, body composition, and musculoskeletal functioning (including flexibility and range of motion). Test items and corresponding standards are designated for specific populations, including individuals with visual impairments, mental retardation, cerebral palsy, spinal cord injury, and amputations. Test selection is also based on classification for each disability, depicting appropriate test items for level of function for each disability type.

Reliability and Validity   The suitability of test items in the Brockport Physical Fitness Test is superior to general physical fitness batteries for school-age individuals with disabilities. Test selection was based on scores of over 1,500 students with various ability levels. Reliability (test-retest and interrater agreement) and validity (content-, criterion-, and construct-related) evidence is reported for the majority of test items within the battery (Table 15.5), and additional evidence of measurement properties is presented elsewhere (Winnick & Short 1998). Reliability evidence for the majority of items is strong. Additionally, criterion-related validity evidence based on functional outcomes is also strong ($r > 0.70$).

Comment   The asset of this manual is the identification of tests that are essential to independence and sufficient health. Although this battery identifies specific target populations, test items could easily be extended to individuals with a variety of ability levels.

Test   Kansas Adapted/Special Physical Education Test

Description   This battery includes muscular fitness, abdominal fitness, hamstring flexibility, and aerobic endurance test options for individuals with multiple types of disabilities.

Reliability and Validity   Acceptable reliability coefficients have been reported for individuals ages 5 to 21 (Johnson & Lavay 1988).

Comment   Test options complement those for able-bodied fitness assessment, enabling this

TABLE 15.4 Brockport Physical Fitness Test Items

	General Population		Mental Retardation		Blind with Assistance		Cerebral Palsy		Spinal cord Injury		Congenital Anomalies/Amputation	
	Test Item	Available Standard	Test Item	Available Standard	Test Item	Available Standard	Test Item	Available Standard	Test Item	Available Standard	Test Item	Available Standard
AEROBIC FUNCTIONING												
PACER (20 m)	O	G	R†	S	R	S					O†	G
PACER (16 m)		G	R†	S								
One-mile run/walk	R	G*	R	G*	O†	S					R†	G
TAMT							R	G*	R	G*	R†	G*
BODY COMPOSITION												
Skinfolds	R	G	R	G	R	G	R	G	R	G	R	G
BMI	O	G	O	G	O	G	O	G				
MUSCULOSKELETAL FUNCTIONING												
Reverse curl							R†	S	R†	S*		
Seated push-up			O†	S			R†	S*	R†	S	R†	S
40-m push/walk							R†/O†	S*				
Wheelchair ramp test												
Bench press	O	G	R†	S			R†/O†	G	O†	G	R†	G
Dumbbell press		G	R†	S					O†	G	R†/O†	G
Extended arm hang		G	O	S								
Flexed arm hang	O	G										
Dominant grip strength		G			O	G	O†	G	R†	G	O†	G
Isometric push-up		G	O†	S								
Push-up	R	G			R	G						
Pull-up	O	G			O	G						
Modified pull-up	O	G			O	G						
Curl-up	R	G			R	G					R†	G

(Continued)

TABLE 15.4 Brockport Physical Fitness Test Items *(Continued)*

	General Population		Mental Retardation		Blind with Assistance		Cerebral Palsy		Spinal cord Injury		Congenital Anomalies/Amputation	
	Test Item	Available Standard	Test Item	Available Standard	Test Item	Available Standard	Test Item	Available Standard	Test Item	Available Standard	Test Item	Available Standard
MUSCULOSKELETAL FUNCTIONING *CONTINUED*												
Modified curl-up	R	G*	R	S								
Trunk lift	R	G*	R	G*	R	G*					R†	G*
Modified Apley test							R†	G*/S*	R†	G*	R†	G*
Shoulder stretch	O	G*	O	G*	O	G*					R†	G*
Modified Tomas test							R†	G*/S*	R†	G*		
Back-saver sit and reach	R	G*	R	G*	R	G*			R†		R†	G*
TST	R	G					R†/O†	G	R†	G	R†	G

Source: From J. P. Winnick and F. X. Short, eds., 1999, *The Brockport Physical Fitness Test Manual: A Health-Related Test for Youths with Physical and Mental Disabilities*, pages 33–34, table 3.1. © 1999 by Joseph Winnick. Reprinted with permission from Human Kinetics (Champaign, IL).

R = recommended test item; O = optional test item; G = general standard; S = specific standard

*Only single standard is available.

†Item is recommended or optional for some, but not all, members of the category.

Note: "Blind with assistance" refers to youngsters who are blind and are being assisted in running activities.

TABLE 15.5	**Reliability and Validity Evidence of Brockport Physical Fitness Test**			
Test Item	**Fitness Component/ Subcomponent**	**Target Population**	**Validity**	**Reliability**
PACER (20 m)	Aerobic capacity	GP, MR, BL, CA/A	High content; moderate concurrent (Cureton, 1994a)	$r = .89$ (GP) (Leger, Mercier, Gadoury, & Lambert, 1988) $\alpha = .97$ (MR) (Short & Winnick, 1999)
PACER (16 m)	Aerobic capacity	MR	$r = .77$ with peak $\dot{V}O_2$ (MR) (Fernhall, Pitetti, Vukavich, Stubbs, Hansen, Winnick & Short, 1996)	$\alpha = .96–.98$ (MR) (Short & Winnick, 1999)
One-mile run/walk	Aerobic capacity	GP, BL, CA/A	$r = .60–.85$ with $\dot{V}O_2$ max (Cureton, 1994a)	Usually highly reliable for adolescents (Safrit & Wood, 1995)
Target aerobic movement test (TAMT)	Aerobic behavior	MR, CP, SCI, CA/A	Logical	$P = .92$ (SCI) (Rimmer, Connor-Kuntz, Winnick, & Short, 1997)
Skinfolds	Body composition	All	$r = .88–.89$ with % body fat (Lohman, 1994)	Interrater reliability is high ($> .95$) (Safrit & Wood, 1995)
Body mass index (BMI)	Body composition	GP, MR, BL, CP	$r = .70–.82$ with % body fat (Lohman, 1992)	Very high (Lohman, 1994)
Reverse curl	Upper-body strength/ endurance	SCI	Logical	No data available
Seated push-up	Upper-body strength/ endurance	CP, SCI, CA/A	Logical	No data available
40-m push/walk	General strength/ endurance	CP	Logical	No data available
Wheelchair ramp test	Upper-body strength/ endurance	CP	Logical	No data available
Push-up	Upper-body strength/ endurance	GP, BL	Logical (Plowman & Corbin, 1994)	Generally reliable (.60–.96) (Plowman & Corbin, 1994)
Pull-up	Upper-body strength/ endurance	GP, BL, CA/A	Logical (Plowman & Corbin, 1994); construct (Winnick & Short, 1982)	Generally reliable (.79–.91) (Plowman & Corbin, 1994)
Modified pull-up	Upper-body strength/ endurance	GP, BL	Logical (Plowman & Corbin, 1994)	Generally reliable (.56–.91) (Plowman & Corbin, 1994)
Dumbbell press	Upper-body strength/endurance	CP, SCI, CA/A	Logical; $r = .81$ (GP) with bench press (Short & Winnick, 1999)	$\alpha = .98$ (MR) (Short & Winnick, 1999)
Bench press	Upper-body strength/endurance	MR, SCI, CA/A	Logical	$\alpha = .91$ (MR); $\alpha = .92$ (GP) (Short & Winnick, 1999)

(Continued)

Test Item	Fitness Component/ Subcomponent	Target Population	Validity	Reliability
Grip strength	Upper-body strength/endurance	MR, CP, SCI, CA/A	Construct (Winnick & Short, 1982); logical	Most coefficients in the .90s (Safrit & Wood, 1995)
Isometric push-up	Upper-body strength/endurance	MR	Logical	$R = .83$ (Eichstaedt & Lavay, 1992) $\alpha = .83$ (MR) (Short & Winnick, 1999)
Extended arm hang	Upper-body strength/endurance	MR	Logical	$\alpha = .85$ (MR) (Short & Winnick, 1999)
Flexed arm hang	Upper-body strength/endurance	GP, MR, BL, CA/A	Construct (Winnick & Short, 1982); logical (Plowman & Corbin, 1994)	$\alpha = .84–.96$ (Daquila, 1982) $\alpha = .93$ (MR) (Short & Winnick, 1999)
Trunk lift	Trunk/abdominal function	GP, MR, BL, CA/A	Logical (Plowman & Corbin, 1994)	$P = .89$ (MR) (Short & Winnick, 1999)
Curl-up	Trunk/abdominal function	GP, BL, CA/A	Logical (Plowman & Corbin, 1994)	$R = .93–.97$ (Robertson & Magnusdottir, 1987)
Modified curl-up	Trunk/abdominal function	MR	Logical (Jette, Sidney, & Cicutti, 1984)	$r = .88$ (Jette et al., 1984) $\alpha = .82$ (Short & Winnick, 1999)
Target stretch test (TST)	Flexibility/ROM	CP, SCI, CA/A	Logical; $P = .85$ with goniometry-based scoring (Short & Winnick, 1999)	$\alpha = .92$ for interrater reliability for similar protocol (Short & Winnick, 1999)
Shoulder stretch	Flexibility/ROM	CP, MR, BL, CA/A	Logical	$\alpha = .83–.94$ (MR) (Short & Winnick, 1999)
Modified Apley test	Flexibility/ROM	CP, SCI, CA/A	Logical	No data available
Modified Thomas test	Flexibility/ROM	CP, SCI, CA/A	Logical	No data available
Back-saver sit & reach	Flexibility/ROM	GP, MR, BL, CA/A	Logical (Plowman & Corbin, 1994)	$\alpha = .95–.97$ (GP) (Patterson, Wiksten, Ray, Flanders, & Sanphy, 1996) $\alpha = .95–.96$ (MR) (Short & Winnick, 1999)

Source: From J. P. Winnick and F. X. Short, eds., 1999, *The Brockport Physical Fitness Test Manual: A Health-Related Test for Youths with Physical and Mental Disabilities,* pages 15–17, table 2.1. © 1999 by Joseph Winnick. Reprinted with permission from Human Kinetics (Champaign, IL).

ROM = range of motion	CP = cerebral palsy	R = intraclass reliability coefficient
GP = general population	SCI = spinal cord injury	α = Cronbach's alpha coefficient
MR = mental retardation	CA/A = congenital anomaly/amputation	P = proportion of agreement
BL = blindness	r = interclass reliability coefficient	

battery to be used in conjunction with alternative test batteries.

Test FITNESSGRAM®

Comment The FITNESSGRAM® was developed to assess physical activity and fitness in the able-bodied population and is not a good option for individuals with disabilities. Test items and administration protocols provide little benefit. Fortunately, adaptations for FITNESSGRAM® items are published in a text called *Physical Best and Individuals with Disabilities* (Seaman 1995). These test modifications enable the FITNESSGRAM® to be administered to a class of students with and without disabilities. The FITNESSGRAM® software is also compatible with the Brockport Physical Fitness software (Meredith & Welk 2004). Regardless of battery choice, scores for students with and without disabilities can be managed in one file.

Test President's Challenge Physical Activity and Fitness Test

Comment The President's Challenge was developed to assess physical activity and fitness in the able-bodied population and is not a good option for individuals with disabilities. The latest version of the President's Challenge (www.indiana.edu/~preschal) addresses testing and award accommodations for students with disabilities, but does not include specific modifications for any test item. Test items and administration protocols provide little benefit for individuals with disabilities, and thus one should select an alternative testing program to the President's Challenge

when measuring youth fitness among individuals with various ability levels.

Youth Field Tests of Aerobic Capacity

Test 20-meter shuttle run (Progressive Aerobic Cardiovascular Endurance Run, PACER)

Reliability and Validity This test is reliable and a valid predictor of $\dot{V}O_2$ peak among individuals with mental retardation. Fernhall et al. (1998) reported a test-retest reliability coefficient (ICC) of 0.97 among 34 children, ages 10 to 17, with mental retardation. Multiple regression equations (Table 15.6) using laps, body mass index, and gender as predictors explained 77% of variability in $\dot{V}O_2$ peak.

Comment This evidence is promising since the PACER is a common test option in many youth physical fitness batteries. Caution is warranted, however, when administering this test because the prediction equation to estimate $\dot{V}O_2$ peak for individuals with mental retardation may overestimate $\dot{V}O_2$ peak among individuals with Down syndrome, at least among adolescents (Guerra, Pitetti & Fernhall 2003).

Test 600-Yard Run

Reliability and Validity This test is reliable and a valid predictor of $\dot{V}O_2$ peak among individuals with mental retardation. Fernhall et al. (1998) reported a test-retest reliability coefficient (ICC) of 0.98 among 34 children, ages 10 to 17, with mental retardation. Time, body mass index, and gender

TABLE 15.6	**600-Yard Run and PACER Prediction Equations for $\dot{V}O_2$ Peak**
600-Yard Run	$\dot{V}O_{2\ peak} = -5.24\ (\text{time}) - 0.37\ (\text{BMI}) - 4.61\ (\text{gender}) + 73.64$
	$R = .86,\ SEE = 4.8\ \text{ml·kg}^{-1}\text{·min}^{-1}$
PACER	$\dot{V}O_{2\ peak} = .35\ (\text{laps}) - 0.59\ (\text{BMI}) - 4.5\ (\text{gender}) + 50.8$
	$R = .88,\ SEE = 4.5\ \text{ml·kg}^{-1}\text{·min}^{-1}$

explained 74% in $\dot{V}O_2$ peak (Table 15.6). Longer distances are not as valid among individuals with mental retardation (Pizarro 1982).

Clinical Tests of Functional Capacity in Youth

Test The Wingate Anaerobic Test

Description The Wingate test is a common laboratory assessment for persons with neuromuscular disease, children in particular (e.g., cerebral palsy, muscular dystrophy).

Objective Skeletal muscle power is more important to motor function among persons with neuromuscular disease than cardiorespiratory fitness; therefore, anaerobic power tests have been instrumental to functional assessment in persons with neuromuscular impairments (Bar-Or 1996; Damiano & Abel 1998).

Reliability and Validity Test-retest reliability coefficients have exceeded .96 for both peak and mean power among children with cerebral palsy (Emons et al. 1991), and strong evidence of test-retest reliability ($r > 0.96$) has been reported for both arm and leg protocols (Unnithan, Clifford & Bar-Or 1998).

Comment Two modifications to the administration of the Wingate are required for special populations. First, wheel resistance should be less than the resistance for the general population. Second, resistance must be manipulated to yield optimal force production. Van Mil et al. (1996) have provided two methods resulting in optimal force identification for children with neuromuscular disease.

Adult Fitness Assessments

Aerobic Capacity

Aerobic capacity is used as a standard of fitness and performance among individuals with disabili-

ties. Although several standardized treadmill and cycle ergometry protocols exist for the able-bodied population, standardized protocols and assessments are lacking for individuals with a variety of disabilities (Durstine et al. 2000). Wheelchair ergometry, cycle ergometry, arm ergometry, and treadmill exercise are modes of assessment for individuals with disabilities, with functional ability dictating appropriate test modes and protocols. Tests of aerobic performance for the able-bodied population may be appropriate for individuals with sensory or cognitive deficits if sufficient practice is provided; however, norm-referenced standards are not appropriate for special populations.

Test Peak Cycle Ergometry Test

Description A cycle ergometry test is used to assess power output by measuring pedal cadence and wheel resistance (see Chapter 11). This test can be performed at a specific submaximal intensity or at a maximal effort, and oxygen consumption is often collected simultaneously with power output.

Validity and Reliability Bhambhani, Holland, and Steadward (1992) reported strong test-retest reliability evidence for $\dot{V}O_2$ max on a cycle ergometer ($r = .93$) among wheelchair athletes with cerebral palsy.

Test Peak Arm Ergometry Test

Description Arm ergometry is a practical testing method for individuals who use wheelchairs for mobility and sport. Participants align the shoulder with the crankshaft and push the ergometer handles in a circular motion at a specific resistance and cadence. Administration protocols (Table 15.7) are similar to cycle ergometry protocols except that resistance increases are less substantial (e.g., 5 watts) and stages are shorter (e.g., 1–2 minutes).

Comment The difficulty with using arm or wheelchair ergometry in special populations lies in the ability to standardize cadence. Individuals with spastic symptoms (e.g., cerebral palsy) may be

TABLE 15.7	Arm Ergometry Protocols for Individuals with Spinal Cord Injury			
Reference	Initial Resistance (W)	Resistance Increase (W)	Speed (rpm)	Stage Duration (min)
Dwyer and Davis (1997)	0	25	50–60	2
Hopman et al. (1998)	80% PO_{Peak}	2–10	60	1
Muraki et al. (2000)	10	20	50	5–6
Raymond (1999)	0	5–10	50	1
Zwiren and Bar-Or (1975)	varied	30	50	2

unable to maintain a regular cadence due to uncontrollable movements and contractions. Essentially, to ensure a reliable power output, computer applications must be used with ergometry protocols to calculate power output relative to variable cadence. Additionally, individuals will need multiple practice attempts to understand and complete submaximal and maximal tests. Individuals with mental retardation, in particular, need multiple familiarization attempts in order to reach maximum effort.

Test   Maximal Wheelchair Ergometry Test

Validity and Reliability   Bhambhani, Holland, and Steadward (1992) reported strong test-retest reliability evidence for $\dot{V}O_2$ Peak max during wheelchair ergometry ($r = .89$) among wheelchair athletes with cerebral palsy. Stewart et al. (2000) demonstrated test-retest ICC values of .82 for power output at peak $\dot{V}O_2$ and peak $\dot{V}O_2$ itself across 8 weeks for arm and wheelchair ergometery among 122 individuals with spinal cord injuries. However, accuracy was not maintained for $\dot{V}O_2$ at rest or at a submaximal workload for the same participants. Additionally, these authors demonstrated that many variables used to estimate $\dot{V}O_2$ max in the general population (heart rate, lactate levels, activities of daily living) did not correlate with $\dot{V}O_2$ max within this population.

Muscular Strength and Endurance

Muscular strength is more important among individuals with disabilities than in the general population (Rimmer 2001). Due to the essential outcomes relative to function and independence, muscular strength and endurance must be developed in order for individuals to independently complete life activities. It is by far more important to document the ability of an individual to move from a wheelchair to a shower than to document a 10-RM score. Strength training and assessment were previously considered taboo for individuals with neuromuscular impairments, but empirical evidence supports the use of both strength training and assessment among individuals with cerebral palsy, spina bifida, and additional neuromuscular disorders (Damiano, Dodd & Taylor 2002).

Among nonathletes, functional improvement is more important than performance improvement; hence, many qualitative assessments of strength are more appropriate for persons with disabilities than standardized, norm-referenced muscular assessments. Clinical isokinetic testing is a reliable and valid mode of assessment, but static field tests of hand and upper body strength provide reasonably similar field estimates of laboratory strength and are therefore more practical for this population (Aronin & Kerrick 1995; Davis, Shephard & Jackson 1981).

Regarding safety, machine weights are suitable test modes because altered sensory recognition or atypical movements will not put the participant at risk. Free weights, however, may be much more problematic, especially for individuals with sensory or physical impairments. Gloves, straps, and spotters may all be needed to secure the weight to the participant. Additionally, atypical blood return may cause blood pressure changes during high-intensity exercise among individuals with various disabilities; therefore, blood pressure should be measured before and after testing (Rimmer 2001).

TABLE 15.8	Review of Physical Fitness Test Choices	
Construct	**Test**	**Appropriate Applications/Comments**
	BPFT	Cognitive, health, physical, and sensory impairments
Youth Fitness	Kansas Adapted/Special Physical Education Test Manual	Documented reliability evidence for individuals ages 5–21; appropriate for many disability types
	FITNESSGRAM®	Appropriate with *Physical Best and Individuals with Disabilities* modifications
	President's Challenge	Not appropriate
Youth Aerobic Capacity	20-Meter Shuttle	Cognitive impairments
	600-Yard Run	Cognitive impairments
Youth Muscular Power	Wingate	Health and physical impairments
	Cycle Ergometry	Cognitive, health, physical, and sensory impairments
Adult Fitness	Arm Ergometry	Physical impairments
	Wheelchair Ergometry	Physical impairments
	Skinfolds	Consider tracking skinfolds rather than estimating body fatness
	Muscular Fitness	Cognitive and health impairments; focus on meaningful outcomes
	Body Composition	Sensory and health impairments, spinal cord injury; consider using skinfold sums rather than estimating body density
	Flexibility	Cognitive, health, physical, and sensory impairments; tests for the able-bodied are often appropriate

Finally, it is essential to address asymmetrical weakness among individuals with physical disabilities. Individuals with cerebral palsy, stroke, or brain injury may have dramatic differences in strength between sides, and assessment records should document this difference over time to determine if overall function is improving or if improvements are specific to one side or one part of the body.

Body Composition

Multiple body composition measures are suitable for individuals with health and sensory disabilities. However, the validity of prediction equations from skinfolds and bioelectrical impedence is influenced by body density changes caused by disease or disability, and therefore these methods are inappropriate for individuals with cognitive and physical disabilities. Skinfold sums are appropriate for documenting change in adiposity among individu-

als with spinal cord injury (test-retest ICC > 0.70; Stewart et al. 2000), but equations should not necessarily be used to document body fatness.

Flexibility

Flexibility assessments used in the general population are appropriate for many disability populations. Flexibility is an important part of fitness for all adults. For individuals with muscular impairments (e.g., cerebral palsy), flexibility can be used to track functional changes over time. In these cases, measurements should target problematic muscle groups (e.g., spastic muscles) and assessment should be performed in a slow, controlled manner (Rimmer 2001). In general, flexibility testing applied to individuals with disabilities is quite similar to administration in the general population.

Table 15.8 provides a review of the physical fitness test choices.

MOTOR FUNCTION

A multitude of assessments are available to measure motor function, especially in school-age children (Burton & Miller 1998; Davies et al. 2004). Assessments are primarily used to identify children with motor deficits (screen individuals needing support services), document performance progress, or plan teaching priorities to remedy deficits. The major focus of the practitioner is to select assessments that have established measurement properties. It is important to choose instruments that are consistent over time—consistently scored by multiple users—and to distinguish between individuals with and without mature motor patterns. Unfortunately, many assessments intended to measure functional deficits demonstrate poor agreement with one another (Tan, Parker & Larkin 2001). In other words, evaluation of motor function/dysfunction varies from test to test despite the fact that function is a stable characteristic. Practitioners must remember that tests do not "diagnose" individuals with delayed motor function; people diagnose or evaluate individuals to determine functional limitations and use motor function tests to assist with this process. It is imperative that practitioners use personal experience and personal judgment in combination with a standardized assessment when evaluating a child's motor performance.

Individuals with Disabilities Education Act

The latest reauthorization of the Individuals with Disabilities Education Act (IDEA; Public Law 108-446), legislation dictating a free and appropriate education for individuals from birth to 21 years, went into effect July 2005. Because the intent of this legislation is to identify children needing educational support services, including physical education, and to ensure progress is made toward annual performance goals, standardized assessments of motor function have become instrumental in school physical education settings. The following field and laboratory assessments may be appropriate to identify individuals with motor delays and document progress toward annual goals.

Assessments Appropriate for Field Use

Test Peabody Developmental Motor Scales-2 (PDMS-2)

Description This battery assesses motor development of children up to five years of age. The instrument includes 249 items grouped into the following domains: (a) reflexes, (b) balance, (c) locomotion, (d) object manipulation, (e) grasping, and (f) visual-motor integration (Folio & Fewell 2000).

Objective This assessment can be used to identify individuals needing further evaluation relative to disability services as well as to document age-specific fine and gross motor skill changes over time.

Validity and Reliability Ample reliability and validity of the PDMS-2 has been established across multiple disability populations (Burton & Miller 1998; Winnick & Short 2000).

Comment This instrument is likely the most common test battery used by occupational therapists within an educational setting (Burtner, McMain & Crowe 2002).

Test Test of Gross Motor Development-Revised (TGMD-2)

Description The TGMD-2 is intended to assess gross motor ability of children. Whereas the PDMS-2 is appropriate for children under five years of age, the TGMD-2 is appropriate for elementary school children. Twelve items contribute to a locomotor subset and an object control subset. Each subset can be scored individually, but the composite score, the Gross Motor Quotient, is intended to be the best measure of gross motor function (Ulrich 2000). The benefit of this battery is the practicality of measurement. Test items can be administered quickly, and all test equipment is readily available in a physical education area (e.g., soccer ball, playground ball, basketball, and beanbag).

Objective   This battery can be used to screen individuals that demonstrate poor motor performance compared to peers, to develop instruction for improvement, and to document improvement in function.

Validity and Reliability   Acceptable internal consistency reliability has been demonstrated (Cronbach's alpha = .76 to .94 across ages 3 to 10 for locomotor, object control, and gross motor quotients). These findings are consistent with subgroups based on gender and ethnicity. Based on a sample of 75 and 30 children, respectively, test-retest reliability ($r = $.84 to .96 across ages and domains) and interrater reliability ($r = $.98 across domains) were also acceptable (Ulrich 2000). Relative to validity, content-related and construct-related evidence has been demonstrated but additional criterion-related evidence is needed (see Chapter 4).

Norms   Scoring norms for this battery were based on a sample of 1,208 students, ages 3 to 10 years, from four demographic regions.

Comment   One difficulty with establishing criterion-related validity evidence with functional tests is the selection of the gold standard. Insufficient data, at this point, are available to conclude that scores are predictive of future gross motor function.

Test   Bruininks-Oseretsky Test of Motor Proficiency (BOTMP)

Description   This test battery assesses multiple gross and fine motor skill items and can be used to identify individuals with motor dysfunction or detect improvement in skill acquisition. Eight subscales contribute to a gross motor, a fine motor, and total score. The battery has an optional short-form assessment (i.e., 14 items compared to 46 for the original), and scoring standards include both age-based norms and percentile ranks (Hattie & Edwards 1987).

Validity and Reliability   Specific to the full battery, Hattie and Edwards (1987) documented test-retest coefficients of eight subscales ranging from .56 (balance) to .86 (upper limb coordination), substantially lower than expected for physical assessment tests. Bruininks (1978) reported similar test-retest reliability values ($.58 \leq r \leq .89$) across subscales, with higher reliability documented for composite scores ($.77 \leq r \leq .89$). Hattie and Edwards also addressed concerns with validity, especially relative to children with disabilities.

Agreement of the short form with other assessments has been mixed. Strong rank-order agreement has been documented between the BOTMP short form and the McCarron Assessment of Neuromuscular Development (*Spearman r = *.86), but the BOTMP was less discriminatory than the former relative to identification of motor impairment. Although the short form of the BOTMP correctly identified all children without motor impairment, only 8 of 26 children with motor impairment were identified correctly (Tan, Parker & Larkin 2001).

Comment   Caution is warranted when considering use of the short or long form of the battery to screen individuals for adapted activity services (Burton & Miller 1998).

Test   I-CAN Instructional Management System (I-CAN)

Description   The I-CAN (Wessel 1981) system can be used as both an instructional and assessment instrument. The instructional component comprises criterion-referenced tasks that are necessary for mature performance, and evaluation is based on the ability to complete/not complete each task.

Objective   This system compiles a multitude of skills necessary for play, activity, and sport performance. Items are designated as preprimary (e.g., play participation), primary (e.g., body management), and sport/leisure/recreation (e.g., team sports). The I-CAN is a skill checklist resource rather than a screening instrument, and checklists can be used to document skill progress over time (Burton & Miller 1998).

Validity and Reliability The measurement properties of this instrument have not been documented.

Test Data Based Gymnasium

Description The data based gymnasium is a model for both curriculum documentation and assessment for individuals with severe disabilities. Detailed by Dunn, Morehouse, and Fredricks (1986), this model enables a practitioner to document activities important to individual performance, evaluate independence with which tasks are completed, and evaluate the effectiveness of chosen behavioral techniques. This model requires direct observation of performance and is similar to the method of physical activity observation. A collection of rubrics and task analyses, described later in this chapter, are used to document progress toward intended outcomes.

Test Project Transition Assessment System (PTAS)

Description The Ohio State Project Transition Assessment System (Jansma et al. 1988) is a battery comprised of factors important for individuals moving from an institutional environment to a community living environment. This battery was developed for individuals with severe mental retardation, and of the various test items included, five address fitness (Table 15.9). The intent of the fitness items is to address function as well as improvement in adaptive skills (e.g., dressing). The score sheets for each skill provide quantitative (i.e., performance score) and qualitative (i.e., level of independence) information. This battery uses task analysis (discussed later in this chapter).

Validity and Reliability Interrater agreement for fitness items exceeds .80, and content validity has been established for this battery.

Assessments Appropriate for Clinical Use

Instrument International Classification of Functioning, Disability and Health (ICF)

Description The World Health Organization's ICF (2002) is a quantitative assessment of individual health and its influence on function. As opposed to addressing causes of morbidity or mortality, the ICF classifies function relative to medical and social conditions. This classification system is holistic in its approach to health and measures function relative to the interaction between medical conditions (disease, injury) and contextual factors (internal feeling about disability, societal expectations). The ICF is intended for clinical or community services use, and its greatest asset in the physical activity field is the ability to document instances when functioning (i.e., activity according to ICF) does not meet the expected capacity to complete a task.

Validity and Reliability Battaglia et al. (2004) have documented good agreement in children and youth with various disabilities between the ICF mobility domain and two functional outcome scales, namely the Gross Motor Function Measure ($r = -.83$) and the Functional Independence Measure ($r = -.87$).

Test Gross Motor Function Measure (GMFM)

Description The Gross Motor Function Measure (Russell et al. 1989) is intended to measure func-

TABLE 15.9	Project Transition Assessment System
Construct	**Test Item**
Cardiorespiratory Endurance	300-yard Run/walk
Abdominal Endurance	Modified Sit-ups
Upper Body Strength	Modified Bench Press
Low Back and Hamstring Flexibility	Modified Sit and Reach
Grip Strength	Hand Dynamometer Test

tion of children with cerebral palsy. Items are scored on a Likert scale ranging from "cannot do" to "task completion." This battery has been validated to distinguish between high and low performers as well as to measure changes over time due to training or intervention. Eighty-five items contribute to the battery, and items are segmented into the following domains: (a) lying and rolling, (b) crawling and kneeling, (c) sitting, (d) standing, and (e) walk, run, jump.

Validity and Reliability   Reliability within (ICC ≥ .92) and between raters (≥ .87) has been high across domains and total score. Additionally, GMFM total scores demonstrated high agreement with video evaluation scored by alternative therapists ($r = .82$), and scores have been sensitive to changes in performance between different ages and ability level (Damiano & Abel 1998; Russell et al. 1989).

Comments   The GMFM is an effective assessment of motor function among individuals with physical disabilities, specifically individuals with various types of cerebral palsy.

Test   Gross Motor Performance Measure (GMPM)

Description   This assessment battery serves to compliment the GMFM and reflects movement quality rather than function. The Gross Motor Performance Measure (Boyce et al. 1995) is criterion-referenced and consists of 20 test items segmented into the following domains: (a) alignment, (b) stability, (c) coordination, (d) weight shift, and (e) dissociation.

Validity and Reliability   Across all five domains, test-retest ICC values have exceeded .89, interrater ICC values have exceeded .84, and intrarater ICC values have exceeded .90. Total battery score reliability has also been high (Gowland et al. 1995). Although 20 items contribute to the instrument, children are only scored on items attempted (or able to attempt) and scores are expressed as a percentage of the maximal points possible for attempted activities. The sensitivity of the instrument seems to be strong. In other words, change scores reflect actual changes

in movement quality. However, criterion-related evidence of the battery relative to parent and therapist evaluation is still lacking (Boyce et al. 1995).

Test   Functional Independence Measure (FIM).

Description   The scoring criteria for this scale reflect a person's independence level on various tasks essential for living, from complete dependence to total independence. Scoring is determined for a total FIM score as well as the subscales of self-care, sphincter control, mobility (transfers), locomotion, communication, and social cognition.

Validity and Reliability   Strong agreement between raters (ICC ≥ .93) has been documented across subscales and total FIM score (Hamilton et al. 1991).

Table 15.10 provides a review of motor function test choices.

SPORT CLASSIFICATION

Seven **disability sport** organizations (DSO) govern disability sport in the United States, and multiple grassroots, national, and international competitions exist for individuals with disabilities (Table 15.11). Classification serves to align individuals with similar function into competition heats as well as ensure that individuals with severe limitations are not excluded from sport opportunities. For instance, wheelchair basketball and quad rugby associations use a point system that enables participants with various functional abilities to compete collectively. Points (0.5 to 4) are awarded based on function (e.g., hand grip control, tricep control), and a maximum point total is allowed on the court at one time (e.g., 12 points for five players). This method ensures that teams will not simply choose high-point, and therefore high-functioning, participants exclusively but rather use a combination of players with high and low function to meet a point total. A **medical classification** system and a **functional classification** system have been the primary models used since the 1940s to classify disability sport competitors.

TABLE 15.10	Review of Motor Function Test Choices
Test	**Comments**
Field Assessments	
PDMS-2	Appropriate for children under six years
TGMD-2	Good reliability and validity evidence for elementary-age children
BOTMP	Weaker reliability and validity evidence than other options
I-CAN	Curricular and assessment guide; lacks measurement evidence
Data Based Gymnasium	Appropriate for individuals with severe disabilities
PTAS	Appropriate for individuals with severe cognitive disabilities
Clinical Assessments	
ICF	Clinical and community use
GMFM	85 items; assesses movement function
GMPM	Criterion-referenced; assesses movement quality
FIM	Good reliability evidence

TABLE 15.11	Disability Sport Organizations	
Organization	**Predominant Populations Served**	**Website Information**
Disabled Sports USA	Individuals with visual impairments, spinal cord injury, dwarfism, multiple sclerosis, head injury, cerebral palsy, neuromuscular conditions, and amputations	www.dsusa.org
Dwarf Athletic Association	Individuals of short stature (≤ 4' 10")	www.daaa.org
National Disability Sports Alliance	Individuals with physical disabilities (cerebral palsy, stroke, brain injury)	www.ndsaonline.org
Special Olympics	Individuals with mental retardation or intellectual disabilities	www.specialolympics.com
USA Deaf Sports Federation	Deaf individuals	www.usdeafsports.org
US Association for Blind Athletes	Individuals who are blind or have visual impairments	www.usaba.org
Wheelchair Sports USA	Wheelchair users	www.wsusa.org

Classification assessments can usually be found through DSO websites.

Medical

A medical classification is based on a specific injury or diagnosis. Originally based on spinal cord injury level, the medical classification was the dominant system used from the impetus of disability sport in the 1940s to the early 1990s. Since its original development, medical classification has been extended to individuals with amputations, individuals with cerebral palsy, and blind athletes (DePauw & Gavron 1995). This model is used by Wheelchair Basketball USA to classify players with spinal cord injury because function varies systematically with the anatomical injury site (see Figures 15-3 and 15-4).

NATIONAL WHEELCHAIR BASKETBALL ASSOCIATION
MANUAL MUSCLE TEST EVALUATION

Muscle Test Administered to: _____ Date: _____

Team or Club: _____ Division or Conference: _____

DIAGNOSIS AND BRIEF CLINICAL HISTORY

LEFT					EXAMINER'S INITITALS				RIGHT				
					DATE								
					N	Flexors		N					
					E	Lateral Flexors		E					
					C	Extensors		C					
					K	Rotators		K					
						Flexors							
					T	R. Ext. Obl. / Rotators / L. Ext. Obl.		T					
					R			R					
					U	L. Int. Obl / R. Int. Obl		U					
					N	Extensors – Thoracic		N					
					K	Extensors - Lumbar		K					
						Quadratus Lumborum							
						Flexors							
						Extensors							
					H	Abductors		H					
					I	Adductors		I					
					P	External Rotators		P					
						Internal Rotators							
						Gludeus Medius							
						Sartorius							
						Tensor Fascia Latae							
					K	Flexor – Outer Hamstring		K					
					N	Flexors – Inner Hamstring		N					
					E	Extensors		E					
					E			E					
					A	Dorsi Flexors		A					
					N	Plantar Flexors		N					
					K	Gastrocnemius		K					
					L	Soleus		L					
					E			E					
					F	Inverter – Ant. Tibial		F					
					O	Inverter – Post. Tibial		O					
					O	Evertor – Peroneus Long.		O					
					T	Evertor – Peroneus Brev.		T					
					H	Flexor		H					
					A			A					
					L	Extensor		L					
					L			L					
					U			U					
					X			X					
						Flexors							
					T	Extensors		T					
					O			O					
					E	Abductors		E					
					S			S					
						Adductors							

(Continued)

Figure 15-3

National Wheelchair Basketball Association medical classification system.

(Source: National Wheelchair Basketball Association, Manual Muscle Test Evaluation, December 18, 2004. www.nwba.org/modules/CmodsDownload/upload/Forms/Classification/manual_muscle_test.pdf. Used with permission.)

		LEFT								RIGHT				
						EXAMINER'S INITIALS								
						DATE								
					S C A P U L A	Abductor – Serratus Ant.	S C A P U L A							
						Adductors – Middle Trapezius								
						– Rhomboids								
						Elevators – Upper Trapezius								
						– Levator Ang. Scap.								
						Lower Trapezius								
						Latissimus Dorsi								
					S H O U L D E R	Flexors	S H O U L D E R							
						Extensors								
						Abductors (ABD, and Elevation)								
						Abductors								
						Horizontal Abductors								
						Horizontal Adductors								
						External Rotators								
						Internal Rotators								
					EL-BOW	Flexors	EL-BOW							
						Extensors								
					FORE-ARM	Supinators	FORE-ARM							
						Pronators								
					W R I S T	Flexors – Radial	W R I S T							
						Flexors – Ulnar								
						Extenxors – Radial								
						Extenxors – Ulnar								
					F I N G E R S	Flexors - MP	F I N G E R S							
						Flexor – Proximal IP								
						Flexor – Distal IP								
						Extensors - MP								
						Extensor – Proximal IP								
						Abductors								
						Adductors								
						Oppens – Digiti Quinti								
					T H U M B	Flexor – MP	T H U M B							
						Flexor – IP								
						Extensors – MP								
						Extensor – IP								
						Abductors								
						Adductors								
						Opponens Policis								

GIRTH MEASURMENTS

					Thigh: Inches above Proximal Patellar Border									
					Calf: Inches below Distal Patellar Border									

K E Y	100%	N	Normal	Complete range of motion against gravity with full resistance
	75%	G	Good	Complete range of motion against gravity with some resistance
	50%	F	Fair	Complete range of motion against gravity
	25%	P	Poor	Complete range of motion with gravity eliminated
	10%	T	Trace	Evidence of slight contractility with no joint movement
	0%	0	Zero	No evidence of contractility

S – Spasm
C – Contracture

If spasm or contracture limit range of motion, place C or S after the grade of a movement that is incomplete for this reason

EXAMINER	ADDRESS
SIGNATURE OF EXAMINER	

Figure 15-3   *Continued*

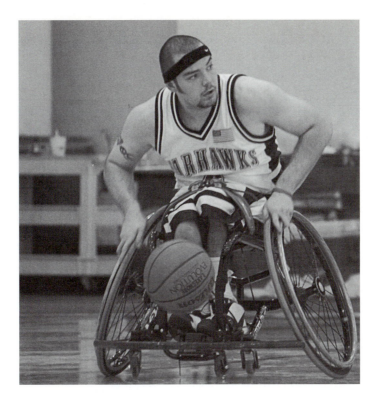

Figure 15-4
Wheelchair basketball is a popular sport for athletes with spinal cord injuries.
(Photo © 2005 Brian Love.)

Functional

The efficacy of the medical model has declined as disability sport opportunities have increased. Due to the inclusion of different disability types within the same competition, the medical classification system resulted in numerous heats with few participants. Paralympic competitions, the elite international competition for athletes with disabilities that immediately follows the Olympic competitions, moved to a functional classification system starting with the 1992 games (DePauw & Gavron 1995). This system enables competitors to be classified relative to function and compete against individuals with different disabilities in the same heat or event (see Figure 15-5). Essentially, sport administrators use criterion-referenced standards to set functional standards that enable fair competition across disabilities. Special Olympics International,

the governing body for athletes with mental retardation, uses a 10% rule to classify participants for competitions. Rather than one outright winner for the long jump, multiple winners are selected from heats of participants grouped by similar precompetition performances. This model enables disability sport organizations to ensure equitable competition at grassroots and elite levels.

Tables 15.12 provides a review of the two types of sport classification models, and Tables 15.13 and 15.14 provide functional classification examples.

AUTHENTIC ASSESSMENT

Although the majority of tests described in this chapter are standardized, many uses exist for nonstandardized, or authentic, assessments within

Figure 15-5

Quad rugby is a contact sport. Athletes are classified based on function rather than injury level.
(Photo © 2005 Brian Love.)

TABLE 15.12	**Review of Sport Classification Models**
Model	**Comments**
Medical	Based on anatomical injury site
Functional	Based on sport function of athlete (e.g., can/cannot use fingers to grip a ball)

disability populations. Authentic assessment enables the tester to develop, administer, and score nonstandardized tests appropriate for an individual's environment (e.g., educational or rehabilitation setting) as well as determine and measure essential outcomes. The variability in function between and within disability types makes authentic assessment a practical option. The content in Chapter 7 helps practitioners to design tests that address realistic school, work, and living outcomes in order to document progress toward necessary functional, work, and educational behaviors. Although the practitioner has latitude in the creation of authentic assessments, this section will address two methods typically employed within disability settings.

Rubrics

A rubric documents specific performance outcomes and the associated score and is thus appropriate for documenting progress toward annual performance goals. The intent of a rubric is to depict actions that range from nonmastery of a skill or behavior to complete mastery. The TGMD-2

TABLE 15.13	National Disability Sports Alliance Functional Classification Example for an Athlete with Cerebral Palsy
Class	**Function**
1	Dependent on motorized chair
2-Lower	Legs primary limbs affected
	Can propel own wheelchair
2-Upper	Arms primary limbs affected
	Lacks grasp but can manipulate a ball
	Limited wheelchair pushing stroke
3	Minimal problems in upper limbs but uses a wheelchair
4	Can ambulate for short distances
5-A	Ambulatory
	Legs primary limbs affected
	May use an assistive device in competition
5-B	Ambulatory
	Strength is good
	Noticeable involvement in upper limbs
	Does not use assistive device in competition
6	Ambulatory
	Coordination and balance problems
7	Ambulatory
	Good function on one side
8	Ambulatory
	Can run and maintain balance

Source: www.ndsaonline.org/class_cp.htm.

TABLE 15.14	United States Association of Blind Athletes Functional Classification Example for an Athlete with a Visual Impairment
Class	**Function**
B1	Cannot recognize shape of hand at any distance
B2	20/600 vision with best visual correction
B3	Above 20/600 to 20/200 vision with best visual correction
B4	Above 20/200 to 20/70 vision with best visual correction

Source: www.usaba.org/Pages/sportsinformation/visualclassifications.html.
Note: 20/600 indicates that an athlete recognizes objects 20 feet away that most people see 600 feet away.

(see earlier in this chapter) is a standardized battery that incorporates rubrics to assess a mature skill performance. The benefit of the rubric is that test items are valid for participants. Variables included in standardized assessments such as kicking a moving ball may not be applicable to a blind athlete or an individual who uses a wheelchair. Rubrics, however, enable multiple users to determine the exact outcomes and variables that are important to measure and evaluate. Table 15.15 provides an example addressing quad rugby performance for an individual with spina bifida.

Task Analysis

Task analysis is a common method used in standardized assessments to document motor skill (e.g., PTSA, I-CAN). This method can also be used within a variety of authentic physical activity settings. Task analysis is an instructor-derived evaluation system documenting tasks that must be performed correctly for a skill, task, or functional outcome to be successfully completed. This method of authentic assessment provides excellent **ecological validity** (see later in this chapter) and is skill- and participant-specific. Task analysis is similar to a performance rubric except that the process of the task is more important than the product (outcome) (see Figure 15-6). Table 15.16 provides an example of a task analysis for a child with spinal cord injury. In this example, the child is participating in a basketball unit. Special Olympics International publishes sport skill programs that utilize task analysis for both instruction and assessment. Camp Abilities, a summer activity camp for individuals with visual impairments, also posts numerous rubric and task analysis assessments to document performance (www.campabilities.com).

Table 15.17 provides a review of authentic assessments.

TABLE 15.15	Example of a Quad Rugby Rubric for an Individual with Spina Bifida

Score

1	Hits a 4-foot target from 8 feet away with a pass while stationary
2	Completes a pass to a teammate 8 feet away while passer and receiver in a stationary position
3	Completes a pass to a teammate 8 feet away while passer in a moving position and receiver in a stationary position
4	Completes a pass to a teammate 8 feet away while passer and receiver in a moving position

Figure 15-6
A rubric or task analysis is appropriate to document performance since activity and sport norms are not readily available for persons with disabilities.
(Photo © 2005 Brian Love.)

TABLE 15.16	Task Analysis for a Child with a Spinal Cord Injury

	No Assistance	Some Assistance	Much Assistance	Complete Physical Assistance
Dribbles a basketball	4	3	2	1
Shoots a basketball	4	3	2	1
Passes a basketball while moving	4	3	2	1
Total				
Total Score:				

ADMINISTRATIVE CONCERNS

Many tests and test items have been described in this chapter. There are several considerations readers should address during the planning phase of assessment. Sufficient practice is probably the foremost administrative concern for disability populations. Individuals with mental retardation may require multiple repetitions to understand intended instructions. Additionally, motivation to complete maximum tests may be lacking for individuals with a variety of cognitive and physical deficits. Essentially,

TABLE 15.17	Review of Authentic Assessments
Item	**Comments**
Rubric	Addresses movement or performance outcome
Task Analysis	Addresses movement or performance quality

an individual may understand the instruction to run but not to run with maximal effort. One must also realize that parents may be overprotective of children with disabilities, discouraging difficult or challenging tasks. Whether an individual is unmotivated or unaware of how to provide maximal effort, multiple practice attempts may be necessary for individuals to reach maximum exertion.

Aside from physical tests, Sherrill (1998) described an important consideration relative to test administration, namely ecological validity. This means that tests should be administered in ways and environments that are participant-specific. For example, self-care skills should be assessed where the skills are performed, namely the home or residential setting. Similarly, sport skills should be assessed in specific disability sport locations where actions are performed. This administrative concern may appear obvious, but it is important to remember that individuals with various disabilities may have difficulty applying skills outside the learned environment. An individual may not be able to apply a self-care skill that was learned in the special education classroom to the actual living environment. Therefore, a test within the special education classroom loses meaning if the application of the skill does not occur in the real-world setting.

Regardless of disability type, test options are more varied than protocols for the able-bodied, making the search for norms more difficult for the test administrator. Also, many disability-specific tests cannot detect changes in disability due to training or activity (Jette 2003). One can measure improvement in aerobic power among individuals with cystic fibrosis, but this finding may not necessarily mean an improvement in symptoms or conditions. Therefore, assessment does not approach the ability of tests for the able-bodied to identify health and performance benefits realized from training. Essentially, testing within a disability population requires that testers provide ample practice time, administer the test within a realistic setting, and carefully consider the validity of a chosen test and test standards.

SUMMARY

Multiple test options specific to physical activity, physical fitness, motor function, and sport classification are available for persons with disabilities. When selecting a test, readers should determine the priority outcome of assessment first and then select a test or authentic assessment with appropriate reliability and validity evidence for the intended population. From a practical standpoint, readers should also recognize that disability will not worsen due to testing and that testing precautions are no different than those used with able-bodied participants. The main distinction in assessment among persons with disabilities is the greater reliance upon criterion-referenced tests compared to the many norm-referenced standards used with the general population.

FORMATIVE EVALUATION OF OBJECTIVES

Objective 1   Select appropriate physical activity assessments.

1. Consider an individual with cerebral palsy. Gait is atypical and inconsistent. What activity assessment is appropriate for this individual and why?
2. Does your decision change if the individual uses a wheelchair? Why?

Objective 2   Recognize the appropriateness of standardized physical fitness test items for persons with disabilities.

1. Consider the Brockport Physical Fitness Test. Describe why one may or may not choose this battery over the FITNESSGRAM® to assess fitness of a student with a visual impairment.

Objective 3   Select motor assessments appropriate for various ages and ability levels.

1. Identify two assessments that would be appropriate for screening school-age children with possible motor delays as well as documenting progress toward improvement.

Objective 4   Distinguish between medical and functional sport classification models.

1. The local Special Olympics event is hosting an event for individuals with mental retardation, brain injury, and alternative cognitive disorders. Describe how a functional classification system could be used to organize softball throw heats.

Objective 5   Develop authentic assessments appropriate for particular outcomes.

1. Design a youth fitness rubric and task analysis for a child who is blind.

Objective 6   Identify environmental factors that impact test scores and interpretation.

1. Describe factors that may prevent a child with a hearing impairment from completing a youth fitness assessment properly.
2. What modifications could be made to ensure the assessment is suitable and meaningful?

ADDITIONAL LEARNING ACTIVITIES

1. Review the physical activity assessment options. Distinguish between appropriate and inappropriate assessment options for an adult dependent upon a manual wheelchair.
2. Consider the test items of the Brockport Physical Fitness Test. Select five test items for a child with a visual impairment and document modifications necessary if the child is blind.
3. Consider the FITNESSGRAM® test battery. Select five test items for a child with a hearing impairment and determine whether test administration modifications are needed.
4. Consider Table 15.1. Determine the appropriate field or clinical test to identify motor deficits appropriate for each disability population.
5. Select three disability sport organizations. Use the Internet to locate the classification assessment for each. Determine if the assessment is based on the functional or the medical model.

BIBLIOGRAPHY

Aronin, P. and P. Kerrick. 1995. Value of dynamometry in assessing upper extremity function in children with myelomeningocele. *Pediatric Neurosurgery* 23: 7–13.

Bar-Or, O. 1996. Role of exercise in the assessment and management of neuromuscular disease in children. *Medicine and Science in Sports and Exercise* 28: 421–427.

Bassett, D. R. 2000. Validity and reliability issues in objective monitoring of physical activity. *Research Quarterly for Exercise and Sport* 71: 30–36.

Battaglia, M. et al. 2004. International classification of functioning, disability and health in a chohort of children with cognitive, motor, and complex disabilities. *Developmental Medicine and Child Neurology* 46: 98–106.

Bhambhani, Y. N., L. J. Holland, and R. D. Steadward. 1992. Maximal aerobic power in cerebral palsied

wheelchair athletes: Validity and reliability. *Archives of Physical Medicine and Rehabilitation* 73: 246–252.

Boyce, W. F. et al. 1995. The gross motor performance measure: Validity and responsiveness of a measure of quality of movement. *Physical Therapy* 75(7): 27–37.

Bruininks, R. 1978. *Bruininks-Oseretsky Test of Motor Proficiency (BOTMP)*. Austin, TX: Pro-Ed.

Burtner, P. A., M. P. McMain, and T. K. Crowe. 2002. Survey of occupational therapy practitioners in southwestern schools: Assessments used and preparation of students for school-based practice. *Physical and Occupational Therapy in Pediatrics* 22: 25–38.

Burton, A. W. and D. E. Miller. 1998. *Movement skill assessment*. Champaign, IL: Human Kinetics.

Busse, M. E. et al. 2005. Quantified measurement of activity provides insight into motor function and recovery in neurological disease. *Journal of Neurology, Neurosurgery, and Psychiatry* 75: 884–888.

Coleman, K. L. et al. 1999. Step activity monitor: Long-term, continuous recording of ambulatory function. *Journal of Rehabilitation Research & Development* 36: 8–18.

Damiano, D. L. and M. F. Abel. 1998. Functional outcomes of strength training in spastic cerebral palsy. *Archives of Physical Medicine and Rehabilitation* 79: 119–125.

Damiano, D. O. et al. 2002. Should we be testing and training muscle strength in cerebral palsy? *Developmental Medicine and Child Neurology* 44: 68–72.

Davies, P. L. et al. 2004. Validity and reliability of the school functional assessment in elementary school students with disabilities. *Physical and Occupational Therapy in Pediatrics* 24(3): 23–43.

Davis, G. M. (1993). Exercise capacity of individuals with paraplegia. *Medicine and Science in Sports and Exercise* 25: 423–432.

Davis, G. M., R. J. Shephard, and R. W. Jackson. 1981. Cardio-respiratory fitness and muscular strength in the lower-limb disabled. *Canadian Journal of Applied Sport Science* 6: 159–165.

DePauw, K. P. and S. J. Gavron. 1995. *Disability and sport.* pp. 119–132. Champaign, IL: Human Kinetics.

Dunn, J., J. Morehouse, and H. Fredricks. 1986. *Physical education for the severely handicapped: A systematic approach to a data based gymnasium.* Austin, TX: Pro-Ed.

Durstine, J. L. et al. 2000. Physical activity for the chronically ill and disabled. *Sports Medicine* 30: 207–219.

Dwyer, G. B. and R. Davis. 1997. The relationship between a twelve-minute wheelchair push test and $\dot{V}O_2$ peak in women wheelchair athletes. *Sports Medicine, Training, and Rehabilitation* 8(1): 1–11.

Emons, H. J. G. et al. 1991. Wingate anaerobic test in children with cerebral palsy. In International Congress on Pediatric Work Physiology (Ed.). *Children and exercise XVI: Pediatric work physiology.* pp. 187–189. Paris: Masson.

Fernhall, B. et al. 1998. Validation of cardiovascular fitness field tests in children with mental retardation. *American Journal on Mental Retardation* 102: 602–612.

Folio, M. and R. Fewell. 2000. *Peabody developmental motor scales.* 2nd ed. Austin, TX: Pro-Ed.

Gowland, C. et al. 1995. Reliability of the gross motor performance measure. *Physical Therapy* 75(7): 21–26.

Guerra, M., K. Pitetti, and B. Fernhall. 2003. Cross validation of the 20-meter shuttle run test for adolescents with Down syndrome. *Adapted Physical Activity Quarterly* 20: 70–79.

Hamilton, B. B. et al. 1991. Interrater agreement of the seven level Functional Independence Measure [abstract]. *Archives of Physical Medicine and Rehabilitation* 72: 790.

Hattie, J. and H. Edwards. 1987. A review of the Bruininks-Oseretsky test of motor proficiency. *British Journal of Educational Psychology* 57: 104–113.

Hopman, M. T. E. et al. 1998. Limits to maximal performance in individuals with spinal cord injury. *International Journal of Sports Medicine* 19: 98–103.

Individuals with Disabilities Education Act of 2004 (P.L. 108-446). 2004. 20 U.S.C. 1400.

Jansma, P. et al. 1988. A fitness assessment system for individuals with severe mental retardation. *Adapted Physical Activity Quarterly* 5(3): 223–232.

Jette, A. M. 2003. Assessing disability in studies on physical activity. *American Journal of Preventive Medicine* 25: 122–128.

Johnson, R. E. and B. Lavay. 1988. *Kansas adapted/special physical education test manual: Health related fitness and psychomotor testing.* Topeka: Kansas State Department of Education.

Kosma, M., B. J. Cardinal, and P. Rintala. 2002. Motivating individuals with disabilities to be physically active. *Quest* 54: 116–132.

McDonald, C. M. 2002. Physical activity, health impairments, and disability in neuromuscular disease. *American Journal of Physical Medicine and Rehabilitation* 81(11, Suppl.): S108–S120.

McKenzie, T. L. 2002. Use of direct observation to assess physical activity. In G. J. Welk (Ed.). *Physical activity assessments for health-related research.* pp. 179–196. Champaign, IL: Human Kinetics.

Meredith, M. D. and G. J. Welk (Eds.). 2004. *Fitnessgram/Activitygram test administration manual.* 3rd ed. Champaign, IL: Human Kinetics.

Muraki, S. et al. 2000. Multivariate analysis of factors influencing physical work capacity in wheelchair-dependent paraplegics with spinal cord injury. *European Journal of Applied Physiology* 81: 28–32.

National Center on Physical Activity and Disability. 2005. Prevalence of disability in America. Retrieved April 30, 2005, from www.ncpad.org/research/fact_sheet.php?sheet=189&section=1385.

Ng, A. V. and J. A. Kent-Braun. 1997. Quantification of lower physical activity in persons with multiple sclerosis. *Medicine and Science in Sports and Exercise* 29: 517–523.

Pizarro, D. C. (1982). Health-related fitness of mainstreamed emr/tmr children. Ed.D. dissertation, University of Georgia, Athens, GA.

Raymond, J. 1999. Cardiorespiratory responses to arm cranking and electrical stimulation leg cycling in people with paraplegia. *Medicine and Science in Sports and Exercise* 31: 822–828.

Rimmer, J. H. 2001. Resistance training for persons with physical disabilities. In J. E. Graves and B. A. Franklin (Eds.). *Resistance training for health and rehabilitation.* pp. 321–346. Champaign, IL: Human Kinetics.

Rimmer, J. H. et al. 2001. A new measure for assessing the physical activity behaviors of persons with disabilities and chronic health conditions: The physical activity and disability survey. *American Journal of Health Promotion* 16: 34–45.

Rimmer, J. H. et al. 2004. Physical activity participation among persons with disabilities. *American Journal of Preventive Medicine* 26: 419–425.

Rose, J. et al. 1989. Energy cost of walking in normal children and in those with cerebral palsy: Comparison of heart rate and oxygen uptake. *Journal of Pediatric Orthopedics* 9: 276–279.

Russell, D. J., P. L. Rosenbaum, D. T. Cadman, C. Gowland, S. Hardy, and S. Jarvis. 1989. The gross motor function measure: A means to evaluate the effects of physical therapy. *Developmental Medicine and Child Neurology* 31: 341–352.

Seaman, J. A. (Ed.). 1995. *Physical best and individuals with disabilities: A handbook for inclusion in fitness programs.* Reston, VA: AAHPERD.

Sherrill, C. 1998. *Adapted physical activity, recreation, and sport.* 5th ed., pp. 6–61. New York: McGraw-Hill.

Stewart, M. W. et al. 2000. The measurement properties of fitness measures and health status for persons with spinal cord injuries. *Archives of Physical Medicine and Rehabilitation* 81: 394–400.

Tan, S. K., H. E. Parker, and D. Larkin. 2001. Concurrent validity of motor tests used to identify children with motor impairment. *Adapted Physical Activity Quarterly* 18: 168–182.

Tobimatsu, Y. et al. 1998. Cardiorespiratory endurance in people with cerebral palsy measured using an arm ergometer. *Archives of Physical Medicine Rehabilitation* 79: 991–993.

Ulrich, D. A. 2000. *Test of gross motor development.* 2nd ed. Austin, TX: Pro-Ed.

Unnithan, V. B., C. Clifford, and O. Bar-Or. 1998. Evaluation by exercise testing of the child with cerebral palsy. *Sports Medicine* 26: 239–251.

Van Mil, E. et al. 1996. Optimization of force in the Wingate Test for children with neuromuscular disease. *Medicine and Science in Sports and Exercise* 28: 1087–1092.

Washburn, R. A. et al. (2002). The physical activity scale for individuals with physical disabilities: Development and evaluation. *Archives of Physical Medicine and Rehabilitation* 83: 193–200.

Winnick, J. P. and F. X. Short. 1998. *Criterion-referenced physical fitness standards for adolescents with disabilities: Project Target final report.* Brockport: State University of New York.

Wessel, J. A. 1981. Effectiveness of the I-CAN physical education instructional system for handicapped individuals, K–12: A summary report. *Canadian Journal of Applied Sport Sciences* 6: 168–175.

Winnick, J. P. and F. X. Short. 1999. *The Brockport Physical Fitness Test manual: A health-related test for youths with physical and mental disabilities.* Champaign, IL: Human Kinetics.

World Health Organization. 2002. *Towards a common language for functioning, disability and health: ICF.* Geneva: Author.

Zwiren, L. and O. Bar-Or. 1975. Responses to exercise of paraplegics who differ in conditioning level. *Medicine and Science in Sports and Exercise* 7: 94–98.

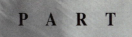

P A R T

IV

Cognitive and Affective Testing

C O N T E N T S

K E Y   W O R D S

completion item

discrimination index

discrimination test

essay item

essay test

item

item analysis

item difficulty

knowledge test

mastery test

matching item

multiple-choice item

objective test

short-answer item

taxonomy

true-false item

OBJECTIVES

The process of evaluating knowledge is threefold: (1) constructing a knowledge test based on the cognitive objectives of the unit, (2) administering it, and (3) analyzing it. Before the actual construction, the type of test and the types of test items must be selected to be sure that the cognitive objectives of the unit are well met. Then the knowledge test is constructed making sure the content of the unit is adequately covered and the items themselves are well constructed. In addition, it is important to administer and score the test so that all people have the same opportunity to do well, and so that the interpretations based on test scores are valid. Finally, it is vital to analyze the test to determine the quality of each item and the test as a whole. This analysis indicates not only the quality of the test, but also how it might be revised. Questionnaires are commonly used in many situations in our disciplines. Constructing a questionnaire is similar to constructing a knowledge test. Before attempting to construct and use a questionnaire, a person must know the basic procedures to follow.

After reading Chapter 16 you should be able to

1. Differentiate among various types of knowledge tests.
2. Define the levels of knowledge most applicable to physical education and adult fitness.
3. Outline the basic procedures used for constructing, administering, and scoring a knowledge test.
4. Evaluate knowledge test items.
5. Analyze knowledge tests in terms of test score reliability and item analysis.
6. Discuss the uses of questionnaires and how to construct them.

INTRODUCTION

Knowledge is one of the objectives of most physical education programs. Teachers want their students to know the rules, etiquette, terminology, procedures, and strategy of various sports and physical activities. Students should understand the role of exercise in health and physical fitness and how to stay fit. Many health-related fitness programs have knowledge objectives. The extent to which these objectives are met can best and sometimes exclusively be determined with a knowledge test.

Knowledge is often retained longer than physical skill and fitness. Obviously, people lose a degree of skill and fitness as they stop participating in sports, but they can continue to enjoy sports as spectators if they have acquired sufficient knowledge. Then, too, as health-related physical fitness programs become more popular, greater emphasis is being placed on the cognitive aspects of physical fitness and health. Knowledge, then, is an objective of physical education programs and should be one of the first areas of attention in any measurement procedure.

Knowledge is also an objective in adult fitness programs and rehabilitation programs. The instructor or clinician wants the program participants to know why fitness is important, how to develop and maintain fitness, the importance of good diet, why stress management is important, the adverse effects of smoking, why they received an injury, and how not to become reinjured. To determine if program participants have this knowledge as they enter the program or are obtaining this knowledge as a result of handouts and verbal presentations during the program, a knowledge questionnaire (test) must be administered. This knowledge questionnaire is scored not to grade each participant, but to determine what information needs to be provided to program participants.

In any class or program that is designed to prepare participants to become certified (in American Red Cross first aid or life saving or CPR, as an American College of Sports Medicine fitness instructor, etc.), there is a knowledge test. The knowledge test must be well constructed based on information presented in this chapter. In fact, there are many purposes of a knowledge test: (1) assigning a grade or summative evaluation, (2) measuring progress or formative evaluation, (3) providing feedback to students or program participants as to their status and what the class or program knowledge expectations are, (4) motivating students or program participants to learn the material tested,

(5) presenting important information, in that students and program participants do learn information by taking a test, and (6) assessing teaching or instructional effectiveness.

LEVELS OF KNOWLEDGE

There are different levels or degrees of knowledge. This is apparent whenever a group of people is tested: their understanding of a given topic can range from superficial to thorough.

Bloom's **taxonomy** of educational objectives (1956) has six levels of behavior arranged in ascending order of complexity: knowledge, comprehension, application, analysis, synthesis, and evaluation. Each level corresponds to a level of knowledge. Bloom then divides the levels of behavior and provides illustrative questions for each subdivision. Listed in Table 16.1 are Bloom's six levels and their subdivisions. Because the two highest levels are quite complex and usually exceed the educational objectives of a typical physical education activity course, adult fitness program, or rehabilitation program, only the first four levels of knowledge in the taxonomy are presented, defined, and illustrated with a test item in Table 16.2. The educational objectives of most courses and programs do exceed Bloom's first level because teachers, exercise specialists, and clinicians want students and participants to acquire more than a superficial knowledge of the topics covered.

Although the majority of items on many physical education knowledge tests require the students only to remember facts, some items should draw on higher levels of knowledge. And certainly, as the class becomes more advanced, the number of knowledge items should be smaller, and the number of items from the higher levels of the taxonomy should be larger.

Test makers don't always use Bloom's six levels. Educational Testing Service nationally distributes many tests. They have a test for certified financial planners with four levels: knowledge, comprehension/application, analysis/synthesis, and evaluation. Educational Testing Service also has a series of Major Field Tests. The one in Education

TABLE 16.1	Bloom's Taxonomy of Educational Objectives

1.00	Knowledge
	1.10 Knowledge of specifics
	1.20 Knowledge of ways and means of dealing with specifics
	1.30 Knowledge of the universals and abstractions in a field
2.00	Comprehension
	2.10 Translation
	2.20 Interpretation
	2.30 Extrapolation
3.00	Application
4.00	Analysis
	4.10 Analysis of elements
	4.20 Analysis of relationships
	4.30 Analysis of organizational principles
5.00	Synthesis
	5.10 Production of a unique communication
	5.20 Production of a plan for operations
	5.30 Derivation of a set of abstract relations
6.00	Evaluation
	6.10 Judgments in terms of internal evidence
	6.20 Judgments in terms of external evidence

has three levels: knowledge, comprehension, and application.

TYPES OF KNOWLEDGE TESTS

Knowledge tests may be essay or objective or a combination of the two types of tests, and they may be either mastery or discrimination tests. Each question on a knowledge test, whether stated as a question or not, is called an **item.** Teachers, exercise specialists, and clinicians must choose the type of test they want before they can begin to construct it.

Essay versus Objective

An **essay test** is any test on which people answer each item with whatever information they choose and write their answers in sentences. The answer to an essay item may be short or long, depending on how much the person knows and how full an answer

TABLE 16.2	The First Four Levels of Bloom's Taxonomy	
Level	Definition	Sample Question for Golf Test
I. Knowledge	Recall of ideas, terms, facts, etc.	What is a slice?
II. Comprehension	The use of translation, interpretation, or extrapolation to understand certain ideas, terms, facts, etc.	What causes a slice?
III. Application	The use of general ideas, rules of procedure, or generalized methods in particular and concrete situations	The following scores were recorded by four golfers on 9 holes. In what order should the golfers tee off on the 8th tee?
IV. Analysis	The separation of a phenomenon into its constituents so that its nature, composition, and organizational principles may be determined	A golf ball is located on a hill above the cup, and the shot will be made downhill onto a very fast green. The ball is best played with what kind of grip and stroke, and off what part of the club face?

Player	1	2	3	4	5	6	7	8	9	Total
A	3	6	3	4	3	4	7	3	6	39
B	4	5	4	4	4	5	4	3	4	37
C	6	6	5	3	3	3	3	3	3	35
D	3	3	4	4	2	4	5	7	3	35

the item requires. **Objective tests**—true-false, multiple-choice, matching, and the like—have potential answers provided with each test item. After reading an item, a person selects one of the provided answers—for example, T or F on a true-false item.

The question of which test to use—essay or objective—raises both philosophical and economic issues. Some educators believe that objective tests encourage students to memorize facts rather than integrate facts together into a total understanding. These people use essay tests on the theory that the students must have a total understanding to answer essay items. Other educators maintain that essay tests allow students to write everything they know about the subject, while objective tests determine if they know only what has been asked. Students frequently complain after objective tests that the teacher did not ask any of the things they knew. We can think of the items on an objective test as a sample from an infinite number of items that could have been used.

Economically, objective tests are time-consuming to construct but quick to score, while essay tests are the reverse. It does not take long to construct three to five general essay-type items, but it takes considerable time to properly read and score each one. Whenever tests are to be used with many people, either in one testing session or over numerous sessions, objective tests are more economical than essays in terms of total time involvement. Once the objective test is developed, it is easy to use and score. This is probably the major reason objective tests are used more than essay tests.

Mastery versus Discrimination

A **mastery test** is used to determine whether the students or program participants have mastered the material. Items on the test pertain to information everyone is expected to know. Many of these items are easy, and often the entire class or group answers them correctly. However, the performance standards for mastery tests tend to be high. Bloom and his associates (1971,1981) recommend that the criterion for passing a knowledge test be 80% to 90% correct answers. Commonly a mastery test is graded pass-fail or proficient-nonproficient for a formative evaluation, but mastery tests can be used for a summative evaluation. It is commonly used in physical education, adult fitness, and other certification programs.

The purpose of a **discrimination test** is to differentiate among students in terms of knowledge. Each test item is written to discriminate among ability groups. Thus, discrimination tests include a larger number of difficult items than do mastery tests. They often do not elicit basic information because they do not discriminate sufficiently. As a result of using a discrimination-type test, a few excellent students will have high scores on the test and the rest of the students will have lower scores. Discrimination tests are only used for a summative evaluation, and they are seldom used outside of education.

Mastery tests tend to include items from the knowledge, comprehension, and application levels of Bloom's taxonomy (1956); discrimination tests tend to include items from the higher levels. Because discrimination tests are more difficult than mastery tests, their performance standards must be lower. The test mean and standard deviation need to be considered in the development of the grading scale (see Chapters 2 and 6).

The decision about which test to use—mastery or discrimination—should depend on how the test scores will be used. For a formative evaluation of student or participant achievement, a mastery test should be used. For a summative evaluation of student or participant achievement, usually a discrimination test should be used. Formative evaluation is on a pass-fail basis; summative evaluation allows the teacher to identify individual differences in achievement by assigning letter grades.

Some teachers use mastery tests to make summative evaluations. The reliability of letter grades based on scores of mastery tests is almost always low because most of the items are too easy to discriminate well. To achieve high reliability, test items must discriminate sufficiently so that the students' scores are spread out. Later in the chapter we

will show that the larger the standard deviation, the higher the Kuder-Richardson reliability. As a result of low reliability, the standard error of measurement (see Chapter 3) is similar in value to the standard deviation for the test.

An example should clarify these points. Assume for a summative evaluation a mastery test is administered in a first aid class and letter grades are assigned based on the test scores. Suppose that the grading standard for a 100-point test is A: 93–100, B: 87–92, C: 78–86, D: 70–77, and F: below 69. If the standard deviation is 8 and the reliability of the test is .44, the standard error of measurement for the test is 6. Thus, the probability is .68 that a student who scored 88 will score between 82 and 94 (88 ± 6) if retested. Notice that 82 is a C and 94 is an A; the assigned grade is not reliable. If criterion-referenced standards are used and a score of 80 or above is considered passing, the large standard error of measurement poses no problem because the student passes whether the score is 82 or 94. This is not to suggest that large standard errors are desirable or will not cause problems for other students. For the student with a score close to the pass-fail cutoff score, the size of the standard error may be quite critical.

Similarly, assume that the instructional objectives for a physical education unit pertain to knowledge of the rules of a sport. The best policy in this situation is probably to use a mastery test with criterion-referenced standards. If a student can correctly answer 80% of the items on the test, the teacher can assume that the student has enough knowledge to play the sport. The mastery test is designed essentially to measure knowledge of basic rules. Similar thinking would apply in an adult fitness program.

Of course, mere knowledge of the rules is not sufficient for playing a sport. The rules must be applied, and several different rules may have to be considered to resolve a situation. To interpret rules, the higher levels of the cognitive domain must be used. The teacher might use a discrimination test for summative evaluation of the students' ability to apply, analyze, and synthesize the rules in a game situation. Although students may know all the basic rules, they are likely to differ in their ability to understand, apply, and interpret them.

CONSTRUCTION

Whenever possible, the teacher, exercise specialist, or clinician should develop her own knowledge tests. A major advantage of instructor-made tests is that they tend to cover the material stressed in the unit in terminology the people understand. Thus, instructor-made tests tend to have validity using the logical approach (see Chapter 4). Another person's test not only may omit important material and include irrelevant material, but also may confuse people with the use of unfamiliar terminology.

Procedure

Typically, there are four general procedural steps to follow in constructing a good knowledge test:

Step 1. Construct a table of specifications.

Step 2. Decide the nature of the test.

Step 3. Construct the test items.

Step 4. Determine the test format and administrative details.

A table of specifications is an outline for the test construction. It lists the areas and levels of knowledge to be tested, as shown in Table 16.3. By adhering to a table of specifications, the test developer ensures that all the material on it is covered and that the correct weight is given to each area.

In deciding which type of test to give, consider the advantages and disadvantages of essay and objective tests, and then, if an objective test is chosen, of true-false, multiple-choice, or other types of items. There is no reason why a test must be composed of a single type of item, although all items of the same type should be grouped together. Tests that include both true-false and multiple-choice items, or some objective and some essay items, are not uncommon.

The third step is writing the test items. Begin this task well in advance of the testing session. It is important to allow enough time to develop items that are carefully conceptualized and constructed. In fact, after constructing the items, the constructor should read them, correct them, and then put them aside for at least a day before reading them again. A fresh look may pinpoint other errors and ambiguities.

Finally the test format is chosen. One important consideration is the directions, which should appear at the top of the test. The directions must clearly indicate how to take the test, what is the policy for guessing, whether a question may have more than one correct answer, and so on. Another consideration is the presentation of the items. They should be typed neatly with enough space to make them easy to read. When several items pertain to information supplied on the test (e.g., a diagram), the information and the items should be on the same page. See the section titled "Sample Tests" later in this chapter for examples of good test format.

Types of Test Items

True-False

A **true-false item** consists of a short, factual statement. If the statement appears to be true, the person marks True or T; otherwise, the person marks False or F. This type of item is quite popular.

TABLE 16.3	Sample Table of Specifications for a Basketball Test		
	Type of Test Items		
Subject Topic	*Knowledge*	*Comprehension*	*Application*
Rules	15%	5%	0%
Player duties	20%	10%	0%
Offensive plays	10%	10%	10%
Defenses	5%	5%	0%
Strategy	0%	0%	10%

The advantages of true-false items are as follows:

1. The rapidity with which people can answer these items makes it possible to include many items on the test.
2. It is easier and quicker to construct true-false items than to construct other types of objective items.
3. Test items can be scored quickly.
4. Factual information is easily tested.
5. Standardized answer sheets can be used.

The disadvantages are these:

1. Probably only the first level of Bloom's taxonomy (1956), knowledge, can be tested by a true-false item.
2. People have a 50% chance of guessing the correct answer.
3. It is easy for a person to cheat by glancing at another person's paper.
4. This type of item can encourage memorization rather than understanding of facts.
5. This type of item is often ambiguous, in that the test taker and the test maker may not interpret an item in the same way.
6. True-false items often test trivial information.
7. To ensure reliability, a true-false test requires more items than does a multiple-choice test.

Construction Procedures   Many people believe that true-false test items are easy to construct. Unfortunately this is not entirely the case. Although they are easier to construct than some other types of objective items, true-false items must be constructed with care, using the following rules:

1. Keep the statement short. If it is long, the test taker may have to read it several times, which means that fewer items can be asked.
2. Use only a single concept in any one statement. This way, if a person answers incorrectly, you can identify the concept he does not know.
3. Keep the vocabulary simple.
4. Do not reproduce statements exactly from the text unless your objective is for the student to identify the passage.

5. Whenever possible, state the items positively rather than negatively.
6. Avoid using words like "always," "never," "all," and "none." Absolute statements are almost always false, and many people know this.
7. Do not allow more than 60% of the items to have the same answer. People expect approximately half the items to be true, which influences their thinking as they take a test.
8. Avoid long strings of items with the same answers.
9. Avoid patterns in the answers like true, false, true, false, and so on.
10. Do not give clues in one item to the answer of another. For example, don't let the statement in item 1 help answer item 14.
11. Avoid interdependent items. They put the person who misses the first item in double jeopardy.

Examples of Poor True-False Items

1. T(F) In soccer, the hands cannot touch the ball except when the ball is thrown in or when the player is the goalie.
   Explanation. The key word "legally" has been omitted. Also, two questions are being asked: (1) Can the hands be used to throw the ball in? (2) Can the goalie touch the ball with her hands?
2. T(F) Never go swimming just after you have eaten.
   Explanation. An absolute like "never" should not be used. A better item would be "It is not recommended that a person go swimming immediately after eating."
3. T(F) Physical fitness is important because a sound body and a sound mind usually go hand in hand, and, further, the physically fit person does not tire as easily as the unfit person and, thus, is usually more productive, but the fit person does not necessarily live longer than the less fit person.
   Explanation. The statement is too long and includes multiple concepts.
4. T(F) A timed run may be used to test aerobic capacity.

Explanation. The statement is ambiguous because the distance of the timed run isn't stated.

Multiple Choice

A **multiple-choice item** is composed of a short complete or incomplete question or statement followed by three to five potential answers. The first part of the item, the question or statement, is called the "stem"; the answers are called "responses." After reading the stem, the person selects the correct response. Complete stems are preferred over incomplete stems. Multiple-choice items are the most popular type of item with professional test makers, and are commonly used by all people who construct knowledge tests.

Among the advantages of this type of item are the following:

1. Because people can answer each multiple-choice item quickly, many items can be included in the test.
2. Test items can be scored quickly.
3. All levels of knowledge in Bloom's taxonomy can be tested with multiple-choice items.
4. The chances of a person guessing correctly are less than for true-false items, and decrease as the number of responses (plausible answers) increases.
5. Standardized answer sheets can be used.

Among the disadvantages of multiple-choice items are these:

1. Fewer items can be asked than with true-false items.
2. The test maker needs considerable time to think of enough plausible responses to each item.
3. There is a certain danger of cheating on multiple-choice items.
4. To some degree, multiple-choice items encourage memorization of facts without regard to their implications. This is more of a problem with items at the lower end of Bloom's taxonomy, and is generally less of a problem than it is with true-false items.

5. People are unable to demonstrate the extent of their knowledge; they can respond only to the items as constructed. Of course, this is a legitimate criticism of all objective test questions.

Construction Procedures Multiple-choice items are not easy to construct. The development of items with good stems and responses takes time, and it can be difficult to think of enough responses for an item. It is not uncommon to spend 15 to 30 minutes constructing a single item. However, if the following few rules are followed, you should end up with an acceptable test.

1. Keep both stems and responses short and explicit.
2. Make all responses approximately the same length. Beginning test constructors have a tendency to include more information in the correct responses than in the incorrect responses, a fact the test takers quickly pick up.
3. Use apparently acceptable answers for all responses. There is no excuse for writing obviously incorrect or sloppy responses.
4. If possible, use five responses for each item. This keeps the guess factors acceptably low (.20), and it is usually hard to think of more. It is desirable that all multiple-choice items on a test have the same number of responses.
5. If the stem is an incomplete sentence or question, make each response complete the stem.
6. Do not give away the correct answer with English usage. If the stem is singular, all responses should be singular. Words beginning with a vowel must be preceded by "an."
7. Do not give away the answer to one item in the content of another.
8. Do not allow the answer to one item to depend on the answer to another. If people answer the first incorrectly, they will answer the second incorrectly as well.
9. Do not construct the stem in such a way that you solicit a person's opinion. For example, do not begin questions with "What should be done?" or "What would you do?"

10. If the items are numbered, use letters (a,b,c,d,e) to enumerate the responses. People tend to confuse response numbers with item numbers if the responses are numbered, particularly when standardized answer sheets are used.

11. Try to use each letter as the correct answer approximately the same number of times in the test. If the constructor is not careful, (c) may be the correct response more often than any other, which could help people guess the correct answer.

12. State the stem in positive rather than negative terms.

Examples of Poor Multiple-Choice Items (∗ indicates the correct answer)

1. What should you do if the right front wheel of your car goes off the pavement as you are driving?
   a. Brake sharply.
   b. Cut the front wheels sharply to the left.
   c. Brake sharply and cut the wheels sharply to the left.
   d. Brake sharply and turn the wheels gradually to the left.
   ∗e. Brake gradually, maintaining control of the car by driving along the shoulder of the road if necessary. Then pull gently back onto the pavement when speed is reduced.
   Explanation. (1) the stem asks for the person's opinion; (2) it is understood, but should be stated in the stem, that the right front wheel went off the right side of the pavement; (3) the longest response is the correct answer.

2. A multiple-choice item is a
   ∗a. very popular and commonly used type of item.
   b. alternative to a true-false item.
   c. important type of knowledge test item.
   d. very easy type of item to construct.
   e. limited application type of item.
   Explanation. Responses b and c can be eliminated because the stem ends in "a"

and they both begin with vowels. The best solution is to end the stem at "is" and to add "a" or "an" to each response.

3. Which of the following does *not* serve on an IEP committee?
   ∗a. Child
   b. Parent
   c. Adapted physical education teacher
   d. Principal
   e. None of the above
   Explanation. It looks like the test constructor could not think of five different responses, so response e was inserted. Does the e response indicate none of the above do not serve on an IEP committee, which means that all of them do serve? Or does the e response indicate that none of the responses above are the correct response? The double negative certainly causes problems in interpreting and answering the item.

4. Pick the incorrect statement from the following:
   a. Only the serving team can score in volleyball.
   ∗b. In badminton, a person cannot score unless he or she has the serve.
   c. In tennis, a set has not been won if the score is 40–30.
   d. In tennis, volleyball, and badminton, a net serve is served again.
   e. In tennis and badminton, a player cannot reach over the net to contact the ball or shuttlecock.
   Explanation. (1) When an incorrect response is to be identified, try to state all responses positively so as not to confuse the students. (2) In response e, it would be preferable to say "it is illegal for a player to reach. . . ." (3) Change the stem to "Pick the *false* statement. . . ," so the person evaluates each response as true or false and is looking for the false response.

Matching

In a **matching-item** test, a number of short questions or statements are listed on the left side of the page and

TABLE 16.4	A Sample Matching Test

Volleyball

For each item on the left-hand side of the page, find an answer on the right-hand side. Place the letter of the correct answer in the space provided at the left side of each item. Each answer can be used only once.

Items

_____ 1. The official height of the net in feet
_____ 2. The number of players on an official team
_____ 3. The number of points needed to win a game
_____ 4. Loss of the serve
_____ 5. Loss of a point
_____ 6. Illegal play

a. 6
b. 8
c. 12
d. 15
e. 18
f. 21
g. Net serve that goes over
h. More than 3 hits by receiving team
i. Reaching over the net to spike the ball
j. Stepping on a side boundary line
k. Serving team carries the ball

Golf

In items 7–10, determine which of the four clubs listed on the right is best suited for the shot described on the left. Each answer can be used more than once.

Items

_____ 7. Tee shot on a 90-yard hole
_____ 8. 100-yard approach to the green
_____ 9. Fairway shot 140 yards from the green
_____ 10. 200-yard shot from the rough

l. Three-wood
m. Two-iron
n. Five-iron
o. Nine-iron

the responses are listed in order on the right. Matching items are a logical extension of multiple-choice items in that both provide the person with several responses from which to choose. Matching items are used less often than true-false or multiple-choice items, but they are very helpful in situations in which the same responses can be used with several test items. A sample matching test is shown in Table 16.4.

Among the advantages of matching items are the following:

1. You can save space by giving the same potential responses for several items.
2. The odds of guessing the right answer are theoretically quite low because there are so many responses from which to choose. In actuality, people will probably be able to detect that no more than five to eight responses apply to any given item.

3. These items are quicker to construct than multiple-choice items.

The disadvantages of matching items are these:

1. Matching items usually test only factual information (the lowest level in Bloom's taxonomy).
2. Matching items are not particularly versatile, and a multiple-choice item often serves just as well.
3. Standardized answer sheets usually cannot be used with these items.

Construction Procedures

To develop a fair test, carefully plan the format and directions using the following rules:

1. State the items and potential responses clearly; neither should be more than two lines long.

2. Number the items and identify the potential responses with letters.
3. Allow a space at the left of each item for the correct answer.
4. Keep all items and potential responses on the same page.
5. Make all items similar in content. It is preferable to construct several sets of matching items rather than to mix content.
6. Arrange potential responses in logical groupings—all numerical responses together, all dates together, and so on. This saves people the time necessary to scan all the potential responses before responding.
7. Provide more responses than items to prevent people from deducing answers by elimination.
8. In the directions, tell the people whether a potential response can be used more than once.
9. Have several potential responses for each item.

Completion

In a **completion item,** one word or several words are omitted from a sentence, and a person is asked to supply the missing information. This type of item has limited usefulness and application, and is less satisfactory than a multiple-choice item. In fact, in many textbooks this type of item is not discussed in detail. Unless completion items are worded carefully, students may be uncertain what information the teacher wants. For example, consider the following item:

Three playing combinations in racquetball are _____, _____ , and _____.

Some people will answer singles, doubles, and cut-throat, while others, thinking about doubles play, will respond side-by-side, front-and-back, and rotation. The acceptable answers to the item "$.02 and $.03 are _____?" must include "$.05," "5," "a nickel," "5 pennies," and "money." Obviously, true-false or multiple-choice items could do the job with less ambiguity.

Short Answer and Essay

Short-answer items and **essay items** are appropriate when the teacher wants to determine the stu-dent's depth of knowledge and capacity to assemble and organize facts. For each item, students answer with whatever facts and in whatever manner they think appropriate.

The advantages of essay items are the following:

1. Students are free to answer essay items in the way that seems best to them.
2. These items allow students to demonstrate the depth of their knowledge.
3. These items encourage students to relate all the material to a total concept rather than just learn the facts.
4. These items are like situations in daily life where the answers are not given, so the student must gather all of the information together and make a decision.
5. The items are easy and quick to construct.
6. All levels of Bloom's taxonomy can be tested with essay items.

Their disadvantages are these:

1. Essay items are time-consuming to grade.
2. The objectivity of test scores is often low.
3. The reliability of test scores is often low.
4. Essay items require some skill in self-expression; if this skill is not an instructional objective, validity for the item may be low.
5. Penmanship and neatness affect grades, which again lowers the validity for the item.
6. The halo effect is present: students expected to do well on the test tend to be scored higher than they may deserve.

Construction Procedures Most teachers can construct reasonably good short-answer or essay items. However, if an item is hastily constructed, the students may not respond in the manner wanted. The biggest disadvantage of this type of item may be its grading. Teachers must key an item carefully to identify the characteristics wanted in the answer and to determine how partial credit points are assigned. Without an answer sheet, the reliability of scores is often low. For example, if a test item is worth 20 points and 5 specific facts should be mentioned in the answer, each fact is worth 4 points. If only 3 of the 5 facts are included, the student receives 12 points. Thus, if the teacher should grade the item again, the student is likely again to receive 12 points. Findings from research that required an instructor to grade a set of essay tests twice have been that the test-retest reliability is usually low. The objectivity of essay test grades has also been investigated by assigning two qualified teachers to grade a set of essays independently. The objectivity has seldom been high.

If the following rules for constructing short-answer and essay items are followed, the items should be satisfactory:

1. State the item as clearly and concisely as possible.
2. Note on the test the approximate time students should spend on each item.
3. Note on the test the point value for each item.
4. Carefully key the test before administration. This is the only way to identify ambiguous items.

Sample Tests

Ideally, teachers should construct their own knowledge tests. Those constructed by others often do not have the terminology or material emphasis needed for every teacher and class. If, for example, two teachers do not use the same technique, the correct answer to a question about that technique will not be the same for both instructors. The content and emphasis of a knowledge test also are influenced considerably by the age, sex, and ability level of the students. Knowledge tests can quickly become outdated as ideas, techniques, and rules change.

There are several sources of knowledge tests. Some have been published in research journals, and most books and manuals about specific sports and skills include sample knowledge tests. McGee and Farrow (1987) published a book of test questions for 15 different activities. Unpublished knowledge tests (theses, dissertations, tests constructed by teachers in your school system) are also available.

Several sample knowledge test items are included here.

Badminton

Part I. True-False. If the answer is true, put a plus (+) to the left of the item number. If the answer is false, put a minus (−) to the left of the item number. Please respond to each item.

_____ 1. In singles play it is poor tactics to return your opponent's drop with another drop unless your opponent is completely out of position in the back court.

_____ 2. Proper position of the feet is more important in the execution of strokes made from a point near the rear boundary line than from a point near the net.

_____ 3. Players A-1 and A-2, a two-person team, are trailing in their game 5–3. They have just broken the serve of Team B, so A-1 will start the serve in the right service court for Team A.

Part II. Multiple-Choice. To the left of the item number, put the letter of the answer that is most correct. Please respond to each item.

_____ 4. During the execution of a stroke, the arm is straightened
   a. at no particular time.
   b. just prior to contact between racket and bird.
   c. at the moment of contact between racket and bird.
   d. just after contact is made between racket and bird.

_____ 5. If your opponent is in the back left-hand corner of his or her court when you play the bird, what number in the diagram (top of page 458) represents your best target?
   a. 1   c. 3
   b. 2   d. 4

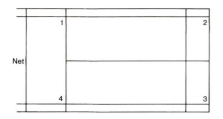

Part III. Identification. Give the official names of the lines of the court that are numbered in the diagram, placing the name next to the number.

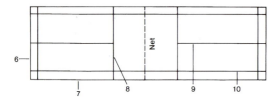

Volleyball

Read the instructions that precede each section of the test before you answer any of the items in that section.

Part I. True-False. If the statement is true, blacken the a on the answer sheet. If the statement is false, blacken b on the answer sheet for that numbered statement.

1. To start the game, Team A serves. Team B's first server will be the player who started the game as the right forward.
2. If the spiker is left-handed, the "ideal" set-up will be on his or her right side.
3. The blocker's jump is begun just before the spiker's jump.

Part II. Matching. Read each numbered statement and choose the best answer from the five responses. Then, on the answer sheet, blacken the letter of the correct response for that numbered statement. Use the same five responses for items 4 through 7.

    a. Point for Team A
    b. Point for Team B
    c. Loss of serve
    d. Legal, play continues
    e. Reserve or serve over

4. While Team B is serving, a player on Team A tries to play the ball, but it bounces off his or her shoulder and a teammate successfully spikes the ball over the net where it strikes the floor inbounds.
5. During the return of B's serve, a player on Team A spikes the ball, which lands inbounds on B's side of the net.
6. Team A serves. Team B sets the ball for its spiker, while Team A sets up a two-person block. During the spike-block play, Spiker B lands over the center line; however, one of A's blockers' hands goes over the net.
7. Team B serves. Team A sets the ball for the spiker, while Team B sets up a two-person block. Player A spikes the ball into Blocker B's hands and the ball bounds over Team A's end line.

Fitness Concepts

Please do not write on this exam. Mark your answers on the answer sheet. Be sure to answer every item.

1. As a result of regular cardiovascular training, resting heart rate
    a. increases.
    b. decreases.
    c. does not change (resting heart rate is unaffected).
    d. changes cannot be predicted.
2. Decreases in lean body mass are
    a. frequently seen in diets below 1200 calories.
    b. rarely seen during periods of starvation.
    c. uncommon in near-fasting diets.
    d. common among smokers.
3. Based on the overload principle
    a. muscles have to be taxed beyond their regular accustomed loads to increase their physical capacity.
    b. the resistance placed on the muscles must be of a magnitude significant enough to cause physiological adaptation.
    c. the load placed on the muscle(s) must be systematically and progressively increased over a period of time.
    d. All are correct choices.

4. The leading cause of death in the United States is
   a. cancer.
   b. cardiovascular heart disease.
   c. coronary heart disease.
   d. hypertension.
5. Which of the following is NOT a component of a successful weight loss program, weight maintenance, and achievement of recommended body composition?
   a. a lifetime exercise program
   b. a diet low in fat and refined carbohydrates
   c. a diet high in complex carbohydrates and fiber foods
   d. a diet high in protein and low in carbohydrates
6. To develop muscular strength, it is recommended that an individual should work between _____ repetitions.

   a. 3 and 8
   b. 9 and 15
   c. 15 and 20
   d. 20 and 30

ADMINISTRATION AND SCORING

Administration Procedures

A test setting should be quiet, well lighted, properly heated, odor-free, spacious, and comfortable. The failure to furnish a comfortable and distraction-free testing site places people at a disadvantage. Physical education teachers often are not careful about the testing atmosphere and setting: the practice of instructing students to lie on the gym floor to take a test while other students participate in another part of the gym leaves much to be desired.

The teacher must also consider test security for objective tests. During a test, students should all face the same direction. They should be sitting close enough to allow the teacher to see everyone, but far enough apart to preclude cheating and whispering. In a classroom, you may assign a student to every other seat or, better still, to every other seat of every other row. Encourage students to keep their eyes on their own papers and their papers covered. Sometimes alternate test forms, with the same items arranged on each form in a different order, are used. Also, a procedure for collecting the papers is essential. If students stand around the teacher waiting to turn in their tests, they can exchange answers while they wait; and students still taking the test can exchange answers while the teacher is busy collecting other students' tests.

If you plan to use the same objective test with several classes, you must ensure that students who have taken the test do not give the test items and answers to those yet to take it. If only two consecutive classes are to take the test, security poses no problem. However, if even as much as an hour elapses between the two administrations, the test's contents will probably be known to the second class. The best approach, then, is to use several forms of the test. Of course each form must cover the same material. A common procedure with multiple-choice tests is to construct parallel items. For example, all forms of the test include an item dealing with aerobic capacity. With true-false tests, a common procedure is to reword some of the items on the second form so that the answer changes.

The teacher must remember that things can go wrong during a test period, so it is good to plan ahead. For example, make sure you have a few extra exams and pencils. Consider what you will do if a student comes in late or misses the test. Also, consider whether you need to make any accommodations, such as special testing location or more time to take the test, for injured students or students with a disability.

Scoring Procedures

Tests are supposed to be a learning experience. Thus, a test should be scored promptly and the students informed of their scores. Also, the test should be discussed so the students will know which questions they missed. On an essay test, remove the person's name from the test paper to increase the validity and objectivity of scoring, and score each student's answer to a single item before going on to the next item. This procedure, and the use of a key, increases the likelihood that the same standards will be applied to all answers. Reliability suffers when an essay test is scored in a hurry. This is one reason essay tests take so much time to score.

The scoring of true-false and multiple-choice items, although usually less time-consuming than scoring of essay items, can be tedious if it is done by referring alternately to the answer key and each person's answers. Standardized answer sheets can speed up the scoring of true-false and multiple-choice items. These answer sheets can be constructed by the teacher or test administrator or purchased commercially. A sample of a commercial, standardized answer sheet is shown in Figure 16-1. These standardized answer sheets have the advantage of being machine-scorable, thus eliminating the time needed to score the items by hand. Machines to score tests vary from the large and expensive ones used by scoring services and universities to the small and inexpensive desktop models used by individual schools or programs. In addition, the use of standardized answer sheets makes it possible to reuse test booklets.

A layover answer key—a standardized answer sheet on which the correct answers are cut or punched out—is used to score standardized tests by hand. To use a layover answer key, first scan the person's answer sheet to make sure there are no multiple responses to any of the test items. Then place the layover answer key on top of the answer sheet, and the number of visible pencil marks is the person's score. A 50-item true-false or multiple-choice test can be scored in 20 to 30 seconds using a layover answer sheet.

To score commercial answer sheets by machine, the person must use a pencil to mark the answer sheets. Many colleges and school districts offer free scoring services to their personnel. The answer key and answer sheets are fed into a machine that scores the tests and stamps a score on each answer sheet.

ANALYSIS AND REVISION

Most objective tests are used more than once. After the test has been administered and scored, it should be examined to determine the merits of the test and of each item, and to identify those items that should be revised or deleted before the test is used again. The failure to analyze a knowledge test after its first administration lowers the reliability of the test scores and the validity of the evaluations based on the test scores.

After administering and scoring a test, the following characteristics should be examined:

1. Overall difficulty
2. Variability in test scores
3. Reliability
4. The difficulty of each item
5. The discrimination, or validity, of each item
6. Quality of each response in a multiple-choice item

Analyzing the Test

Difficulty and Variability

The overall difficulty of a test is determined by calculating the mean performance for the group tested. The higher the mean, the easier the test. The variability in test scores is determined by calculating the standard deviation. The larger the standard deviation, the more reliable the test, and the more the test discriminates among ability groups.

Reliability

The reliability of a knowledge test is influenced by whether the test is mastery or discrimination, the number of students who took the test, the number of items on the test, the number of responses to each item (2 for true-false to 5 for multiple choice), and so on. Discrimination tests tend to be more reliable than mastery tests. Generally, as the number who took the test, the number of items on the test, and the number of responses to each item increase, the reliability of the test increases. For these reasons it is difficult to set a minimum acceptable reliability value. Maybe a reliability of at least .70 is the goal. The author of this chapter has seen reliability values of .50 to .55 for a 30-item multiple-choice test with 4 responses for each item administered to 92 students.

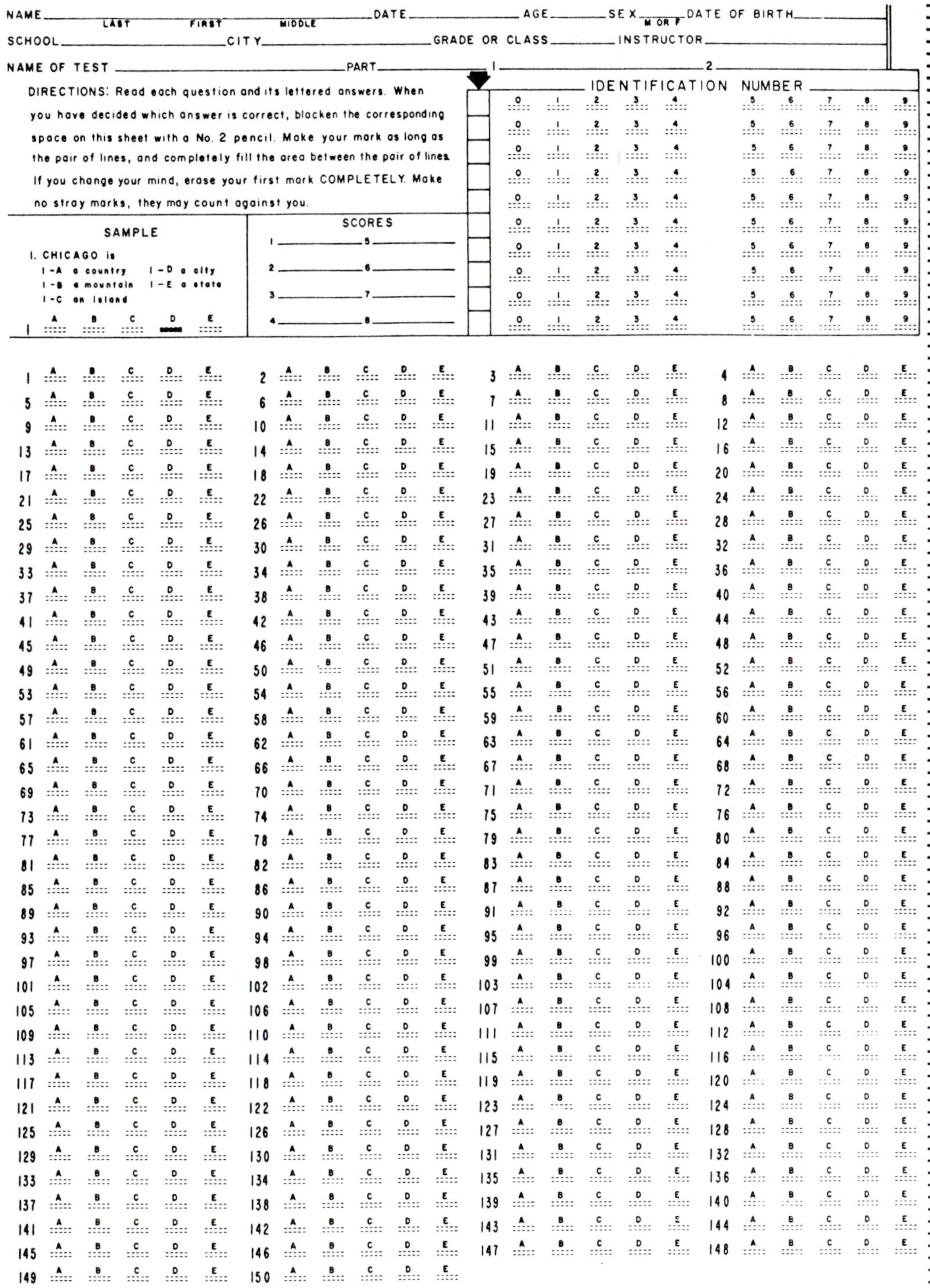

NAME_____ LAST ____ FIRST ____ MIDDLE _____DATE_____ AGE_____ SEX___ M OR F ___DATE OF BIRTH_____

SCHOOL_____CITY_____ GRADE OR CLASS_____INSTRUCTOR_____

NAME OF TEST _____PART_____ 1 _____ 2

DIRECTIONS: Read each question and its lettered answers. When you have decided which answer is correct, blacken the corresponding space on this sheet with a No. 2 pencil. Make your mark as long as the pair of lines, and completely fill the area between the pair of lines. If you change your mind, erase your first mark COMPLETELY. Make no stray marks, they may count against you.

IDENTIFICATION NUMBER

SAMPLE

I. CHICAGO is
I—A a country   I—D a city
I—B a mountain   I—E a state
I—C an island

SCORES

Figure 16-1

Standardized commercial answer sheet.

The reliability of knowledge test scores is usually estimated using either the Kuder-Richardson or the coefficient alpha method. As indicated in Chapter 3, coefficient alpha is the same as an intraclass reliability coefficient. The administration of the test twice on different days to estimate stability reliability, as discussed in Chapter 3, is inappropriate, because persons would be expected to do better the second day due to a carryover of knowledge and an exchange of information about the test.

The Kuder-Richardson Formulas 20 and 21 are typically used to estimate the reliability of knowledge test scores. Nunnally and Bernstein (1994) state that with dichotomous items (items scored as either right or wrong), the Formula 20 reliability coefficient is the same as coefficient alpha. (In Chapter 3 we illustrated coefficient alpha.) Formula 20 (commonly used in computer programs) is time-consuming to use, because the percentage of the class answering each item correctly must be determined. On the assumption that all test items are equally difficult, Formula 20 can be simplified to Formula 21. Although Formula 21 is commonly used, it underestimates the reliability coefficient when test items vary in difficulty, which they usually do. Formula 21 should be considered an estimate of the minimum test score reliability. The Kuder-Richardson Formula 21 is as follows:

$$r_{21} = \frac{k(s^2) - \bar{X}(k - \bar{X})}{(k - 1)(s^2)} \qquad \textbf{(16.1)}$$

where k is the number of test items, s^2 is the test's standard deviation squared, and $\bar{X}$ is the test mean.

Problem 16.1 Use the information in Table 16.5 to calculate the Kuder-Richardson Formula 21 reliability coefficient of the test.

Solution Where k is 10, s^2 is 3.70, and $\bar{X}$ is 6.2, the reliability coefficient using Formula 21 is .40:

$$r_{21} = \frac{(10)(3.70) - (6.2)(10 - 6.2)}{(10 - 1)(3.70)}$$

$$= \frac{3.70 - (6.2)(3.8)}{(9)(3.70)}$$

$$= \frac{3.70 - 23.56}{33.30} = \frac{13.44}{33.30} = .40$$

Remember that—all other factors being equal—the larger the standard deviation, the higher the reliability coefficient. If in Problem 16.1 the scores had been 9, 8, 6, 5, and 4; $\bar{X}$ was 6.4; and s^2 was 4.3, the reliability coefficient r using Formula 21 would have been .52. Thus, high reliability is harder to obtain with homogeneous groups than it is with heterogeneous ones.

As noted above, coefficient alpha is the same as Kuder-Richardson Formula 20 with dichotomous items. If the items have more than two possible answers (like answers A, B, C, D, E on a knowledge test or scores 1 to 5 on an attitude scale), Kuder-Richardson formulas are not appropriate, but coefficient alpha can be utilized. Coef-

TABLE 16.5	Kuder-Richardson Formula Scores										
					Item						
Person	1	2	3	4	5	6	7	8	9	10	X
A	1	1	1	1	0	1	1	1	1	1	9
B	1	0	0	0	0	1	1	0	1	1	5
C	0	1	0	0	0	0	1	1	0	1	4
D	1	1	0	0	0	1	0	1	1	1	6
E	1	1	0	0	0	1	1	1	1	1	7

$\bar{X} = 6.2$
$s^2 = 3.70$

ficient alpha is commonly provided when computer analysis of a knowledge test is conducted.

Item Analysis

The last three relevant characteristics of a test—the difficulty of the items, the discrimination of the items, and the efficiency of responses—can be determined by an item analysis, a procedure that is important but tedious to do by hand. This analysis should be conducted whenever a test is used the first time.

For the results of an item analysis to be reliable and interpretations of the item analysis valid, a large number of people (over 100) must have taken the test. There are several reasons a large number is essential, one being that all ability levels are apt to be represented. Also, some estimates of correlation coefficients are used in the item analysis procedure, and coefficients based on small groups are often uncommonly high or low and thus untrustworthy.

The first step in an item analysis is to identify a top and bottom group using the total test scores. We will use the top and bottom 27% of the scores. Use only the tests of people in these ranges in the analysis. The next step is to make a chart on which to record the answer each person in the top and bottom groups chose for each item. Presented in Figure 16-2 is a sample chart using the test papers of the top and bottom 16 students in a class of 60. You can see that 12 students in the top group and 5 students in the bottom group answered item 1 correctly. By using only the top and bottom 27% of the test papers in the analysis, we minimize the work of constructing the chart and can also determine how well each item discriminates between the best and worst students. With the information in the chart, it is possible to determine the difficulty and discrimination for each test item, and whether all responses functioned.

Item Difficulty

Because each person answers each item correctly or incorrectly, we can calculate the percentage of people who chose the right answer. This percentage, called the **item difficulty** (D), is large when the test item is easy, and small when it is hard. We use the following formula to determine item difficulty:

$$D = \frac{\text{number right in top group} + \text{number right in bottom group}}{\text{number in top group} + \text{number in bottom group}} \quad (16.2)$$

ITEM	CORRECT ANSWER		a	b	c	d	e	OMIT
					RESPONSE			
1	b	top		𝖳𝖧𝖫 𝖳𝖧𝖫 //	///	/		
		bottom	//	𝖳𝖧𝖫	𝖳𝖧𝖫	//	//	
2	e	top	//	//	/	///	𝖳𝖧𝖫 ///	
		bottom	//	///	//	𝖳𝖧𝖫	////	
3	c	top			𝖳𝖧𝖫 𝖳𝖧𝖫 𝖳𝖧𝖫 /			
		bottom		///	𝖳𝖧𝖫 𝖳𝖧𝖫 ///			
4	a	top	𝖳𝖧𝖫	𝖳𝖧𝖫 ///	///			
		bottom	𝖳𝖧𝖫 𝖳𝖧𝖫	//	////			

Figure 16-2

Chart showing answers selected by top and bottom groups in a class of students taking a given test.

Problem 16.2 Determine the difficulty of item 1 in Figure 16-2.

Solution Where the number right in the top group is 12, the number right in the bottom group is 5, and the number of students in each of the groups is 16, the item difficulty, D, is .53, or 53% of the students answered the question correctly.

$$D = \frac{12 + 5}{16 + 16} = \frac{17}{32} = .53$$

Discrimination Index

Item discrimination, or item validity, indicates how well a test item discriminates between those who performed well on the test and those who did poorly. If, as is wanted, an item is answered correctly by more of the better performers than the worse performers, it discriminates positively; if more of the worse performers answer the item correctly than do the better performers, the item is a poor one and discriminates negatively. The first time a test is used, it is not uncommon to find that a few items discriminate negatively. These items should be revised or rejected before the test is used again.

The **discrimination index** (r) is essentially a correlation coefficient between scores on one item and scores on the whole test. Thus its value ranges from +1 to −1; +1 corresponds to the best possible positive discrimination. The calculation of the correlation between scores on each item and scores on the total test is too time-consuming, but we can estimate it, using the top and bottom 27% of the class, with the following formula:

$$r = \frac{\begin{array}{c} \text{number right} \\ \text{in top group} \end{array} - \begin{array}{c} \text{number right} \\ \text{in bottom group} \end{array}}{\text{number in each group}} \quad \textbf{(16.3)}$$

Problem 16.3 Determine the discrimination index of item 1 in Figure 16-2.

Solution Where the number right in the top group is 12, the number right in the bottom group is 5, and the number of students in each group is 16, the discrimination, or validity, index r is .44:

$$r = \frac{12 - 5}{16} = \frac{7}{16} = .44$$

The discrimination index is quite easy to compute with a calculator; it can be tedious if done by hand.

It is apparent from the discrimination index formula that a positive value is obtained when more people in the top group than in the bottom group answer an item correctly; a zero value is obtained when the same number of people in both groups answer correctly.

We assume in determining item discrimination that the total test score is the best measure of knowledge, and evaluations based on it are valid. Therefore, validity for the total test must be determined, usually by using the logical approach, before the item analysis. Item discrimination has no meaning if the validity for the total test is not high. Also, as noted earlier, all other factors being equal, the larger the standard deviation, the more reliable the test scores. The more a test discriminates, the larger the standard deviation tends to be.

It is worth noting as well that the difficulty of a test item affects the maximum attainable discrimination index. Suppose there are 40 people in each group. If, for example, all people in the top group and none in the bottom group answer the item correctly, D = 40/80 =.5, and r = 40/40 = 1.0. If, however, the difficulty of a test item is .60, the best possible discrimination (.80) is obtained when 100% of the top group and 20% of the bottom group respond to the item correctly: D = (40 + 8) /80 = .60; r = 32/40 = .80. The maximum possible discrimination if item difficulty is .40 is also .80: D = (32 + 0)/80 = .40; r = 32/40 = .80. As item difficulties go up or down from .50, the maximum possible discrimination index decreases. For this reason teachers who want to develop discrimination tests, rather than mastery tests, try to write as many test items whose difficulty is approximately .50 as possible—a difficult task.

Response Quality

Ideally, each response of a multiple-choice item should be selected by at least some of the people whose test papers are analyzed. The instructor can use the chart developed to do the item analysis to determine whether all responses were indeed selected. As seen in Figure 16-2, all responses were selected in item 1, but only responses b and c were selected for item 3. Thus item 3 might as well have been a true-false item.

Item Analysis by a Computer

The **item analysis** just presented is time-consuming to do by hand. The computer can be used to complete an item analysis. When standardized answer sheets are used, the process is quite easy. As noted previously, many schools offer machine scoring. As each answer sheet is scored, the machine can record the student's name, test score, and response to each item. This information for the entire group is then submitted to the computer for item analysis. Computer analysis is more complete than the item analysis undertaken by hand because all the students' scores are used. At many colleges, universities, and public school districts, the item analysis service is free.

A sample of the data from a computer printout of an item analysis appears in Table 16.6. The test was administered to 52 people and was composed of 15 multiple-choice items. Notice that much useful information accompanies the analysis. Having the raw score, percent of items correctly answered, and percentile rank for each person plus the mean, median, and standard deviation for the test provided can save the instructor a lot of calculations.

In the item analysis section of the printout, the correct answer for each item is starred (∗). Because all calculations are done so quickly by the computer, frequencies and percentages are reported for each answer to each item. For item 6, of the 13 people in the upper quarter of the group in terms of total test score, 10 people selected answer C, 2 people selected answer D, and 1 person selected answer E. Similar information is reported for the 13 people in the lower quarter of the group in terms of total test score. Under the total count heading, the number of people in the total group (n = 52) who selected each answer is reported. Thirty-four people, which is 65% of the

total group, selected answer C, the correct answer. A discrimination index is reported for each answer to each item based on the discrimination index formula used when calculating by hand and the frequencies under upper and lower quarter. For item 6, answer C, the discrimination index reported to one decimal place is .4 [(10 − 5)/13]. The difficulty factor reported to one decimal place is based on the total count and total percent for the correct answer. For item 6, the difficulty factor is .7. Item 6 is a good item since all five answers functioned (see under total count heading) and the item discrimination and difficulty factor are acceptable. Notice that a negative item discrimination is desirable for the incorrect answers since it indicates that more of the lower-quarter than the upper-quarter people selected the answer. Item 6 also fulfills this standard with the exception of answer B, which was not selected by any of the people in the upper and lower quarters. In looking over the item analysis, item 3 was very difficult (.4) with fabulous discrimination (.8), but it was basically a true-false item with answers B and C selected. Although item 5 was easy (difficulty = .9), it discriminated well (.4) and all answers functioned. Item 4 was not as good as item 5 due to low discrimination (.2). Item 8 was not good due to low difficulty factor (.4) and two answers with similar positive discrimination indexes. Item 10 is too hard. The reliability of the test is not provided, but it can be quickly calculated from the information on the computer printout using the Kuder-Richardson 21 Formula.

Problem 16.4   Determine the reliability of the knowledge test using the information in Table 16.6.

Solution   Where K is 15, s is 2.52 so s^2 = 6.35, and $\overline{X}$ is 9.9, the reliability coefficient using Kuder-Richardson Formula 21 is .50:

$$r = \frac{(15)(6.35) - (9.9)(15 - 9.9)}{(15 - 1)(6.35)}$$

$$= \frac{95.25 - 50.49}{88.9} = \frac{44.76}{88.9} = .50$$

TABLE 16.6 Sample Item Analysis Printout

Student ID	Student Name	Raw Score	% Right	Percentile Rank
1234	AC	8	53	22
2562	BZ	9	60	42
2981	CC	13	87	87
3324	DF	12	80	75
•	•	•	•	•
•	•	•	•	•
•	•	•	•	•
2617	GJ	5	33	3

No. of Respondents = 52
No. of Items = 15

Mean Score = 9.9
Median Score = 9.0
Stand. Dev. = 2.52

High Score = 14
Low Score = 2

Item Analysis

Question		Upper Quarter	Lower Quarter	Total Count	Total %	Discrim. Index	Diff. Factor
1	A	0	0	1	2	0.0	0.8
	B*	13	8	42	81	0.4	
	C	0	0	1	2	0.0	
	D	0	3	4	8	−0.2	
	E	0	2	4	8	−0.2	
2	A	1	4	11	21	−0.2	0.6
	B*	12	5	29	56	0.5	
	C	0	0	1	2	0.0	
	D	0	2	3	6	−0.2	
	E	0	2	8	15	−0.2	
3	A	0	0	0	0	0.0	0.4
	B*	11	1	22	42	0.8	
	C	2	12	29	56	−0.8	
	D	0	0	0	0	0.0	
	E	0	0	1	2	0.0	
4	A*	13	10	45	87	0.2	0.9
	B	0	2	2	4	−0.2	
	C	0	1	2	4	−0.0	
	D	0	0	1	2	0.0	
	E	0	0	2	4	0.0	
5	A	0	1	1	2	−0.0	0.9
	B	0	2	3	6	−0.2	
	C*	13	8	45	87	0.4	
	D	0	1	2	4	−0.0	
	E	0	1	1	2	−0.0	
6	A	0	2	2	4	−0.2	0.7
	B	0	0	3	6	0.0	
	C*	10	5	34	65	0.4	
	D	2	4	7	13	−0.2	
	E	1	2	6	12	−0.0	

* = correct answer.

(Continued)

TABLE 16.6   **Sample Item Analysis Printout**   *(Continued)*

Item Analysis

Question		Upper Quarter	Lower Quarter	Total Count	Total %	Discrim. Index	Diff. Factor
7	A	0	1	2	4	−0.0	0.9
	B	0	0	0	0	0.0	
	C*	13	9	46	88	0.3	
	D	0	0	0	0	0.0	
	E	0	3	4	8	−0.2	
8	A*	7	3	19	37	0.3	0.4
	B	0	2	6	12	−0.2	
	C	4	8	20	38	−0.3	
	D	2	0	7	13	0.2	
	E	0	0	0	0	0.0	
9	A	0	0	0	0	0.0	0.7
	B*	12	11	37	71	0.0	
	C	0	0	0	0	0.0	
	D	1	1	6	12	0.0	
	E	0	1	9	17	−0.0	
10	A*	6	0	7	13	0.5	0.1
	B	6	10	36	69	−0.3	
	C	1	0	3	6	0.0	
	D	0	3	4	8	−0.2	
	E	0	0	2	4	0.0	
11	A	2	3	8	15	−0.0	0.5
	B*	9	4	26	50	0.4	
	C	1	1	6	12	0.0	
	D	1	2	4	8	−0.0	
	E	0	3	8	15	−0.2	
12	A	0	8	11	21	−0.6	0.8
	B	0	0	1	2	0.0	
	C*	13	5	39	75	0.6	
	D	0	0	0	0	0.0	
	E	0	0	1	2	0.0	
13	A	0	2	3	6	−0.2	0.8
	B	0	3	6	12	−0.2	
	C	0	1	1	2	−0.0	
	D	0	1	2	4	−0.0	
	E*	13	6	40	77	0.5	
14	A	0	0	0	0	0.0	0.7
	B	0	8	14	27	−0.6	
	C*	13	5	37	71	0.6	
	D	0	0	0	0	0.0	
	E	0	0	1	2	0.0	
15	A	0	0	0	0	0.0	0.9
	B*	12	11	45	87	0.0	
	C	0	1	3	6	−0.0	
	D	1	1	4	8	0.0	
	E	0	0	0	0	0.0	

Total in Upper Quarter = 13   Number of Respondents = 52
Total in Lower Quarter = 13   Number of Test Items = 15

* = correct answer.

Revising the Test

After calculating the difficulty of and discrimination index for each item, the overall quality of the test and of each item must be determined so the test can be revised as necessary. A set of standards for evaluating discrimination-type multiple-choice tests appears in Table 16.7. Some easy items are desirable to avoid having really low or zero scores on the test. Also, easy items may be needed to determine whether the students know basic information. However, some difficult items are necessary to discriminate between the superior and above-average students.

Using these standards, we can evaluate the four items in Figure 16-2.

Item 1. D is .53; r is .44. All responses functioned; a good item.

TABLE 16.7	**Standards for Evaluating a Discrimination-Type Multiple-Choice Test**

1. The total test
   a. The validity of the test is acceptable.
   b. The reliability of the test is acceptable.
   c. The mean performance of the class approximates that wanted by the teacher.
   d. At least 90% of the class finished the test (not applicable to speed tests).
2. Each test item
   a. Difficulty: No more than 5% of the test items have difficulty indexes above .90, and no more than 5% are below .10.
   b. Discrimination:
      (1) More than 25% of the test items have discrimination indexes above .40.
      (2) More than 25% of the test items have discrimination indexes between .21 and .39.
      (3) More than 15% of the test items have discrimination indexes between .0 and .20.
      (4) Less than 5% of the test items have zero or negative discrimination indexes.
   c. Responses: On each test item, each response was selected by at least 5% of the students whose test papers were used in the item analysis.

Item 2. D is .38; r is .25. All responses functioned; an acceptable but difficult item.

Item 3. D is .91; r is .19. Only two responses functioned; essentially an easy true-false item. Revision might improve the responses. If left as is, it should be changed to a true-false item.

Item 4. D is .47; r is –.31. Three responses functioned. Revise or reject the item. Either the item itself or response b misled many of the top group. If this problem is corrected by revision, most students will probably answer correctly, because ten of the bottom group did so this time. However, because it is unlikely that the item will ever discriminate and because two responses do not function, the item probably should be rejected.

QUESTIONNAIRES

The construction of questionnaires follows procedures and strategies very similar to those for knowledge tests. Questionnaires are commonly utilized by teachers, exercise specialists, therapists, and researchers to quickly and economically collect information from a group. Often in research the group is widely dispersed, so the questionnaire is sent and returned by mail. In any situation when the group is locally available, the questionnaire is handed out to the group and returned to the person in charge. Information such as beliefs, practices, attitudes, knowledge, and so forth are commonly obtained by the use of a questionnaire. Student evaluation of instructor and course, participant evaluation of an exercise program, participant recall of exercise adherence or barriers to exercise, people's attitudes toward exercise, smoking, or drugs, and people's knowledge about the benefits of exercise and tension reduction are all examples of the use of a questionnaire. Several attitude questionnaires, rating scales, and inventories are presented in Chapter 17. Presented in Table 16.8 is a questionnaire that was used to evaluate physical education courses and fitness programs.

TABLE 16.8	**Example Questionnaire to Evaluate an Instructor and the Course or Program**

Instructor and Course or Program Evaluation Form

Please provide your views on the instructor and course or program you just completed. The information you provide will be kept anonymous. So, do NOT place your name on the form. This form will take less than 5 minutes to complete. The information provided by individuals who have completed the course or program will help the instructor improve the course or program.

Please answer each item below by circling the letter for your answer.

1. The instructor was well prepared each day.
   - a. Almost never
   - b. Infrequently
   - c. Occasionally
   - d. Often
   - e. Almost always
2. The instructor seemed knowledgeable about what was presented in the course or program.
   - a. Almost never
   - b. Infrequently
   - c. Occasionally
   - d. Often
   - e. Almost always
3. The instructor was enthusiastic about the course or program.
   - a. Almost never
   - b. Infrequently
   - c. Occasionally
   - d. Often
   - e. Almost always
4. The course or program content was appropriate for my needs.
   - a. Strongly agree
   - b. Mildly agree
   - c. Mildly disagree
   - d. Strongly disagree
5. How would you rate the overall instructional ability of the instructor?
   - a. Poor
   - b. Fair
   - c. Good
   - d. Very good
   - e. Excellent
6. Was there any course or program material that you would eliminate from the course or program?
   - a. No
   - b. Yes (please list below)

7. Are there any course or program materials that you would add to the course or program?
   - a. No
   - b. Yes (please list below)

8. How would you rate the overall value of the course or program?
   - a. Poor
   - b. Fair
   - c. Good
   - d. Very good
   - e. Excellent
9. Although optional, indicating your sex may help us better interpret your response to the item on this evaluation form.
   - a. Female
   - b. Male

Many things influence the success of obtaining information with a questionnaire. Of concern here is getting people to complete and return the questionnaire, particularly if it is mailed to them. Recommendations for constucting and using a questionnaire can be found in research books like Baumgartner and Hensley (2006). A few things that influence the success of any questionnaire are appearance, form, and length. A questionnaire should be typed, on good paper, with a neat and professional appearance to improve the return rate. The form of the questionnaire in regard to people understanding the directions and easily or quickly responding to the questions influences the return rate. If the questionnaire looks short, people are more likely to return it than if it looks long. Using small type and both sides of the paper makes a questionnaire look short.

In Table 16.8, responses to each item are identified with numbers rather than letters. Usually the volume of data (1,000 scores if 100 people each respond to a 10-item questionnaire) requires that the computer be used for the analysis of questionnaire data. The computer always can analyze numbers, whereas letters (a, b, etc.) for the responses to each item may cause problems. Also in Table 16.8, the last item is used to obtain demographic information. Generally, it is best to place demographic items at the end of the questionnaire.

The minimum data analysis for a questionnaire is frequency counts for the responses to each item. For example, in Table 16.8 the number of individuals selecting each of the five responses to item 1 is determined. Often each of the demographic items is cross-tabulated with each of the nondemographic

items to see if different classifications of the people (in terms of a demographic item) responded differently to a nondemographic item. For example, does gender (item 9) influence response to program materials to add (item 7) in Table 16.8? The outcome of this cross-tabulation is as follows:

Item 7

		Yes	No
Gender	Female	25	35
	Male	78	12

The number in each cell (square) is a frequency for a combination of the two items; so we see that 25 females responded Yes to item 7, whereas 78 males responded Yes. Gender influenced response to item 7, since most males responded Yes, but less than one-half of the females responded Yes. If gender were cross-tabulated with each of the other eight items, there would be eight cross-tabulations, which is too many to do by hand. All packages of statistical computer programs have a cross-tabulation program.

A more comprehensive discussion of questionnaire construction and use is not possible in the space provided in this book. The interested reader should consult any of a number of good texts on the subject, such as Weisberg and Bowen (1977) and Sudman and Bradburn (1988), or research books with a chapter on the subject, such as Baumgartner and Hensley (2006). Lawrence Erlbaum Associates (2006) and Sage Publications (2006) list in their catalogs many excellent publications dealing with developing and administering questionnaires.

SUMMARY

Knowledge testing should be a component of most measurement programs. Before trying to construct a knowledge test, you must be aware of the types of knowledge tests and items, the advantages and disadvantages of each, and the construction process.

Certain techniques are necessary in administering a knowledge test, and their use can help you obtain reliable scores whose interpretations are valid. It is also important to be aware of the different techniques you can use in grading a knowledge test after it is administered.

You should understand the importance of analyzing a knowledge test after it has been administered and should master the techniques used in item analysis. Improving the quality of knowledge tests through item analysis should be every teacher's goal.

Finally, the value and many uses of questionnaires must be recognized. Information that allows valid interpretations can be obtained easily and quickly using questionnaires, provided they are correctly constructed and analyzed.

FORMATIVE EVALUATION OF OBJECTIVES

Objective 1   Differentiate among various types of knowledge tests.

1. Knowledge tests can be classified as either essay or objective tests. Differentiate between these two basic test types.
2. Knowledge tests can also be classified as either mastery or discrimination tests. Differentiate between these two categories in terms of the difficulty and the objectives of the tests.

Objective 2   Define the levels of knowledge most applicable to physical education and adult fitness.

1. The taxonomy for educational objectives lists six classes, or levels, of knowledge. Ranging from low to high, the levels are knowledge, comprehension, application, analysis, synthesis, and evaluation. Define the first four of these levels and write a test item for each.

Objective 3   Outline the basic procedures for constructing, administering, and scoring a knowledge test.

1. Listed below are basic steps that a teacher or program instructor can follow in constructing a knowledge test. Summarize the major decisions made at each step.
   a. Construct a table of specifications.
   b. Decide what type of test to give.
   c. Construct the test items.
   d. Determine the test format and administrative details.
2. When administering a test, a person must consider the basic problems and procedures of test administration.
   a. What types of considerations should be given to the testing environment and test security?
   b. Is it advantageous to have alternate forms of the same test on hand?
3. Differentiate between the procedures used to score an essay test and those for an objective test.
4. Listed in the chapter are basic rules that professional test makers follow in constructing various types of test items. Briefly summarize these basic procedures, being sure to list the key points.

Objective 4   Evaluate knowledge test items.

1. In constructing a test, you can choose from several types of items. Each type has its advantages and disadvantages, as discussed in the chapter. Briefly summarize these advantages and disadvantages for each type of item listed below.
   a. true-false
   b. multiple-choice
   c. matching
   d. completion
   e. short answer and essay
2. What is wrong with the following multiple-choice item?
   a. The score of a student on a multiple-choice test is the number of correct answers minus some fraction of the number wrong. On a 50-item, 5-response test, a student had 30 items correct and omitted 5. The student's score should be (1) 26; (2) 27; (3) 28; (4) 29; (5) 30.
3. What is wrong with the following two multiple-choice items that were together on an archery test?
   a. What is the term that designates a bow made of several pieces of wood and/or other materials? (1) Self-bow; (2) Laminated bow; (3) Multiple bow; (4) Chrysal bow.
   b. Which of the following is the smoothest shooting wood for a self-bow? (1) Birch; (2) Lemonwood; (3) Hickory; (4) Yew.

Objective 5   Analyze knowledge tests in terms of test score reliability and item analysis.

1. Test score reliability is useful for evaluating knowledge tests. Assume that a 50-item multiple-choice test was administered to 225 students. Calculate the test score reliability from the following:
   a test mean of 37 and a standard deviation of 3.5.

2. It is difficult to write a knowledge test with reliable scores on the first try. A test's quality will improve if an item analysis is conducted after the first administration and the test is revised accordingly. An item analysis consists of item difficulty and item discrimination.
   a. Define the term "item difficulty" and interpret the following item difficulties: (1) .68 and (2) .21.
   b. Define the term "item discrimination" and interpret the following discrimination indices: (1) .45, (2) .15, (3) .03, and (4) −.67.
3. Outline the basic procedures involved in an item analysis.

Objective 6   Discuss the uses of questionnaires and how to construct them.

1. What are at least five uses of questionnaires in your area of interest?
2. What are at least six desirable characteristics of a questionnaire?

ADDITIONAL LEARNING ACTIVITIES

1. Several of the books referenced in the text offer complete discussions of knowledge test construction and analysis. Read some of them to increase your familiarity with the subject.
2. Construct a knowledge test composed of some true-false and some multiple-choice items. Administer the test and do an item analysis.
3. As noted in the text, an item analysis can be obtained by using a standardized answer sheet and a test-scoring service on campus. Determine the type of standardized answer sheet to use and the procedures to follow in using your school's service.

BIBLIOGRAPHY

Baumgartner, T. A. and L. D. Hensley. 2006. *Conducting and reading research in health and human performance.* 4th ed. New York: McGraw-Hill.

Bloom, B. S. (Ed.). 1956. *Taxonomy of educational objectives: Cognitive domain.* New York: McKay.

Bloom, B. S. et al. 1971. *Handbook on formative and summative evaluation of student learning.* New York: McGraw-Hill.

Bloom, B. S. et al. 1981. *Evaluation to improve learning.* New York: McGraw-Hill.

Lawrence Erlbaum Associates. (2006). Publication catalog. Lawrence Erlbaum Associates, Inc., 10 Industrial Ave., Mahwah, NJ 07432-2262.

McGee, R. and A. Farrow. 1987. *Test questions for physical education activities.* Champaign, IL: Human Kinetics.

Nunnally, J. C. and I. H. Bernstein. 1994. *Psychometric theory.* 3rd ed. New York: McGraw-Hill.

Sage Publications. (2006). Publication catalog. Sage Publications, Inc., P.O. Box 5084, Thousand Oaks, CA 91359-9924.

Sudman, S. and N. Bradburn. 1988. *Asking questions: A practical guide to questionnaire design.* San Francisco: Jossey-Bass.

Weisberg, H. F. and B. D. Bowen. 1977. *An introduction to survey research and data analysis.* San Francisco: W. H. Freeman.

EXERCISE PSYCHOLOGICAL MEASUREMENT

C O N T E N T S

K E Y   W O R D S

activity factor
affective domain
anorexia nervosa
attitude scale
binge-eating
body image
bulimia nervosa
eating disorders
evaluation factor
potency factor
psychophysical
rating of perceived exertion (RPE)
semantic differential scales
silhouette figure ratings
trait

O B J E C T I V E S

Measuring psychological dimensions is of interest to physical education teachers, exercise specialists, sport psychologists, and researchers. However, psychological dimensions are difficult to measure in a reliable and valid manner. As discussed in Chapter 1, regular vigorous exercise has a positive influence on cardiovascular health and longevity, but many who start exercise programs will quit. Affective behavior—interests, attitudes, appreciations, values, and emotional sets or biases—are not only difficult to measure, but also difficult to teach (Krathwohl et al. 1964). As Ebel (1972) has noted,

> Feelings . . . cannot be passed along from teacher to learner in the way information is transmitted. Nor can the learner acquire them by pursuing them directly as he might acquire understanding by study. Feelings are almost always the consequences of something—of success, of failure, of duty done or duty ignored, of danger encountered or danger escaped.

Physical educators have always valued affective objectives, and the development of affective instruments that can be used by teachers in school settings is an important area of research. While there are limited affective instruments useful to physical education teachers, the instruments available in exercise and sport psychology are growing at an accelerated rate. There are so many exercise and sport psychology scales that it becomes difficult to select representative examples. Ostrow (1996) published a book that evaluates over 300 sport psychological instruments and places them into one of 16 different categories. An electronic version of this information is available at www.fitinfotech.com. His system is presented to aid the interested reader in selecting exercise and sport psychology measures. The primary purpose of this chapter is to describe the process by which exercise and sport psychology instruments are developed. We give special focus to exercise- and sport-related psychological instruments. These include psychological instruments designed to measure self-motivation toward exercise, exercise and self-esteem, psychophysical perceived exertion, eating disorders, and body image.

After reading Chapter 17 you should be able to

1. Evaluate the validity of physical education attitude scales.
2. Outline the procedures used to develop semantic differential scales.
3. Describe the nature of the Self-Motivation Inventory (SMI).
4. Describe the nature of instruments designed to relate exercise and self-esteem.
5. Describe the nature of eating disorder scales.
6. Describe the nature of body image instruments.
7. Evaluate the validity and value of the psychophysical rating of perceived exertion scales (RPE).

MEASUREMENT IN EXERCISE AND SPORT PSYCHOLOGY

The psychology of exercise and sport is a developing academic discipline, dependent on having reliable and valid instruments. Initially, general psychological scales (e.g., Spielberger's Trait and State Anxiety Scale) were used in exercise and sport psychology, but the more recent trend has been to develop exercise- and sport-specific scales. The exercise- and sport-specific scales have their roots in the more general psychological scales. The publication of these specific scales reflects the evolution of exercise and sport psychology as a discipline independent of the general area of psychology.

Ostrow (1996) published a comprehensive summary of over 300 psychological scales, questionnaires, and inventories in the area of exercise and sport sciences, in 20 different categories. The instruments were found through computer literature searches of more than 45 journals and conference proceedings over a 30-year period. The summary contains the following information on each of the instruments:

1. Source—Bibliographical listing of most recent version
2. Purpose of the instrument
3. A general description of the instrument, with example items and response format
4. The methodology used to construct the instrument

5. The reported reliability estimates for populations studied
6. Validity evidence for the instrument
7. Normative data on the populations tested
8. Who to contact to obtain the instrument, including e-mail address when available
9. Articles in which the scale has been used

Ostrow's directory is a valuable resource for anyone attempting to find a psychological instrument for use in sport and exercise science settings. Listed next are the 20 categories. Following each category is Ostrow's description of each general category and the number of instruments reviewed.

Achievement Orientation   Number of instruments reviewed: 18. Instruments measure achievement orientations of sport participants in terms of competitiveness, the desire to win, striving for goals, task versus ego orientation, motives to approach/avoid success and to avoid failure, and perceptions of motivational climate and effort.

Aggression   Number of instruments reviewed: 7. Instruments measure the aggressive tendencies of sport participants in terms of instrumental and reactive aggression, physical and nonphysical aggression, and perceptions among players and spectators of the legitimacy of aggressive behavior.

Anxiety   Number of instruments reviewed: 31. Instruments measure anxiousness among sport participants in terms of cognitive and somatic trait and state anxiety, worry cognitions, and concerns regarding concentration disruption, social evaluation, and fear of injury. Coping strategies for dealing with anxiety are examined. Athlete burnout and sources of stress experienced by youth sport participants, officials, coaches, and cheerleaders are also assessed.

Attention   Number of instruments reviewed: 5. Four of the five instruments are sport-specific versions of Nideffer's test of attention and interpersonal style, which is based on a two-dimensional conceptual framework of attention, containing broad/narrow and internal/external components. The remaining instrument examines attention among elite rifle shooters from a multidimensional perspective.

Attitudes toward Exercise and Physical Activity   Number of instruments reviewed: 17. Instruments measure attitudes of children, college students, physical education teachers, and other groups toward participating in exercise and related physical activities. Enjoyment of physical activity, attraction to being physically active, pathological attitudes toward exercise, and the attitudinal beliefs among nonexercisers are also evaluated.

Attitudes/Values toward Sport   Number of instruments reviewed: 29. Instruments measure the attitudes and values of sport participants regarding sport participation, professional versus play orientations expressed during sport participation, sportsmanship attitudes, and the values youth sport coaches hold regarding the potential outcomes of competitions for children. Tests assess children's beliefs about the purposes of sport, perceptions of coaching behaviors, attitudes toward sport officials, and the value of professional sport to the community as perceived by spectators. Also included are role expectancies for female versus male participation in sport, attitudes toward female involvement in sport, and perceived and experienced role conflict among female athletes.

Attributions   Number of instruments reviewed: 9. Instruments measure the explanations sport participants give for their successes and failures in sport and related physical activities.

Body Image   Number of instruments reviewed: 17. Instruments measure the attitudes of individuals toward their body appearance and structure, and confidence in movement. Tests assessing individual difference in body esteem and body satisfaction are also prominent. One scale determines the extent to which people become anxious when others observe or evaluate their physiques.

Cognitive Strategies   Number of instruments reviewed: 13. Instruments measure the cognitive skill that athletes employ prior to and during sport competition. These strategies include self-talk, coping with anxiety, imagery, association/dissociation, and concentration. Instruments also assess thoughts during running, coping strategies that athletes employ to adjust to pain, task-irrelevant cognitions, and thoughts that occur following mistakes during athletic competition.

Cohesion   Number of instruments reviewed: 7. Instruments measure attraction to the group, interpersonal interactions, group integration, and team unity across sport team members and coach.

Confidence—Exercise   Number of instruments reviewed: 18. Instruments measure perceptions of movement competence, physical fitness capacities, and the physical self-concept. The strength of perceived self-efficacy in relation to exercise participation and one's confidence in overcoming barriers toward exercising are also assessed.

Confidence—Sport   Number of instruments reviewed: 19. Instruments measure perceptions of sport performance competence and perceptions of competence in the coaching role. The strength of perceived self-efficacy in relation to sport performance, and perceptions of self-acceptance within the sport domain, are also evaluated.

Imagery   Number of instruments reviewed: 5. Instruments measure individual differences in visual imagery of movement, the imagery of kinesthetic sensations, and imagery utilization.

Leadership   Number of instruments reviewed: 4. Instruments measure the perceptions/preferences of athletes for specific leader behaviors from the coach, the coach's perceptions of his or her own leader behavior, and satisfaction with various aspects of leadership in sport. Tests also assess the leadership tendencies of soccer players and the leadership qualities of athletic administrators.

Life Adjustment   Number of instruments reviewed: 5. Instruments measure life events and stressors, such as injury, that are experienced by athletes and that necessitate adjustment.

Locus of Control   Number of instruments reviewed: 6. Instruments measure individuals' perceptions of internal and/or external factors that control their reinforcements in relation to exercise, behavior, sport performance, injury rehabilitation, and career choice.

Miscellaneous   Number of instruments reviewed: 21. Instruments measure a variety of psychological constructs, including the affective responses of athletes to experiencing injury, the athletic identity, attitudes toward sport psychological services, psychological factors related to spectator attendance and allegiance to sport teams, sportsmanship attitudes, officials' role satisfaction, and athletes' superstitious beliefs.

Motivation—Exercise   Number of instruments reviewed: 37. Instruments measure reasons for adherence to exercise and injury rehabilitation programs, commitment to exercise and running, perceived benefits/barriers to exercise participation, and the motives/incentives that individuals express for participating in running and other forms of exercise. Also reviewed are perceived exertion, feeling states that stem from exercising, negative addiction to exercise/running, and stages of exercise behavior change.

Motivation—Sport   Number of instruments reviewed: 20. Instruments measure the motives individuals express for participating in sport, the degree of satisfaction derived from sport participation, and the reasons people give for not engaging in sport. Tests also assess spectator motivation, sport commitment, flow states in sport, and perceptions of psychological momentum.

Multidimensional   Number of instruments reviewed: 26. Instruments measure multiple personality traits, attitudes, motives, beliefs, or psychological skills evident among individuals participating in sport or exercise.

Another useful, and more recent, directory of psychological measurements is that of LeUnes (2002). The text is divided into the following four sections:

1. Measures of enduring traits (aggression, authoritarianism/Machiavellianism, burnout, eating disorders, locus of control, omnibus personality inventories, optimism/pessimism, self-concept/self-esteem/self-actualization, sensation seeking, sex-role orientation)
2. Measures of temporary states (anxiety/depression)
3. Sport-specific measures (aggression, anxiety, attributions, group cohesion/leadership, mental skills in sport, motivation, self-concept/self-confidence/self-efficacy, miscellaneous sport inventories)
4. Measures of response tendencies

LeUnes also provides a list of instrument authors and a list of sports.

MEASURING ATTITUDES

Much of the physical education research in the **affective domain** has focused on attitudes (see Figure 17-1) and their measurement. "Attitudes concern feelings about particular social objects—physical objects, types of people, particular persons, social institutions, government policies" (Nunnally 1978). Attitudes are generally measured with scales that require a student to agree or disagree with a series of statements, worded both positively and negatively. Several types of scales are used to determine a respondent's degree of affect. The most common offer two alternatives, Disagree-Agree, or five alternatives: Strongly Disagree, Disagree, Undecided, Agree, Strongly Agree. A 7-step scale can be created by adding Very Strongly Disagree and Very Strongly Agree to the 5-step scale.

Nunnally (1978) recommended the use of a graphic scale demarcated with numbers, like that shown below, to clearly convey degrees of feeling. A graphic scale also allows greater flexibility in selecting the number of steps offered.

Completely disagree $\underline{1} : \underline{2} : \underline{3} : \underline{4} : \underline{5} : \underline{6} : \underline{7} :$ Completely agree

An **attitude scale** lists various statements that elicit one's feelings about the attitude object. The individual's attitude is determined by adding the scores of the statements. In scoring them, the positive statement scores are simply added as they appear; the point values for the negative statements, however, must be reversed by subtracting the score from the total number of levels plus 1. Using a 7-step scale like the one shown here, the marked score of a negative statement is subtracted from 8. For example, assume that a student marks a 2 next to the following statement: "If for any reason a few subjects must be dropped from the school program, physical education should be one of the subjects dropped." Notice that this is a negative statement in terms of an attitude toward physical education and that by scoring it with a low number the student is actually showing a positive attitude toward physical education. In contrast, assume that a student marks a 2 next to the following statement: "Participation in physical education activities establishes a more wholesome outlook on life." Because the statement is positive,

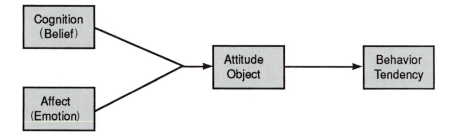

Figure 17-1

Attitudes are a function of beliefs and emotion. An attitude scale is used to measure a person's feelings toward the object. The true validity of the attitude scale is determined by the individual's behavior. Many have a positive attitude toward physical fitness but lead a sedentary lifestyle.

a score of 2 on the 7-step scale indicates a negative attitude.

Most psychological instruments use positively worded and negatively worded statements. Negatively worded statements must be reverse scored in order to reflect the intended response. This is accomplished by subtracting the recorded score from a value of one point higher than the highest possible response value. This would be the value 8 for the illustrated graphic scale. The formula is

$$\text{Reverse Scoring an Item} \qquad \textbf{(17.1)}$$

$$\text{Final Value} = [(1 + \text{Highest Scale Value}) - \text{Record Value}]$$

Calculation Example

To illustrate, assume the 7-step scale was used, and a student marked the score of 2 for a negative statement. Since the student tended to disagree with the negatively worded statement, reverse scoring results in a value reflecting a positive attitude. The calculation would be

$$\text{Final Value} = [(1 + 7) - 2] = 6$$

The process can be completed with computer programs such as Microsoft Excel and SPSS.

Validity of Attitude Scales

An attitude scale is a self-report measure and suffers from the weaknesses typical of this type of instrument. Its principal limitation is that it reflects only what individuals know and are willing to relate about their attitudes. Students who like a teacher tend to respond more favorably than their true attitudes warrant, and often favorable responses on a self-report scale are accompanied by contrary behavior. For example, students may express a favorable attitude toward physical activity, yet be inactive.

Because it is impractical to establish an attitude scale's concurrent validity with actual behavior, most scales claim face validity. This involves defining the content area to be measured and devising attitude statements that logically relate to it. Usually an individual's attitude toward the content area is represented by the total score on the scale. Unfortunately this has created a serious problem of validity

on physical education attitude scales. If you sum all the scores on the scale, it is essential that all statements measure the same general attitude.

Several physical education teachers and exercise specialists have published attitude scales. The targeted objects have included physical education (Adams 1963; Carr 1945; Edington 1968; Kappes 1954; Kneer 1971; Mercer 1971; O'Bryan & O'Bryan 1979; Penmon 1971; Seaman 1970; Wear 1951, 1955); athletic competition (Harris 1968; Lakie 1964; McCue 1953; McGee 1956; Scott 1953); creative dance (Allison 1976); and sportsmanship (Johnson 1969). These published scales report high reliability estimates (≥ 0.85), but their validity has not been established. In addition, the development of scales has not led to widespread use by public school physical education teachers, exercise specialists, or researchers.

Attitude toward Physical Activity (ATPA)

The attitude scale developed by Kenyon (1968b) is especially important and an excellent example of sound measurement procedures. The publication of the ATPA scales marked a departure from using physical education as the attitude object. Rather, Kenyon's scales were designed to measure the reasons why individuals exercised. He recognized that exercise motives were multidimensional, that there were different reasons for people being physically active. The methods used to develop the six scales of the ATPA provide an excellent example of the pursuit of construct validity.

Kenyon (1968) demonstrated that attitude must be considered to be multidimensional. That is, there are several different types of attitudes toward an object, and the composite score must be split into several scores to provide a valid measure of each dimension. For example, assume that a scale measures two factors in a child's attitude toward physical education: (1) the value of physical education for social development, and (2) the value of physical education for health and fitness. By simply summing all the scores, two individuals with very different attitudes might receive the same total score. One may highly value physical education for social development; the other may consider it valueless for social development but important for health and fitness. Thus, the total score is not a valid representation of the true feelings of either person.

The ATPA scale for men consists of 59 items, and the parallel scale for women consists of 54 items. Following is a description of the six dimensions. The complete instrument with instructions is provided in other sources (Baumgartner & Jackson 1982; Kenyon 1968; Safrit 1981). The six dimensions measured by the ATPA and sample statements are given next. Examples of positively worded (+) and negatively worded (–) statements are presented.

Dimension 1. Physical Activity as a Social Experience

Physical education teachers and exercise specialists maintain that physical activity meets certain social needs. Individuals who score high on this factor would value physical activities "whose primary purpose is to provide a medium for social intercourse, that is, to meet new people and to perpetuate existing relationships." The internal consistency reliability estimates for this scale are about .70. These are examples of items used to measure physical activity as a social experience:

(+) The best way to become more socially desirable is to participate in group physical activities.

(–) Of all the kinds of physical activities, I don't particularly care for those requiring a lot of socializing.

Dimension 2. Physical Activity for Health and Fitness

The importance of physical activity for maintaining health and fitness is generally recognized. Individuals who score high on this factor would value physical activity for its "contribution to the improvement of one's health and fitness." The internal consistency reliability estimates are about 0.79. These are examples of items used to measure physical activity for health and fitness:

(+) Physical education programs should stress vigorous exercise since it contributes most to physical fitness.

(–) Of all physical activities, those whose purpose is primarily to develop physical fitness would not be my first choice.

Dimension 3. Physical Activity as the Pursuit of Vertigo

The pursuit of vertigo is the search for excitement: "those physical experiences providing, at some risk to the participant, an element of thrill through the medium of speed, acceleration, sudden change of direction, exposure to dangerous situations, with the participant usually remaining in control." The internal consistency reliability estimates are 0.88 for men and 0.87 for women. These are examples of items used to measure pursuit of vertigo:

(+) Among the best physical activities are those which represent a personal challenge, such as skiing, mountain climbing, or heavy-weather sailing.

(–) I would prefer quiet activities like swimming or golf rather than activities such as waterskiing or sailboat racing.

Dimension 4. Physical Activity as an Aesthetic Experience

Many people value the beauty or artistry of human movement. People who score high on this factor perceive the aestheticism of physical activity. The internal consistency reliability estimates were 0.82 and 0.87 for men and women, respectively. These are examples of items used to measure physical activity as an aesthetic experience:

(+) The most important value of physical activity is the beauty found in skilled movement.

(–) I am not particularly interested in those physical activities whose sole purpose is to depict human motion as something beautiful.

Dimension 5. Physical Activity as a Catharsis

Many believe that physical activity can provide a release from the frustrations of daily living. The validity of this factor has not been fully established. A negative relationship was reported between catharsis scores and preference for "physical activity for recreation and relaxation." The internal consistency reliability estimates were 0.77 and 0.79 for men and women, respectively. These are examples of items used to measure physical activity as a catharsis:

(+) Practically the only way to relieve frustrations and pent-up emotions is through some form of physical activity.

(–) There are better ways of relieving the pressures of today's living than having to engage in or watch physical activity.

Dimension 6. Physical Activity as an Ascetic Experience Individuals who score high on this scale value the type of dedication and intense physical challenge involved in championship-level performance. Such activity demands long, strenuous, often painful training and competition, forcing a deferment of many of the gratifications of general physical activity. The internal consistency reliability estimates were 0.81 for men and ranged from 0.74 to 0.78 for women. These are examples of items used to measure physical activity as an ascetic experience:

(+) I would gladly put up with the necessary hard training for the chance to try out for the U.S. Women's Olympic Team.

(–) A sport is sometimes spoiled if allowed to become too highly organized and keenly competitive.

Semantic Differential Scales

A flexible device for measuring attitudes is the **semantic differential scale,** which asks the subject to respond to bipolar adjectives to measure attitude (Osgood et al. 1967; Snider & Osgood 1969). An example is shown in Table 17.1. The approach is flexible, in that many different attitude objects can be measured without revising the scale. In Table 17.1, for example, the object "Physical Fitness" could be replaced with others, such as "Intramural Football," "Physical Education Class," "Interschool Athletics," or some other concept.

When originally developed, the object being measured was stated in global, neutral terms such as "Intramural Football." A limitation of stating the attitude object in global terms is that the scale lacks the sensitivity to make strong behavior predictions. There is a major trend in sports psychology to move from the measurement of general to that of more specific traits (Ajzen & Fishbein 1980). This can be easily accomplished with semantic differential scales by including the intended behavior with the attitude statement. For example, the general attitude object "Intramural Football" could be replaced with the more specific phrase "My participation this year in the football intramural program."

TABLE 17.1	**Semantic Differential Scales Illustrated**

Physical Fitness

(E) pleasant	____:____:____:____:____:____:____	unpleasant
(A) relaxed	____:____:____:____:____:____:____	tense
(A) passive	____:____:____:____:____:____:____	active
(E) unsuccessful	____:____:____:____:____:____:____	successful
(P) delicate	____:____:____:____:____:____:____	rugged
(A) fast	____:____:____:____:____:____:____	slow
(E) good	____:____:____:____:____:____:____	bad
(P) weak	____:____:____:____:____:____:____	strong
(A) lazy	____:____:____:____:____:____:____	busy
(P) heavy	____:____:____:____:____:____:____	light
(E) unfair	____:____:____:____:____:____:____	fair

Note: Any concept may be used. The concept "Physical Fitness" is illustrated. E = Evaluation; P = Potency; A = Activity

Semantic Dimensions

The process of developing semantic differential scales involves first defining the object to be evaluated and then selecting the bipolar adjective pairs. Numerous studies using various concepts have concluded that three major factors are measured by the semantic differential technique: evaluation, potency, and activity. Table 17.2 provides the bipolar adjective pairs that measure these three dimensions.

The **evaluation factor** is the most common factor. It involves the degree of "goodness" the subject attributes to the object being measured. For most instances, evaluation is the only factor of interest. The most common adjective pair is "good-bad." The **potency factor** involves the strength of the concept being rated. Common potency factors are "hard-soft" and "strong-weak." The **activity factor** is measured by adjective pairs that describe action, like "fast-slow." These factors and adjective pairs provide a flexible method for evaluating attitudes toward an object.

Construction of Semantic Differential Scales

The first step in constructing a semantic differential scale is the selection of concepts relevant to the general attitude being evaluated. The second step is the selection of appropriate adjective pairs. Two criteria

determine the pairs: how well they represent the factor, and their relevance to the concept in question.

Certain adjective pairs have demonstrated validity for measuring the evaluation, potency, and activity factors. Because a minimum of three adjective pairs is suggested to measure a factor reliably, at least nine adjective pairs are needed to measure all three factors. Finally, the adjective pairs must be at the reading comprehension level of the individuals being tested and must relate logically to the concept in question.

The letters E, P, and A in Table 17.1 identify the factor measured by the adjective pair (these letters would not appear on the instrument itself). The various adjective pairs are randomly ordered to prevent those relating to a single factor from being clustered together. It is also essential that both negative and positive adjectives appear in each column.

Scoring and Interpretation

The respondent places a mark at that point between the two adjectives that best reflects his or her feeling about the concept. There are several ways to score semantic scales, but perhaps the easiest is to develop a key, with the lowest point value assigned to the first space on the left side and the highest

TABLE 17.2	Bipolar Adjective Pairs for the Evaluation, Potency, and Activity Factors of Semantic Differential Scales	
Evaluative Factor	**Potency Factor**	**Activity Factor**
good-bad	deep-shallow	excitable-calm
new-old	heavy-light	stable-unstable
healthy-unhealthy	strong-weak	happy-sad
beautiful-ugly	full-empty	hot-cold
fresh-stale	light-dark	fast-slow
valuable-worthless	smooth-rough	tense-relaxed
pleasant-unpleasant	dominant-submissive	active-passive
fair-unfair	hard-soft	changeable-stable
successful-unsuccessful	thick-thin	lazy-busy
honest-dishonest	rugged-delicate	dynamic-static

assigned to the last space on the right side. The scoring system would be

unsuccessful   1 : 2 : 3 : 4 : 5 : 6 : 7   successful

pleasant   1 : 2 : 3 : 4 : 5 : 6 : 7   unpleasant

Since the adjectives "successful" and "pleasant" are the positive ends of the scale, the pleasant-unpleasant scale scoring is reversed by subtracting x from 8 for the obtained score (i.e., 8 − 1 = 7). The student's score on a factor is the sum for all bipolar adjectives that measure that factor. Thus, if all three factors are measured, each scale yields three scores. The reverse scoring and summing of scale scores can be easily completed by computer.

Because these data can be analyzed statistically, it is possible to develop norms from them. The semantic differential scale was designed to measure an individual's feelings about a given concept. Nunnally (1978) reported that the evaluation factor serves as a definition of attitude, so that responses to this factor's adjective pairs are excellent measures of verbalized attitudes. Often, just the evaluation factor is used. The potency and activity factors tend to be partly evaluative, but they also tend to reveal the respondent's interpretation of the concept's physical characteristics. Assume, for example, that two groups of students are administered a semantic differential scale for the concept "Physical Education Class." One group is enrolled in a 12-week basic course in archery; the other, in a basic body-conditioning course that involves distance running and weight training. Although both groups might rate the physical education class "good" on the evaluation factor, their responses are likely to differ on the potency and activity factors. The archery students are apt to respond to the potency adjectives "delicate" and "weak." Students in the conditioning class are more likely to rate their class "strong" and "hard," and the activity adjectives "active," "fast," and "busy." Thus, all three factors would be useful to determine how the students feel about the concept.

Sample Semantic Differential Scale

The Children's Attitude toward Physical Activity Inventory (CATPA-I) is a good example of the use of semantic differential scales to measure attitude. The instrument was developed by Simon and Smoll (1974) and adapted by Schutz and associates (1985) to measure Kenyon's dimensions of physical activity. The general design of the CATPA-I is shown in Figures 17-2 and 17-3. The normative information of the scale is provided in other sources (Schutz et al. 1985).

PSYCHOLOGICAL DETERMINANTS OF PHYSICAL ACTIVITY

It is well established that being sedentary is a risk factor for many chronic diseases, and for premature mortality. Yet in 1997, the Centers for Disease Control established that 40% of adults engaged in no leisure-time physical activity (United States Department of Health and Human Services 2000). The typical dropout rate from supervised exercise programs is about 50% (Dishman 1990). Of major companies that provide employee fitness programs, only 20% to 40% of eligible employees participate, but of these only 33% to 50% exercise on a regular basis at a vigorous intensity—a small fraction of those eligible to participate.

The reasons individuals adhere to exercise programs are complex and not fully understood. Past and present personal attributes, environmental factors, and physical activity characteristics are determinants of the exercise habits of adults. Some of the determinants of exercise behavior reported by Dishman (1990) are as follows:

- *Smoking behavior.* Smokers are more likely than nonsmokers to drop out of exercise programs and less likely to utilize worksite exercise facilities.
- *Occupational level.* Blue-collar workers are more likely than white-collar workers to drop out of exercise programs and less likely to utilize worksite exercise facilities.
- *Body composition.* Overweight individuals are less likely to stay with a fitness program. Even in easy walking programs, 60% to 70% of obese individuals drop out.
- *Exercise history.* Past exercise participation is the best predictor of physical activity.

Physical activity for social growth
    Taking part in physical activities that give you a chance to meet new people.

Physical activity to continue social relations
    Taking part in physical activities that give you a chance to be with your friends.

Physical activity for health and fitness
    Taking part in physical activities to make your health better and to get your body in better condition.

Physical activity as a thrill but involving some risk
    Taking part in physical activities that could be dangerous because you move very fast and must change direction quickly.

Physical activity as the beauty in movement
    Taking part in physical activities that have beautiful and graceful movements.

Physical activity for the release of tension
    Taking part in physical activities to reduce stress or to get away from problems you might have.

Physical activity as long and hard training
    Taking part in physical activities that have long and hard practices. To spend time in practice you need to give up other things you like to do.

Figure 17-2

Children's Attitude toward Physical Activity Inventory (CATPA-I) inventory subdomain descriptions.
(Schutz et al. 1985).

How Do You Feel about the Idea Below?

Physical Activity for Social Growth
Taking Part in Physical Activities that Give You
a Chance to Meet New People

Always Think about the Idea in the Box

If You Do Not Understand This Idea, Mark This Box ☐
and Go to the Next Page.

1. Good					Bad
2. Of No Use					Useful
3. Not Pleasant					Pleasant
4. Nice					Awful
5. Happy					Sad

Figure 17-3

Scale format for the Children's Attitude toward Physical Activity Inventory (CATPA-I), grades 7 through 11.

- *Self-motivation.* The personality trait of self-motivation (Dishman 1980) is related to exercise behavior. The self-motivated individual often leaves a supervised program, but continues a personal exercise program.
- *Level of knowledge.* Knowledge and belief in the health benefits of physical activity motivate individuals to initiate exercise programs and return following relapse.
- *Positive affect.* Feelings of enjoyment and well-being are strong motives of regular participation in physical activity.
- *Perceived exercise capacity.* Specific efficacy beliefs about the ability to exercise tend to increase exercise compliance in medically supervised rehabilitation and free-living exercise programs.

Provided in this section are psychological instruments used to assess the motives of exercise. The Self-Motivation Inventory (SMI) (Dishman & Ickes 1981) is provided in its entirety. The SMI correlates with exercise behavior and identifies those most likely to drop out of an exercise program. Norms for the SMI, based upon University of Houston students participating in a required personal health–related fitness course, can be found in Jackson and Ross (1997). The second section reviews Sonstroem's Physical Estimation and Attraction Scales (PEAS). The PEAS is important because it is the first exercise-specific instrument to evaluate the importance of the physical self as a motivator of exercise behavior (Fox 1997; Sonstroem 1997).

Self-Motivation Inventory (SMI)

Self-motivation is a personality trait that is related to exercise behavior. A psychological trait is a construct that tends to be stable. This means that someone who scores high on the SMI will likely be self-motivated in many different situations. Being a stable psychological construct, it provides a means of predicting future behavior. Dishman (1990) described the self-motivation trait in the following way:

> It is believed that self-motivation reflects willpower or self-regulatory skills such as effective goal setting, self-monitoring of progress, and self-reinforcement. These factors are believed to be important for maintaining physical activity and intentions to change behavior. Successful endurance athletes have consistently scored high on self-motivation, and self-motivation has discriminated between adherents and dropouts across a wide variety of settings, including athletic conditioning, adult fitness, preventive medicine, cardiac rehabilitation, commercial spas, corporate fitness, and free-living activity in college students. (p. 83)

Dishman and Ickes (1981) developed the Self-Motivation Inventory (SMI) to measure the self-motivation trait. The psychological **trait** measure is a 40-item scale, which consists of 20 positively keyed and 20 negatively keyed statements. Using a sample of over 400 undergraduate men and women, the internal consistency reliability was estimated to be 0.91. Stability reliability has been found to be high, exceeding 0.86 (Dishman & Ickes 1981).

Dishman and Ickes's initial analysis produced ten different factors, suggesting that self-motivation consisted of ten different dimensions. This suggests that one would need ten different subscale scores to adequately measure self-motivation. Merkle (1997) examined the construct validity of the SMI with over 1,600 college students enrolled in a required health-related fitness course. Her factor analysis of the 40-item SMI produced eight factors that were similar to those found in the initial analysis. Further analysis showed that six of the eight factors were highly correlated, demonstrating that the self-motivation construct consisted of six related dimensions. The six correlated factors were consistent with Dishman's interpretation of self-motivation. The six factors are presented below, with a sample item for each:

> *Commitment*—I'm not very good at committing myself to do things.
>
> *Lethargy*—I don't like to overextend myself.
>
> *Drive*—Sometimes I push myself harder than I should.
>
> *Persistence*—I can persevere at stressful tasks even when they are physically tiring or painful.
>
> *Reliability*—I'm not very reliable.
>
> *Discipline*—I'm good at keeping promises, especially ones I make to myself.

Notice again that some of the items are negatively worded and need reverse-scoring. For example, the item "I'm not very reliable" would be reverse-scored so that a higher score would correspond to "more reliable," not "less reliable."

Finding that the six self-motivation factors were correlated supported the practice of using a single SMI score, which is the sum of the items represented by the six factors. This reduced the SMI from the original 40 items to 35 items. The revised SMI is provided next.

Scale   Self-Motivation Inventory (35 items)

Purpose   Measure the personality trait of self-motivation, which has been shown to be a consistent predictor of exercise adherence.

Reliability   The internal consistency reliability of the original and revised forms was 0.91 and 0.88, respectively. The 40-item scale was found to be stable, and the test-retest reliability was .92. The time between test administrations was one month.

Validity   The factor analyses supported the subscale structure of the SMI. The predictive validity of the scale was examined by determining if the scale predicted the likelihood that female college students would quit the physically demanding college crew team. Scores between dropouts and those who adhered were compared at three points in time: the first 10 days; 8 weeks; and 32 weeks, when the final team cuts were made. The analysis showed that the mean SMI of the dropouts was significantly lower than that of the adherents at each of the points in time (Dishman 1980). The SMI was found to predict adherence to a medically supervised cardiovascular and muscular endurance training program (Dishman 1980). The predictors of exercise adherence were percent body fat, body weight, and SMI. The SMI was the only psychological instrument that was found to predict exercise adherence. Using the three predictors, it was possible to correctly classify 80% of adherers and dropouts. The profile of dropouts was high body fat, high body weight, low SMI. With college students, the SMI is significantly correlated with self-reported exercise habits, but not body composition (Merkle 1997).

Scoring   The point values for each response are these: (1) extremely uncharacteristic of me; (2) somewhat uncharacteristic of me; (3) neither characteristic nor uncharacteristic of me; (4) somewhat characteristic of me; (5) extremely

TABLE 17.3	Percentile-Rank Norms for the Self-Motivation Inventory		
Percentile	SMI Level	Women	Men
90	High	150	149
75	Above average	140	140
50	Average	129	127
25	Below average	116	113
10	Low	103	101

Source: Jackson, A. S. and R. M. Ross, *Understanding Exercise for Health and Fitness*, 1997.

characteristic of me. Items negatively keyed are scored 6 – X, where X is the assigned value (1 to 5). SMI score is the sum of all items.

Norms   Table 17.3 provides percentile-rank norms for men and women. The norms were developed on over 1,600 University of Houston students who completed a required personal fitness course (Jackson & Ross 1997).

35-Item SMI Instructions and Items   Read each of the following statements. Respond to each statement using the "bubble sheet." Mark the letter that best describes how characteristic the statement is when applied to you. The choices are as follows:

A: Extremely Uncharacteristic of Me
B: Somewhat Uncharacteristic of Me
C: Neither Characteristic nor
    Uncharacteristic of Me
D: Somewhat Characteristic of Me
E: Extremely Characteristic of Me

Be sure to answer every question. Be honest and complete in your responses.

1. I'm not very good at committing myself to do things.
2. Whenever I get bored with projects I start, I drop them to do something else.
3. I can persevere at stressful tasks even when they are physically tiring or painful.
4. If something gets to be too much of an effort to do I am likely to just forget it.
5. I'm really concerned about developing and maintaining self-discipline.

6. I'm good at keeping promises, especially ones I make to myself.
7. When I take on a difficult job I make a point of sticking with it until it is completed.
8. I'm willing to work for the things I want as long as it's not a big hassle.
9. I have a lot of self-motivation.
10. I'm good at making decisions and standing by them.
11. I generally take the path of least resistance.
12. I get discouraged easily.
13. If I tell someone that I will do something, you can depend on it being done.
14. I don't like to overextend myself.
15. I'm basically lazy.
16. I have a hard-driving aggressive personality.
17. I work harder than most of my friends.
18. I can persist in spite of pain or discomfort.
19. I like to set goals and work toward them.
20. Sometimes I push myself harder than I should.
21. I seldom if ever let myself down.
22. I'm not very reliable.
23. I like to take on jobs that challenge me.
24. I change my mind about things quite easily.
25. I have a lot of willpower.
26. I'm not likely to put myself out if I don't have to.
27. Things just don't matter much to me.
28. I avoid stressful situations.
29. I often work to the point of exhaustion.
30. I never force myself to do things I don't feel like doing.
31. It takes a lot to get me going.
32. Whenever I reach a goal, I set a higher one.
33. I can persist in spite of failure.
34. I have a strong desire to achieve.
35. I don't have much self-discipline.

Exercise and Self-Esteem Instruments

There is a growing interest in the study of exercise and self-esteem (Sonstroem 1997). This interest stems from the growing importance of the physical self as a motivator of exercise behavior and a contributor to mental health and well-being (Fox 1997). These scales are state instruments, or scales that reflect change from one situation to the next. How one feels in one situation or environment is not predictive of how one feels in others. When the situation changes, so does the psychological state. Some of the more common exercise-related psychological state measures (Fox 1997) are the following:

> *Perceived competence*—A statement of personal ability that generalizes across a domain, such as sport or exercise.
>
> *Perceived ability*—A more specific statement of competence restricted to a limited set of behaviors, such as playing soccer or other sports.
>
> *Body image*—The mental representation an individual has of his or her body.
>
> *Self-efficacy*—A statement of expectancy about one's ability to accomplish a specific task.

Physical Estimation and Attraction Scales (PEAS)

Sonstroem (1974) is credited with developing the first social psychological scale designed to measure the components of the physical self as a motivator of physical activity. His global scale, Physical Estimation and Attraction Scale (PEAS), provided the theoretical basis for many of the newer state instruments.

The Physical Estimation and Attraction Scales (PEAS) developed by Sonstroem (1974) were incorporated into a model (see Figure 17-4) explaining the psychological benefit of physical activity and motivation to participate in physical activity (Sonstroem 1978). The 33 "estimation" items measure self-perceptions of (attitudes toward) one's own physical abilities. Estimation is conceived to be a component of general self-esteem. The 54 "attraction" items assess interest in or attraction to vigorous physical activity. Of the 100 items, 2 pertain to the social aspects of physical activity, and 11 neutral items (not scored) are included to hide the nature of the scale. Examples of estimation and attraction items are presented on page 487. The

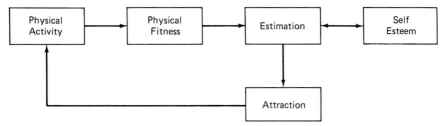

Figure 17-4

Sonstroem's psychological model for physical activity.

(Sonstroem, R. J. 1974. Attitude testing examining certain psychological correlates of physical activity. *Research Quarterly* 45: 93–103.)

entire PEAS may be obtained from Baumgartner and Jackson (1982) or Safrit (1981).

The estimation items ask students to affirm or deny their own physical characteristics, fitness, athletic ability, or potential in motor performance. Examples of items include the following:

I am stronger than a good many of my friends.

It is difficult for me to catch a thrown ball.

I am in better physical condition than most boys my age.

Even with practice I doubt that I could learn to do a handstand well.

The attraction items ask students to affirm or deny their personal interests or likes for certain forms of physical activity. Sample items are as follows:

Sports provide me with a welcome escape from present-day life.

I love to run.

Playing tennis appeals to me more than golfing does.

I enjoy the discipline of long and strenuous physical training.

Reliability and Validity of PEAS

Reliability and validity research has been conducted with boys in grades 8 through 12. Internal consistency reliability estimates of 0.87 and 0.89

and stability reliability estimates of 0.92 and 0.94 have been reported for the estimation and attraction scales, respectively (Sonstroem 1974, 1976).

Construct validity research has supported the two scales (Sonstroem 1974). Both estimation and attraction were found to be correlated with height, weight, and athletic experience and unrelated to intelligence quotient (Sonstroem 1974). Sonstroem (1976) found the scales to be relatively free of response distortion. Dishman (1980) identified a tendency for subjects to "fake bad" on the attraction scale under instructions to do so.

Repeated research has shown that self-perceptions of physical ability (estimation scores) correlate well with actual physical fitness scores and with measures of self-esteem, as Sonstroem's model hypothesizes (Dishman 1978; Fox, Corbin & Couldry 1985; Sonstroem 1978). Estimation scores have been significantly related to mental health scales of the Tennessee Self-Concept Scale (Sonstroem 1976). Physical fitness seems to bear no direct association with self-esteem, which suggests that what people think about their fitness and bodies is more closely related to positive mental adjustment than is their actual fitness level. Estimation scores have been shown to increase following exercise experiences (Dishman & Gettman 1981; Kowal, Patton & Vogel 1978). Attraction scores have been found to be related to self-reports of participation in sport-type activities (Neale et al. 1969; Sonstroem 1978; Sonstroem & Kampper 1980). Sonstroem and Kampper (1980) administered the PEAS to boys in grades 7 and 8 at the beginning of a school year. They found that attraction, first, and estimation, second, predicted those boys who would subsequently try out for the touch football and soccer teams. Scores, however, failed to predict staying with a team for the entire season. The PEAS has not been found to predict exercise adherence.

Evolving Research Applications

Sonstroem and Morgan (1989) have proposed a model that explains how exercise program experiences influence self-esteem by means of such variables as physical self-efficacy and physical competence. They suggest that physical competence can be assessed by the estimation scale. The current trend is to develop specific self-efficacy and perceived competence scales.

To illustrate, Garcia and King (1991) developed an exercise self-efficacy scale. Self-efficacy is based on Bandura's social psychological theory (Bandura 1977) and is the belief that one can execute a specific behavior to achieve a specific outcome. The Garcia-King instrument consisted of 16 items in which the respondents rated their confidence that they could exercise under 16 different conditions. The confidence rating ranges from 0% (I cannot do it at all) to 100% (I am certain that I can do it). The individual's score is the average of the 16 responses. Some examples of the conditions specific to exercise used by Garcia and King are these:

> I could exercise when tired.
>
> I could exercise during bad weather.
>
> I could exercise when I have a lot of work to do.
>
> I could exercise when I have no one to exercise with.

Many self-perception scales are theory-based, multidimensional, and situation-specific. For example, Fox and Corbin (1989) developed a physical self-perception profile consisting of four dimensions of physical self-worth. The dimensions were perceived sport competence, physical condition, attractive body, and strength.

EATING DISORDERS

Eating disorders[1] are extremely complex problems and have been historically documented. Cases of self-inflicted starvation and weight loss were noted as early as the fourth century when it was recorded that pale, thin, fasting women died of the regimen (Foreyt et al. 1998). Biological, family, and cultural factors are associated with eating disorders. Eating disorders are much more prevalent among young women than men. It is estimated that about 90% of individuals with eating disorders are women (Foreyt et al. 1998). The incidence of these disorders appears to be on the rise and corresponds to societal pressure for women to be thin.

Nature of Eating Disorders

The common eating disorders are anorexia nervosa, bulimia nervosa, and binge-eating. **Binge-eating** is a less well defined eating disorder and often judged to be a behavioral trait of bulimia nervosa. The causes of anorexia nervosa and bulimia nervosa are complex and not well understood. In American society, women associate thinness with beauty. Advertisements in the mass media constantly reinforce this notion. Anorexics and bulimics tend to judge their self-worth in terms of shape and weight. Table 17.4 summarizes the recognized characteristics used to diagnose anorexia nervosa (APA 1994; Foreyt et al. 1998).

The central characteristic of **anorexia nervosa** is "drive for thinness." Persons with anorexia strive to lose weight beyond the point of social desirability, attractiveness, and good health. Individuals with this disorder are highly motivated to adhere to socially derived notions of beauty and femininity, which in our society has become thinness (Foreyt et al. 1998). Mass advertising with female models constantly reinforces this notion. Anorexia nervosa begins in early to late adolescence, with the greatest risk for onset between the ages of 14 and 18 years. It is estimated that about 1% of young women are

---

[1]This section was written with the assistance of John Foreyt, Ph.D., and Carlos Poston II, Ph.D., from the Nutrition Research Center, Baylor College of Medicine, Houston, TX.

TABLE 17.4	The Recognized Characteristics Used to Diagnose Anorexia Nervosa
Anorexia Nervosa	**Bulimia Nervosa**
Refusal to maintain body weight at or above a minimally normal weight for one's age and height.	Recurrent episodes of binge eating that includes eating a large amount of food within a discrete period of time (e.g., 2-hour period); and a sense of lack of control over eating.
Denial of the seriousness of their current low weight.	Recurrent inappropriate compensatory behavior designed to prevent weight gain. These may include self-induced vomiting, misuses of laxatives, fasting, or excessive exercise.
Intense fear of gaining weight or becoming fat, though underweight.	The binge eating and inappropriate compensatory behaviors occur regularly, at least twice a week, for an extended time period, e.g., three months.
Amenorrhea, or the absences of at least three consecutive menstrual cycles in postmenarcheal females.	The bulimic's self-evaluation is unduly influenced by body shape and weight.

Source: Foreyt et al. (1998).

anorexic. Anorexia nervosa has potentially lethal consequences. This disorder has a 20% mortality rate, the highest of any psychological disorder.

The essential characteristic of **bulimia nervosa** is an excessive intake of food, usually high in calories, in a relatively short period. Although this varies considerably, as many as 30,000 calories may be consumed during a binge. This binge-eating is accompanied by recurrent methods to prevent weight gain, such as vomiting or using laxatives. The average age of onset for bulimia is 17–19 years. The prevalence of bulimia nervosa is approximately 1–3%. It has been estimated that 4–19% of young women engage in significant levels of bulimic behavior. The bulimic needs psychological counseling to develop self-esteem and overcome serious concerns about body image. Unlike the anorexic, the bulimic may not experience serious weight loss; many maintain a normal weight.

Eating Disorder Scales

Psychological inventories are used to help identify those at risk of developing eating disorders. While these paper-and-pencil tests provide useful information, the diagnosis of eating disorders can be made only by professionals after intensive evaluation.

The first instruments used to assess anorexic behavior were behavioral rating scales (Slade 1973). The Eating Attitudes Test (EAT) was the first objective self-report measure of anorexia nervosa (Garner & Garfinkel 1979). A more recent scale is the Eating Disorder Inventory (Garner 1984).

Eating Disorder Inventory (EDI)

The EDI is the most comprehensive eating disorder scale. The scale was constructed to assess both psychological and behavioral traits associated with both anorexia nervosa and bulimia nervosa. The 64-item scale consists of eight subscales. Table 17.5 provides a summary of the scales. The EDI is a comprehensive scale used to help diagnose eating disorders. The scale was developed by psychological professionals and was not intended to be used by nonprofessionals. The EDI illustrates the complexities of an eating disorder.

Eating Attitudes Test (EAT)

The most popular scale is the Eating Attitudes Test or EAT. The original EAT consisted of 40 items that the subject rated on a Likert scale that ranged from never to always. Further research (Garner et al. 1982) with a large sample of female anorexia

TABLE 17.5	A Description of the Eating Disorder Inventory (EDI) Scales and the Reliability of Each Scale
Scale	**Scale Description**
Drive for thinness ($r_{xx} = 0.92$)	Excessive concern with dieting, preoccupation with weight and entrenchment in an extreme pursuit of thinness
Bulimia ($r_{xx} = 0.90$)	The tendency toward episodes of uncontrollable overeating, binge-eating, and recurrent methods to prevent weight gain such as self-induced vomiting.
Body dissatisfaction ($r_{xx} = 0.92$)	The belief that parts of the body are too large, e.g., hips, thighs, buttocks.
Ineffectiveness ($r_{xx} = 0.85$)	A feeling of general inadequacy, insecurity, worthlessness, and not being in control of one's life.
Perfectionism ($r_{xx} = 0.88$)	Excessive personal expectations for superior achievement.
Interpersonal distrust ($r_{xx} = 0.81$)	A sense of alienation and general reluctance to form close relationships.
Interoceptive awareness ($r_{xx} = 0.85$)	The lack of confidence in recognizing and accurately identifying emotions and sensations of hunger or satiety.
Maturity fears ($r_{xx} = 0.96$)	A wish to retreat to the security of the preadolescent years because of the overwhelming demands of adulthood.

Source: Garner (1984); Rhea (1995).

nervosa patients produced a 26-item form of the EAT. The correlation between the 26- and 40-item tests was very high, 0.97. The 26-item scale was found to measure three general factors. Table 17.6 gives the three factors and sample items. Women with eating disorders were found to differ significantly from controls on the 26-item scale.

A possible limitation of the EAT is that it was developed as a screening test for detecting previously undiagnosed cases of anorexia nervosa in populations at high risk for the disorder (Garner & Garfinkel 1979; Garner et al. 1982). Koslowsky and associates (1992) examined the validity of the 26-item EAT with a sample of over 800 young, female Israeli soldiers. Over 90% of the women were 18 or 19 years of age, an age group at risk for eating disorders. Since military service in Israel is mandatory, this sample was representative of the total Israeli female population of this age group. Their analysis showed that the scale measured four different factors. Table 17.6 gives these factors and sample test items.

The Israeli Army study demonstrated that the EAT is a reliable instrument for the general population. While research (Garner & Garfinkel 1979;

Koslowsky 1992) shows that the EAT consists of several factors, the first factor (dieting) was the predominant, most important factor. Additional analyses showed that the other factors tended to be correlated with the dieting factor.

College Student EAT Screening Version

Both the 40- and 26-item versions of the EAT were developed by psychological professionals to use for identifying individuals at risk for eating disorders and help in the diagnosis of eating disorders. Eating disorders is a topic of the University of Houston personal fitness course required of all students (Jackson & Ross 1997). One objective of the course is to help students be aware of eating disorders and help determine if they may be at risk. The 26-item EAT (Garner et al. 1982) was administered to over 2,300 students who were enrolled in the course. These data were factor analyzed (Suminski et al. 1998), and the analysis produced the same four factors found in the Israeli Army study (Koslowsky 1992). The goal of this analysis was to develop a shortened version of the EAT that measured just the principal factor, dieting. This analysis produced a 10-item screening version of the scale.

TABLE 17.6	**Factors and Sample Items of the Eating Attitudes Test (EAT) from Two Studies**
Factor	**Sample Items**
26-Item EAT Study (Garner et al. 1982)	
Dieting ($R_{xx} = 0.90$)	I eat diet foods.
	I am preoccupied with the thought of having fat on my body.
Bulimia and food preoccupation ($R_{xx} = 0.86$)	I have an impulse to vomit after meals.
	I have gone on eating binges where I feel that I may not be able to stop.
Oral control ($R_{xx} = 0.84$)	I cut my food into small pieces.
	I feel that others pressure me to eat.
Israeli Army Study (Koslowsky et al. 1992)	
Dieting ($R_{xx} = 0.90$)	I engage in dieting behavior.
	I am preoccupied with the thought of having fat on my body.
Oral control ($R_{xx} = 0.74$)	I enjoy eating new and rich foods.
	Other people think I am too thin.
Awareness of food content ($R_{xx} = 0.76$)	I avoid foods with sugar in them.
	I eat diet foods.
Food preoccupation ($R_{xx} = 0.56$)	I feel that food controls my life.
	I give too much time and thought to food.

Scale   10-Item EAT

Purpose   The purpose of the scale is to provide students with a general assessment of the EAT dieting factor.

Reliability   Using a sample of 2,327 male and female college students, the internal consistency reliability was found to be 0.95.

Validity   The scale has construct validity for the EAT dieting factor. The factor has been shown to discriminate between eating-disordered females and controls (Garner & Garfield 1979) and to correlate with body image ($r = 0.40$) and the number of diets in the past year ($r = 0.55$) (Koslowsky 1992).

Scoring   The scoring method is a 5-response Likert scale. The scoring method was established to facilitate machine scoring on bubble sheets. The choices and point values are: A, Always (5); B, Usually (4); C, Sometimes (3); D, Rarely (2); E, Never (1). The subject's score is the sum of their responses on the 19 items.

10-Item EAT Instructions and Items *Eating Behavior.*   Please read each item below. Most of the statements relate to food or eating, although other types of statements have been included.

Place a mark on your bubble sheet for each of the numbered statements using the letter description that best applies to you. The choices are

A: Always
B: Usually
C: Sometimes
D: Rarely
E: Never

1. I vomit after I have eaten.
2. I feel extremely guilty after eating.
3. I am preoccupied with a desire to be thinner.
4. I am preoccupied with the thought of having fat on my body.
5. I eat diet foods.
6. I feel that food controls my life.
7. I give too much time and thought to food.
8. I engage in dieting behavior.
9. I like my stomach to be empty.
10. I have the impulse to vomit after meals.

A Note of Caution   It is important to understand that the diagnosis of an eating disorder can be confirmed only through a comprehensive assessment by a competent professional. The purpose of the 10-item scale is to provide students with normative data to compare their status with other college students. Most colleges and universities have psychological services available to students who want more comprehensive information. The students are confidentially given their 10-item EAT score and use the normative information to interpret their score. Students are also given information about the services provided at the university counseling center to seek additional help if concerned.

BODY IMAGE

The term **body image** has been used loosely in the psychological literature, as an umbrella term to describe several different psychological traits relating to the appearance, structure, and function of a person's body. The multitude of different instruments all bearing the label "body image" has led to some confusion in this area of research. The study of body image is nevertheless important to exercise science and physical education professionals for several reasons.

The Importance of Body Image

The role of body image disturbance in the development of eating disorders such as anorexia nervosa and bulimia, and the connection between body image and body weight problems, are well documented, both in the general population (Thompson 1996a) and in a significant minority of exercise professionals and exercise participants (Moriarty, Ford & Rawlings 1991). Several research studies have been designed to demonstrate a connection between exercise and body image. For example, Holmes, Chamberlin, and Young (1994) reported a significant relationship between self-reported exercise frequency and overall body satisfaction in 212 college students, measured with the Body Cathexis scale (Secord & Jourard 1953). Koff and Bauman (1997) found significant improvements in various subscale scores from the Body Self-Relations Questionnaire (Cash 1990) in 33 college women enrolled

in a wellness course and 60 college women enrolled in a fitness course, but no significant changes in 47 women who were enrolled in college sport skill classes. Conversely, in a study comprising 88 exercising men and 112 exercising women of varying ages, Davis and Cowles (1991) found a relationship between amount of habitual exercise and body dissatisfaction only in the younger (under 25 years old) group of men, as measured by the Body Image Inventory (Myers et al. 1985). Imm and Pruitt (1991) compared 28 high-frequency exercisers, 26 moderate-frequency exercisers, and 20 nonexercising women, using the Body Shape Questionnaire (Cooper et al. 1987), which was designed to measure feelings of fatness. Despite no differences in actual body weight, the high-frequency exercisers reported significantly greater levels of dissatisfaction with their body shape than either the moderate-frequency exercisers or the nonexercisers.

In other research, exercise participants with higher levels of body dissatisfaction were more likely to report participating in exercise in order to bring about changes in body weight or overall appearance, rather than for health and fitness reasons (Cash, Novy & Grant 1994; McDonald & Thompson 1992). In extreme cases, excessive exercise (or exercise obsession) and use of steroids are connected to clinical conditions such as body dysmorphia (obsession with an imaginary flaw in the physical appearance) and muscle dysmorphia (Pope et al. 1997). Muscle dysmorphia is found primarily in males, and is characterized by an obsession with muscularity and body size.

The Nature of Body Image

Interestingly, there is very little mention in the body image measurement literature of the theoretical works of authors such as Schilder (1950), Shontz (1969), and Fisher (1990). A simple theoretical definition of body image was provided by Schilder (1950) as "the picture of our own body which we form in our mind" (p. 11). This belies the complexity of body image. Fisher (1986), for example, listed as many as 14 separate dimensions that he theorized were a part of body image. There is a general consensus that body image is multidimensional. The prevailing model is of two major facets of body image: a sensory-perceptual facet and a cognitive-affective facet. The sensory-perceptual facet involves the objective feedback (sensory) and processing (perception) of various types of information about the body (although the overwhelming body of research evidence is restricted to feedback regarding the size and shape of the body). The cognitive-affective aspect is more subjective in nature, and includes thoughts and opinions about one's own body or the bodies of others (cognitive), and feelings and emotions relative to the body (affective). Bane and McAuley (1998) extended this description recently, to include behaviors related to the body, such as avoidance of situations in which attention is drawn to the body.

Measurement Methods

There is a multitude of instruments currently available to measure body image, using a wide range of methods. These methods include image distortion techniques (e.g., Rowe et al., 2005); silhouette figure ratings (e.g., Fallon & Rozin 1985; Thompson & Psaltis 1988); photograph ratings (e.g., Counts & Adams 1985); computer-generated reproductions of perceived body shape and size (e.g., Dickson-Parnell et al. 1987); and paper-and-pencil questionnaires measuring a variety of unidimensional (e.g., Garner, Olmstead & Polivy 1983) and multidimensional (e.g., Cash 1990; Rowe, Benson & Baumgartner 1999) conceptions of body image. A detailed discussion of all of these methods is beyond the scope of this book, although readers are directed to a comprehensive summary written by Thompson (1996b). In recent years, body image research has focused primarily on figure ratings and questionnaire measures, so these will be the focus in this section.

Figure Ratings

Silhouette figure ratings have been used to measure the degree of satisfaction (or dissatisfaction) with one's bodily appearance. The concept of "self-ideal discrepancy" involves the participant's assessment of her actual body shape, usually from the perspective of a fatness-thinness continuum, and the

assessment of ideal or desired shape, using the same scale. The self-ideal discrepancy rating is used to indicate the degree of dissatisfaction with bodily appearance (a greater discrepancy between actual and ideal appearance equating to a greater degree of dissatisfaction with one's body). A positive self-ideal discrepancy score reflects a desire to be thinner, or smaller, whereas a negative self-ideal discrepancy score reflects a desire to be fatter, or larger. A series of silhouettes, ranging from extremely thin to extremely fat, are arranged above a line that is marked with numbers at equal intervals. Each whole number corresponds with the figure drawn directly above it, but participants may mark anywhere along the line, according to the specific instructions given. Thus, if a participant thought that his body corresponded to a position somewhere between two figures, the line would be marked somewhere between the two whole numbers corresponding to the two figures. An example nine-figure silhouette rating scale called the Contour Drawing Rating Scale, from Thompson and Gray (1995), is shown in Figure 17-5. Seven-day test-retest reliability for self-ideal ratings using the Contour Drawing Rating Scale was .79; published test-retest reliability for these types of instruments is generally above .70.

Silhouette figure ratings may be used to measure several aspects of body dissatisfaction, depending upon the directions given by the administrator. For example, in a study by Fallon and Rozin (1985), their Figure Rating Scale of nine figures scored from 1 (thinnest figure) to 9 (fattest figure) was used to measure perception of actual body size and a variety of "ideal" body sizes (personal ideal, most attractive to the opposite sex, and the opposite-sex figure considered most attractive by the participant). Instructional format used with such scales can affect the way in which people respond to the scale. Thompson and Psaltis (1988) demonstrated that college-age females scored differently when asked to describe the size they *felt* (affective rating) their body was than when asked to describe the size they *thought* (cognitive rating) their body was.

Similar scales have employed varying numbers of figures. Examples are the Body Image Silhouette (Powers & Erickson 1986), which used seven figures; the Body Image Assessment (Williamson et al.

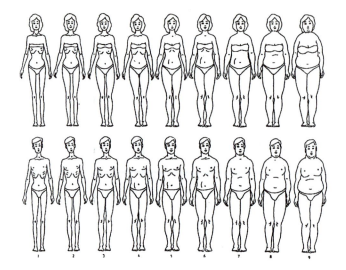

Figure 17-5

The Contour Drawing Rating Scale, an example nine-figure silhouette rating.

(From Thompson M. A. and J. J. Gray, Development and validation of a new body image assessment scale, *Journal of Personality Assessment* 84, 1995.)

1990), which used nine; and a scale by Buree, Papageorgis, and Solyom (1984), which used 19 female silhouettes. Some ingenious variations on this type of scale include that of Counts and Adams (1985), in which a photograph of the participant was used as the basis for silhouettes that were 2.55, 5.05, and 7.55 percent smaller and larger than the original. Another technologically inventive scale was the Body Build Assessment Program devised by Dickson-Parnell and associates (1987). This computer-driven program allows the participant to create a figure by manipulating the size of its various body parts, thus providing versatility in adjusting for different shapes and proportions. At least one age-appropriate version has been produced for use with children (Collins 1991).

Questionnaires

By far the most common format for assessment of the cognitive-affective dimensions of body image has been the questionnaire. Available questionnaires range from independent scales, such as the Body Attitude Scale (Kurtz 1969), to subscales on larger inventories devoted to related constructs,

such as the Body Dissatisfaction Scale of the Eating Disorders Inventory (Garner, Olmstead & Polivy 1983). Some questionnaires have been designed to measure a broad, multidimensional conception of body image, while others are explicitly intended as measures of some specific subdimension of body image, or of constructs closely related, considered to be almost synonymous with body image. Examples of the latter three types are the Body Self-Relations Questionnaire, or BSRQ (Cash 1990), the Body Image Automatic Thoughts Questionnaire (Cash, Lewis, & Keeton 1987), and the Body Esteem Scale (Franzoi & Shields 1984).

Perhaps the most continuous and comprehensive line of body image research has been that in which variations of the Body Self-Relations Questionnaire have been utilized. In its initial form, the BSRQ consisted of a 140-item questionnaire based upon nine conceptualized dimensions, arranged in a three (Attitudes) by three (Somatic Domains) matrix. In the test manual, Cash (1990) described three somatic domains of physical aesthetics (Appearance), physical competence (Fitness), and biological integrity (Health), which were each measured originally by three separate attitude subscales of an affective (Evaluation), cognitive (Attention or Importance), and behavioral (Action or Activity) form. In most subsequent research, a shortened version consisting of 54 items was used, and two of the attitude dimensions (cognitive and behavioral) were collapsed to form a single dimension (subsequently labeled Orientation); thus, the 54-item BSRQ became based on six conceptualized dimensions. These were Appearance Evaluation (6 items), Appearance Orientation (12 items), Health Evaluation (6 items), Health Orientation (12 items), Fitness Evaluation (6 items), and Fitness Orientation (12 items). This latter change was made, according to its author, on "conceptual and empirical grounds" (Cash 1990, p. 1). Interestingly, neither a conceptual explanation nor any empirical evidence is provided in the test manual, and a comprehensive review of the available literature has so far not uncovered the basis for these particular changes to the questionnaire.

In 1985, the BSRQ was administered to over 30,000 respondents from among readers of the popular magazine *Psychology Today* (Cash, Winstead & Janda 1986). The data from a stratified random sample of 2,000 people were factor analyzed five years later (Brown, Cash & Mikulka 1990). The results concurred somewhat with the previously conceptualized structure, but several items loaded on factors other than those from the conceptualized scale structure, such that only two of the subscales retained their original form. Additionally, a completely separate factor emerged. The new factor consisted of a number of items previously contained in the Health Orientation subscale, and was labeled "Illness Orientation." Although primary factor loadings of 14 example items were reported, a complete table of factor loadings (including any cross-loadings) was not presented. Subsequent to these findings, it was suggested in the test manual that the questionnaire may be scored in either of two ways: according to the originally conceptualized six-dimensional structure, or according to the seven-dimensional structure arising from the factor analysis. This was not an appropriate interpretation of the research evidence. No subsequent research

has sought to clarify the puzzling inconsistencies in the empirical evidence, and the BSRQ has been used by its authors in both its originally conceptualized form and the form that resulted from the exploratory factor analysis. It seems that no researcher has sought to confirm or disconfirm these previous factor analysis findings, yet the BSRQ continues to be the most widely used instrument in body image research to date. Example items from the BSRQ are presented in Table 17.7.

Future Use of Body Image Instruments

Body image is an important consideration for exercise and sport science professionals, and for physical educators. There are many body image measurement instruments to choose from, and it seems that the number of new instruments being designed has not slowed in recent years. The lack of construct validity evidence for existing instruments has been recognized in recent reference texts (Bane & McAuley 1998; Thompson 1996c), and this will hopefully result in further investigation and either refinement or rejection of these existing instruments. Selection of instruments to measure body image in applied and research settings should include only those instruments with strong validity and reliability evidence. Future uses of these instruments should include avoidance of the umbrella term "body image" in favor of the specific dimensions being measured (e.g., appearance evaluation, body size dissatisfaction, physique anxiety). In this way, we will gain a better understanding of the exact relationship between exercise and body-centered attitudes, emotions, and behaviors.

PSYCHOPHYSICAL RATINGS

Individuals are able to perceive and rate strain during physical exercise. The **rating of perceived exertion (RPE)** is a simple method supported by good validity evidence for determining exercise intensity. The RPE is a **psychophysical** scale that was developed by the Swedish psychologist Gunnar Borg (1962, 1978, 1982a, 1982b) and is used extensively for exercise testing

TABLE 17.7	Example Items from the Body Self-Relations Questionnaire
Subscale	**Example Items**
Appearance Evaluation (7 items)	I like the way I look without clothes
	I dislike my physique
Appearance Orientation (12 items)	Before going out, I usually spend a lot of time getting ready
	It is important that I always look good
Health Evaluation (6 items)	I often feel vulnerable to illness
	I am seldom physically ill
Health Orientation (8 items)	I know a lot about things that affect my physical health
	I have deliberately developed a healthy lifestyle
Fitness Evaluation (3 items)	I easily learn physical skills
	I am very well-coordinated
Fitness Orientation (13 items)	I work to improve my physical stamina
	I try to be physically active
Illness Awareness (5 items)	If I am sick, I don't pay much attention to my symptoms
	At the first sign of illness, I seek medical advice

Source: Cash, T., *The Multidimensional Body Self-Relations Questionnaire*, 1990.

and exercise prescription (Borg, 1998). It is Borg's opinion (1982a) that perceived exertion is the single best indicator of the degree of physical strain, because the overall perception rating integrates many sources of information elicited from the peripheral working muscles and joints, central cardiovascular and respiratory functions, and central nervous system. "All these signals, perceptions and experiences are integrated into a configuration of a 'Gestalt' perceived exertion" (Borg 1982a).

Borg has published two RPE scales. The first is a category scale with values ranging from 6 to 20, which assumes a linear relation between exercise heart rate and RPE rating (Borg 1962). The second scale was developed to be consistent with the nonlinearity of psychophysical ratings (Borg 1972, 1982a, 1982b).

Borg's Linear RPE Scale

Borg's linear RPE scale was the first developed to measure perceived exertion of aerobic exercise. The Borg RPE scale increases linearly with exercise heart rate. The scale values range from 6 to 20. This was proposed to denote heart rates rang-

ing from 60 to 200 beats/min. For example, a rating of 15 was meant to correspond with a heart rate of 150 beats/min. Borg did not intend that the heart rate–RPE rating be taken literally, because many factors can affect exercise heart rate. Age, exercise mode, environment (e.g., heat, humidity), anxiety, and drugs (e.g., beta-blocker drugs that are used to control high blood pressure) all can affect exercise heart rate. The influence of aging on RPE is illustrated in Figure 17-6. The scale has been shown to correlate between 0.80 and 0.90 with heart rate, $\dot{V}O_2$, and lactic acid accumulation (Borg 1982a).

The RPE scale (Figure 17-7) is very popular and very easy to use. Research by Pollock, Jackson, and Foster (1986) showed that the scale provides an excellent estimate of exercise intensity and can be used to prescribe exercise and to regulate exercise testing. RPE values of 12 and 13 represent exercise intensities at about 60% of heart rate reserve[2] and $\dot{V}O_2$ max. Ratings of 16 and 17 correspond to about 90% of heart rate reserve and

[2]Percent Heart Rate Reserve = [X × (Max HR – Rest HR)] + Rest HR, where X is the desired percentage and HR is heart rate (Pollock, Wilmore & Fox 1984).

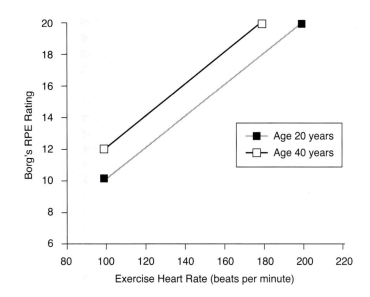

Figure 17-6

Graph shows the linear change in the heart rate and rating of perceived exertion (RPE). The RPE scale was initially used to duplicate exercise heart rate (i.e., HR = RPE × 10), but maximum heart rate decreases with age. RPE ratings for older individuals can be expected to be associated with lower exercise heart rates than the same RPE ratings for younger individuals. RPE ratings ≥ 18 are typically an indication that the person has reached his maximum. The RPE scale has become a standard for most exercise testing laboratories.
(Graph from CSI Software Company, Houston, TX.)

6	
7	Very, very light
8	
9	Very light
10	
11	Fairly light
12	
13	Somewhat hard
14	
15	Hard
16	
17	Very hard
18	
19	Very, very hard
20	

Figure 17-7

The 15-grade category scale for rating perceived exertion (RPE scale).
(Dr. G. Borg, Dept. of Psychology, University of Stockholm, Stockholm, Sweden.)

85% of $\dot{V}O_2$ max. Values of 18 or more are considered to be an indication that the person has reached her maximum. These ranges have been valid for both leg and arm exercise and for subjects on beta-blocker drugs that lowered $\dot{V}O_2$ max and maximal heart rate (Pollock, Jackson & Foster 1986). The instructions used for the RPE scale during exercise testing follow:

Instructions—15-grade RPE Scale

You are now going to take part in a graded exercise test. You will be walking or running on the treadmill while we are measuring various physiological functions. We also want you to try to estimate how hard you feel the work is; that is, we want you to rate the degree of perceived exertion you feel. By perceived exertion we mean the total amount of exertion and physical fatigue. Don't concern yourself with any one factor such as leg pain, shortness of breath, or work grade, but try to concentrate on your total, inner feeling of exertion. Try to estimate as honestly and objectively as possible. Don't underestimate the degree of exertion you feel, but don't overestimate it either. Just try to estimate as accurately as possible.

Borg's Category Scale with Ratio Properties

The assumption of Borg's linear RPE scale is that the perception of physical exertion changes at a linear rate. Figure 17-6 shows this. Changes in exercise heart rate (X variable) are assumed to produce a linear change in RPE (Y variable). Stevens's classic psychophysical work (Stevens 1975; Stevens & Galanter 1957) showed that sensory perception often changes at a linear rate, rather than nonlinearly. Stevens's work provides the theoretical and mathematical basis for Borg's ingenious Category (C)–Ratio (R) scale, or CR-10 scale (Borg 1972; Borg 1982b). Figure 17-8 gives Borg's CR-10 scale.

The CR-10 scale is one that uses an accelerating power function to model the physical stimulus with its psychophysical perception. Figure 17-9 shows the theoretical basis of the category scale with ratio properties. The X-axis, physical stimulus, is a category scale, while the Y-axis is the psychophysical scale with ratio properties. As the physical stimulus (e.g., the person's exercise intensity) increases from low to maximum, the psychophysical perception rating increases at an accelerated rate. Note the CR-10 change for a 1-unit change on the category scale (X). A change from 1 to 2 produces a CR-10 change from about 0.2 to 1.2, but changes from 2 to 3 and 3 to 4 produce CR-10 changes from 1.2 to 3.1, and 3.1 to 6.3, respec-

tively. Mathematically, this accelerated curve is called a power function.

The instructions[3] for the ratio RPE scale are as follows:

Instructions—CR-10 Scale

We would like you to estimate the exertion you feel by using this scale. The scale starts with 0 "Nothing at all" and goes on to 10, "Extremely strong" that is "Almost max." For most people this corresponds to the hardest physical exercise they have ever done, as for example the exertion you feel when you run as fast as you can for several minutes till you are completely exhausted, or when you are lifting or carrying something which is so heavy that you nearly can't make it. Maybe it is possible to imagine exertion or pain that is even stronger, and that is why the maximum value is somewhat over 10. If you feel the exertion or pain to be stronger than "Extremely strong" (almost max) you can use a number that is over 10, for example 11, 13 or an even higher number.

If the exertion is "Very weak" you should answer with the number 1. If it is only "Moderate" you say 3 and so on. Feel free to use any number you wish on the scale, as well as half values, as, for example, 1.5 or decimals such as 0.8, 1.7 or 2.3. It is important that you give the answer that you yourself feel to be right and not that which you think you ought to give. Answer as honestly as possible and try neither to overestimate nor underestimate the degree of exertion that you feel.

The feature of the ratio RPE scale is that numbers anchor verbal expressions that are simple and understandable. The expressions are placed in a position on the ratio scale where they belong according to their quantitative meaning. A simple range of 0 to 10 is used to anchor the verbal expressions. It is permissible to use fractional ratings (e.g., 2.5 or 3.8) and values above 10. The CR-10 scale has been shown to correlate highly with both blood lactate and muscle lactate level, which are the biochemical markers of cardiorespiratory and muscle fatigue (Borg 1982a). The CR-10 scale has been shown to

0	Nothing at all	
0.5	Extremely weak	(just noticeable)
1	Very weak	
2	Weak	(light)
3	Moderate	
4	Somewhat strong	
5	Strong	(heavy)
6		
7	Very strong	
8		
9		
10	Extremely strong	(almost max)
•	Maximal	

Figure 17-8

Borg's category scale with ratio properties (CR-10).
(Dr. G. Borg, Dept. of Psychology, University of Stockholm, Stockholm, Sweden.)

[3]Personal communication with Dr. Gunnar Borg, Department of Psychology, University of Stockholm, Stockholm, Sweden, November 1985.

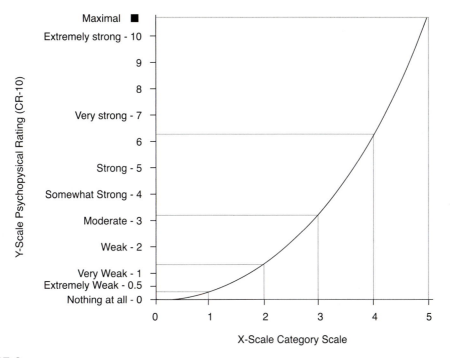

Figure 17-9

The theoretical basis of Borg's CR-10 scale. A linear increase in the physical stimulus produces a ratio increase in the perception of the stimulus.

(Graph from CSI Software Company, Houston, TX.)

be useful for evaluating an individual's capacity to perform common industrial tasks, such as lifting heavy objects (Chin, Bishu & Halbeck 1995; Hidalgo et al. 1997; Jackson et al. 1997; Resnik 1995). Psychophysically defined demanding lift loads increase the risk of back injury (Snook, Campanelli & Hart 1978; Snook & Ciriello 1991; Waters et al. 1993). The scale is used as a basis for helping individuals define safe lifting weights for their physical capacity (Jackson et al. 1997).

Borg provided convincing evidence that the CR-10 scale is useful for describing aerobic and anaerobic levels of exercise intensity (Borg 1998). Ergonomic research (Chin, Bishu & Halbeck 1995; Hidalgo et al. 1997; Jackson & Ross 1997; Resnik 1995) shows the CR-10 scale is extremely useful for rating the difficulty of industrial lifting tasks. Figure 17-10 graphically shows the accelerated increase in psychophysical perception (ratio) associated with the linear increase in lift weight (cate-

gory). Shown are the curves produced by stronger and weaker subjects. These curves show that while lift weight increases at a linear rate, the perception of lift difficulty increases at an accelerated rate. As expected, the CR-10 rating for a common lift load (e.g., 60 pounds) is higher for the weaker person than for the stronger person (CR-10 rating of 6.1 vs. 3.0), but both groups produce accelerated curves. When both the weak and the strong subjects approach their maximum, the psychophysical rating increases at an accelerated rate.

Uses of Psychophysical Ratings
Exercise Testing

Psychophysical ratings are used for many different purposes. Some of the more common uses follow.

The RPE scale is used to judge exercise intensity when administering a graded exercise test on a treadmill or cycle ergometer. The objective of an

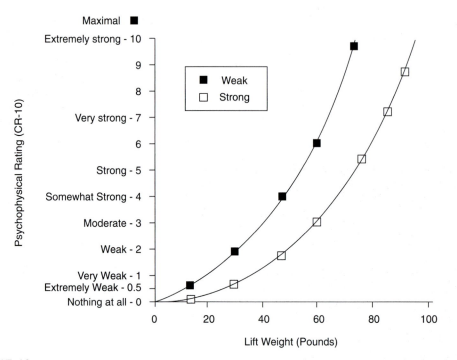

Figure 17-10

Graphic representation of the nonlinear relationship between changes in lift weight and psychophysical rating of lift difficulty. The lift task was lifting boxes that varied with weight from floor to knuckle height. The psychophysical rating is the subject's CR-10 rating of lift difficulty. The stronger group were those who were able to lift at least 95 pounds, and the weaker group were individuals with a maximum lift of 75 pounds.

(Data from Jackson 1997 and graph from CSI Software Company, Houston, TX.)

exercise test is to slowly and systematically increase the exercise intensity from submaximal to maximal levels. Often, percent of maximal heart rate is used to quantify exercise intensity. But in most instances maximal heart rate is not known and must be estimated from age (Max HR = 220 – age). However, there tend to be errors in this estimate of as much as ± 10 to 15 beats per minute. Additionally, many adults take medication for common health problems, such as hypertension. Often these drugs lower resting and exercise heart rate, but do not affect RPE. The RPE ratings are used to determine when a subject is reaching his maximal tolerance (≥ 18 on the 6–20 RPE scale and > 7.0 on the CR-10 scale).

Exercise Prescription

Percentage of $\dot{V}O_2$ max is the most valid method of prescribing exercise, but this is typically not known. Therefore, percentage of maximal heart rate reserve is recommended. A difficulty with this method is that maximal heart rate must be known, and some individuals are taking medications that affect heart rate. It has been found that RPE ratings (see Figure 17-11) are an excellent method of selecting the proper intensity for exercise and can be used to supplement heart rate estimates (Pollock, Jackson & Foster 1986).

Quantification of Energy Expenditure

Many adult fitness programs seek to quantify energy expended through exercise, which is often expressed in kilocalories. This can be done very accurately with aerobic exercise modes such as walking, jogging, or cycling because external work can be quantified (see Chapter 11). There are other popular aerobic exercise modes, such as aerobic dancing or

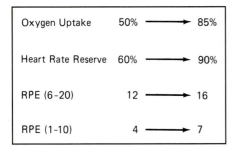

Figure 17-11
Recommended training zone for exercise prescription.
(Adapted from Pollock, Wilmore & Fox 1984.)

playing tennis, where external work cannot be quantified. Individuals vary in the intensity to which they exercise. Many fitness centers use commercial computer software to quantify exercise by caloric expenditure. This software uses psychophysical ratings to estimate exercise intensity when external work cannot be measured. To illustrate, more calories would be expended when playing tennis at an RPE rating of 7, Very strong, as compared to a rating of 3, Moderate. This method is illustrated in another source (Jackson & Ross 1997).

Rating Work Difficulty

Psychophysical methods are used to define the difficulty of industrial jobs, such as lifting. Psychophysical criteria are used to define acceptable workloads for industrial populations (NIOSH 1981; Waters et al. 1993). Acceptable workloads are defined as those one can perform without undue strain.

Injury Prevention

Demanding lift loads increase the risk of back injury. Epidemiological data (Snook, Campanelli & Hart 1978) estimate that about 67% of industrial back injuries could be eliminated if workers lifted loads psychophysically judged to be acceptable. Using this logic, the CR-10 scale is used as a basis for helping individuals define safe lifting weights for their level of fitness (Chin, Bishu & Halbeck 1995; Hidalgo et al. 1997; Jackson et al. 1997; Resnik 1995).

Uses of Psychological Scales

Psychological scales are readily available and easy to administer and score. This enhances their use, but also presents a potential danger. Psychological instruments, especially personality inventories, can be threatening and potentially harmful when administered and interpreted by the untrained or naive. The legitimacy of using psychological instruments can be clarified by asking two simple questions:

1. Do you have a need and right to secure such data?
2. Are you capable of correctly interpreting and using the test results in a way that will help the person being tested?

Psychological scales such as personality inventories and behavior rating scales may have limited application to physical education and exercise settings, but other psychological inventories have legitimate educational and research purposes. Some specific examples follow.

Achievement of class objectives. A common objective of physical education programs is the development of a positive feeling toward class activities and physical activity in general. Semantic differential scales would be especially useful to evaluate this.

Administrative planning, curriculum development, and evaluation of teaching methods. Again, semantic differential scales could provide data that could be used to evaluate the effectiveness of instruction units and methods of instruction. Children may improve their physical fitness, but they could develop negative feelings toward physical activity in general. Psychological scales could be used for these purposes.

Individual diagnosis and remediation. The identification of children with a low self-concept, self-esteem, or body image could be very important. Altering a child's attitude in a positive direction could enhance his or her mental health.

Screening. Psychological scales can be used to identify individuals at risk for eating disorders. Care must be taken to help interested individuals find professional services.

Research. A current problem in physical education and exercise science is a lack of understanding of the psychological motives of sports participation and exercise adherence. Although medical research has clearly established that lack of exercise and obesity are major cardiovascular disease risk factors (see Chapter 1), we still do not know why some people are physically active and others are not. This will be a major area of research in the future. Trait instruments, such as the SMI, can be useful to identify those at risk of dropping from exercise programs. State instruments will likely be useful for creating favorable environments that will enhance exercise behavior.

SUMMARY

Most of the published physical education attitude scales were developed on the assumption that a single factor was being measured. Scales that gauge attitudes toward physical education report high reliability, but the construct validity of what factors are measured is yet to be determined. The Kenyon and Sonstroem scales are multidimensional instruments that have established construct validity. Semantic differential scales that use bipolar adjectives to measure feelings about concepts are a flexible technique for measuring attitude. Many adults who start exercise programs will quit. It has been shown that adherence to exercise is related to self-motivation as measured by the SMI. There is a growing group of researchers who are examining the influence of exercise on self-esteem. These state instruments have their roots in Sonstroem's global scale, Physical Estimation and Attraction Scale (PEAS). The "estimation" items ask students to affirm or deny their own physical characteristics, fitness, athletic ability, or potential in motor performance, and the "attraction" items ask students to affirm or deny their personal interests or likes for certain forms of physical activity. Eating disorders are a growing, serious problem. The prevalence of eating disorders, anorexia nervosa and bulimia nervosa, is highest among young women between the ages of about 14 and 19 years. The incidence of these disorders appears to be on the rise and corresponds to societal pressure for women to be thin. The psychophysical RPE scales have been shown to be useful for determining exercise intensity. Borg has developed two scales, either of which can be used for exercise testing, exercise prescription, quantification of energy expenditure, rating work difficulty, and injury prevention. The area of exercise and sport psychology is expanding rapidly. Ostrow (1996) has developed a comprehensive system to categorize and evaluate exercise psychological instruments.

FORMATIVE EVALUATION OF OBJECTIVES

Objective 1   Evaluate the validity of physical education attitude scales.

1. Attitude scales are self-report instruments designed to measure attitudes by the way one responds to statements. In terms of validity, what is the basic weakness of this type of measurement?
2. Kenyon's attitude scale offers a valid method of measuring attitudes toward physical activity. The scale measures six different types, or dimensions, of attitudes. Identify and briefly describe each.

Objective 2   Outline the procedures used to develop semantic differential scales.

1. Semantic differential scales provide a flexible method for evaluating attitudes. Research indicates that three basic factors are measured with these scales: evaluation, potency, and activity. Define these concepts and list three adjective pairs that measure each of them.
2. Outline the process you would follow to develop semantic differential scales.

3. Outline the procedure for scoring semantic differential scales that would calculate a score for each of the three factors.
4. What are the concepts being measured by the Children's Attitude Toward Physical Activity Inventory? What semantic dimensions are being used with the CATPA-I?

Objective 3   Describe the nature of the Self-Motivation Inventory (SMI).

1. What does the SMI predict?
2. How might one use the SMI?

Objective 4   Describe the nature of instruments designed to relate exercise and self-esteem.

1. The Physical Estimation and Attraction Scales were developed to explain motivation toward physical activity. Identify and briefly describe each scale.
2. Why are scales related to exercise self-esteem considered to be state instruments?

Objective 5   Describe the nature of eating disorder scales.

1. What are the most common types of eating disorders?
2. What is the nature of eating disorder instruments?
3. What is the EAT?

Objective 6   Describe the nature of body image instruments.

1. What is body image?
2. What are the most common types of body image measures?
3. What is the BSRQ?
4. What is a self-ideal discrepancy rating?

Objective 7   Evaluate the validity and value of the psychophysical rating of perceived exertion scales (RPE).

1. What are the similarities and differences between the two Borg RPE scales?
2. How can the RPE scales be used?
3. In order to improve aerobic fitness, one should exercise at what level on the RPE scales?

ADDITIONAL LEARNING ACTIVITIES

1. Several studies have sought to determine the correlation between attitude and physical fitness. Review articles published in the Research Quarterly to determine whether a positive attitude is associated with a high level of physical fitness. How was attitude measured? How was physical fitness measured?
2. Select either the CATPA-I or the PEAS and administer it to a group of students. Can you develop a spreadsheet to score the scale?
3. Select a concept (e.g., physical fitness, athletics, aerobic dance) of particular interest to you and develop semantic differential scales to measure attitude toward the concept. Administer the scales to various groups and determine whether the groups' means differ. You might use male and female physical education majors as your groups. You may want to consult a basic statistics text to determine whether the means between the groups are significantly different.
4. Administer the CATPA-I to a group of children. Be sure to read the proper instructions (Schutz et al. 1985) and administer either the scale for third graders or the scale for older children.
5. What are the reasons adults do not continue exercise programs? Conduct a review of the exercise science literature to answer this question. A good place to start is to conduct a computer search for research published by R. K. Dishman.

6. Learn how to use either of the Borg RPE scales. This can be accomplished several ways. If you take a maximal exercise test, relate the submaximal ratings with percent of heart rate reserve, or $\dot{V}O_2$ max. A second method is to exercise at an exercise intensity that will produce an aerobic training effect and rate this intensity by either the 6 to 20 or the 1 to 10 scale.

7. Take the SMI and compare your score with that of a friend or fellow student who does not exercise as much as you do (or who exercises more than you do). Were the results what you expected? Discuss why or why not.

BIBLIOGRAPHY

Adams, R. S. 1963. Two scales for measuring attitude toward physical education. *Research Quarterly* 34: 91–94.

Ajzen, I. and M. Fishbein. 1980. *Understanding attitudes and predicting social behavior.* Englewood Cliffs, NJ: Prentice-Hall.

Allison, P. R. 1976. An instrument to measure creative dance attitude of grade five children. Ph.D. dissertation, University of Alabama, Tuscaloosa, AL.

Bandura, A. 1977. Self-efficacy: Toward a unifying theory of behavioral change. *Psychological Review* 84(2): 191–215.

Bane, S. and E. McAuley. 1998. Body image and exercise. In J. L. Duda (Ed.). *Advances in sport and exercise psychology measurement.* pp. 311–322. Morgantown, WV: Fitness Information Technology.

Baumgartner, T. A. and A. S. Jackson. 1982. *Measurement for evaluation in physical education.* 2nd ed. Dubuque, IA: Wm. C. Brown.

Borg, G. 1962. *Physical performance and perceived exertion.* Lund, Sweden: Gleerup.

Borg, G. 1972. A ratio scaling method for interindividual comparisons. University of Stockholm 12: Reports from the Institute of Applied Psychology.

Borg, G. 1978. Subjective effort in relation to physical performance and working capacity. In *Psychology: From research to practice.* New York: Plenum.

Borg, G. 1982a. Psychophysical bases of perceived exertion. *Medicine and Science in Sports and Exercise* 14: 371–381.

Borg, G. 1982b. A category scale with ratio properties for intermodal and interindividual comparisons. In H. G. Geissler and P. Petzold (Eds.). *Psychophysical judgment and the process of perception.* Berlin: VEB Deutscher Verlag der Wissenschaften.

Borg, G. 1998. *Borg's perceived exertion and pain scaling method.* Champaign, IL: Human Kinetics.

Brown, T., T. Cash, and P. Mikulka. 1990. Attitudinal body-image assessment: Factor analysis of the Body Self-Relations Questionnaire. *Journal of Personality Assessment* 55: 135–144.

Buree, B., D. Papageorgis, and L. Solyom. 1984. Body image perception and preference in anorexia nervosa. *Canadian Journal of Psychiatry* 29: 557–563.

Carr, M. G. 1945. The relationship between success in physical education and selected attitudes expressed in high school freshmen girls. *Research Quarterly* 16: 176–191.

Cash, T. 1990. *The Multidimensional Body Self-Relations Questionnaire.* Unpublished test manual, Old Dominion University, Norfolk, VA.

Cash, T. F., R. J. Lewis, and P. Keeton. 1987. *Development and validation of the Body-Image Automatic Thoughts Questionnaire: A measure of body-related cognitions.* Paper presented at the meeting of the Southeastern Psychological Association, Atlanta, GA.

Cash, T. F., P. L. Novy, and J. R. Grant. 1994. Why do women exercise? Factor analysis and further validation of the Reasons for Exercise Inventory. *Perceptual and Motor Skills* 78: 539–544.

Cash, T. F., B. A. Winstead, and L. H. Janda. 1986. Body image survey report: The great American shape-up. *Psychology Today* 24: 30–37.

Chin, A., R. R. Bishu, and S. Halbeck. 1995. Psychophysical measures of exertion. Are they muscle group dependent? *Proceedings of the Human Factors Society* 39: 694–698.

Collins, M. E. 1991. Body figure perceptions and preferences among preadolescent children. *International Journal of Eating Disorders* 10: 199–208.

Cooper, P. J. et al. 1987. The development and validation of the Body Shape Questionnaire. *International Journal of Eating Disorders* 6: 485–490.

Counts, C. R. and H. E. Adams. 1985. Body image in bulimic, dieting, and normal females. *Journal of Psychopathology and Behavioral Assessment* 7: 289–300.

Davis, C. and M. Cowles. 1991. Body image and exercise: A study of relationships between physically active men and women. *Sex Roles* 25: 33–44.

Dickson-Parnell, B. et al. 1987. Assessment of body image perceptions using a computer program. *Behavior Research Methods, Instruments, and Computers* 19: 353–354.

Dishman, R. K. 1978. Aerobic power, estimation of physical ability, and attraction to physical activity. *Research Quarterly* 49: 285–292.

———. 1980. The influence of response distortion in assessing self-perceptions of physical ability and attitude toward physical activity. *Research Quarterly for Exercise and Sport* 51: 286–298.

———. 1990. Determinants of participation in physical activity. In C. Bouchard et al. (Eds.). *Exercise, fitness, and health: A consensus of current knowledge.* pp. 75–102. Champaign, IL: Human Kinetics.

Dishman, R. K. and L. R. Gettman. 1981. Psychological vigor and self-perceptions of increased strength. *Medicine and Science in Sports and Exercise* 15: 118.

Dishman, R. K. and W. Ickes. 1981. Self-motivation and adherence to therapeutic exercise. *Journal of Behavioral Medicine* 4: 421–436.

Ebel, R. L. 1972. What are schools for? *Phi Delta Kappan* 54: 3–7.

Edington, C. W. 1968. Development of an attitude scale to measure attitudes of high school freshmen boys toward physical education. *Research Quarterly* 39: 505–512.

Fallon, A. E. and P. Rozin. 1985. Sex differences in perceptions of desirable body shape. *Journal of Abnormal Psychology* 94: 102–105.

Fisher, S. 1986. *Development and structure of the body image* (Vols. 1 & 2). Hillsdale, NJ: Erlbaum.

Fisher, S. 1990. The evolution of psychological concepts about the body. In T. F. Cash and T. Pruzinsky (Eds.). *Body images: Development,*

deviance, and change. pp. 3–20. New York: Guilford Press.

Foreyt, J. P. et al. 1998. Anorexia nervosa and bulimia nervosa. In E. J. Mash and R. A. Barkley, Treatment of childhood disorders. (2nd ed.), pp. 647–691. New York: Guilford Press.

Fox, K. R. (Ed.). 1997. *The physical self: From motivation to well-being.* Champaign, IL: Human Kinetics.

Fox, C. R. and C. B. Corbin. 1989. *The Physical Self-Perception Profile: Development and preliminary validation.* Journal of Sport and Exercise Psychology, 11: 408–443.

Fox, K. R., C. R. Corbin, and W. H. Couldry. 1985. Female physical estimation and attraction to physical activity. *Journal of Sport Psychology* 7: 125–136.

Franzoi, S. L. and S. A. Shields. 1984. The Body Esteem Scale: Multidimensional structure and sex differences in a college population. *Journal of Personality Assessment* 48: 173–178.

Garcia, A. W. and A. C. King. 1991. Predicting long-term adherence to aerobic exercise: A comparison of two models. *Journal of Sport and Exercise Psychology* 13: 394–410.

Garner, D. M. 1984. *The eating disorder inventory manual.* Odessa, FL: Psychological Assessment Resources.

Garner, D. M. and P. E. Garfinkel. 1979. The Eating Attitudes Test: An index of the symptoms of anorexia nervosa. *Psychological Medicine* 10: 273–279.

Garner, D. M., M. A. Olmstead, and J. Polivy. 1983. Development and validation of a multidimensional eating disorder inventory for anorexia nervosa and bulimia. *International Journal of Eating Disorders* 2: 15–34.

Garner, D. M. et al. 1982. The Eating Attitudes Test: Psychometric features and clinical correlates. *Psychological Medicine* 12: 871–878.

Harris, B. 1968. Attitudes of students toward women's athletic competition. *Research Quarterly* 39: 278–284.

Hidalgo, J. et al. 1997. A comprehensive lifting model: Beyond the NIOSH lifting equation. *Ergonomics* 40(9): 916–927.

Holmes, T., P. Chamberlin, and M. Young. 1994. Relations of exercise to body image and sexual desirability among a sample of university students. *Psychological Reports* 74: 920–922.

Imm, P. S. and J. Pruitt. 1991. Body shape satisfaction in female exercisers and nonexercisers. *Women and Health* 17(4): 87–96.

Jackson, A. S. and R. M. Ross. 1997. *Understanding exercise for health and fitness.* 3rd ed. Dubuque, IA: Kendall/Hunt.

Jackson, A. S. et al. 1997. Role of physical work capacity and load weight on psychophysical lift ratings. *International Journal of Industrial Ergonomics* 20: 181–190.

Johnson, M. L. 1969. Construction of sportsmanship attitude scales. *Research Quarterly* 40: 312–316.

Kappes, E. E. 1954. Inventory to determine attitudes of college women toward physical education and student services of the physical education department. *Research Quarterly* 25: 429–438.

Kenyon, G. S. 1968. Values held for physical activity by selected urban secondary school students in Canada, Australia, England, and the United States. Washington, DC: U.S. Office of Education.

Kneer, M. E. 1971. Kneer attitude inventory and diagnostic statements. In *A practical approach to measurement in physical education.* Philadelphia, PA: Lea & Febiger.

Koff, E. and C. L. Bauman. 1997. Effects of wellness, fitness, and sport skills programs on body image and lifestyle behaviors. *Perceptual and Motor Skills* 84: 555–562.

Koslowsky, M. et al. 1992. The factor structure and criterion validity of the short form of the Eating Attitudes Test. *Journal of Personality Assessment* 58(1): 27–35.

Kowal, D. M., J. F. Patton, and J. A. Vogel. 1978. Psychological states and aerobic fitness of male and female recruits before and after basic training. *Aviation, Space, and Environmental Medicine* 49: 603–606.

Krathwohl, D. R. et al. 1964. *Taxonomy of education objectives handbook II. The affective domain.* New York: McKay.

Kurtz, R. M. 1969. Sex differences and variations in body attitudes. *Journal of Consulting and Clinical Psychology* 33: 625–629.

Lakie, W. L. 1964. Expressed attitudes of various groups of athletes toward athletic competition. *Research Quarterly* 35: 497–503.

LeUnes, A. D. 2002. *Bibliography on psychological tests used in research and practice in sport and exercise psychology.* Lewiston, NY: Mellen Press.

McCue, B. F. 1953. Constructing an instrument for evaluating attitudes toward intensive competition in team games. *Research Quarterly* 24: 205–210.

McDonald, K. and J. K. Thompson. 1992. Eating disturbance, body dissatisfaction, and reasons for exercising: Gender differences and correlational findings. *International Journal of Eating Disorders* 11: 289–292.

McGee, R. 1956. Comparison of attitudes toward intensive competition for high school girls. *Research Quarterly* 27: 60–73.

Mercer, E. L. 1971. Mercer attitude scale. In *A practical approach to measurement in physical education.* Philadelphia: Lea & Febiger.

Merkle, L. A. 1997. Factor analysis of the self-motivation inventory. Doctoral dissertation, Department of Health and Human Performance, University of Houston, Houston, TX.

Moriarty, D., C. Ford, and J. Rawlings. 1991. *Recent research on eating disorders and body image distortion among aerobic instructors and exercise participants.* Paper presented at the Prevention North Conference of the Ontario Fitness Association, Sudbury, Canada.

Myers, A. M. et al. 1985. *Body images: Cohort and age differences across the lifespan.* Paper presented at the Canadian Psychological Association Annual Meeting, Halifax, Canada.

Neale, D. C. et al. 1969. Physical fitness, self-esteem and attitudes toward physical activity. *Research Quarterly* 40: 743–749.

NIOSH. 1981. *Work practices guide for manual lifting.* Washington, DC: U.S. Department of Health and Human Services.

Nunnally, J. C. 1978. *Psychometric theory.* New York: McGraw-Hill.

O'Bryan, M. H. and K. G. O'Bryan. 1979. Attitudes of males toward selected aspects of physical education. *Research Quarterly* 40: 343–382.

Osgood, C. E., G. J. Suci, and P. H. Tannenbaum. 1967. *The measurement of meaning.* 2nd ed. Urbana, IL: University of Illinois Press.

Ostrow, A. C. 1996. *Directory of psychological tests in the sport and exercise sciences.* 2nd ed. Morgantown, WV: Fitness Information Technology.

Penmon, M. M. 1971. Penmon physical education attitude inventory for inner-city junior high school girls. In *A practical approach to measurement in physical education.* Philadelphia: Lea & Febiger.

Pollock, M. L., A. S. Jackson, and C. Foster. 1986. The use of the perception scale for exercise prescription. In *The perception of exertion in physical work.* pp. 161–176. Wenner-Gren Center, Stockholm, Sweden.

Pollock, M. L., J. H. Wilmore, and S. M. Fox III. 1984. *Exercise in health and disease.* Philadelphia: W. B. Saunders.

Pope, H. G., Jr. et al. 1997. Muscle dysmorphia: An underrecognized form of body dysmorphic disorder. *Psychosomatics* 38: 548–557.

Powers, P. D. and M. T. Erickson. 1986. Body image in women and its relationship to self-image and body satisfaction. *Journal of Obesity and Weight Regulation* 5: 37–50.

Resnik, M. L. 1995. The generalizability of psychophysical ratings in predicting the perception of lift difficulty. *Proceedings of the Human Factors Society* 39, 679–682.

Rhea, D. J. 1995. Risk factors for the development of eating disorders in ethnically diverse high school athlete and non-athlete urban populations. Doctoral dissertation, Department of Health and Human Performance, University of Houston, Houston, TX.

Rowe, D. A. et al. 2005. Validation of Digital Image Manipulation using the multitrait, multimethod design. *Research Quarterly for Exercise and Sport* 76: 407–415.

Rowe, D. A., J. Benson, and T. A. Baumgartner. 1999. Development of the Body Self-Image Questionnaire. *Measurement in Physical Education and Exercise Science* 3: 223–247.

Safrit, M. J. 1981. *Evaluation in physical education.* Englewood Cliffs, NJ: Prentice-Hall.

Schilder, P. 1950. *The image and appearance of the human body.* New York: International Universities.

Schutz, R. W. et al. 1985. Inventories and norms for children's attitudes toward physical activity. *Research Quarterly for Exercise and Sport* 56: 256–265.

Scott, P. M. 1953. Attitudes toward athletic competition in elementary school. *Research Quarterly* 24: 353–361.

Seaman, J. A. 1970. Attitudes of physically handicapped children toward physical education. *Research Quarterly* 41: 439–445.

Secord, P. F. and S. M. Jourard. 1953. The appraisal of body cathexis and the self. *Journal of Consulting Psychology* 17: 343–347.

Shontz, F. C. 1969. *Perceptual and cognitive aspects of body experience.* New York: Academic.

Simon, J. A. and F. L. Smoll. 1974. An instrument for assessing children's attitudes toward physical education. *Research Quarterly* 45: 407–415.

Slade, P. D. 1973. A short anorexic behavior scale. *British Journal of Psychiatry* 122: 83–85.

Snider, J. G. and C. E. Osgood. 1969. *Semantic differential technique: A sourcebook.* Chicago, IL: Aldine.

Snook, S. H., R. A. Campanelli, and J. W. Hart. 1978. A study of three preventive approaches to low back injury. *Journal of Occupational Medicine* 20: 478–481.

Snook, S. H. and V. M. Ciriello. 1991. The design of manual handling tasks: Revised tables of maximum acceptable weights and forces. *Ergonomics* 34: 1197–1213.

Sonstroem, R. J. 1974. Attitude testing examining certain psychological correlates of physical activity. *Research Quarterly* 45: 93–103.

———. 1976. The validity of self-perceptions regarding physical and athletic ability. *Medicine and Science in Sports* 8: 126–132.

———. 1978. Physical estimation and attraction scales: Rationale and research. *Medicine and Science in Sports* 10: 97–102.

———. 1988. *Psychological models in exercise adherence: Its impact on public health.* Champaign, IL: Human Kinetics.

———. 1997. Chapter 1. The physical self-system: A mediator of exercise and self-esteem. In K. R. Fox (Ed.). *The physical self: From motivation to well-being.* Champaign, IL: Human Kinetics.

Sonstroem, R. J. and K. P. Kampper. 1980. Prediction of athletic participation in middle school males. *Research Quarterly for Exercise and Sport* 51: 685–694.

Sonstroem, R. J. and W. P. Morgan. 1989. Exercise and self-esteem: Rationale and model. *Medicine and Science in Sports and Exercise* 21: 329–337.

Stevens, S. S. 1975. *Psychophysics: Introduction to its perceptual, neural, and social prospects.* New York: Wiley.

Stevens, S. S. and E. Galanter. 1957. Ratio scales and category scales for a dozen perceptual continua. *Journal of Experimental Psychology* 54: 377–411.

Suminski, R. R. et al. 1998. Construct validation of a 10-item eating attitudes screening test for college students. Unpublished manuscript.

Thompson, J. K. 1996a. Introduction: Body image, eating disorders, and obesity—an emerging synthesis. In J. K. Thompson (Ed.). *Body image, eating disorders, and obesity: An integrative guide for assessment and treatment.* pp. 1–20. Washington, DC: American Psychological Association.

Thompson, J. K. 1996b. Assessing body image disturbance: Measures, methodology, and implementation. In J. K. Thompson (Ed.). *Body image, eating disorders, and obesity: An integrative guide for assessment and treatment.* pp. 49–81. Washington, DC: American Psychological Association.

Thompson, J. K. (Ed.). 1996c. *Body image, eating disorders, and obesity: An integrative guide for assessment and treatment.* Washington, DC: American Psychological Association.

Thompson, J. K. and K. Psaltis. 1988. Multiple aspects and correlates of body figure ratings: A replication and extension of Fallon and Rozin (1985). *International Journal of Eating Disorders* 7: 813–818.

Thompson, M. A. and J. J. Gray. 1995. Development and validation of a new body image assessment scale. *Journal of Personality Assessment* 64: 258–269.

United States Department of Health and Human Services. 2000. *Healthly People 2010: Understanding and improving health.* Washington, DC: United States Government Printing Office.

Waters, T. R. et al. 1993. Revised NIOSH equation for the design and evaluation of manual lifting tasks. *Ergonomics* 7: 749–766.

Wear, C. L. 1951. The evaluation of attitude toward physical activity as an activity course. *Research Quarterly* 22: 114–216.

———. 1955. Construction of equivalent forms of an attitude scale. *Research Quarterly* 26: 113–119.

Williamson, D. A. et al. 1990. Development of a simple procedure for assessing body image disturbances. *Behavioral Assessment* 11: 433–446.

APPENDIX A

SPSS 14.0 FOR WINDOWS BASICS

1. Getting into SPSS (several methods possible)
   A. You should save your data on floppy disk. So insert a floppy disk in the disk drive now.
   B. Click on **Start** in the lower left-hand corner of the screen and then click on **Program** in the drop-down menu.
   C. Click on **SPSS 14.0 for Windows** in the next menu.
   D. In the SPSS Windows dialog box:
      1. Click on **Tutorial** and then **OK** if you want information on using SPSS.
      2. Click on **Type in Data** and then **OK** if you want to enter data.
      3. Click on **Open an Existing File** and then **OK** if the data is already saved on disk.
   E. Alternative to D:
      1. **SPSS Data Editor** window is displayed.
      2. Click on **File.**
      3. Select the data entry option desired.

2. Entering the data (see one of the guides in the Reference section)
   A. Click on the **SPSS Data Editor** window title bar to make it the active window if it is not already highlighted. At the bottom of the window are two tabs: (1) Data View—to enter the data, edit the data, and see the data; and (2) Variable View—to name variables and define variables. When you click on a tab it is displayed in dark letters. Define all variable names before entering the data.
   B. To define all variable names, click on the **Variable View** tab. Or to define one variable name, double click on the dimmed title *var* at the top of the column you want to name. This displays the headings (Name, Type, etc.) under which information can be entered.
   C. Enter a name for each variable under **Name.** [*Note:* The following rules apply to valid variable names and file names: (1) one word, (2) maximum 8 characters, (3) no special characters (!, *, ?, -, etc.).] You may backspace to correct typos. Make sure for each variable under Type the term is Numeric. Click on the right side of the cell if you need to change it. Also, for each variable it is suggested that under Width the number is 8 and under Decimals the number is 2. Then click on the **Data View** tab and the entered names appear at the top of the columns. [*Note:* The first column you have not named is labeled **var00001.**]

D. After defining all variable names, put the cursor on the first empty cell (square) in the first column and click once. Type a score which is displayed in the space below the **SPSS Data Editor** menu. Each time you press **Enter**, the value appears in the cell with the default or selected number of decimal places, and the cursor will move down. If you press **Tab** rather than **Enter** the cursor will move to the right.

E. If a person has no score for a variable (score is missing), enter it as a blank (enter no score and press **Enter** or **Tab**). The missing score is represented by a period(.).

F. After entering all the data for a column or row, select the first cell in the next column (the next defined variable) or row (next person) by using the mouse to click on the cell or using the arrow keys on the keyboard or using the arrow keys on the right and bottom margin of the **SPSS Data Editor** to move to the cell.

G. Do steps D and E until all data are entered.

H. Additional information: in the SPSS Data Editor window, note the buttons at the top of the window for doing special things like inserting cases and variables.

I. Additional information: when naming a variable, in addition to a title for the variable, labels for each level of the variable, changing the position of the decimal point, etc. are possible.

J. Example: variable is sex with 1 = female and 2 = male.
   1. In the Data Editor window click on the **Variable View** tab or click twice on **var** to name a column.
   2. The headings (Name, Type, etc.) are displayed
   3. Click on **Name** and type in the name of the variable: Sex
   4. Click on **Label** and type in the title of the variable: Sex of Person
   5. Click on **Values**, then the button for Values, and then type in the following:

Value: 1
Value Label: Female
click on **Add**
Value: 2
Value Label: Male
click on **Add**
click on **OK**
   6. This information will be shown in the output of any analysis (Frequencies used).

Sex of Person	
Frequency	
Female	35
Male	45

K. Additional information: to remove a variable (column) or case (row) in a data file, first highlight the column or row, then click on **Edit** on the menu bar, then click on **Cut.**

3. Saving the data
   A. To save the entered data in a file, Save does not have to be after the last score is entered. Click on **File** in the **SPSS Data Editor** menu and then click on **Save.** This opens the **Save Data As** dialog box. Enter a name for the data file (see rules in 2-C) in the **File name:** text box. Select the **a:** drive in the **Save in:** dialog box.
   B. At the **Save as type:** make sure the file is **SPSS (*.sav).** Click on **Save.**
   C. [*Note:* The untitled window will be changed to the drive and file name which you entered in 3-A.] The **SPSS Data Editor** window is still displayed. If this does not happen, save the data again.
   D. After a file is named, more data can be saved in it by clicking on **Save File** in the **SPSS Data Editor** menu.

4. Editing the data
   A. You can change data values that are incorrect, so the data entered should be still displayed on the screen.
   B. Where there are mistakes, click on the cell with the incorrect score or use the arrow

keys to move to the incorrect score. Type in the correct value and press the **Enter** key. After editing, save the data again by clicking on **File** in the **SPSS Data Editor** menu and then clicking on **Save.** Make sure the **SPSS Data Editor**, and not an **Output** or **Syntax** window, is active because **Save** will save the active window. The light on the disk drive comes on while the data is being saved. Save again if the data is not saved to the disk. The **SPSS Data Editor** window is still displayed.

C. If you type in a score twice you may want to delete it rather than change it. If you leave out a score you may want to insert it. This may require deleting or inserting a row of data. To delete a row, click on the row to be deleted. The entire row will be highlighted. From the **SPSS Data Editor** menu click on **Edit** and then **Clear.** To insert a row (case) click on the row where you want to insert a row. Click on **Data** in the **SPSS Data Editor** menu. Click on **Insert Case**, the row you clicked on and all rows below it will be moved down, then enter the data. [*Note:* See the SPSS guides in the Reference or the SPSS Help menu for more details.]

5. Analyzing the data
   A. After doing steps 2–4 to enter the data, or the existing data file has been identified, click the analysis you want and then click on what options you want in the drop-down menus. For data analysis, click **Analyze.** For graphs of the data, click **Graph.** For transformation of the data, click **Transform.**
   B. Since usually data analysis (Analyze) is desired, the options for Analyze are Report, Descriptive Statistics, Compare Means (3 t-tests, etc.), etc. [*Note:* Put the cursor (no need to click) on any of these options and the screen will display a drop-down menu of available options.]
   C. For specific information on using the options, see the SPSS 14.0 for Windows

Statistical Procedures later in this document.
   D. The results of the analysis are displayed on the screen. After this you can print the output if desired or do another analysis on the same data. You can also enter another set of scores and analyze it or retrieve another set of scores on disk and analyze it.

6. Printing output of the analysis
   A. To print the contents of the output of the analysis, make sure the **SPSS Output Viewer** is the active window at the top left of the screen. If it is not the active window, click on **Window** in the menu bar and then **SPSS Output Viewer.** The content of the active window is displayed on the right-hand side of the screen (content pane) and the output objects on the left-hand side of the screen (outline pane). Use the arrow keys to move around the screen.
   B. Before printing, indicate whether the entire contents (**All Visible Output**) (the default) or just part of the contents (**Selection**) of **Output Viewer** are to be printed. SPSS tends to produce many partially full pages of printout. To decrease the number of printed pages, select just the output desired.
      1. In the left pane of **Output Viewer** highlight what contents of Output Viewer are to be printed.
      2. From the Output Viewer click on **File** and then click on **Print.**
   C. The name of the file is shown in the dialog box. The printer name is also displayed. Click on the print option desired (All Visible Output or Selection). By default, one copy is printed. If you want multiple copies, enter the number of copies you want to print. If there are too many columns (>7–8) to get on one vertical page (Portrait), or a line for the output can't be seen in full on the screen, select **Landscape** to print a horizontal page. To

select Landscape print, click on **Properties**, click on **Basics,** click on **Landscape**, and then click on **OK.** To print the contents, click on **OK.**

D. Example:

1. Suppose the Descriptives and Frequencies programs have been run on scores for each person called jump, pullups, and run. The output from both programs is in Output Viewer.

2. The left pane of Output Viewer will look like this:

SPSS Output
  Descriptives
    Title
    Notes
    Descriptive Statistics
  Frequencies
    Title
    Notes
    Statistics
    Jump
    Pullups
    Run

3. If SPSS Output is clicked on, everything will be highlighted and the entire output will be printed.

4. If Descriptives is clicked on, the Descriptives title and the three things under it will be highlighted and only that content will be printed.

5. If Run which is under Frequencies is clicked on, it will be highlighted and that content will be printed.

E. Situations for the Example in D

1. If Descriptives is run, the Descriptives output is printed, and then Frequencies is run, all that needs to be printed is the Frequencies output by highlighting Frequencies in the left pane of Output Viewer.

2. If Descriptives is run, and Frequencies is run, all of the output needs to be printed by highlighting **SPSS Output** in the left pane of Output Viewer.

F. Useful Information and Hints on Printing

1. What is highlighted in the left pane is enclosed with a dark line box in the right pane of Output Viewer. If only part of the contents of Output Viewer is selected to be printed in the print menu, make sure Selection is highlighted as the print range.

2. If both the Data Editor and Output Viewer are on the screen, be sure to click **File** or **Print** under Output Viewer to print the output.

3. At the bottom of the screen both of the windows, Data Editor and Output, are shown. Click on one of them to make it the active window displayed on the screen.

4. The content of the Output Viewer window can be eliminated by clicking on **File** for the Output Viewer window, then **Close**, and finally **No** (don't save content). This is usefull when there is a lot of content no longer needed. The same thing can be accomplished by clicking on the **X** box in the upper right-hand corner of the Output Viewer window.

G. If you want to print the contents of the **SPSS Data Editor** window, do steps B and C after activating the **SPSS Data Editor** window (see A and F-3).

7. Getting out of SPSS

A. To end an SPSS session, click on **File** under the **SPSS Data Editor** or **Output Viewer** and then click on **Exit** in the drop-down menu.

B. [*Note:* SPSS will ask whether you want to save the contents of the **Output Viewer** and **SPSS Data Editor** windows. If you want to save them, click on **Yes.** If not, click on **No.** Only if you want to keep the output on disk and/or you have not previously saved the data do you need to click on **Yes.**]

8. Retrieving data saved on disk (Data entered using **SPSS for Windows**)

A. If just getting into SPSS, see 1-D-(3).
B. If opening a saved data file, from the **SPSS Data Editor** menu click on **File** and then on **Open.**
C. Click on the drive **a:** or the drive to use from the **Look in:** dialog box and then click on **SPSS(*.sav)** in the **Files of type** list. You can click on a file from the list to use it or you can type in a filename. Then click on **Open.**
D. The retrieved data file is displayed on the screen.
9. Importing and exporting data
   A. Importing data is using data not entered in SPSS (e.g., a word processing program).
   B. Exporting data is using data entered in SPSS in some other program (e.g., Excel).
   C. A file format may have to be selected when importing or exporting data. The file format can be either fixed field or free field. With fixed field the scores must be kept in specified columns and decimal points do not have to be entered, whereas with free field the scores only have to be separated by one blank space and decimal points must be entered.
   D. [*Note:* For more detailed procedures on importing and exporting data, see the guides in Reference below.]

Reference

SPSS (2006). *SPSS 14.0 brief guide.* Upper Saddle River, N.J.: Prentice-Hall. (Short and inexpensive.)

Pavkov, T. W., and Pierce, K. A. (2007). *Ready, set, go! A student guide to SPSS 13.0 and 14.0 for Windows.* New York: McGraw-Hill. (Short and inexpensive.)

Green, S. B., and Salkind, N. J. (2005). *Using SPSS for Windows and Macintosh: Analyzing and understanding data* (4th ed). Upper Saddle River, NJ: Prentice-Hall. (It has 458 pages, with good coverage of topics.)

The SPSS website has a wealth of information about the program, manuals, etc.: www.spss.com.

Prentice-Hall distributes SPSS Student Version for Windows and other SPSS publications. At the website the local Prentice-Hall representative can be identified. At the website, search on SPSS to identify many SPSS publications: www.prenhall.com.

The present Macintosh version of SPSS is SPSS 11 for Mac OS X.

Acknowledgment

Instructions for using SPSS were developed for earlier versions of SPSS by Suhak Oh and Ted Baumgartner. This document is an edited version of these instructions for SPSS 14.0.

SPSS 14.0 FOR WINDOWS STATISTICAL PROCEDURES

Table of Contents for the SPSS 14.0 programs described in this document.

1. Frequencies
2. Descriptives
3. One-Sample T Test
4. Independent-Samples T Test (two independent groups)
5. Paired-Samples T Test (dependent groups and repeated measures)
6. One-Way ANOVA
7. Two-Way Factorial ANOVA
8. One-Way Chi-Square
9. Two-Way Chi-Square
10. Correlation
11. Linear Regression
12. Reliability Analysis
13. Percentiles
14. Percentile Ranks
15. Standard Scores (z-scores)
16. Transformation
17. Histograms
18. Line Chart (similar to frequency polygon)
19. Scatterplot

NOTE, click on **Analyze** or **Graphs** or **Transform** under the **SPSS Data Editor** menu and all of the subheadings for it will be displayed.

Click on one of the subheadings and all procedures under the subheading will be displayed.

SPSS has a **Help** feature that can be clicked on from the **SPSS for Windows** menu or any procedure menu. **Help** is excellent for learning about a statistical procedure or what to do in a procedure. To quit **Help**, click on **Cancel.**

1. Frequencies
   A. Click on **Analyze** under the **SPSS Data Editor** menu. Click on **Descriptive Statistics.** Click on **Frequencies** which opens the **Frequencies** dialog box.
   B. Click on one or more variables from the left variable box. The variable(s) is highlighted. Click on the arrow button and the variable(s) will show in the variables box. By default, frequency tables are displayed with the data listed in ascending order (small to large). If small score is a good score, the data should be displayed in descending order. Click on **Format**, then on **Descending** (value), and finally click on **Continue** when through.
   C. To get optional descriptive and summary statistics, click on **Statistics** in the **Frequencies** dialog box. Click on the statistics desired. The **median** statistic is not provided by the Descriptives program, but is provided here. Many people use the Frequencies program to get descriptive statistics. Click on **Continue** when through. When using Frequencies to get descriptive statistics, if you don't want frequencies for each variable, turn off the **Display Frequencies Tables** option before analyzing the data.
   D. To get optional bar charts or histograms, click on **Charts** in the dialog box. Click on the charts or histograms desired in the dialog box. Click on **Continue** when through.
   E. Click on **OK** when ready to analyze the data.
2. Descriptives
   A. To get descriptive statistics, click on **Analyze** under the **SPSS Data Editor** menu. Click on **Descriptive Statistics.**

Click on **Descriptives.** This opens the **Descriptives** dialog box.
   B. Click on one or more variables from the left variable box. The variable(s) is highlighted. Click on the arrow button and the variable(s) will show in the variables box. By default, mean, standard deviation, minimum score, and maximum score will be calculated.
   C. If you want to get additional statistics, click on **Options** under the Descriptive dialog box. This opens the **Descriptives: Options** dialog box.
   D. Click on one or more options from the box. [*Note:* The **median** statistic is not an option, but it can be obtained under optional statistics in the Frequencies program (see directions for Frequencies).] Click on **Continue** when through.
   E. Click on **OK** when ready to analyze the data.
3. One-Sample T Test
   A. Click on **Analyze** under the **SPSS Data Editor** menu. Click on **Compare Means.** Then click on **One-Sample T Test.**
   B. Click on one or more variables from the left variable box to use in the analysis. The variable(s) is highlighted. Click on the arrow button to put the variables in the **Test Variable(s)** box. Click on the value in **Test Value** and enter a number which is the value against which the variable mean is tested (the hypothesized population mean).
   C. By default, the confidence interval is 95%. If you want to change this value, click on **Options** in the dialog box, then type the numeric value for the confidence interval. Click on **Continue** when through.
   D. Click on **OK** when ready to analyze the data.
   E. The variable mean is provided automatically in the analysis output.
4. Independent-Samples T Test (2 independent groups)
   A. Click on **Analyze** under the **SPSS Data Editor** menu. Click on **Compare Means.** Click on **Independent-Samples T Test.**

B. Click on one or more variables from the left variable box to use in the analysis. The variable(s) is highlighted. Click on the arrow button to put the variable(s) in the **Test Variable(s)** box.

C. Click on a variable to form the two groups and then click on the arrow button for **Grouping Variable.**

D. You must define a value of the grouping variable for each group. To define groups, click on **Define Groups.** Enter a value of the **Grouping Variable** which identified (is the code for) **Group 1.** Click on **Group 2** and enter a value for the grouping variable. Click on **Continue** when through.

E. By default, the confidence interval is 95% (alpha = .05). Click on **Options** to change it (see 3-C).

F. Click on **OK** when ready to analyze the data. Landscape print is suggested.

G. The means for the groups are provided automatically in the analysis output.

5. Paired-Samples T Test (dependent groups and repeated measures)

A. Click on **Analyze** under the **SPSS Data Editor** menu. Click on **Compare Means.** Click on **Paired-Samples T Test.**

B. Click on (highlight) one of the variables from the left variable box and click on the arrow button. It appears as **Variable 1** under **Current Selections.** Click on another variable from the left variable box and click on the arrow button to move the pair to the **Paired Variables:** dialog box. Other pairs can be entered.

C. To change the confidence interval, click on **Options** (see 3-C).

D. Click on **OK** when ready to analyze the data. Landscape print is suggested.

E. The means for the repeated measures are provided automatically in the analysis output.

6. One-Way ANOVA

A. Click on **Analyze** under the **SPSS Data Editor** menu. Click on **Compare Means**. Click on **One-Way ANOVA**.

B. Click on (highlight) one or more variables from the left variable box to test (analyze). Click on the arrow button to put the variable(s) in the **Dependent List:** box.

C. Click on a variable for forming groups and click on the arrow button to put it in the **Factor** box.

D. Click on **Options**. This opens the **One-Way ANOVA: Options** dialog box. Click on **Descriptive,** and any other options desired. You *must* select **Descriptive** to get the mean and standard deviation for each group. When through click on **Continue.**

E. If you want post hoc tests, click on **Post Hoc** and click on one of the 18 tests. When through, click on **Continue.**

F. Click on **OK** when ready to analyze the data.

7. Two-Way Factorial ANOVA

A. Click on **Analyze** under the **SPSS Data Editor** menu. Click on **General Linear Model.** Click on **Univariate.** (Only Univariate is in the student version.)

B. On the left side, the variables available in the data set are listed in a box.

C. On the right side are: Dependent Variable, Fixed Factors, Random Factors, and Covariance boxes.

D. Put the variable to be the data analyzed in the Dependent Variable box.

E. Put the variables for the rows and columns in the Fixed Factors box.

F. Example: If the variables in the data set are named Row, Column, and Score, put Score in the Dependent Variable box, and Row and Column in the Fixed Factors box.

G. Click on **Options** to get the means for rows, columns, and cells.

1. On the left side, in the Factors box, are listed Overall, the name of the row variable, the name of the column variable, and the name of the row × column interaction.

2. On the right side is the Display Means box.

3. Put everything from the Factors box into the Display Means box.

4. Click on **Continue** to return to the Univariate menu.

H. Also, post hoc tests, effect size, observed power, etc. are available. If post hoc tests are selected, it must be identified whether the post hoc tests are for rows, columns, or both.

I. Click on **OK** to analyze the data.

8. One-Way Chi-Square

A. Click on **Analyze** under the **SPSS Data Editor** menu. Click on **Nonparametric Tests.** Click on **Chi-Square.** This opens the **Chi-Square Test** dialog box.

B. Click on (highlight) a variable from the left variable box and then click on the arrow button to put it in the **Test Variable List.** Do this for each variable to be analyzed.

C. Under **Expected Range** the **Get from Data** should already be selected (marked; the default). If it is not selected, click on it.

D. Under **Expected Values, All Categories Equal** will be marked (the default). If you do not want all categories equal, click on **Values** and enter an expected value for each category by typing in a value and then clicking on **Add.** The expected values are used with all the variables in the **Test Variable List.**

E. Click on **Options** and then click on **Descriptives** in the dialog box. When through selecting values you want, click on **Continue.**

F. Click on **OK** when ready to analyze the data. If the output is more than five columns, landscape print is suggested.

9. Two-Way Chi-Square (Crosstabs)

A. Click on **Analyze** under the **SPSS Data Editor** menu. Click on **Descriptive Statistics.** Click on **Crosstabs.** This opens the Crosstabs dialog box.

B. Click on (highlight) the variables in the left variable box you want to use as the row and column variables. Click on a variable to highlight it and then click on the arrow button for **Row(s)** or for **Column(s).**

C. Click on **Statistics** in the **Crosstabs** dialog box. Click on Chi-square, Contingency coefficient, Correlation, and anything else you want. When through, click on **Continue.**

D. Click on **Cell** in the **Crosstabs** dialog box. Click on **Observed, Expected,** and all three options under **Percentages.** When through, click on **Continue.**

E. Click on **OK** when ready to analyze the data.

10. Correlation

A. Click on **Analyze** under the **SPSS Data Editor** menu. Click on **Correlate.** Click on **Bivariate.**

B. Click on (highlight) two or more variables from the left variable box in the **Bivariate Correlations** dialog box. Click on the arrow button and the variable(s) will show in the **Variables** box.

C. Click on one or more of the correlation coefficients in the Correlation Coefficients box (usually Pearson).

D. If you want a significance test, click on the type of significant test: **One-tailed** or **Two-tailed** (usually two-tailed).

E. Click on **Options** and then click on Means and Standard Deviations. Then click on **Continue.**

F. Click on **OK** when ready to analyze the data.

11. Linear Regression

A. Click on **Analyze** under the **SPSS Data Editor** menu. Click on **Regression.** Click on **Linear**.

B. Click on (highlight) a variable from the left variable box for the dependent score (the Y-score). Click on the arrow button to put the variable in the **Dependent** box. Click on (highlight) a variable(s) from the left variable box for the independent variable (the X-score(s)). Click on the arrow button to put the variable(s) in the **Independent** box.

C. Click on one of the regression models (usually **Enter**).

D. Click on **OK** when ready to analyze the data.
12. Reliability Analysis
   A. This analysis is in the SPSS standard version and now in the SPSS student version.
   B. Click on **Analyze** under the **SPSS Data Editor** menu. Click on **Scale.** Click on **Reliability Analysis.**
   C. Click on (highlight) a variable from the left variable box and then click on the arrow button to put it in the **Items:** box. Do this for at least two variables. These are the repeated measure like trials or days.
   D. The **Model:** box should have **Alpha** in it. If it does not, click on the down arrow in **Model:** and click on **Alpha.**
   E. Click on **Statistics** in the **Reliability Analysis** dialog box. Click on **Item** under **Descriptives** to get item means and **F Test** under **ANOVA Table** to get the ANOVA summary table.
   F. Also, in **Statistics,** click on **Intraclass Correlation Coefficient.** Set Model to One-Way or Two-Way Mixed depending on which ANOVA model is desired. **Confidence Interval** and **Test Value** can be changed but usually the default values are used. Click on **Continue** when through.
   G. Click on **OK** when ready to analyze the data.
13. Percentiles
   A. Analyze the data using the Frequencies procedure (see number 1 in this document). Click on **Analyze.** Click on **Descriptive Statistics.** Click on **Frequencies.**
   B. After getting into **Frequencies,** if frequency tables are not desired, click on **Display Frequency Tables** to eliminate that option.
   C. Click on **Statistics** and then on **Percentile(s):.**
   D. The percentiles are calculated as if large score is good. If small score is good, the calculated percentiles will have to be corrected by hand using the formula:

Corrected Percentile = 100 − Calculated Percentile

   E. The percentiles desired must be indicated by typing a number between 0 and 100 into the percentile box and then clicking on **Add.** Do this for each percentile desired. After indicating the percentiles desired, click on **Continue** to get out of **Statistics.**
   Example: if the percentiles 5th, 10th, 15th, . . . , 100th are desired

Percentile Box	Add
5	click
10	click
•	•
•	•

   F. The default for **Cut Points,** which is an alternative to typing in percentiles, is 10 equal groups yielding the 10th, 20th, etc. percentiles.
   G. Click on **OK** when ready to analyze the data.
14. Percentile Ranks
   A. Analyze the data using the **Frequencies** procedure (see number 1 in this document). Click on **Analyze.** Click on **Descriptive Statistics.** Click on **Frequencies.**
   B. After getting into **Frequencies,** make sure that the scores are listed from worst to best (ascending order if large score is good).
   C. The output from the analysis will look like this example.

Value	Frequency	Percent	Valid Percent	Cum. Percent
15	4	20	20	20
16	6	30	30	50
17	8	40	40	90
19	2	10	10	100
	20	100	100	

D. Calculate percentile ranks for a score (Value) by the formula:

PR = (Cum. Percent above the score)
    + (.5) (Percent for the score)

PR for score = 15:
PR = 0 + (.5) (20) = 10

PR for score = 16:
PR = 20 + (.5) (30) = 35

15. Standard Scores (z-scores)
    A. See the guides in the Reference section for more information.
    B. A z-score for each variable analyzed is calculated assuming a large score is good whether or not the data is listed in ascending or descending order. If a small score is good, the sign of the z-score is reversed (e.g. –2.0 should be 2.0).
    C. Analyze the data using the **Descriptives** procedure (see number 2 in this document) by clicking on **Analyze,** then **Descriptive Statistics,** and finally **Descriptives.**
    D. Click on **Save standardized values as variables** in the **Descriptives** dialog box. Highlight the variables you want z-scores for in the left variables box. Click the arrow to move the variables into the variable box. Click on **OK** when ready to analyze the data. The z-scores are calculated, and added to the file containing the original data. A message does appear in the output that this occurred. The names of the z-scores will be the names of the original data with a z in front of them (e.g., for the original variable CAT the z-score is ZCAT). Z-score can be seen by displaying the data file on the screen and printing it if desired. The data file must be saved again for the z-scores to be saved with the data. In most cases, saving the z-scores is not necessary. If saving the z-scores, it might be good to save them as a new file so the original data file is retained as one file, and the original data with z-scores are another file. When saving the z-scores as a new file, use **Save As.**

E. Sum of the z-scores can be obtained by using the Transformation procedure (presented in this document) and writing the formula for obtaining the sum of the z-scores, allowing for the fact that some z-scores have the wrong sign (z-scores for scores when small score is good will have the wrong sign.) For example, if the original data were X1, X2, and X3 the z-scores are ZX1, ZX2, and ZX3, and if ZSUM is the name used for the sum of the z-scores:

ZSUM = ZX1 + ZX2 − ZX3
(for X3, small score is good)

16. Transformation
    A. See the guides in the Reference section for more information.
    B. Many things can be done with transformations such as changing the values of variables, grouping variables, creating new variables, etc. First, creating a new variable is presented. Then other examples are presented.
    C. Click on **Transform** and then **Compute.** In the **Compute Variable** dialog box the name of the variable to be computed is typed in the **Target Variable:** box and the numeric expression or equation for calculating the target variable is typed in the **Numeric Expression:** box. Click on **OK** when ready to do the analysis. The computed variable is displayed on the screen and saved with the original data.
    D. Example 1, creating a new variable: There are 3 scores named X1, X2, and X3 on each person and for all three scores a large score is good.
       1. The sum (to be named SUMX) of the 3 scores is desired.
          Target Variable: SUMX
          Numerical Expression: X1 + X2 + X3
       2. The data have already been analyzed calculating z-scores for each score (see Standard Score in this document). These z-scores are named ZX1, ZX2,

and ZX3. The sum of the z-scores (to be named ZSUM) is desired.
Target Variable: ZSUM
Numerical Expression: ZX1 + ZX2 + ZX3
[*Note:* The target variable is added to the file containing the original data (and z-scores in the case of ZSUM). The data file must be saved again for the target variable to be saved with the rest of the file (see 15-D for save procedures).]

E. Example 2, creating new variables by computing and by recoding: Each person has an X, Y, and ZZ score. X score values are from 1 to 10; Y score values are from 0 to 3; and ZZ score values are from 10 to 29.

1. Analysis 1: Calculate a new score for each person (Ratio) where Ratio = X/Y.
   a. Click on **Transform** and then on **Compute**
   b. Fill the Boxes:
      1. Target Variable Box: type in Ratio (name of new score)
      2. Numeric Expression Box: click on the box and type in X/Y or highlight X, click on the right arrow to put it in the box, click on /, highlight Y, and click on the right arrow to put it in the box.
      3. Click on **OK**
   c. The new score (Ratio) is added to the data file as the last score for each person, so now each person has an X, Y, ZZ, and Ratio score.
   d. [*Note:* (1) When Y is zero, Ratio = X/Y will be set to missing value (period)(.) since division by zero is undefined; (2) the Ratio score is not saved on the data disk at this time. If Ratio should be saved, save the file (File, Save) or save the file with a new name (File,

Save As) to preserve the original data file. If multiple transformations are to be done, saving could be done after doing all the transformations.]

2. Analysis 2: Calculate a new score for each person (Newz) using the ZZ scores and the Recode option as follows: (1) if ZZ = 10–14, Newz = 1; (2) if ZZ = 15–19, Newz = 2; (3) if ZZ = 20–24, Newz = 3; and if ZZ = 25–29, Newz = 4.
   a. Click on **Transform** and then on **Recode.**
   b. Click on **Into Different Variable.**
   c. Fill the Boxes:
      1. Input Variable Box: click on ZZ (the variable recoded), and click on the right arrow to put it in the box. The box name changes to Numeric Variable.
      2. Output Variable Box: click on it, and type in Newz (the name of the new variable)
   d. Click on **Old** and **New Values**
      1. Under Old Value, click on **Range,** enter 10, tab or click to the **Through Box,** and enter 14
      2. Under New Value, click on **Value** and enter 1
      3. Click on **Add**
      4. Do this for each variable change

ZZ	Newz
15–19	2
20–24	3
25–29	4

      5. Click on **Continue**
      6. Click on **Change**
      7. Click on **OK**
   e. The new score (Newz) is added to the data file as the last score for each person.

f. [*Note:* The Newz score is not saved on the data disk at this time. Save it if necessary.]

17. Histogram
    A. See the Help feature or the guides in the Reference section for more information.
    B. Click on **Graphs,** and then on **Histogram.**
    C. In the **Histogram** dialog box, click on (highlight) a variable from the left variable box and then click on the arrow button so the variable is listed under the **Variable:** box. Note a variable can be removed from the **Variable:** box by clicking on it and then on the arrow button.
    D. If the default format for histogram is acceptable, click on **OK** to obtain the graph. The histogram is displayed in the **SPSS Viewer.** If you want to display the normal curve with the histogram, click on **Display normal curve** before clicking on **OK.** A normal curve will be superimposed over the histogram.
    E. [*Note:* Double click on a graph in the **SPSS Viewer** to bring it in the **SPSS Chart Editor.** Double clicking on a graph created from interactive graphics activates the chart manager. The **SPSS Chart Editor** on the chart manager can be used to edit the chart.]
    F. By default the histogram has bars showing the data divided into about 10 evenly spaced intervals. Usually 10–20 intervals are used with continuous data putting 2–5 different scores in an interval (e.g., 15–17 is interval size = 3). The base intervals of the histogram in the **SPSS Chart Editor** can be changed.
18. Line Chart (similar to frequency polygon)
    A. See the Help feature or the guides in the Reference section for more information.
    B. Click on **Graphs** and then on **Line.**
    C. In the Line Charts dialog box click on **Simple** line chart and **Summaries for Groups of Cases.** Then click on **Define,** click on (highlight) the variable from the left variable box to use, click on the arrow button to put the highlighted variable in the **Category Axis:** box, and click on **N of cases.** Click on **OK** when ready to obtain the graph. The line chart is displayed in the **SPSS Viewer** (see Histogram for details on the editing chart).
    D. By default the line chart has the data divided into about 15 intervals for the X-axis. Usually 10–20 labels (intervals) are used with continuous data putting 2–5 different score values in an interval (e.g., 15–17 is interval size = 3). The labels (intervals) for the X-axis can be altered.
19. Scatterplot
    A. See the Help feature for more information.
    B. Click on **Graphs,** then **Scatter,** and then **Simple** in the **Scatterplot** dialog box.
    C. Now click on **Define.** Click on (highlight) a variable from the left variable box and then click on the arrow button to put it in the **X Axis:** box. Do the same thing for a second variable to put it in the **Y Axis:** box.
    D. Click on **OK** when ready to obtain the graph.
    E. The scatterplot is displayed in the **SPSS Viewer** (see Histogram for details on the editing charts).

Acknowledgment

Instructions for using SPSS were developed for earlier versions of SPSS by Suhak Oh and Ted Baumgartner. This document is an edited version of these instructions for SPSS 14.0.

Presented here are some instructions for using Excel 2003 for Windows. The appendix was written referencing manuals exclusive to the 2003 version of Excel. Previous versions of Excel are extremely similar, and versions change quite rapidly. No matter what version you are using, most of the information in this appendix is relevant to your version. Additional help can be found at Microsoft's homepage (www.microsoft.com).

EXCEL 2003 FOR WINDOWS BASICS

Click with the left mouse button unless otherwise indicated.

1. Getting into Excel
   A. You should have a designated drive space or appropriate removable media (such as a disk) to save your data to. Prior to starting Excel, ensure that a space to save data is readily available.
   B. Click on Start in the lower left-hand corner of the screen and then click on All Programs in the drop-down menu.
   C. Click on Excel 2003. If you do not see it in the drop-down menu, look for a subfolder entitled Microsoft Office. Once located, click on Microsoft Excel 2003 in the next menu.
   D. Within the Excel Spreadsheet Program:
      1. Click on Help in the menu bar if you would like to receive online training.
      2. Click on an empty cell if you want to start typing in data.
      3. Click on File ⇒ Open if you have data already saved on disk.

When you start Excel, you begin with a screen which is an empty grid. This grid is called sheet1 and the default name of the file is Book1. Notice at the bottom of the screen there are three tabs entitled "sheet1, sheet2, sheet3"; these are separate worksheets.

Collectively these sheets are saved in one file, which is called a workbook. This is where the name Book1 comes from.

When you begin with a new document, Excel starts you on sheet1, Book1. It is recommended that you save your data at the very beginning. To do this, go to File ⇒ Save As and create a name for your data set—it will replace the name Book1. If you like, you can also go to the three tabs at the bottom (sheet1, sheet2, sheet3) and rename them. To accomplish this, click on the tabs until they become highlighted and type the new sheet name. A teacher might use Excel to manage the grades of her classes. The overall file or workbook might be called Grades, and the separate tabs at the bottom might be named for different class sections. These features are included to help better organize your work.

Now that you have a saved workbook, the next step is to add data to it. Notice on the spreadsheet that you have letters going across the top of the grid. These letters represent columns, and the name "Column" will be used throughout this appendix.

Remember that when referring to the letter portion of the spreadsheet, you are referencing a column. Running down the side of the spreadsheet will be numbers. These numbers represent rows, and the name "Row" will be used throughout this appendix. Remember when referring to the number portion of the spreadsheet, you are referencing a row.

The spreadsheet in Excel is designed to work as a grid with columns and rows. The columns and rows in Excel are merely used as reference points to guide data being entered into the cells. To identify a cell, first identify the column letter it is located in, followed by the row number it is located in. For example, if you need to enter your name in cell B5, simply find the column labeled "B" and count down 5 cells. Now simply type your data into the cell.

2. Entering Data
   A. Always use Row 1 as the header row for each variable you wish to enter. Often, the first variable in a data set is "Person ID." To enter Person ID, simply go to Row 1, Column 1 (A1) and type in whatever term you want to use to represent Person ID. In creating variable names, remember that it is easier if you keep the names short and concise (8 or fewer characters). Also SPSS doesn't allow the use of all characters and symbols. It is recommended that you use only numbers and letters. In creating your variable names, remember to make a list of all the variable names you create; this can later be used as a key. All variable names should be entered in Row 1, starting with cell A1 and continuing horizontally across the grid (B1, C1, etc.).
   B. When defining categorical or nominal variables, it is important to note that SPSS allows the import of text only when used in the header row; therefore, you cannot define your terms until after they are imported into the SPSS programs. For example, if gender is one of the variables in your data, you would have to predefine the numbers you want to use to represent males and females. You may choose to define males as "1" and females as "2." For any variable, the data are entered vertically. If cell A1 is defined as "Person ID," then the first person's ID would be entered into cell A2, and the next person's into cell A3, and so on. If you do not have data for a variable, simply leave the cell empty: DO NOT ENTER A ZERO. A zero is much different from no response. In entering data, remember that you are working with a grid and that each row represents a series of responses for one particular person. Therefore, if you fail to skip cells when no response is given, you can throw off the entire data set.
   C. In order to make entering data more accessible, Excel offers an advantage over SPSS in that the user has the ability to hide both rows and columns. This feature allows data to be more easily entered and verified. To hide a column, or a set of columns, click your mouse on the column letter (drag the mouse across columns if you want more than one) and, while the column is still highlighted, click the right mouse button and select "Hide." The column will disappear. The column is not deleted but simply out of sight. To make the column reappear, click the mouse on the column letter prior to the hidden column and drag it across to the next adjacent column (e.g., if column B is hidden, click on column A and drag the mouse across to column C). Once this is done, click the right mouse button and select "Unhide"; the column will reappear. The process to hide a row is similar. The only difference is the direction you drag the mouse when selecting the row to hide, or the adjacent rows to unhide a row. It is important to note that when a row is hidden, it still remains in the spreadsheet. This means that if you hide a column or row and then import the data into SPSS or another program, the hidden column or row also is imported.

3. Importing Excel Data into SPSS
   A. To import data into SPSS, first open SPSS, then click File ⇒ Open and select Data. A box will pop up for you to select your data file. At the bottom of the box there is an

option to select the file type. The default setting is SPSS (*.sav) data. Click the pull-down menu of this box and change the setting to Excel (*.xls). Once this is done, locate your Excel file and click Open.

B. At this point, a second box pops up that reads "Opening Excel Data Source." There is a box beside the statement: "Read variable names from the first row of data." Make sure this box is clicked so the option is selected. Next, there is a pull-down menu for Worksheet. When working with multiple worksheets, you need to select which worksheet you want Excel to open. You will also notice a box entitled "Range"; this box can be used if you are working with data that has a header at the top of the sheet. If this is the case, enter the rows/columns that contain the range of data you are working with into this box.

4. Conducting Analyses within the Excel Spreadsheet Program.

A. Excel has the ability to conduct many statistical analyses that are readily available in SPSS. However, a considerable amount of work is involved in conducting some of the analyses, and directions for this are beyond the scope of this appendix. It is recommended that SPSS be used as the primary program for statistical analyses. However, if you cannot find an available copy of SPSS, Excel spreadsheets can be modified to conduct almost any analysis. To give you an idea of how this works, a few examples are included. In the following section are the instructions for each set of example programs.

B. **Before beginning to reproduce any of the programs, be sure the statistical data analyses tools are installed in the copy of Excel you are working with.** To see if they are installed, go to "Tools" in the menu bar; you should see an option for "Data Analyses." If you do not see an option for "Data Analyses," there will be an

option for "Add-Ins." Click this option, then click the checkbox beside "Analysis ToolPak." This option will install the "Data Analyses" components. *Note:* You may be prompted for the Microsoft Office installation CDs as well as the program's installation key. Once the tools are installed, proceed to the next section for detailed descriptions of two statistical programs.

EXCEL 2003 FOR WINDOWS STATISTICAL PROCEDURES

The Excel 2003 programs described in this document are (1) Frequencies and (2) Descriptives. Note that every analysis within Excel can be conducted either by using the point-and-click method (as in SPSS) or by typing in Excel commands. Also note that Excel has a Help feature that can be accessed from the Excel menu or by pressing F1. Help is an excellent resource for learning about a procedure or to receive general Excel training.

1. Frequencies (*Note:* This has to be done using mostly Excel commands.)

A. FREQUENCY calculates the number of times values occur within user-specified ranges.

B. To conduct a series of frequency analyses, the data must be arranged using a two-column format. One column contains the data, the other column contains the values you want to group your data into. The FREQUENCY command works by examining the column of data and sorting the scores into specified ranges (or groups) provided by the user. Because of the format Excel uses, it is not capable of completing simple frequency distributions (providing frequencies when groups are not defined). The Excel command is as follows: FREQUENCY (scores of interest, grouping values).

C. "Scores of interest" is the column of data you wish to count frequencies on. In an Excel spreadsheet, it is the column of data representing your scores.

D. "Grouping values" is the column containing the groups Excel will sort the scores into. The user selects the size and number of the groups.

E. An example is provided below. In the example, the groups are < 50, 50–59, 60–69, 70–79, etc.

	A	B	C
1	**Scores**	**Groups**	**Results**
2	95	50	
3	78	60	
4	80	70	
5	60	80	
6	40	90	
7	79	100	
8	70		
9	100		
10	95		

F. Enter the Scores in column A and Groups in column B. Go to cell C2 and select the same number of cells that you have for groups. In this example, cells C2 through C7 (C2:C7) will be selected. Once the cells are selected, press F2 and type in the FREQUENCY command [in this example the Excel command is as follows: FREQUENCY (A2:A10,B2:B7)]. Then press CTRL+SHIFT+ENTER. In columns C2 through C7 the frequency counts for Groups B2 through B7 will appear. Specifically, C2 will contain the number of scores less than 50 (in the example, this is one score). C3 will contain the number of scores between 50 and 59 (one score). C4 will contain the number of scores between 60 and 69 (one score), and this will continue for all of the groups you create. If the situation is one where lower scores are better, the groups can be set up in reverse order (100, 90, 80, etc.) and the frequency counting is the same as before.

2. Descriptives
   A. The descriptive statistic option in Excel provides the Mean, Standard Error, Median, Mode, Standard Deviation, Variance, Range, Sum, Count, and a few other values.
   B. Set up the data using the same format as before with rows as the subjects and

columns as the variables (see section 2 under Excel 2003 for Windows Basics). The first row of data will be the header row and should contain the variable names; each column should represent a different variable.

C. Once you have entered the data, go to the menu bar and select "Tools" and then click on "Descriptive Statistics." A window will pop up with multiple options.

D. Select the cells that contain your data and enter them into the "input range." This can be done by typing in the cell values (A2:A10 in the frequency example) or by dragging the mouse over the cells you wish to select.

E. If you want to select multiple columns or rows of variables that are not adjacent, you can select the first column of data using the mouse and then hold the CTRL key and select additional columns or rows of data.

F. One Option you select is whether the data are analyzed by rows or columns. Whether you choose rows or columns depends on what you are examining. If you want to look at the descriptive statistics for each variable, choose the column option. If you want to look at descriptive statistics for the repeated measures of a test for each person, choose the row option.

G. Also in Options, be sure "Summary Statistics" and "Labels in the first row" are checked.

H. Select your output range. The output can be placed in specific columns on the same sheet, as a separate sheet, or as a separate workbook. When doing multiple analyses, it is recommended that you save the output to a separate worksheet and keep a master sheet that contains data only. Using this method allows a sheet to always be accessible for import to other statistics programs such as SPSS.

Acknowledgment

Instructions for using Excel were developed by Mathew Gregoski.

GLOSSARY

A

AAHPERD Health-Related Fitness Test (HRFT)   One of the first health-related fitness tests sponsored by AAHPERD

AAHPER Youth Fitness Test (YFT)   A youth fitness test developed by a group of physical educators who met and selected tests on the basis of logic

Absolute Endurance Test   An endurance test that uses a weight load constant for all subjects tested

Accuracy Test   A test in which the student projects an object at a target for a score

Activity Factor   A semantic differential factor that involves motion; measured by adjective pairs such as fast-slow and excitable-calm

ACTIVITYGRAM®   A physical activity recall instrument, used within the FITNESSGRAM® program, that is designed to provide information about children's normal physical activity patterns

Aerobic Capacity   A dimension of physical fitness that relates to the ability to perform sustained exercise; a laboratory measure of maximal oxygen consumption ($\dot{V}O_2$ max) is considered the best index of aerobic capacity.

Aerobic Fitness   Physical working capacity or $\dot{V}O_2$ max

Affective Domain   A system used to categorize affective behavior to help teachers formulate affective objectives

Age-Appropriate Physical Activity   Activity of a frequency, intensity, duration, and type that leads to optimal growth and development in children and contributes to development of a physically active lifestyle

Agility   The ability to change the direction of the body or body parts rapidly

Alternative Assessment   Nontraditional assessments often resulting in students creating a product for the teacher to grade

Analysis of Variance   A statistical technique for dividing total test variance into parts

Android Obesity   Central or upper body adiposity, referred to as apple-shaped

Anorexia Nervosa   Excessive diet and exercise resulting in extreme weight loss

Attitude Scale   A list of various statements that elicit one's feelings about the attitude object

Authentic Assessment   Evaluating students in a real-life setting

B

Balance   The ability to maintain body position

Basic Physical Ability   A trait, more general than a psychomotor skill, that provides the foundation for the successful execution of many different psychomotor skills; also called *psychomotor ability*

Bell-Shaped Curve   See *normal curve*

Binge-eating   Consumption of large quantities of food in a short time

Bioelectrical Impedance Analysis (BIA)   Technique used to estimate body composition, based on the principle that the resistance to the flow of a low-level electrical current is related to total body water

Body Composition   The classification of the body into fat weight and fat-free weight

Body Density   A value used to calculate percent body fat; calculated with the underwater weighing method, it is determined by the following formula:

$$\text{Body density} = \frac{\text{weight}}{\text{volume}}$$

Body Image   The attitude one has toward the body and the manner in which one's own body is perceived

Body Mass Index (BMI)   The ratio of weight and height, defined as BMI = Weight/Height^2, where weight is in kilograms and height is in meters

Brockport Physical Fitness Test   Youth health-related physical fitness test for individuals with visual impairments, mental retardation, cerebral palsy, spinal cord injury, and amputation

525

Bulimia Nervosa   An eating disorder involving episodes of binge-eating and associated feelings of guilt or depression

C

Cardiovascular Disease   The leading cause of death of Americans. The most common are heart disease and strokes

Central Tendency   The tendency of scores to be concentrated at a central point; measures of central tendency are the mode, median, and mean

Circumferences   Girth measurements around specific body sites

Classification Index   A mathematical formula used to combine age, height, and weight to predict excellence in the ability to perform a wide variety of motor tasks

Closed Kinetic Chain   Situation in which the end segment or joint meets with external resistance that prevents or restrains free movement

Coefficient of Determination   The amount of variability in one measure explained by the other measure

Completion Item   A knowledge test item that requires students to complete or fill in the blanks in the item

Concurrent Validity   Validity for the present

Confidence Limits   Indicate the degree of confidence that the population value is between certain values; used in reference to confidence limits for a reliability coefficient

Construct Validity Evidence   The degree to which a test measures some part of a whole skill or an abstract trait

Content Validity Evidence   See *logical validity evidence*

Continuous Scores   Scores with the potential for an infinite number of values

Coronary Heart Disease   A major form of cardiovascular disease that affects coronary arteries, the arteries that deliver oxygen and nutrients to the heart muscle (myocardium). A build up of plaque restricts the blood flow through the coronary arteries

Correlation   A mathematical technique for determining the relationship between two sets of measures

Correlation Coefficient   A value between –1.0 and 1.0 that indicates the degree of relationship between two sets of measures

Criterion-Referenced Standard   A standard that explicitly defines the task to be achieved

Criterion Score   An individual's recorded score; the score used to represent a person's ability

Criterion Validity Evidence   The degree to which scores on a test correlate with scores on an accepted standard

Criterion Variable   See *dependent variable*

Cross-Sectional Method   A method used to study the rate at which fitness declines with age; a large sample who are tested once and vary greatly in age

Cross-Validation   If the prediction formula and standard error seem acceptable, the prediction formula should be proven on a second group of individuals similar to the first

Curvilinear Relationship   A relationship between two measures that is best described by a curved line

Cycle Ergometer   A machine that regulates the work performed while cycling; workload can be accurately altered by increasing or decreasing the resistance on the ergometer

D

Decision Validity   An indication of the validity of a criterion-referenced test using logic

Dependent Variable   The Y variable of a regression equation, often called the criterion variable

Difference Scores   Change in individuals' scores from the beginning to the end of an instructional program or training program. Also called *change scores* or *improvement scores*

Disability Sport   Competitions sanctioned by sport organizations organized for individuals with disabilities

Discrete Scores   Scores with the potential for a limited number of specific values

Discrimination Index   A value indicating how well a knowledge test item differentiates between the high- and low-scoring students

Discrimination Test   A test designed to identify different ability groups based on test scores

Distance Run Tests   Tests that require the participant to cover a specific distance as quickly as possible (e.g., 1 mile) or to cover as much distance as possible in a specified time (e.g., 12 minutes) for the purpose of estimating aerobic fitness

Domain-Referenced Validity   An indication of the validity of interpretations based on criterion-referenced test scores expressed as a numeric value

E

Eating Disorders   A variety of disorders often associated with eating excessive or insufficient quantities of food

Ecological Validity   Test selection is meaningful to the individual and is appropriate for a given living, work, or school environment

Essay Item   A knowledge test item for which students write a several-paragraph response to the item

Essay Test   A knowledge test that requires students to respond to test items in writing

Evaluation   A decision-making process that involves (1) the collection of suitable data (measurement), (2) a judgment of the value of these data against a standard, and (3) a decision based on these data and standards

Evaluation Factor   A semantic differential factor that involves a degree of "goodness"; measured by adjective pairs such as good-bad and beautiful-ugly

Exercise   Any physical activity that is planned, structured, and designed to improve fitness

F

Fat-Free Weight   See *lean body weight*

Fat Weight   In measuring a person's body, the weight in pounds that is body fat

Final Grade   The grade assigned at the end of a unit or grading period

FITNESSGRAM®   A youth health-related fitness and physical activity assessment program and computerized reporting system

Flexibility   The range of motion about a joint

Formative Evaluation   The process of judging achievement at the formative stages of instruction to determine the degree of mastery and to pinpoint that part of the task yet to be mastered; often used as a form of student feedback

Frequency Polygon   A graph of a frequency distribution with scores along the horizontal axis and frequencies along the vertical axis

Functional Adult Fitness   Fitness that is specific to performance of everyday functions such as standing up, walking up stairs, and dressing

Functional Classification   Sport classification for persons with disabilities based on an individual's ability to complete specific sport tasks

G

General Motor Ability   The theory that individuals who are highly skilled on one motor task will be highly skilled on other motor tasks

Generalized Equations   Equations that can be validly used with heterogeneous samples

Gynoid Obesity   Lower body obesity that results when excess fat is deposited in the hips and thighs, referred to as pear-shaped

H

Health-Related Physical Fitness   Physical fitness as it pertains to health promotion and disease prevention. Includes components of aerobic fitness, body composition, muscular strength and endurance, and flexibility

Healthy Activity Zone   The level of physical activity deemed healthy by the ACTIVITYGRAM®. The Healthy Activity Zone is set at three bouts of activity (total of 45 minutes) for children and two bouts of activity (total of 30 minutes) for adolescents

Healthy Fitness Zone   Standards of fitness set by the FITNESSGRAM® that offer some degree of protection against diseases that result from sedentary living

Healthy Weight   A body weight determined for a specified percent body fat

Hydrostatic Weighing   The underwater weighing method used to determine body volume, which is then used with dry land body weight to calculate body density

I

Independent Variable   The X variable of a regression equation, often called the predictor variable

Intermittent Physical Activity   Relatively short bursts of movement (several seconds or minutes) interspersed with periods of rest

Internal-Consistency Reliability Coefficient   The degree to which an individual's scores are unchanged within a day

Interval Scores   Scores that have a common unit of measure between consecutive scores but not a true zero point

Intraclass Correlation Coefficient   A correlation coefficient that estimates test reliability; derived with analysis of variance values

Isokinetic Strength   Strength that is measured by recording the force exerted through the entire range of motion

Isometric Strength   Strength that is measured by recording the force exerted against an immovable object

Isotonic Strength   Strength that involves moving an object through a defined range of motion; often measured with a 1-RM test, which is the maximum weight that can be lifted during one repetition

Item   A question or statement on a knowledge test; one of the tests in a battery of physical performance tests

Item Analysis   An item-by-item analysis of a knowledge test to identify good questions

Item Difficulty   The difficulty of a knowledge test item; the percentage of a group that correctly answers an item

K

Kappa Coefficient   An indication of the reliability of criterion-referenced test scores; one of two coefficients commonly used

Kinesthesis   The ability to perceive the body's position in space and the relationship of its parts

Knowledge Test   A paper-and-pencil test that measures knowledge

L

Lean Body Weight   The weight of the body with the fat tissue removed; also called *fat-free weight*

Line of Best Fit   See *regression line*

Linear Relationship   A relationship between two measures that is best described by a straight line

Logical (content) Validity Evidence   A validity technique based on the subjectively established fact that the test measures the wanted attribute

Longitudinal Method   A method used to study the rate at which fitness declines with age; for each age group a large sample are tested

M

Mass Testability   The degree to which a large number of students can be tested in a short period of time

Mastery Test   A test that determines how well students have mastered the material

Matching Item   A knowledge test item for which students match columns of questions and answers

Maximal Exercise Test   Test whose objective is to increase systematically exercise intensity until the subject reaches exhaustion

Maximal Oxygen Uptake ($\dot{V}O_2$ max)   The amount of oxygen one utilizes during exhausting work; the criterion for validating field tests of cardiorespiratory function

Mean   A measure of central tendency, or average; obtained by dividing the sum of the scores by the number of scores

Measurement   The collection of information on which a decision is based

Median   A measure of central tendency, or average; the score below which 50% of a group scored

Medical Classification   Sport classification for persons with disabilities based on an individual's anatomical injury site

MET   A unit used to quantify oxygen consumption. A MET equals a $\dot{V}O_2$ of 3.5 ml·kg^{-1}min^{-1} and is the oxygen uptake at rest

Mode   A measure of central tendency, or average; the most frequent score for a group of people

Moderate Exercise   Activities performed at an intensity between 3 and 6 METs ($10.5–21$ ml·kg^{-1}·min^{-1}), with an intensity 40% to 60% of $\dot{V}O_2$ max

Moderate Physical Activity   An intensity equivalent to brisk walking

Morbidity   Disease

Mortality   Death

Motor Educability   The ability to learn motor skills easily and well

Motor Fitness   A category of the psychomotor domain that is defined by the component's strength, power, and endurance

Motor Skill   The level of proficiency achieved on a specific motor task; also called *psychomotor skill*

Multicomponent Model   The method used to measure percent body fat from the underwater weighing method. The model assumes that the density of fat is 0.9 g·cc^{-1} but also uses total body water and bone density to adjust density estimate of the fat-free weight component

Multiple-Choice Item   A knowledge test item for which students select an answer from three or more provided answers

Multiple Correlation   The correlation between a criterion and two or more predictors that have been mathematically combined to maximize the correlation between the criterion and predictors

Multiple Prediction   The prediction of the value of one measure based on the performance of two or more other measures; also called *multiple regression*

Multiple Regression   See *multiple prediction*

Multi-Stage Exercise Test   A method used to estimate $\dot{V}O_2$ max from two or more submaximal workloads and heart rates

Muscular Endurance   The ability to persist in physical activity or to resist muscular fatigue

Muscular Power   Traditionally, the maximum force released in the shortest possible time; more appropriately, the rate at which work can be performed by involved muscle groups

Muscular Strength   The maximum force a muscle group can exert during a brief period of time

N

Natural Breaks   A grading technique that assigns grades by breaks in the distribution of scores

Negatively Skewed Curve   A curve with a long, low tail on the left, indicating few individuals received low scores

Nominal Scores   Scores that cannot be ordered from best to worst

Nonexercise Models   Equations used to estimate maximal oxygen consumption ($\dot{V}O_2$ max) from variables obtained without exercise testing

Normal Curve   A symmetrical curve centered around a point that is the mean score; also called *bell-shaped curve*

Norm-Referenced Standard   A standard that judges a performance in relation to the performance of other members of a well-defined group

Norms   Performance standards based on the scores of a group of people

O

Obesity   The excessive accumulation of fat weight

Objective   Describing a test that two or more people score and to which they assign similar scores

Objective Evaluation   A test in which the student's performance yields a score without a value judgment by the scorer (see *subjective measure*); also, a test for which students respond to questions by selecting one of two or more provided answers

Objective Tests   True-false, multiple-choice, matching, and similar knowledge tests

Objectivity   The degree to which multiple scorers agree on the magnitude of scores

Open-Circuit Spirometry   A system to measure oxygen consumption by analyzing the oxygen content, carbon dioxide content, and volume of expired air

Open Kinetic Chain   Situation in which the limb segment is free in space

Ordinal Scores   Scores that can be ordered from best to worst but that do not have a common unit of measure

Overweight   That weight that exceeds the "normal" weight based on gender, height, and frame size

Oxygen Consumption   The volume of oxygen consumed by the body under given conditions

P

Percent Body Fat   That proportion of total weight that is fat weight

Percentile   A score that has a specified percentage of scores below it

Percentile Rank   A value that indicates the percentage of scores below a given score

Physical Activity   Any behavior that involves movement and results in an increase in energy expenditure above resting levels

Physical Activity Readiness Questionnaire (PAR-Q)   A short questionnaire used before exercise testing to screen for individuals who should not exercise or should not take an exercise test

Physically Dependent   When used to describe adult functional fitness status, dependent on help from someone else to perform activities of daily living (washing, dressing, etc.)

Physically Elite   When used to describe adult functional fitness status, master athletes who are very fit

Physically Fit   When used to describe adult functional fitness status, well above average in ability to perform all necessary activities of daily living, and also engaging in strenuous physical activities and/or regular exercise

Physically Frail   When used to describe adult functional fitness status, able to perform some activities of daily living, but requiring help with others

Physically Independent   When used to describe adult functional fitness status, able to perform all necessary activities of daily living, but sedentary and possibly borderline physically frail

Pilot Study   The testing of a small group that is representative of a larger group; used in reference to estimating reliability in a pilot study

Plethysmograph   A device, or "body box," used for measuring the volume of air in the body

Positively Skewed Curve   A curve with a long, low tail on the right, indicating few individuals received high scores

Posttest Procedures   The analysis and recording of test scores

Potency Factor   A semantic differential factor that involves the strength of the concept; measured by adjective pairs such as strong-weak and smooth-rough

Power   The rate at which work is performed; calculated with the following formula:

$$Power = \frac{work}{time}$$

Power Output   The rate of work used to define exercise intensity. The power output for a cycle ergometer is increased by placing more resistance on the flywheel and increasing the cycle pedaling rate. The power output for treadmill exercise is increased by increasing treadmill speed and increasing the grade

Prediction   The estimating of the value of one measure based on the value of one or more other measures; see also *multiple regression*

Predictive Validity   The degree to which one measure can predict future performance on a second measure

Predictor Variable   See *independent variable*

Presidential Active Lifestyle Award   An award from the President's Challenge that recognizes the benefits of a physically active lifestyle

President's Challenge Health Fitness Test   A youth fitness test, from the President's Council on Physical Fitness and Sports, that measures health-related fitness

President's Challenge Physical Fitness Test   A youth fitness test, from the President's Council on Physical Fitness and Sports, that measures both health-related fitness and motor fitness components

Pretest Planning   The procedures that must be followed before a test is administered; includes knowing the test, developing test procedures and directions, and preparing the students and the testing facility

Prevalence   The percentage of individuals within the group affected; refers to the disease rate within a defined group of people (cohort)

Program Evaluation   Determination of the extent to which a program achieves the standards and objectives set forth for it

Proportion of Agreement Coefficient   An indication of the reliability of criterion-referenced test scores; one of two coefficients commonly used

Psychomotor Ability   See *basic physical ability*

Psychomotor Skill   See *motor skill*

Psychophysical   A term used to describe scientific methods used to integrate psychological and physical parameters. An example of a psychophysical test is Borg's RPE scale

R

Range   A measure of the variability or heterogeneity in a set of scores; the difference between the largest and smallest scores

Rank Order Correlation Coefficient   *Rho or Spearman's rho;* calculated when the scores for the two sets of scores are ranks

Rank Order Grading   A straightforward, norm-referenced method of grading that assigns grades after ordering the scores

Rating of Perceived Exertion (RPE) Scale   A scale developed by Dr. G. Borg of Stockholm, Sweden, that is used to rate the intensity of exercise

Rating Scale   A set of standards or a checklist for measuring performance subjectively

Ratio Scores   Scores that have a common unit of measure between consecutive scores and a true zero point

Reactivity   A phenomenon whereby a person's normal behavior is influenced by a measurement instrument. An example would be children jumping up and down after being fitted with pedometers

Regression   See *prediction*

Regression Line   Often termed the "line of best fit," the line that is defined by predicting the dependent variable from the independent variable

Reliability   The degree to which a measure is consistent, unchanged over a short period of time

Residual Lung Volume   The amount of air remaining in the lungs after a full expiration. This measurement is used when estimating body density by the underwater weighing method

Rubric   A criterion-referenced scoring instrument for a given task performance; may or may not be standardized

S

Semantic Differential Scales   A method of measuring attitude by having someone react toward an object or concept by responding to bipolar adjective pairs

Short-Answer Item   A knowledge test item for which students write a short answer to the item

Silhouette Figure Ratings   A method of measuring the degree of satisfaction or dissatisfaction with one's bodily appearance

Simple Frequency Distribution   An ordered listing of a set of scores, complete with the frequency of each score

Simple Prediction   The prediction of the value of one measure, the dependent variable, using another measure, the independent variable

Single-Stage Exercise Test   A method used to estimate $\dot{V}O_2$ max from one submaximal workload and heart rate

Skill Test   A test that measures physical skill, not fitness

Skinfolds   A double layer of skin and fat pinched to provide an estimate of percent fat

Social Desirability   A sometimes subconscious tendency to answer questionnaries in a way that makes us seem more commendable than we really are. An example would be an overestimate of how active we are

Speed The ability to move rapidly

Stability Reliability Coefficient The degree to which individuals' scores are unchanged from day to day

Standard Deviation A measure of the variability, or spread, of a set of scores around the mean

Standard Error of the Mean A value indicating the amount of variation to expect in the mean if individuals were tested again

Standard Error of Measurement The amount of error expected in a measured score

Standard Error of Prediction A value indicating the amount of error to expect in a predicted score

Standard Score A test score calculated using the test mean and standard deviation; usually expressed as a z or T

Steady State Exercise Responses to exercise that are relatively constant from one minute to the next; defined as two successive heart rates within 6 beats·min^{-1}

Step Activity Monitor Pedometer that accounts for atypical gait

Subjective A test lacking a standardized scoring system, which introduces a source of measurement error

Subjective Evaluation A test in which the scorer must make a value judgment before assigning the performer a score

Submaximal Exercise Test A test used to evaluate cardiorespiratory function by measuring one's ability to perform work at submaximal workloads and then predicting $\dot{V}O_2$ max from submaximal heart rate

Submaximal $\dot{V}O_2$ The volume of oxygen consumed ($\dot{V}O_2$) at a submaximal exercise level

Summative Evaluation The process of judging achievement at the end of instruction

T

Task Analysis A scoring instrument that addresses the process of a given skill; identifies components necessary for satisfactory completion of a skill

Taxonomy A classification for parts of a system; the educational taxonomies for the cognitive, affective, and psychomotor domains are used to formulate educational objectives

Teacher's Standards A grading technique that compares students' scores to a standard developed by the teacher

Test-Retest Method Administering a test on each of two days to establish stability reliability

Trait A stable psychological characteristic such as extroversion or independence

Treadmill A machine that regulates the work performed during walking or running by regulating the treadmill speed and or elevation

True-False Item A knowledge test item for which students answer either *True* or *False*

T-Scores Standard scores used to combine different tests together with mean 50 and standard deviation 10

t-Test An inferential statistical test used to determine if two means are equal in value

Two-Component Model The method used to measure percent body fat from the underwater weighing method. The model assumes that the density of fat is 0.9 g·cc^{-1} and the fat-free weight is 1.0 g·cc^{-1}

U

Underwater Weighing Determining a person's body weight in water; one method used to determine body density. See also *hydrostatic weighing*

Useful Scores Test scores that can be used immediately or inserted into a formula with little effort

V

Validity The degree to which interpretations of test scores lead to correct conclusions

Variability The degree of heterogeneity in a set of scores; measures include the range and the standard deviation

Variance The square of the standard deviation

Vigorous Exercise Activities performed at an intensity greater than 6 METs (21 ml·kg^{-1}·min^{-1}), with an intensity greater than 60% of $\dot{V}O_2$ max

Vigorous Physical Activity Movement that expends more energy than brisk walking

$\dot{V}O_2$ max See *maximal oxygen uptake*

W

Wall Volley Tests Skill tests that require the student to repeatedly volley a ball against a wall

Watt A unit to quantify power output during cycle ergometer exercise; equal to 6.12 kg·m·min^{-1}

Z

z-Score A standard score used to combine different tests together with mean 0 and standard deviation 1

NAME INDEX

A

Abel, M. F., 427, 433
Adams, H. E., 493, 494
Adams, R. S., 478
Ainsworth, B. E., 184, 185
Ajzen, I., 480
Algina, J., 88, 96
Allison, P. R., 478
Alsawalmeh, Y. M., 87
Anderson, K. V., 7
Aronin, P., 428
Åstrand, I., 263, 270
Åstrand, P.-O., 278, 279
Ayoub, M. A., 230

B

Baker, A. B., 98
Baker, E. L., 151
Balke, B., 275, 276
Ball, T. E., 358
Bandura, A., 488
Bane, S., 493, 495
Baranowski, T., 203
Barfield, J. P., 195
Bar-Or, O., 427
Barrow, H. M., 136, 224
Bassett, D. R., 203, 209, 210, 418
Bassey, E. J., 213
Battaglia, M., 432
Bauman, C. L., 492
Baumgartner, T. A., 60, 70, 77, 80, 81, 84,
          85, 88, 89, 91, 101, 103, 225, 251,
          355, 470, 479, 487, 493
Baun, M., 407
Baun, W. B., 407
Beam, W. C., 402
Beckett, M. B., 312

C

Campanelli, R. A., 499, 501
Campbell, E. J. M., 274

Behnke, A. R., 312
Bender, J. M., 196
Benson, J., 493
Berger, R. A., 70
Bernauer, E. M., 225
Bernstein, I. H., 86, 88
Bernstein, I. R., 96, 100
Bhambhani, Y. N., 427, 428
Bishu, R. R., 234, 499, 501
Blair, S. N., 6, 9, 265, 266, 300, 381, 384, 407
Blakley, B. R., 387
Blomqvist, G., 263
Bloom, B. S., 5, 450
Bohnenblust, S. E., 27
Boileau, R. A., 309
Bonanno, J., 225
Booth, M. L., 196
Borg, G., 234, 495–96, 499
Bourdeaudhuij, I., 197
Bouthier, D., 152
Bowen, B. D., 470
Boyce, W. F., 433
Bradburn, N., 470
Bray, M. S., 200
Brown, T., 495
Brožek, J., 306, 307, 308
Bruce, R. A., 275, 276, 384
Bruininks, R., 431
Bryant, H. E., 204
Buree, B., 494
Burger, D. L., 151
Burger, S. E., 151
Burtner, P. A., 430
Burton, A. W., 430, 431
Buskirk, E. R., 9, 381, 382
Busse, M. E., 418

Cardinal, B. J., 417
Cardon, G., 197
Carr, M. G., 478
Cascio, W. F., 232
Cash, T., 492, 493, 494, 495
Casperson, C. J., 13, 179, 212
Castelli, W. P., 7
Chamberlin, P., 492
Chapman, C. B., 263
Chasan-Taber, L., 202, 208
Chin, A., 234, 499, 501
Ching, L. Y. H., 196
Chung, H., 84, 85, 101
Ciriello, V. M., 499
Clarke, H. H., 339
Clifford, C., 427
Cohen, J., 58
Cohen, P., 58
Coleman, K. J., 199, 418
Collins, D. R., 157
Collins, M. E., 494
Considine, W., 225
Consolazio, L. J., 274
Cooper, K., 283, 407
Cooper, P. J., 492
Corbin, C. B., 19, 20, 193, 200, 358
Corbin, C. R., 487, 488
Cornoni-Huntley, 379
Costill, D. L., 325, 386
Cotten, D. J., 358
Couldry, W. H., 487
Counts, C. R., 493, 494
Courneya, K. S., 204
Cousins, G. F., 225
Cowles, M., 492
Craig, C. L., 202, 206
Crocker, L., 88, 96
Crocker, P. R. C., 200
Crowe, T. K., 430
Cucina, I. M., 152
Cumbee, F., 225
Cureton, K. J., 9, 105, 284, 318, 346
Cyarto, E. V., 212, 213

SUBJECT INDEX

A

AAHPERD
functional fitness test, 399–402
Health-Related Fitness Test (HRFT), 340
Sport Skills Test Series, 168–70
Youth Fitness Test (YFT), 338, 339
Abdomen
abdominal strength and endurance, 99, 251
curl-up test, 353, 364
1-minute half sit-up, 393–94, 395
sit-up test, 98, 99, 397
skinfold test, 314, 316
Absolute endurance test, 247
Absolute strength, 236–37
Abstract test measures, 100, 101
Accelerometers, 186, 188, 194
for children and adolescents, 193–94
for older adults, 212
validity, 204, 206
Accuracy tests, 157
Achievement orientation, 475
Actigraph accelerometer, 186, 196
Activity factor, 481
ACTIVITYGRAM®, 198
Activity monitors, 418
Actiwatch accelerometer, 197
Adult fitness. *See also* Elderly fitness
aging and decline, 379–88
evaluation model, 11
Adult fitness testing, 4, 223
AAHPERD test, 399–402
aerobic fitness, 381–84, 388–90, 401–2, 404–5, 406
body composition, 384–86, 390–91
computer applications, 407–9
flexibility, 394–96
functional fitness, 398–407
Groningen Fitness Test for the Elderly, 405–7
muscular endurance, 393–94
muscular strength, 387, 391–94
reliability evidence, 201–4

Senior Fitness Test, 402–5
U.S. Army Fitness Test, 396–98
validity evidence, 205–11
Y's Way to Fitness program, 279, 379, 388–96
Adult-onset diabetes, 299
Aerobic capacity tests
youth fitness tests, 344–49
Aerobic fitness. *See also* $\dot{V}O_2$ max
adult evaluation, 381–84, 388–90, 401–2, 404–5, 406
age-adjusted standards for health promotion in adults, 267
average values for normal adults and elite endurance athletes, 266
comparison of methods used to estimate, 292
defined, 263–65
and health, 265–66
Aerobic fitness tests, 9
evaluation of, 266–67
field tests of, 282–87
laboratory-based, 269–72
laboratory-based maximal tests, 272–76
maximal treadmill tests, 274–76
multi-stage exercise test, 279–81
nonexercise estimates of, 287–89
open-circuit spirometry, 272–74
for persons with disabilities, 426
single-stage exercise test, 277–79
single-stage treadmill walking test, 281–83
submaximal tests of, 276–87
submaximal treadmill protocols, 281
walking and jogging tests, 286–87
youth tests, 8
Affective domain, 477
African Americans, body composition measurement, 307
Age-appropriate physical activity, 20
Aggression, 475
Agility/dynamic balance, 401
adult evaluation, 405, 407
Agility run test, 226

Aging. *See also* Adult fitness testing and fitness, 379–88
"All-around" athlete, 224
Alpha level, 61
Alternative assessment, 141
examples of, 149
measurement concerns with, 151–53
types of, 146–51
American Alliance for Health, Physical Education, Recreation and Dance, 399
American College of Sports Medicine, 181, 193
guidelines for exercise testing and prescription, 11
standards for $\dot{V}O_2$ max, 267
American Heart Association, 13, 180, 181
Americans with Disabilities Act, 227–28
Analysis of variance (ANOVA), 60
one-way, 64, 74–77
two-way, 65, 78–82
Analytical rubrics, 142, 143–44, 145
Android obesity, 313
Anorexia nervosa, 301, 488, 489
Anthropometric assessment
body circumferences, 312–13
body mass index (BMI), 9, 310–11, 351–52, 370, 405
skinfold measurement, 313–24, 328–29, 350–51
waist-hip ratio (WHR), 312–13
Anxiety, 475
Apple-shaped bodies, 299–300, 313
Archery
criterion-referenced test for, 105
performance evaluation, 166
Archimedes principle, 304
Arm tests
arm lift, 239
curl test, 403
flexed arm hang test, 358–59, 365, 367
pull-up test, 356–58
push-up test, 355–56, 396
right angle push-up test, 364, 365